MW00781152

Non dilexerunt animam suam usque ad mortem.

The Latin, *Non dilexerunt animam suam usque ad mortem*, translates, "... they loved not their lives unto the death." Revelation 12:11

On The Cover: *Massacres at Salzburg* took place in 1528 when Prince-Archbishop Cardinal Matthaus Lang of Salzburg issued mandates sending police in search of Anabaptists. Many were captured and killed. This engraving illustrates the sufferings and sacrifices these Dissenters endured when their government, in conjunction with established religion, attempted to coerce and impose uniformity of religious belief. Hence, this picture is a reminder of the cost of religious liberty and the ever-present need to maintain the separation of church and state. We use this art to represent our Dissent and Nonconformity Series.

HISTORY

OF

The Evangelical Churches

SAMVEL MORLANDIVS. SEP.[.] D.^I   PROTECTORIS. AD REGEM
GALLIÆ. DVCEMQ, SABAVDIÆ,   DE REBVS VALLENSIVM
INTERNVNTIVS. ET DEINDE   EXTRA ORDINĒ. COMMISSARIVS

SAMUEL MORLAND
1625-1693

THE
H I S T O R Y
OF
The Evangelical Churches
Of the VALLEYS of
PIEMONT.

CONTAINING

A most exact *Geographical* Description of the Place, and
a faithfull Account of the Doctrine, Life, and Persecutions of
the Ancient Inhabitants.

TOGETHER,

With a most naked and punctual Relation of the late
BLOUDY MASSACRE, 1655. And a Narrative of
all the following Transactions, to the Year of Our LORD, 1658.

All which are justified, partly by divers Ancient *Manuscripts*
written many hundred Years before CALVIN or LUTHER, and
partly by other most Authentick Attestations: The true
Originals of the greatest part whereof, are to be seen in their proper Languages
by all the curious, in the Publick Library of the famous University
of *CAMBRIDGE*.

Collected and compiled with much pains and industry,
By *S A M U E L   M O R L A N D* , Esq;
During his abode in *Geneva*, in quality of HIS
HIGHNESS *Commissioner Extraordinary* for the Affairs
of the said VALLEYS and particularly for the
Distribusion of the *Collected Moneys*, among the remnant of those poor distressed People.

REVEL. 6.9.
And when he had opened the fifth seal, I saw under the Altar the souls of them that were slain for the word of God,
and for the testimony which they held; And they cried with a loud voice saying, How long O Lord, holy and
true, dost thou not judge and avenge our bloud on them that dwell on the earth?

BOOKS 1 & 2 of 4

LONDON.
Printed by *Henry Hills*, one of His Highness's Printers, for
Adoniram Byfield, and are to be sold at the three Bibles in *Cornhill*, next to *Popes-head Alley*, 1658.

he Baptist Standard Bearer, Inc.

NUMBER ONE IRON OAKS DRIVE • PARIS, ARKANSAS 72855

Thou hast given a *standard* to them that fear thee;
that it may be displayed because of the truth.
-- *Psalm 60:4*

Reprinted
by

THE BAPTIST STANDARD BEARER, INC.
No. 1 Iron Oaks Drive
Paris, Arkansas 72855
(501) 963-3831

THE WALDENSIAN EMBLEM
lux lucet in tenebris
"The Light Shineth in the Darkness"

ISBN #1-57978-541-7

THE
Authors Epiſtle Dedicatory

To His moſt Serene Highneſs,

OLIVER,

By the Grace of God, *Lord Protector of England, Scotland,* and *Ireland,* &c.

May it pleaſe **YOUR HIGHNESS,**

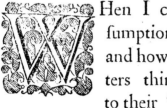Hen I conſider the great preſumption of the *Age* we live in, and how even the meaneſt Writers think it an undervaluing to their Works, if they have not the Greateſt of *Princes* for their *Patrons,* I am loth to preſs in with the crowd to importune *Your Highneſs* by a *Dedication* of the following *Hiſtory* ; But when I call to minde how exceeding precious in *Your* thoughts the lives and liberties

berties of thofe poor diftreffed *Members of Chrift*
have been (who are the onely fubject of my
Difcourfe) and how deeply their bleeding condition hath always affected *Your* very heart, I
cannot but hope *You* will vouchfafe to own
the weak endeavours (though of the unwor-
thieft of *Your* fervants) for preferving the name
and memory of thofe Ancient and *Primitive
Profeffors* to future Generations : Efpecially
confidering that my defign herein is very fubfervient to that great end, which *You* have propofed to *your Self* ever fince *Providence* bleft
thefe *Three Nations* with *Your* happy Government, Namely, the promoting of the general
intereft of Gods people throughout the *Chriftian*
world. It is an obfervation of that Excellent
Prince, the *Duke* of *Rohan*, that *The Intereft of
the chief Magiftrate of England is, by all means to
become Head of the Reformed Party throughout
Europe* ; And it is *Your Highnefs* Glory and
Crown, that *You* have formed all *Your* Counfels in Order thereunto, and laying afide all o-
ther Reafons of *State*, have adhered onely to
this, that *Your own Intereft may appear one and the
fame with the Univerfal Intereft of the Evangelical Churches in their refpective Nations.* The Piety of which Refolution *The Lord* himfelf hath
born

born witneſs to, by a continued ſeries of wonderfull Providences and Heavenly benedictions
that have alwayes accompanied *You* in *your* moſt
honourable and Heroick Enterpriſes ; Whereas
thoſe other *Princes* that went before *You,* who
had little regard in the adminiſtration of their
Government, either to the honeſt Maximes of
Humane Policy, or to the wholeſome Rules of
the *Holy Scriptures* (which they ought to have
bound about their necks, and to have graven upon the
Tables of their hearts) but miſerably ſpent the
beſt of their powerfull Intereſts, and precious
talents in perſecuting tender conſciences in their
own Dominions, and moſt treacherouſly betraying the *Proteſtant Cauſe* in *Germany, France,*
and other Countries, did at laſt to their great a-
ſtoniſhment, even in the height of thoſe their
oppreſſions, and in the midſt of all their jollities,
behold with their eyes a *MENE TEKEL*
upon *the Walls* of their *Palaces* and *Banqueting*
Houſes, and of late years in all the branches of
their *Families* have taſted the bitter fruits of
their own unrighteous doings. This is a Doom
which was long ſince pronounced againſt them
by the moſt pious *Paſtors* and *Profeſſors* of for-
reign *Churches,* who oft times heretofore have
been heard to ſay, *That God would one day render*

a

a recompence to that House *for all their perfidious dealings towards his poor servants,* and now many of those godly men, who have lived to see the execution of those his righteous judgements, considering on the other side the wonderful passages of *Divine Providence* leading the way to the extirpation of *that Family,* and to the placing of *your Highness* in the *Princely Dignity,* have of late frequently declared (as I my self have been divers times an ear witness)with tears of joy in their eys,*that they looked on You as a man miraculously raised up by God, and endowed with an extraordinary spirit of Wisdome and Courage, to plead the Cause of his afflicted ones against the Mighty, that they may no more oppress.*

Who is there so ignorant in these Our dayes who knows not, that all the Peace, Tranquillity, and Priviledges, which those of the *Reformed Religion* enjoy at present in any part of the *European* World, does some way or other own *your Patronage* and *Protection*? And who is there likewise that knowes not that when first You were call'd forth in the view of the World, and singled out as a chosen Instrument to *go forth to the help of the Lord against the Mighty, and to fight His Battels a-*
gainst

gainft the great Perfecutors, the eftate and condition of the *Church Militant* was but at a very low ebb? The mighty flouds of *Popery* and *Atheifme* were broken in upon the *Ifles* of *Great Britain* and *Ireland*, and the poor *Proteftants* in all other parts were even finking down under the *heavie burdens* laid upon their fhoulders by thofe cruel *Task-mafters* of the *Church of Rome* ; Yea the *Plowers* were almoft every where *plowing and making long furrowes upon the backs* of the faithfull ones in all the Quarters and Corners of their Habitations! It was a time when *the Enemies of the Lord took crafty counfel together againft His people, and were confederate againft His hidden ones (The Tabernacles of Edom and the Ifhmaelites! Amaleck and the Philiftims, with them that dwell at Tyre!) They faid one to another, Come and let us cut them off from being a people, that fo their name may be had no more in remembrance.*

And the truth is, they had undoubtedly compaffed their hellifh defigns, had not the *Shepheard of Ifrael awoke as a man out of fleep, and found out a man* (I mean *your Highnefs*) *to ftand in the gap, girding You with ftrength unto the Battel, and putting his own fword into Your hand, to fmite thofe his*

his enemies in the hinder parts, and put them to a perpetual reproach.

The *Spaniard*, that old Enemy of *England* and *Religion*, is sufficiently able even already to give the world a very clear account of the blessed fruits and happy success of Your Noble and Princely undertakings; For here indeed You seemed *to lay the axe to the root of the tree,* when that ancient *Quarrel* revived again, which had lain asleep ever since the days of *Queen Elizabeth* of glorious memory. *That Princess,* looking upon this branch of *The House of Austria* as the main pillar of the *Romish* power and persecution, did set her whole shoulder to the work of overturning it, in hope to have put an end to the great *Mystery of Iniquity* and Tyranny exercised upon the bodies and consciences of mankinde; But the measure of their iniquity being not yet filled up, *She* was not permitted by *God* to accomplish her design: And now after the long Reigns of *two unhappy Kings,* the *Martial* spirit and renown of *Our Nation* being raised again under the auspicious Name and Counsels of *Your Highness,* equal to the best and most victorious of Our Ancestors , all things seem to work , as if the final accomplishment of what she intended, were reserved

for

for Your Triumph and Trophees. You have with *Your Naval Forces,* in a manner held him shackled, and shut him up within his own Dominions for several years, In a word his treasures are almost exhausted, and the *Veins* which should supply him, are intercepted, besides in credit he is almost become bankrupt; so that if it please the *Almighty* to crown Your endeavours with a few more successes, a fair stroke will be given in a short time for excluding him from any considerable interest or influence in these *North* parts of the World. The fear of this, is that which made him of late betake himself to the same ignoble practises and attempts by *Assassinations,* and plotted *Insurrections* against the person and Government of *Your Highness,* as He practised of old against the person and Government of *That Renowned Queen ;* But as God was graciously pleased to make *Her* fortunate in the discovering and apprehending such *Assassinats* and *Traitors* from time to time, and to continue her in a long and prosperous Reign, so Your *HIGHNESS* having hitherto been no less remarkably happy in having always Your eys as it were miraculously enlightned, by the *God of Light and Truth,* to *foresee the mischief, and pass by,* while the intended A-

ctors

ctors thereof have happily perifhed upon the points of their own fwords, and *fallen headlong into that very pit of deftruction which they had digged for others,* We are encouraged to hope, that the fame *God* will vouchfafe to us this great blefsing, that You likewife may long fway the Scepter of thefe Nations, and go in and out before us, for the perfecting of thofe bleffed purpofes, which he has put into Your heart for the good of his people, both here and in foreign parts ; that fo You may (as You have done upon all occafions) *deliver the poor that cry, and the fatherlefs, and him that hath none to help him* ; that You may continue to be *eyes to the blinde, and feet to the lame* ; to *break the jawes of the wicked,* and to *pluck the prey out of his teeth* ; *to loofe the heavie burden, and to let the oppreffed go free.* Though Your *Highnefs* delights more to do thefe things than to hear of them, yet give me leave to tell You, that thefe *Your actions of Mercy and Righteoufnefs* are the true *Walls* and *Bulwarks* of thefe Your Iflands ! thefe are the very *Weapons* wherewith you have fo oft *run through a* Troop, and *broken the gates of brafs, and cut the barrs of iron in funder !* Yea I am bold to add, that *the blefsing of the poor Waldenfes* which were *ready to perifh,* together with *that of the Po-*
lonian

lonian and *Bohemian Exiles,* is already visibly come upon You, and had no small influence in all Your late successes. *May the God and Father of Mercies still go on to open the Treasures of his Grace, and rain down his blessings upon* Your Princely Person *and pious undertakings, for the honour of his great Name, and the good of his poor afflicted* Church *and* People: *for which end and purpose all honest and true hearted* English *souls ought to bow their knees daily to the Father of Our* Lord Jesus Christ, *that so (if it be his good pleasure that Our eyes shall see those happy days) the glory of his* Gospel *may by* Your *means be more highly advanced, and that the* Top stone *of that Heavenly building being at last laid, all the people may cry* Grace, Grace *unto it.* This is the unfeigned prayer of,

Your Highness most humble and
most faithfull Subject and
Servant,

SAMUEL MORLAND.

An Advertiſement to the

READER.

THough it be the cuſtome of *Printers* to prefix their *Errata* to the Books they publiſh, I hope the want thereof here, will not make this be thought the more imperfect. Where the *Reader* findes a different *Orthography* in ſome of the *French* and *Italian Manuſcripts,* from that of later times, his judgement will tell him that its an Argument of their *Antiquity*; where he meets with any real miſtake, (which will be no wonder in ſuch variety of matter, and Languages) his ingenuity will eaſily prompt him to correct them.

The Authours

INTRODUCTION

To the following

HISTORY

By way of Apology for the

EVANGELICAL CHURCHES

in the Valleys of *Piemont*.

Againſt the bitter Calumnies and Reproaches of their bloudy Perſecutours.

Directed principally to all the faithful and compaſſionate Souls of the *Engliſh* Nation, who have been grieved for the Afflictions of *Joſeph*.

But withall intended for the enlightening and edifying of the more moderate and ingenuous Spirits among the *Roman* Catholicks.

Chriſtian and courteous Reader,

 Am not ignorant, that both the nature of my Employ-ment, and the principles which I profeſs, may at the firſt fight beget ſome prejudice in the ſpirits of divers againſt the enſuing Treatiſe, and cauſe them to look upon it as a thing compoſed and brought forth upon the Stage of the World, by one, whoſe intereſt (as they will ſuppoſe) being always in his eye like the Yellow Jaundis, muſt needs make him judg all Ob-jects to be of the ſame colour with it, and whoſe affection hath an in-fluence upon his hand, and leads him unawares to draw now and then

an

an oblique and unpleafing Line, notwithftanding, fo much do I prefume upon the generous difpofition of the candid and ingenuous Reader, that when he fhall have throughly weighed in the *Ballance of the Sanctuary* thofe moft authentick Atteftations, whereby the truth of each effential part of the following Difcourfe is fo manifeftly juftified, that he that runs may reade it, I fhall finde fo much favour in his eys, as to be accounted by him, in the number (though not of the moft able, yet) of the moft fincere and faithfull Hiftorians, (I except the Pen-men of the holy Scriptures) that ever yet appeared in publick. Yea, that which I defire of thee, whoever thou art, is but to proportion and meafure out thy Cenfure, according to the Evidence of the Matter therein contained. And then, if thou thinkeft that I ow thee ten thoufand Talents of Truth, onely have patience with me, and I will pay thee all.

There are now more than nineteen Moneths paft, fince the voice of the Bloud of the poor *Proteftants* in the Valleys of *Piemont* was heard in all the Corners of the *Chriftian* World, efpecially throughout the *Englifh* Nation, where there then arrived Letters upon Letters, juft like *Job*'s Meffengers, one at the heels of another, with the fad and dolefull Tidings of moft ftrange and unheard of Cruelties, for which I almoft dare to challenge the beft furnifht Hiftorians, (as well ancient as modern) to finde me their Parallels. Some of their Women were ravifht, and afterwards ftaked down to the ground through their Privities; others ftrangely forced, and then their Bellies rammed up with Stones and Rubbifh: the Brains and Breafts of others fodden and eaten by their Murderers, (as if the Defign of thofe bloudy *Canibals* and barbarous *Anthropophagi* had been not onely to extirpate thofe poor Creatures out of this World, but alfo as much as in them lay, by fuch a ftrange commixtion and confufion of fubftances, to hinder them from having a being in the World to come.) Others had their Flefh fliced from off their Bones, while they were yet alive, till fuch time as they were become meer Skeletons or Anatomies. Many impotent and aged perfons of ninety and an hundred years of age moft cruelly burnt in their Beds, without any refpect had to their fnowy Heads and hoary Hairs, upon which notwithftanding the All-wife Creatour has fet fo frequent Marks of Honour in his facred Word. And if two She Bears out of the Wood were commanded to tear in pieces *fourty and two little Children* for abufing the *old Prophet*, barely by the term of *Bald Pate*, Lord, what fhall be the end of thefe Murderers of riper years, who took fo much pleafure and delight in torturing and tormenting fo many poor, impotent and aged perfons, by Fire and Sword?

There is none, there is none, who knows what it means, to be *grieved with the Afflictions of* Jofeph, but will here eafily conceive how nearly this bloudy and barbarous Maffacre then touched all the tender hearts of the *Englifh* Nation, efpecially the heart of that moft ferene Prince and *Heroick* Captain, the dimenfions of whofe moft *Chriftian* bowels of compaffion for the poor afflicted

Saints

Saints of *Jeſus*, are in no wiſe to be meaſured by any of my ſlender
and ſhort Expreſſions.

The truth is, he has been a victorious Prince in all his undertakings, yet I am confident it would be much eaſier to outgo him in
any thing than in tenderneſs and compaſſion towards the poor Members of *Chriſt* in miſery and affliction. The News of this *Maſſacre* no
ſooner came to his Highneſs ears, but he *aroſe like a Lion out of his
place*, and by divers pathetical and quickening Letters, awoke the
whole *Chriſtian* World, and moved their hearts to pity and commiſeration. Of theſe his Highneſs Letters, the meaneſt of his Servants
had the honour to be the Bearer of Two, the one to the King of
France, to engage (if poſſible) his *moſt Chriſtian Majeſty* to improve
his Power and Intereſt in the behalf of the Remainder of thoſe miſerable People. And the other to the *Duke* of *Savoy*, which I according to his Highneſs Commands delivered, together with an earneſt
Interceſſion by word of mouth in his Highneſs Name, That the ſaid
Duke would be pleaſed to recall thoſe mercileſs and inhumane Edicts,
and reſtore his poor afflicted Subjects to their ancient Liberties and
Habitations.

Now when I had according to my weak and ſlender capacity executed his Highneſs (my Maſter's) Commands at *Turin*, I retired my
ſelf to the City of *Geneva*, a place not more pleaſant by reaſon of its
lovely ſituation, than eminent for the ſincere, conſtant, and painfull
Preaching of the *Word*, and Adminiſtration of the Sacraments, in no
leſs than three ſeveral Languages, (*French, Italian,* and *High Dutch*)
the which alſo, to make up the heavenly Harmony, is accompanied
with a ſingular Piety and *Chriſtian* Behaviour in general, both of Governours and People.

I had not remained many Moneths in this place, before I received a
Letter from the Right Honourable Mr. Secretary *Thurlo*, wherein he
was pleaſed to intimate unto me, *how uſefully both for the preſent Age
and future Generations, I might imploy my vacant hours during the time
of my Retirement ; namely, by drawing into an exact Hiſtory all that had
lately happened to the poor Proteſtants in the Valleys of* Piemont, *beginning with the Order of* Gaſtaldo, *and ſo proceeding and ſetting down all
particulars in a diſtinct and clear method.*

Now when I had ſate down and ſeriouſly conſidered the Contents
of this Letter, joyned to the ſtrict Charge given me by the late deceaſed *Lord Primate* of *Ireland*, one of the Wonders of this our later
Age, touching the ſame ſubject, I began to perſwade my ſelf, that as
there were many ſincere hearted *Chriſtians* of the *Engliſh* Nation, ſo
were there alſo many ingenuous Souls in other parts of the World,
yea and that among the more moderate Party of the Adverſaries
themſelves, who were exceeding curious in inquiry, and almoſt
impatient to know more particularly *who* thoſe People were, *and
what was their fathers houſe*, whoſe Lives and Liberties have been ſo
exceeding precious in the thoughts of *His Highneſs*, and whoſe
bleeding miſeries effectually ſo moved him to improve his utmoſt
Intereſt

Intereft both at home and abroad for their Deliverance.

And indeed upon thefe and the like Confiderations (Providence having then bleft me with a fingular Opportunity) I knew not how better to ferve my Generation, or fucceeding Ages, than in the collecting and reducing into an exact and entire Hiftory, whatfoever concerns either the Antiquity, Doctrine, Life, or Perfecutions of thofe poor *Evangelical Churches*, even from the Days of *Chrift* and his *Apoftles*, to this very time ; and the truth is, I promifed my felf no fmall pleafure and fatisfaction in the beginning of this my undertaking. But alas, I had no fooner made a confiderable entrance into the work, but I found it to be, even from one end thereof to the other, one of the faddeft Tragedies that ever has been acted in the *Chriftian* World ; a Story fo lined and interwoven with horrible Attempts, fuch bloudy Edicts, fuch profound Stratagems, and barbarous Perfecutions, againft the poor harmlefs and innocent Flock of that great Shepherd of our Souls, that the Reader cannot fix his eye almoft upon any part thereof, without finding matter of weeping and lamentation ; I fay, which way foever he turns he fhall finde Treacheries complotted, Defolations fore-determined, the *Pit digged*, and the *Net* of *Deftruction fpread* ; in conclufion, whole Families miferably ruined, and the innocent *Bloud of the Saints powred out and fpilt as Water upon the Ground*. In fo much that my fpirit has oft waxed cold within me, and my heart even failed me, yea my very hand has trembled as with a Fit of the Palfie in the writing thereof. And the truth is, I fhould foon have been difheartened from proceeding in this my Defign, had it not been a Work that I knew might juftly be expected from me by his Highnefs, and all the good People of the *Englifh* Nation, to whom I am bound by all the Obligations, both of Nature and Confcience, to give an Account of my Time and Opportunities : as likewife I knew it to be a Work that would be moft acceptable, fatisfactory, and ufefull to the whole *Chriftian* World, both as to themfelves, their Children, and their Childrens Children in future Generations : yea befides all this, the Example of *Mofes* and the Prophets, of the Evangelifts and Apoftles, as likewife of the greateft Doctours, as well ancient as modern, who have publifhed to the World, and left in writing the feveral Difpenfations of Divine Providence towards his People in this World, are more than abundantly fufficient to authorize and encourage me, (how unequal foever I be to follow them) in fo important an undertaking. Sure I am, whofoever fhall reade with an anfwerable underftanding and due attention, the treacherous Stratagems and horrid Cruelties therein contained, muft have an Heart of Adamant and Bowels of Brafs, fhould they not be touched with a fellow-feeling of their Brethrens mifery : yea I am much miftaken if they remain not aftonifhed and amazed to think, that a Prince (or rather indeed his royal Mother)who ought to be as a nurfing Father and a nurfing Mother of their Subjects, fhould fo miferably comply with the fpirits of malicious men, wholly tranfported with rage and paffion, and inflamed with a vehement thirft after

Bloud,

Bloud ; And should so far do violence to their more moderate inclinations, as to lend an ear , yea and countenance those importunate
Sollicitations, which tend to the ruine of their Countrey, and the division of their people ; which has not only rendred them unlovely to
all the Princes and States of the Reformed Churches , but has also
procured unto themselves no small blame from those of the very same
Religion with themselves.

Not to mention any other then that of *France*, who certainly cannot but see, that this late Attempt in the Valleys, was a meer Stratagem to gain *Pragela* in possession, and thereby to stop his *most Christian Majesties* passage into *Italie* ; As likewise the more easily to deprive him of those places which he holds in *Piemont*, and all this by
the subtill suggestion of the *Spanish Monks* and *Friers*, who know how
to palliate their politique Designs under false pretexts, as cunningly
as *Rachel did her Fathers Images* , and disguise their murtherous practices, with the mask of Religious, and zealous intentions.

Gen. 31.34.

Neither is it probable that such Actions of violence committed by
the *Pope* and his *Emissaries* are offensive to *France* alone , but that it is
as ill taken likewise by all the politick Catholiques themselves , who
know right well that this can do no less then unite the *Protestant* party
more firmly, and consequently, when there shall be a fair opportunity
offered, may very probably put all into a confusion, and prove their
utter overthrow. However it be, it cannot but melt the bowels of
all tender and compassionate souls towards the poor afflicted Saints of
Jesus.

This is that O ingenious Reader, this is that which I am bold to present thee with at present, and that out of a real affection to thy immortal soul) though it's possible thy Principles and mine may be different)
hoping that the undoubted truths herein contained, may prove as a precious *ey-salve* to annoint thine eyes, that so thou maist see and discover
the many remarkable passages of Divine Providence towards his poor
Church militant in this world, and likewise that it may perswade thee *in
this thy day of visitation, to come out of* Babylon, *that so thou maist not be
partaker of her sins , nor receive at length of her plagues* ; I mean that
generation of Vipers, who by their barbarous and unheard-of cruelties ,
have plainly discovered themselves to be the Firebrands of Hell it self,
and Fiends of Infernal darkness. *Longè diversa sunt carnificina & pi-
etas , nec potest aut veritas cum vi , aut justitia cum crudelitate conjun-
gi, there is a vast difference between Butchery and godliness, neither has
truth any concord with violence, or cruelty with righteousness* , as *Lactan-
tius* elegantly expresses himself upon this Subject. Believest thou this
O tender-hearted Reader ? I know that thou dost believe it, and therefore it is that I am desirous to lay before thee the ensuing History, beseeching the God of Truth and Righteousness to remove all the stum-
bling-blocks , and prejudicial thoughts, which either the frailty of the
Authors understanding and youth, or the seeming inconsiderableness
of the poor people of the Valleyes , who are the subject of his discourse, may at the first sight suggest unto thee.

Revel. 18 4.

*Lactant. In-
stit. l. 5. c. 10.
pag. 418. Ex-
cus. Coloniæ
Allobrog. apud
Joa. Tornesium
cIↃIↃcxlvi.*

The

The truth is, if thou regardeft the outfide only of thefe poor wretches, and the form of their countenance, thou wilt be ready to cry out, *Lord, what are thefe men, that thou fhouldeft be mindful of them?* or their pofterity, *that thou fhouldeft have any regard unto them?* As like-wife, if thou vifiteft their ancient houfes and habitations in fo dark and blinde a corner of the world (being as it were divided from the reft of the habitable earth) in Defarts and folitary places, among the craggy Rocks and fnowy Mountains ; They may feem unto thee to have been lightly efteemed by the great Creatour of the world, as the moft inconfiderable part of his handy-work ; But when thou fhalt *enter into the Sanctuary of God*, and confider ferioufly the man-ner of thefe peoples life and converfation, together with their Principles and practice of Religion, in all Ages and Generations, and that from the Ample teftimony of their profeft enemies ; when thou fhalt confider their Loyal fubmiffion to their Soveraign Prince, their Chriftian patience and magnanimity in their afflictions, and the redoubling of their Heroick zeal in the deepeft of their tribulations, (as not efteeming the fame *worthy to be compared with the joyes which are to be revealed*) when likewife thou fhalt confider on the other fide, how the Lord has many times chofen thefe *foolifh things to con-found the wife : and thefe weak things to confound the mighty, and thefe bafe things, and things which were defpifed, yea,* and *which* in a manner *were not, to bring to nought things that were* ; When thou fhalt have feen how they have been alwaies preferved *as Lambs amongft Wolves*, though they have been oft times moft furioufly affaulted by the *Ana-kims* and fons of violence, infomuch that neither the deliverance of the *Ifraelites* in the Red Sea, nor of *Jonas* in the Whales belly, nor of *Daniel* in the Den of Lions, nor of the three *Children* in the fiery Furnace, was ever more miraculous; I fay when thou fhalt have well confidered and laid to heart all thefe things, Then it may be thou wilt conclude with me, that thefe are not the people that have been reprefented to thee by their black-mouth'd enemies, and that they have not in any wife deferved to be fo cruelly handled by their perfe-cutours. Thou wilt then conclude with me, that all the bitter ac-cufations both of their Doctrine and Manners, are no other then meer impoftures. And that the defcription of this late Maffacre hath fallen very fhort of what it ought to exprefs the rage and horrour of the fame; As likewife that fubtilty hath not been wanting in any kinde of artifice, nor is there any contrivance of falfhood, nor paffionate part of fury, which the Court of *Rome* and their adherents have not devifed and acted for the total extirpation of *Chriftian Religion:* which fhould be a ftrong motive for us to unite our felves the bet-ter to refift their bloudy force, and countermine their Stratagems ; then alfo thou wilt conclude with me, that the All-wife Creator did certainly from the beginning, defign this remote and obfcure part of the world, to hide and lock up therein fome Rich and Ineftimable Treafure ; That this is the *Defart whither the woman fled* when fhe was perfecuted by the Dragon with feven heads and ten horns. And *where*
fhe

*Revel.*12.6.
*Revel.*12.3.

she had a place prepared of God, that they should feed her one thousand two Revel. 12 3 6.
hundred and sixty daies: That here it was that the Church *fed, and where*
she made her Flocks to rest at noon , in those hot and scorching seasons Cant. 1 7.
of the nine and tenth Centuries; Then it may be thou wilt begin to
believe with me , that it was *in the clefts of these Rocks, and in the se-*
cret places of the stairs of these Valleys of *Piemont* , that the *Dove* of Cant. 2. 14.
Christ then *remained* , where also the *Italian Foxes* then began to
spoil the Vines with their tender Grapes , although they were never able Cant. 2. 15.
utterly to destroy or pluck them up by the roots , according to that
excellent Character which the learned *Beza* gives of them in his Treatise of the Famous Pillars of Learning and Religion, in these following words,

Valdenses liceat mihi veteris Christianæ purioris Ecclesiæ semen vocare, Icones Theod. Bizæ, de Vald. GENEVÆ apud Joan. Laonium An. Dom. 1580. Excuf.
utpote quos constet verè admirabili Dei Providentiâ , neque illis infinitis
tempestatibus , quibus est per tot secula Christianus Orbis concussus , &
occidens tandem à pseud-Episcopo Romano miserè oppressus , neque adver-
sus illos propriè excitatis horribilibus persecutionibus, eò potuisse adduci ,
ut Idolomaniæ & Romanæ tyrannidi assentirentur ;

As for the Waldenses , give me leave to call them the very seed of the
Primitive and purer Christian Church , being those who have been so up-
held (as is clear and manifest) by the admirable Providence of God , that
neither those infinite storms and tempests whereby the whole Christian
World has been shaken for so many Ages together , and at length the We-
stern parts so miserably oppressed by that Bishop of Rome, *falsely so called,*
nor those horrible persecutions which have been directly raised against
them , were ever able so far to prevail upon them, as to make them bend
or yield a voluntary subjection to the Roman Tyranny and Idolatry.

Here thou shalt finde, besides the Arguments which may be drawn
from the Ancient confessions of Faith , and several other Authentick
Manuscripts, which have been in former times so miraculously preserved from the flames during their hottest persecutions , I say, besides
all these, thou shalt finde even the most eminent and the most bitter of
their profest enemies , to have let fall many seasonable passages in
those their very writings, which were directly composed against these
poor faithful ones, whereof some by a manifest deduction , others in
plain terms avow the Antiquity of their Religion under the name of
Heresie, even from the Apostles time; So that now *what need we*
any further witness ? we have heard themselves speak , and justifie sufficiently what we assert.

They will certainly henceforward blush, and be ashamed to upbraid us as formerly, by demanding of us where our Religion was before the daies of *Calvin* and *Luther* ? If they doe, we call *Jonas*
Aurelianensis, Prior Rorenco, Samuel de Cassini, Rainerius Sacon, Bel-
vedere, Bellarmin, and other most renowned Catholicks, to witness
for us, that it was in the Valleys of *Piemont.* Yea, I am bold to proceed and affirm (as before) that it is very probable that this was
the *place prepared of God for the persecuted Woman and the Remnant of*
her feed in those dark and gloomy daies, when *the smoak out of the bot-* Revel. 9. 2.
tomless

Rev.9.2.

Rev.12.9.
Rev.20.2.
Rev.13.7.
Rev.13.16.

tomlefs Pit had fo darkened the face of the Univerfe, that it was not eafie to diftinguifh with the eyes of flefhly reafon the Little Flock of Chrift Jefus, and when *that great Red Dragon, and old Serpent called the Devil and Satan, had power given him to make War with the Saints, and to overcome them, and to compell all, both fmall and great, Rich and Poor, Bond and Free, whofe names were not written in the Book of Life, to recieve a mark in their Right Hand and in their Foreheads.*

The truth is, if we had no other Light to guide us in this dark and cloudy night, yet the fires wherewith thofe Cadmeans or *generation of Vipers* have burnt the bodies of the Saints, would ferve us as fo many Torches to keep us from lofing our way between the daies of the Apoftles, and thofe of *Calvin* and *Luther.*

I befeech you, O ye worfhippers of the *Beaft and Antichrift*, fuffer me that I may fpeak, and after that I have fpoken, then mock on ! May it not be righteoufly faid of you, that *ye have gone in the way of Cain,* that you have *flain your Brother Abel as he was talking with you in the Field,* and that now ye make ftrange of it, as though ye had never feen him, or at leaft knew not at all what was become of him.

Gen.4.8.

I fay you have *flain your Righteous brother Abel,* becaufe *his Sacrifice* of a broken Spirit, *was more acceptable to God,* then your Idolatrous and Humane Inventions : and by this means you had thought to have even blotted out the very name and memory of the true Church of Chrift Jefus, in the world. But let me tell you, that as the Church which was then in part flain by that murderer in the perfon of *Abel,* was by Divine providence revived in the perfon of *Seth* (whofe very name in the *Hebrew* fignifies *fubftituted*) fo the Church which you have fo cruelly maffacred in part, in the perfons of fo many Noble and Renowned Martyrs in thofe dark Intervalls after the *number of the Beaft 666.* God has alwaies renewed in the perfon of others his chofen Saints and Servants, according to that of the Poet ———

Gen.4.25.

———*Uno avulfo haud deficit alter*

Aureus———

I fay there have been famous Worthies in all Ages, ever fince the firft rife of our main differences, during the Reign of *Charls* the Great, who like the ancient Heathen Race-runners, having finifht their courfe, have alwaies delivered the Lamp of their Doctrine to the next runner. Thus in the Valleys of *Piemont, Claudius Arch-Bifhop of Turin,* and he to his Difciples, and they to their fucceeding Generations in the ninth and tenth Centuries: in another part of the World, *Bertram* to *Berengarius, Berengarius* to *Peter Brus, Peter Brus* to *Waldo, Waldo* again to *Dulcinus, Dulcinus* to *Gandune* and *Marfilius,* they to *Wickleif, Hus* and *Jerome of Prague,* and their Schollars the *Thaborites* to *Luther* and *Calvin.*

Wherefore I pray you fuffer me a little, and hearken to my words, you that have *liv'd in pleafure on the earth, and been wanton and have nourifht your hearts as in a day of flaughter, you have condemned and killed the juft, and he has not refifted you,* you have *perfecuted* the poor Saints in thofe dark ages of the World from *City to City,* yea, ye *have*

Jam.5.5.

Jam.5.6.

have ftoned them, ye have fawn them afunder, ye have tempted them, ye have flain them with the Sword, ye have caufed them to wander in Deferts, and in Mountains, in Dens and in Caves of the earth, and now ye demand of us a *Sign* to prove their Succeffion and glorious vifibility. May not we juftly anfwer you, as our Saviour did the *Scribes* and *Pharifes* (and yet not exceed the bounds of modefty or charity) *A wicked and adulterous Generation feeketh after a Sign, and there fhall be no fign given unto it, but the fign of the Prophet* Jonas (a true Embleme in this cafe of the Church!) For as God fuffered *Jonas* for a time, becaufe of his unbelief in flying to *Tarfhifh*, to be *caft forth into the Sea* & to be *fwallowed up by a mighty Whale,* but yet afterwards commanded the Fifh to *vomit him out upon the dry Land,* even fo has he fometimes dealt with his Church, in fuffering her to be expofed to the violence of the boifterous Waves of the See of *Rome,* yea fometimes for her back-flidings and unbelief to be *fwallowed up* by that *Leviathan* of *Popery* the *Antichrift* : But yet ftill he has commanded that huge *Fifh to vomit out the fame upon the dry Land* : neither has he fuffered her to be digefted by that cruel Monfter. According to that excellent paffage in *Hofea, Come and let us return unto the Lord, for he hath torn us, and he will heal us, he hath fmitten, and he will bind up ; after two daies he will revive us, and the third day he will raife us up, and we fhall live in his fight.*

Heb. 11. 37, 38.

Mat.16. 4,11.

Jonah 1.3.15.

Jon. 2. 10.

Hof. 6. 1, 2.

True it is I fay, that the Church of Chrift, as it has been *travelling* from Jerufalem *to* Jericho, *has oft-times fell among Theeves* who have *robb'd* her, and *ftript* her, *and left* her *naked, and wounded, and half dead ;* But yet ftill the *good Samaritan* has *paft* by, and had *pittie* on her ; *and bound up* her *Sores, and powred Oyl into* her *Wounds.* And by that means faved her from perifhing in her mifery ; And thus fhe has been *troubled on every fide, but yet not diftreffed : perplexed, but not to defpair ! perfecuted, but yet never forfaken ! caft down, but yet not deftroyed ! Thus many have been the afflictions of the* poor Church Militant of Chrift in this world, but *ftill the Lord hath delivered* her *out of all !* Alas fhe has alwaies had her converfation in this world, *in much wearinefs and painfulnefs, in hunger and thirft, in cold and nakednefs, in ftripes and imprifonments, in labours, in watchings, in faftings, in perills of waters, in perills of robbers, in perills by the Heathen, in perills among falfe brethren* : She has been *reviled,* when fhe has *bleffed !* fhe has been *defamed,* when fhe has *entreated !* yea fhe has *been made as the Filth and Off-fcouring of all things.* But yet behold *he that has carried* her *down to the Grave,* has *brought* her *back again !* and has never *fuffered the gates of Hell to prevail againft* her. *When her Children have forfaken the Law of their God, and not walked in his judgments, then he has vifited their Tranfgreffions with a rod, and their iniquity with ftripes* : although as for *his loving kindnefs he never hath utterly taken it from them, nor fuffered his faithfulnefs to fail.*

Go to now therefore ye that boaft of the vifibility of the true Religion in all Ages ! Com e, let us reafon together, and fee whether

in

in truth and reality, this external Pomp and glory has been alwaies an inseparable companion of the Church !

Let us first look back into the old World before the *Floud* (which yet we have sufficient ground to believe to be as well peopled as ever it has been since) and see how many more we can finde then *Abel*, *Seth*, and *Enoch* , who had the Characters of men of uprightness. Yea, on the contrary, we have God himself complaining (before whom all things are naked, and open, and who certainly had reason to know the number of his faithful ones) That *all flesh had corrupted his way upon the earth* , yea, there was only found *Noah* and his Family that were accepted by him ! which certainly was no more to the whole world, then a small dust to the Ballance, or the Grape-gleaning to the Vintage.

Again, after the *Floud*, when the Face of the Universe was more cleanly washt from its filthiness, we finde no other Church for several hundreds of years, then what was confined within the single Families of the Ancient *Patriarchs*. Yea when the Common-wealth of the *Jews* was very much setled in all appearance, it was not certainly for nothing that the good Prophet *David* cryed out, *Help Lord for there is not one godly man left , for the faithfull are failed from among the Children of men*. Where, I pray you was the glory of the *Jewish* Church , when *they were for a long season without the true God, and without a teaching Priest, and without a Law* ?

Thou that boastest of the constant visibility of the Church,

Dic quibus in terris,& eris mihi magnus Apollo ;

Tell me what was the external glory thereof, when *Uriah the Priest built an Altar according to all that King* Ahaz *had sent to* Damascus. And when the *Children of* Israel *walked in the Statutes of the Heathen,* and *built them high places in all their Cities , from the Tower of the Watchmen, to the fenced City*, and *set them up Images*, and *Groves in every high Hill*, and *under every green Tree, and made them Molten Images*, and *worshipped all the Host of Heaven, and served* Baal, *and caused their Sons and Daughters to pass through the fire, and used Divinations and Inchantments, and sold themselves to doe evil in the sight of the Lord, and to provoke him to anger. When they shut up the doors of the Porch, and burnt not Incense in the holy place* ?

I beseech you where was the visibility of the Church, (if ye can answer me, and set your words in order before me) then when the Prophet *Elias wrapped his face in a Mantle , and went out and stood at the entering of the Cave* , and made such bitter complaints before the Lord, *That the Children of* Israel *had forsaken his Covenant , thrown down his Altars, and slain his Prophets with the sword, and he, even he alone was left, and they sought his life to take it away* ?

Again, what means the Prophet *Isaiah*, when he cryes out in so lamentable, and as it were a despairing manner , *The whole head is sick, and the whole heart is heavy, from the sole of the Foot , even unto the head, there is nothing whole therein*. Neither doe I believe that the good Prophet *Jeremiah* was distracted, or besides himself, when

Gen.6.12.

Psal.12.1.

2 Chron.15.3

2 King.16.11

2 King.17.8, 9,10,16,17.

2 Chro.29.7.

1 King.19. 13,14.

Isa.1.5,6.

when he used those strange expressions in the following words, *Run ye to and fro by the streets of* Jerusalem, *and behold now and know, and seek in the broad places thereof, if ye can finde a man that executeth judgment, and seeketh the truth.* Again, what ails the Prophet *Micah* to complain so grievously, *Woe is me, for I am as the Summer gatherings, and as the Grapes of the Vintage. There is no cluster to eat, the good man is perished out of the Earth, they all lye in wait for blood, every man hunteth his neighbour with a Net.* Nay, have we not the Lord himself complaining by the mouth of his Prophet, that he sought *for a man to stand in the Gap before him in the Land, that he should not destroy it, but he found none.* *Jer.* 5.1.
Micah 7. 1,2.
Ezek. 22.30.

To all this we may adde the divers bitter complaints throughout the whole Book of Psalms, touching the sad and declining condition of the Church, in one place, That *the Lord himself looked down from Heaven upon the children of men, to see if there were any that did understand and seek after God :* And that *they were all gone aside, and that there was none that did good, no not one !* In another place, That *they had cast fire into his Sanctuary, and burnt up all the Synagogues of God in the Land.* In another, That *the Heathen were come into his Inheritance, and had laid* Jerusalem *on heaps.* That *they had given the dead bodies of his Servants to be meat to the Fowls of Heaven, and the flesh of his Saints unto the Beasts of the Earth.* That *they had shed their bloud like water round about* Jerusalem, *and that there was none to bury them,* and that the Remnant of his servants *were become a reproach to their neighbours, and a scorn to them that were round about them.* In another place, That *the hedges of his Vine that he had brought out of* Egypt *were broken down,* That *the Boar out of the wood had wasted it, and the wild Beast of the Field devoured it.* In another, That *they sat down and wept* (as they had good reason) *by the waters of* Babylon, *when they remembred* Sion. *Psal.*14.2,3.
*Psal.*74. 7, 8.
*Psal.*79.1,2,3.4.
*Psal.*80.8,12.13.
*Psal.*137.1.

I beseech you what means such expressions, if the Sun of the visible Church had not at least seemed in those Intervalls to have been Eclipsed.

True it is, that the Lord had even in those daies many of his chosen servants, whom he reserved in secret, and covered with the skirts of his Garment, as he did those seven thousand in *Israel* in the daies of *Elias*, whom neither their enemies, nor the Prophet himself were able to discern. But alas, what doth this speak to external pomp and glory of the Church, when as both Princes and people had corrupted their waies, and the very Temple was now become a meer sink of sin and prophanation. 1 *Kin.*19.18.
*Rom.*11.4.

Neither is it here sufficient for the Adversaries of the Truth to answer us, that these were only the Old Testament Dispensations, and so shuffle all the abovesaid instances out of doors, let me tell you, that there are many and large promises under the Old Testament for the lasting of the *Jewish* Church, till the coming of *Messias*, as there are in the New, for the *Evangelical Churches* duration till the end of the world.

For

For example, it is faid of *Jerufalem* (which faving the Babylonifh Captivity was the only fet place of Gods eminent Worfhip and publick Service) *This is my reft for ever, here will I dwell, &c.* And in another place, *In Jerufalem fhall be my name for ever.* The like whereof I hardly believe is promifed to the City of *Rome* in any part from the firft of *Matthew*, to the laft of the *Revelation.*

But however for a better fatisfaction of the unintereffed Reader, it will not be amifs to examine a little this Queftion, and beat up the Quarters of our gainfaying Adverfaries throughout the New Teftament, as we have already through the Old.

Upon the Birth of our Saviour, is it not faid, That *all Jerufalem was troubled at it?* Had not *Annas* and *Caiphas* the higheft Spiritual promotions? VVere not *the Scribes and Pharifees Hypocrites in the uppermoft feats in the Synagogues?* VVere they not men of this gang

who had the Law and the Altars, and all the Sacred things in their cuftody? Yea, was not the Priefthood long before bought and fold? And not long after that, is it not faid that the *Jews had agreed that if any did confefs that Jefus was the Chrift, he fhould be put out of the Synagogue?* You that are fo fharp fighted to difcern things that are not, noi ever were, tell me of whom do ye finde mention in thofe days, upon whom you can righteoufly faften the Character of Saints and Believers, unlefs *Simeon* and *Anna*, who had each of them one foot in the grave? As alfo *Jofeph, Mary, Zachary, Elizabeth*, and a few *Shepheards in the field* abiding in their Tents.

When our bleffed Lord and Saviour had felected out his Apoftles, he himfelf ftiles them by the name of *a little Flock.* At his death, when his Body *hung on the Crofs*, and *his Difciples were all fled*, alas, *Jofeph and Mary and a few women* were all the faithfull that appeared then upon the earth.

After the daies of Chrift and his Apoftles, during the ten bloudy Perfecutions, till the converfion of the Emperour *Conftantine*, for the fpace of three hundred years, we fhall finde no other then an invifible vifibility of the Church.

Again, when the *Arrian* perfecution began, how fad a pofture was the Church then in, when St. *Jerome* fticks not to fay, that after the Council at *Rimini, all the world groaned and wondered to fee it felf become Arrian.* And *Athanafius* in his Epiftle *ad vitam folitariam agentes*, gives but a mournfull defcription of the calamity of his time, Ποία ἐκκλησία νῦν + χεισὸν μετ' ἰλδ.Ͻεριας ωρσκωνῖ; ἐάν τε ͵β ἐυσεβὴς ἧ κινδυνεύει, &c. ἐάν θ' ὑποκρίνηται ρο᷉εῖται, &c. *What Church* (faies he) *is there now a dayes that worfhips Chrift with Liberty? for if any make a profeffion of piety, he is thereby expofed to danger, &c.*

And in another place of the fame Epiftle, 'Ω τίς ἂν ᷍ψοῖτο τύτων λογογεⳇᷳ; τίς ἀπαͻγτίλη ταῦτα εἰς ͵ψοιὰν ἐτέϸας; τίς ἄϸα πιστεύσειεν ἀκύων ὅτι ωαδ'όντες οἱ εἰκⱦαϰὰς ὑπηϸεσίας μόγις πιςδιόͻⱱοι, ὕτοι νῦν τῆς ἐκκλησίας κατάϸχυσι. *O who is able to write this Hiftory? or who is he that will undertake to declare thefe things to Pofterity? Who can poffibly believe that thofe Eunuchs who are not capable of the charge of a private Family, fhould come to be Governeurs of the Church!* St. *Am-*

St. *Ambroſe* likewiſe in a certain Oration of his, makes a bitter complaint in the following words. *Whither can I turn me to finde a place that is not fill'd with mourning and tears, when they begin to caſt out of doors the Catholique Prieſts, and to put to the ſword all thoſe who make reſiſtance, &c.* It were not difficult to run through all Ages and Generations, and to ſhew that very oft the Church has been brought to a very low ebb. I ſhall only content my ſelf with this one, which is confirmed by our Adverſaries themſelves, I mean in the ninth and tenth Centuries, during which time the corruption of the Church was ſo great, that *Baronius* himſelf calls the year 900. the true *Iron Age* as to the ſterility of goodneſs, and the *Leaden Age* as to the abundance of heavy and enormous crimes, and alſo gives the reaſon thereof, in the following words, *Ne quid ſcandali puſillus animo patiatur, ſi quando videre contigerit abominationem deſolationis in Templo.* Baronius An.

Leaſt any of the weak ones ſhould be troubled, when he ſhould ſee the abomination of deſolation ſtanding in the holy place. And again, *Intruſi in Cathedram Petri, ſolium Chriſti, tum homines monſtroſi, vitâ turpiſſimi, moribus perditiſſimi, uſq; quaq; fœdiſſimi.* Now a dayes there are thruſt into the Chair of Peter, the Seat of Chriſt himſelf, even monſtrous men, of a moſt baſe life, and moſt corrupt manners, and altogether filthy And *Genebrard* in his Chronicle of the year 907. complains that *this Age had been unhappy, that for the ſpace of* 150. *years, about* 50. *Popes had degenerated from their Anceſtors, being rather Apotacticks and Apoſtates, then Apoſtolicks.* Wherefore I ſhall conclude this point with the ſame argument for our Religion that *Baronius* brings for his in his Annals 897. 5. *Licèt ſit ſemper idem Sol, eademq; Luna ſemper exiſtat, interdum tamen obice rubium, eadem ſydera minus lucent, & eclipſibus intercurrentibus redduntur obſcura. Noli igitur nimis rigidé in Apoſtolicâ ſede majora requirere, quam quæ in ſymbolicis ſignis fuerint divinitùs demonſtrata.* Although the Sun and the Moon be alwaies the ſame, yet ſometimes by the interpoſition of Clouds, the very ſame Starrs ſhine with leſs ſplendour, and by the Eclipſes become more obſcure. Doe not therefore with overmuch rigour exact more from the Apoſtolical See, then what has been divinely revealed in the Symbolicall Signs. So ſay I, doe not, O ye profeſſours of the Roman Catholick Religion, exact more of our Religion then what *Baronius* pleads for yours. Genebrard in his Chronicles. Baron. An. 897.

Neither are theſe things at all diſconſonant to the alluſions and Predictions of the New Teſtament: Mark I pray you what a tacit deſcription *Chriſt* himſelf gives of the faithful ones under the notion of his own perſon. *I was an hungred, I was thirſty, I was a ſtranger, I was naked, I was ſick, and I was in priſon.* So again he deſcribes them in another place, to be ſuch as have no other habitation nor abode then *in the high waies and Hedges?* And in a third he ſeems to deſcribe the men of the world by a *certain rich man clothed in purple and fine Linnen, and fairing deliciouſly every day,* And the Saints by a *certain Begger lying at the Rich mans Gates full of Sores, and the Dogs licking the ſame.* Neither does he only ſpeak theſe things in Parables, but alſo Math. 25. 35, 36. Matth. 22. 9. Luke 16 19; 20, 21.

also in plain terms he forewarns his Disciples upon several occasions, *That whosoever would come after him*, they must of necessity *take up his Cross and follow him.* And that upon this account *he sent them forth as Lambs among Wolves :* He told them plainly that they *should be delivered up to be afflicted, and to be killed, and should be hated of all Nations for his Names sake* ; (which expression intimates an universal defection from the true Religion) yea, that *the time should come, that whosoever should kill them, should think to do God an acceptable Service.*

This was the Language of our blessed Saviour, and this was the Language of his Disciples after him, as appears by many Pathetical expressions of theirs to this purpose, wherein they labour to fortifie all believers against suffering times, exhorting them *not to think it at all strange concerning the fiery tryal* ; As likewise minding them, that *all that will live godly in Christ Jesus must suffer persecution :* and that if *in this Life only we had hope , we were of all men most miserable.*

By this time, I hope the ingenuous Reader is fully perswaded, that misery and affliction is much rather the mark of the true Church, then outward glory and prosperity, according to that saying of *Athanasius* τὸ μὲν τύπτεσχ χεισιανῶν ἴδιόν ἔςι. And by consequence that the Religion which both the poor *Waldenses* and we profess, has much better evidences for its truth and Antiquity, then that of our Adversaries and Antagonists. And if after all we should as boldly demand of them , as they have done of us , where was their Religion during the first six Centuries ; I say, if we should demand of them *where their Church then fed ,and where she caused her Flocks to rest at noon ?* I much fear they would be extreamly confounded,and not able to give a categorical & distinct answer. Certainly it was not on *mount Sion,* but rather on *Mount Gerazim,* and *Mount Seyr* , in the Pastures of Paganisme, Judaisme, &c. whence they had raked and scraped together whatsoever the Rabble of the *Pharisaical* Tribe had formerly brought into the *Synagogue* , or the vain Philosophy of the *Greeks* into the *Academy.*

The Pope had his *Holiness* given him by that *Parricide Phocas,* who permitted *Boniface* to assume the Title of *Universal Bishop,* and by vertue of his Commission to pardon sins, and give Laws to mens Consciences in the year 606. Though *Gregory* his Predecessour had declared openly, that whosoever should presume to arrogate the title of *Universal Bishop,* was the forerunner of *Antichrist* ; see his own very words, *Ego fidenter dico, quisquis se universalem sacerdotem vocat,vel vocari desiderat, in elatione suâ Antichristum præcurrit, quia superbiendo se cæteris præponit.* And in another place *in isto scelerato vocabulo consentire , nihil est aliud quàm fidem perdere.*

Their *Adoration of Images* was only established in the second *Nicene Councel* in the year 767.

As for their Doctrine of *Transubstantiation,* I am bold to say that there passed more then 1200. years before there was any mention

Mark 8. 34.

*Matth.*24.9.

John 16.2.

1 *Pet.*4.12.
2 *Tim.*3.12.
1 *Cor.*15.19.

Athan Ep. ad
Vit. sol. agent.
ex Officin.
Commel.
cɔɔɔc cum
gr. & priv. P.
647. D.

Greg.lib.6.ep.
30.

Ibid. cp 39.

tion made thereof. For all agree in this, that was only brought in by *Innoc.* 3. in the Council of *Lateran* in the year 1215. where was eſtabliſhed the following Article, *Chriſti corpus et ſanguis in Sacramento Altaris ſub ſpeciebus panis et vini veraciter continentur, tranſubſtantiatis pane et vino in corpus Chriſti.*

The *Communion under one ſpecies* onely was not before the *Council of Conſtance,* where in the 13. Seſſion they deprived the people of the *Cup,* contrary to Chriſts Inſtitution.

It was onely in the year 1220. that Pope *Honorius* ordained, *That in the celebration of the Maſs the Hoſt ſhould be lifted up, and the people do low obeyſance.* The which ſuperſtition *Gregory* 9. his ſucceſſor skrewed a peg higher, and made a Decree, that *at the lifting up the Hoſt, a Bell ſhould be rung, and that all thoſe which heard the ſound thereof ſhould fall down upon their knees, and lifting up their hands towards Heaven, worſhip the ſame.*

Their *Doctrine of Purgatory* never paſt for an Article of Faith before the Council of *Florence,* under *Eug.* 4. in the year 1439.

It was onely in the *Council of Trent* that it was decreed that their Traditions ſhould be obſerved *pari pietatis affectu, with the ſame pious affection and reverence* with the Holy Scriptures.

The Jeſuit *Coton* confeſſes plainly, That the *Canonization of Saints* began 800. years after Chriſt.

Coton Inſtitut. Cath. l. 1. ch. 18.

Laſtly, the pretended Empire of the *Pope,* which his Paraſites the *Jeſuits* (who may well be ſo called from the Sorcerer Bar-Jeſus) would fain give him over all the Kings and Emperours of the Earth, not onely to excommunicate them, but alſo to diſpenſe their Subjects from the Oath of fidelity. Which is much contrary to the ſtile of the ancient Biſhops of *Rome,* who ſtiled themſelves the Emperours *Humble and obedient Servants,* and ſubmitted to their Laws. And is quite of another ſtrain then that profeſſion of *Tertullian* in the name of the Chriſtians, *Colimus Imperatorem ut hominem a Deo ſecundum, et ſolo Deo minorem. Ipſe omnibus major eſt, dum ſolo Deo minor eſt.* And that of *Optatus* likewiſe in his 3. Book, *Super Imperatorem non eſt niſi ſolus Deus, qui fecit Imperatorem.* The foundation of this tyranny was indeed laid in the 8. and 9. Century, but it brake forth by the fury of Pope *Hildebrand,* who deprived the *Emperour Henry* of His Empire, and abſolved his Subjects of their fidelity. And then it alſo was, that the ſame who took on him the name of *Greg,* 7. aſſembled a Council at *Rome* in the year 1076. where among other Articles, theſe were concluded ; That there was no other name under Heaven but that of the Pope. That *no Book was Canonical without the Popes Authority. That all Kings ought to kiſs the Popes feet. That the Pope ought to judge all the world, and to be judged by none. That he had power to depoſe Kings, Emperours,* &c. Nay I have horrour to blaſpheme the blaſphemy of *Bellarmine* in this particular, *That He may make that which is ſin to become no ſin, and that which is no ſin to become ſin.*

Tertull. ad Scap. c. 2.

Bell. contr. Barcl. c. 13.

Thus were it very eaſie to demonſtrate the diſproportion of the Pret. Cathol. Religion with that of the Primitive Church in an infinity

finity of points, which the Ring-leaders thereof have foifted in from time to time, And by confequence that their Religion compared with ours is but a thing of yefterday, and no ways derived either from the Doctrine or Practice of Chrift and his Apoftles.

The truth is, I deny not but they may challenge fome fort of Antiquity for their Religion, and that a great part of their Traditions have been a long time practifed in the world, whereby they have beguiled many millions of poor fouls: Which I cannot better exprefs then by that fubtilty of the *Gibeonites*, who when they had defigned to betray the men of *Ifrael*, and to make them believe that they came

Jefh. 9. 4,5,6.

from a very far Country, *They did work wilily, and made as if they had been Ambaffadours, and they took old Sacks upon their Affes, and Wine-bottles old and rent, and bound up, and old Shooes clouted upon their feet, and old garments upon them, and all the bread of their provifion was dry and mouldy; And* in this pofture, *They went to* Jofhua *unto the Camp at Gilgal, and faid unto him, and to the men of Ifrael, We be come from a far Country, now therefore make ye a League with us.* So fay I, Thefe *Gibeonitifh* Catholiques have taken the *old Sacks of Jewifh Ceremonies*, and the *old clouted Shooes of Paganifm*, together with *the dry and mouldy bread of the Arrian Herefie*, whereof they have made a Medley of Religion; And now to the end that they may daily gain more and more Profelytes, they pretend with confidence, yea and would fain make us believe, that thefe their traditions are derived from *Chrift* and his Apoftles, whereas the contrary is as clear as the Noon-day.

Whence is it that *Pope John* 22. affumed the title of *Dominus Deus nofter*, as in the following Verfes ——

Oraclo vocis mundi moderaris habenas,
Et meritò in terris diceris effe Deus,

If not from *Domitian?* Who as *Sueton* obferves, was ftiled *Dominus Deus nofter*, in the very fame terms.

The Adoration of the Pope, and kiffing his foot.

From whence, if not from the Pagans, comes *the Adoration of the Pope*, and the *kifsing his foot*, as alfo his being *carried upon mens fhoulders?* For even they alfo after the election of their *Soveraign Pontifex*, clothed him with their *Pontificalibus*, and put a *Mitre* upon his head, and worfhipped him, as *William du Choul* obferves in his difcourfe con-

William du Choul in his difcourfe concerning the Religion of the Ancient Romans. pag. 337. Polyd. Virg. 4 Book de Invent. Rer. cap. 10.

cerning the Religion of the Ancient *Romans*. In like manner for the ceremony of *kifsing his foot*, *Polyd. Virg.* obferves that the very fame was done to the *Pontifex* of the *Pagans*, and that fome Emperours caufed the fame honour to be done them; as for Example; *Caligula* thruft out his left foot to *Pompeius Pennus* (a perfon of honour, and invefted with the *Confular* dignity) and made him *kifs the fame*. As likewife *Dioclefian* fet forth a folemn Edict; whereby he commanded all men of what quality or degree foever, *That they fhould fall down before him and kifs his feet.*

The Canonization of Saints.

Again as for the *Canonization* and *Invocation of Saints*, what is it but purely in imitation of the Heathen's *Dii minorum gentium?* to whom they dedicated their Temples, erected their Altars, confecrated their Images, committed the protection of their Kingdoms, Commonwealths,

monwealths and families, addreſſed their prayers and ſupplications, &c. *Lud. Vives* cannot hold from confeſſing ſo much in his learned Comment upon *Auguſt. de Civ. Dei. Multi Chriſtiani in re bonâ plerumque peccant, quòd Divos, Divaſque non aliter venerantur quam Deum, nec video quòd ſit diſcrimen inter eorum opinionem de Sanctis, et id quod Gentiles putabant de Diis ſuis.* h. e. *Many Chriſtians do for the moſt part err in a good matter, becauſe they worſhip the Saints of both Sexes no otherwiſe then God ; I do not ſee that there is any difference between their opinion concerning the Saints, and that which the Heathen conceived touching their Gods.*

Thus Idolatry remains ſtill upon the ſtage of the world, but it is preſented under other diſguiſes. *Janus* has ſurrendred his charge of the Gates and Keyes of Heaven to St. *Peter!* *Lucina* has ſurrendred her care of women in child-bearing to St. *Margaret!* St. *George on horſe-back* has ſupplanted *Mars*, as to conducting warlike Affairs! St. *Margaret* ſucceeds *Minerva* for the Sciences! The Phyſitians have renounced *Æſculapius*, and received St. *Coſme*, and St. *Damian!* And thus every place, perſon and family, have ſome Saint or other for their *Guardian*, or *Tutelary Diety.*

Demand of *William du Choul*, whether or no your *Nuns*, or Religious Virgins, be not the ſame with the *Virgines veſtales* among the Heathen? And the Ceremonies to which they were obliged, the very ſame with yours?

Whence comes that cuſtome of whipping and laſhing your ſelves on *Good Friday*, &c. if not from the Prieſts of *Baal*, 1 *King*. 18. *Who cut themſelves with Knives and Lances till the bloud guſhed out upon them?* Or from the Prieſts of the Goddeſs *Cybele*, of whom *Apuleius* makes mention, who *whipped themſelves till the very bloud ran down*. I am ſure you have not learned it from the Holy Scriptures, neither have you any command of God for it, who has commanded to the contrary, *Lev*. 19. 28, *Ye ſhall not make any cuttings in your fleſh, nor print any marks upon you.*

The Heathens of old, in the buildings of their Temples, placed them towards the *Eaſt*, and ſo likewiſe their Altars, as *Polyd. Virg.* obſerves ; And do not ye the ſame?

From whence have you received the Doctrine of *Purgatory*, if not from the ſame Source and Fountain? *Plato* in his Dialogue of the ſoul intituled *Phædon*, ſpeaks plainly in this point, as alſo *Euſebius* obſerves in his laſt Chapter of his 11. Book, *de præp. Evang*. οἱ μ̈ ἂν δόξωσι μέσως βεβιωκέναι ὅτι τῦτον ἀφικνῦνται εἰς λίμνͅ, ⁊ ἐπ̈ οἰκῦσί ⸆ ⁊ καθαρόμͅοι νῦν ⸆ ἀδͅικημάτων διδόν͠ες δίκας ἀπολύονται. *Thoſe who have lived indifferently well, come to this Pool and abide there, And after they have been purged, and ſuffered the penalties of their ſins, they are diſmiſſed ;* Virgil likewiſe perſues this point in the 6. Book of his *Æneads.*

——— ——— *Aliæ panduntur inanes*
Suſpenſæ ad ventos, aliis ſub gurgite vaſto
Infectum eluitur ſcelus, aut exuritur igni.

It is more then clear that the Heathens were the firſt that kindled the

L. Vives Com. upon Aug. de C.D. l.8. c. 27.
Baſil. 1522.

The Nuns or Religious Virgins.
Will. du Choul. pag. 236.

The Papiſts Diſcipline on Good Friday, &c.
1 Kings 18.
Apuleius.

Levit. 19. 28.

The building their Temples toward the Eaſt.
Polyd. Virg. l. 5. c. 9.
Purgatory.

Euſeb. l. 1. de præp. Evang.

Virg. 6. Æn.

Bell. de Purg.
l.1.c.11.

Their Prayers
for the Dead.

Polyd.Virg.
lib.6. c. 10.

Decr. Grat.
dist.44.Can.
Nullus.
Their Feasts.

Their Feast of
Candles.

Tertull. contra
Marcion.
Their Lent-
Masques.
Their Roga-
tions and Pro-
cessions.
Their Agnus
Dei.

Baronius An.
Tom.1.An.56.

What the Pa-
pists have bor-
rowed of the
Jewish Cere-
monies.

the fire of *Purgatory* in the world ; And the truth is, *Bellarmine* himself confesses so much, when he proves the Doctrine of *Purgatory* from the testimony of *Plato*, *Cicero* and *Virgil*.

If we do but consider a little your Prayers and Services for the dead, we shall finde that you are as much beholding to the Heathen for them, as any of the former (as the same *Polyd. Virg.* observes:) For as the Heathen had very solemn services performed the ninth day after their friends decease, and entertained the Priests of their false Gods with much magnificence ; Even so do you seven days after the decease of yours, ye solemnize the Service of trespasses, and entertain the Priests so liberally, that there was once a *Canon* made, whereby Priests are prohibited to be drunk, when they are called to such meetings.

From whence have you the Institution of all your Feasts ? True it is, many of them are in imitation of those of the *Jews*, but your own Doctors will not deny,but that a great part of them are borrowed from the *Heathen*.

The *Feast of Candles*, or the *Purification of our Lady*, had it ye not from the *Februal Ceremonies* of the *Romans*, which was the *Feast of the Purification* of *Februa* Mother to *Mars* ? from whence comes also that word *Februarius*, i. e. purging the Reins, as is manifest in one of the Books of *Tertullian contra Marcionem*.

The *Lent-Masques* with other fopperies of that nature, have succeeded the *Bacchanalia* and *Saturnalia*.

The *Rogations and Processions* , &c. have succeeded the *Ambanalia*.

Your *Agnus Dei* hanging on the neck, is no other then in imitation of the Heathens, who were wont to hang little Balls or Bottles upon the necks of their Children, to preserve them from enchantments, and sorceries, as *Baronius* himself grants in his *Annals*.

I should never make an end, if I should run over all the instances that might be brought upon this subject ; and therefore what I have already said, shall suffice : Now let us see whether they have not been as bold with the ancient *Jewish* Ceremonies, which yet notwithstanding have been long since abolished by *Christ* himself. True it is, that he hath *rent the veyl of the Temple*, and also declared by the mouth of his *Apostles*, That the *shadow* ought to give place to the *substance*, and the *figures* and *types* to the real truth, That it was not reasonable to light the Candles of the *Law*, when the light of the *Gospel* shined so bright, by the *rising of the Sun of righteousness*. But however there has been no hindring the Devil from foisting in several things into the Church, and to attire the Christian Religion after the *Mosaique* Mode, thereby to diminish the vertue of the *Cross of Christ*, and corrupt the simplicity of the Gospel. Regard I pray you the *Roman* worship, and see if it does not smell of the *Law*, and the ancient *Pedagogie* ! As for example, who is there that when he well observes those huge swarms of your Ceremonies, the glittering Ornaments of your Chappels, and your *Altars*, your great *Wax Candles*, and your *Sacrifices*, your *Salt*, your *Water*, your *Oyl*, with a thousand other devices, that would not
immedi-

immediately think you had revived the *Mofaical* worſhip, or at the leaſt counterfeited the ſame. And thus you will needs rake out of the grave the body of the *Synagogue*, that was ſo glorioufly buried by *Chriſt* himſelf.

In the third and laſt place, if we confider the ancient Herefies which have troubled the Church, we ſhall finde that a great part of your Religion is very near of kind to the moſt of them. Where have you any foundation for your *diſtinction of Meats*, your *regular Faſts*, your *Law for Virginity*, unleſs from the *(a) Montaniſts*, the *Manichees*, the *Encratits*, the *Tatiens*, and the *Euſtatiens*, which both taught and practiſed the ſame thing ? To whom will you attribute your *Monaſtique vows*, if not to the *(b) Euchetes*, and *Pattalorintehites*, and thoſe whom they call *Apoſtoliques*, and *Nudipedales* ? To whom do ye owe the *Service* of *Angels*, of the *Bleſſed Virgin*, and of the *Croſs*, if not to the *(c) Angelicks*, the *Collyridians* and the *Staurolatres* ?

It is from the *(d) Carpocratians* and the *Baſilidians* that ye have received the *uſe of Images* ! From the *(e) Oſſenians* the unknown language of your ſervices ! From the *(f) Cathares* the prefumption of your *merits, and works of ſupererogation*! From the *Pelagians* and the *Demipelagians* your *Free-will*, the *perfection of Righteouſneſs*, and the *exaltation of Nature* above *Grace*. From the *(g) Manichees* and *Nazarens* the prohibition of the *Cup in the Sacrament* of the Lords Supper and Communion under one *ſpecies*. From *(h) Simon the Magician* that infamous Simony, which is practiſed in the diſtribution of your *Eccleſiaſtical* charges, infomuch that *Durand* complains openly, *Simoniam regnare in Eccleſiâ Rom. ac ſi nullum eſſet peccatum.* And *Bapt. Mantuan, de Calamit. ſuorum temp. l.* 3. does the like.

————— *Venalia nobis*

Templa, Sacerdotes, Altaria, Sacra, Coronæ,
Ignis, Thura, Preces ; Cælum eſt venale, Deuſque.

From the *(i) Marcionites* and *Pepuſians* it is that you have learned the *baptizing of Women*. From the *(k) Cnoſimachi* the praiſe of Ignorance, the exaltation of blinde Obedience ; And in ſum, of all the Hereticks in General, the neceſſity of Traditions, and the decrying of the Scriptures, as not ſufficient to Salvation.

See now I pray the goodly Antiquity of your Church, after that you have with ſo much confidence demanded of Us where was Ours before *Luther*, and tell me if it be not a thing meerly borrowed, partly of the *Jews*, partly of the Heathens, and partly of the Ancient Hereticks, whoſe corrupt Doctrines and Practices you have compounded together, and made up the *Myſtery of Iniquity*.

Lo, theſe are the righteous Grounds upon which you have proceeded miſerably to murder and maſſacre ſo many poor innocents, of all Nations, tongues, and people, and amongſt others, the poor *Proteſtants of the Valleys* ! Yea, the Lord knows how many millions of thoſe innocent Lambs you have moſt cruelly ſlaughtered in ſeveral parts of the World, *the ſouls* of whom are now *under the Altar, crying, How long O Lord, holy and true, wilt thou ceaſe to avenge our bloud upon them who*

What the Papiſts have borrowed of the ancient Hereticks.
(*a*) *Epiphan. hær.* 46, 47. *Par.* 1622. *Aug. de hær. c.* 25.
Euſeb. hiſt. l. 5. *c.* 16.
Aug. Ep. 74.
(*b*) *Aug. de hær. c.* 40. *& c.* 68.
(*c*) *Aug. de hær. c.* 39.
Epiph. hær. 79.
Niceph. l. 18. *c.* 54.
(*d*) *Iren. lib.* 1. *c.* 27.
Epip. Hær 27.
(*e*) *Epiph .hær.* 19.
(*f*) *Aug. de bon. perf. l.* 2. *c.* 5. *& de hær.* 7. *c.* 88.
(*g*) *Leo* 1. *ſer.* 4. *de quadrage.*
(*h*) *Act.* 8. 18.
Durand. Tract. de modo celebr. con.
Bapt. Mant. de Calam. ſuor. temp. l 3.
(*i*) *Epiph. hær.* 42.
(*k*) *Damaſc. de hæreſ. fol.* 467. *Pariſiis apud Guil. Chaudiere* 1577.

who dwell upon the earth? It's more then evident that thofe bloudy men are too clearly convinc'd in their mindes and underftandings of the vanity of their Ceremonies, and Superftitions, and know well enough, That fuch like fopperies of themfelves are never able to prevail upon mens confciences, and by confequence they might hazard the lofing and depriving themfelves of the pleafures and profits of this world (which are their chiefeft aym,) if they fhould not endeavour to force their way by fire and fword, as they have always hitherto done; juft like the *Mahometans*, the *Heathens*, and ancient *Hereticks*; Againft the laft of which St. *Hilary* complains in the following words againft the *Arrians*: *Quibus adjuti poteftatibus Chriftum prædicaverunt Apoftoli? &c. Edictis ne Regis Paulus, cum in Theatro fpectaculum ipfe effet, Chrifto Ecclefiam congregabat? Nerone fe, credo, aut Vefpafiano, aut Decio patrocinantibus tuebatur, &c. Cum tanto magis Chriftus prædicaretur, quanto magis prædicari inhiberetur. At nunc, proh dolor, Divinam fidem fuffragia terrena commendant : inopsque virtutis fuæ Chriftus, dum ambitio nomini fuo conciliatur, arguitur: Terret exiliis & carceribus Ecclefia, credique fibi cogit, quæ exiliis et carceribus eft credita : pendet à dignatione communicantium, quæ perfequentium eft confecrata terrore : fugat Sacerdotes, quæ fugatis eft Sacerdotibus propagata : diligi fe gloriatur à mundo, quæ Chrifti effe non potuit, nifi eam mundus odiffet, &c. Neceffe eft in ipfam nos ætatem Antichrifti incidiffe.* What powers did affift the Apoftles in the preaching of Chrift? Did Paul gather a Church unto Chrift under the countenance of a royal Edict, when as he himfelf was made a fpectacle to the world? He defended himfelf (I warrant you) by the patronage of Nero, or Vefpafian, or Decius, &c. when the more he preached Chrift, the more he was forbidden to preach. But now, alas, faith in things Divine is carried by moft voices in the world; and Chrift is reproached, as if he had no power of his own, while his name is fupported by Ambition. The Church terrifieth men with Exiles and Imprifonments, and fo fhe compelleth them to believe in her, who her felf was left expofed to the danger of Banifhments and Bonds. She who was founded under the terrour of Perfecutors, fubfifteth now by the dignity and greatnefs of thofe that hold Communion with her : fhe who was propagated by Priefts in banifhment, now banifheth Priefts: fhe glorieth in being loved by the world, who could not have belong'd unto Chrift, if the world had not hated her, &c. It muft needs be, that we are faln into the very time of Antichrift.*

St. *Athanafius* in like manner obferve that the true Church has always fuffered perfecutions, but it felf has perfecuted none, thereby to force them to embrace their Religion; And that this was the practice of the *Arrians*, the Ecclefiaftick Hiftory affures us! And *Athanafius* himfelf confirms the fame in the following words.

Εἰπάτωσ᾽ ἡμῖν πόθεν ἔμαθον αὐτοὶ τὸ διώκειν. ἀπὸ μὲν ᾖ τῆς ἁγίων ἂκ ἂν εἴποιεν, ἀπὸ δ᾽ τῆ διαβόλε τοῦτο αὐτοῖς περιείλημπται τῆ λέγοντ᾽, Διάξας καταλήψομαι; ᾗ τὸ μ᾽ φεύγῳν ὁ κύει᾽ προσέταξε, ᾗ οἱ ἅγιοι ἔφυγον, τὸ ᾖ διώκειν διαβολικὸν ὅτιν ἀπιχείρημα. i. e.

Let them tell us from whence they learned to perfecute; for, they cannot fay they received this from the Saints, but from the Devil, who faid, I will

Marginal notes:

D. Hilarii Pictav. Epift. contra Arrian. vel. Anxent. lib. pag. 295. Froben. Bafilcæ 1550.

Athan. Apol. de fug. fuâ. latter end pag. 557.

pursue and overtake ; whereas truly the Lord hath commanded to flie, and the Saints have fled, but persecution is a device of the Devil. Again, in his Epistle *ad vit. fol. ag.*

Ath. Ep. ad Vit. fol. ag. lib. 1. pag. 661.

ἡ μυσαρὰ τέτων αἵρεσις, ὅταν ὑπ' αὐτῆς τ̃ ἀληθείας αἰχμωθεῖσα πέσῃ, λοιπὸν, ὃς μὴ δεδύνηται πεῖσαι λόγοις, τέτυς τῆ βία κỳ πληγαῖς κỳ δεσμωτηρίοις ἕλκην δηχρεῖν· γνωείζυσα ἑαυτὴν, κỳ ὅτως, ὡς πάνῖα μᾶλλόν ἐσιν ἢ θεοσεβὴς θεοσεβείας μ̃ γὸ ἴδιον μὴ ἀναγκάζην ἀλλὰ πείθειν, κỳ γὸ ὁ κύειⓈ αὐτὸς ὐ βιαζόμυⓈ ἀλλὰ τῇ προαιρέσι διδὺς ἕλεγε πᾶσι μ̃· Εἴ τις θέλει ὀπίσω μυ ἐλθεῖν, αὕτη παιτελῶς ἀλλοτρία τ̃ θεοσεβείας ὅτι, τὸ ποιεῖν αὐτὴν ἔχειω, ἢ ἐναντία τῦ ΣωτῆρⓈ, ὡς χειρόμαχον, ἡγεμόνα τ̃ ἀσεβείας, διηγεφομένην Κωνσάντιον ὡς αὐτὸν τὸν ἀντίχρισον. h. c.

Filthy and abhominable is the Heresie of these men when it falleth, being put to shame by Truth it self ; then those whom she cannot perswade by reasons, she endeavoureth to draw by force, and stripes, and imprisonments, knowing her self, and so, that she is any thing rather then godly : For truly, it is the property of godlines not to necesitate, but to perswade, even as the Lord himself, not using force, but offering himself with good will, hath said ; If any man WILL *come after me ; whereas she is utterly a stranger to godliness, and knoweth not what she ought to do, besides such things as are contrary to our Saviour, being as a Fighter against Christ, a Ringleader of impiety, and who hath entituled or characterized* Constantius *as it were the Antichrist himself.* And before that in the same Epistle.

Pag. 643.

μᾶλλον ἀπρεπέσερον τὸ βιάζεθι κỳ ἀναγκάζην τὼ μὴ βυλομνύυς, ὅτως ὁ μ̃ διάβολⓈ ἐπεὶ μηδὲν ἀληθὲς ἔχει, ἐν πελέκει κỳ λαξάτηείῳ ἐπιβαίνων καθεσον τὰς θύρας τ̃ δεχομνύων αὐτόν. Ὁ ὁ Σωτὴρ ὅτως ὅτι πρᾷος ἐσι διδάσκη· Εἴ τις θέλει ὀπίσω μυ ἐλθεῖν, ἐρχόμωθον ὁ πρὸς ἕκασον μὴ βιάζεθι· ὐ γὸ ξίφεσιν ἢ βέλεσιν ὐδὲ, διὰ σερτιωῖ ἡ ἀλήθεα καθαγγέλλεται, ἀλλὰ πειθοῖ κỳ Συμβυλία· ποία ἂν πειθω̃ ἔνθα βασιλέως φόβⓈ· ἢ ποία Συμβυλία ἐν ἧ ὁ ἀντιλέγων τὸ τέλος ἐξοεισμὸν ἔχει ἢ θάνατον ; i. c.

It is a very unbeseeming course to force and compel such as are not willing, for so the Devil who hath nothing of Truth, making his attempts with the Axe and Iron Crow, breaketh open the doors of them that receive him. But our Saviour is so gentle, that he teacheth ; If any WILL *come after me, but that when he cometh to any man the man is not forced: For, Truth is not propagated by Swords or Spears, nor by Souldiers, but by Perswasion and Counsel. What kinde of perswasion therefore is there where there is the fear of a King ? or what Counsel, wherein he who gain-sayeth findes the end to be banishment, or Death ?*

Again, τὸ μὼ τύπῆεθ χρισιανῶν ἴδιόν ἐσι, τὸ ὁ μασίζειν χρισιανὸς Πιλάτυ κỳ Καϊάφα τὸ τόλμημα. i. c.

It is indeed the manner of Christians to be beaten ; but to scourge Christians ; It is the bold act of a Pilate, *or* Caiphas.

And in the same place, *That the* Arrian *Bishops, forasmuch as they persecuted the true Christians, to make them renounce their Religion, were not* ἐπίσκοποι, *Bishops, but* κατάσκοποι *Spies : And that such proceedings against the Church, were* παρόιμιον, κỳ παρασκυὴ τῦ Ἀντιχρίσυ *the Proem and Preparation of Antichrist : And that* Constantius *the Persecutor deserved not the name of a Christian, but was rather,* εἰκὼν Ἀντιχρίσυ, *the Image of Antichrist.*

Pag. 629.

Pag. 663.

Pag. 665.

Du Haillan, *an ancient Historian, and exceedingly renowned among the Papists, describes the horrible butcheries executed by the*

Du Haillan.

Popes

Popes Order againſt the poor *Albigenſes*, having publiſhed the *Croiſade* againſt them, promiſing thoſe who would aſſiſt in this Perſecution, the remiſſion of all their ſins, (as the Hiſtorian *Gaguinus*, and the Catholick *Rouyian*, obſerves,) And likewiſe *Bellarmin, de Notis Eccleſiæ*, amongſt other Bravado's of the *Church* of *Rome*, boaſts, that the *Papal* Army ſlew at one time *An hundred thouſand poor Albigenſes.* And as touching the Maſſacres done in *France* in the year 1572. *Pope Gregory* 13. was not onely the Author of them, but alſo glories in it, as thoſe of whom the Prophet *Ezekiel* ſpeaks, That they *powred it forth upon the top of a rock, and not upon the ground to cover it with the duſt.* This is he, who cauſed his *money* to be *ſtamped* with his own picture and name on the one ſide, and the picture of an *Angel* on the other ſide, holding in one hand a *Croſs*, and in the other a *Sword*, killing a multitude of men and women with this Motto [*Ugonothorum Strages* .] And *P. Matthieu*, although a *Roman* Catholick, yet in one place of his Hiſtory obſerves, that in the war of the Catholick League for the extirpation of the Reformed Religion, Three *Spaniards* made them a *Chappelet* of an hundred *Lutherans* ears, to ſhew their extraordinary devotion.

The aboveſaid *Haillan*, amongſt other horrible cruelties exerciſed againſt the *Albigenſes, Many Prelats* (ſays he) *Knights and others, received the* Croiſade *to go againſt the Hereticks,* the Albigenſes, *with a potent Army, their Enſignes being adorned with the Croſs. They went to beſiege the City of* Beziers, *wherein lived the Lord* Roger, *a famous Abettor of theſaid Hereticks. In the end the ſaid City was taken, and ſixty thouſand of them that were found therein put to the ſword;* The ſame Author likewiſe obſerves, that fifty men of *Caſtelnaudarri* were burned alive : That *Vaur alſo was taken by aſſault, where certain obſtinate Hereticks were burnt, the Captain of the City* Amaulri, *a brave Souldier, hanged, and* 80. *Gentlemen beheaded. Neither was the female Sex at all ſpared!* Girarde *a certain Lady of the ſame City was caſt into a deep Well, and afterwards a multitude of ſtones thrown upon her: In ſum, there was very great cruelty exerciſed in that City.* And a little after, ſays he, *Our forces were a a long time before* Moiſſac, *which at length was taken and great butcheries were there committed. The City of* Thoulouſe *was taken with great ſlaughter of men, where a great number were ſlain by the ſword, and yet a greater caſt into the River, whereof there periſhed above twenty thouſand ;* which is confirmed by *Will.* Brito a Roman Catholick, *Philipidos Lib.* 8.

> *Quam virtus modico ſub tempore Catholicorum*
> *Frangit, et ingreſsi ſexus utriuſque trucidant,*
> *Millia bis triplicata decem* — — —

As alſo by *Paulus Æmilius*, who ſaith, *nè mulieribus quidem temperatum !* to ſhew, That this their cruelty was not un-accompanied with ſuch like ſordid actions committed upon the bodies of the female Sex, The aboveſaid *Sieur de Haillan* in the place formely cited, ſpecifieth, *That ſeveral Prelates, Knights, and others, having received the* Croiſade, &c. *after that they had taken the City of* Beziers, *and exerciſed their cruelty, went from thence to* Carcaſſonne, *whither all the Inhabitants*

of

Marginal notes (left column):

Gaguinus.
Rouyan.
Bellarm. de Notis Eccleſ. pag. 285.

Ezek. 24 7.

Pet. Matth. lib. 1. *pag.* 117.

Du Haillan. Philip. Aug. 2. *lib.* 10. *p.* 824. *Tom.* 1. *Imprim. par. S. Andre. L'an.* 1577.

Will. Brito Philip. l 8.

Paul. Æmil.

Du Haill. Tom. 2. *Phil. Aug.* 2. *Lib.* 10. *p.* 824. *Imprime par S. Andre. L'an.* 1557.

of the Country (*men, women, and children*) had retired themselves, And the City being surrendred, it was concluded by a Treaty, that all that were within, should retire out of the City stark naked, their very privities being uncovered. This *Gagnin*, in his History, also confirms, in these very words ; *Inde abire nudi omnino compelluntur.* Let the ingenuous Reader here judge, whether this were according to the *Chastity* of the *Spouse* of *Christ*, or of her whom St. *John* calls the *great Whore*, and the mother of *Whoredomes*. See the lively Description which *Petrarcha* gives thereof in his Sonnets.

Compend.Rob. Gaguini super Francor. gestis impres.in Offic. Bellovisiana & in inclyto Paris. Gymnas.An. 1504. Ab.Ibib.Aug.lib. 6. fol. 56.

Sonnet. 108.

Fiamma dal ciel sù le tue treccie piova
Malvagia, che dal fiume, e da le giande !
Per l' altrui impoverir se' ricca, & grande !
Poiche di mal oprar tanto ti giova.
Nido di tradimenti, in cui si cova,
Quanto mal per lo mondo hoggi si spande :
Di vin serva, di letti, e de vivande,
In cui lussuria fa' l'ultima prova:
Per le Camere tue, fanciulle, et vecchi,
Vanno tres cando, e Belzebub in mezzo.
Con mantici, col fuoco, et con gli specchi,
Gia non fosti nudrita in piume al rezzo,
Ma nuda al vento, e scalza, fra li stecchi,
Hor vivi si ch'a Dio ne venga'l lezzo.

Sonetti del Petrarcha 108. Stampati in Venetia, per Augustino de Zanni de Portese nel MDxv finito à stampar. à di 20. Maggio.

Sonetto 109.

L'avara Babilonia ha' colmo il sacco ——
D'ira di Dio, et divitii empi, et Rei,
Tanto che Scoppia, et hà fatti suoi Dei,
Non Giove et Palla, ma Venere, et Bacco.

Sonetto 109.

Sonetto 110.

Fontana di dolore —— albergò d'ira !
Schola d'errori ! et tempio de heresia !
Gi' Roma hor Babilonia, falsa et ria,
Percui tanto si piagne, et si sospira.
O fucina d'inganni ! O pregion d'ira !
Ou' el ben more, e'l mal si nutre et cria !
Di vivi inferno ! un gran miracol sia,
Se Christo teco al fine non s'adira :
Fondata in casta, et humil povertate,
Contra tuoi fondator alzi le corna,
Puta sfacciata ! et dove hai posto spene ?
Ne gl' adulteri tuoi, nelle mal nate,

Sonetto 110.

Richezze

Richezze tante? Hor Conſtantin non torna,
Ma tolga il Mondo triſto, ch' il ſoſtenne!

And *Mantuan* the *Carmelite*, in his Verſes touching the calamities of his times, deplores the ſame in the following Verſes.

Mantuan.

—— —— —— *Per oppida ſævit*
Martis opus, Petrique domus polluta fluenti
Marceſsit luxu, nulla hic arcana revelo.
Non ignota loquor! Liceat vulgata referre.
Sanctus ager ſcurris, venerabilis ara cynædis
Servit, honorandæ divum Ganymedibus ædes.
Quid miramur opes recidivaque ſurgere tecta?
Thuris odorati globulos et cynnama vendit
Mollis Arabs, Tyrii veſtes et muricis imbrem,
Indus ebur, croceum Cilices, et Tmolus odorem,
Mel Siculi, ferrum chalybes, tenuiſsima Seres
Vellera, Cretenſes molliſsima vina, Tanager
Pernices mercatur equos. Venalia nobis
Templa! Sacerdotes! Altaria! Sacra! Coronæ!
Ignes! thura! preces! Cælum eſt venale, Deuſque.

But alas! What need we ſearch any further then the *late* bloudy *Maſſacre* to furniſh the Reader abundantly, as touching theſe two points of cruelty and luxury, the like whereof I can hardly perſwade my ſelf can be found in any Hiſtory: Certainly, The ancient *Hereticks,* *Mahometans* and *Pagans,* had they now lived, would have been very much aſhamed to have ſeen themſelves ſo out-ſtript by the bloudy butchers of theſe our days, in the invention of ſo ſtrange and unheard of cruelties! yea ſuch, as *the Lord the righteous judge* will moſt certainly one day repay into the Authors boſome, with as great variety of puniſhments, either in this world, or that which is to come! *Shall not* *God avenge his choſen Elect, that cry day and night unto him?* I tell you, that he will avenge them, and ſhall ſpeedily! Though *the Kings of the* *earth may* for a time *ſet themſelves, and the Rulers take counſel together,* *againſt the Lord, and againſt his Anointed,* yet he ſhall one day *break them* *with a rod of iron, and daſh them in pieces like a Potters veſſel.* Though *the wicked in his pride* may for a time *perſecute the poor,* and though they *may eat up the Saints, as they eat bread, and call not upon the Name of* *the Lord,* yet *when he maketh inquiſition for bloud, he will ſurely remem-* *ber them;* yea *upon the wicked he ſhall rain ſnares, fire, and brimſtone,* *and an horrible tempeſt,* and this ſhall *be the portion of their cup:* when *they ſpring up as the graſs, and flouriſh as the green herbe,* alas! it is, that *they ſhall be deſtroyed for ever! For lo, thine Enemie (O God) for lo, thine* *enemies ſhall periſh; And all the workers of iniquity ſhall be ſcattered,* but *the Righteous ſhall flouriſh like the Palm-tree, and grow like the Cedar in* *Lebanon.*

Moſt certain it is, though it be not a thing ſo commonly taken notice

tice of, that God seldome lets go unpunished the shedding of bloud (especially the bloud of his Saints)even in this world ! and if we search narrowly into History, and trace the foot-steps of Divine Providence, we shall really finde, that few of the eminent and bloudy Persecutors of his Church and people have *gone down to their graves in peace, But God has cast the fury of his wrath upon them, and their end has been miserable. Though their excellency* has *mounted up to the heavens, and their glory to the clouds,* yet they have *perished like their own dung, and their remembrance from off the earth : Their branches above* have been *cut off, and their roots beneath* have been *dried up : their candle* has been *put out,* and the *light* has been *dark in their tabernacles : they have flown away as a dream,* and been *chased as a vision of the night : their eyes* have *seen their own destruction,* and they have *drunk of the wrath of the Almighty : Terrors have made them afraid on every side,* and *brimstone* has been *scattered upon their habitations :* they have been *driven from light into darkness, and chased out of the world.* And thus God *avenges at length his elect, that cry day and night unto him, Though he bear very long* with their Persecutors. That passage in the *Revelation* is exceeding remarkable, When *the voice went out of the Temple to the Angels to pour out the Vials of the wrath of God upon the earth. The first went, and poured out his Vial upon the Earth, and there fell a noisom and grievous sore upon the men which had the mark of the Beast, and upon them which worshipped his image. The second Angel poured out his Vial upon the Sea, and it became as the bloud of a dead man : and every living soul died in the sea. The third Angel poured out his Vial upon the Rivers and Fountains of Waters, and they became bloud. And I heard the Angel of the waters say, thou art righteous O Lord, which art, and wast, and shalt be, because thou hast judged thus. For they have shed the bloud of thy Saints and Prophets, and thou hast given them bloud to drink, for they are worthy.*

But to come more closely to what we have in hand, let us see what has been the end of the famous Persecutors of the Church of *Christ Jesus ! Cain slew his righteous brother Abel,* but what was his end ? He fell into the hands of the living God, and was *cursed from the earth, and became a fugitive and a Vagabond !* yea (which was a thousand thousand times more) he was tormented, and wracked by his own conscience, till such time as he *went to his proper place. Pharaoh dealt cruelly with the Egyptians,* but God dealt as cruelly with him in the end, *overwhelming both him and his,* after ten remarkable plagues, *in the midst of the Red Sea. Ahab* was a most vehement murderer, but he was in the end most miserably slain, yea *the very Dogs licked up his bloud at the Pool of* Samaria *where they also licked the bloud of* Naboth ! Yea, *the Lord brought evil upon him, and took away his posterity, and cut off from* Ahab *him that pissed against the Wall, and him that was shut up and left in* Israel ; *And made his house like the house of* Jeroboam *the son of* Nebat, *and like the house of* Baasha *the son of* Abijah ; *And as for* Jezebel, *the Dogs did also eat her by the walls of* Jezreel.

Antiochus the Noble, was so swollen with anger against the Jews, that he threatned *to make* Jerusalem *their burial place, but the Lord smote him*

Rev. 16. 2, 3, 4, 5, 6.

Gen. 4. 8, 12.

Exod. 14. 27, 28.

1 Kin. 22. 38.
1 Kin. 21. 19.

1 Kin. 21. 21, 22, 23.

2 Kin. 9. 36.

2 Maccab. 9.

him immediately after he had uttered thefe words with an incurable difeafe in his bowels ; And as he was haftning thither he fell from his Chariot, and bruifed his body ; And afterwards the very Worms rofe out of his body, and the filthinefs of his fmell was noifome to all his Army, and he was conftrained to confefs (fays the Story) when he could not abide his own fmell, in the following words. *It is meet to be fubject to God.* And thus the grievous pains of this murderer and blafphemer increafing every moment, at length *he died a moft miferable death in a ftrange Country in the Mountains. Herod the Great* ftunk alive! *Herod Antipas* was miferably confined ! And *Herod Agrippa* was eaten up of Wormes !

Jofeph. Art. l. 17, 19.
12 Acts 23.
Su<rb>et<rb>on. Dion. and other Hiftorians.

Nero.

That grand Perfecutor *Nero,* when he had filled up the meafure of his wickednefs, Not onely all his Provinces revolted from him, but even his own Life-guard forfook him, and in this forlorn condition, as he was flying for his life (being already fentenced to fuffer an ignominious death, as an enemy to the *Roman* Empire) he confeffed to thofe few which bare him company, That *as he had lived a wicked life, fo now he muft dye a wretched death.* And the words were no fooner out of his mouth, but he thruft his Dagger into his throat, with this expreffion, *Ecce fidem*! And that he might not go to Hell without company, the ftory tells us, that there were in thofe days no lefs then thirty thoufand of his faithful and true fubjects, fwept away with the Peftilence.

*Aug. De Civ. Dei,l.*18 *c.*52.
Egefip. l. 3.
*Eufeb. Hift. Eccl.l.*2.*c.*25.

Suet. in Ner. c. 16, 38,40, 42,47,49.
Tacit. An. lib. 15,16,& 17.
Orof.l.7.c.7.

At this time were elected Emperours, *Galba* in *Spain* ; in *Germany Vitellius* ; and *Vefpafian* in *Syria* ; the firft whereof was flain by *Otho,* who afterwards ftab'd himfelf ! The *fecond,* after he had fuffered an ignominious death, had his carkafs thrown into the River *Tiber*! The brethren of the *Third,* together with the *Flavii* his Allies, were burnt alive in the *Capitol* !

Galba.
Tacit. l. 1,2,3, & 4.
Suet.in Galba.
Vitellius.
Suet. in Vitel. c. 17.
Vefpafian.
The judgment of God upon the Jews for perfecuting Chrift.
Matth.27,25.
*Orof. l.*7. *c.*9.
*Jofeph. Belli Jud.l.*7.*c.*16, & 18.

Matth.24,2.

The Jews had indeed a reward for crucifying their *Saviour,* and fuch a one as they themfelves defired ! but what was it ? That *his bloud might be on them, and on their children* ! And indeed they were not bated an ace, as to the performance of what they had bargain'd for, of Divine Vengeance ! there being deftroyed of them in *Vefpafian's* days during that long fiege, no lefs then eleven hundred thoufand fouls by famine and peftilence, and an hundred thoufand of them taken captives, and their goodly City alfo, *Jerufalem,* was burnt down to the ground, according to the prediction of *Chrift,* and the *Prophets*! And as for the remnant of them, who were left alive, with their feed, and their feeds feed, they have been from that time to this, no other then a fcorn and by-word to all Nations ; yea they have been as Vagabonds upon the face of the earth, and in moft places driven from the fociety of men.

Domitian.
*Orof.l.*7. *c.*9.
Suet. in Dom. c. 17,& 23.
Eutrop.
Aurelius.

Victor Trajan.

What was the end of *Domitian, Vefpafian's* fon ? He perfecuted the *Chriftians* without mercy, and was himfelf buried without honour! For he was not onely flain by his own people, but the *Senat* likewife ftrictly commanded, that his very name fhould be blotted out, and all his ftatues thrown to the ground, and broken in pieces.

In the time of *Trajan* the Emperour, the very River *Tiber*, was
fwollen

fwollen with anger againft the *Romans*, for fo much *Chriftian* bloud which they had fpilt, over-flowing in a moft furious manner their goods and houfes! The gilded houfe of *Nero* was turned into afhes! Lightning fell upon the *Pantheon* and burnt the Temple with the Idols! Four Cities in *Afia*, two in *Greece*, and three in *Galatia* were ruined by an horrible Earthquake! *Antiochia* became almoft a ruinous heap! And the whole Empire was punifht with Famine and the Peftilence, as *Orofius* relates.

Orof.l.7. c.12.
Eufeb. in Hift.
& Chronico.
Xiphilin. in
Trajano.
Eutropius.
Caffiodorus.

In the time of the Emperours, *Antonin* furnamed *The True*, and *Lucius*, a great number of Towns and Villages in *Italy*, were depopulated by an horrible plague, and became a meer defolate Wildernefs.

Antoninus
and Lucius,
Orof.l.7. c.15.
& 16.
Capitol.
Lamprid.

The Emperour *Severus* was worfe then his name to the *Chriftians*, but it coft the City of *Rome* three ftrange Civil Wars by *Julian*, *Pefcenius Niger*, and *Claudius Albinus*, which fent an incredible number of thofe murderers to their proper places.

Eufeb.in Chro.
& Hiftor. l.5.
c.1, & 5.
Ammian.
Marcel.
Severus.

Julius Maximinus a famous Butcher of the poor *Chriftians*, had fo often fhown his people the way, that at laft they cut their own Mafters throat, at the fiege of *Aquila*; And that in fuch a rage, that feveral in the Camp were heard to fay, *there ought not any foul of that wicked race (great or fmall) to be left alive.* Whereupon they cut off his head, and the head of his fon *Maximian the younger*, and fixing them upon the ends of their Pikes, fhewed them firft in a publike manner to thofe of that City, and afterwards fent them to *Rome*, where they were burnt with great difdain and mockery.

Orof. l.7.c.17.
Spartianus.
Xiphilin.
Herodian.
Maximinus.
Orof.l.7. c.19.
Capitolin.
Herodian.

What was the end of that wicked *Decius* for all the innocent bloud that he fhed? Hiftorians credibly report, that he was flain by the *Barbarous Scythians*, or *Tartars*, and that his body was immediately after, conveyed away by the *Devil* ('twas but equal, that he who had fuch an intereft in the foul of *Decius*, fhould lay claim to his body alfo!) *Paul Orofius* adds further, and fays, That at that very time there was fuch an horrible Plague throughout the whole *Roman* Empire, that there was neither Province, City, nor Houfe free from it. And indeed thefe and the like judgements upon *Decius*, and his fucceffor *Gallus*, (who was likewife maffacred by *Æmilian*) occafioned St. *Cyprian* to write that excellent *Treatife of Death and Mortality*, which is at this day extant amongft the reft of his Works. In this Treatife, he fpeaks of the Perfecution of *Decius* in the following terms. *We know affuredly, That what we fuffer, will not laft always, but by how much more terrible the perfecution is, fo much more notorious, and terrible fhall be the vengeance. We need not trouble our felves to fearch Antiquity for this truth; the experience of latter times may fuffice, Namely that in one inftant, and that in an admirable manner, the equity of our caufe has appeared by the horrible death of Kings, ruines of States, death of Souldiers, and lofs of Battles!*

Decius.
Orof. l.7.c.21.
Eutrop.l.9.
Sext. Aurel.
Orof.l.4. c.21,
Eufeb.

Gallus.
Eufeb.
Victor.

Cypr. de Mort.

Valerian, the Author of the eighth Perfecution, who rode upon the backs of fo many good men, was at laft fain himfelf to become *Sapores* his foot-ftool, or at leaft, to hold the Reins, when he got on horf-back.

Valerian.
Orof. 7.c.22.

Trebellius Pol-lio in vit.Val. *Eufeb.*

back. And after a long imprifonment in his *Cage*, was at laft by *Sapores* commandment, flead alive, as *Eufebius* writes.

Neither did the judgement of God reft here, but immediately after the Captivity of *Valerian*, the whole Empire was embroiled in a thoufand troubles and diftractions! At one and the fame time, there were no lefs then thirty feveral perfons in feveral places, which took upon them the Title and Authority of *Emperour*! The *Perfians, Germans, Goths, Sarmatians* and others, pillaged and ruined divers Countries! Many Cities bordering upon the Sea-coafts, were fwallowed up! and *Galienus, Valerian's fon,* together with a fon or brother of his, was flain in the City of *Milan.*

Claudius.

Claudius, one of *Valerian's* creatures, and a great Perfecuter of the Church, was afterwards poffeffed with an evil fpirit, which having torn his tongue in pieces, choaked him.

Aurelian. *Eufeb l.7.c.30.* *& in Chronic.* *Orif.l.7. c. 23,* *& 27.* *Vopifcus.* *Eutrop.* *Aurelius.*

Aurelian, when as a Thunderbolt from Heaven falling juft in his way before him, could not reftrain him from his bloudy refolutions againft the Church of *Chrift,* and his poor members, The Lord turned the fword of his own domeftiques againft him, (as fome Hiftorians report) by whom he was flain between *Byzance* and *Heraclea.* Though others fay, that he fell down dead fuddainly, in the very inftant that he was figning a Letter againft the *Chriftians.* A judgement not inferiour to this, befel likewife *Antiochus* one of *Aurelians* Provofts, having

Antiochus.

tortured *Agapetus,* a faithfull witnefs of the truth, fell fuddainly from his judgment feat, crying out in a moft fearfull manner, *My bowels are on fire! My bowels are on fire!* and fo gave up the ghoft.

Dioclefian and *Maximilian.* *Enfeb. Hift.* *Eccl.l.8.c.1,2,* *& 3.* *Orof. l.7.c.25,* *26, 27, 28.*

In the days of *Dioclefian* and *Maximilian,* there were put to death in the fpace of feventeen days, (befides a world of other inhumane ufage) no lefs then 30000. *Chriftians,* and as many more bound in chains, and fetters, and condemned to work in their Mines, and Quarries (torments much refembling the *Galleys* which are at this day ufed by the *Turks!*) yea fome fay, that *Dioclefian* was in fuch a rage againft them, that he put to death his own Wife, becaufe fhe was a *Chriftian. Maximinian* commanded to fet fire on a Church where were twenty thoufand *Chriftians* affembled together, and fo burnt alive every mothers childe of them. The City of *Phrygia* was likewife confumed to afhes with all its inhabitants, not fparing the very Magiftrates, Captains, or Governours under the Emperour, and all becaufe they owned the true doctrine of *Chrift,* and would not yeild to abjure the fame. When they faw this availed nothing for the abolifhment of their Profeffion, they caufed them to affemble by thoufands, and

Eufeb. Hift. *Eccl.l.8.c.18.* *Colonia Allobr.* *excudebat Pet.* *de la Roviere* *CIƆIƆCXII.* *Cum grat. &* *priv.facraCaf.* *Majeftatis.* *Eufeb. Hift.* *Eccl. l. 8.c.16.* *& l.9.c. 8, 9.* *Orof. l.7.c.28.*

putting out each mans right Eye, and burning his left knee with an hot iron, they fent them to work in their Mines. This was the daily work of thofe two Tyrants! But now mark their wages! *Dioclefian's* body being wafted with a violent flux, became as a dry ftick, and the vermin bred in his tongue with fuch a noyfom fmell, that no man durft approach him, and in this manner he departed this life, with horrible blafphemies in his mouth. And as for *Maximinian,* being driven out of *Rome* by his own fon *Maxence,* he fled to *Marfeille,* where he was

hanged

hanged for conspiring the death of his son in Law *Constantin.*

During the persecution above-mentioned, there happened a very great Earthquake in *Tyre* and *Sidon,* where many thousands were slain by the fall of Houses. The like also happened at *Rome,* and in divers other places of *Italy. Flaccus, Provost* of *Spolette,* after he had put to death *Gregory* Bishop of the place, was smitten by God in a very remarkable manner, his soul and his bowels quitting his body at the same time. And *Dioscorus* was smitten to death with a Thunderbolt, soon after he had put to death his own daughter.

Galerius Maximinus that Horf-leech of the *Eastern* Churches, was at last smitten with an incurable disease, his guts being strangely swollen, and the Worms continually creeping out of all parts of his body, insomuch that he became so noysom, that his own very Physicians chose rather to suffer death (as by his special command several of them did) then to abide the stench of his rotten carkass.

His Lieutenant General *Maximinus,* was so enraged against the *Christians,* that he caused their condemnation to be graven in Tables of Brass, and fixed upon Pillars in all the publike places of his Dominions, which caused such a fearfull havock of those poor Churches, that there were numbred in those days no less then eighty thousand Martyrs, who suffered for the name of *Jesus.* At the length, as he had prepared his Army against *Constantin,* and *Lucinus,* and was upon the very point to assault them, he was surprised with such horrible pains in his bowels, that he could take no rest, and ever and anon threw himself against the ground in despairing fits. In the end the extremity of his torment, made him loath both the sight of meat, and the smell of wine, and so his body being by little and little consumed, he closed his eyes, being forced to acknowledge frequently in his sickness, *that it was the just judgement of God upon him for his cruelties.*

Julian the *Apostat,* (President of the *Devils* Privy-Council) was a sworn enemy to the *Christians,* whom he called *Galileans* in derision. The truth is, many Persecutors had done famously, but this surpassed them all! He restored to the *Heathens* all their *Temples,* which *Constantin* had caused to be shut up! He rob'd both the Churches and Ministers of the *Christians* of all those Priviledges which *Constantin* had granted them! He prohibited their Schools, for the instructing of their youth, and wrote himself many Books against their Religion. He confiscated all the goods belonging to their Churches, saying by way of scoff, that *Jesus Christ* had prohibited the *Christians* from *laying up treasures in this world,* and had commanded, *if any took away their Coat, they should give him their Cloak also,* and that they should *suffer all manner of reproaches patiently,* because their *Master* had so commanded them: He caused the Images of *Jupiter, Mars,* and *Mercury,* to be put in the Standard of the Empire, and suffered none to go to the Wars, except they had first done sacrifice to *Idols,* And ordered that no *Christian* should be admitted into any charge whatsoever. He permitted the *Jews* to return to *Jerusalem,* and there to rebuild their *Temple,* (which they would have done, had not Lightning from Heaven

Flaccus Provost of Spolette.

Dioscorus.

GaleriusMaximinus.

Euseb. Hist. Eccl. l.8. c.16, & 17. Oros.l.7. c.28.

Maximinus Lieut. Gen. to Gal. Max. Euseb. Hist. Eccl.l.9. c. 7.

Euseb. Hist. Eccl.l.9.c.10.

Julian the Apostat.

Oros.l. 7. c.30. Amm. Marcel. l. 22. Eutrop. Aurel.

Theodor.Hift.
Eccl. l.3. c.20.
Soz. l.6. c. 1.
Niceph. l.10.c.
34.

Oros.l.7. c. 30.

Greg.Naz. O-
rat.cont. Jul.

ven hindered them, and flew a great number of them.) Having thus fought againſt *Jeſus Chriſt*, he went to make a War with the *Perſians*, ſwearing that at his return he would extirpate all the *Chriſtians* ; But as the Proverb is, *he reckoned without his Hoſt :* For he was ſmitten with a deadly ſtroak, no man knowing whence it came, but the greateſt part thinking that it was rather an Angel then a man. And as he was dying, he took with his hands the bloud that ran down his ſide from his wound, and in deſpight towards *Jeſus Chriſt* once for all, he threw the ſame in a great rage againſt Heaven, with theſe words *O Galilean* (meaning *Jeſus Chriſt*) *thou haſt overcome.* And thus he died moſt deſperately in the 32. year of his age as ſome report, though *Greg. Nazianz.* writes in his Oration againſt *Julian*, That he had heard by ſome, that *the Earth opened her ſelf, and ſwallowed up the carkaſs of this miſerable wretch.*

His Uncle and
Servants.
Theod. Eccl.
Hiſt.l.3. c.11,
& 12.
Niceph.l.10 c.
29.

Sozomene.

The uncle of this *Apoſtat* named alſo *Julian*, having out of ſcorn piſſed upon the Table on which the Chriſtians of *Antioch* uſed to celebrate the *Lords Supper*, and beaten with his Fiſt the Biſhop named *Euzoius*, who reprov'd him for this Villany; was a little afterwards ſeized with a grievous and lothſome diſeaſe in his bowels, inſomuch that he could by no means make Water nor void his Ordure, any otherwiſe then through his filthy mouth, and ſo ended his wicked days. *Sozomene* adds, that his fleſh was corrupted and turn'd into Worms, which never left gnawing his body, till they had conſumed it. In like manner, A certain Treaſurer of *Julian*, ſeeing the Veſſels of this Church of *Antioch*, which were uſed in the adminiſtration of the *Lords Supper*, began to mock, ſaying, *Theſe are the Goblets wherewith they ſerve that ſon of Mary :* But ſoon after all the bloud of his body came out at his mouth in a little ſpace of time, and ſo he died, being indeed worthy to be inſerted among the number of *Apoſtats*, together with his Maſter. As alſo did *Elpidius* a great man in the Court of *Julian* the *Apoſtat*, Who after many blaſphemies uttered againſt *Jeſus Chriſt* in divers manners, and upon divers occaſions, was accuſed of being too highly intereſſed in the Affairs of State, whereupon he was clapt up cloſe priſoner, and there tormented to purpoſe, and at length died an ignominious death. Theſe judgements are deſcribed at large by *Theodoret, Sozomene*, and *Nicephorus*, in their *Eccleſiaſtick* Hiſtories, ſpeaking of *Julian* and his followers.

Elpidius.
Theod.
Sozom.
Niceph.

Valens.

Valens the *Arrian* Emperour, cauſed to be drowned at one time no leſs then fourſcore Miniſters of ſeveral Churches by a ſtratagem, as *Socrates* relates, and this he did about the year of Our Lord 371. *Theodor.* tells us, that he would have forced the *Chriſtians* to become *Arrians*, but was puniſhed accordingly ; For, they ſay, he was wounded with an Arrow in the Battle which he loſt againſt the *Goths*, and thinking to ſave himſelf in a certain little Hut in the field, was there ſurpriſed by his Enemies, and burnt alive.

Socrat. Hiſt. l.
4. c. 16.
Theod.
Sozom. Hiſt.
l. 6. c. ult.
Oros.l.7. c.33.

The Vandals,
Huns, and
Goths.
Evag.l.2. c.13,
14, &c.

It's almoſt incredible, how much *Chriſtian* bloud was ſpilt by the *Vandals, Huns, Goths*, and other ſavage, and barbarous people, within the compaſs of thoſe 80. or an hundred years, wherein they over-ran

Africa,

Africa, and *Europe.* But in the fifth year of *Gilimer* their laſt King, *Bel-liſarius* Lieutenant General to the Emperour *Juſtinian,* diſcomfited, and wholly extirpated them, to their great ignominy and everlaſting confuſion, in the year of Our Lord 533. And likewiſe, during the time of this their tyranny, their Kings and Governours, did not al-ways eſcape the ſtroke of Divine vengeance.

Eucherius the ſon of *Stilicon,* in hopes to be one day made Empe-rour, according to his fathers promiſe, engaged himſelf to the *Van-dals* to ruin and extirpat all the *Chriſtians,* and what was his reward? no other then this! that both he and his father were murdered by the Souldiers of *Honorius.*

Croſcus King of the *Vandals* after *Stilicon,* as he would have beſie-ged *Arles,* was taken priſoner, and after he had been caried openly through all the Cities and places, where he had perſecuted the faith-full, and endured great variety of torment, he ſuffered an ignomini-ous death.

Gunderic was poſſeſſed with an evil ſpirit! in the ſecond year of the Emperour *Valentinian,* and *Theodoſius* the younger.

Hunneric after a good part of his rotten carkaſs had been gnawn by the Worms while he was yet alive, the reſt was torn in pieces by the Devil, as *Sigebert Victor* and *Gregory de Tours* do relate.

Proculus Lieutenant to *Genſeric* ſucceſſor to *Gunderic,* a notorious ranſacker of Churches, and burner of Bibles, grew mad, and having bitten his tongue to pieces, died with rage.

Rhadagaiſus King of the *Goths,* a profeſt enemy and horrible Perſe-cutor of the *Chriſtians,* as he was making ſtrange preparations to de-ſtroy them and their Churches, was delivered up himſelf with his whole Army into the hands of his Enemies, who after a thouſand diſ-graces, put him to a cruel death; And the priſoners taken with him, were ſo many, that a great company of them were ſold but for a Crown, as *Paul. Diac.* and *Oroſius* relate.

Attila that fearfull *Rod of God,* and terrible Tyrant (if ever there was any) to whom *Theodoſius* the younger, was for a time tributary, to preſerve the *Eaſtern Churches,* after the ſhedding of a Sea of bloud, in the ſixth year of his Raign, and upon his very Wedding day, ha-ving made himſelf drunk, was ſtricken with an Apoplexy, and choked (by a juſt and viſible judgement of God) with his own bloud, having been all his life ſo thirſty of other mens.

Theodoric King of the *Weſt Goths,* an *Arrian,* and great enemy of the faithfull, ſeeing one day a Fiſh upon his Table with its mouth open and gaping, did really beleive it to be the head of one of thoſe whom he had unjuſtly put to death, and thereupon fell into an extream fit of melancholy and deſpair, and died not long after.

Amalarick, a Prince amongſt thoſe Nations, and a vehement Perſe-cutor of his own Wife, for being a *Chriſtian,* was overthrown and kill'd, with the moſt part of his Army by *Childebert* the King of *France* his Brother in Law, as *Procopius* and *Gregory de Tours* ob-ſerve.

The)

Niceph. l. 17. c. 11.
Baſilcæ An. Dom. 1533.

Eucherius. Crinitus. Volateranus.

Croſcus.

Gunderic. Chron. Sigeb. Hunneric. Greg. Turo-nenſis. Sigeb. Victor. Proculus.

Rhadagaiſus. Oroſ. l. 7. c. 37. Aug. de Civ. Dei, l. 5. c. 23.

Attila.

Paul. Diac. lib. 15.

Theodoric.

Paul. Diac. lib. 17. Procop. in Go-thicis. Amalarick.

Greg. de Tours.

Judgements of God upon the *Germans* for perfecuting the Church.

Lutarius *and* Bultinus.

Antharis.
Paul. Diac.l.3. de geft. Lomb.

Mahomet.

Phocas.
Cedrenus.
Zonaras.

The Saracens.

Abdiram.]

Athin.

Amorrheus.

Paul. Jovius in his Hiftory of our times.

The *Germans* who were confederate with the *Goths*, after they had deftroyed and defolated the Churches of *Italy*, part of them were killed in the War, part of them being laden with booty, were flain and caft head-long down the Mountains by the *Huns*, and others ; And the remainder died of the Plague in thofe places whither they had retired: As for their Captains likewife, namely *Lutarius* and *Bultinus*, The *firft* grew mad, and having with his own teeth torn himfelf, died drunk with his own bloud ; The *fecond*, was overthrown and flain with his Army of thirty thoufand men, whereof five onely efcaped, who fled betimes.

Antharis King of the *Lombards*, a great adverfary of the *Chriftians*, was poyfoned in *Pavia*, as a juft judgement of God for his cruel actions.

If I fhould here undertake to reckon up all the fearfull judgements of God upon the Perfecutors of his Church and people, in the fourth, fifth, fixth, and feventh Centuries, I mean the *Perfians*, *Greeks*, *Romans*, and other Nations, it would require a Volume as big as that of the Book of *Martyrs*.

What fhall we fay of *Mahomet* the Eaftern, and *Phocas* the Weftern *Antichrift* ? The *firft* whereof left nothing but an abhominable ftink behinde him, and though he boafted that his body fhould have no need of burial, forafmuch as it was to rife the third day, yet notwithftanding his carkafs rotted upon the earth, that none were able to endure it. The *fecond*, after he had moft traiteroufly put to death the Emperour *Maurice* his Wife, the *Senat* of *Rome* and his own fon in Law confpired againft him, and cutting off his hands, feet, privities and head, they put him into a brazen Oxe, together with all his children and kinred. And this was the end of this execrable murderer, who had granted to *Boniface* the third, Bifhop of *Rome*, the title of *Primat* and *Supreme* over all the Churches, about 600. years or thereabouts after the death of *Chrift*.

I beg the Chriftian and Courteous Readers patience to add a word concerning the Difciples and followers of the above-mentioned Mahometans, I mean the *Saracens*, who being a moft cruel people towards the *Chriftians*, were fometimes rewarded and that feven-fold for their actions. To inftance but that one Battle of *Abdiram* with *Charls Martel* near *Tours*, where there were flain 300 feventy five thoufand upon the place, which happened in the year of *Our Lord* 730. After this, in the year 736. *Athin* King of the *Saracens* got into *France* with an innumerable company, but *Charls* overthrew him and his Army near *Avignon*. Finally, *Amorrheus* another of their Kings, bringing fuccour to *Athin*, was killed, and his troups utterly defeated. The truth is, it is a fearfull thing to read of the end of the Kingdom of the *Saracens*, wherein may be feen, as in a glafs, an evident teftimony of the wrath of God : *Selym* the firft, father to *Solyman*, who was the man that deftroyed and extinguifhed that Kingdom, firft of all won two Battles againft the *Sultan Tomumbei* under the conduct of *Synan Bafcha*, one near *Gaza* in *Syria*, the other in *Egypt* near *Grand Cairo*.

After-

Afterwards *Selim* led all his forces to *Cairo*, where was another Battle in the very City, which continued two dayes and two nights, before he could get all the Forts thereof: It is hard to believe how great the effusion of bloud then was, and how horrible the cruelties acted upon the *Saracens* ! The Castle of the Town above-mentioned being won the 25th. of *January* in the year 1517. The *Sultan* fled, and hid himself amongst the Reeds in the *Moors*, from whence he was drawn, and brought before *Selym*, and after many exquisite tortures, was put upon a Camel, and led thorough all the streets of the Town, for greater ignominy, and at last hanged at one of the Gates. This happened in the year 1517. upon the 13. of *April.* I leave the Reader to think how wofull a spectacle it was then to see that mighty Emperour of *Syria* and *Egypt*, so ignominiously hanged in the sight of his own people. (This *Sultan* was the last Prince of the *Saracens* and proud *Mamalucks* :) So did the just and righteous God make them feel the power of his hand, in revenging upon them the bloud of his beloved ones ! And he will certainly one day remember the *Turks* themselves, *when he makes inquisition for bloud,*for all their inhumane Butcheries of his faithfull servants. — The Mamalucks.

But here it may be, the *Popes* of *Rome*, and successors of *Boniface* may take offence, that in so prolix a discourse of Gods judgements against the Persecutors of the Church, there should be no notice taken of their *Holinesses.* The truth is, they have a long time been a scourge to the true Professors of the Gospel, yet they have not always scap'd scot-free, but have felt the heavy hand of vengeance upon them ; yea, when they have wanted enemies from abroad to mischief them, they have run one against another with their *Bulls* horns, which have begotten all kinds of violence, wars, murthers, and other strange confusions : *Onuphrius* in his abridgement of the History of the *Popes*, enumerateth from *Gregory* the seventh till *Urban* the sixth (in the space of 294. years) seven great Schismes in the *Roman* Church, during which time there were no less then seven times, two *Popes* at once, and towards the latter end three, every one notwithstanding calling himself the true *Pope*, and accordingly excommunicating, and condemning the other his Competitors. — The Popes of Rome. — *Onuphrius Panuinus.*

After that came the eighth and great Schism, which began in the time of *Urban* the sixth, and *Clement* the seventh, and lasted thirty nine years, until the Council of *Constance* : During which time, the *Popes* bandied themselves one against another, with such impudence and fury, by *Bulls*, *Briefs*, and defaming *Libels*, that if any other had done so, he had indangered his life ; calling one another Schismaticks, Hereticks, and other odious names. If any has a desire to see their doings, let him read *Theod.* his 5.Books, who was a servant, and very familiar with the *Popes*, & consequently a man whose relation is the more to be credited. But neither is this all! if we cast our eys upon the Histories of the *Popes*, we shall finde that a great number of them have not been very long liv'd ; for, from *Gregory* the 7. to *Gregory* the 13. there were near 68. Popes, during which time, from *Henry* 4. to *Maximilian* 11. — *Theodoricus.* — That the Popes have been for the most part but short liv'd.

there

there were but 26. Kings or Emperours of the *Romans* : thus were their lives extreme short, but yet not very sweet, for we finde that most part of them were tormented with grievous diseases, and many surprised by sudden death ! Some were driven out of their seats, and taken prisoners ; others made away by poyson : *Lucius* the second was stoned by his own people. *Lucius* the third was banisht the City, and his domesticks beaten to death ; *Adrian* the fourth, was choaked by a flye. Pope *John* the eighth, or rather *Joan* the first (if we may give any credit to *Platina,* and many other of their own Writers of note) after she had made a very apt and complete exposition upon the 17th. of the *Revelation,* concerning the GREAT WHORE and THE MOTHER OF HARLOTS, that is to say, after she had been in travel and brought forth a childe, in the time of a *Procession,* as she was going to the Church of *Lateran,* in the view of the people, she died immediatly, and that with as much ignominy, and disgrace, as she had lived in villany and wickedness. This accident (as the same Historians tell us) occasioned the making of that *Trying-stool* called the *Porphyrie Chair,* for her successors ; although the truth is, the greatest part of them ever since, have given sufficient proofs of their abilities in that kinde, by a multitude of *Nephews,* who have call'd them *Fathers. John* the twelfth was stab'd by a *Roman* who by chance caught *His Holiness* in bed with his Wife (a great Argument without doubt of the Popes *peccability,* to commit such a sin, and a greater of his *fallibility,* to be so caught in the manner ! Pope *John* 21. was slain with the fall of a Vault. *Boniface* the eighth who came to the Popedome like a Fox, and governed like a Lion, at last died like a Dog.

I suppose it is now high time to draw to a conclusion, I shall therefore onely make a very brief reflection upon some few of those cruelties that have been exercised against the Professours of the Gospel, in our neighbouring Countries.

It is observed that *Henry* the second of *France,* being incensed against the Protestants by the Dutchess of *Valentinois* his Concubine, took once an oath that he would see with his own eys the burning of *Du Bourg* ; But the wise God had otherwise disposed of affairs, for a splinter of *Count Montgomeries* Lance, as he was running with him at Tilt, rebounding, and glancing into his eye, wounded him so sorely, that he died within a few days after. And which is yet more remarkable, as they carried him off the place, he turned his face toward the Bastille, and with a deep sigh confessed, that *he had most unjustly persecuted and afflicted the honest and good people that were within that place.*

Philip the second of *Spain,* who married *Elizabeth* of *France,* daughter of *Henry the second,* after the death of *Charls the fifth* his Father, being arrived in *Spain,* caused a summons to be made of all the prisoners in all parts of *Spain,* upon the account of Religion, caused them all to assemble by two Acts, the first whereof was promulgated at *Valdolid,* where a certain Doctour *Caca,* preacher to the Emperour *Charls the fifth,* in all his *German* expeditions, and one of his Advisers in his

Retire-

Margin notes:

Lucius 2.

Lucius 3.

Adrian 4.

Platin. and others.

John 12.

John 21.
Boniface 8.

Henry 2. of France.
D' Aubigny in his Histoire universelle, Edition d' Amsterdam.

Philip 2. of Spain.

Retirement was degraded, and had his mouth gag'd in a moſt cruel manner, as likewiſe a multitude of other eminent perſons, being diſguiſed in yellow habits painted with Croſſes and Devils (which they call St. *Benedicts* habits) were burned alive in the Month of *May.*

The ſecond Act was proclaimed at *Seville,* in the Kings preſence, where were burnt *Pome* of *Lions,* ſon to *Roderic* Count of *Bayley, John Bayley* a Divine of *Seville, Garſias Arias,* a man eſteemed the moſt excellent and able Doctour of *Spain,* together with a great number of men and women ; amongſt others, *Conſtantin* Biſhop of *Droſſe,* Confeſſour to the Emperour, and alſo his privy companion in his Retirement, dying with the cruel torments which he endured in priſon, was carried about *in effigie,* in the habit of a Miniſter, and thus preſented to publick view.

This King having raigned about 40. years, cauſed to be put to death his onely ſon, and his Wife *Elizabeth,* by the advice of the Inquiſition ! But now mark his end ! he was ſeized by four Apoſtemes in the four corners of his ſtomack, which being opened, caſt forth ſuch a prodigious quantity of Lice, that the Chirurgions could never finde any remedy for him ; and thus he died moſt miſerably, being eaten up of lice.

Francis the ſecond, ſon to *Henry the ſecond,* having by the inſtigation [Francis 2.] of the *Guiſars* perſecuted the *Proteſtants,* as alſo ſeiz'd upon the *Prince* of *Conde,* and was very near cutting off his head, after he had made a vow (which he intended to confirm by oath to the *Virgin Mary*) for the extirpation of the *Proteſtants,* and all their Abettours, or who any way had favoured that party, being ſurpriſed by a feaver, and having an Apoſteme broken in one of his ears, died ſuddenly in the Month of *December.*

Charls the ninth, ſon to *Francis the ſecond,* having contrary to the [Charls 9.] faith of his promiſe, cauſed the execution of the Maſſacre of St. *Bartholomew* (which they call the *Pariſian Matins*) about eight days after, there came ſuch a prodigious multitude of Crows making an hideous noiſe upon the great *Lanthorn* of the *Louvre,* that both the King and all the Court were not a little affrighted ; And the very ſame night, the *King* about two hours after he had been in his bed, leapt up on a ſuddain, cauſed thoſe of his Chamber to riſe immediatly, and call his Brother in Law amongſt others, to hear a ſtrange and hideous noiſe in the ayr, being as it were a great multitude of voices, ſome crying and groaning in a moſt lamentable manner, others threatning and blaſpheming, being not unlike that confuſed noiſe that was heard the night when the *Maſſacre* was executed.

After this *Bartholomew-tide* this Prince took no true reſt, but was [*Thuanus l.* 57. *pag.* 990.] always interrupted with ſtartings, and groanings, which ended in words of diffidence and deſpair, and moſt extreme pains of a diſeaſe which ſeized on him ; yea the very bloud was obſerved to ſpring forth from almoſt all the paſſages of his body, inſomuch that he died thus wallowing and weltring in his own gore.

It's ſaid, that he had reſolved a little before his death, to have baniſht
out

out of his Council, all the Authors of the *Maſſacre*, together with his Mother, however ſome of them were met with as followeth.

Henry *the* 3d.

Henry the third, his Brother, received his deaths wound by *James Clement*, a *Jacobin*, in the very ſame houſe, chamber, and place of the chamber, as alſo the very ſame Month, that 17. years before he had treacherouſly plotted, violently ſollicited, and abſolutely determined the above-ſaid *Maſſacre* of St. *Bartholomew*.

Francis *of* Lorrain.

Francis of Lorrain, Duke of *Guiſe*, having executed the *Maſſacre* of *Vaſsi*, and afflicting *Orleans*, to the end he might exterminate the Proteſtants, was aſſaſinated by one *Poltrot*.

Henry *his ſon*.

Henry, his ſon, one of the Authors of the Maſſacre of St. *Bartholomew*, together with the *Cardinal* his Brother, were both put to death at *Blois*, by the commandment of King *Henry the third*.

Du Haillan in the life of Charls *the*9th. *De Serres in the life of* Charls *the* 9.

Du Haillan reports in the life of *Charls the ninth*, that the King viſibly declined in thoſe days, and that in the very flower of his age. And after the departure of the King of *Polonia*, he was found to be as much altered in minde as body, being in an eſpeciall manner provoked and incenſed againſt the Authours and contrivers of the *Maſſacres*, as he alſo plainly told ſome of his Court, who were enemies of injuſtice, and as appeared likewiſe by ſeveral Letters which he wrote into foreign parts, for which Authours of the *Maſſacres* he had preſcribed a very ſtrange Potion, if Divine Providence had not prevented him, who reſerved them as inſtruments of thoſe after-chaſtiſements which he had appointed to bring upon the Kingdom.

The ſame Authour obſerveth a little after, that having languiſhed during the Months of *February*, *March*, and *April*, he was ſo waſted in his body by ſuch furious ſtorms and tempeſts, that his bed became irkſom to him, and the 30. of *May* he took his laſt ſleep in his Caſtle *du Bois de Vincennes*, after a ſtrange effuſion of bloud, which forced its way through ſeveral parts of his body, during the two laſt Weeks of his ſickneſs, in all which time he endured all the moſt violent aſſaults and combats, that the vigour and force of his age could poſſibly furniſh him with ſtrength to undergo.

De Serres in the life of Charls *the* 9.

Du Serres relates of him, that raging and raving under the juſt judgements of God, he was ſeen to wallow in his own bloud, (the juſt recompence and reward of one, who had wallowed all his life-time in the bloud of his ſubjects throughout all his Dominions.)

Staniſlaus *of* Znoyme. *The French Book of Martyrs, printed* 1570. Count Felix *of* Wartenberg. *Illiricus cites this.*

Staniſlaus of *Znoyme*, as he was going to *Conſtance* to bear falſe witneſs againſt *John Hus*, was remarkably ſmitten by the hand of God himſelf.

Count *Felix* of *Wartenberg* one of the Emperours Captains, as he was ſitting at Supper with many of his companions and brethren in iniquity, in the year 1530. ſwore in the preſence of all that were at Table, that before he died he would ride *aux eſperons* up to the horſe-belly in the bloud of the Lutherans; But that very night, he was choaked with his own bloud, and wallowed miſerably in the ſame.

John Menier. *Fren.Book of Martyrs l.* 3. *p.* 75, *and* 76.

John Menier, after a thouſand miſchiefs which he had done to the poor *Proteſtants*, was ſeized by a bloudy flux, which did ſo afflict his

privy

privy members, and engendred such a retention of urine, that he died thereof with most horrible and despairing cries, feeling also a fire already in his body, as an earnest of those eternal flames that are prepared for such fire-brands of the *Church.*

Gaspar de Renialme one of the Magistrats of the City of *Antwerp*, having adjudg'd to death certain poor *Protestants*, was smitten by God in the very place, insomuch that being led home as it were almost desperate, he died in a terrible manner, often crying out and saying, that *he had condemned innocent bloud.*

Gaspar de Re-
nialme.
Id. l. 6. p. 512.

The Chancellour *du Prat,* who was the first that gave jurisdiction to *Parliaments* to proceed against the poor *Protestants,* died in his own house, swearing and cursing against God himself; But his very stomack was afterwards found to have been gnawn and eaten through by Worms.

Du Prat.
Id. l. 6. p. 473.

John Morin, Lieutenant de la Prevosté de Paris, a strange and cruel monster, having put to death a great number of Martyrs, was smitten with the disease called the *Wolf* in both his legs, of which he died, blaspheming and renouncing God in a most hideous manner.

John Morin.
Ibid.

The same Author makes mention of a certain Counsellour who having had a hand in certain Processes which were made by the *Lieutenant du Chastelet de Paris,* died a very strange death, and in his sickness he would often cry out to those that visited him, in the following terms; *Why do we put to death these poor people, who pray to God so well?*

Pag. 535.
A certain
Counsellour.

During the cruel executions at *Amboise,* issued out against those who assembled themselves to discover to the King the secret machinations that were then plotting against him, *Oliver* the *Chancellour,* who had drawn the Process against these poor people, and who also had proceeded in the former persecutions directly against his own conscience (which for a long time had been inlightened by the knowledge of the truth) was at length seized by a grievous disease, during the which he sent forth most lamentable sighs and bitter groans. In this torment he was visited by the *Cardinal of Lorrain,* to whom he cried out in these words, *Ha! Cardinal! Tu nous fais tous danner, thou causest us all to be damned:* It is said moreover, that he mentioned with profound regret the death of *M. Ann du Bourg,* who not long before, had been burnt for the testimony of the truth.

Ibid.
Oliver *the*
Chancellour.
Id. l. 7. *p.* 558.

The *Baillif of Nancy* in *Lorrain,* having without any form of legal proceeding, caused to be hanged one *Florentin,* a native of *Cologne,* a faithfull servant and Minister of *Jesus Christ,* and likewise demolished the Church where the said *Florentin* was wont to preach and administer the Sacraments, It happened that as he was walking out after dinner, (not knowing the place where this poor Martyr had been executed) he lighted just upon the very place where he was hanging; But as soon as he beheld him, he was struck with such a dismal affrightment, that it accompanied him to his grave. His Body not long after became dry as parchment rolled upon wood; Besides this, he was grievously tormented in his conscience, insomuch that he often demanded

The Bailiff de
Nancy *in*
Lorrain.
Id. l. 7. *p.* 579.

manded of divers honest people during the time of his languishment, *Whether God would pardon unto a man those sins that he repented of, without confessing at all the cause of this his remorse?* (it is likely out of fear of displeasing the Princes and great ones.) However, when he came to make his last Will and Testament, he plainly discovered the cause of this his torment and horrour of conscience, assigning 500. *Francks* to the daughter of the above-said Martyr *Florentin,* which was also afterwards really given her by His Executors.

John de Roma, an Inquisitor in *Provence,* who had found out a strange invention to torment the poor Saints, which was to cause them to draw on a certain kinde of Boots filled with boyling grease, thereby (if possible) to make them despair through excessive pains, Was afterwards surprized by a terrible and loathsome disease, insomuch that none durst approach him by reason of the stench and putrifaction of his malady ; And all his consolation was a desire to die, in the mean time uttering nothing but words of despair. His complaints were such as these. *Alas, to what a miserable state and condition am I brought! What is it that I suffer! I remember indeed the evils that I have done to those poor people, and know full well for what cause I am thus afflicted on every side. Who shall deliver me from this distress? O kill me speedily, that I may no longer languish in this misery.*

One Dr. *Lambert* Priour of the *Augustin Friers,* as he was preaching with open mouth against the faithfull flock of Christ, (whom he called by the name of *Calvinists,* and *Lutherans,*) all of a suddain became mute in his Pulpit, and his sences failed him in an odd and strange manner, insomuch that he was immediately carried out of the Assembly, and a few days after he was found dead in a ditch.

Poncher Archbishop of *Tours,* pursuing the execution of a famous Martyr, was burnt by a fire from Heaven, which began at his heel, and he was forced to cut off one member after another, till at last he died most miserably, no man being ever able to know the cause of his disease.

Thomas Arundel , Archbishop of *Canterbury ,* that gave sentence against the *Lord Cobham* (that ancient witness of the Truth) died notwithstanding before him, having his tongue so swollen in his mouth, before his death, that he could neither eat, nor speak.

Dr. *Foxford* Chancellour to *Stokesley* Bishop of *London,* had his guts fallen out of his body as he sate in his Chair.

Morgan Bishop of St. *Davids,* who sate upon *Farrar* the Martyr, and usurped his place, was smitten with a lothsome disease, his meat that he ate still rising up again, sometimes through his mouth, sometimes through his nose, till he died.

Justice Morgan, who sate upon the *Lady Jane,* fell mad, and cried out alwaies in his raging fits, *Take away the Lady Jane! Take away the Lady Jane!* and so he died.

The Wife of *John Fettie* betrayed her own husband, and then fell mad.

Alexander

Alexander the Keeper of *Newgate* in the days of the Martyrs, died in a moſt formidable manner, his Body being ſwollen, and become as monſtrous as his Actions, and as rotten as his Principles.

Gardiner the Biſhop of *Winchester*, the Devils chief *Courier du Cabi net*, would by no means go to dinner that day that *Ridley* and *Latimer* were burnt at *Oxford*, till ſuch time as his Man came Poſt from thence, with the News that he ſaw Fire ſet to them at the Stake, but ere this curſed Murderer had ſate long at the Table, he was taken with ſuch an intolerable Pain in his Bowels, and the Heat within his Body was ſo violent, that his Tongue was ſwollen, and become black in his Mouth. This wicked Wretch when he was put in minde by one of the Biſhops that ſtood by him, of the Death and Merits of *Christ*, made anſwer thus, *Open that Door to the People, my Lord, and all's gone ! You may speak it to such as are in my condition, but open that Door to the People, and all's gone.*

I ſhall end all with that Reproach of her Sex, Queen *Mary*, who never proſpered after once ſhe began to perſecute the Saints, and at laſt died of a Tympany. This miſerable Wretch told one of her Maids of Honour, that *if they opened her after she was dead, they should finde* Calais *lying at her heart.* But I am perſwaded ſhe was miſtaken, and that it was rather the *Fire*, the *scalding Lead,* and *red hot Irons*, wherewith ſhe had put to death the poor Martyrs.

The truth is, the inſtances that might be alleged for the confirmation of this truth, are almoſt innumerable, And I do verily believe that there hath hardly been any famous Perſecutour of the Church almoſt in any Age, or Place of the World, that hath gone down to his Grave without ſome remarkable Tokens of Divine Vengeance upon him, in ſome reſpect or other.

I might here in the concluſion of this Diſcourſe (and it would not be at all beſides my purpoſe if I ſhould) deſcend to ſome particular Inſtances in *Savoy* it ſelf, whereby it would plainly appear to all the World, That even they alſo, as they have in a very eminent manner acted their parts in the Perſecution of the Saints, have likewiſe been met with by Judgments from Heaven. I ſay, I might inſtance in ſeveral perſons of quality and note, ſome whereof had had their *Candles* ſtrangely *put out,* and others who are now living, and have already taſted in ſome meaſure the firſt fruits of their bloudy Deeds, as an earneſt of a heavier Curſe, without a ſerious and timely Repentance. I would not be here miſtaken or thought bluntly to ſtrike at, or fall foul upon the princely perſons of their *Royal Highnesses*, (I mean the *Duke* and his *Mother* now reigning) the tender years of the one, and thoſe few Obſervations I my ſelf have ſometimes made of the candour and mildneſs of the natural tempers and diſpoſitions of both, forbidding me to believe them to be otherwiſe, or any further guilty of thoſe horrid Cruelties and Perſecutions, than by giving ear (the more's the pity) to the black calumnies of malicious men, and by ſuffering themſelves to be made believe, that whoſoever kills and deſtroys thoſe their poor *Protestant* Subjects, do thereby ſave their own Souls, and do
God

Alexander the *Keeper of* Newgate, 1003.
Gardiner *Bish.* of Winchester 1824.

Queen Mary.

God a fingular and meritorious fervice ; and upon thofe grounds moft unhappily fet their hands to many a cruel and bloudy Edict. No! they are a generation of Jefuitical Spirits to whom I direct this Difcourfe, who love Cruelty in the Abftract, and hunt after Bloud as naturally as the Eagle after her Prey. But I fhall rather be fparing and tender in this regard, and onely pray for them, as *Stephen* did for his Murderers; *Lord lay not this Sin to their Charge!* Or in the words of our *Saviour* for the *Jews*, *Father forgive them, for they know not what they do.* But withall let me tell them, That ftrong and loud is the Cry of thofe *Souls* who are now *under the Altar,* whom they have fo cruelly and barbaroufly *flain for the teftimony of* Jefus ; And let them take heed that they prevail not at length with the *Lord Holy and true, to judg and avenge their bloud upon them that dwell on the Earth.*

Thefe are the Introductory (and I hope feafonable) thoughts and intimations

(Chriftian and Courteous Readers)

O F

Your faithfull Servant in
CHRIST:

SAMUEL MORLAND.

The Contents and Heads of the following History of the *Evangelical Churches* in the *Valleys* of *Piemont*.

The Contents of the First BOOK.

The Contents of the following History.

The Contents of the Second BOOK.

The Contents

Here followes a Catalogue of the *Manuscripts*, and other
pieces inserted, or at least mentioned in the following *History of the Evangelical Churches of the Valleys of Piemont*; The greatest part and
most essential whereof are either *Originals*, or otherwise most Authen-
tickly *Vidimated* for the justification of that Work to Po-
sterity.

Presented by the Author (together with divers other Manuscripts relating to the late troubles of *Switzerland*
upon the Accompt of *Religion*) as his free gift,
to the publick Library of the famous University of *Cambridge*, in *August* 1658.

THe Volume marked with the Letter *A*, contains in it the following Treatises.

1 *The History of the Creation and Deluge, written in their own Language.*

2 *An excellent Treatise of sundry profitable Instructions which a man
ought to learn from the nature of divers Animals.*

3 *Lo tracta di la pecca, or a Treatise of Sin, which is an allegorical and
moral Explanation of the* Beast *described,* Rev. 13.

4 *A Treatise of the Word of God, and the power and efficacie thereof; as
also how it ought to be received; at the end whereof there is affixed the
Date, either of the Work, or at least of the Copy of it,* viz. Anno Domini
1230.

5 *Several* Latin *Pieces, which are certain Rhapsodies concerning Priests
and Friers.*

6 *A Treatise against* Tramettament, *or Traditions and Ordinances of
Men, as not consonant to the Holy Scriptures.*

7 *An Exhortation to* Herman, *to convert himself to God, and not to the
creatures.*

8 *Concerning Pharisaical Plantations which the Father hath not planted,
viz. the Orders and Sects of* Monks, Franciscan Friers, Dominicans,
and the like, which are not ordained by God.

9 *A* Latin *Treatise,* De Officiis Conjugum, Viri & Uxoris.

10 *A* Latin *Treatise,* De Symbolo Apostolico.

11 *A* Latin *Treatife*, De Ædificatione Urbium, Idololatriæ ortu & progreffu, ejufque everfione per Evangelii predicationem.

12 *A* Latin *Treatife*, Quibus Modis peccatum fiat.

13 *A* Latin *Treatife*, De vera peccati purgatione.

14 *A* Latin *Treatife entituled*, Uni Deo placere ftudeamus.

15 *A* Latin *Treatife entituled*, Tres Veritates. 1 Doctrinæ. 2 Juftitiæ. 3 Vitæ.

16 *A* Latin *Treatife entituled*, Sola Dei Lege fcripta definiri Fidei Controverfias.

In the Volum marked with the Letter *B.* are contained the following Treatifes, all written in that which is called the *Waldenfian* Language, in Parchment, and that in a very ancient, but excellent Character.

1   Glofa Pater, *or the Explication of the Lords Prayer.*

2   Trecenas, *or divers paffages of the Evangelifts, and Epiftles.*

3   Doctor, *that is, divers Sentences and Teftimonies of the Fathers, touching Repentance.*

4   Penas, *or a Treatife concerning the punifhment of fin.*

5   Li Goy de Paradis, *a Treatife concerning the Joys of Paradife.*

6   *An Epiftle to all the Faithfull.*

7   *A Poeme entituled,* Novel Confort.

8   *A Poeme entituled,* Novel Sermon, *containing many wholefome Inftructions to the People.*

9   *A Poeme entituled,* La Noble Leyçon.

10   *A Poeme entituled,* Pair eternal.

11   *A Poeme entituled,* Barca, *concerning the mifery and fhortnefs of mans life, and his arriving at the haven of Salvation.*

12   *An Explanation of the Ten Commandments.*

13   *An Explanation of the Articles of the Apoftles Creed.*

14   *A Treatife concerning Vice, and Mortal Sins.*

15   *A Treatife concerning the feven Gifts of the Spirit,* Ifai 11.

16   *A Treatife concerning the three Theological, and the four Cardinal Virtues.*

17   *A Treatife concerning the Goods of Fortune, Nature, and Grace.*

18   *A Treatife concerning the fix honorable things in this World.*

19 *Several Sermons upon feveral Texts of Scripture ; Namely,*

    1   *A Sermon upon the fecond of* Matthew *touching idle words.*

    2   *A Sermon upon* Ephef. 4. *touching the putting on of the New Man.*

    3   *A Sermon* Del Fantin Jefus, *or concerning the little Childe* Jefus, *during his abode in* Jerufalem, Luk.2.

    4   *A Sermon touching Chrifts being tempted in the Defert,* Matth. 4. *and* Luke 4.

    5   *A Sermon upon* Mat. 8.25. Save us, *or elfe we perifh.*

    6   *A Sermon touching the Rich Man,* Luke 16.

    7   *A Sermon upon the fixth of* John.

    8   *A Sermon upon the Parable of the Sower,* Matth.13.

In

The Contents

In the Volume marked with the Letter *C.* are contained the following Treatises.

In the Volume *D,* are many excellent and Heavenly Meditations, touching the Miseries, Tribulations, and Shortness of this Life; as likewise of Repentance, Good works, and the like; written in the language of the ancient Inhabitants of the Valleys, in Parchment, but the Letter almost worn out with age, which according to many probable circumstances of the place and manner of its preservation, is judged to have been written at least six or seven hundred years ago.

In the Volume marked *E.* are contained.

In the Volume *F,* are collected and written in Parchment, in that which is called the *Waldensian* Language, of a very ancient, but fair and distinct Character.

The

The Volume marked with the Letter *G*, containeth the following Manuscripts.

In the Volume *H*, are contained the following Manuscripts.

In the Volume *J*, are contained the following Manuscripts.

5 *The*

The Contents

The Contents

In the Volume *O*, are contained the following Edicts, all printed by the Printers to their respective Highnesses, excepting onely the Court of *Savoy's Factum* and *Reasons*.

In

The Contents

In the Volume *R*, are contained the following Manufcripts.

1 *An ancient* Italian *Manufcript, Entituled,* Hiftoria breve e vera de gl'Affari de i Valdefi delle Valli.
2 *A brief Confefsion of Faith publifhed by the Reformed Churches of* Piemont, An. Dom. 1655.
3 *The fentence of the Arbitrators and Judges* Catholicks, *of the two Cities of* Fryburg, *and* Soleure, (*in* High-Dutch *and* French) *given at* Olten *the* 30 *of* Jan. 1657.

The Volume *S,* is the *French Bible,* printed by the people of the *Valleys* at *Neuf Chaftel,* in *June* Anno Dom. 1535. mentioned in the firft Book, and third Chapter of the following *Hiftory.*

In the Volume *T,* are contained the reft of thofe Original pieces which are mentioned in the following *Hiftory of the Evangelical Churches,* which yet are not fpecified in the fore-going *Catalogue,* nor in that *Black Box* hereafter mentioned, marked *W.*

In the Volume *V,* are contained the following Manufcripts.

1 *A brief but exact Relation in Englifh, of the occafion and grounds of the late War in* Switzerland, *between the* Proteftant *and the* Catholick Cantons, *bearing date the* 14 *of* Dec. 1655.
2 *A large Hiftory written in the* French *Tongue, of all paffages and Tranf-actions between the* Evangelical, *and the* Catholick Cantons *of* Switzerland, *in relation to the* Nicodemites, *or poor Exiles of the* Cantons *of* Switz, *compiled with much pains and induftry, by* Sam. Morland *Efq; during his abode at* Geneva, *the which Hiftory confifts of the following parts or branches ;*

   1 *The beginning of the troubles in* Switzerland, *in the year* 1655. *upon account of* Religion, *with their feveral Affemblies upon that occafion.*
   2 *The Rupture.*
   3 *The effects of the faid Rupture.*
   4 *The Peace concluded at* Baden, *the* 26 Feb. / 7 March, 1656.

In the Volume *W,* are contained the following Authentick *High-Dutch* Manufcripts, for the juftification of the abovefaid *Hiftory,* concerning the differences in *Switzerland,* about the poor Exiles of *Switz.,* &c. All figned by Mr. *Andrew Schmidt,* Under-Secretary of *Zuric.*

1 *Their Citation, in* September 1655.
2 *The* Nicodemites *Letter to thofe of* Switz, *written from* Zurich *the* 15 *of* September 1655.
3 *A Letter from the* Canton *of* Zurich *to thofe of* Switz, *in favour of the faid* Nicodemites, *the* 15 *of* Septemb. 1655.

4 *A*

of the following Hiſtory.

In

The Contents

In the black Boxe marked *X*, are contained the feveral printed Tickets and other Papers and Pictures, which were found in the pockets of fome of the fouldiers in *Piemont*, who had before maffacred the *Proteftants*.

Namely,

In the Paper *A*, are feveral forms of bleffing, confecrated to be carried about them for preservation ; As for example.

1 *Potentia Dei Patris, Sapientia Dei Fili, Virtus Spiritus Sancti, per intercefsionem Sanctifsimæ Virginis Dei genitricis Mariæ, Sancti Francifci, & Beatorum Didaci, & Salvatoris liberet te Dominus ab omni Febre, Pefte, & improvisâ morte.* Amen.
2 *Facite homines difcumbere, ex Cathed. Cafalenf.* 1649.
3 *Eft puer unus hic, ex Cathed. Cafalenf.* 1648.

In the Paper *B*, is a certain Powder which they call *Latte della Madonna* ; Or, *The Milk of the Virgin Mary.*

In the Papers *C, D, E, F, G, H, I, K*, are inclofed fmall pieces of the dead bones of feveral Martyrs, *&c.* with the following infcriptions on the backfide of the Papers.

C, Sancti Fuftine Vierge Martyre.
D, Sancti Lucii Eremitæ.
E, Sancti Dindari Martyris.
F, Sancti Blafii Epifcopi Martyris.
G, Sancti Antonii Abbatis.
H, Sancti Antonni Martyris.
I, Sancti Pancratii.
K, De la Sancta Sepulcra.

In the Paper *L*, are the Pictures of feveral Saints, as alfo of *Chrift* and the *Virgin Mary*, among which there is one remarkable, whereof the Title or Superfcription is, Pro Conversione Hæreticorum ; all painted in a bloudy colour.

Befides thefe Papers and Tickets, there are in the faid black Box, thefe Original pieces.

1 *The Marquefs of* Pianezza's *grant of Indemnity, and divers Priviledges, to a certain perfon for renouncing his* Religion.
2 *The Certificate of* Profpero da Tarano, *delivered to the Marquefs of* Pianezza, *that the perfon abovefaid had certainly abjured his* Religion.

Books

Books Printed, and are to be sold by *Adoniram Byfield*, at the three Bibles in Cornhil ; next door to Popes-head Alley.

DIvine Characters, *in two Parts, acutely distinguishing the more secret and undiscerned differences ; Between,* 1 *the Hypocrite in his best dress of seeming virtues and formal duties, and the true Christian in his Real Graces and sincere Obedience. As also between,* 2 *the blackest weeds of daily infirmities of the truly Godly, eclipsing saving grace, and the reigning sins of the unregenerate that pretend unto that godliness they never had : By that late burning and shining Lamp, Master* Samuel Crook, B. D. *late Pastor of* Wrington *in* Somerset, *in* Fol.

2 *A Commentary upon the three first Chapters of* Genesis, *by that Reverend Divine Mr.* John White, *late Preacher of Gods Word, at* Dorchaster, *in* Fol.

3 *An Exposition upon the* 6, 7, 8, 9, 10, 11, 12, *and* 13. *Chapters of* Ezekiel, *by Mr.* Williams, *being the second Volume, in* Quarto.

4 *An Exposition upon the* 15, 16, 17, 18, *and* 19. *Chapters of* Ezekiel, *by the same Author, the third Volume, in* Quarto.

5 *The humbled Sinner resolved what he should do to be saved, or, Faith in the Lord* Jesus Christ, *the onely way of Salvation : By Mr.* Obadiah Sedgwick, *in* Quarto.

6 *The Riches of Grace displayed, in the offer and tender of Salvation to poor sinners, upon* Rev. 3 10. *By the same Author, in* 12°.

7 *The Fountain opened, and the Water of Life flowing forth, for the refreshing of thirsty sinners, in several Sermons Preached at* Covent Garden *on* Isa. 55. 1, 2, 3. *by the same Author, in* Quarto.

8 *A short Catechisme b the same Author.*

9 *Hidden Manna, or the Mystery of saving Grace, by Mr.* William Fenner, *in* 12°.

10 *Safe Conduct, or the Saints guidance to Glory, at the Funeral of Mrs.* Thomasin Barnardiston: *By Mr.* Ralph Robinson, *in* Quarto.

11 *The Saints longing after their heavenly Country. A Sermon by the same Author, in* Quarto.

12 *A Sermon at a Fast, by Mr.* Nathaniel Ward, *in* Quarto.

13 *A full Discovery and Confutation of the wicked and damnable Doctrines of the* Quakers : *By Mr.* Jonathan Clapham, *in* Quarto.

14 Moses *his Death, opened and applied in a Sermon at* Christ-Church, London, *at the Funeral of Mr.* Edward Bright *Minister there, by Mr.* Samuel Jacomb, M. A. *Pastor of* Mary Woolnoth, London, *in* 4°.

15 *A*

THE

THE
HISTORY
OF THE
EVANGELICAL CHURCHES
IN THE
VALLEYS
OF
PIEMONT.

BOOK I.

CHAP. I.

The Situation and Extent of the Valleys *of* PIEMONT.

Or as much as it is my purpose in the ensuing Discourse to make a faithfull and exact Relation of those many signal and remarkable Passages of Divine Providence, which have almost in all Ages accompanied the poor Protestants of *Piemont,* (otherwise known by the name of *Waldenses,)* and especially of that bloudy and cruel *Massacre,* in the Year of our Lord, 1655. (the wofull cry whereof has been heard throughout all the Christian World) I shall intreat the courteous Reader to spend with me a few minutes in
viewing

viewing the situation of those *Valleys*, where not onely those poor people then inhabited, but where, in all humane probability, their Forefathers and Ancestours have both had their abode, and profest the same Religion, ever since the days of the *Apostles.*

The pleasant situation and great fruitfulness of the Province of *Piemont.*

Now because the said valleys are for the most part inclosed within the Confines of *Piemont*, it will not be amiss in the first place to give a brief Description of the whole *Province*, which indeed is but a little Spot of Earth in comparison, and of a very small Extent, yet as pleasant for situation, and likewise by its incredible fruitfulness, bringing in as great a Revenue (in proportion) to its Prince, as any Province of *Europe.*

The derivation or etymology of the word *Piemont.* The Confines of *Piemont.*

This Province of *Piemont* (so called, because situated *a pede montium*, or at the feet of the *Alps*, which separate *Italie* from *France*) the County of *Nizza* being thereto adjoyned, has for its Confines, on the East, the Dutchy of *Milan*, *Montferrat*, and the Common-wealth of *Genoa* ; on the South-side it has for a Trench, the *Mediterranean Sea* ; on the West and the North part, it has the *Alps* for a Wall or Bulwark, and is by them separated on the West-side from *Provence* and *Dauphine*, and on the North-side from *Savoy*, and the Countrey of *Valley.*

The extent of the whole Province of *Piemont.*

Its longest extent from East to West, is from the Valley of *Barcellonette*, (which is three Leagues from *Ambrun*) to *Cairo*, which is upon *Bornia*, towards *Montferrat* and *Gennois*. It is almost all covered with high Mountains, and the *Alps*, *Penines*, *Graies*, or *Greques*, and *Cotionnes*, (which now have their name *de la Val d' Aosta*,) *Mont Senii, Mont Geneure*, as also the *Appenin* Hills.

The four great Rivers that traverse *Piemont*, viz. 1. *Po.* 2. *Tanaro.* 3. *Stura.* 4. *Dora.*

It is traversed with four great Rivers, namely the River *Po,* (which has its source or head near *Mont Visol*, one of the highest Mountains of *Europe*) the River *Tanaro*, the River *Stura*, and the River *Dora*. But besides these four, there are about eight and twenty other Rivers great and small, wherewith it is watered like a pleasant Garden, and which render it exceeding fruitfull in Cattel, Wine, Corn, Hay, Nuts, and almost all other things in great abundance.

The truth is, this is a part of the World where are many things very remarkable, and which, if particularly treated of, would swell into a large Volume. But my Design being not to enlarge much upon this subject, I shall content my self, for brevity sake, to give onely a general Description of the *Valleys* of *Piemont* ; and this to prepare the ingenuous Reader the better to comprehend the situation of that part of them, which before the late *Massacre*, was inhabited by the Protestants.

The principal Valleys that enrich *Piemont.*

The principal *Valleys* which enrich *Piemont*, are on the North part, those two of *Aosta* and *Susa*, on the South-side the Valley of *Stura*, and certain others, and in the mid-land, *Lucerna*, *Angrogna*, *Roccapiatta*, *Pramol*, *Perosa*, and *S. Martino.*

The situation of the Valley of *Clusone.*

The Valley of *Clusone* otherwise called *Pragela*, that is to say, the High and the Low Communalty, (although it be at the descent of the *Alps* on the East-side, and discharge its River *Clusone* in the Valley of *Perosa*, which is on the West-side of *Pignerolio*) in ancient times has been, and yet is a part of *Dauphine*, as far as *La Capella*, which is seated at the
lower

lower end thereof, and divides it from *Perofa*. As likewife it was the ordinary Paffage of the *French* Armies into *Italie*.

These Valleys, efpecially that of *Angrogna, Pramol*, and *S. Martino*, are by nature ftrongly fortified, by reafon of their many difficult Paffages, and Bulwarks of Rocks and Mountains, as if the All-wife *Creatour* had from the beginning defigned that place as a Cabinet, wherein to put fome ineftimable Jewel, or (to fpeak more plainly) there to referve many *thoufands of fouls*, which fhould not *bow the knee before Baal*.

How the Valleys of Piemont are by nature moft ftrongly fortified.

But to come more clofely to our purpofe ; of thefe Valleys of *Piemont*, there were feveral inhabited and peopled by thofe Proteftants, who have now, for fomething above five hundred years, been ftiled *Waldenfes*, as namely *Lucerna, Perofa*, and *S. Martino*.

What Valleys have been heretofore inhabited by the Proteftants.

The Valley of *Lucerna*, (which alfo bears the name of a County) contains in length fifteen miles of *Piemont*, or feven *French* miles, that is to fay, from the loweft part thereof Eaftward, which is bounded by *Garcigliana* and *Campiglione*, to the higheft part Weftward, where is the Fort of *Miraboco*. The higheft Communalty thereof, (*viz.*) *Bobio, Villaro*, and *La Torre*, are the greateft part of them mountainous, the Valley being not very large ; but the loweft parts thereof, namely, *Lucerna, S. Giovanni, Fenile, Campiglione*, and *Garcigliana*, although they have both on the North and South-fide a little of the Mountains, do extend themfelves into a very fair Plain.

A defcription of the Valley of Lucerna,

Angrogna which is but a little Valley by it felf on the North-fide of *Lucerna*, as alfo *Rorata* and *Vallon*, which are Meridional to the Valley of *Lucerna*, are wholly within the Mountain : fo is alfo *Roccapiatta* and *Pramol*, which are inclofed between the Valleys of *Lucerna* and *Perofa*.

Angrogna, Rorata, Vallon, Roccapiatta, Pramol.

The Communalty of *La Torre*, took its name from an ancient and high Tower, which ftood upon a little Hill near *Bourg*. *Francis* the firft, King of *France*, confidering the great prejudice that this *Citadel*, being fo near the conflux of the two Rivers of *Lucerna* and *Angrogna*, in the very centre of the faid Valley of *Lucerna*, might bring to the affairs and intereft of *France*, and the fafety of *Pignerole*, caufed it to be demolifhed. And this is the place where the *Duke* of *Savoy* did rebuild that *Citadel*, 1652. which ferved before as a Slaughter-houfe to murder and make away fo many innocent Souls.

A defcription of the Communalty of La Torre.

Bricheras being adjoyned to the Valley of *Lucerna*, is on the Eaft of *Angrogna*, and *S. Giovanni*, and on the South-fide of *Roccapiatta*, almoft all in the Plain.

Bricheras.

The Valleys of *Perofa* and *S. Martino* are on the North of *Lucerna*, *Angrogna*, and *Roccapiatta*, fituated in fuch fort, that the Valley of *Perofa*, being at the lower end, and on the Eaft of the Valleys of *S. Martino* and *Pragela*, receives their two Rivers, namely, *Clufone* and *Germanacha*.

Perofa, S. Martino.

The Valley of *Perofa*, being about fix miles long, is diftributed part in Mountains, part in fair Plains, and very fruitfull Hills. At the lower part thereof it hath the Communalties of *Porte*, *S. Germano*, and *Villaro* ;

A defcription of the Valley of Perofa.

laro; in the middle, *Pinachia*, and in the higher part, that of *Perofa*, where there is the City and *Citadel* of *Perofa*, from whence the Valley takes its name, this Valley of *Perofa* being divided by the River into two parts. The Duke, upon Agreement, put the King of *France* in poffeffion of the North part, which is the greater, and more fertile, by reafon of the paffage and *Appenage* of *Pignerolio*, and referved for himfelf the South-part, to which is annexed *Pramol* in the Mountain.

A defcription of the Valley of *S. Martino*.

The Valley of *S. Martino* containing eight miles in length, is on the Weft of the Valley of *Perofa*, inclofed between the Valley of *Lucerna* and *Clufone*, in the higheft part of the *Alps*, which Confine with the Valley of *Queyras*, and comprehend eleven Communalties, namely, *Rioclaret, Faet, Prali, Rodoreto, Salfa, Macel, Maneglia, Chabrans, Traverfes, Bovili*, and *S. Martino*, which gives the name to this Valley. This is the pooreft of all, but yet the strongeft by reafon of its fituation, wherein for this reafon the *Barbes* or Minifters, (of whom we fhall hereafter fpeak) had anciently their chief refidence, or abode, for fecurity and prefervation againft the rage of their malicious Adverfaries, who were always hunting them with a Net, and thirfting after their bloud.

CHAP. II.

A Defcription of the Evangelical Churches in the Valleys of Piemont.

The fourteen Churches in the Valleys of *Piemont*, diftinguifhed into two *Claffes*.
The firft *Claffis* comprifing the 7 churches.
1. *S. Giovanni*.
2. *La Torre*.
3. *Villaro*.
4. *Bobio*.
5. *Rorata*.
6. *Angrogna*.
7. *Roccapiatta*.
The other *Claffis* comprifing the feven Churches.

Efore the late horrible difperfion of thofe poor Proteftants in the Year, 1655. There were in the faid Valleys which were peopled with *Waldenfes*, fourteen *Churches*, which compofed two *Claffes* or *Colloques*, and thofe two *Claffes* one *Synod*.

The one of thefe two was called the *Colloque* of the Valley of *Lucerna*, comprifing the Churches of *S. Giovanni, La Torre, Villaro, Bobio, Rorata*, and *Angrogna*, which belong to the Valley of *Lucerna*, and the Church of *Roccapiatta*, which is between the Valley of *Lucerna*, and *Perofa*, fituated upon thofe little Hills which feparate the two Valleys, and is annexed to the faid *Colloque* of the Valley of *Lucerna*.

The other *Colloque* which was called the *Colloque* of the Valley of *Perofa*, and *S. Martino*, contained the other feven Churches, namely, four in the faid Valley of *Perofa*, and three in the Valley of *S. Martino*.

Thofe

Thofe of *Perofa* were *Villaro* and *S. Germano*; joyned together and making one onely Church, *Pinachia, La Capella,* and *Pramol*; And thofe of *S. Martino* were *Villa Secca, Maneglia,* and *Prali.*

The Church of *S. Giovanni* contains within it felf a very fair Plain, and little Hills, very fertile and abounding in Grain, Vines, Cheftnuts, Figs, Olives, and all forts of Fruits. But for as much as the whole is thus employed in Husbandry, there is want of Paftures and Woods, which is the reafon that they have not there much Cattel, fave onely Oxen to till their Ground, and to carry their Wine to *Turin,* and other places of *Piemont,* to fell.

The faid Church has yet annexed unto it the places of *Lucerna, Lucernetta,* the Vineyards of *Lucerna, Fenile, Bubiana,* and *Bricheras.* In the City of *Lucerna,* which gives the name to the whole Valley, a third part of the Inhabitants were of the Reformed Religion. As alfo in *Lucernetta,* in the Vineyards of *Lucerna* almoft all the Inhabitants, profeffed the Reformed Religion time out of minde.

Fenile alfo is yet lower on the other fide of the River *Pelice* towards the South, being a more fat and fertile Soil, than any place of *S. Giovanni,* in all forts of Fruits and Grain.

Bubiana as to the Plain, is the fame with *Fenile,* and clofe adjoyning to it. But the Proteftants have heretofore been chafed and driven out of a great part thereof by little and little; And that which they then poffeffed in this Communalty, was for the moft part in Hills, which were terminated at *Fruzzafca, Bagnolo,* and *Barge,* where grows but little Corn or Wine, being all covered with Cheftnuts; The Proteftant Inhabitants of this place, (which were about fifty five Families) were the greateft part of them poor, chiefly living upon meer induftry, and of the profit they made by Wood, which they carried to fell at the Towns of *Bubiana* and *Lucerna.*

The Hills of *Bricheras,* (where there have always been Proteftant Families) are like to thofe of *S. Giovanni.*

The Church of *La Torre* is the fame for fituation and quality with that of *S. Giovanni,* containing one Plain, where is the Town of *La Torre,* and alfo Hills adorned with the fame kindes of Fruits as the faid Church of *S. Giovanni.*

The Church of *Villaro* is adjoyned to that of *La Torre,* but is a little higher towards *Dauphine,* containing a little Plain, where the Town is feated, and the refidue of Hills abounding with Vines and Cheftnuts.

The Church of *Bobbio* confineth with that of *Villaro,* being a little higher towards the Mountain on the Weft, but as fertile every way as that of *Villaro.* And as the faid places are environed with a multitude of Mountains and fat Paftures, fo the Inhabitants had a very great number of Oxen, Kine, and fmaller Cattel, together with Milk and Wool in abundance, which returned them a confiderable profit, as alfo the Cheftnuts which they dried and cleanfed to fell, or exchange for other Commodities.

The Church of *Rorata* is a little Dale or Valley fituated on the other fide

1.*Villaro,* and *S. Germano.* 2.*Pinachia.* 3.*La Capella.* 4.*Pramoli.* 5.*Villa Secca.* 6.*Maneglia.* 7.*Prali.* A defcription of the Church of *S.Giovanni.*

The places annexed to the Church of *Lucerna.*

A defcription of the Church of *La Torre.*

A defcription of the Church of *Villaro.*

A defcription of the Church of *Bobbio.*

side of the River *Pelice*, on the West of *Lucerna*, being bounded by the Mountains of *Villaro*. The said place abounds in Pastures, and is otherwise very fertile, especially in Cheſtnuts.

The Church of *Angrogna* is North-weſt to that of *S. Giovanni*, inclining towards *Perofa*, in a mountainous Countrey, but fertile in Cheſtnuts, Grain, and Paſtures, incompaſſed with very beautifull and fertile Mountains for Paſturage in the Summer ſeaſon.

The Church of *Roccapiatta* contains four parts or parcels, namely the said place of *Roccapiatta*, *S. Bartholomeo*, *Peruſtine*, and *L' Inverſo delle Porte*. In the three latter, which are lower towards the Plain of *S. Secondo*, grows abundance of rich Wines, Cheſtnuts, and other good Fruits. In *Roccapiatta*, which is ſomewhat higher inclining towards *Angrogna*, they have Grain, Paſture and other Fruits, but no Wine.

The Church of *Villaro* and *S. Germano*, is ſituated in the loweſt part of *Perofa*, about a mile from *Pignerolio*; the Weſt and North part of *Villaro* being on this ſide the River *Cluſone*, within the obedience of the King of *France*, and *S. Germano* on the South and Eaſt of *Villaro*, within the Duke of *Savoy*'s Dominion, on the other ſide of the ſaid River, which running along the whole length of the ſaid Valley, ſeparates the *Kings* Territories from thoſe of the *Duke*. Theſe two places of *Villaro* and *S. Germano* contain a little Plain both on the one ſide and the other, the reſt is in Hills, generally affording Corn, Wine, and other Fruits.

The Church of *Pinachia* ſtands within the *French* Dominion, being on the Weſt part thereof contiguous to that of *Villaro*, and contains a very fair and beautifull Plain, fenced on the North-ſide with pleaſant little Hills, having on the Weſt the Town and Fort of *Perofa*, on the South the River *Cluſone*, and on the other ſide thereof in the ſame South-ſide, other Hills, but ſcarce any Plain at all, belonging to his *Royal* Highneſs. It generally abounds in Grain, Wines, Nuts, Graſs, and all ſorts of Fruits.

The Church of *La Capella* is Weſt to that of *Pinachia*, in the uppermoſt part of the Valley of *Perofa*, cloſe adjoyning on the Weſt part thereof to the Valley of *Pragela*, or *Cluſone*, (which belongs to the King of *France*, and ſo has done from all antiquity) and to the Burrough or Citadel of *Perofa*, on the Eaſt. This *La Capella* has ſeveral little Hills exceeding fertile in all things, in a manner juſt like unto that of *Pinachia*, and it has annexed unto it *Pomare*, and another called *Inverſo de Perofa*, ſeparated from the ſaid Confines of *Perofa*, the one by the River *Cluſone*, the other by the River *Germanaſca*, which comes from the Valley of *S. Martino*. Moreover, it has other ſmall Villages called *Le Mean*, conſtituting a little Communalty, at the foot of the Valley of *Pragela*, and having its dependance upon it, but in reference to all Eccleſiaſtical Affairs, always adjoyned to the Church of *Capella* or *Perofa*.

The Church of *Pramol*, is ſituated upon a Mountain, between the Valley of *Lucerna* and *Perofa*, at the feet whereof grows a little quantity of Wine, and very good Fruits, but in the higheſt part thereof grows nothing but Grain, and abundance of Wood, and there is alſo

Paſture-

Pasture-ground ; this is the Native Countrey of Captain *Faber*, of whom we shall hereafter speak at large, as one whose name ought to be very memorable to posterity.

The Church of *Chiotti* or *Villa Secca*, is at the lowest part of the Valley *S. Martino*, where there is almost no Plain, save onely there where the River *Germanasca* takes its course. The little Hills which lie South from the said River side are very cold, so that there grow no Vines near them. But those that lie North, whose sides open towards the South, are hot, and by that means have on them store of Vines. In sum, all the parts thereof are tolerably fruitfull in Grain, Fruits, and Pasture. *A description of the Church of Chiotti, or Villa Secca.*

The Church of *Maneglia*, which is on the West part of that of *Chiotti*, comprehends three little Communalties, namely, *Maneglia*, *Macel*, and *Salsa*. The whole is in a Mountainous place, but exceeding fruitfull in Grain, Pasture, and the like, save onely in the highest parts thereof. *A description of the Church of Maneglia.*

The Church of *Prali*, is situated in the upmost part of the Valley of *S. Martino*, and contains two Communalties, namely, *Prali* and *Rodoret*, which are confined on the South, by the *Alps*, with the Valley of *Lucerna*, on the West by the Valley of *Queyras* in *Dauphine*, and on the North by the Valley of *Pragela* : there grows here nothing but Hay, and a great quantity of Herbage. *A description of the Church of Prali.*

Generally in all these Churches (unless it be on the tops of the Mountains) there is found great plenty of Fruits, but especially Chestnuts ; yea, there are some places thereof where are vast spaces of Ground yielding almost nothing else ; as for example, in the little Hills of *Bubiana*, and all along the Valley of *Lucerna*, and the South parts of the Valley of *Perosa*, which look towards the North ; in so much that the Inhabitants of those places dry and cleanse great quantities of them, a part whereof they lay up for their own spending, and the rest they sell or exchange for Corn, and that, quantity for quantity, with the Inhabitants of the Plain (this being a great part of their food in *Piemont*.) They likewise make of these Nuts, dried in an Oven, or upon a Kiln, an excellent sort of Bisquet, which in *France* they call *Marrons*, which they first of all string, as they do their *Chapelets*, or Beads, and then hang them up in some humid place the better to preserve them ; These they frequently make use of, instead of *Macqueroons*, or such other kinde of Confects.

CHAP.

CHAP. III.

The Antiquity of the Evangelical Churches in the Valleys of Piemont, from the days of Christ and his Apostles, down to the present Age.

THe fore-going Chapter prefents to the *Readers* eye, the beautiful Situation of the *Valleys* of *Piemont*, with the great abundance of Fruits which the Earth there brings forth, both for the neceffity and convenience of the body: This gives him as pleafant a profpect of the heavenly fituation of thofe Evangelical Churches, together with the fpiritual and divine *Fruits* of *Faith*, *Hope*, and *Patience*; which were long fince planted by *Chrift* and his *Apoftles*, and cultivated by their Succeffours in following Generations, down to this prefent Age.

True it is, That a great part of the moft ancient Records, and Authentick Pieces, treating of, and difcovering the Antiquity of thofe Churches, have been induftrioufly fought after, and committed to the flames, by their bloudy Perfecutors, in the Years 1559, and 1560. that fo the truth of their affairs might lie for ever fmother'd under thofe afhes, and be buried in perpetual filence ; neverthelefs God has been fo gracious to his Church, both in preferving, as it were by miracle, many Authentick Pieces relating to this particular, compiled and written by the ancient Inhabitants in their own proper Language, as alfo by fuffering even the moft eminent and bitter of their Adverfaries, ever and anon unwarily to let fall many remarkable paffages to this purpofe, in thofe very Writings which they compofed exprefly againft them ; That by the help of thefe two *Mediums*, it will be eafie to produce fuch Arguments for the antiquity of that Religion, which both they and we at this day profefs, as are fufficient to convince any fober perfon, who does not wilfully fhut his eys againft a noon-day truth.

But before we fall directly upon this point, it will be neceffary to premife this, namely, that it is a truth generally received by all thofe who profefs to be verfed in *Ecclefiaftical* Hiftory, that before the year 800, the differences between the *Catholick* and *Reformed* Churches (excepting fome few *clouds* of *Ceremonies* which were yet no bigger then a *mans hand*) did not at all publickly appear, (at leaft, fo as to be eftablifhed by *General Councils* or decrees) in any part of *Italy*. As for the firft 500 years, Bifhop *Jewel* will undertake, that not any one clear fentence can be produced out of any one *Father* or *Council* for the *Papifts* againft the *Proteftants*. And therefore we may take the generality of the *Fathers* and Writers in thofe Ages to be on our fide, in all points then controverted & now maintained by us againft *Rome*. So that the main of the *Quere* will fall upon the 2 next *Centuries*, which was a period moft barren of Authors, and of thofe few that wrote, *Italy* had but a fmall proportion, yet we may inftance in one or two of note. *Gregory* the firft entituled the *Great*, who died *A. D.* 605. (befides

Whitaker and *Humphry* in anfwer to *Campians* firft reafon, *in fine*.

Gregor. 1.

sides his detesting and rejecting the title of *Occumenical Bishop*, which was the next year after his death, claimed by *Boniface* the third, consented to by *Phocas* the Emperor, and confirmed by a Council at *Rome A. D.* 607) is ours in very many points against the present Church of *Rome*, some whereof *Illyricus* in his *Catalogus Testium* hath collected, and more might be gathered, had not the *Papists* so abominably corrupted him, as Dr. *Thomas James* in his *Bellum Gregorianum* hath made to appear in some hundreds of places. Also *Paulinus* Bishop of *Aquileia* in the year 790, held the truth in many of the controverted points, as appears out of the same *Illyricus*. In the year 794, the Synod of *Franckfort*, at which were present many *Italian* Bishops, condemned the second *Nicene Council* for decreeing *Image-worship* (though *Binius* and others would fain evade it) for confirmation whereof there are cited *Aventinus l. 4. Aimonius l. 4. c. 85. Hincmarus in Lugd. Episcop. c. 20. Abb. Urspergensis*, whose testimonies are related by *Hospinian de Origine Imaginum, c. 10.* printed *Tiguri* 1603, and partly by *Vignier* in his *Recuel de l' Histoire de l' Eglise*, ad *An.* 794.

Illyricus Cat.
Testium p. 558
ex Officin. Fac.
Stoer. 1608.

Illyr. Cat. Test.
l, 8. p. 650.

   These things being premised, in the first place therefore it may be affirmed, That these Churches of the *Valleys* of *Piemont* remained united with the other *Christian Churches*, and particularly with that of *Rome*, so long as it retained the true Religion, which was planted throughout all *Italy*, by the *Apostles*, their *Disciples*, and *Successours*. But when as the Church of *Rome* began to corrupt it self, and would by no means be perswaded to retain the purity of that *Apostolical Doctrine* and Divine worship, then those of the *Valleys* began to separate themselves from them, and to *come out from amongst them, that so they might not be partakers of their sins, nor receive of their plagues.* And this is evident by divers very ancient Manuscripts, long since laid up and preserved in the Valley of *Pragela*, which do directly strike at and oppose the Errors of the *Church of Rome.* Among these Manuscripts there are three very considerable: The first is intituled, *Qual cosa sia Antichrist?* that is to say, *What thing is Antichrist?* which was written in the year 1120. The second was written (as is supposed) much about the same time, Entituled, *Purgatori Soima*, that is to say, *The Dream of Purgatory:* The third is as ancient as the other two, and Entituled, *La causa del nostre departiment de la Gleisa Romana*, That is to say, *The cause of our separation from the Church of Rome.* These Manuscripts are not onely made mention of by that famous and learned Mr. *Paul Perrin* in his History *Des Vaudois*; but likewise averred by Mr. *Thomas Tronchin* the chief Minister of *Geneva*, (a person of known probity and learning) whose formal Attestation is here inserted.

The first
Ground or E-
vidence of a
notable Argu-
ment to prove
the Antiquity
of the Prote-
stant Church-
es in the Val-
leys of Pie-
mont from the
days of Christ
and his Apo-
stles down to
the present
Age.
The titles of
three famous
Manuscripts
written by the
ancient Inha-
bitants of the
Valleys of
Piemont in
their own pro-
per Language.
Paul Perrin
des Vaudois,
Geneve pour
Piere & Ja-
ques Chouet.
CID.ID.XIX.

The Attestation of Mr. Thomas Tronchin, *the chief Minister of* Geneva, *a person of known probity and learning, concerning certain Manuscripts touching the ancient Doctrine and Worship of the Evangelical Churches in the Valleys of* Piemont, *inserted in Mr.* Paul Perrin's *History.*

The true Original of which Attestation, is to be seen, together with the rest of the Original Papers and Pieces of this present History, in the publick Library of the famous University of Cambridge.

I Whofe Name is here under-written, Minifter of the Holy Gofpel, and Divinity Profefsor at *Geneva,* do atteft, that Sieur *Jean Paul Perrin* coming into this City to prin the Hiftory of the *Waldenfes* and *Albigenfes* by him compiled, did then communicate to me that his Work, and divers Original Manufcripts, out of which he had extracted the ancient Doctrine and Difcipline of thofe People, which Manufcripts I then faw and perufed, in faith whereof I have given this prefent Atteftation, to the end that it may ferve and bear witnefs to the truth, when and where ever there fhall be occafion. Made at *Geneva, Nov.* 19. 1656.

THO: TRONCHIN.

The illuftra-
tion of the
firft Argu-
ment.

Now then I fay, Thefe Churches of the *Valleys* of *Piemont,* feparating from the Church of *Rome,* do not upon this account either begin or ceafe to be the true Church of God; but rather did hereby manifeft their perfeverance in that ancient Doctrine of *Chrift* and his *Apoftles,* from which the Church of *Rome* was now departed. Even as the *Jewifh* Church of old feparated it felf from the ten idolatrous *Tribes*; and fo, the faithful *Jews* believing in *Jefus Chrift,* and retaining the ancient Doctrine of the *Patriarchs* and *Prophets,* when they were perfecuted by the *High Priefts* of the unbelieving *Jews,* feparated themfelves from them; But yet neither did the one or the other by this feparation, lofe their ancient right of fucceffion; nay, on the contrary, they did hereby retain the fame in its firft chanel, and primitive purity.

The fecond
Ground of a
notable Argu-
ment to prove
the Anti-
quity of the
Waldenfian
Churches in
the Valleys of
Piemont, from
the days of
Chrift and his
Apoftles down
to the prefent
age.
*Jo. Tilius E-
pifcopus Mel-
denf. in Pra-
fat. in Lib. Ca-
roli Magni de
Imaginibus.*

In the fecond place, and in confirmation of the former, the *Ecclefia-ftical* Hiftory that treats of *Charls* the Great and his Followers, tells us, That both that Emperour and the *Weftern Churches* did joyntly ftrive and ufe their utmoft endeavour in the Council held at *Francfort* in the Year *794.* to have drawn Pope *Adrian* and the Church of *Rome* out of that Gulph of Superftition, into which it had precipitated it felf, by perfwading them to imbrace the true Doctrine of *Chrift* and his *Apoftles.* Moreover, that one of the chief Counfellours of the faid Emperour, (by name *Claudius* Archbifhop of *Turin,* and confequently of the Valleys of *Piemont*) was exceeding active, and did very much ftickle in this bufinefs. This *Claudius* was one of the moft learned and renowned Worthies of his Age, he was one of the chief Founders of the Academy of *Paris,* (as the Bifhop *de Meaux* in his Preface to the Books of *Charls* the Great touching *Images,* abundantly teftifies.) And about the Year of our Lord 815. the Emperour *Louis Le Debonair* Son of *Charls* the Great, preferr'd him to the Archbifhoprick of *Turin,* that fo he might furnifh his Diocefs with the Doctrine devoted *Italicæ plebi, to the people of Italy :* the which he in truth did with all his might, (as his famous Adverfary *Jonas Aurelianenfis* confeffeth) as well by frequent

quent Writings, as by painfull and conftant preaching to, and inftruct-
ing the Flock committed to his charge: for, indeed, this holy man
finding that he was not able to withftand that mighty torrent of the
Romiſh Superftitions in other parts, imployed all his endeavours, to preferve his own Diocefes from being infected with thofe idolatrous principles ; and to this end he ceafed not to inftruct his people by all ways
and means, That *they ought not to run to* Rome *for the pardon of their ſins,*
nor have recourſe to the Saints or their Reliques ; That *the Church is not*
founded upon St. Peter, *much leſs upon the Pope, but upon the Doctrine of*
the Apoſtles ; That *they ought not to worſhip Images, nor ſo much as have*
them in their Churches. And this he obferved throughout his whole
Diocefes, as is confeſſed by the abovefaid *Jonas Aurelianenſis,* in a
Book that he wrote expreſly againft him, in the Year 820. The fame is
likewife reported by *Bellarmine,* from whence I conclude, (and it is exceeding remarkable as to the proof of the matter in hand) that the fame
Belief which was publickly taught & profeft in thofe Valleys of *Piemont*
in the Year 820. was the very fame that is at this day profeft and owned by the *Reformed Churches* ; that is to fay, the true, ancient and
Evangelical Doctrine. To this I ſhall add, that not the moft bitter Adverfaries of this *Claudius* Arch-biſhop of *Turin,* were ever able to lay to
his charge any fundamental Errour, for as much as he always retained
Fidei Catholicæ Regulam, the Rule of the Catholick Faith ; and did not
expreſs any oppofition, fave onely againft the (pretended) *Traditiones*
Eccleſiaſticas, Eccleſiaſtick Traditions. Thefe are *Jonas Aurelianenſis*
his own expreſſions, yet in the mean time he dexteroufly gives himfelf
the Lie, for that calumny of *Arrianiſm* wherewith in other parts of his
Writings he had unjuſtly branded that worthy Biſhop and his Difciples,
meerly for their not complying with the idolatrous and fuperftitious Inventions of the Church of *Rome.* And this is all likewife that *Raineri-*
us Saccon has to object againft the *Waldenſes,* who fucceeded this Archbiſhop and his Difciples ; For faith he, *All other Sects render themſelves*
horrible, by reaſon of their Blaſphemies againſt God himſelf, but on the con-
trary, this hath great appearance of pietie, for as much as they live juſtly in
the ſight of men ; *they believe well, as concerning God, in all things, and*
hold all the Articles of the Creed;there is onely one thing againſt them,that is,
they hate and blaſpheme the Church of Rome, *and hereby they eaſily gain*
credit and belief among the people. In like manner *Samuel de Cafsini* a
Frier of the *Franciſcan* Order, writing againft the *Waldenſes,* inhabiting
the Valleys of *Piemont,* declares plainly in the beginning of his Book,
intituled, *Vittoria Trionfale,* printed at *Coni cum privilegio,* in the Year
1510. *That all the* (pretended) *Errours of thoſe* Waldenfes *conſiſted in*
this, that they denied the Church of Rome *to be the holie Mother Church,*
and would not obey her Traditions. As touching other points, he confeffeth, that the *Waldenſes* did acknowledg the *Chriſtian* Church, whereof
likewife he reckons and efteems them as true members.

By this then, fay they, Firft, it plainly appears, that the Inhabitants
of thofe *Valleys* have profeft and taught the fame *Evangelical* Doctrine
which they now own, before the Dukes of *Savoy* had any poffeffion of
Piemont ;

*Jonas Aureli-
anenſis his re-
lation of the
chief Heads
of the Do-
ctrine of Clau-
dius Arch-bi-
ſhop of Turin.*

*Rainerius
Saccon his
chief Objecti-
on againſt the
Waldenſes.*

*Samuel de Caſ-
ſini his chief
cavil againſt
the Waldenſes
in his Vittoria
Trionfale,
printed at Co-
ni 1510.*

1. Corollary.

Piemont ; and therefore he has no juſtifiable pretext to deprive them of their ancient Liberties and Privileges, upon the account of Religion.

2. Corollary.

Again it is as manifeſt, and neceſſarily follows, that the *Waldenſes* who eſcaped the Maſſacres in *France*, in the Year 1165. and came from thence into the Valleys of *Piemont*, were not the firſt Founders of that Religion, but rather that they joyned themſelves to thoſe their faithfull Brethren, for the better fortifying and mutual edification of each others Faith, juſt as thoſe other *Waldenſes* did, who having recourſe to *Bohemia*, cloſed with the faithfull Profeſſours of the *Greek* Church there, who had retained the ancient and true Religion, (not the *Papal)* as

Stranchi Reip. Bohem.

Stranchi Reip. Bohem. teſtifies.) Neither is it at all probable, that it could be otherwiſe ; for the *Waldenſes* knew right well, that the ſeat of their chief Adverſary was in *Italie* ; and therefore they would not have been ſo void of all ſenſe and common prudence, as to have undertaken ſo long and tedious a Journey over the *Alps,* had they not been well aſſured that the Natives of thoſe Valleys who profeſſed the ſame Religion with them, would receive and embrace them as their Brethren.

D' Aubigné. Mr. Perrin.

D' Aubigné a very judicious Hiſtorian ſeems to be clearly of this opinion. And Mr. *Perrin* amongſt his other Manuſcripts makes mention of a certain Epiſtle of the *Waldenſes,* inſcribed, *La Epiſtola al ſereniſsimo Rey Lancelau, à li Ducs, Barons, & à li plus veil del Regne, Lo petit tropel de li Chriſtians appella per fals nom falſament P. O. V.* That is to ſay, *An Epiſtle to the moſt ſerene King* Lancelau, *the Dukes, Barons, and moſt ancient Nobilitie of the Realm. The little troop of Chriſtians falſly called by the name of poor people of* Lions, *or* Waldenſes. By which it is moſt evident, that they had not their original from the ſaid *Waldo,* but that this was a meer nick-name or reproachfull term put upon them by their Adverſaries, to make the world believe, that their Religion was but a Novelty, or a thing of yeſterday. Thus thoſe who eſcaped the Maſſacres

The reaſon of the ſeveral opprobrious and ignominious titles put upon the *Waldenſes* by their popiſh Adverſaries. Why they were called *Waldenſes.* *Albigenſes.* The poor of *Lyons. Chaignards. Tramontani. Lollards. Siccars. Fraticelli. Gazares.* *Turlepins.*

in *France,* were by the *popiſh* party ſirnamed either according to the places where they inhabited, or the chief of their Leaders ; for example, from *Waldo* a Citizen of *Lyons,* they were named *Waldenſes,* and from the Countrey of *Albie, Albigenſes.* And becauſe thoſe who did adhere to the doctrine of *Waldo* came out of *Lyons,* naked and ſtript of all their Goods and Eſtates, they were in deriſion, ſtyled, *The Poor of Lyons.* In *Dauphine* they were nick-named in mockery *Chaignards.* And for as much as part of them went over the *Alps,* they were called *Tramontani.* In *England* they were known by the name of *Lollards,* from one *Lollard* who was one of their chief Inſtructours in that Iſle. In *Provence* they were uſually termed *Siccars,* from a vulgar word then in uſe, which ſignified *Cut-purſes.* In *Italie* they had given them the title of *Fraticelli,* or *Men of the Brotherhood,* becauſe they lived together like Brethren. In *Germanie* they were named *Gazares,* a word which ſignifies *execrable,* and *wicked in the higheſt degree.* In *Flanders* they went under the name of *Turlepins,* that is to ſay, *Men inhabiting with, or companions of Wolves,* becauſe thoſe poor people were oft times conſtrained in the heat of perſecution, to inhabit in Woods and Deſerts, amongſt wilde and ſavage beaſts. Sometimes to render them more execrable,

crable, their Adverfaries borrowed the names of feveral ancient Hereticks to brand them with. Thus for as much as they made profeffion of purity in their Life and Doctrine, they were called *Cathares,* that is, *Puritans.* And becaufe they denied the *Hofte* which the Prieft holds up at *Mafs,* to be God, they were called *Arrians,* as thofe who denied the Divinity of the eternal Son of God. And becaufe they maintained that the Authority of the Kings and Emperours of the World, did not depend upon the Jurifdiction of the Pope, they were called *Manichæi,* as men afferting *two firft Principles.* And for fuch like caufes as thefe they were firnamed *Gnoftiques, Cataphrygians, Adamites,* and *Apoftolicks.* Yea fometimes their Adverfaries were outragious, *Matthew Paris* calls them *Ribaux,* that is, *Rogues, Rafcals, Scoundrels, Varlets,* or *bafe Fellows.* The Authour of the *Threfor des Hiftoires,* calls them *Bougres,* that is, *Buggerers* or *Sodomites.* *Rubis* reports, that the word *Sorcerer* was in thofe days expreffed by the term *Valdenfis.*

Now the lapfe of time between *Claudius* Arch-bifhop of *Turin,* and *Waldo,* does not at all hinder the continual Succeffion of thofe Churches and that Religion, no more than thofe dark Intervalls which were in the Church before and after the Deluge, thofe Intervalls of the *Egyptian* Bondage, the Judges, the *Babylonifh* Captivity, and the like in afterages, did hinder or interrupt the continual Succeffion of the *Jewifh* Religion; no more than the *Sun* or *Moon* do ceafe to be, when their light is eclipfed or withdrawn from the eye by the interpofition of other Bodies; no more than the Rivers, *Po,* the *Rhene,* or *Guadiana* in *Spain,* do lofe their continual current, becaufe for fome time they run under ground, or among the Rocks, and appear not; fo for the Church of God, though fometimes it has not been fo vifible to the eys of men, it hath notwithftanding continued in a conftant uninterrupted Succeffion through all Ages and Generations. Thus the good Prophet *Eliah* in his days thought he had been *left alone,* but yet God had referved at that very time feven thoufand fouls of the very fame principles and profeffion with himfelf.

Although this be a truth that is by many thought fufficient of it felf againft the fierceft objections of the gain-faying Adverfaries, yet I fhall proceed a ftep further, and make bold to allege moreover, that *Marc. Aurelio Rorenco* Priour of *Lucerna* in his *Narratione del Introduttione de gl' heretici nelle Valle di Piemonte,* printed at *Turin, Anno Dom.1632.* with approbation and privilege, confeffes that it continued to the ninth and tenth Century, which is the very intervall between the faid *Claudius* and *Peter Waldo,* or rather the retreat of certain of his Difciples into the faid *Valleys.* For the faid *Rorenco* teftifies in exprefs terms *pag.16. Nel nono è decimo fecolo continuarono l' herefie antecedenti,* that is, *The abovefaid Herefie continued throughout the ninth and tenth Centuries.* And to remove all fcruples, that this Doctrine which he calls Herefie, (as S. *Paul* fpeaks *Acts* 24. 14. and which the Enemies of the *Chriftian Religion* call Herefie) continued in the Valleys of *Piemont,* the fame *Rorenco* in his *Hiftorical Obfervations* printed at *Turin,* 1649. with approbation, and dedicated to the *Duke* himfelf, confeffeth *pag.3.* That the

Cathares.

Arrians.

Manichæi.

Gnoftiques.
Cataphrygians.
Adamites.
Apoftolicks.
Ribaux.
Bougres.

The third Ground of a notable Argument to prove the Antiquity of the Proteftant Churches in the Valleys of *Piemont* from the days of *Chrifti* and his Apoftles down to the prefent Age.

Marc. Aurelio Rorenco in his *Narratione del Introduttione de gl' Heretici nelle Valle di Piemonte,* printed at *Turin cum privilegio* 1632. *p.16.*

The continual Succeffion of the Reformed Religion through the feveral Centuries from our blefled Lord and Saviour down to the prefent Age.
1,2,3,4,5,6,7, 8,9,10,11,12, 13,14,15,16.

the faid *Claudius* Arch-bifhop of *Turin,* (and confequently of the *Valleys,* which were within that Diocefe) maintained this very Doctrine in the ninth Century. Wherefore feeing the Succeffion of the *Evangelical Religion* is manifeft from the time of the *Apoftles* to that of *Claudius* Arch-bifhop of *Turin,* which was in the eighth Century, and that his Doctrine continued in the ninth and tenth Centuries; and that in the beginning of the eleventh Century the *Waldenfes* or Difciples of *Peter Valdo* came into the *Valleys* to refide with their Brethren, where they have profeft and taught the fame ever fince; The profeffours of the *Reformed Religion* may clap their hands in token of an abfolute Triumph for ever againft all the Difciples of the Church of *Rome,* and fay, that they are now able manifeftly and undeniably to prove and make good the continual Succeffion of their *Religion* from the days of *Chrift* and his *Apoftles* down to this prefent Age.

2. Argument to prove the Antiquity of the Proteftant Churches in the Valleys of *Piemont* from the days of *Chrift* and his *Apoftles* down to the prefent Age.

In the fecond place, the faithfull people of the *Valleys* in the Year 1535. being at that time poffeffed of their ancient Hiftories and Manufcripts, teftifying the Antiquity of their Churches, which were afterwards confumed to afhes by their Perfecutours in the Years 1559. and 1560. caufed to be printed at their own proper coft and charges the firft *French* Bible that ever was put forth, or came to light, and that for the benefit of the *Evangelical Churches* where this Language was in ufe, and dedicated the fame to God himfelf by the Pen of their Interpreter *Robert Olivetan,* in the Preface of the faid Bible; which was a Piece moft folemnly confecrated, and fpeaking as it were to God himfelf, wherein they mention, that they have always had the full enjoyment of that heavenly Truth contained in the holy Scriptures, ever fince they were enriched with the fame by the *Apoftles* themfelves. And for as much as it is a Piece fo exceeding rare, and to be found in very few places of the World, I have here inferted the fame at length, in the original Language, and their own words as followeth.

The

The Preface of *Robert Olivetan* to his Tranflation of the *French Bible*, Printed at *Neuf Chaftel*, and publifhed, *June* 3. *Anno Dom.* 1535.

LA bonne Couflume à obtenu de toute ancienneté que ceux qui mettent en avant quelque livre en publique, (foit qu'ils l'ayent compilé de leur propre induftrie & invention , ou qu'ils l'ayent tranflaté d'une langue en autre) le viennent à defdier & prefenter à quelque Prince, Roy, Empereur, ou Monarche, ou s'il y a quelque Majefté plus Souveraine : A celle fin (comme ils fçavent bien dire) que l'oeuure fe trouue plus franchement, & hardiment entre les mains des hommes comme ayant fauf-conduit, & eftant mis en la fauvegarde du Prince, auquel il eft offert , & dedié : Et ce voyons nous eftre fait & pratiqué de jour en jour. Laquelle maniere de faire, n'eft point totalement maintenue fans caufe : Car avec ce que on eft invité & affriandé à ce par l'expectation d'un Royal remerciement, (c'eft à dire ample & liberal recompenfement) aucuns ont bien telle prudence & efgard, que leurs inventions ne feroyent pas bien receües du peuple, fi elles ne portoyent la livrée de quelque Tres Illuftre, Tres Excellent, Tres Haut, Tres Puiffant, Tres Manifique , Tres Redouté , Tres Victorieux, Tres Sacre, Beatiffime & Sanctiffime *Nom.*

Parquoy apres avoir eu le tout bien confideré & veu courir & trotter tous les autres efcrivains & tranflateurs, l'un deçà l'autre delà, l'unà fon Mecenas,

IT has been a laudable Cuftome in all Ages, for fuch as have caufed Books to be publifht, (whether they have been the true Authours thereof , or the Tranflators onely) to dedicate and prefent the fame to fome Prince, King , Emperour, or Monarque, or to a more fupreme Power, if there were any fuch, to the end (as they themfelves freely confefs) that their Work might appear with the more boldnefs and confidence before men, having as it were a fafe conduct, and being under the protection of that Prince, to whom it is dedicated. And this we fee daily practifed, and indeed not altogether without ground : For befides that the expectation of fome Royal thanks, (that is to fay, of a noble and Princely Reward) does allure and invite men thereunto: There are thofe who do verily believe , that their Inventions would not finde acceptance with the People, unlefs they were adorned with the Livery of fome moft *Illuftrious , Excellent , High , Mighty, Magnificent, Dreadfull , Invincible, Sacred , Bleffed, and moft Holy* Name.

Therefore having throughly confidered thefe things, and obferved how all other Authours and Tranflators have their feveral addreffes, the one to his moft magnificent *Mecænas,*
the

the other to his moſt Worſhipfull Patron, and a third to his moſt Reverend, I know not what, I thought it not fit to comply ſo much with Cuſtome, in the ſetting forth of this preſent Tranſlation of the Bible, which I have in hand, (notwithſtanding that I have been much flattered, tempted, yea importuned by her) as to binde and oblige my ſelf to pay her that tribute which ſhe claims and requires, I mean to entitle ſome Lordly, Majeſtick, and immortal Guide to this Book, which I now ſend forth, not at all intending that it ſhould follow thoſe *ways of the Gentiles*, neither indeed would it become a Work of this nature to play the Paraſite, what glorious *Thraſo* ſoever it meets with, for as much as it is quite of another nature than all other Books whatſoever, whoſe Authours ſeek ſo much after profit and merit in the dedication of them, craftily exchanging the ſame for rich Preſents and advantageous Grants, which manner of game I hunt not after, as not ſtanding in need thereof, thanks be to God, who abundantly furniſhes me with contentment. Now it had been alſo in my power to have made a fair and ſingular preſent of this Tranſlation, but not to ſuch as I might have been willing to chuſe and nominate, though never ſo Great, Mighty, and Abſolute ; for this Book needs neither the favour, ſupport, or protection of humane Powers or Principalities, nor indeed any Patronage though never ſo ſovereign, but thine onely, *O poor little Church*, together with thoſe thy faithfull ones, who have truly learned and known God in *Jeſus Chriſt*, his onely Son and our Lord ; I mean not that Church which triumphs with pomp and riches ; neither do I mean the Church Militant which defends it ſelf by force of Arms: No, it is Thee

liberaliſsime, l' autre à ſon patron colendiſsime , l' autre à ſon, je ne ſçay quel , Reverendiſsime , Je ayant en main ceſte preſente tranſlation de la Bible preſte à mettre en avant, n'ay pas tant fait pour icelle Dame Couſtume, (ja ſoit qu'elle m'ait moult enhorté, flatté, tenté, voire auſſy importuné) que je me ſoye voulu aſſervir & aſſuiettir, au droit qu'elle exige & requiert, affin de nommer & donner quelque Seigneurialle, auguſte, & immortelle guide à ceſtuy livre, que j'envoye en publique, duquel le chemin ne s'addreſſe point en telle voye des Gentils, auſſy ne luy appartient il point faire du Paraſite, quelque glorieux Thraſo qu'il recontre. Car il eſt bien d'autre eſtoffe que tous autres livres quels qu'ils ſoyent , les Autheurs d'eſquels en font offrandes ſi proffitables & meritoires, & ſi cauteleux eſchanges contre riches dons, & plantureux octroys. Apres leſquelles beſtes , je ne chaſſe point : car je me paſſe bien de cel gibier , la grace à Dieu qui me fournit de contentment à ſuffiſance. Or eſtoit il bien en moy de faire auſſy quelque beau & ſingulier preſent de la preſente tranſlation : mais non pas à qui que j'euſſe bien voulu choiſir & nommer tant grand, puiſſant, & Souverain fut il, car tel livre de ſoy meſme n'a que faire de faveur, ſupport, ny adveu humain quel qu'il ſoit , ne de puiſſance principauté, ou paternité, quelconque, tant Souveraine ſoit elle, fors que de toy, O pauvre petit Egliſes, & de tes vrays fideles, ſçavans & ayans la cognoiſſance de Dieu par Jeſus Chriſt ſon ſeul filz noſtre Signeur. Je ne di point celle Egliſe triumphante en pompes & richeſſes : ne militante, c'eſt à dire guerroyante par faits d'armes. C'eſt à toy ſeule
à nbi

à qui s'addreſſe ce precieux threſor (du quel tu en pourrois dire מזהוא comme les enfans d'Iſrael, n'eſperant toutes fois que jamais il te ſoit en faſcherie) & ce de par un certain pauure peuple le tien amy & frere en Jeſus Chriſt : Lequel, depuis que jadis il en fut doue & enrichy par les Apoſtres ou Ambaſſadeurs de Chriſt en a touſiours eu l'entiere jouiſſance & fruition. *Et maintenant Iceluy te voulant faire feſte de ce que tant tu deſire & ſouhaite : m'à donné cette charge & commiſsion de tirer & deſployer iceluy threſor hors des armaires & coffres* Ebraicques *&* Grecz, *pour (apres l'avoir entaſſé & empacqueté en bougettes* Francoiſes, *le plus convenablement que je pourroye, ſelon l'addreſſe & le don que Dieu ma donné) en faire un preſent à toy ò pauure Egliſe, à qui rien on ne preſente. Et certes je ne voyoie raiſon aucune pourquoy il ſe deuſt donner à autre qu'à toy, Car que voudroit on donner à ceux qui ont tout, & auxquels tout de tous ſe donne ? Or cecy qui vaut bien autant & plus que le tout des chevances & richeſſes mondaines, eſt pour* toy pauurette Egliſe, *à qui (las) on oſte pluſtoſt qu'on ne donne, & qui es tellement deſſaiſie de tous biens, qu'és tant mince, aſſadie, & amagrie, qu'il ne te reſte que la parole. Urayement il ne te reſte que la parole, la parole (di je) de verité & de vie,* la parole de Dieu, laquelle demeure Eternellement. *Par laquelle tu as eſté crée & engendrée. Ainſy tu n'as que les biens de ta naiſſance & generation : car tu es nue, & deſpourveue de toutes autres richeſſes, des quelles le monde eſtant fardé & reparé ſe glorifie tant en ſoy meſme. Ceſt offre donc t'eſtoit proprement deüe (qui ne t'euſt*

alone to whom I preſent this precious Treaſure (whereof thou mayſt ſay מזהוא as the Children of *Iſrael*, yet hoping that it ſhall never create thee any trouble) in the name of a certain poor People thy Friends and Brethren in Jeſus Chriſt, *who ever ſince they were bleſſed and enriched therewith by the Apoſtles and Ambaſſadours of* Chriſt, *have ſtill enjoyed and poſſeſſed the ſame :* and being now willing to gratifie thee with what thou deſireſt ſo earneſtly, they have given me a Commiſſion to draw this precious Treaſure out of the *Hebrew* and *Greek* Cabinets, and having wrapt up the ſame in a *French* Mantle, to the beſt of my skill, and according to that talent which the Lord hath given me, forthwith to preſent thee with it (O poor Church) on whom no man beſtows any thing. And indeed I ſee no reaſon why it ſhould be preſented to any but thy ſelf, For what can be given to thoſe that have all things, and to whom every one gives what he hath? As for this, which is of as great, yea of much greater value than all worldly wealth or riches, I ſay it is for thee, *O poor Church*, whoſe ſubſtance they would much ſooner diminiſh than increaſe. To thee, I ſay, who art ſo unprovided of all things, who art ſo thin and lean, and out of heart, and haſt nothing left thee but the voice onely, no I ſay, Thou haſt nothing left thee but voice and words (yet) the Word of Truth and Life, *The Word of God, which endureth for ever*, and whereby thou haſt been created and begotten : and ſo thou haſt onely the Goods which are thine by Birth-right and Inheritance, being unprovided of all other Riches, wherewith the Men of the World are painted and adorned, and wherein they ſo much glory. This therefore was properly due to thee, (to do thee no wrong) becaufe it contains all thy Patrimony, thy Eftate, and all that belongs to thee, that is to fay, that very fame Word, by virtue whereof, and through the confidence and affurance which thou repofeft in it, thou doft efteem thy felf rich in poverty, happy in misfortune, in folitude well-accompanied, fetled in doubts, undaunted in perils, at perfect eafe in the midft of torments, honoured in reproaches, profperous in adverfities, not at all diftempered in ficknefs, and even quickened and raifed to life in death it felf: Accept therefore I pray thee (*O poor little Church*) this gift which I offer thee in the name of that poor People, with as much joy, & with as good a heart (notwithstanding thine afflictions, griefs and troubles) as it is fent and dedicated unto thee. Why fhould we be afhamed to prefent thee with fuch a royal gift? notwithstanding that thou art fo defolate, fo deformed and defpifed, and very often (yea and for the moft part) haft in thy Family the blinde, the lame, the halt, the deaf and the dumb, the fick of the Palfie, ftrangers, widows, orphans, the fimple and the ignorant, all ftanding in great need of the confolations of *Chrift*; feeing the Lord has given and communicated himfelf to fuch a *meek, lowly* and *humble* generation, and hath freely *declared unto them the great myfteries of the Kingdom; which have been hidden in all Ages*, as alfo ftyling himfelf their Evangelift, and affuring them that *the Kingdom of Heaven belongs unto them*. This is his little inexpugnable Canton, his little invincible Brigade and victorious Army, to whom he *gives a fpirit of power*, and whom he animates and imboldens (like a noble General) by his own prefence, and likewife difpoffeffes them of all fear by the force and virtue of his *living and powerfull Word*.

voulu faire tort) en tant qu' elle contient & comprend tout ton patrimoine ton droict proprietaire, & tout tant qu'il t' appartient, affavoir icelle mefme parole, par laquelle & par la foy & affeurance que tu as à Icelle: en pauureté, tu te repute trefriche ; en malheureté, bien heureufe ; en folitude, bien accompagnée ; en doute, accertainée ; en perils, affeurée ; en torments, allegée ; en reproches, honnorée ; en adverfités, profperée ; en maladie, faine ; en mort, vivifiée. *Tu accepteras donc* O pauurette petite Eglife *ceftuy prefent que je te prefente pour & en nom d' iceluy pauure peuple, d' auffy joyeufe affection (non obftant tes afflictions, angoiffes, & douleurs) que de bon coeur il t' eft envoyé & dedié. Pourquoy aurions nous honte de t' addreffer un tel prefent Royal: combien que tu fois fy defolée, maloftruë, & deboutée, & aye le plus fouvent & pour la plus part en ta famille aveugles, boiteux, impotents, manchots, fourds, paralyticques, eftrangers, vefues, & orphelins, fimples & idiots, tous ayans finguliercment befoin de la confolation de Chrift, veu que Iceluy s' eft donné & communiqué foy mefme à telle maniere de gens, abjects, petits, & humbles, & leur à familierement* declaré les grands fecrets du Royaume cachez de tout temps, *defquels auffy il fe dit & renomme eftre l' Euangelifte, & auxquels il protefte* le Royaume des cieux appartenir: C' eft fon petit Canton inexpugnable, fa petite bande invincible, fa petite armée victorieufe, à laquelle, (comme un vray chef de guerre) il donne courage & hardieffe par fa prefence, &. chaffe toute frayeur & crainte par fa vive & vigoureufe parole.

Mais

Mais ne te voudrois tu point volon-
tiers enquerir & enquester, qui est cest
amy incogneu & estrange bien faiteur,
qui se mesle ainsy de te donner le tien,
quant a ce qu'il te donne le tien,
i'estime que tu ne luy en sçauras pas
moins de gré, que s'il te donnoit quel-
que autre chose, (combien qu'il ne te
sçauroit rien donner meilleur) veu que
de sy long temps voire (comme je croy)
jamais, (au moins si pleinement &
franchement) on ne t'à donné le loisir
d'en pouuoir jouyr, comme mainte-
nant tu feras, le bien est tien, & sy
le te donc tellement, qu'il est aussy sien,
& luy demeure entierement, tant est
feconde & heureuse la communication
d'une telle chevance. O la gracieuse
denrée de charité, de laquelle on fait
marchandise par telle convenance sub-
tile & proffitable ! O la benigne pos-
fefsion de grace qui rend au donnant
& à l'acceptant une mesme joye & de-
lectation ! Quel autre don ou quelle
parcille pourroyent donner les hommes
entre eux dont ils ne puissent avoir
faute quelque fois, & en donnant ne
craignent estre dommagez, & en avoir
puis apres besoing ? Quelque beau sem-
blant qu'ils facent, quand ce vient à
offrir, & quelque propos qu'ils ayent
en la bouche, pour vouloir colorer &
faire entendre de combien bon cœur
ils donnent : si à il coufiours en quel-
que anglet de ce cœur une prudence
poureuse, qui crie, Regarde que tu
feras, garde que tu n'ayes faute de ce
dont tu es prodigue. Or ne va il pas
ainsi de ceste besongne, & de ce don
lequel est bien d'autre nature & feli-
cité que tout autre don. Car (affin
que tu le sçache) il n'est fait que pour
estre donné & communiqué à un chaf-
cun, & veut le gracieux donnateur,

But now, It may be thou wouldest willingly know who this thy concealed Friend and unheard of Benefactor is, who undertakes to prefent thee with that which is thine own,(though as for giving thee what is thine own, I prefume that thou efteemeft thy felf no lefs beholding unto him, than if he fhould have given thee fomething elfe, and yet he can give thee no better thing) feeing it is now a long time fince thou hadft, nay (I believe) thou never hadft leave and leafure (at leaft not fo full and free) to enjoy it, as thou now fhalt; the Treafure is thine, and yet he gives it fo to thee, that it is his alfo, and remains his wholly. So fruitfull and advantagious is the communication of fuch a good. O the bleffed Trade of Charity, wherewith one may make Traffick in fo convenient, wife and profitable way ! O happy poffeffion of grace, which fills and replenifhes the giver and the receiver with the fame joy ! what other, or what equal gift can men give one to another and not fometimes want it, or not be afraid both to fuffer dammage by giving it, and likewife want it afterwards? I fay, As for other gifts, let the giver thereof make never fo fair a fhew, or colour the bufinefs with never fo fine words, and endeavour to perfwade his Friends that it comes moft willingly and from the heart, yet there is ftill in fome corner or other of that heart, a relučating kinde of prudence which thus whifpers in his ears, Have a care of what thou doft, and take heed left thou come one day to want thofe things whereof thou art now fo prodigal: but now it is not fo in this bufinefs, and with this gift, which is of a far better nature and virtue than other gifts whatfoever, for thou muft know, that it is to be given and communicated to every one, and that it is
the

the pleasure of the gracious giver, (who of his free will has given it) that it should be *freely given, and without expectation of reward*; for it is of such a nature, that it makes rich those to whom it is given, and does not impoverish in the least those that are the givers of it, but rather they finde and are perswaded, that they have made a good bargain, and have been no losers in finding an occasion to present it unto thee, and to give thee the possession thereof. *This poor People who presents thee with it, was driven away and banisht out of thy company above three hundred years ago, and was dispersed up and down in the four Quarters of* France, and have been ever since accounted and reputed to be (though without ground, onely for the sake of *Chrift,* and according to his Word) the most *wicked, execrable, and ignominious Generation* that ever was, in so much that their very name has been a *Proverb* and *By word* to other People. Nevertheless, of late time, a certain person of eternal renown (having been truly informed of the holy behaviours and integrity of that People, and understood those false and calumnious accusations wherewith they were branded by their Enemies) hath of late years taken away their name of reproach by publick Proclamation, and bestowed on them a noble and royal Title, even such as he bore himself, and it is this, *The true patient People,* who by silence and hope has overcome all the assaults and violences of their Enemies, neither could those lapses and intervalls of time any ways rob their just cause of its undoubted right, to the fruition whereof he now invites thee, and to the enjoyment of a sure conquest obtained by *Jesus Chrift.* Dost thou not know who this person is? I tell thee, It is thine own

lequel de son gré l'à donné, que gracieusement sans guerdon on le donne, & si l'à doüé d'une telle bien heurance qu'il enrichit ceux aux quels il est donné, & n'appauurit aucunement ceux qui le donnent, mais se tiennent pour avoir fait un grand gain, & bonne emplette, quand ils ont trouué occasion de le te presenter & le mettre en ta possession. Ce pauure peuple qui te fait le present fut deschasse & banny de ta compagnie plus de trois Cents ans y a, & espars aux quatre parties de la Gaule, tenu depuis & reputé (à tort & sans cause toutes fois pour le nom de Chrift, & selon sa promesse) le plus meschant, execrable, & ignominieux que jamais fut, voire tant que le nom d'iceluy à esté comme en fable & proverbe aux autres nations & usurpé pour extreme injure & reproche. Toutes fois que depuis peu de temps quelque personnage de renom immortel, ayant cogneu certanement les Sainctes meurs & la prend homie d'iceluy & experimenté le contraire de fausse & calomnieuse renommée: luy changea par edict publicq son laid nom, & luy en donna un beau & Royal tel qu'il le portoit. C'est le vray peuple de patience, lequel en silence & esperance à vaincu tous assaux & efforts que l'on à sceu faire à l'encontre de luy, & sa juste querelle par quelque laps ou intervalle de temps, n'à sceu perdre son bon droit, dont maintenant il l'invite à la fruition & jouissance de la certaine victoire conquestée par Jesus Chrift. Ne le cognois tu point? C'est ton Frere, le-

quel

quel comme le pitoyable Joseph ne se
peut plus contenir qu' il ne se donne
a cognoistre a toy:*C' est ton* ami tel que
Jonathan *le plus parfait, constant &
entier que tu aye jamais eu , lequel à
porté sa part en son coeur douloureux du
rude traitement, qui t' á esté fait souf-
frant beaucoup en soy mesme , pour
l' estrange & dure servitude en laquelle
il t' à veu estre par cy devant , at-
tendant tousiours que tu vinsse à re-
cognoistre ton droit qui t' est commun
avec luy, duquel il luy desplaisoit en
jouir sans toy . Touchant lequel il te
veut bien advertir & remonstrer , à
celle fin que tu vienne quelque fois à
reconfermer la fraternité , & re-
spondre à la charité & dilection, dont
il t' a si parfaitement aymée , J'a çoit
qu' il te fust incognen, & que plustost
l' eusse à mespris et desdain, et le nom
d' iceluy en horreur et abomination , à
l' exemple et au plaisir de tes maistres,
aux quels miserablement tu servois et
sers encore . Au service desquels tant
rigoureux et* difficiles maistres *enjoin-
gnans et commandans mille choses à
faire l' une sur l' autre, il ta veu (non
pas certes sans grands regrets et compassions) aller , venir, courir, trotter
et tracasser, mal traittée , mal accou-
strée, mal menée , deschirée, crotteé,
esgratinée, deschevelée , morfonduë ,
meurtrie, mutilée , batuë , deffigurée,
et en si piteux estat que on t' eust plustost jugeé estre quelque pauure serve,
esclave , ou souillarde que la fille e t
l' heritiere du Dominateur et Possesseur
universel , et la bien aymée amie de
son fils unique, telle que tu és. I celuy
donc ton frere et amy auquel ta vie
tant miserable faisoit pitié s' est sou-
ventesfois ingeré en passant et repas-
sant de t' appeller par le nom de soeur,*

Brother, who *Joseph*-like *can hide himself no longer from thee ;* 'tis even such
another Friend as *Jonathan,* the most
perfect, constant and sincere that thou
ever hadst , who has been touched
with the feeling of thy sufferings and
hard usage , lamenting the strange
and heavy bondage which thou hast
formerly lived under, longing still to
see thee come to the knowledg of
that right, which thou hast in common
with him, and which he was loth to
enjoy without thee, whereof he would
not have thee to be ignorant, to the
end that thou mayst be enabled one
day to strengthen the Brethren, and
mutually to answer that love and affection which he has shewn unto thee,
notwithstanding that he was unknown to thee, and that thou hadst
him in scorn and contempt, yea that
his very name was odious and abominable unto thee, conforming thy self
to the example and pleasure of thy
masters, to whom thou wert and art
yet enslaved; for the service of which
rigid and *hard masters* (commanding a
thousand several things one after another) he has observed thee, (and that
indeed not without great grief and
fellow-feeling) to trot up and down
here and there, being evilly treated,
ill accounted, and cruelly handled, all
besmeared, torn, and scratcht, thy hair
hanging about thy shoulders, ready
to starve for cold, bruised and beaten,
lamed and disfigured, and in so pitifull and sad a condition , that thou
mightest sooner have been taken for
some poor silly and dirty drudg than
for the daughter and heir (as indeed
thou art) of the Lord and Possessour
of the whole World, or for the well-
beloved Spouse of his onely Son.
Therefore this thy Brother and Friend
pitying thy sad and afflicted life, has
many times called in, as he has passed
by, saluting thee by the name of Sister,

fter, and endeavouring to make thee underſtand and know thy birth-right, and to give thee the (Word) by virtue whereof thou mightſt freely paſs to the enjoyment of a perfect and happy liberty: but thou wert grown ſo ſtupid through the many blows, pains, and troubles, wherewith thou wert tormented by thy cruel and *hard Maſters,* that thou wenteſt on without regarding me, and didſt purſue that unacceptable, painfull, yea beaſt-like imployment, which they had ſet thee about: O what *Loads of heavy Ordinances* has he ſeen thee take up and bear, in the preſence of thoſe thy moſt ſuperſtitious Maſters, notwithſtanding thy weakneſs, and yet they pitied not thy pain and the ſweat of thy brows ſo much as to *help thee with one of their fingers*! nay not ſo much as to try in a way of paſtime the weight of thoſe burdens which thou didſt groan under! Thou wert no ſooner freed of one, but immediately they did load thee with another, and would ſcarce give thee time and leaſure to eat or drink, nay theſe pious pretenders would have thee to faſt for the moſt part, onely to pleaſe and ſatisfie the inſatiable appetite of ſuch like Gluttons, and to fill the *ſlow bellies* of ſuch like *evil beaſts.* Wherefore ſince thou art now come to thy ſelf again, and knoweſt in ſome meaſure of what quality and extraction thou art, and in what a ſervile condition thou art detained, and what honour and dignity thou art called unto, This People hath thought fit to draw near unto thee, and treat thee gently according to their duty, kindly preſenting thee all they have: Go then *O poor little Church,* that art yet in the garb and attire of a mean Servant and handmaid, ſubject to furious frowns and imperious threats of ſo many ſower and ill-lookt Maſters! Go I

ſe parforceant de te faire entendre le droit qui t' appartient et donner le mot *du* guet *de parfaite & heureuſe liberté. Mais toy eſtant toute hebetée, aſſomée & allourdie de tant de coups, peines & travaux, que te donnoient tes rudes &* mal gracieux maiſtres, *paſſois outre & allois ton chemin, pour faire & achever la tant ingrate, faſcheuſe, & ſalle beſongne d'iceux, ſelon qu'elle t'eſtoit enchargée & enjoincte. Quelles charges &* fardeaux de peſantes conſtitutions, (*non obſtant que tu fuſſe linge & tendrette) t'a il veu lever porter & trainer devant iceux tes Religioſiſſimes Maiſtres, leſquels n'avoyent pas tant de pitié de la ſueur & travail, qu'ils te voyoient endurer en leur preſence qu'ils te daignaſſent ſecourir & aider tant ſeulement du petit doigt! non pas meſme, eſſayer par maniere de paſſetemps la peſanteur de tels fardeaux ſous leſquels tu eſtois garrotée & accablée. Tu n'avois pas deſchargé l'un qu'ils te rechargeoient l'autre. Et à peine te donnoyent ils le loiſir de boire & de manger: ains vouloyent, entendoyent, & commandoyent, ces gens de bien que tu jeuſnaſſe la plus part du temps, & le tout pour fruyr & valoir à l'inſatiable appetit de tels gloutons, & pareſſeux ventres de telles mauvaiſes beſtes. Puis donc maintenant que tu és un petit revenue à toy, & que tu commence à cognoiſtre aucunement de quelle race & anceſtres tu es partie, la ſervile condition en laquelle tu es detenuë, & l'honneur & eſtat auquel tu es appellée, ce Peuple s'eſt voulu avancer à te faire favorable recueil ſelon ſon devoir & vouloir en te faiſant amiablement offre de ſon tout. Or avant donc* pauure petite Egliſe, *qui és encore en eſtat de Chambriere & Servante, ſoubs les furieuſes trongnes et Magiſtrales menaces de tant de maiſtres refrongnés et rebarbatifs que tu as, va deſfay, scrotter tes haillons tout poudreux & terreux, d' avoir couru, viré, & tracafsé par le marché fangeux de vaines traditions : Va laver tes mains qui font toutes falles de faire l' oeuure fervile d' iniquité ; Va nettoyer tes yeux tout chafsieux, à caufe de la negligence qu' il t'a fallu avoir de toy, pour courir & eftre plus diligente apres la befongne de fuperftition & hypocrifie, affin que tu reçoiue ton bien honneftement, ainfi qu' il le vaut : par la jouïfsance duquel tu delibereras en toy mefme qu' elle fin tu as intention de faire. Veux tu tous jours ainfy eftre à maiftre ? N' eft il pas temps que tu entende à ton Efpoux Chrift, qui à tant & plus enduré que un loyal amant pour ton amour ! aura il perdu les peines qu' il à pris pour toy ? t' aura il aymé en vain ? Veux tu point prendre efgard aux precieux & finguliers joyaux, que luy mefme (Si tu le fçais entendre) t' envoye en loyauté de mariage ? Car ainfy fait il traiéter l' affaire par fes amis & par les tiens, fon Sainét Efprit faifant la pourfuite : Ayme tu mieux de tes Maiftres vindicatifs la fervile crainte, que de ton benin Efpoux lamitié liberale ? Defire tu plus de te trouuer où l' on te vienne à reprocher, que tu fafche la Court, que en la joyeufe compagnie de celuy qui te fouhaite tant ? Prife tu plus les crieries fophiftiques & troubles d' efcervelez, que les plaifans deuis & propos de ton amy ? Prefere tu les umbres & tenebres Clauftrales, (ou tu es conftrainte vueille ou non de tenir filence) aux fumptueax tabernacles & deleétables Palais d' iceluy ? Appete*

fay, and fhake off the filth from off thy fordid garments, which are fo nafty and beaftly, by reafon of thy long walking to and fro through the dirty Market of vain Traditions : Go and wafh thy hands that are fo foul with doing the *fervile work* of iniquity. Go wafh thy foreand mattery eys, which thou haft not had leifure to cleanfe in former times, becaufe thou wert wholly taken up and bufied about thy *works of Superftition and Hypocrifie* ; that fo thou mayft be fit to receive thine own in a decent manner, anfwerable to the value thereof : and when thou haft once enjoyed it, thou mayft do well to advife with thy felf, what courfe thou oughteft to fteer : what wilt thou ftill lie under bondage, and flavery ? Is it not time for thee to look after *Chrift thy Hufband,* who like a faithfull Lover hath fuffered fo much for thy fake ? Muft he at laft lofe the fruit of all his labours ? Is it altogether in vain that he hath loved thee ? Haft thou no regard to thofe precious and incomparable Jewels, he himfelf fends thee (if thou canft but apprehend it) as an earneft of Mariage ? For thus does he manage the bufinefs by means of his Friends and thine, his holy Spirit being the Solicitour) Doeft thou love better the flavifh fear of thy revengefull Mafters, than the free love of thy gracious Husband ? Is it more pleafant for thee to be where they reproach thee for difpleafing the Court, than to be in his delightfull company who fo longs after thee ? Doeft thou like fophiftical brawlings and confufed noifes more than the pleafing and fweet Difcourfes of thy Friend ? Doeft thou prefer the fhadows and darkneffes of Cloifters (where thou muft neceffarily be in perpetual filence) before his fumptuous Tabernacles and delightfull palaces ? Are

the

the secret drunken meetings of thy Masters, and the filthy Dregs of their tippling Cups more pleasing to thee than the abundant and delicious Table of thy rich Husband? Wilt thou not give him thy love and thy faith? What means this thy Delay? Wilt not thou trust him? Or is there not *enough in his Fathers House* to entertain thee? Doest thou fear he should deceive thee, who never knew fraud or malice? Canst thou fear to be evilly treated by one so milde and so gracious? Art thou afraid he should not love thee, who languishes for love? Canst thou suspect him of ever abandoning thee, who is so jealous and faithfull? Will he not be able to succour and help thee, who *has power given him over all things?* Will he suffer thee to be trampled upon, who has already *exposed himself to death for thy sake?* Will he suffer thee to die, who gives immortal life? Will he leave thee one day a Widow, who lives for ever? Defer no longer this *Mariage with the Kings Son,* how poor soever thou art, considering he is willing to take thee for his Spouse: Take no notice of thine own meanness, seeing he considers not (in this particular) his own greatness: If so be he be willing to favour thee, wilt thou ingratefully resist him? It is his good pleasure to *chuse low things to confound and bring to nought the high!* The truth is, if the question were to match him according to his degree and quality, where should we finde his equal? He is pleased to chuse thee, who art nothing, for to make thee something. *Thou art a Bond-woman, he will make thee free:* Thou art *naked* and *torn,* he will *clothe thee:* Thou art *despised,* and he will *exalt* thee: Take no care, do but *forget thy kindred and his house,* whom thou hast called *Father,* & that base Step-mother whom thou hast

tu plus les ords & salles reliefs & secrets choppinements soubs tes Maistres, que la plantureuse & delicieuse table de ton riche Espoux? Luy veux tu point donner ton amour & ta foy? Que attends tu? ne te veux tu pas fier en luy: N'y à il pas asses de bien en la maison de son pere *pour t'entretenir? As tu peur qu'il te deçoiue, luy en qui n'y à nulle fraude ou malice? As tu doute qu'il te traitte mal, luy qui est tant doux & tant de bonne sorte? As tu soucy qu'il ne te vueille aymer, luy qui languit d'amours? As tu suspicion qu'il t'abandonne, luy qui est tant jaloux & fidele? Doute tu qu'il ne te puisse secourir, luy a qui est donnee puissance sus toutes choses? Crains tu qu'il endure qu'on te foulle, luy qui s'est ja expose a la mort pour toy? As tu doute qu'il te laisse mourir, luy qui donne vie immortelle? As tu peur qu'il te delaisse quelque jour vefue luy qui vit Eternellement? Ne differe donc point t'allier au fils du Roy, quelque pauurette que tu sois, puis qu'il te veut pour son Espouse. N'aye esgard à ta petitesse, puis qu'il ne considere en ce sa hautesse. Sil te veut faire grace y dois tu resister par ingratitude? Il luy plaist* d'eslire les choses basses, pour confondre & faire honte aux choses hautes: *S'il estoit question de luy cercher party selon luy & son estat, où le trouueroit on? Et pourtant luy plaist il de te choisir, toy qui n'es rien, pour te faire estre quelque chose.* Tu es serve & il t'affranchira: *tu es d'eschiree & nue, il te revestira: tu es mesprisee, il t'exaltera. Ne te chaille,* oublie *tant seulement* les tiens, *& la maison de celuy que tu as tenu pour ton pere, & celle traistre marastre que tu as* *fy long temps* appellée Mere : *Aban-donne tes Maiſtres, prens congé d'eux, & leurs mets en avant par bonne rai-ſon, qu'il eſt temps que tu face ton proffit, que tu trouue ton party & ad-dreſſe, & que tu ſuive & face la vo-lomté de* Chriſt *ton amy &* Eſpoux, *le quel te demande, duquel pour la be-ſongne d'autry tu ne veux pas perdre la grace ny l'occaſion de trouuer ton bien* ; *Quitte leur tout ton ſalaire, & tout ce que tu pourrois avoir gagné & merité avec eux, ſelon leur conte & marché, Car le tien* Eſpoux *n'à que faire de ces biens là, & ne veut point auſſy que tu luy apporte ton trouſſeau de vieux pattons & drapeaux que tu as amaſſé au ſervice d'iceux, pour le meſler avec ſes tant precieuſes, nettes & pures Richeſſes : car tu luy ferois deſhonneur. Il eſt bien vray que de ta part tu ne luy pourrois apporter en ac-quit choſe qui vaille : mais qu'y ferois tu ? Viens hardiment avec tous les plus braves & mignons de ta court, tous faits execration pour* Chriſt, *non pour leurs mesfaits, desquels les til-tres ſont ceux cy, aſſavoir,* Injuriez, Blaſmez, Chaſſez, Deſcriez, Deſa-vouez, Abandonnez, Excommuniez, Anathematiſez, Confiſquez, Empri-ſonnez, Gehennez, Banniz, Echellez, Mitrez, Decrachez, Chaffaudez, Eſ-fourillez, tenaillez, fleſtriz, tirez, trainez, Grillez, Roſtiz, Lapidez, Bru-ſlez, noyez, Decapitez, Demembre z, *& autres ſemblables titres glorieux & Magnificques du Royaume des cieux, Tous leſquels il n'à point à deſdain, luy qui eſt tout au contraire des autres Princes & Rois, leſquels ne veulent perſonne à leur court & ſervice, s'il n'eſt noble, bien accouſtré, gorgias, miſte, ſain, & en bon point. Mais il les veut tels* comme luy meſme a eſté

haſt hitherto owned for thy *Mother* ! Abandon thy Maſters; Take thy leave of them, and give them to under-ſtand by ſolid Reaſons, that it is high time for thee to look after thine own profit, and to follow and obey the will of *Chriſt* thy Friend and *Husband,* who calls after thee, and whoſe favour thou muſt not loſe, to do any bodies work ; nor do thou let ſlip ſuch an occaſion to purſue thine own intereſt; I ſay, quit them freely, thy wages, and ſalary, and all thou mayſt have gotten or deſerved of them, according to their own bargain, For thy Husband needs no ſuch Goods, neither will he ſuffer thee to bring all that bag and baggage which thou haſt gotten in ſerving them, or to lay it up together with his precious and pure riches; For as much as this would be a diſgrace to him. It is true, that of thine own thou canſt bring him nothing of any value: But what of that ? Come notwith-ſtanding boldly with all the Gallants and Favourites of thy Court, who have been all made an execration for *Chriſt,* and not for their miſdeeds, and whoſe Titles of Honor are theſe, *viz.* injured, reproacht, fugitives, forſaken, deſpiſed, abandoned, excommunicated, anathematized, confiſcated, impriſoned, tortured, baniſhed, publickly diſgraced, wearing Miters in deriſion, ſpit upon, ſhewn upon Scaffolds, their ears cut off, their fleſh pluckt off with Pinchers, decay-ed, drawn with Horſes, dragged up and down, broil'd, roſted, ſtoned to death, burnt, drowned, beheaded, diſmembred, & other like glorious and honourable Titles of the Kingdom of Heaven, which he doth not deſpiſe, being not like to o-ther Kings and Princes, who will ſuffer none in their Courts, unleſs they be nobly deſcended. well accoutred, in a good garb, well-favoured, and in good plight: But for his part, he will have his Courtiers *to be like him-*

ſelf

self while he was in this life, and he *calls* them friendly to him,*to eafe them,* and to make them rich, to advance and exalt them, and to make them *triumph with him in his celeftial Court.*

Now then, O noble and worthy Church, that art the happy Spoufe of the Kings Son, accept and receive this *Word, Promife,* and *Teftament,* which thou haft here written, word for word, and no where elfe: and where thou maift fee and learn the will of *Chrift,* thy Husband, and of God his Father; according to which Word thou fhalt govern thy Family, then fhalt thou be *called His beft Beloved,* whereas before thou didft not at all feem to have any relation to him. To prefent thee with a larger Preface than the Title and Face of the Book can bear, (as the abovefaid arrogant cuftome requires) I believe it would not onely be fuperfluous, but alfo temerity; For his Name, who here fpeaks, and who defires to be known and heard, is of fuch authority, that there is no ear but ought to be open to receive *the true and living Word* of his *Eternal and Immutable will, by which Word all things do fubfift;* which bleffed and holy will of God he will have to be entertained by the ears of our hearts, there to remain and dwell, that fo in ftead of our wicked and depraved lufts, we may here be furnifhed with the holy and immutable will of God, to whofe favour *(O poor little Church)* we heartily recommend thee; From the *Alpes, Febr.* 12. 1635.

En ce monde, & amiablement les appelle pour les foulager, & leur bailler nouuelles Richeffes pour les auancer, eflever & faire triumpher avec luy en fa cour celeftielle.

Maintenant donc O noble & digne Eglife, heureufe efpoufe du fils du Roy, accepte & reçoy cefte Parole, Promeffe & Teftament, lequel tu as icy par efcrit de mot à mot, & non ailleurs: ou tu pourras voir la volonté de Chrift le tien Efpoux, & de Dieu fon pere, felon laquelle tu gouverneras ta famille, fy feras dite la mieux aimee, au lieu qu'il fembloit que tu ne luy fuffe rien. De te faire plus de preface que le tiltre & face du liure ne porte, (comme auffy le requerroit Icelle arogante Couftume) j'eftime que ce ne feroit pas feulement fuperflu: mais auffy temerité, Car le nom de celuy qui parle icy, qui fe veut faire ouyr & donner à cognoiftre, eft de telle authorité: qu'il n'y à aureille, qui ne doive eftre entencive, pour efcouter la vraye & vive parole de *fon* Eternelle & immutable volonté, par laquelle toutes chofes confiftent, *laquelle il nous vueille faire entendre des oreilles de noftre coeur, & la faire habiter en nous, fy que au lieu de la noftre, mefchante & depravée, nous y trouuions icelle Saincte & Infaillible volonté de Dieu,* lequel O pauure petite Eglife *te maintienne en fa grace;* Des Alpes *ce* xii. *de* Feburier, 1635.

God is all fufficient.

Fear not little Flock, for it is your Fathers good will to give you the Kingdom. Luke 12.32.

En Dieu tout.

Ne craignez point petit trouppeau, Car il a pleu a voftre pere, vous donner le Royaume. *Luc.* 12.32.

At the end of the faid Bible is added, That it was perfected and printed at *Neufchaftel* by *Peter de Wingle, dict. Pirot Picard,* the fourth of *June,* 1635.

There

There is likewise this Divine MOTTO and following VERSES.

Lecteur, Entends, Si Verité Addreſſe,
Viens, Donc Ouyr Inſtamment Sa Promeſſe,
Et Vif Parler, Lequel En Excellence,
Veut Aſſeurer Notre Grelle Eſperance.
L'Eſprit Jeſus Qui Viſite & Ordonne,
Nos Tendres Meurs, Icy Sans Cry Eſtonne
Tout Haut Raillart Eſcumant ſon Ordure.
Remercions Eternelle Nature,
Pour nous Vouloir Bien-Faire Librement
Jeſus Querons Voir Eternellement.

That is to ſay by a ראשי תינור
Les Vaudois Peuple Evangelique,
Ont mis che threſor en Publique.

Engliſhed thus :
The Evangelical Waldenſian *Flock,*
Have giv'n this Treaſure to the publick Stock.

In the third and laſt place, for the more ample confirmation of this Truth, I ſhall here bring and inſert the Teſtimonies of their moſt famous Adverſaries themſelves touching this point, *Marc Aurelio Rorenco* Prior of *Lucerna,* and *Theodore Belvedere* chief of the *Miſſionaries* of the Valleys, and others, having undertaken to ſhew the Original of the ſaid Religion in thoſe Valleys, were never able to ſhew the very Age,

The third Argument to prove the Antiquity of the Reformed Churches in the Valleys of Piemont.

Rorenco p. 60.

Age, even from the Days of the Apostles, when it was there introduced. The abovesaid *Rorenco* in a Book of his composed expresly to shew their Original, after he had tormented himself to prove that it was not as ancient as the Apostles, confesses *Pa.*60, *Non si puo haver certezza del principio del suo ingresso.* That is to say, *There can be no certainty had of its first entrance,* Because he was ashamed to confess the true Original, to wit, the Preaching of the Apostles ; and the truth is, there cannot be found or produced an Edict made by any Prince, who gave permission at any time for its introduction. But *all the ancient Concessions import onely thus much, that the said Princes have permitted their Subjects to continue in the same Religion that they had received from their Ancestours,* the which had been conveyed to them from Father to Son, *&c.* even from the Apostles themselves. Yea the said Adversaries (falling short in this their Design of convicting the Belief of the *Waldenses* of Novelty) have been forced to confess the quite contrary ; as for Example, *Belvedere* in his Relation to the Congregation *De Propaganda Fide,* printed at *Turin* by priviledge and approbation of his Superiours, *Anno* 1638. was so convinced by palpable evidence of this Truth, that he confesses *Page* 37. that the Religion which he calls Heresie, had been always in *Angrogna,* La *Valli di Angrogna sempre ò in un tempo, ò in un altro, ha havuto heretici.* So likewise, the Frier *Rainerius Saccon* writing against the *Waldenses,* above four hundred years ago ; namely 1254. confesses the Antiquity of their Religion which he calls a Sect ; see his very words taken out of the *Bibliotheque des Peres* printed at *Paris* 1624. the Author whereof was *Jac. Gretsero, Inter omnes Sectas quæ sunt vel fuerunt, non est perniciosior Ecclesiæ Dei quàm pauperum de Lugduno ; tribus de causis, Prima, quia diuturnior, quidam dicunt quod duraverit à tempore Silvestri, alii dicunt, quod à tempore Apostolorum,* &c. That is to say, *Amongst all the Sects which are or ever were, there is none more pernicious to the Church of God, than that of the poor people of* Lyons, *for three Reasons, First, because it is of a longer duration. Some say that it has remained from the time of* Silvester, *others, from the time of the Apostles.* And although *Gretserus* endeavors to shift off the force of the fore-going passage by this evasion, namely, that what *Reinerius* there speaks, he speaks *not as his own opinion, but as the opinion of others.* For if *Reinerius* had not believed *that Sect* (as he calls it) had not been more ancient then the preaching of *Waldo* (which was not, as *Gretserus* himself says, above 94 years before his writing that Book) it had been a very ridiculous thing to have at all mentioned the Antiquity thereof in such a manner as he there do's. This is the learned and famous *Bishop Usher's* own Observation and Comment upon that place of *Reinerius,* in his Book *De Christianarum Ecclesiarum successione & statu, Chap.* 8. *fol.* 211. in the following expressions. *Frustra autem est* Gretserus *cum opponit,* Reinerium non ex sua sed ex aliorum sententia *affirmare* Sectam Waldensium a temporibus Silvestri Papæ, vel etiam ipsorum Apostolorum durasse. *Nam, ut hoc demus, ex aliorum sententia fuisse dictum : illud tamen apparet eum dixisse ex sua ; inter omnes sectas, quæ sunt vel fuerunt, nullam fuisse diuturniorem*

Belvedere de propaganda fide, printed at *Turin,* 1638. *Rainerius Saccon.*

Gretf. Proleg. in Script. edit. contr. li all. cap. 8. *pag.* 39.

Gretser. ibid. pag. 39.

Jacob. Usserius de Christianarum Ecclesiarum successione & statu cap. 8. *pag.* 211. *excudebat Bonham Norton, Lond.* 1613.

turniorem *quam Leoniſtarum hanc ſive Waldenſium: quod ſatis oſtendit, primam eorum originem ab omni memoriâ fuiſſe remotiſſimam, evincit certè (quod oſtendi ſibi poſtulat Jeſuita) novam doctrinam non fuiſſe à* Waldenſibus & Albigenſibus circa Annum Chriſti M C L X. primitùs in mundum introductam, & poſtea miris incrementis multiplicatam. *Cùm enim inter Annum Chriſti* M C L X *& Annum* M C C L I V *quo fratrem* Reinerium *claruiſſe ex* Antonii Senenſis *Bibliotheca docet ipſe* Gretſerus, *tantùm 94 annorum ſpatium interceſſerit: omnibus ludibrium debuiſſet. qui talia de* diuturnitate *proferret Sectæ, quam non ampliùs uno ante ſeculo exortam conſtitiſſet.* Gretſerus ibid. pag 38. And indeed this is the true Original of their Religion, which the People of the Valleys always conſerved without a publick ſeparation from the Church of *Rome* during ſeveral ages, that is to ſay, ſo long as ſhe did not attempt to force them to embrace her Errours; but when once ſhe began to offer violence to their conſciences, and its tyranny became intolerable: then they *went out of* Babylon, and *ſeparated themſelves* from the others impieties: and from the time that the ſame has made any noiſe in the World, Hiſtorians have likewiſe made mention thereof in their Books of Antiquity. To this purpoſe, I finde a certain paſſage in a Manuſcript (which is to be ſeen together with the reſt, in the publick Library at *Cambridge*) concerning the Religion of the *Waldenſes, An. Dom.* 1587. where, in the firſt Article, when it is demanded, *Quanto tempo è, ch'è ſtata predicata la pura dottrina nelle Valli?* That is, *How long ſince is it, that the pure Doctrine has been preached in the Valleys?* It is anſwered, *Circa cinque cento anni come ſi pno raccoglier per alcune Hiſtorie, ma ſecondo l'opinione de gl'habitatori delle Valli il tempo è immemoriale è di Padre à figliuoli.* That is, *About* 500 *years, as near as can be gathered from any Hiſtories, but according to the opinion of the Inhabitants, from Father to Son time out of minde.* Now the reaſon of this is, becauſe Hiſtorians have not made any particular mention of theſe Valleys before the time that they were abſolutely ſeparated from the Hereſies and abominations of the Church of *Rome.* However the Inhabitants of the Valleys have preſerved the entire memory of the great benefit beſtowed on them by God himſelf from the beginning, and which they and their Predeceſſors have enjoyed from generation to generation ever ſince the days of the Apoſtles.

CHAP. IV.

The ancient and modern Belief of the Evangelical Churches in the Valleys *of* Piemont.

After all the authentick proofs that have been alledged to make good the Antiquity of the *Evangelical Churches* in the *Valleys* of *Piemont*, even from the time of the *Apoſtles*, if there yet remains any ſcruple in the mind of the *Chriſtian Reader* concerning this Truth, their own Language in their Confeſſions of Faith from time to time, which I have here inſerted in the following Form, will eaſily diſcover whether they be *Jews* or *Galileans*, the true

*Rom.*4. 9,11.
Greg.Naz. in
his Oration
in magnum
Athanasium.

feed of *Abraham*, or a counterfeit generation. For, if they have the Doctrine of the Prophets and Apostles of *Jesus Christ*, then they are the true successors and the legitimate *Children of Abraham*, for as much as they have the *Faith of Abraham*, *Rom.* 4. and 9. and 11. as *Gregory Nazianzen* observes in his Oration, *in magnum Athanasium.*

An ancient Confession of Faith of the *Waldenses*, Copied out of certain Manuscripts, bearing date *Anno Dom.* 1120. That is to say, near 400 years before the time of either *Calvin* or *Luther.*

Article 1.

Nos cresen & fermament tenen tot quant se conten en li doze Articles del Symbolo, loqual es dict de li Apostol, tenent esser heresia tota cosa laqual se discorda, & non es convenent à li doze Articles.

Article 1.

WE believe and firmly hold all that which is contained in the twelve Articles of the Symbol, which is called the Apostles Creed, accounting for Heresie whatsoever is disagreeing, and not consonant to the said 12 Articles.

Article 2.

Nos cresen un Dio Paire, Fil, & Sanct Esperit.

Article 2.

We do believe that there is one God, Father, Son, & Holy Spirit.

Article 3.

Nos reconten per Sanctas Scripturas Canonicas, li Libres de la Sancta Bibla.

viz. { *Moyse autrament Genesi.*
Moysi dict Exodi.
Moyse dict Leviric.
Moyse dict Nombre.
Moyse dict Deuteronome.

Josué.
Juges.
Ruth.
1 *Samuel.*
2 *Samuel.*
1 *De li Rey.*
2 *De li Rey.*
1 *De las Chroni.*
2 *De las Chroni.*
1 *Esdras.*
Nehemia.
Esther.

Article 3.

We acknowledg for the holy Canonical Scriptures, the Books of the holy Bible, *viz.*

The Books { Genesis.
of *Moses* { Exodus.
called—— { Leviticus.
Numbers.
Deuteronomy.

Joshua.
Judges.
Ruth.
1 Samuel.
2 Samuel.
1 Kings.
2 Kings.
1 Chronicles.
2 Chronicles.
1 Ezra.
Nehemia.
Esther.

Job

Job.

Pfalms.

The Proverbs of Solomon.

Ecclefiaftes, or the Preacher.

The Song of Solomon.

The Prophefie } Ifaiah.

    of   } Jeremiah.

The Lamentations of Jeremiah.

    Ezekiel.

    Daniel.

    Hofea.

    Joel.

    Amos.

    Obadiah.

    Jonas.

    Micah.

    Nahum.

    Habakkuk.

    Zephaniah.

    Haggai.

    Zechariah.

    Malachi.

Here follow the Books *Apocryphal,* which are not received of the *Hebrews.* But we reade them (as faith St. *Hierome* in his Prologue to the *Proverbs*) for the inftruction of the People, not to confirm the Authority of the Doctrine of the Church. *viz.*

    3. Efdras.

    4. Efdras.

    Tobit.

    Judith.

    Wifdom.

    Ecclefiafticus.

Baruch with the Epiftle of Jeremiah.

Efther from the tenth Chapter to the end.

The Song of the three Children in the Fornace.

The Hiftory of Sufanna.

The Hiftory of the Dragon.

    1. Maccabes.

    2. Maccabes.

    3. Maccabes.

Job.

Lo libre de li Pfalmes.

Proverbis Solomon.

Ecclefiaftes, autrament lo predicator.

Cantic de Solomon.

Propheti a d' Efaia.

De Jeremia.

Lamentation de Jeremia.

    Ezekiel.

    Daniel.

    Ozea.

    Joel.

    Amos.

    Abdias.

    Jonas.

    Michea.

    Nahum.

    Abacuck.

    Sophonia.

    Aggea.

    Zacharia.

    Malachia.

Ara fenfegon li libres Apocriphes, *liqual non font pas receopù de li* Hebrios, *Ma nos ligen (en ayma dis* Hierome *al Prologo de li Proverbi)per l' enfeignament del Poble, non pas per confermar l' authorità de las* Doctrinas *Ecclefiafticas en aimi.*

    Lo ters D' Efdras.

    Lo quatre D' Efdras.

    Tobias.

    Judith.

    Sapientia.

    Ecclefiaftic.

Baruch con la Epiftola de Jeremiah.

Efther defpois el 10. *cap. daqui à la fin.*

Le Cant de li trei Fantin en la Fornais.

L' Hiftoria de Sufanna.

L' Hiftoria del Dragon.

Lo premier de li Machabei.

Lo fecond de li Machabei.

Lo ters de li Machabei.

Ara senſegon li libres del Novel Teſtament.

L' Euangeli Sanct Matheo.
L' Euangeli Sanct Marc.
L' Euan. Sanct Luc.
L' Euan. Sanct Johan.
Actes de li Apoſtols.
Epiſtola Sanct Paul à li Rom.
    1. *A los Corinthios.*
    2. *A los Corinthios.*
    A li Galatiens.
    A li Epheſiens.
    A li Philippiens.
    A li Coloſsiens.
La 1. A li Theſſaloniciens.
La 2. A li Theſſaloniciens.
La 1. A Timotheo.
La 2. A Timotheo.
    A Tito.
    A Philemon.
    A li Hebrios.
Epiſtola Sanct Jaco.
La 1. Epiſt. Sanct Peire.
La 2. Epiſt. Sanct Peire.
La 1. Epiſt. de Sanct Joan.
La 2. Epiſt. de Sanct Joan.
La 3. Epiſt. de Sanct Joan.
    Epiſt. de Sanct Juda.
    Apocalis de Sanct Joan.

Los libres ſobre dict enſeignan aizò, Que l' es un Dio tot poiſſant, tot ſavi, & tot bon, loqual per la ſoa bontà à fait totas las coſas. Car el à formà Adam à la ſoa imagena & ſemblança, ma que per l' envidia del Diavol, & per la deſobediença del dict Adam, lo peccà es intrà al mond, & que no ſen peccadors en Adam & per Adam.

Que Chriſt es iſtà promes à li paire, liqual an receopù la ley, aiço que per la ley conoiſſent lor peccàs,

Here follow the Books of the New Teſtament.

The Goſpel according to S. ⎱ Matthew.
              Mark.
              Luke.
              John.
The Acts of the Apoſtles.
The Ep. of S. Paul to the Romans.
    1. Corinthians.
    2. Corinthians.
    Galatians.
    Epheſians.
    Philippians.
    Coloſſians.
    1. Theſſalonians.
    2. Theſſalonians.
    1. Timothy.
    2. Timothy.
    Titus.
    Philemon.
The Epiſtle to the Hebrews.
The Epiſtle of St. James.
The 1. Epiſt. of St. Peter.
The 2. Epiſt. of St. Peter.
The 1. Epiſt. of St. John.
The 2. Epiſt. of St. John.
The 3. Epiſt. of St. John.
The Epiſtle of St. Jude.
The Revelation of St. John.

Article 4.

The Books aboveſaid teach this, That there is one God, Almighty, all wiſe, and all good, who has made all things by his goodneſs, For he formed *Adam* in his own image and likeneſs, but that by the envy of the Devil, and the diſobedience of the ſaid *Adam,* Sin has entred into the World, and that we are Sinners in *Adam* and by *Adam.*

Article 5.

That *Chriſt* was promiſed to our Fathers who received the Law, that ſo knowing by the Law their ſin, unrighteouſneſs

ousness and insufficiency, they might desire the coming of *Christ*, to satisfie for their sins, and accomplish the Law by himself.

Article 6.

That *Christ* was born in the time appointed by God the Father. That is to say, in the time when all iniquity abounded, and not for the cause of good works, for all were Sinners: but that he might shew us grace and mercy, as being faithfull.

Article 7.

That *Christ* is our life, truth, peace, and righteousness, as also our Pastour, Advocate, Sacrifice, and Priest, who died for the salvation of all those that believe, and is risen for our justification.

Article 8.

In like manner, we firmly hold, that there is no other Mediatour and Advocate with God the Father, save onely *Jesus Christ*. And as for the Virgin *Mary*, that she was holy, humble, and full of grace: and in like manner do we believe concerning all the other Saints, *viz.* that being in Heaven, they wait for the Resurrection of their Bodies at the Day of Judgment.

Article 9.

Item, we believe that after this life, there are onely two places, the one for the saved, and the other for the damned, the which two places we call *Paradise* and *Hell*, absolutely denying that *Purgatory* invented by *Antichrist*, and forged contrary to the truth.

Article 10.

Item, we have always accounted as an unspeakable abomination before God, all those Inventions of men,

& la non justitia, & la lor non abastança desiresson l' advenament de Christ per satisfar de li lor pecca & accomplir la ley per luy meseime.

Que Christ es nà al temp ordonnà de Dio lo seo Paire soes à saber à l' hora que tota eniquità abondiè, & non pas per las bonàs obras solament. Car tuit eran peccadours, ma açò qu' el nos se gratia & misericordia en aima veritadier.

Que Christ es la nostra vita, & verità, & pacs, & Justitia, & Pastor, & Avocat, & Hostia, & Preyre, loqual es mort per la salut de tuit li cresent, & resuscità per la nostra justificatiòn.

Et semeillament nos tenen fermament non esser alcun autre Mediator & Advocat en apres Dio Paire si non Jesu Christ, ma que la Vergena Maria es istà sancta, humil & plena de gratia & en aimi crefen de tuit li autre Sanct, qu' illi speran en li cel la resurrectiòn de lor corps al Judici.

Item, nos crefen en apres àquesta vita esser tant solament duoi luoc, un de li salvà, loqual appellen per nom Paradis, & l' autre de li damnà, lo qual appellen Enfern, denegant alpostot à quel Purgatori soimà de l' Ante-Christ, & enseint contra la verità.

Item, nos haven totavia cresù esser abomination non parlivol devant Dio totas las cosas atrobàs de li homes en aima

aima ſon las feſtas, & las vigilas de li Sanĉt, & l' aigua laqual diſon benietta, & ſe abſtenir alcuns jorns de la carn & deli autres maniars, & las ſemeillant coſas, & principalment las Meſſas.

namely, the Feaſts and the Vigils of Saints, the Water which they call holy. As likewiſe to abſtain from Fleſh upon certain Days, and the like; but eſpecially their Maſſes.

Nos abominèn li atrobament humàn, en aima Anti-Chriſtian per liqual ſon contorbà & que prejudican à la libertà de l' Eſprit.

Article 11.
We eſteem for an abomination and as *Anti-Chriſtian,* all thoſe humane Inventions which are a trouble or prejudice to the liberty of the Spirit.

Nos creſen que li Sacrament ſon ſignal dela coſa Sanĉta, ò forma veſibla, de gratia non viſibla, tenent eſſer bon que li fidel uzan alcune vecs d' à quiſti diĉt ſignal, ò forma veſibla, ſi la ſe po far. Ma emperço nos creſen, & tenen que li prediĉt fidel pon eſſer fait ſalfs non recebent li prediĉt ſignal quand non hà lo luoc nilo modo de poer uſar deli prediĉt ſignal.

Article 12.
We do believe that the Sacraments are ſigns of the holy thing, or viſible forms of the inviſible grace, accounting it good that the faithfull ſometimes uſe the ſaid ſigns or viſible forms, if it may be done. However, we believe and hold, that the aboveſaid faithfull may be ſaved without receiving the ſigns aforeſaid, in caſe they have no place nor any means to uſe them.

Nos non aven connegù autre Sacrament que lo Baptiſme, *& la* Euchariſtia.

Article 13.
We acknowledg no other Sacrament but *Baptiſm* and *the Lords Supper.*

Nos deven honor à la poteſtà ſecular, en ſubjeĉtion, en obediença, en prompteza & en pagament.

Article 14.
We ought to honour the ſecular powers, by ſubjeĉtion, ready obedience, and paying of Tributes.

A very

A very ancient Confeſſion of Sins oommonly uſed among the *Waldenſes* and *Albigenſes.*

Tranſlated out of their own Language.

O Dio de li Rey & Segnor de li Segnor, yo me con-
feſſo a tu car yo ſoy a quel peccador que tay mot
offendu, &c.

O God of Kings, and Lord of Lords, I make my Confeſſion to
thee, for I am a Sinner which have grievouſly offended thee
by my ingratitude: Excuſe my ſelf I cannot, for thou haſt
ſhewed me what is both the good and the evil. I have underſtood thy
power, I have not been ignorant of thy wiſdom, I have known thy
juſtice, and taſted of thy goodneſs. And yet notwithſtanding all the
evil that I do proceeds from mine own naughtineſs ; Lord pardon
me, and give me repentance, for I have ſlighted thee by my great pre-
ſumption, and have not believed thy wiſdom, nor thy Commandments, but have tranſgreſſed the ſame, for which I am heartily ſorry.
I have not feared thy Juſtice nor thy Judgments, but have committed
many evils from the very beginning of my life, neither have I had
that love to thy great goodneſs which I ought to have had, and as I
was commanded, but I have too much complied with the Devil
through mine own perverſneſs ; I have been delighted in pride, rather than in humility. If thou doeſt not pardon me, I am utterly undone, ſo much is covetouſneſs rooted in my heart, ſo much do I love
avarice, and ſeek after applauſe, and bear ſo little love to thoſe who
have obliged me by their kindneſs. I ſay, if thou doeſt not pardon
me, my ſoul muſt needs go down into perdition. Anger likewiſe
reigns in my heart, and envy gnaws upon me, for I have no charity
at all ; Lord pardon me for thy goodneſs ſake. I am raſh, ſlow to do
good, but bold and induſtrious to do evil ; Lord grant of thy grace
that I may not be numbered among the wicked. I have not returned
thee thanks as I ought, and as thou haſt commanded, for the good
which thou haſt out of love given and beſtowed upon me ; yea I
have been diſobedient through my naughtineſs. Lord pardon me,
for

for I have not ferved thee, but on the contrary, I have offended thee. I have too much ferved mine own body, and mine own will, in many vain thoughts and wicked defires, wherein I have taken pleafure. I have blinded my felf, and I have had many evil thoughts againft thee, and have hunted after many things contrary to thy will. Have pity on me, and give me humility. I have caft mine eys upon vain delights, and have feldom lifted them up towards thy face. I have lent an ear to empty founds, yea and to many evil fpeakings, but to hear and *underftand thy Laws and thy Statutes* has been grievous and irkfome to me. I have committed great faults as to my underftanding, having taken more pleafure in the noifome fink of fin and evil, than in divine fweetnefs and heavenly honour, having worfhipped fin, and taken more contentment therein, whereby I have committed many evils, and left undone much good : I have endeavoured to conceal mine own guilt, and caft it upon another. I have not been moderate as I ought to have been in my eating and drinking. I have often recompenfed violence for violence, and therein taken immoderate pleafure ; both my body and minde are wounded. I have ftretched forth my hands to take hold of vanity, and moft perverfly laboured to gain anothers goods, and to fmite my Neighbour, and do him a difpleafure; yea my heart has been delighted in thefe things that I have mentioned, and much more in very many foolifh and unprofitable objects : Lord pardon me and give me chaftity. I have evilly imployed the time which thou haft given me in vanity, and the days of my youth in pleafures. I have turned afide into by-paths, and have by my lightnefs given an ill example unto others. I finde in my felf no good, but much evil. I have difpleafed thee by my naughtinefs, and have condemned mine own foul, and have reproached my Neighbour. Lord preferve me from condemnation. I have loved my Neighbour onely becaufe of temporal Goods. I have not behaved my felf faithfully in matters of giving and receiving, but have had refpect to perfons according to my affection. I have too much loved the one, and hated the other. I have rejoyced for the profperity of the good, and been too much lifted up at the adverfity of the wicked . And over and above all the evils which I have committed for the time paft to this prefent moment, I have not had a repentance or remorfe proportionable to the offence. I have oftentimes by my tranfgreffion returned to the fame fin which I had confeffed, for which I am exceedingly grieved. Lord God, thou knoweft that I have not confeffed all, and that there are yet many evils in me which I have not reckoned up. But thou knoweft all the evil thoughts, and all the evil words, and all the perverfe actions which I have ever been guilty of: Lord pardon me, and give me fpace to repent in this prefent life, and grant me of thy grace, that for the future I may hate thofe evil things, and commit them no more, as likewife that I may love the good, and preferve them in my heart. That I may love thee above all things, and that I may fear thee in fuch a manner, that at the Day of my Death I may have done that which is acceptable unto thee. And give me fuch a firm
hope

hope concerning the Day of Judgment, that I may not fear the Devil, nor any other thing that may affright me, but that I may be received at thy right hand without spot or blemish. Lord accomplish all this, according to thine own good pleasure. *Amen.*

Another Confession of Faith of the *Waldenses*, extracted out of *Charles du Moulin de la Mon : des Francois.* *Pag.*65.

Article 1.

WE believe, that there is but one God, that he is a Spirit, Creatour of all things, God of all, who is over all, and through all, and in us all, who ought to be worshipped in spirit and in truth, whom alone we serve, and to whom we give the glory of our life, food, raiment, health, sickness, prosperity, and adversity; and we love him as one who knoweth our hearts.

Article 2.

We believe that *Jesus Christ* is the Son and Image of the Father. That in him dwells all the fulness of the Godhead, by whom we have knowledg of the Father. That he is our Mediatour and Advocate. And that there is no other name under Heaven given unto men, by which we can be saved; in whose Name alone we call upon the Father, and use no other Prayers than those which are contained in the holy Scripture, or such other as are conformable unto them for substance.

Article 3.

We believe that the Holy Spirit is our Comforter, proceeding from the Father and the Son, by whose Inspiration we make our Prayers, being by him renewed, who works in us all good works, and by whom we have the knowledg of all truths.

Article 4.

We believe that there is one Holy Church, which is the Congregation of all the Elect and faithfull ones from the very beginning of the World to the end, whereof our Saviour *Christ* is the Head: the which is governed by his Word, and conducted by his Spirit, wherewith all good *Christians* ought to hold Communion: for, she prays for all without ceasing, and the Word which she hath is agreeable

able to God himfelf ; without which Church no man can be faved.

Article 5.

We hold that the Minifters of the Church, as Bifhops and Paftours, ought to be irreprehenfible, as well in their life as Doctrine. And that otherwife they ought to be deprived of their Office, and others fubftituted in their places. As likewife, that none ought to prefume to take upon him this honour, but he who is called by God as was *Aaron*, feeding the Flock of God, not for the fake of difhoneft gain, nor as having any Lordfhip over the Clergy, but as being fincerely an Example to his Flock, in Word, in Converfation, in Charity, in Faith, and in Chaftity.

Article 6.

We confefs, that Kings, Princes, and Governours, are ordained and eftablifhed as Minifters of God, whom we ought to obey. For they bear the Sword for Defence of the Innocent, and for the punifhing of evil Doers, for which caufe we are bound to give them honour, and to pay them tribute ; from whofe power none can exempt himfelf ; it being likewife forbidden by the Example of our Lord *Jefus Chrift*, who was willing to pay tribute, not pretending jurifdiction over the temporal powers.

Article 7.

We believe, that in the Sacrament of Baptifm, Water is the vifible and external Sign, which reprefents unto us that which (by the invifible virtue of God operating) is within us ; namely, the renovation of the Spirit, and the mortification of our members in *Jefus Chrift* ; by which alfo we are received into the holy Congregation of the People of God, there protefting and declaring openly our faith and amendment of life.

Article 8.

We hold, that the holy Sacrament of the Table or Supper of our Lord *Jefus Chrift* is an holy commemoration, and giving of thanks for the benefits which we have received by his Death and Paffion ; that we ought to affemble together in Faith and Charity, examining our felves, and fo *to eat of that Bread*, and communicate of *that his Bloud*, in the very fame manner as he hath prefcribed in the holy Scripture.

Article 9.

We confefs, that Mariage is good, honourable, holy, and inftituted by God himfelt ; which ought not to be prohibited to any perfon, provided that there be no hindrance fpecified by the Word of God.

Article 10

Article 10.

We confefs, that thofe who fear God follow thofe things which are well pleafing to him, and do thofe good works which he hath prepared, to the end that we fhould walk in them; which are Love, joy, peace, patience, meeknefs, goodnefs, brotherly kindnefs, temperance, and other the like works contained and commended in the holy Scriptures.

Article 11.

On the contrary, we confefs, that we ought to take heed and beware of falfe Teachers, whofe fcope and aim is to turn afide the People from the true Worfhip, which belongs to our onely God and Lord, and to lean upon Creatures, and to truft in them : as likewife to forfake thofe good works, which are contained and required in the holy Scriptures, and to do thofe which are onely invented by men.

Article 12.

We hold for the Rule of our Faith, the Old and New Teftament, and agree to the general Confeffion of Faith, with the Articles contained in the Apoftles Creed, namely, *I believe in God the Father Almighty, &c.*

A brief Confeffion of Faith,

Made with general confent by the Minifters, and Heads of Families of the Churches of the Valleys of *Piemont*, affembled in *Angrogne* the 12. of *September* of the Year 1532.

THe following Articles having been then framed, read, approved, and figned by all that were prefent, they with one accord did fwear to believe, hold and obferve them inviolably, as agreeing with the holy Scriptures, and containing the fum of the Doctrine, which was taught them from father to fon according to the Word of God, as was done by the faithfull in the time of *Efdras* and *Nehemiah*, *Efdr.chap.*10. *Nehem.*9. *& 10.*

Article 1.   That Divine Service cannot be performed but in fpirit and in truth : becaufe God is a Spirit, and whofoever will fpeak to him, muft do it in fpirit.

2. All

2. All thofe that have been, and fhall be faved, have been elected of God, before the Foundation of the World.

3. It is impoffible that thofe that are appointed to falvation, fhould not be faved.

4. Whofoever upholds Free-will denieth abfolutely *Predeftination*, and the *Grace of God.*

5. No work is called good, but that which God hath commanded, and no work is bad but that which he forbiddeth.

6. A *Chriftian* may fwear by the Name of God without contravention to what is written, *Matth. ch.5.* provided that he that fweareth doth not take the Name of God in vain. Now it is not in vain, when the Oath tendeth to Gods glory, and the falvation of a mans Neighbour: moreover, one may fwear before Magiftrates, becaufe he that exercifeth the Office of a Magiftrate, whether a believer or unbeliever, holdeth his power from God.

7. Auricular Confeffion is not commanded of God, and it hath been determined according to holy Scriptures, that the true Confeffion of a *Chriftian* is, to confefs to God alone, to whom belongeth honour and glory: there is another kinde of Confeffion, which is, when one reconcileth himfelf to his Neighbour, of the which mention is made in St. *Matthew* and in St. *James, chap.5.* The third manner of Confeffion is, when one having offended publickly, and to every mans knowledg, doth alfo publickly confefs and acknowledg his offence.

8. We ought to ceafe on the Lords Day from our Works, as men zealous of the honour and glory of God, alfo out of Charity towards our Servants, and to apply our felves to the hearing of the Word of God.

9. It is not lawfull for a *Chriftian* to take Revenge upon his Enemy in any manner whatfoever.

10. A *Chriftian* may exercife the Office of a Magiftrate over *Chriftians*.

11. There is no certain Determination of time for any *Chriftian* Faft, and it cannot be found in the Scripture, that God hath commanded and appointed any fpecial Days.

12. Mariage is not forbidden to any, of what quality and condition foever he be.

13. Who-

13. Whofoever forbiddeth Mariage teacheth a Diabolical Doctrine.

14. Whofoever hath not the gift of Chaftity is bound to marry.

15. The Minifters of the Word of God ought not to remove from place to place, except it be for fome great good to the Church.

16. It is not a thing repugnant to the Apoftolical Communion, that Minifters fhould poffefs fome Eftate proper to themfelves, for the fubfiftence of their Families.

17. Concerning the matter of the Sacraments, it hath been determined by the holy Scripture, that we have but two Sacramental Signs left us by *Jefus Chrift*, the one is *Baptifm*, the other is the *Eucharift*, which we receive, to fhew that our perfeverance in the Faith is fuch as we promifed when we were baptized being little children, and moreover, in remembrance of that great benefit given to us by *Jefus Chrift*, when he died for our Redemption, and wafhed us with his precious Bloud.

A Declaration of the *Waldenfes* of the Valleys, Maties, and Meane, and Marquifate of *Saluces, &c.* made in the Year, 1603.

WHereas our Predeceffours, from Father to Son, time out minde, have been taught and brought up in the Doctrine and Religion of which we from our childhood have made open profeffion, and in the fame have inftructed our Families, as we learned it from our Fathers, yea and which, while the King of *France* held the Marquifate of *Saluces*, it was permitted us to make profeffion of without being troubled or molefted, as well as our Brethren of the Valleys of *Lucerne, Perouze*, and others, who by a fpecial Treaty made with our fovereign Prince and Lord have enjoyed to this day the free exercife of the Reformed Religion ; and whereas his Highnefs led rather by evil counfels and paffionate men, than by his own will, hath refolved to moleft us, and to that end hath fet out an Edict : therefore to the end it might appear unto all men, that it is not for any crime committed, either againft the perfon of our Prince, or for Rebellion

againft

againſt the Laws, or that we have been guilty of Murders or Thefts, that we are ſo tormented and ſpoiled of our Houſes and Goods. We declare, that being very confident and certain, that the Doctrine and Religion taught and followed by the Reformed Churches of *France,* *Swiſſerland, Germany, England, Scotland, Geneve, Denmark, Swede-* *land, Holland,* and other Kingdoms, Nations, and Dominions, of which we hitherto have made open profeſſion under the obedience of our Princes and ſovereign Lords, is the onely true Doctrine and Religion ordained and approved of God, which alone can render us acceptable to God, and bring us to ſalvation, we are reſolved to ſtand to it to the hazzard of our Lives, Honours, and Eſtates, and to continue in it the remnant of our Days ; and if any body pretendeth that we are in an Errour, we intreat any ſuch to let us ſee our Errour, offering to abjure it without delay, and to follow whatſoever ſhall be ſhewed us to be more excellent, deſiring nothing more than with ſafe conſcience to render that true and lawfull ſervice which we poor Creatures ow to our Creatour, and by this means to obtain true and everlaſting felicity : but if by meer violence and conſtraint, they will compell us to leave and forſake the true way to ſalvation, to go after Errours, Superſtitions, and falſe Doctrines, invented by men, we chuſe rather to part with our Houſes, Eſtates, and Life it ſelf ; right humbly beſeeching his Highneſs (whom we acknowledg to be our lawfull Prince and Lord) not to ſuffer us to be moleſted without cauſe, but rather to grant that we may continue the remnant of our Lives, and our Children and Poſterity after us, in that obedience and ſervice which we have hitherto yielded unto him, as his true & faithful Subjects ; ſince we intreat nothing elſe at his hands, than that yielding faithfully to him whatſoever we are bound to, by expreſs commandment of God, we may be alſo ſuffered to give to God that homage and ſervice we ow unto him, and which he requireth of us in his holy Word. And in the mean while in the midſt of our calamities and exile we requeſt the Reformed Churches to hold and acknowledg us, as true Members of theirs, being ready to ſign with our own Bloud, (if God calleth us to it) the Confeſſion of Faith by them made and publiſhed, which we acknowledg every way agreeing with the Doctrine taught and regiſtred by the holy Apoſtles, and therefore truly Apoſtolical, promiſing to live and die in it ; and if for ſo doing we be afflicted and perſecuted, we return our thanks unto God, who hath vouchſafed us the honour to ſuffer for his Names ſake, committing the iſſue of our affairs, and the juſtice of our cauſe into the hands of his Divine Providence, who will deliver us when and by what means it ſhall pleaſe him ; moſt humbly praying, that as he hath the hearts of Kings and Princes in his hands, he will be pleaſed to bend the heart of his Highneſs to pity, towards thoſe who never offended him, and are reſolved never to offend him, that ſo he may hold and acknowledg us more true and faithfull to his ſervice, than thoſe that endeavour to perſwade him to ſuch Perſecutions : and for our ſelves, that he will be pleaſed to ſtrengthen us in the midſt of theſe temptations, and give

us

us patience and conftancy to perfevere in the profeffion of the truth to our lives end, and our Pofterity after us. *Amen.*

An Abbreviation of that Confeffion of Faith

which was prefented to *Ladiflaus* King of *Bohemia, &c. Anno Domini* 1508. **By** his Subjects falfly called *Waldenfes,* wherein they declare the Reafon of their Separation from the Church of *Rome.*

And fince that time amplified and explained by the fame People. And prefented to *Ferdinand* King of *Bohemia, &c. Anno Domini* 1535.

The Preface.

Quanquam retroactis temporibus, ab Ecclefiaftis noftris, hujus quam tenemus fidei, &c.

ALthough our Minifters and Ecclefiafticks in former Ages have oft times given an account of that Faith, Religion, and Doctrine which we now hold and profefs, to feveral Kings and Princes, and in a word, to all who by virtue of either their Ecclefiaftical or fecular power have demanded a Reafon thereof; yet notwithftanding it feems to us to be a thing very needfull, (and that for many confiderable Reafons) to prefent your royal Majefty in as brief and compendious a method as the nature of the thing will permit, an account of that Doctrine which we have received from thofe our Anceftours, in the following Articles, which we look upon, and efteem (efpecially in this conjuncture of time) to be of the more general concernment, and of greateft confequence. And this we do, to the end that all men may know and fee, how unjuftly we have been hitherto perfecuted by the Adverfaries of this Doctrine, and are now wrongfully accufed before your Royal Majefty, by this means to render both us and ours obnoxious to further fufferings and violence.

Article 1.

ARTICLE I.

Concerning the holy Scriptures.

Principio, noſtri omnes unanimi conſenſu docent Scripturas ſacras, &c.

In the firſt place, all thoſe of our profeſſion do with an unanimous conſent teach and hold forth, that the holy Scriptures which are contained and comprehended in the *Bible,* and which have been received by the Fathers, and eſtabliſhed by *canonical* Authority, are to be accounted as undeniably and without all controverſie, moſt true and certain ; and in all things and upon all accounts ought to be preferred before any other Writings whatſoever, as far as holy things ought to be preferred before profane, and divine before humane, as likewiſe to be entirely and abſolutely believed, and all the Rules of Truth which concern our Juſtification and Salvation by Faith, are to be ſought for there, and to be derived thence. And furthermore, that they were delivered and inſpired by God himſelf, as is affirmed by *Peter, Paul,* and others, and are publickly read and recited in all our Churches (eſpecially the Epiſtles and Goſpels) and that in our mother and vulgar Tongue, after the manner and cuſtome of the *Primitive* Churches, to the end chiefly that they may be underſtood by all ; and laſtly, that from thence ariſe points of Doctrine and Exhortation anſwerable to all affairs and occaſions ; and Sermons are frequently made in publick to the People.

ARTICLE II.

Concerning Catechiſms.

Hinc Catechiſmum docent, hoc eſt Catholicam hanc & Orthodoxam Patrum, &c.

Fom hence they derive the Catechiſm, that is, the Catholick and Orthodox Doctrine of the Fathers, which is one and the ſame with the Decalogue of Gods Commandments, and with the *Apoſtles Creed,* digeſted into *twelve Articles,* and delivered in the *Symbol* by the Council of *Nice,* and ſo likewiſe expounded and confirmed by others ; and laſtly, it contains alſo the *Lords Prayer.* Now all theſe things they conſtantly affirm to be moſt holy, good, and well-pleaſing in the eys of God.

Moreover they teach that all theſe things ought to be obſerved in deed and with the whole heart, ſeeing the Law is ſpiritual ; as alſo
that

that the Articles of Faith ought undoubtedly to be believed, and confessed with the mouth, and to be manifested by works, which Articles they likewise enforce and corroborate by the Scriptures with all their might, endeavouring to teach the genuine sense of them; and where there occurrs any thing abstrufe or difficult, to unfold the true scope and meaning thereof fully and plainly.

They teach likewise, that God alone is to be prayed to, and invoked onely through the Name of *Christ* the Mediatour. As also that Prayers and Supplications ought to be made for all Governours of the Church, and all others who are conftituted in places of Eminency and Authority for the Government of others.

ARTICLE III.

Of Faith in the Holy Trinity.

Præterea fide nosci Deum Scripturis docent, &c.

Furthermore they teach, that God is known by Faith in the Scriptures, to be one as to the fubftance of the Divinity, and three persons, *viz.* Father, Son, and Holy Spirit. That as to the persons there is a difference; but as to the effence and fubftance, coequality and indiftinction: and this the Catholick Faith, the confent of the Council of *Nice,* with the Decrees and Sanctions of other Councils, and *Athanafius* his Confeffion or Creed do clearly teftifie.

Hence they alfo teach the great power, wifdom, and goodnefs of this one onely God, as likewife thofe his three moft excellent works agreeable to him alone, and which are applicable to none but him, *viz.* the work of Creation, Redemption, and Confervation or Sanctification: Moreover they teach, that this true God in one effence of Divinity and bleffed Trinity of perfons, is alone to be worfhipped, *Deut.6, &c.*

ARTICLE IV.

Of Sin, and the Fruit thereof, and the knowledg of ones felf.

Hic docent, ne peccata ignoremus quæ cum in proximos, tum in Deum, &c.

Here they teach, that fo we may not be ignorant of our fins which are committed and acted both againft God and our Neighbour;

First, that men ought to acknowledg themfelves to be conceived
and

and born in fin, and fo to be finners forthwith and naturally from the womb, and thus prevaricating from their childhood againft the Law of God in heart and deed, to be preffed and burdened with the weight of fin, as it is written, *The Lord looked down from Heaven to fee whether there was any one that was wife,* or *fought after God : but they are all gone out of the way, they have all corrupted themfelves, there is none that doth good, no not one.* Again, *God faw that the wickednefs of man was great upon the earth, and that all the thoughts and imaginations of his heart were wholly evil, and that continually.* And again the Lord faith, that *the conception and thought of mans heart is evil from his youth.* And *Paul* likewife, *We were* (faith he) *by nature the Children of wrath even as others.*

In the next place, they teach from the Scriptures, that men ought to acknowledg that for this their depravation and corruption, and for the fins arifing and fpringing up from this Root of Bitternefs, the fearfull vengeance of God and utter perdition defervedly hangs over their heads ; and that according to thofe their deeds the Pains of Hell are moft juftly laid before them ; For (as *Paul* faith) *the wages of fin is death.* And the Lord in the Gofpel, *They that have done ill fhall go into eternal punifhment , where fhall be weeping and gnafhing of teeth.* They teach further, that it is neceffary all fhould confider and know their infirmity, with their extreme want, and the mifchiefs into which they are fallen for their fins, and that they can no way fave or juftifie themfelves by any works or endeavours of their own, nor have any thing to truft unto but *Chrift* alone, whereby to redeem and free themfelves from fin, Satan, the wrath of God, and eternal death. As alfo, that there is nothing in man whereby one may help another before God, feeing all are equally void of the righteoufnefs of God, and obnoxious to his wrath by fin.

ARTICLE V.

Of Repentance.

Hoc loco docent Pœnitentiam effe; quæ ex peccatorum & irâ divinâ agnitione nafcitur, &c.

In this place they teach Repentance to be that which cometh from the acknowledgment of fin and Gods anger, which through the Law of God firft ftrikes the confcience with forrow and terrour : for as much as by the Word of God they are inwardly convinced of fin, and the minde becomes affected with an evil confcience, unquiet, exceeding forrowfull and defpairing ; the heart anxious, broken, and contrite, fo that a man by himfelf can by no means be raifed up, or get comfort, but is altogether afflicted, his fpirit being dejected, trembling, fhaken and fhatter'd with exceeding great horrour through

the

the fight of Gods wrath, (as *David* faith of himfelf) *There is no health in my flefh becaufe of thine indignation, neither is there any reft in my bones by reafon of my fin.* I am become miferable, *and am bowed down, and go mourning all the day long.* But yet notwithftanding they teach, that being thus affrighted, they ought neverthelefs not to defpair, but rather to return to God with the whole heart, by faith in *Chrift*, which is alfo a part of Repentance, taking hold of Mercy, and grieving that they have finned : for although they be void of Righteoufnefs, yet ought they to implore Divine Grace and Mercy, that he would have mercy on them, and that he would pardon their fins for *Chrift* and his merits fake, *who for our fake was made fin, and a curfe that he might fatisfie the juftice of God for our fins, &c.*

ARTICLE VI.

Of the Lord *Chrift*, and Faith in him.

Omnium primò docent, certam firmámque fidem habendam de Chrifto Domino, &c.

Firft of all, they teach, that we ought to have a certain and firm Faith concerning the Lord *Chrift, viz.* that he is true God by nature, and alfo true man, by whom all things were made, vifible and invifible, in Heaven and Earth ; whom *John* calling the *Eternal Word*, interprets to be *God, Light, the onely begotten, abiding in the bofome of the Father, full of grace and truth.* The fame in his former Epiftle and fifth Chapter, faith, *This is the true God* and *Eternal Life.*

They alfo declare concerning his works fhewed forth for our Salvation, his Incarnation, Nativity, Paffion, Death, Burial, Refurrection, Afcenfion into Heaven, fitting at the right hand of God, and his returning to judg the Quick and the Dead ; and that by the Word and Sacraments good fruits are derived to us, through which we may be faved, as the Scriptures fhew.

They teach further, that *Chrift* is not now in the World, nor will he ever appear untill the World be ended, in the fame fenfible and corporal manner, wherein he heretofore converfed as man upon the Earth, and fuffered himfelf to be betrayed, tormented, crucified, put to death, and afterwards rifing again in a glorious manner, made his way through the hard Rock, and the fealed Door of the Sepulcher. But that now he is in fuch a manner in Heaven, that every tongue ought to confefs, and all the godly to worfhip him together with the Father. To this the Article of Faith clearly beareth witnefs ; *He afcended into Heaven, where he fits at the right hand of God the Father Almighty, from whence he fhall come to judg both the Quick and the Dead.* Even as faith *Paul* in the 4. to the *Theffalonians, The Lord himfelf fhall defcend from Heaven with a fhout, and the voice of an Arch-angel, and the Trump of God.*

God. *Peter* likewife in the *Acts,* faith, *Whom the Heaven muft receive untill the times of the reftitution of all things.* And in the laft of *Mark, Therefore the Lord, after he had fpoken to them, was received up into Heaven, and fat on the right hand of God.* And the Angels which ftood by, faid unto them, *This fame* Jefus, *which is taken up from you into Heaven, fhall fo come, as ye have feen him going into Heaven, &c.*

They teach alfo, that the Lord *Chrift,* in this his other manner of Being, which we call Invifible, is prefent in the Minifters of his Church, the Word, and the Sacraments, and through thefe means all men hereafter ought fo to receive him by faith, that he may dwell in them, and abide in them by the Spirit of Truth, concerning whom he hath faid, *He fhall be in you.* And again, *I will come unto you, &c.*

Moreover alfo they hold, that by faith in *Chrift* men are, through mercy, freely juftified, and attain Salvation and Remiffion of fins by *Chrift,* without any humane help and merit, *&c.*

They hold likewife, that all confidence and hope is to be fixed in him alone, and that all our care ought to be caft upon him; and to thefe they further add, that for his fake onely, and for his merits alone, God is pacified and reconciled, doth love and preferve us, and adopt us to be his Children; and that Life Eternal is in him, and as many as believe in him fhall through him enjoy it. *John 6. He that believeth on me, hath Life Eternal, &c.*

They teach alfo, that no man can have this Faith by any power, will and pleafure of his own : it is indeed the gift of God, who when, and where it pleafeth him, worketh it in man by his Spirit, to the end he may receive whatfoever fhall be rightly adminiftred to him by the outward Word, and the Sacraments inftituted by *Chrift,* in order to Salvation.

Of this faith *John* the Baptift, *Lord, no man can have any thing, unlefs it be given him from above.* And, faith *Chrift* himfelf, *No man can come unto me, unlefs the Father, who fent me, draw him.* And a little after he addeth, *Unlefs it be given him of my Father ;* that is to fay, by the Holy Spirit.

Furthermore, they teach, that men are juftified before God, by faith alone, or confidence in *Jefus Chrift,* without their endeavours, merits and works, according to that faying of *Paul, Moreover, to him which worketh not, but believeth on him who juftifieth the ungodly, is his faith reckoned for righteoufnefs.* Again, *But now the righteoufnefs of God is manifefted without the Law, being witneffed by the Law and the Prophets. And this righteoufnefs is through the faith of* Jefus Chrift.

ARTICLE VII.

ARTICLE VII.

Of good Works.

His addunt, ut qui sola Dei gratia, fidéque in Christum, justificati sunt, &c.

To these they add, that those men who are justified onely by the grace of God, and through faith in *Christ*, do perform those good works which God commandeth, and do every man walk therein as becomes them according to their Calling, in any kinde of life, condition, and age whatsoever: for so saith the Lord in *Matthew*, *Teach them to observe all things which I have commanded you*. But seeing there are many things in several places of the Scriptures concerning this matter, we forbear to enlarge.

Yea and they teach also, upon what account especially and with what purpose, good works are to be done; not to such an end, as that men should conceive they can obtain Justification, Salvation or Remission of sins by them: for even the Lord himself saith, *When ye shall have done all things which are commanded you, say ye, We are unprofitable Servants*. Again, *Paul* saith, *By the works of the Law shall no flesh be justified in his sight*. So also saith *David*, *Lord, enter not into judgment with thy Servant, for in thy sight shall no man living be justified*.

But they teach, that good works are therefore to be done, that faith may be approved by them: for, good works are sure Testimonies, Seals, and Evidences of a lively faith lying hid within, and fruits of the same, whereby the Tree is known to be good or bad, *Matth.*7. Also, to the end that men may by them make their Calling sure and certain, and be saved therein without sin; according to what *Peter* saith, Epist.2. Chap.1. *Brethren give diligence that ye may make your Calling and Election sure.*

But they teach, that we should know there is a difference between works ordained by men, and works which are commanded by God, and by what means both may be done and observed, for as much as the works commanded by God, are in no wise to be neglected for the sake of humane Traditions; for, the Lord severely reproveth them that do the contrary, *Wherefore do ye transgress the Commandment of God for your Traditions?* And, *In vain do they worship me, teaching for Commandments the Doctrines of men.*

They teach moreover, that there is no man that can indeed perform the works commanded by God. Also, that there is no man who sinneth not, although he carefully exercise himself in good works and in the Law of God; as it is written, *There is none upon earth who doth good, and sinneth not, &c.*

ARTIC.

ARTICLE VIII.

Of the Holy Catholick Church.

*Docent primùm, Chriſtum Dominum ſuo merito, gratiâ & veritate, Ec-
cleſiæ caput & fundamentum eſſe, &c.*

They teach firſt, that the Lord *Chriſt,* by his own merit, grace, and
truth, is the Head and Foundation of the Church, in whom ſhe is built
up through the Holy Spirit, by the Word and Sacraments; as *Chriſt*
ſaith unto *Peter, And upon this Rock (that is, my ſelf) I will build my
Church.* And *Paul* 1 *Cor.*3. *Other Foundation can no man lay, beſide
this which is laid, that is* Jeſus Chriſt. So ſaith the ſame Apoſtle in another place, *He is the Head of the Church, who filleth all in all.*

They teach likewiſe, that we muſt believe and confeſs, that the
holy Catholick Church, as it is at preſent collected, conſiſteth of all
Chriſtian men throughout the world, in what Nations ſoever they
live, or whereſoever they be diſperſed, who by the ſacred Word of
the Goſpel are gathered together, out of all Nations, People, Tribes,
and Languages, of what Degree, Age, or Condition ſoever they be,
into the ſame Faith of *Chriſt,* and the holy Trinity; according to
what is written by *John* in the *Apocalypſe, After theſe things I beheld,
and lo, a great multitude, which no man was able to number, &c.* And
the Lord ſaith, *Where two or three ſhall be gathered together in my Name
(in any Nation or People whatſoever) there am I in the midſt of them :*
for, whereſoever *Chriſt* is preached and received, whereſoever his
Word and Sacraments are, and are diſpenſed and received according
to his appointment and will, there is a holy Church and *Chriſtian* Society, and the People of God, whatſoever their number be. But
where *Chriſt* is abſent, and his Word rejected, there can be neither a
true Church, nor People pleaſing God.

But as touching their own Congregation, they thus conceive and
teach, that it, even as other Congregations, be they great or ſmall, is
not the holy univerſal Church, but onely a part and member thereof,
as the *Corinthians* were, of whom ſaith the Apoſtle, 1 *Co.*12. *Now ye
are the body of* Chriſt, *and members in particular, &c.*

Beſides, they teach, that thoſe who are manifeſtly impious, impenitent, and obſtinate, that is to ſay, who do not give ear to the Admonitions of the Church, may be conſtrained by that her Cenſure and
Puniſhment, which in the uſual acception is called *Anathema,* or Excommunication. And that this ought to be done without reſpect of
perſons, againſt all thoſe whoſe impiety is known, and who are addict-
ed to the more notorious ſins, and who having been often admoniſhed
do yet perſiſt in their ſins.

But they teach, that *Antichriſt,* that man of ſin, doth ſit in the
Temple of God, that is, in the Church, of whom the Prophets, and
Chriſt

Chriſt and his Apoſtles foretold, admoniſhing all the godly, to beware of him and his Errours, and not ſuffer themſelves to be drawn aſide from the Truth, *&c.*

ARTICLE IX.

Of the Eccleſiaſtical Order, or the Overſeers, or Miniſters of the Church.

Docent Miniſtros Eccleſiæ, quibus adminiſtratio Verbi & Sacramentorum demandatur, ritè inſtitutos eſſe opportere, &c.

They teach, that the Miniſters of the Church, to whom the Adminiſtration of the Word and Sacraments is committed, ought to be rightly ordained, according to the Rule preſcribed by the Lord and his Apoſtles. And that for the undertaking this Office, there may be called from among the godly and faithfull People, men full of faith and without blame, ſuch as have gifts neceſſary for this Miniſtry, being alſo of honeſt life and converſation; and that theſe be firſt of all tried, then after Prayer made by the Elders, that they be by Impoſition of Hands for this Office, confirmed in the Congregation, *&c.*

Wherefore indeed, no man among us is permitted to perform the Office of a Prieſt, unleſs he ſhall, as is meet, be called, and ordained according to this kinde of Rule. Next they teach, that it is the duty of thoſe who are thus choſen to the Miniſtry of the Church, to have a diligent care of the ſouls committed to their charge, and faithfully to adminiſter to them the Word of the Goſpel, and the Sacraments, according to *Chriſt's* Inſtitution, and to ſhew forth themſelves a good Example unto all men for Imitation, and to pray for them unto God, that they may be delivered from their Errours and Offences, *&c.*

ARTICLE X.

Of the Word of God.

Deinde docent, quod verbi Dei, ſeu Evangelii prædicatio eſt Miniſterium à Chriſto inſtitutum & præceptum, Matthæi ultimo: &c.

Furthermore, they teach that the preaching of the Word of God or the Goſpel is a Miniſtration appointed and commanded by *Chriſt,* in the laſt of *Matthew, Go ye into all the World, and preach the Goſpel to every Creature. Peter* alſo ſaith, *Acts* 10. *The Lord commanded us that we ſhould preach, &c.*

They teach alſo, that we ought to hold a difference betwixt the
power

power and efficacy of the Law and of the Gofpel, that the former is indeed the Adminiftration of Death, but the latter the Adminiftration of Life and Glory by *Chrift*, 2 *Cor.*3. *The Letter killeth, but the Spirit maketh alive.* And *John* 6. *The words which I fpeak unto you are Spirit and Life.*

They believe moreover, that no man can attain true Faith, unlefs he hear the Word of God, according to that of *Paul*, *Faith comes by hearring, and hearing by the Word of God.* And again, *But how fhall they believe on him, of whom they have not heard?* Therefore ours do ufe all their endeavour, to teach and preach in the Church, the Word of the Gofpel without any mixture of humane Traditions : for that caufe they in their Churches do reade the Gofpels themfelves, and the other Scriptures alfo in the vulgar Tongue.

ARTICLE XI.

Of the Sacraments.

Docent imprimis, Sacramenta per Chriftum inftituta, ad falutem neceffaria effe, &c.

Firft, they teach, that the Sacraments ordained by *Chrift* are neceffary to falvation, by means whereof Believers are made fellow-partakers of the merits of *Chrift :* but in cafe any man fhall wilfully contemn, or not worthily efteem them, or ufe them in any other manner whatfoever, than as *Chrift* hath willed and commanded, they declare that he grievoufly finneth againft *Chrift* the Authour of them.

But if it fo come to pafs, that any man truly defire to communicate by the Sacraments, according to the minde and command of *Chrift*, yet being hindered by fome ficknefs, or carried away captive into foreign parts, or being oppreffed by the Adverfaries and Enemies of the Faith, *&c.* he be not able to fatisfie his own pious defire, then in fuch cafes without doubt he fhall, if fo be he fincerely and entirely believe the Gofpel, be faved by the Faith of *Chrift* alone.

They teach next, that the Sacraments of themfelves, or (as fome fpeak) *ex opere operato,* do not confer grace, nor juftifying faith, upon thofe who are not firft endued with good inclinations, and inwardly quickened by the Holy Spirit, *&c.*

ARTIC.XII

ARTICLE XII.

Of Baptifm.

Docent item, quod Baptifmus fit falutaris adminiftratio, à Chrifto inftitu-
ta, &c.

They teach alfo that Baptifm is a faving Adminiftration, inftituted
by *Chrift*, and added to the Gofpel, by which he purifieth, cleanfeth,
and fanctifieth his Church in his own Death and Bloud, as *Paul* faith,
Chrift loved his Church, and gave himfelf for it: that he might fanctifie it,
being cleanfed by the wafhing of water through the Word, &c.
   Likewife they teach, that Children are to be baptized unto Salvation, and to be confecrated to *Chrift*, according to his Word ; *Suffer*
little Chidren to come unto me, and forbid them not, for of fuch is the
Kingdom of God, &c.

ARTICLE XIII.

Of the Lords Supper.

Dominicam Cœnam, feu Sacramentum Euchariftiæ, Minifterium effe à
Chrifto, &c.

They teach, that the Lords Supper, or Sacrament of the Euchariſt,
was a Miniftration appointed by *Chrift*, afterward by his Apoftles, and
by them, through his grace and goodnefs, delivered to the whole
Church, for the common ufe and Salvation of all men, as the Evangelifts do bear witnefs, and the Apoftle, whofe words are ufed by all
the Church, *For I have received from the Lord, that which alfo I have*
delivered to you, how that the Lord Jefus, *in the fame night wherein he*
was betrayed, took Bread, &c. And a little after, *Therefore my Bre-*
thren, when ye come together to eat, (to wit, this Supper) ftay one for ano-
ther.
   Yea and they teach here alfo, that men muft believe with the heart,
and confefs with the mouth, that the Bread of the Lords Supper is the
true Body of *Chrift*, which was delivered for us, and that the Cup is
his true Bloud, which was fhed for us for the Remiffion of fins, as the
Lord *Chrift* exprefly faith, *This is my Body, This is my Bloud, &c.*
   They further teach, that in the Adminiftring this Sacrament nothing elfe is to be done, but what is fet forth and commanded by
thefe exprefs words of *Chrift*, who giving Bread to his Difciples,
faid, *Take, eat, This is my Body. And taking the Cup, he gave thanks*
and faid, Drink ye all of this, for, This is my Bloud of the New Tefta-
ment,

ment, which is shed for many for the Remission of sins. And so, according to this Command of the Lord, they teach, that his Body and Bloud ought to be taken by all promifcuoufly, under both kindes, even as they were apart and by themfelves by him inftituted and ordained, and as the Primitive Church alfo ufed this whole Sacrament. But if any man, out of prefumption attempt any thing contrary to this Inftitution of *Chrift,* he finneth againft *Chrift* the Authour thereof, and againft his will exprefly revealed in the Scripture.

ARTICLE XIV.

Of Ecclefiaftical Power, or the Keys.

Et hic docent, ut credatur Claves à Chrifto Ecclefiæ traditas effe, &c.

And here they teach, how it ought to be believed, that the Keys were delivered by *Chrift* to the Church, concerning which he faid unto *Peter,* inftead of all, *I will give thee the Keys of the Kingdom of Heaven.* And that thefe were an Adminiftration delivered to the Church of *Chrift* and the Minifters thereof, which continueth therein to this prefent day, and is not to have an end before the diffolution of the World.

The duty and authority of this Adminiftration, according to the Command and Intent of *Chrift,* is, as the Scriptures do exprefs, to correct and binde fuch as are wicked and impenitent in the Church, and to fhut the Kingdom of Heaven againft them, which is, to exclude them from *Chrift,* and from the ufe and communion of the Church. And on the contrary, to abfolve fuch as are truly penitent, reftore them to peace of Confcience, place them in a fure hope and belief of Salvation, and fo to open unto them the Kingdom of Heaven, and inftruct and ftrengthen them againft all the Temptations, Affaults, and cunning Devices of that Enemy. And this they ought to do, not by their own power and pleafure, but as Difpenfers of the Myfteries of God, Minifters and Servants of *Chrift,* by his authority, through the Word and Sacraments, *&c.*

ARTICLE XV.

Of humane Traditions.

Humanas traditiones, ritus & confuetudines, quæ nihil pietati adverfantur, in publicis conventibus fervanda docent, &c.

They teach, that humane Traditions, Rites, and Cuftoms, which
are

are not againſt piety, are to be obſerved in publick Congregations, *&c.*

But they teach, that ſuch Traditions, Rites, and Ceremonies, which
obſcure the glory of *Chriſt* and his grace, lead the People away, and
draw them back from the truth and faith, and are made equal or preferred to Divine Inſtitutions, or if any man tranſgreſs theſe upon the
account of the other, and relinquiſh the ſincere uſe of the Word of
God, are to be avoided and rejected, *&c.*

They teach next, that becauſe of the Differences of Ceremonies,
Cuſtoms, and Rites, which are to be ſeen in ſeveral Churches among
Chriſtians, and are not prejudicial or hurtfull to piety, they ought not
to be offended one with another, or contemn, hate, and perſecute one
another, *&c.*

ARTICLE XVI.

Of the Secular Power.

Docetur hic apud nos juxta Scripturas, quod ſublimior poteſtas, ſeu Magi-
ſtratus ſecularis, Dei ordinatio ſit, &c.

We teach here according to the Scriptures, that the higher Power
or Secular Magiſtrate, is an Ordinance of God, to the end the People
may be governed in thoſe things which are Political and Temporary.
Concerning this, excellent is that place of *Paul, For there is no Power*
but of God, the Powers which are, are ordained of God.

They teach moreover, that thoſe who are in power, or bear publick
Office and Magiſtracy, of what degree ſoever they be, ſhould underſtand, that they do not their own, but the work of God, and that he
is ſovereign Lord and King over them and others ; to whom alſo they
ought to remember that they are to give an account of their Steward-
ſhip at the laſt Day.

They teach alſo, that it is commanded in the Word of God, that
all men ſhould in all things be ſubject to the higher Powers, provided
they be ſuch, as are not contrary to God and his Word, *&c.*

But as touching thoſe things which concern Souls, and Faith, and
Salvation, they teach, that we ought to give ear unto Gods Word
onely, and his Miniſters, as *Chriſt* himſelf ſaith, *Give ye unto* Cæſar
the things that are Cæſar's, *and to God the things that are God's* .

And if any man endeavour to compell them unto ſuch things as are
againſt God, and repugnant to his Word, which endureth for ever,
they teach, that we ought to follow the Example of the Apoſtles,
who gave this Anſwer to the Magiſtrate at *Jeruſalem, We ought* (ſay
they) *to obey God rather than men.*

ART.XVII.

ARTICLE XVII.

Of the Worshipping of Saints.

Initio docent quòd post creatos homines nullus eorum unquam extitit, nec nunc quoque est, nec aliquando futurus est, &c.

They teach first, that since the Creation of Mankinde, there never was any one of them, nor is there now, nor ever will there be here-after, who can be holy or righteous, by any strength, merits, endeavours, and works of his own. Even as holy *Job* saith, *What is man, that he should be pure, and he that is born of a woman, that he should appear righteous?*

But what good things soever there are in the Saints, they ought to be acknowledged as received from the bounty and goodness of God. For, in that they are holy and acceptable to God, it is a matter that befalls them without all merit, through his divine will and pleasure onely, *&c.*

They teach moreover, that the Honour and Worship due unto God, is not to be transferred unto the Saints, nor to their Images; as it is written in *Isaiah, I am the Lord, This is my Name, I will not give my glory to another, &c.*

ARTICLE XVIII.

Of Fasts.

Jejunia nostri cultum quendam externum in piis esse, Deo soli exhibendum, &c.

The men of our perswasion teach, that Fasts are a kinde of outward Worship among the Godly, to be given onely to God himself, and such as are to be observed, according to the circumstance of persons, nations, places, and affairs, by all, and by every man also, without Superstition and Hypocrisie.

They teach next, that Fasting doth not consist in a difference of Meats, but in a sparing use of them, Sobriety, and Temperance, and afflicting of the Body, and Humiliation before God. But it is a matter altogether of concernment, with what minde or purpose any man doth fast, for as much as Fasting is then good, when it is pleasing and acceptable to God, as you may reade *Matth. 6.* and *Isai 58.*

ART. XIX.

ARTICLE XIX.

Of Celibate, or, The Unmarried State.

Ad cælibatum docent, neminem cogendum, aut ab eo retrahendum esse, &c.

They teach, that no man ought to be conftrained unto a fingle Life, or withdrawn from it, becaufe God hath commanded, or forbidden it to no man, but hath left it to every mans will and pleafure, to live unmarried, or to marry.

They teach moreover, that no man ought to chufe a fingle Life with this intent, that he fhould think thereby to merit Remiffion of Sins and Eternal Life, for himfelf or others. For, neither Single Life, nor any work of ours procureth thefe things for us, but onely the Death and Grace of *Chrift* alone.

ARTICLE XX.

Of the Time of Grace, wherein the Favour of God ought to be fought, and may be found.

Hoc demùm loco docent, ut sciant homines tantifper dum in vivis funt, tempus à Deo, quod gratiæ eft, &c.

Laftly, they teach in this place, that men are to underftand, that fo long as they live in this World, there is a time given them by God, which is a time of grace, to the end they may feek him, and his grace, goodnefs, mercy, and gentlenefs, and fo through his promife may finde, and by that means attain bleffednefs and falvation, &c. to the end alfo that every man, while this time of grace doth laft, may repent of his life paft, be reconciled to God, and pacifie, quiet and fecure his own confcience through faith in *Chrift*, and by his Miniftry in the Church. Hereupon firmly believing, that his fins are pardoned, and that God is reconciled for the fake of *Chrift*, in whofe grace being eftablifhed, walking and perfevering in good works, he ought affuredly to expect, that his Soul being loofed from the Prifon of the Body, he fhall pafs, not into any punifhment, but be carried like poor *Lazarus* into eternal happinefs, and there remain with the Lord *Chrift* for ever, &c.

A Teftimony

A Testimony taken out of Dr. *Martin Luther's* Preface before the Confession of the *Waldenses*, *Anno Domini* 1533.

Inter hos autem occurrebant & isti Fratres, quos Pighardos vocabant, jam mihi non ita invisi, &c.

But among these I observed also those Brethren, whom they called *Fratres Pighardi* or *Picardi*, who are not now odious to me, as they were in the days of my Popery. In a word, I found among them that one great and wonderfull thing, scarce ever so much as heard of in the Popes Church, to wit, that laying aside the Doctrines of Men, so far as they were able, they meditated in the Law of the Lord night and day: and that they were skilled and ready in the Scriptures, whereas in the Papacy our Masters themselves wholly neglected the Scriptures; with the name of which they were puffed up, but some of them had not so much as seen the *Bible* at any time. But yet it could not otherwise be, but that divers places must needs remain obscure to them, because not onely the *Greek* and *Hebrew* Tongues, but the *Latine* also, were in a manner lost. And that continued a fault among them, that while they endeavoured to avoid the Briars and Bogs wherein the Sophisters and Monks were entangled, they wholly abstained from all study of the Arts, being withall pinched by poverty, which they relieved by the labour of their hands.

But now they appear, not a little better instructed and more free, I may say also more enlightened and better, so that I hope they will be neither unwelcome nor unpleasing to such as are truly *Christian*; wherefore it behoveth us to give very great Thanks to God the Father of our Lord *Jesus Christ*, who according to the Riches of his Glory, hath commanded this Light of his Word to shine out of Darkness, thereby to destroy Death in us, and restore Life; and we ought to rejoyce also, both on their behalf and our own, that we who were among our selves also at a distance, are now, upon throwing down that partition-wall of Jealousie, whereby we seemed Hereticks to each other, made near, and reduced together into one Sheep-fold, under that one Shepherd and Bishop of our Souls, who is blessed for ever. *Amen.*

The

The Testimony given by *Philip Melancthon* to the *Waldenses*, in an Epistle of his inscribed:

To the Reverend Brother in *Christ* Mr. *Benedict*, and the rest of the *Waldensian* Brethren in *Bohemia.*

Gratia & pax, &c. Existimo, vir eximie, Fratres tuos in hoc nostro congressu in multis rebus melius meam sententiam cognovisse, &c.

Grace and Peace, *&c.* I suppose, worthy Sir, that your Brethren in this our Meeting, have known and throughly discerned my opinion in many things, better I think than I my self understood your affairs heretofore. Wherefore seeing we are agreed about the chief Articles of the *Christian* Faith, let us mutually imbrace each other in love, for as much as no difference and variety of Rites and Ceremonies ought to disunite our mindes. The Apostle *Paul* speaketh often touching Ceremonies, and forbiddeth *Christians* to disagree, because of the variety of Ceremonies, although the World quarrels vehemently about Ceremonies. Indeed, I do not dislike that severer way of Exercise or Discipline used in your Churches; I would to God it were a little more severely observed also in our Churches: As concerning mine own affection towards you, I would have you so to think, that I earnestly wish that those who love the Gospel, and desire the Name of *Christ* may be glorified, would follow one another with mutual love, and so with joint-endeavours improve their Learning to the glory of *Christ*, lest they destroy themselves by mutual and private Enmities or Dissensions, especially about those things, for which there needeth no contention. Farewell, pray for me, and for the Glory of *Christ*.

Given at *Wittenberg*, in the year 1533.

Philip Melancthon.

Another

Another out of *Bucer*'s Book, entituled, *Scripta duo Adverſaria Latomi, &c.* in that Chapter which treateth of the Authority of the Church, *p.* **159.**

Illa certe ratio optima eſt quam obſervant Fratres Picardi, &c.

That certainly is a very good courſe which is obſerved by our Brethren the *Waldenſes,* who have ſet forth in Print that Confeſſion of their Faith which they lately preſented to King *Ferdinand, Anno* 1533. together with a Preface. They have alſo retained the Diſcipline of *Chriſt* among them; which commendation the thing it ſelf conſtraineth us to give them, to the end we may praiſe the Lord, who ſo worketh in them, although thoſe Brethren be deſpiſed by ſome men perverſly learned. But the courſe which they obſerve in this matter is this.

Beſides Miniſters of the Word and Sacraments, they have a certain College of men, excelling in prudence and gravity of ſpirit, whoſe Office it is to admoniſh and correct offending Brethren, to compoſe ſuch as diſagree, and judg in their Cauſes, *&c.*

A brief

A brief Confeſſion of Faith publiſhed by the Reformed Churches of PIEMONT, *Anno Domini* 1655.

The Original whereof is to be ſeen, together with the reſt, in the publick Library of the famous Univerſity of *CAMBRIDG.*

Avendo inteſo che li noſtri Avverſarii non contentandoſi d' haverci crudelmente perſeguitati e ſpogliati de noſtri beni, per renderci vie più odioſi, vanno ancora ſeminando de falſi rumori, tendenti non ſolo à macchiare le noſtre perſone, mà principalmente ad' infamare con calunnie attroci, la ſanta e ſalutare dottrina laquale profeſsiamo: Noi ſiamo obligati per chiarire lo ſpirito di quelli, che potrebbono eſſere preoccupati di tali ſiniſtri penſieri, di fare una breve dichiaratione della noſtra fede, quale habbiamo per l' addietro havuta, & la teniamo ancora hoggidi, conforme alla parola di Dio, acciò chè ogn' uno vegga la falſità di quelle calunnie, e con quanta ingiuſtitia ſiamo odiati, e perſeguitati per una ſi innocente dottrina.

Aving underſtood that our Adverſaries, not contented to have moſt cruelly perſecuted us, and robbed us of all our Goods and Eſtates, have yet an intention to render us odious to the World, by ſpreading abroad many falſe Reports, and ſo not onely to defame our perſons, but likewiſe to aſperſe with moſt ſhamefull calumnies that holy and wholeſome Doctrine which we profeſs, we look upon our ſelves as obliged, for the better information of thoſe, whoſe mindes may perhaps be preoccupied with ſiniſter opinions, to make a ſhort Declaration of our Faith, ſuch as we have heretofore profeſſed and held, and do at this day profeſs and hold, as conformable to the Word of God; that ſo every one may ſee the falſity of thoſe their calumnies, and alſo how unjuſtly we are hated and perſecuted upon the account of our Profeſſion.

Noi crediamo.

1. *Che v' è un ſolo Iddio il quale è una eſſenza ſpirituale, eterna, infi-*

We believe.

1. Firſt, that there is one onely God, who is a ſpiritual Eſſence, Eternal,

nal, Infinite, All-wife, Mercifull, Juft, and in fum, All-perfect, and that there are three perfons in that one onely and fimple Effence, *viz.* the Father, Son, and Holy Spirit.

2. That the fame God has manifefted himfelf unto us by the Works of Creation, and Providence, as alfo in his Word revealed unto us, firft by Oracles in feveral manners, and afterwards by thofe written Books which are called *The holy Scriptures.*

3. That we ought to receive thofe holy Scriptures (as we do) for facred and canonical, that is to fay, for the conftant Rule of our Faith and Life: as alfo to believe, that the fame is fully contained in the *Old* and *New Teftament*; and that by the *Old Teftament* we muft underftand onely fuch Books as God did intruft the *Judaical* Church with, and which that Church always approved and acknowledged to be from God; namely, the five Books of *Mofes, Jofuah,* the *Judges, Ruth,* 1. and 2. of *Samuel,* 1. and 2. of the *Kings,* 1. and 2. of the *Chronicles,* the 1. of *Efra, Nehemiah, Efther, Job,* the *Pfalms,* the *Proverbs* of *Solomon, Ecclefiaftes,* the *Song of Songs,* the four great, and the twelve *minor* Prophets: the *New Teftament* contains onely the four *Evangelifts,* the *Acts* of the *Apoftles,* the *Epiftles* of St. *Paul,* 1. to the *Romans,* 2. to the *Corinthians,* 1. to the *Galatians,* 1. to the *Ephefians,* 1. to the *Philippians,* 1. to the *Colofsians,* 2. to the *Theffalonians,* 2. to *Timothy,* 1. to *Titus,* 1. to *Philemon,* and his *Epiftle* to the *Hebrews,* one of St. *James,* 2. of St. *Peter,* 3. of St. *John,* 1. of St. *Jude,* and laftly the *Revelation.*

4. We acknowledg the Divinity of thefe Books, not onely from the Teftimony of the Church, but more

2. *Che quello Iddio s' è manifeftato à gli huomini nelle fue opere della creatione; e della providenza, e di più nella fua parola, revelata dal principio con oracoli in diverfe maniere, poi meffa in ifcritto nè libbri chiamati la Scrittura Santa.*

3. *Che conviene ricevere, come riceviamo, quefta fanta Scrittura per Divina, e Canonica cio è per regola della noftra fede, e vita; e ch' ella è pienamente contenuta nè libri del Vecchio e Nuovo Teftamento, che nel Vecchio Teftamento deono effer folo comprefi i libri, ch' Iddio fidò alla Chiefa Giudàica, da lei fempre approvati e riconofciuti per Divini, cio è i cinque libri di Moïfe, Jofue, li Giudici, Ruth, 1. & 2. di Samuel, 1. & 2. de Rè, 1. & 2. delle Croniche, il 1. di Efdra, Nehemia, Efther, Job, i Salmi, i Proverbi di Salomone, l' Ecclefiafte, il Cantico de' Cantici, i quattro gran Profeti, i dodici Piccioli, e nel Nuovo, i quattro Evangelii, i Fatti delli Apoftoli, le Epiftole di St. Paolo, una à Romani, due à Corinti, una à Galati, una alli Efefi, una à Filippefi, una à Coleffefi, due à Theffalonicefi, due à Timoteo, una à Tito, una à Filemone, l' Epiftola à gli Hebrei, una di St. Giacopo, due di St. Pietro, trè di S. Giovanni, una di S. Giuda, e l' Apocaliffe.*

4. *Che riconofciamo la Divinità di quefti libri facri, non folo dalla teftimonianza della Chiefa, mà principalmente*

palmente dall' eterna, & indubitabile verità della dottrina contenuta in efsi, d' all' eccellenza, fublimità, e Maeftà del tutto Divina che vi fi dimoftra; e dall' operatione dello Spirito Santo, che ci fà ricevere con riverenza la tefti-monianza, laquale cene rende la Chie-fa, che ci apre gli occhi per ifcuoprir i raggi della celefte luce che rifplendono nella Scrittura, e corregge il noftro gufto, per difcernere quefto cibo col fuo Divino fapore.

5. Ch' Iddio hà fatto tutte le cofe di nulla, colla fua volontà del tutto libera, e colla potenza infinita della fua parola.

6. Ch' egli le conduce, e governa tutte colla fua providenza, ordinando & addirizzando tutto ciò che nel mon-do accade, fenza che pure egli fia ne autore, nè caufa del male che fanno le Creature, ò che la colpa ne gli poffa, ò-debba in alcuna maniera effer impu-tata.

7. Che gli Angeli effendo ftati tutti creati puri, e fanti, alcuni fono ca-duti in una corruttione, & perditione irreparabile, mà che gli altri fono per-feverati per un' effetto de la Divina bontà, che gli hà foftenuti, e confir-mati.

8. Che l' huomo il quale era ftato creato puro, e Santo all' imagine di Dio, per fua colpa s' è privato di quello ftato felice, preftando fede à difcorfi in-gannevoli del Diavolo.

9. Che l' huomo nella fua tranfgref-fione hà perduta la giuftitia, e la fan-tità che haveva ricevuto, ed è in-corfo nell' indignatione di Dio, nella

especially becaufe of the eternal and undoubted Truth of the Doctrine therein contained, and of that moft divine Excellency, Sublimity, and Majefty, which appears therein; be-fides the teftimony of the Holy Spi-rit, who gives us to receive with re-verence the teftimony of the Church in that point, and opens the eys of our underftanding to difcover the beams of that celeftial Light, which fhines in the Scripture, and prepares our tafte to difcern the divine favour of that fpiritual Food.

5. That God made all things of nothing by his own free will, and by the infinite power of his Word.

6. That he governs and rules all by his providence, ordaining and ap-pointing whatfoever happens in this world, without being Authour or caufe of any evil committed by the Creatures, fo that the defect thereof neither can nor ought to be any ways imputed unto him.

7. That the Angels were all in the beginning created pure and holy, but that fome of them are fallen into irreparable corruption and perdition; and that the reft have perfevered in their firft purity by an effect of divine goodnefs, which has upheld and con-firmed them.

8. That man was created clean and holy, after the Image of God, and that through his own fault he depri-ved himfelf of that happy condition, by giving credit to the deceitfull words of the Devil.

9. That man by his tranfgreffion loft that righteoufnefs and holinefs which he received, and is thereby ob-noxious to the wrath of God,
Death,

Death, and Captivity, under the Jurisdiction of him who has the power of Death, that is, the Devil; in so much that our free will is become a Servant and a Slave to Sin; and thus all men (both *Jews* and *Gentiles*) are by nature the Children of wrath, being all dead in their trespasses and sins, and consequently incapable of the least good motion, or inclination to any thing which concerns their salvation; yea incapable to think one good thought without Gods special grace, all their Imaginations being wholly evil, and that continually.

10. That all the Posterity of *Adam* is guilty of his disobedience, and infected by his corruption, and fallen into the same calamity with him, even the very Infants from their mothers womb, whence is derived the word of *original sin.*

11. That God, saves from that corruption and condemnation those whom he has chosen from the foundation of the world, not for any disposition, faith or holiness that he foresaw in them, but of his meer mercy in *Jesus Christ* his Son; passing by all the rest, according to the irreprehensible Reason of his free will and Justice.

12. That *Jesus Christ* having been ordained by the eternal Decree of God, to be the onely Saviour, and Head of that Body which is the Church, he redeemed it with his own Bloud in the fulness of time, and communicates unto the same all his benefits, together with the Gospel.

13. That there are two natures in *Jesus Christ*, *viz.* Divine and Humane, truly united in one and the same person, without either confusi-

---

morte, & nella cattività sotto la potenza di colui, ch' hà l' imperio della morte, ciò è del Diavolo, à tal segno ch' il suo libero arbitrio è divenuto servo, e schiavo del peccato: cosi che di natura tutti gli huomini, e Giudei, e Gentili sono figliuoli d' ira, tutti morti nè loro falli, e peccati, & conseguentemente incapaci d' havere alcun buono muovimento per la salute, etiandio di formar un buon pensiero senza la gratia, tutte le loro imaginationi non essendo altro che male in ogni tempo.

10. Che tutta la posterità d' Adamo è col penale in esso lui della sua disobbidienza infetta della sua corruttione, e caduta nella medesima calamità infino alli piccoli fanciulli fin dal ventre della madre onde viene il nome di peccato originale.

11. Che Iddio cava da quella corruttione, & condannatione le persone ch' egli hà elette dinanzi la fondatione del mondo, non perche egli prevedesse in essi alcuna dispositione alla fede o alla santità, mà per la sua misericordia in Giesu Christo suo figliuolo, lasciandovi gli altri secondo la raggione irrepreensibile della sua libertà, e giustitia.

12. Che Giesu Christo essendo stato da Dio ordinato nel suo eterno decreto, per esser il solo Salvator, e l' unico capo del suo corpo ch' è la Chiesa, egli l' hà riscattato col suo proprio sangue nel compimento de tempi, e le communica tutti li suoi benefici coll' Euangelio.

13. Che vi sono due nature in Giesu Christo, la Divina, e l' humana, veramente unite in una stessa persona, senza con-

confusione, senza separatione, senza divisione, senza cangiamento, l'una, e l'altra natura servando le sue distinte proprietà; e che Giesu Christo è insieme vero Dio, e vero huomo.

on, separation, division, or alteration; each nature keeping its own distinct proprieties; and that *Jesus Christ* is both true God and true man.

14. Che Iddio hà tanto amato il mondo, ciò è quelli ch'egli hà eletti dal mondo ch'egli hà dato il suo figlivolo per salvarci colla sua perfettissima ubbidienza: quella specialmente ch'egli ha dimostrata sofferendo la morte maledetta della croce, e colle vittorie ch'egli ha riportate sopra'l Diavolo, il peccato, & la morte.

14. That God so loved the world, that is to say, those whom he has chosen out of the world, that he gave his own Son to save us by his most perfect obedience, (especially that obedience which he expressed in his Suffering the cursed Death of the Cross) and also by his Victory over the Devil, Sin, and Death.

15. Che Giesu Christo havendo fatta l'intiera espiatione dè nostri peccati co'l suo perfettissimo sacrificio una volta offerto nella croce, non può, ne deve esser reiterato sotto qualunque pretesto, come si pretende fare nella Messa.

15. That *Jesus Christ* having fully expiated our sins by his most perfect Sacrifice once offered on the Cross, it neither can, nor ought to be reiterated upon any account whatsoever, as they pretend to do in the *Mass*.

16. Ch'il Signor Giesu havendoci pienamente reconciliati à Dio con il sangue della sua croce, in virtù del suo solo merito, e non delle nostre opere, noi siamo assolti, e giustificati nel suo cospetto, e che non v'è altro purgatorio, che nel suo sangue, il quale ci purga da ogni peccato.

16. That the Lord having fully and absolutely reconciled us unto God, through the Bloud of his Cross, by virtue of his merit onely, and not of our works, we are thereby absolved and justified in his sight, neither is there any other *Purgatory* besides his Bloud, which cleanses us from all sin.

17. Che noi habbiamo unione con Giesu Christo, e communione à suoi benefici per la fede, la quale si appoggia sopra le promesse di vita, che ci sono fatte nell'Evangelio.

17. That we are united with *Christ*, and made partakers of all his benefits by Faith, trusting and confiding wholly to those promises of life which are given us in the Gospel.

18. Che quella fede viene dall'operatione gratiosa, & efficace dello Spirito Santo, che illumina le anime nostre è le porta ad appoggiarsi sopra là misericordia di Dio, per applicarsi i meriti di Giesu Christo.

18. That that Faith is the gracious and efficacious work of the Holy Spirit which enlightens our Souls, and perswades them to lean and rest upon the mercy of God, and so thereby to apply unto themselves the merits of *Jesus Christ*.

19. Che Giesu Christo è il nostro ve-

19. That *Jesus Christ* is our true and

and onely Mediatour, not onely re-
deeming us, but alſo interceding for
us, and that by virtue of his merits,
and interceſſion we have acceſs unto
the Father, for to make our Supplications unto him, with a holy confidence and aſſurance that he will grant
us our Requeſts, it being needleſs to
have recourſe to any other Interceffour beſides himſelf.

20. That as God has promiſed us,
that we ſhall be regenerated in *Chriſt*;
ſo thoſe that are united unto him by
a true Faith, ought to apply, and do
really apply themſelves unto good
works.

21. That good works are ſo necef-
ſary to the faithfull, that they cannot
attain the Kingdom of Heaven without the ſame, ſeeing that God hath
prepared them that we ſhould walk
therein, and therefore we ought to
avoid vice and to apply our ſelves to
Chriſtian virtues, making uſe of Faſt-
ing, and all other means which may
conduce to ſo holy a thing.

22. That although our good works
cannot merit any thing, yet the Lord
will reward or recompenſe them with
eternal life, through the mercifull continuation of his grace, and by virtue
of the unchangeable conſtancy of his
promiſes made unto us.

23. That thoſe, who are already in
the poſſeſſion of eternal life by their
faith and good works, ought to be
conſidered as Saints, and as glorified
perſons, and to be praiſed for their
virtue, and imitated in all good actions of their life, but neither worſhip-
ped nor prayed unto, for, God onely
is to be prayed unto, and that through
Jeſus Chriſt.

ro ed unico *Mediatore*, non ſolo di Re-
dentione, mà anche d' interceſsione,
& che per li ſuoi meriti, e per la ſua interceſsione noi habbiamo introduttione
al Padre, per invocarlo con ſanta fi-
ducia d' eſſer eſauditi, ſenza che ſia ne-
ceſſario il ricorrere ad alcun altro inter-
ceſſore che lui.

20. *Che come Iddio ci promette la
regeneratione in Gieſu Chriſto, coloro che
ſono uniti con eſſo lui per una viva fede,
deono adoperarſi, e realmente s' adope-
rano à buone opere.*

21. *Che le buone opere ſono tanto neceſſarie à fedeli, che non poſſono giun-
gere al Regno dè cieli ſenza farle, at-
teſo che Iddio le hà preparate acciochè
in eſſe noi caminiamo, che coſi dobbiamo
fuggire i vitii, & applicarci alle virtù
Chriſtiane, impiegando i digiuni, &
ogn' altro mezzo che può ſervirci in
una coſa ſi ſanta.*

22. *Che quantunque le buone opere
noſtre non poſſano meritare, il Signore
non laſcierà di ricompenſarle della vita
eterna, per una miſericordioſa conti-
nuatione della ſua gratia, ed in virtù
della conſtanza immutabile delle promeſſe ch' egli cci hà fatte.*

23. *Che quelle che poſſeggono la vita eterna in conſeguenza della fede, e
delle buone opere loro, deono eſſer conſi-
derati come Santi e glorificati, lodati
per le loro virtù, immitati in tutte le bel-
le attioni della loro vita, mà non ado-
rati ne invocati, poi che non ſi deve
pregar ſe non un ſolo Iddio per Gieſu
Chriſto.*

24. *Che*

24. *Che Iddio s' è raccolta una Chiesa nel mondo per la salute degli huomini, e ch' ella non hà se non un solo capo, e fondamento, ciò è Giesu Christo.*

25. *Che quella Chiesa è la compagnia dè fedeli, i quali essendo stati da Dio eletti avanti la fondatione del mondo, e chiamati d' una santa vocatione, vengono ad unirsi per seguitare la parola di Dio, credendo ciò ch' egli vi ci insegna, e vivendo nel suo timore.*

26. *Che quella Chiesa non puole mancar, ed esser ridotta al niente ; mà che deve esser perpetua, e che tutti gl'eletti sono sostenuti e conservati per la virtù di Dio, in tal modo che essi tutti perseverano nella vera fede fin' al fine, uniti nella santa Chiesa, come membra di essa*

27. *Che ogn' uno a quella deve congiungersi, e tenersi nella sua communione.*

28. *Che Iddio non ci ammaestra solo colla sua parola, mà che di più egli hà ordinati dè Sacramenti per congiunger ci li ad essa, comme mezzi per unirci a Christo; e participar alli suoi benefici, e che non ve nè sono più di due communi à tutte le membra della Chiesa sotto' l Nuovo Testamento, ciò è il Battesimo, e la santa Cena.*

29. *Ch' egli hà stabilito quello del Battesimo per una testimonianza della nostra adottione, e che vi siamo lavati de nostri peccati nel sangue di Giesu Christo, e rinovati in santità di vita.*

30. *Ch' egli hà stabilito quello della Santa Cena od Eucharistia per il nodri-*

24. That God has chosen unto himself one Church in the World for the Salvation of Mankinde, and that same Church to have one onely Head and Foundation, which is *Christ.*

25. That that Church is the Company of the Faithfull, who having been elected before the Foundation of the World, and called with an holy Calling, come to unite themselves to follow the Word of God, believing whatsoever he teaches them, and living in his fear.

26. That that Church cannot err, nor be annihilated, but must endure for ever, and that all the Elect are upheld and preserved by the power of God in such sort, that they all persevere in the Faith unto the end, and remain united in the holy Church, as so many living members thereof.

27. That all men ought to joyn with that Church, and to continue in the communion thereof.

28. That God does not onely instruct and teach us by his Word, but has also ordained certain Sacraments to be joyned with it, as a means to unite us unto *Christ,* and to make us partakers of his benefits ; and that there are onely two of them belonging in common to all the members of the Church under the *New Testament,* to wit, *Baptism,* and the *Lords Supper.*

29. That God has ordained the Sacrament of *Baptism* to be a testimony of our Adoption, and of our being cleansed from our sins, by the Bloud of *Jesus Christ,* and renewed in holiness of life.

30. That the *Holy Supper* was instituted for the nourishment of our souls,

fouls, to the end that eating effectual-ly the Flesh of *Chrift*, and drinking effectually his Bloud, by the incom-prehenfible virtue and power of the Holy Spirit, and through a true and living Faith ; and fo uniting our felves moft clofely and infeparably to *Chrift*, we come to enjoy in him and by him the Spiritual and Eternal Life. Now to the end that every one may clearly fee what our Belief is as to this point, we have here inferted the very Expreffions of that Prayer which we make ufe of before the Communion, as they are written in our Liturgy or Form of Celebrating the holy Supper, and likewife in our publick Catechifm, which are to be feen at the end of our Pfalms: thefe are the words of the Prayer.

Seeing our Lord has not onely once offered his Body and Bloud for the Remiffion of our fins, but is wil-ling alfo to communicate the fame unto us as the Food of Eternal Life, we humbly befeech him fo to give us of his grace, that in true fincerity of heart, and with an ardent zeal we may receive of him fo great a benefit ; that is, that we may be made partakers of his Body and Bloud, or rather of his whole felf, by a fure and certain Faith.

The words of the Liturgy are thefe, Let us then believe firft, the promifes which *Chrift*, (who is the in-fallible Truth) has pronounced with his own mouth, *viz.* that he will make us truly partakers of his Body and Bloud, that fo we may poffefs him intirely, and in fuch fort that he may live in us, and we in him. The words of our Catechifm are the fame, *Nella Dominica* 53.

31. That it is neceffary the Church fhould have Minifters, known by thofe who are imployed for that pur-pofe, to be learned, and of a good life,

mento dell' anime noftre, acciochè con una vera, e viva fede, per la virtù incomprehenfibile dello Spirito Santo, mangiando effettivamente la fua carne, e beendo il fuo fangue, e congiungendoci ftrettifsimamente ed infeparabilmente à Chrifto, in lui, e per lui habbiamo la vita fpirituale, ed eterna. Ed accio-chè ognuno vegga chiaramente ciò che crediamo in quefto capo, aggiugniamo qui le medefime efprefsioni, che fi tro-vano nella preghiera che facciamo a-vanti la communione, nella noftra Li-turgia, ò forma di celebrar la fanta Cena, e nel noftro Catechifmo publico, i quali fcritti fi veggono dietro à noftri Salmi : quefte fono le parole della preghiera :

Si come il Signor noftro non folo ci hà una volta offerto il fuo corpo, ed il fuo fangue per la remifsione dè noftri pec-cati, mà vuole etiandio communicarce-gli in nudrimento di vita eterna ; facci etiandio quefta gratia, che in vera fince-rità di cuore, & con zelo ardente, ri-ceviamo dà lui un fi grande beneficio, ciò è che con ficura fede, noi godiamo del fuo corpo & del fuo fangue, anzi di lui tutto intero.

Le parole della Liturgia fono tali, Primo dunque crediamo alle promeffe che Giefu Chrifto la verità infallibile, hà pronontiate colla fua bocca, cio è ch' egli ci vuol far veramente partecipi del fuo corpo, e del fuo fangue, accioche lo poffediamo intiramente, in modo ch' egli viva in noi, e noi in effo lui : Quelle del noftro Catechifmo fono le me defime, Nella Domenica 53.

31. *Ch' egl' è neceffario che la Chie-fa habbia dè Paftori, giudicati bene inftrutti, e di buona vita, dà coloro che*

che ne hanno la raggione, tanto per predicar la parola di Dio, come per amminiſtrar i Sacramenti, e vegghiare ſopra la greggia di Chriſto, ſecondo le regole d' una buona, e ſanta Diſciplina, inſieme cò Antiani, e Diaconi, conforme all' uſanza della Chieſa antica.

32. Ch' Iddio hà ſtabilito i Rè, & i Prencipi e Magiſtrati per il governo dè popoli, ch' i popoli deono eſſer loro ſoggetti ed obbidienti in virtù di quella ordinatione, non ſolo per l' ira, mà ancora per la conſcienza in tutte le coſe conformi alla parola di Dio, il quale è il Rè, dè Rè e 'l Signore dè Signori.

33. Finalmente che convien ricevere il ſimbolo degli Apoſtoli, l' oratione Dominicale, e 'l Decalogo come ſcritti fondamentali della noſtra fede, e delle noſtre devotioni.

E per una più diſteſa dichiaratione di quanto crediamo, reiteriamo quì la proteſtatione che già dal 1603. fecimo ſtampare cio è, Che conſentiamo nella ſana dottrina con tutte là Chieſà Rifformate di Francia, della gran Brettagna, dè Paèſi Baſsi, Alemagna, Suizzeri, Boëmia, Polonia, Ongaria, & altre, com' ella è rappreſentata nelle loro Confeſsioni, etiandio nella Confeſſione d' Auguſta, ſecondo la dichiaratione datane dall' autore; e promettiamo di perſeverarui colla gratia di Dio inviolabilmente, e nella vita, e nella morte, eſſendo apparecchiati di ſottoſcrivere à queſta eterna verità di Dio col noſtro proprio ſangue, come l' hanno fatto i noſtri Maggiori fin dal tempo de gli Apoſtoli, particolarmente in queſti ultimi ſecoli.

E però preghiamo humilmente tutte le Chieſe Evangeliche, e Proteſtanti

as well to preach the Word of God, as to adminiſter theSacraments, and wait upon the Flock of *Chriſt,* (according to theRules of a good and holy Diſcipline) together with Elders and Deacons, after the manner of the Primitive Church.

32. That God hath eſtabliſhed Kings and Magiſtrates to govern the People, and that the People ought to be obedient and ſubject unto them, by virtue of that ordination, not onely for fear, but alſo for conſcience ſake, in all things that are conformable to the Word of God, who is the King of Kings, and theLord of Lords.

33. Finally, that we ought to receive the Symbole of the Apoſtles, the Lords Prayer and the Decalogue, as Fundamentals of our Faith, and of our Devotion.

And for a more ample declaration of our Faith, we do here reiterate the ſame Proteſtation which we cauſed to be printed in the year 1603. that is to ſay, that we do agree in ſound Doctrine with all the Reformed Churches of *France, Great Brittain,* the *Low Countreys, Germany, Switſerland, Bohemia, Poland, Hungary,* and others, as it is repreſented by them in their Confeſſions; as alſo we receive the Confeſſion of *Augsbonrg,* and as it was publiſhed by the Authour, promiſing to perſevere conſtantly therein with the help of God both in life and death, and being ready to ſubſcribe to that eternal truth of God, with our own Bloud, even as our Anceſtours have done, from the days of the Apoſtles, and eſpecially in theſe latter Ages.

Therefore we humbly intreat all the Evangelical and Proteſtant Churches to look upon us as true Members of the myſtical Body of *Chriſt*, ſuffering for his Name ſake, notwithſtanding our poverty and lowneſs; and to continue unto us the help of their Prayers to God, and all other effects of their charity, as we have heretofore abundantly found and felt; for the which we return them our moſt humble thanks, intreating the Lord with all our heart to be their Rewarder, and to powre upon them the moſt precious Bleſſings of Grace and Glory, both in this Life and that which is to come. *Amen.*

****

A ſhort Juſtification, relating to thoſe Points, whereof the Doctours of the *Roman* Church are wont to accuſe us and other Reformed Churches, which nevertheleſs are condemned by us all, as being full of impiety, and to be abominated of all *Chriſtians.*

Firſt, we are ordinarily accuſed:

1. That God is the Authour of ſin.
2. That God is not Omnipotent.
3. That *Chriſt* was not impeccable.
4. That *Jeſus Chriſt* being upon the Croſs fell into Deſpair.
5. That Man is like a Stock or a Stone in the Actions whereunto he is moved by the Holy Spirit for his own Salvation.
6. That upon the account of Predeſtination, it is an indifferent thing whether we live well or no.
7. That good works are not neceſſary to Salvation.
8. That Repentance and Confeſſion of Sins are abſolutely condemned amongſt us.

Breve giuſtificatione intorno a quei capi de' quali i Dottori della Religione Romana ſono ſoliti d' accuſare le noſtre Chieſe, e le altre Riformate: i quali pure da tutte ſono condannati come pieni d' empieta, e degni dell' abominio de' Chriſtiani.

Siamo ordinariamente accuſati di credere.

1. *Ch' Iddio è autore del peccato.*
2. *Ch' Iddio non è Onnipotente.*
3. *Che Gieſu Chriſto non fù impeccabile.*
4. *Che Gieſu Chriſto nella croce cadè in diſperatione.*
5. *Che'l huomo è come un ſtecco od una pietra nelle attioni, alle quali egli è moſſo per la ſalute, dallo Spirito di Dio.*
6. *Ch' in virtù della predeſtinatione egli è indifferente di vivere bene,ò male.*
7. *Che le buone opere non ſono neceſſarie alla ſalute.*
8. *Che la penitenza, e la confeſſione de' peccati,ſono tra noi aſſolutamente condannate.*

9. *Che*

9. *Che conviene ributtare i digiuni & altre mortificationi per vivere in diſ-ſolutione.*

10. *Ch' egli è licito ad ognuno di ſpiegar a ſuo ſenno la Scrittura, e ſecondo i movimenti d' un ſpirito particolare.*

11. *Che la Chieſa può del tutto mancare ed eſſer ridotta al niente.*

12. *Ch' il Batteſimo non è d' alcuna neceſsità.*

13. *Che nel Sacramento del l' Euchariſtia non v'è alcuna communione reale a Gieſu Chriſto ma ſolo delle figure.*

14. *Che non conviene ſottoporſi alli Rè, & Principi, e Magiſtrati ne ubbidirgli.*

15. *Perche non invochiamo la Santa Vergine, & gli huomini già glorificati, ſiamo accuſati di ſprezzargli, la dove noi gli ſtimiamo Beati, degni de laude, & d' immitatione ; & particolarmente teniamo la glorioſa Vergine, benedetta ſopra tutte le donne.*

Queſti capi che ci ſono imputati, ſono tenuti dalle noſtre Chieſe per eretici dannabili : E con tutto 'l cuore dinunciamo Anatema, à chiunque vorrà mantenergli.

9. That Faſtings and other Mortifications ought to be rejected , and that we ought to live diſſolutely.

10. That it is lawfull for every one to interpret the Scripture according to his own minde, and the motions of a private ſpirit.

11. That the Church may fall abſolutely, and be reduced to nothing.

12. That Baptiſm is a thing not at all neceſſary.

13. That in the Sacrament of the Lords Supper we have no real communion with *Jeſus Chriſt*, but onely in figure or type.

14. That we ought not to ſubmit our ſelves to any Kings, Princes, or Magiſtrates whatſoever, nor yield obedience to them.

15. Becauſe we do not pray to the Virgin *Mary* and the Saints, we are accuſed of deſpiſing them, whereas on the contrary, we account them happy, and alſo worthy of praiſe, and imitation ; and do more eſpecially eſteem the glorious Virgin to be bleſſed above all other Women.

All theſe things being falſly imputed unto us, are held for heretical and damnable by our Churches : and we do with all our heart denounce *Anathema* againſt all thoſe who maintain and hold the ſame.

CHAP.

CHAP. V.

The ancient Discipline of the Evangelical Churches in the Valleys *of* P I E M O N T.

Extracted out of divers Authentick Manuscripts, written in their own Language several hundreds of Years before either *Calvin* or *Luther.*

ARTICLE I.

Concerning Discipline.

Discipline contains in it self all moral Doctrine, according to the teaching of *Christ* and his *Apostles,* shewing after what manner each one ought to live in his Calling by Faith, and walk worthily in present righteousness.

The holy Scripture reciteth divers Doctrines touching this Discipline, and sheweth not onely how every one in particular ought to live, of what estate, age, or condition soever he be, but also what ought to be the union, consent, and bond of love in the Communion of the Faithfull. Now if so be any one desire to have a knowledg of these things, let him reade what the *Apostle* saith in his *Epistles,* and he shall finde it there

LA Disciplina contenen si tota doctrina Moral segond l' enseignament de Christ, & de li Apostolat, en qual maniera un chascun del seo appellament vivent per se, poissa anar degnament en la present justitia.

Et d' aquesta Disciplina las Sacras Scripturas reciton abondiant enseignamens, & non solament en qual modo un chascun depersi debia viore, d' un chascun stat, aita & condition: ma qual debia esser la unita, la unanimosita, lo ligam d' amor en la communita de li fidel. Et daisso si alcuno vol conoisser legissa l' Apostol en las Epistolas & ou trobare pausa abondiament & special-

ment

*ment en qual maniera un chafcun en-
tengu confervar fi mefeime en unita, &
anar degnament quel non fia fcandol, &
occafion de la ruina de li proyme, per
mal ditto per mal faitt ; & en qual
modo non folament es entengu fugir lo
mal, ma & la occafion del mal & la
fpecie del mal : & fi alcun aure erra
en qual modo reforma, poiffa effer ef-
menda.*

*Per moti aitals univerfals enfeigna-
mens de li qual lo poble domefti de la fe
debia effer enfeigna, afin quelli con-
verfon degnament en la maifon del
Seignor, & non façan del temple del
Seignor balma de lairons, per mala &
perverfa converfation, & per fuffrença
de li mal.*

amply fet down, efpecially in what
manner every one is bound to keep
himfelf in unity, and to walk in fuch
fort, that he be not an occafion of
fcandal and ruine to his neighbour,
either by finfull words or actions ;
and in that fort he is bound not onely
to avoid evil, but the occafion alfo
and appearance thereof ; and when
any is fallen, to ufe his beft endeavour
to reftore him, and to bring him to
amendment of life.

By divers fuch general Doctrines,
thofe who are of the houfhold of
faith ought to be inftructed, that fo
they may walk worthily in the houfe
of the Lord, and not make it *a Den of
Thieves* by their profane and perverfe
converfation, and by their toleration
of evil.

ARTICLE II.

Concerning Paftors or Minifters.

*Tuit aquelli liqual devon effer receo-
pu Paftor dentre de nos quant illi fon en-
car cum lor gent, ille pregon, fi plai a
noftra gent que li recipian al menestier,
& lor plaça de pregar en apres Dio aço
quilli fian fait digni de tant grand offici : ma li predict requerent non fan
las predittas cofas per autra fin, finon
que per demonstrar humilità.*

*Nos lor enfeignan leçons & fafen
empenre de cor tuit li capitol de Sanct
Mattheo, & de Sanct Foan, & tot as las
Epistolas lafquels fon dittas Canonicas :
una bona part de Salomon, de David, &
de li Prophetas.*

*Et pois filli auren bon tefti-
moni, fon receopu com l' impofition*

All thofe which are to be received
as Paftours amongft us, while they
remain with their Brethren they are to
intreat our People to receive them into the Miniftry, as likewife that they
would be pleafed to pray to God for
them, that they may be made worthy
of fo great a Charge ; and this they
are to do, to give a proof or evidence
of their humilty.

We alfo appoint them their Lectures, and fet them their Tasks, that
they may get by heart all the Chapters of St. *Matthew* and St. *John*,
with all the *Epiftles* which are called
Canonical, and a good part of the
Writings of *Solomon*, *David*, and the
Prophets.

And afterwards having good Te-
ftimonials, and being well approved
of

of, they are received with Imposition (or *laying on*) of hands and preaching.

He that is received the last ought to do nothing without the permission of him that was received before him ; and in like sort the former ought to do nothing without the consent of his Associate, that so all things may be done amongst us in good order.

Our daily food, and that rayment wherewith we are covered, we have ministred and given to us freely and by way of alms, sufficient for us, by the good People whom we teach and instruct.

Amongst other Privileges which God hath given to his Servants, he hath given them this, to chuse their Leaders and those who are to govern the People, and to constitute Elders in their Charges, according to the diversity of the work in the unity of *Christ*; which is clear by that saying of the *Apostle* in the Epistle to *Titus chap* I. *For this cause left I thee in* Crete, *that thou shouldest set in order the things that are wanting, and ordain Elders in every City, as I had appointed thee.*

When any one of us the foresaid Pastours falls into any gross sin, he is both excommunicated and prohibited to preach.

de las mans, en l' offici de la predica-tion.

Lo sequend non Deo far alcuna cosa senza la licentia del devant pausa: & semillament li devant pausa non devon far alcuna cosa senza la licentia de lor compagnon, afin que totas cosas sian faitas entre nos cum bon orde.

Lo nuriment & de la qual cosa sian cubert, son administra a nos, & dona de gra, & en luoc d' almositas, mot aba-stantament, del bon poble loqual nos en seignan.

Entre las autras potestas Dio donné a li serf, competent quilli eslegissan Re-gidors del poble & Preires en li lors of-ficis, segond la diversità de l' obrament en l' unita de Christ. Et l' Apostol en-semp prova aço, Tit.I. Yo laissai a tu en Creta per la gratia d' aquestas cosas que defaillan, & ordonnes preyres per las Citas, enaimi yo ordonnei a tu.

Quand alcun de nos predict Pastor es tomba en pecca de la deshonnesta, es de-gietta fora de la nostra compagnia, & prohibi de l' offici de la predication.

ARTICLE III.

Of the Instructing of their Youth.

Those Children which are born of Carnal Parents, ought to be made Spiritual towards God by Discipline and Instruction, as it is said in *Ecclesiasticus*, *He that loveth his Son causeth him oft to feel the Rod, that so he may have joy of him in the end, and may not be ashamed before his Neighbour.* He

Li filli liqual naisson li pairons car-nals, devon esser rendu de lor spirituals a Dio per disciplina, & per ama estra-ment, enaimi es dict en Ecclesiastico. Aquel loqual ama lo seo filli, souvendeia a luy la verga, quel s' alegre en la der-rairia, & non palpe li hus del preyme. *Aquel*

Aquel loqual enseigna lo seo filli sere lauva en lui, & se gloriarè en luy al mez de li domesti. Aquel loqual enseigna lo seo filli, met en jelosia l' ennemic, & se gloriare en lei al mez de li amic. Lo paire de luy es mort, & quasi non es mort, & laissa apres si semblant a si. El vec & se alegre en luy en la soa vita: car el non es confus ni contrista en la soa mort devant la seo ennemic. Car el laissa defendedor de la maison contra li ennemic, & rendent gratias a li amic.

Enseigna lo teo filli en la temor del Seignor, & en la via de las costumas, & de la fe.

Non teo desperar de luy si el non volrè recebre viazament lo teo corregiment, & si el non sere viazament bon: car lo cohotivador non recevilli viazament, li fruc da la terra pois quel aure semena, ma speita temp convenivol, &c.

Dereço: l' home deo corrigir & gardar las fillas. Fillas son a tu garda lo corps de lor que ellas non vaguejan. Car Dina filla de Jacob fo corrotta per mostrar se a li olli strang, &c.

that instructeth his Son, shall have praise in him, and shall gain commendation in the midst of his houshold. He that teacheth his Son maketh his Enemy jealous, and getteth honour among his Friends. Though his Father die, yet he is as though he were not dead, for he leaveth behinde him one like unto himself: while he lived, he saw and rejoyced in him, and when he died he was not confounded or sorrowfull before his Enemies: For he left behinde him such as shall uphold his house against his Enemies, and Children that shall requite kindness to his Friends.

Instruct thy Son in the fear of the Lord, and in the ways of the Customes, and of the Faith.

Despair not of thy Childe, when he will not receive willingly thy correction, and though he be not speedily good, for the Labourer gathereth not all the Fruit of the Earth so soon as he casts the seed into the ground, but waiteth the appointed time.

In like manner, a man ought to correct and keep in his Daughters. Hast thou Daughters? keep their Bodies that they wander not, for *Dina* the Daughter of *Jacob* was ravished by shewing her self abroad to strangers.

ARTICLE IV.

The Catechism of the ancient *Waldenses* for the Instructing of their Youth.

Lo Barba.

Si tu fosses demandà qui si es tu. Respond.

L'enfant. *Creatura de Dio rational & mortal.*

Lo Barba. *Per que dio te à creà?*

Resp. *Afin que yo conoissa lui mesei*

The Minister.

If one should demand of you, who are you, what would you answer?

Childe. A Creature of God, reasonable, and mortal.

Min. Why has God created you?

Answ. To the end that I might
know

know him and serve him, and be saved by his grace.

Min. Wherein consists your salvation?

Answ. In three substantial virtues, which necessarily belong to salvation.

Min. Which are they?

Answ. Faith, Hope, and Charity.

Min. How can you prove that?

Answ. The Apostle writes 1 Cor. 13. *Now abideth, Faith, Hope, and Charity, these three.*

Min. What is Faith?

Answ. According to the Apostle, *Hebr.* 11. It is the *substance of things hoped for, and the evidence of things not seen.*

Min. How many sorts of Faith are there?

Answ. There are two sorts, *viz.* a Living and a Dead Faith.

Min. What is a Living Faith?

Answ. It is that which works by charity.

Min. What is a Dead Faith?

Answ. According to St. *James,* It is *that which without works is dead.* Again, Faith is null without works. Or, a Dead Faith is, to believe that there is a God, to believe on God, and not to believe in him.

Min. What is your Faith?

Answ. The true Catholick and Apostolick Faith?

Min. What is that?

Answ. It is that which in the Result (or Symbole) of the Apostle, is divided into twelve Articles.

Min. What is that?

Answ. I believe in God the Father Almighty, &c.

Min. By what way can you know that you believe in God?

Answ. By this, that I know and I observe the Commandments of God.

Min. How many Commandments of God are there?

---

me, *& cola, & avent la gratia de luy mesesime sià salvà.*

Lo Barb. *En qve ista la toa salut?*

Resp. *En tres vertus substantials de necesità pertinent à salù.*

Lo Barb. *Quals sont aquellas?*

Resp. *Fè Esperança & carità.*

Demanda. *Per que cosa proveràs aizò?*

Resp. *L' Apostol scri 1 Corinth.* 13. *Aquestas cosas permanon. Fè Esperança & Carità.*

Dem. *Qual cosa es Fè?*

Resp. *Second l' Apostol Heb.* 11. *Es una subsistentia de las cosas de esperar, & un argument de las non appareissent.*

Dem. *De quanta maniera es la fè?*

Resp. *De doas manieras, zo es viva & morta.*

Dem. *Qual cosa es fè viva?*

Resp. *Lo es aquella que obra per carità.*

Dem. *Qual cosa es fè morta?*

Resp. *Second Sanct Jaques la fè s' illi non à obras es morta, & dereço, la fè es ociosa senza las obras, O Fè morta es creire esser Dio creire de Dio, & non creyre en Dio.*

Dem. *Dela qual fè sies tu?*

Resp. *Dela vera fè Catholica & Apostolica.*

Dem. *Qual es aquella?*

Resp. *La es aquella laqual al conseil de li Apostol es despartia en doze Articles.*

Dem. *Qual es aquella?*

Resp. *Yo creo en Dio la Paire tot Poissant, &c.*

Dem. *Per qual cosa poyes tu cognoser que tu crees en Dio?*

Resp. *Per aizo, car yo say & garde li commandament di Dio.*

Dem. *Quanti son li commandament de Dio?*

Resp.

Resp. *Dies coma es manifest en Exode & Deuteronomio.*

Dem. *Quals son aquilli?*

Resp. *O Israel au lo teo Segnor non aurès Dio strang devant mi, non farès à tu entaillament ni alcuna semblança de totas aquellas cosas que son al cel, &c.*

Dem. *En que pendon tuit aquisti commandament?*

Resp. *En dui grand commandament, ço es amar Dio sobre totas cosas, & lo proyeme enaima tu meseime.*

Dem. *Qual es lo fondament d'aquesti commandament per loqual un chascun deo intrar à vita, sença loqual fondament non se po degnament far ni complir li commandament?*

Resp. *Lo Segnor Jesu Christ, delqual di l'Apostol I Corinth. alcun no po pausar altre fondament stier aquel qu'ès pausà loqual es Jesu Christ.*

Dem. *Per qual cosa po venir l'home à aquest fondament?*

Resp. *Per la fè disent Sanct Peire, Ve vos yo pauseray en Sion sobrirana peira cantonal eslegia & pretiosa, aquel que creyrà en luy non sere confondu. Et lo Segnor dis. Aquel que cree en mi à vita eterna.*

Dem. *En qual maniera postu conoiser que tu crees?*

Resp. *Ca yo conoisso luy meseime veray Dio & veray home nà & passionna, &c. per la mia redemption, justification, & amo luy meseime, & desiro complir li commandament deluy.*

Dem. *Per qual cosa & se perven à las vertùs essentials, zo es à la Fè, l'Esperança & la Carità?*

Resp. *Per li dondel Sanct Esperit.*

Dem. *Crees tu al Sanct Esperit?*

R. *Yo y creo. Car lo Sanct Esperit pro-*

Answ. Ten, as is manifest in *Exodus* and *Deuteronomy.*

Min. Which be they?

Answ. Hear O Israel, I am the Lord thy God. Thou shalt have none other Gods before me. Thou shalt not make any graven Image, or any likeness of any thing, that is in Heaven, &c.

Min. What is the sum (or drift) of these Commandments?

Answ. It consists in these two great Commandments, *viz.* Thou shalt love God above all things, and thy Neighbour as thy self.

Min. What is that Foundation of these Commandments, by the which every one may enter into life, and without the which Foundation none can do any thing worthily, or fulfill the Commandments?

Answ. The Lord *Jesus Christ*, of whom the Apostle speaks in the I *Cor.* Other foundation can no man lay, than that is laid, which is Jesus Christ.

Min. By what means may a man come to this Foundation?

Answ. By Faith, as saith St. *Peter*, I *Pet.*2.ch. 6. v. Behold, I lay in Sion a chief corner stone, elect, precious, and he that believeth on him shall not be confounded. And the Lord saith, He that believeth, hath eternal life.

Min. Whereby canst thou know that thou believest?

Answ. By this, that I know him to be true God, and true Man, who was born, and who hath suffered, &c. for my Redemption, Justification, And that I love him, and desire to fulfill his Commandments.

Min. By what means may one attain to those essential Virtues, Faith, Hope, and Charity?

Answ. By the gifts of the Holy Spirit.

Min. Do'st thou believe in the Holy Spirit?

Answ. Yes, I do believe. For the Holy

Holy Spirit proceeds from the Father and the Son, and is one Perfon of the Trinity: and according to the Divinity, is equal to the Father and the Son.

Min. Thou believeft God the Father, God the Son, and God the Holy Spirit, thou haft therefore three Gods.

Anfw. I have not three.

Min. Yea, but thou haft named three.

Anfw. That is by reafon of the difference of the Perfons, not by reafon of the Effence of the Divinity. For, although there are three Perfons, yet notwithftanding there is but one Effence.

Min. In what manner doft thou adore and worfhip thatGod on whom thou believeft ;

Anfw. I adore him with the adoration of an inward and outward worfhip. Outwardly, by the bending of the knee, and lifting up the hands, by bowing the body, by hymns and fpiritual fongs, by fafting and prayer But inwardly, by an holy affection: by a will conformable unto all things, that are well pleafing unto him. And I ferve him by Faith, Hope, and Charity, according to his Commandments.

Min. Do'ft thou adore and worfhip any other thing as God ?

Anfw. No.

Min. Why ?

Anfw. Becaufe of his Commandment, whereby it is ftrictly commanded, faying, *Thou fhalt worfhip the Lord thy God, and him onely fhalt thou ferve.* And again, *I will not give my glory to another.* Again, *As I live, faith the Lord, every knee fhall bow before me.* And *Jefus Chrift* faith, *There fhall come the true worfhippers which fhall worfhip the Father in fpirit and in truth.* And the Angel would not be worfhipped by St. *John,* nor St. *Peter* by *Cornelius.*

cedent del Paire, & del filli, es una perfona de la Trinità, & fecond la Divinità, es aigal al Paire & al filli.

Dem. Tu crees Dio Paire, Dio Filli, Dio Sperit Sanct effer tres en perfonnas. Donc tu as tres Dios ?

Refp. Non ay tres.

Dem. Emperzò tu n' as nommà tres ?

Refp. Aiçò es per rafon de la differentia de las perfonnas : ma non per rafon de la effentia de la Divinità. Car iafiaçò que el es tres en perfonas emperçò el es un en Effentia.

Dem. Aquel Dio al qual tu crees en qual modo, l' adores tu & coles.

Refp. Yo l' adora per adoration de latria exterior & interior,exterior per plegament de genovilli, eflevation de mans per enclinament,per hymnis,per cant fpirituals, per Dejunis per Envocations, ma interiorament per piatofa affection, per voluntà appareillà à totas cofas ben placent à fi, ma yo colo per Fè, per Efperança, & per Charità en li feo commandament.

Dem. Adores tu alcuna otra cofa & coles coma Dio ?

Refp. Non.

Dem. Per que ?

Refp. Per li feo commandament loqual el mende deftreitament difent : Tu adoreràs lo teo Segnor Dio & ferveràs à luy fol, Encara la mia gloria non la donnarey à li autre. Et dereço yo vivo dis lo Seignor, & tot genoil ferè plegà à mi, & Jefu Chrift dis, lo feren vrays adoradors liqual adorarèn lo Paire en Efperit & en la verità. Et l' Angel non vole effer adorà de Sanct Johan, ni Peire de Cornelli.

Dem.

Dem. *En qual modo oras?*

Resp. *Yo orò de la oration liorà per lo filli de Dio difent, Noiftre Paire qui fies en li cel.*

Dem. *Qual es l' autra vertù fob-ftantial de necefsità pertinent à falu?*
Resp. *Lo es Charità.*
Dem. *Qual cofa es Charità?*
Resp. *Lo es un don del Sanct Efpe-rit ; per loqual es Reformà l' arma en volontà, enlumenà per Fè, per laqual creo totas cofas de creyre, fpero totas cofas d' efperar.*

Dem. *Crees tu en la Sancta Gleifa?*

Resp. *Non car illi es creatura ma yo creo de ley mefeima.*
Dem. *Qual cofa crees tu de la Sancta Gleifa?*

Resp. *Yo demando de ley mefeima que la Gleifa es de doas manieras, l' una de la part de la fubftantia, l' autra de la part de li minifteri. De la part de la fubftantia Sancta Gleifa Catholica fon tuit li efleit de Dio, del commençament entro à la fin, en la gratia de Dio : per lo merit de Chrift, congregà per lo Sanct Sperit, & devant ordennà à vita eter-na, li nombre & li nom de liqual aquel fol conec loqual eflegic lor. Et finalment en aquefta Gleifa non remanneon pro-fcrit : ma la Gleifa fecond la verità mi-nifterial fon li miniftres de Chrift cum lo pople foject ufant de li meneftier par Fè, Efperanza, & Carità.*

Dem. *Per qual cofa deves conoiffer la Gleifa de Chrift?*
Resp. *Per li miniftres convenivols & lo poble participant en verità en li meneftier.*

Min. After what manner prayeft thou?

Anfw. I pray, rehearfing the Pray-er given me by the Son of God, fay-ing ; *Our Father which art in Hea-ven, &c.*
Min. What is the other fubftantial virtue appertaining to falvation?
Anfw. It is Charity.
Min. What is Charity?
Anfw. It is the gift of the Holy Spirit by which the foul is reformed in the will, being enlightened by faith, whereby I believe all that ought to be believed, and hope all that ought to be hoped.
Min. Do'ft thou believe in the Ho-ly Church?
Anfw. No, for it is a creature, but I believe that there is one.
Min. What is that which thou be-lievest concerning the Holy Church?
Anfw. I fay, that the Church is confidered two manner of ways, the one Subftantially, and the other Mi-nifterially. As it is confidered Sub-ftantially, by the Holy Catholick Church is meant all the Elect of God, from the beginning of the World to the end, by the grace of God through the merit of *Chrift*, gathered together by the Holy Spirit, and fore-ordained to eternal life ; the number and names of whom are known to him alone who has elected them ; and in this Church remains none who is repro-bate ; but the Church, as it is confi-dered according to the truth of the Miniftery, is the company of the Mi-nifters of *Chrift*, together with the People committed to their Charge, ufing the Miniftry, by Faith, Hope, and Charity.
Min. Whereby doft thou know the Church of *Chrift*?
Anfw. By the Minifters lawfully called, and by the People participating in truth of the Miniftery.

Min. But by what Marks knowest thou the Ministers?

Answ. By the true sense of Faith, by sound Doctrine, by a Life of good Example, by the preaching of the Gospel, and a due Administration of the Sacraments.

Min. By what Mark knowest thou the false Ministers?

Answ. By their fruits, by their blindness, by their evil works, by their perverse Doctrine, and by their undue administration of the Sacraments.

Min. Whereby knowest thou their blindness?

Answ. When, not knowing the truth, which necessarily appertains to salvation, they observe humane Inventions as Ordinances of God. Of whom is verified what *Isaiah* says, and which is alleged by our Lord *Jesus Christ, Matth.*15. This People honour me with their lips, but their heart is far from me. But in vain they do worship me, teaching for Doctrines the commandments of men.

Min. By what Marks knowest thou evil works?

Answ. By those manifest sins of which the Apostle speaks, *Gal.*5. saying, That *they which do such things, shall not inherit the Kingdom of God.*

Min. By what Mark knowest thou perverse Doctrine?

Answ. When it teacheth contrary to Faith and Hope; such is Idolatry of several sorts, *viz.* towards a reasonable, sensible, visible or invisible Creature. For, it is the Father alone with his Son and the Holy Spirit, who ought to be worshipped, and not any creature whatsoever. But when on the contrary they attribute to man and to the work of his hands, or to his words, or to his authority in such a manner, that men ignorantly believe that they have satisfied God by a false Religion, and by satisfying the covetous Simony of the Priests.

Dem. *Ma per qual cosa conoisses li ministres?*

Resp. *Per lo veray sen dela Fè & per la sana doctrina, & per vita de bon exemple, & per Evangelization, & per debita ministration deli Sacrament.*

Dem. *Per qual cosa conoisses li fals ministres?*

Resp. *Per li fruc de lor, per l'encequetà, per mala operation, per perversa doctrina, per indebita administration deli Sacrament.*

Dem. *Per qual cosa se conois lencequetà?*

Resp. *Cum non sabent la verità de necessità pertinent à salù, gardan li attrobament human en aimi commendament de Dio, de liqual es verificà aquel dict de Esaia que Christ à dict Matth. 15. Aquest poble honra mi cum labias, ma locor de lor es long de mi, ma illi colon mi senza caison, enseignant las doctrinas & li commandament de li homes.*

Dem. *Per qual cosa es conoissua la mala operation?*

Resp. *Per li manifest peccà de liqual di l'Apostol Galat. 5. Aquilli que fan aital cosa non consegren lo regne de Dio.*

Dem. *Per qual cosa es conoissua la perversa doctrina?*

Resp. *Cum la enseigna contra la Fè, & l'esperança, en aima idolatrie fait de mota maniera à la creature rational sensibla ò vesiblà, ò non vesiblà. Car lo sol Paire cum lo seo filli & lo Sanct Esperit, se deo coler, & non autre qual que qual se sia creatura. Ma contra aizò attribuissen à l'home, & a l'obrà de las soas mans, ou à las paralas, ou à la soà authorità, enaimi que l'home cresent cequament estiman lor esse aiosto à Dio per falsa Religion, & per avara Simonia de li Sacerdot.*

D m.

Dem. *Per qual cofa es conoiſſü a la non debita adminiſtration de li Sacrament.*

Reſp. *Cum li Sacerdot non aven lo fen de Chriſt, ni conoiſſent l' entention de luy meſeime en li Sacrament diſon la gratia & la verità eſſer encloufa, per las folas ceremonias exteriors, & amenon li home ſenza la verità de la fè , de l' eſperanza, & de la charità, à receber lor meſeime Sacrament. Et lo Seignor devant garda li ſeo d' aitals fals Sacerdots diſent, garda vos deli fals Prophetas, Item guarda vos de li Phariſæi, ço es del levam delor, zo es dela doctrina, Item non voill creire, non voilla anar en apres lor, Et David airè la Gleiſa d' aitals diſent, Yo ayen odi la Gleiſa de la malignant. Et lo Seignor commanda Saillir d' aitals , Nomb. 16. Departe vos de li tabernacle de li felon, & non voilla tocar à las cofas que pertenon à lor, que non ſià enveloppà en li peccà de lor. Et Apoſtol 2 Corin. Non volla menar joug cum li non fidel: car qual participation de la juſticia cum la iniquità, & qual compagnia de la lux à tenebras, qual convention de Chriſt al Diavolo, ò qual partia del fidel cum li non fidel, qual conſentiment del Temple de Dio cum las Idolas? Per laqual cofa iſſe del mez de lor, & ſia departi dis lo Seignor. Non tocare lo non mond, et yo recebray vos. Item 2 Theſſ. O fraires nos annuncien à vos que vos vos gardes de tot fraire anant de for dannament. Item Apocal.18. Iſſe lo meo poble de ley, et non ſia perçonnier de li peccà de ley, et non recebe de las plagas de lor.*

Dem. *Per qual cofa es conoiſſü lo poble , loqual non es en verità en la Gleiſa?*

Min. By what Marks is the undue Adminiſtration of the Sacrament known?

Anſw. When the Preiſts not knowing the intention of *Chriſt* in the Sacraments, ſay, that the grace and the truth is included in the external Ceremonies, and perſwade men to the participation of the Sacrament without the truth, and without faith. But the Lord chargeth thoſe that are his to take heed of ſuch falſe Prophets, ſaying, *Beware of the Phariſees,* that is to ſay, *of the Leaven of their Doctrine.* Again, *Believe them not, neither go after them.* And *David* hates the Church or the Congregation of ſuch perſons, ſaying, *I hate the Church of evil men.* And the Lord commands *to come out from the midſt of ſuch* people, Numb.16 *Depart from the tents of theſe wicked men, and touch nothing of theirs, leſt you be conſumed in their ſins.* And the Apoſtle 2 Cor.6.14. *Be ye not unequally yoaked with unbelievers. For what fellowſhip hath righteouſneſs with unrighteouſneſs, and what communion hath light with darkneſs, and what concord hath* Chriſt *with* Belial, *or what part hath he that believeth with an Infidel. And what agreement hath the Temple of God with Idols? Wherefore come out from among them, and be ye ſeparate, ſaith the Lord, and touch not the unclean thing, and I will receive you.* Again, 2 Theſſ. *Now we command you, Brethren, that you withdraw your ſelvs from every Brother that walketh diſorderly.* Again, Revel. 18. *Come out of her my people, that ye be not partakers of her ſins , and that ye receive not of her plagues.*

Min. By what Marks are thoſe People known who are not in truth within the Church?

Anſw.

Answ. By publick sins, and an erroneous faith. For, we ought to fly from such persons, left we be defiled by them.

Min. By what ways oughteft thou to communicate with the Holy Church?

Answ. I ought to communicate with the Church in regard of its substance, by Faith and Charity, as also by observing the Commandments, and by a final perseverance in well doing.

Min. How many things are there which are ministerial?

Answ. Two. The *Word* and the *Sacraments.*

Min. How many Sacraments are there?

Answ. Two, namely, *Baptism* and the *Lords Supper.*

Min. What is the third virtue neceffary to salvation?

Answ. Hope.

Min. What is Hope?

Answ. It a waiting for Grace and Glory to come.

Min. How does a man wait (or hope) for Grace?

Answ. By the Mediatour *Jesus Christ,* of whom St. *John* faith, *Grace comes by* Jesus Christ. Again, *We have seen his Glory, who is full of Grace and Truth.* And *we all have received of his fulness.*

Min. What is that Grace?

Answ. It is Redemption, Remission of sins, Juftification, Adoption, and Sanctification.

Min. Upon what account is this Grace hoped for in *Christ?*

Answ. By a living Faith, and true Repentance, saying, *Repent ye, and believe the Gospel.*

Min. Whence proceedeth this Hope?

Answ. From the gift of God, and the promises of which the Apoftle

Resp. Per li public peccà et per la Fè erronien, car la es de fugir d'aitals, que non vegna fozura de lor mefeimes.

Dem. Per qual cofa deves communiquar a la Sancta Gleifa?

Resp. Yo devo communiquar à la Gleifa per rafon de fubftantia per Fè, per Charita e per obfervanza de li commandament, et per final perfeveranza en ben.

Dem. Quantas fon las cofas minifterials?

Resp. Doas, la parola et li Sacrament.

Dem. Quanti fon Sacrament?

Resp. Dui, ço es Baptifme et l'Euchariftia.

Dem. Qual cofa es la terça vertù neceffarià à falù?

Resp. Efperança.

Dem. Qual cofa es Efperança?

Resp. Lo es certa fperança de gratia, et de la gloria avenador.

Dem. Per qual cofa fe fpera la gratia?

Resp. Per lo Mediator *Jefus Chrift* del qual di Sanct *Johan* 1. Gratia es faita per *Jefus Chrift.* Et dereço, Nos veguen la gloria de luy plen de gratia et de verità, & nos tuit aven receopù de la plenetà de luy.

Dem. Qual cofa es aquella gratia?

Resp. Lo es Redemption, Remifsion de li peccà, Juftification, Afillament, Sanctification.

Dem. Per qual cofa es fperà aquellà gratià en Chrift?

Resp. Per fè viva, & per vera penitentia difent Chrift, Pentè vos & creè à l'Evangeli.

Dem. Dont procedis l'Efperança?

Resp. Del don de Dio & de las promifsions dont dis l'Apoftol, Et es poif*(fant*

fant complir qual que qual cofa el pro-
met, Car el mefeime à promès. Si al-
cun aurè conoiffù luy, & fe ferè pentì,
& aurà fperà, Car el vol aver miferi-
cordia perdonnar, juftificar, &c.

Dem. *Quals cofas dévian dá que-*
fta Efperançà ?

Refp. *La fè morta, la feduction de*
l' Anti Chrift, creire en autre que à
Chrift, ço es en li Sancts & en la foa po-
teftà, & authorità, parolas, en benedi-
ctions, en Sacraments, Reliquias, de li
mort, en Pugatori foimà, & en feint, en
enfeignar aver quefta fperança per li
mez liqual van dreitament contra la ve-
rità, & contra li commandament de
Dio, enaima fer idolatria de molta ma-
niera, & per fimoniaca pravità, &c.
Abandonnant la fontanna de laiga vi-
va, donà de gratia per corre à las cifter-
nas devant dictas, adorant, honorant,
colent la creatura enaima lo Creator, fer-
vent à lei per orations, per Dejunis, per
Sacrificis, per donas, per offertas, per
pelegrinations, per envocations, &c.
confidant lor aquiftar gratia, laqual neun
non à de donar fi non lo fol Dio en Chrift,
Enaimi lavorant vanement, laiffon la
pecunia & la vita, & acerta non fola-
ment la vita prefent, ma el lavenador,
per la qual cofa lo es dict, l' efperança
de li felon perire.

Dem. *Et qual cofa dis de la beata*
Vergena Maria ? Car illi es plena de
gratia, come teftifica l' Angel, Yo te fal-
ve plena de gratia.

Refp. *La beata Vergena, fo & es*
plena de gratia, enquant à la foa be-
fongna, ma non enquánt à la commu-
nication à li autre, car lo fol feo filli es
plen de gratia, en quant à la particpa-
tion, coma es dict de fi mefeime & nos
tuit receopen gratia per gratia de la ple-
netà de luy.

mentioneth, *He is powerfull to perform*
whatfoever he promifeth. For he hath
promifed himfelf, that whofoever
fhall know him, and repent, and fhall
hope in him, he will have mercy upon, pardon, and juftifie, &c.

Min. What are the things that put
us befide this hope ?

Anfw. A dead faith, the feduction
of *Antichrift* to believe in other things
befide *Chrift,* that is to fay, in Saints,
in the power of that *Antichrift,* in his
authority, words, and benedictions, in
Sacraments, Reliques of the Dead, in
Purgatory, which is but forged and
contrived, in teaching that faith is obtained by thofe ways which oppofe
themfelves to the truth, and are a-
gainft the Commandments of God.
As is Idolatry in divers refpects. As
alfo by wickednefs and Simony, &c.
Forfaking the fountain of living water given by grace, and running to
broken cifterns, worfhipping, honouring, and ferving the creature by Prayers, by Faftings, by Sacrifices, by Do-
nations, by Offerings, by Pilgrimages,
by Invocations, &c. Relying upon
themfelves for the acquiring of grace,
which none can give fave onely God
in *Chrift.* In vain do they labour, and
lofe their money and their lives, and
the truth is, they do not onely lofe
their prefent life, but alfo that which
is to come ; wherefore it is faid, that
the hope of fools fhall perifh.

Min. And what doft thou fay, of
the bleffed Virgin *Mary ?* For fhe is
full of grace, as the Angel teftifies, *I*
falute thee full of grace.

Anfw. The bleffed Virgin was and
is *full of grace,* as much as is neceffary
for her own particular, but not to
communicate to others, for, her Son
alone is full of grace, and can communicate the fame as he pleafeth, and
We have all received of his fulnefs,
grace for grace.

Min.

Min. Believeſt thou not the Communion of Saints?

Anſw. I believe that there are two ſorts of things wherein the Saints communicate, the firſt Subſtantial, the other Miniſterial. As to the Subſtantials, they communicate by the Holy Spirit, in God through the merit of *Jeſus Chriſt*; as to the Miniſterials or Eccleſiaſtiques, they communicate by the Miniſtery duly performed, namely, by the Word, by the Sacraments, and by Prayer: I believe both the one and the other of theſe Communions of Saints. The firſt onely in God, and in *Jeſus Chriſt*, and in the Holy Ghoſt by the Holy Spirit. The other in the Church of *Chriſt*.

Min. Wherein conſiſts eternal life?

Anſw. In a living and operating faith, and in perſeverance in the ſame. Our Saviour ſays *John* 17. *This is life eternal to know thee the onely true God, and Jeſus Chriſt whom thou haſt ſent.* And *he that endures to the end ſhall be ſaved.*

Dem. *Tu non crees la communion de li Sanct?*

Reſp. *Yo creo que lo ſon doas coſas en laſquals communicon li Sanct, alcunas ſon ſubſtantials, alcunas ſon Miniſterials. Illi communicon à las Subſtantials per lo Sanct Eſperit en Dio per lo merit de Jeſu Chriſt. Ma illi communicon à las Miniſterials ò Eccleſiaſticas per li Miniſtier fait debitament, en aima ſont per las parolas, per li Sacrament, per las orations, yo creo l' una & l' autre d' aqueſtas communions de li Sanct. La premiera ſolament en Dio, & en Jeſu Chriſt, & al Sanct Eſperit per Sperit, l' autra en la Gleiſa de Chriſt.*

Dem. *En qual eſta vita eterna?*

Reſp. *En la fè viva, & obrivol en perſeverança en luy meſeima, lo Salvador dis Joan 17. Aqueſta es vita eterna quilli conoiſſan tu ſol veray Dio, & Jeſu Chriſt lequal tu trames, Et à quelque perſeverarè entro à la fin aqueſt ſerè ſalvà.*

ARTICLE V.

Concerning Elders, the Diſtribution of Alms, and Eccleſiaſtical Aſſemblies.

Rulers and Elders are choſen out of the People, according to the diverſity of the work, in the unity of *Chriſt*. And the *Apoſtle* proveth it in the Epiſtle to *Titus*, ch. I. *For this cauſe I left thee in* Crete, *that thou ſhouldeſt ſet in order the things that are wanting, and ordain Elders in every City, as I had appointed thee.*

The Money which is given us by the People, is by us carried to the general Council, and there delivered publickly in the preſence of all; and

Regidors ſon eſlegi del poble & Preire ſegond la diverſita de l' obrament en l' unita de Chriſt. Et l' Apoſtol enſemp prova aiço. Tit. 1. Yo laiſſay a tu a Creta per la gratia d' aqueſtas coſas que defaillon, & ordonnes Preyres per las Citas, enaima yo ordonney a tu.

Las pecunias laſquals ſon donnas a nos del poble ſon porta de nos el predict Concili general, & lioras en commun

devont

devant tuit nos lasquals son ceuillius de li nostre Major, & part de lor es despartia en aquilli que an a far camin enaima est vist esser besongnivol a lor, & part de la dicta pecunia es dona a li paure.

Nos Pastor nos aiosten tuit ensemp una vez lan, azo que ensemp tratten las nostras facendas per Concili general.

afterwards the same is taken and distributed by our Stewards, part thereof being given to such as are sent upon Journeys for occasion, and part thereof to the poor.

We that are Pastours, assemble once a year, to treat of our affairs in a general Council.

ARTICLE VI.

Of Ecclesiastical Correction or Discipline.

Semeillament devon esser faict corrections per enduction de temors. Que li non fidel poissan esser puni, & desparti, o la sola vita del mal, o la doctrina del mal, o sia contra la Fe, o sia contra la Charita, o sia contra l' Esperança, o d' un chascun modo de mal en temp. Et que aiço deo esser faict en correction, lo Seignor Jesus o enseigna. Si lo teo fraire peccarè, vay tu & corrigis luy entre tu & luy meseime sol: si el auvirè, tuas gagna lo teo fraire. Aiço meseime confirma l' Apostol disent a li Galat. Si l' home serè devant pres en alcun forfaict, o pecça vos liqual se spiritual enseigna luy d' aquesta maniera en sperit de soivessa.

Ma car tuit non recebon charitativament la correction, lo Seignor enseigna qual cosa li regidors spirituals debian far dizent. Si el non auvirè tu, adiosta cun tu un o dui, que tota parola iste en bocha de duy & de trey testimoni.

Et lo Seignor entent aizo aqui ont

In like manner, Correction (or Discipline) is to be used to retain the People under a reverence, that so those which are not faithfull, may be punished, and excommunicated, either for their ungodly conversation, or erroneous Doctrine, or transgressing the Rules of Charity, or for failing in point of Hope, or for being guilty of any of those the fore-mentioned evils, which may possibly be all found together in some one particular person. Now that the use of such Correction as this is necessary, the Lord *Jesus Christ* teacheth us, saying, *If thy Brother sin, go and rebuke him between thee and him alone, if he hearken to thee thou hast gained thy Brother.* The Apostle likewise in his Epistle to the *Galatians* confirmeth this, saying, *If a man be taken in a fault (or sin) you that are spiritual, instruct such an one in the spirit of meekness.*

But for as much as all receive not correction in love, the Lord teacheth what the spiritual guides ought to do in this case, saying, *But if he hearken not unto thee, then take with thee one or two, that so every word may be established in the mouth of two or three witnesses.*

And this is the Lords meaning in
case

case the fault be not known to many; but it's to be understood otherwise, when the sin is manifest and known to every one, as a sin; for in such a case, the chastisement ought to be publick. And this the Apostle sheweth, saying, *Rebuke those that sin in the presence of all, that so others may fear.*

fossa la colpa non conoissua a moti. Ma mot majorment es autre aqui ont alalcun pecca manifestament, & es manifesta tuit en pecca. Sobre aital deo esser faict corregiment manifest. L' Apostol mostro aiço disent. Repren li peccant devant tuit que li autre ayan temor.

ARTICLE VII.

Of Excommunication.

But in case all these Chastisements produce no amendment of life, nor forbearance of evil, *Christ* himself teacheth us how we ought to proceed against such an one, *If he hear not those, tell it to the Church, (that is, to the Rulers by whom the Church is governed and conserved) that so he may be afflicted with punishment, especially because of his contumacy.* Which the Apostle also confirmeth, *For, I verily, as absent in body, but present in spirit, have judged already as though I were present, in the Name of our Lord Jesus Christ, when ye are gathered together, and my spirit with the power of our Lord Jesus Christ, to deliver such an one to Satan for the destruction of the flesh, that the spirit may be saved in the day of the Lord Jesus Christ. And if any man that is called a Brother amongst you be a Fornicator, or covetous, or an Idolater, or a Railer, or a Drunkard, or an Extortioner, with such an one you shall not eat, therefore put away from among your selves that wicked person. Also, if there be any that obeyeth not our word, mark such a one by Epistle, and have nothing to do with him, that he may be ashamed, (and yet count him not as an Enemy, but admonish him as a Brother.)* And as the Lord saith, *Let*

Ma car tuit en aital reprennament, non volon avec assai esmendament ni abandonnar lo mal: Christ enseigna que debian far cum aitals, si el non auvire aquilli de la Gleisa, ço es li endreiçador, de liqual la Gleisa es regia & conserva, quel sia afflageli de pena, specialment per la contumacia. Et ço meseime conferm l' Apostol. Acer yo desistant per corps, ma present per Sperit, ja jugey enayma present luy loqual obra enaima, al nom del nostre Seignor Jesu Christ, vos aiostas & lo meo Sperit cum la vertu del Segnor Jesus liorar l' home d' aquesta maniera a Satanas en destruiment de la carn, & l' Esperit sia salf al dia de nostre Seignor Jesus Christ. Et dereço: Si aquel ques nomma fraire entre vos, & es fornicador, o avar, o servent a las Idolas, o mandiçador, o ubriach, o robador, non peure maniat cum luy loqual es d' aquesia maniera: hosta lo mal del mey de vos. Et dereço. Si alcun non obedire a la nostra parola, nota aquest per Episole, & non sia mescla cum luy, quel sia confundu, & non voilla estimar luy ennemic, ma corrige luy enaima frayere, & coma diu lo Seignor,

quel

quel te fia enaima Publican et Pagan, ço es quaital fia privâ de tot adjutori de la Gleifa, et del meneftier, et de la confortia de l' unita.

him be to thee as an *heathen man, or a* Publican, *that is,* let him be deprived of all benefit from the Church, of Miniftery, and from the Affembly of the Church, and the Communion of Saints.

ARTICLE VIII.

Of Marriage.

Le Mariage fe deo far fecond li gra liqual Dio a permes non fecond li gra liqual el a deffendu : ma la non fe deo gis far de confcientia d' aquilli del Papa, ja cia ço que non ly aya gis donna d' or o d' argent per aver difpenfation. Car ço que Dio non a deffendu fe po far fen luy.

La ligança maritivol del Sanct Mariage non fe deo far fenza lo confentiment de li parens de totas las doas partias : car li filli appartenon al paire, & a la maire.

Marriage ought to be performed according to the Rules prefcribed by God, and not within thofe degrees which he hath forbidden. And there need no fcruple of confcience be made concerning what the Pope hath forbidden, although we give him no money for a Difpenfation; for that which God hath not forbidden may very well be done without his permiffion.

The bond of holy Marriage ought not to be made without the confent of Friends on both fides, for as much as Children ought to be wholly at the difpofal of their Parents.

ARTICLE IX.

Of Taverns.

La Taverna es fontana de pecca : Efchola del Diavol : fay foy miracols tal qual li taignon de far. En la Sancta Gleifa a Dio coftuma de moftrar fas virtus, o feo miracle, enlumenar li cec, far anar li fop, parlar li mut, auvir li ford : ma lo Diavol fay en la Taverna tot lo contrari. Car quand lo glot va a la Ta-

The Tavern is a Fountain of fin, and School of the Devil, which worketh his Miracles after his own manner. God ufeth to fhew his power in the Church, and there to work his Miracles, *viz.* by opening the eys of the blinde, and making the lame to walk, and the dumb to fpeak, and the deaf to hear, but the Devil doth the clean contrary in the Tavern. For
when

when the Drunkard goeth to the Tavern, he goes upright, and when he returneth, he reels and staggers, and hath as it were lost his sight, hearing, and speech. Behold the Miracles which the Devil worketh in the Tavern. The Lessons which are learned in this School of the Devil are Drunkenness, Swearing, Lying, Perjury, Blasphemy, to deny God, and commit many other sins. This is the place where for the most part are raised all quarrels, slanders, contentions, and murders; and those which keep the Taverns, and suffer this, are partakers of all those sins and evils there committed. For certainly, if any should offer to speak so reproachfully of their Father and Mother in the presence of those men, as they suffer to be spoken of God, the glorious Virgin, and the Saints in Paradise, for to sell a Penny-worth of Wine, they would never suffer them so peaceably to abide in their houses. And therefore its said in *Ecclesiasticus*, that *he that keepeth a Tavern shall not be held guiltless.*

verna el y va dreit, & quand s' entorna souvent non se po sostenir, & a quasi perdu lo veser, l' auvir & lo parlar, lo sen, la rason, & la memoria. Aital son li miracle que lo Diable sap far en la Taverna. Las leçons que se legisson en aquesta eschola del Diavol son glotonias, jurar, perjurar, mentir, blestemar, & reniar Dio & de dir & far molti aultre pecca: car en la Taverna sappareillan breas, detractions, contentions, homicidis: & li tavernier que o suffren son parçonniers de tuit li pecca & li mal que si fan. Car qui lo diria tanti vituperier de paire o de maire, o de moller coma illi en suffren de Dio & de la gloriosa Vergena, & de li Sanct & Sanctas de Paradis per vendre un denier de vin, illi non o suffririan enaimi en paz. Dont es dict en Ecclesiastico que lo Tavernier non sere justifica de pecca.

ARTICLE X.

Of Dancings or Balls.

A Ball is the Devils Procession, and whosoever entreth in there, entereth into his Procession. The Devil is the Leader, the Middle, and the End of the Dance. So many Paces as a man maketh in a Ball, so many Leaps he maketh towards Hell. They sin in Dancing sundry ways, first, in walking, for all their Paces are numbered, they sin in touching, in their ornaments, in hearing, and seeing, in speaking, in singing, in lyes and vani-

Lo Bal es la procefsion del Diavol, & qui intra al Bal intra en la soa procefsion. Del Bal lo Diavol es la guia, lo mez & la fin. Tanti pas quant l' home fay al Bal, tanti saut vay en enfer. Al Bal si pecca en moltas manicras. En anar, car tuit li pas son nombra; en tocar, en ornament, en auvir, en veser, en parlar, en cants, en mesconias, & en vanetas. Lo Bal non es autre que

miseria,

miseria , pecca & vaneta. Donc nos volen monstrar de li Bal. Premierament per testimonis de l' Escritura, & daquienant per motas razons quant si mal cosa balar. Lo premier testimoni loqual nos pausen aizi es zo que se legis en l' Evangeli que la sauteiris & Baleiris say taillar la testa a Sanct Johan Baptista. Lo second es en Exodi cum Moises se so appropia a la compagnia, vic lo vedel, & gitté las taulas de las soas mans, & las rompé al pe des mont, daquienant pres li silli de Levi cum ci oeciseron del poble vinguetrey millia. Dereço li ornament que portan las senas al Bal son enaima coronas per plusiors victorias que lo Diavol a agu de li silli de Dio per lor. Car lo Diavol non a solament un glai en li Bal, ma tanti quanti y a de personas bellas & orna. Car la parola de la senna es glai fogueiant. Donc lo es forment de temer lo luoc alqual son vist tanti glai de iennemic, cum solament un de li glai de luy sia de esser forment temi. Encara fier aqui lo Diavol cum lo glay emola , car las sennas non venon legierament en li Bal, si ellas non se polisson premierament, & se ornan, loqual poliment & ornament , es coma aymolar lo glai del Diavol, & la roa que se say al Bal, es enaima una mola del Diavol, cum laqual el agusa lo seo glai. Aquilli que ornan las lors sillas, son enaimi aquellis que metton la legnas seccas al suoc azo quel arcta meilli. Car aitals sennas abrason lo suoc de luxuria en li cor de li home ; coma las volps de Samson embraseron li bla de li Philistio, enaimi aquestas sennas an suoc en las lors facias & en li lor act, ço es en regardar & vezer, & parlar cum loqual ellas brusan li ben de li

ties. A Ball is nothing but misery, sin , and vanity ; and therefore we will shew as touching Balls ; first by testimony of Scripture, and afterwards by Reasons, how wicked a thing it is thus to dance. The first testimony we produce is out of the Gospel, where the dancing Damosel caused *John* Baptist's head to be cut off. The second is in *Exodus,* when *Moses* drawing near to the Congregation saw the Calf, and the Dancing, *Exod.* 32. 19. *He cast the Tables out of his hands, and brake them beneath the Mount,* and afterwards *were slain of the People about three thousand men.* Besides the Ornaments which Women wear in Balls, are as so many Crowns, signifying the several Victories which the Devil hath obtained by them against the Children of God, for the Devil hath not onely a Sword in these Balls, but also comely persons, and well adorned ; for the Tongue of a Woman is a glittering Sword ; and therefore certainly that place is much to be feared where the Enemy hath so many Swords , seeing that any one of his Swords is exceedingly to be dreaded ; moreover the Devil in this place smiteth with a very sharp Sword, for the Women come not willingly to Balls without painting and adorning themselves, which paint and ornaments are like the whetting of the Devils Sword, and the Rings which are made in Balls, as the round stones whereon he sharpens them. Those which thus attire and adorn their Daughters are as they which lay dry wood upon the fire, that it may burn the better ; for such Women do kindle the fire of lust in the hearts of men : and as the Foxes of *Sampson* burn'd the Corn of the *Philistims,* so have these women fire in their faces, and in their actions, *viz.* it's in their looks, features, and words, by which they consume fume mens Eſtates. The third Reaſon is, that the Devil maketh uſe in Balls of his beſt Armour of proof. Now the ſtrongeſt Weapons the Devil hath, are Women ; which is ſhewen in that the Devil made choice of the Woman to deceive the firſt Man by. And ſo *Balaam* made choice of Women to make the children of *Iſrael* to be rejected. By a Woman the Devil made *Sampſon, David* and *Abſalom* to ſin. The Devil tempted the Man by a Woman three manner of ways, *viz.* by touching, ſight, and hearing. By theſe three ways he tempts at Balls thoſe men which are unwiſe, that is to ſay, by touching of the hands, by a beautifull look, and by the ſweetneſs of the voice. The fourth Reaſon is, that they which thus dance break that agreement which they made with God at their Baptiſm, when their God-fathers & God-mothers promiſe for them, to renounce the Devil and all his pomp. Balls are the pomp and the maſs of the Devil, & who ſo entreth into Balls entreth into the Devils pomp and Maſs. For the Woman that ſingeth at the Ball, is the Prioreſs of the Devil, and they that anſwer are Clerks, and they which look on are the Pariſhioners. As likewiſe the Cimbals and the Flutes are the Bells, and the Muſicians are the Miniſters of the Devil. For as when the Swine are ſcattered abroad, and the Swineherd makes one cry, ſtraitway the other flock together to him ; ſo the Devil cauſeth one Woman to ſing at the Bal, or play on the Muſick, that ſo all the Swine, (that is, the Dancers) may ſtraitway draw together into a knot.

Item, at the Balls they violate the ten Commandments of God, *viz.* the firſt, *Thou ſhalt have no other Gods but me.* But,

At the Ball they adore that perſon whom they ſtudy to ſerve, and there-

home. La terça razon es, car lo Diavol uſa en li Bal de la plus fort armadura quel aya. Car la plus fort armadura que lo Diavol aya ſon las fennas, laqual coſa es demonſtra, car lo Diavol eſtegic la fenna a decebre lo premier home. Et Balaan acer eſtegic aqueſtas a degittar lo filli d' Iſrael. Cum la fenna fey peccar Samſon, David, Abſalon. Lo Diavol tenta l' home au las fennas per tres manieras, ço es per tocar, per veſer, & per auvir. Cum aquiſti trey modi el tenta li home non ſavi en li Bal, ço es per lo tocament de las mans, per lo demoſtrament de la belleza, & per la ſoveſſa de li cant & de li ſon. La quarta razon es, car aquilli que Balan rompon la convenenza laqual illi an faict cum Dio al Baptiſme, cum li Parrin de lor ayan dict per lor yo renoncio lo Diavol & totas las pompas de luy. Lo Bal es la pompa & la Meſſa del Diavol, & qui intra al Bal, intra en la ſoa pompa & en la ſoa Meſſa. Car la fenna cantant al Bal es Prioreſſa del Diavol, & aquilli que reſpondon ſon Clercs, & aquilli quis ſon a regardar ſon li perrochian, & li ſon & las calamelas ſon las campanas, & li joglar liqual ſonan ſon Miniſtre del Diavol. Car enàima quand li porc ſon ſpars, & lo Paſtor de lor en fay quialar un, aço que li autre auven ſajoſton. Enaimi lo Diavol fay cantar una fenna al Bal, o quiallar la calamella aço que tuit li ſeo porc, ço es, Balador ſajoſtan.

Dereço al Bal ſe trepaſſan li dies Commandaments de la Ley de Dio. Contra lo premier. Non aures autre Dio que mi.

Al Bal la ſe col la perſonna laqual s' eſtudian de ſervir: dont di Sanct Hieroſme,

Hierofme, que lo Dio d' un chafcun es ço que ce col, & ama fobre totas cofas.

Contra lo fecond Commandament fe pecca al Bal quand lo fe fay idola del que chafcun ama.

Contra lo ters. Non recebres lo nom del teo Seignor Dio en van. Al Bal fe fervis a la vanita de la càrn.

Contra lo quart. Per lo Bal la Diamengea es çoça en Ballar.

Contra lo quint. Honora lo teo paire, &c. En li Bal li pairon fon fouvent defhonnora: car moti paCt fon faiCt en li Bal fenfa la confeilli de lor.

Contra lo fezen. Non occires. Lo es fouvent occi al Bal: car tota perfona que s' eftudia a plaçer a autruy, nauci tanti en l'ama quanti el en fay cu cubitar.

Contra lo fepten. Non avoortares, es pecca en li Bal: car la perfona o fia mafclè o fia fenna avootra cum tanti quanti illi en cubita. Difent lo Seignor. Tot aquel que veiray la fenna a cubitar ley a jay avootra ley al feo cor.

Lo huiCten. Non fores furt. Lo fe pecca al Bal contra aqueft Commandament, quand l' una perfona foftray lo cor de l' autra, de Dio.

Lo noven. Non dires fals teftimoni. Contra loqual es pecca quand difon falfament contra la verita.

Lo defen. Non cubitares, &c. Lo es pecca contra aqueft Commandment, quand las fennas cubiton l' ornament de las autras. Et quand li home cubiton la moller, las fillas, las ferventas del feo proyme.

Dereço la fe po monftrar quant mal fia Balar en la monteza de li pecca que commetton aquilli que Balan. Car illi peccan en avar, car illi non fan pas

fore St. *Hierome* faith, that the God of every one is that which he ferveth, and loveth above all things.

They fin in Balls againft the fecond Commandment, when they *make idols* of that which each one loveth.

Againft the third Commandment, *Thou fhalt not take the Name of the Lord thy God in vain.* When at the Balls they ferve the vanity of fin.

Againft the fourth, for by Balls the Sabbath Day is profaned.

Againft the fifth, *Honour thy Father and thy Mother.* For in Dancing the Parents are often difhonoured, while many contraCts and agreements are there made without their knowledg or confent.

Againft the fixth, *Thou fhalt not kill.* For perfons are often killed at Balls; fince every perfon who ftudieth to pleafe another killeth the foul in moving her to luft.

They fin in Balls againft the feventh, *Thou fhalt not commit Adultery.* For the perfon, Male or Female, commits Adultery fo often as they luft; for *He that looketh upon a Woman to luft after her, hath already committed Adultery with her.*

Againft the eighth, *Thou fhalt not fteal.* They fin at the Ball againft this Commandment, when one fteals the heart of another away from God.

Againft the ninth, *Thou fhalt not bear falfe witnefs.* When one fpeaketh falfly at the Ball, contrary to truth.

The tenth, *Thou fhalt not covet.* They fin againft this, when the Women covet the Ornaments of others; and when Men covet the Wives, Daughters, and Servants of their Neighbours.

Moreover it might be fhewed how great an evil thefe Balls are by the multitude of fins which they that dance commit. For they do all by

mea-

measure and number. And therefore St. *Augustine* said, *The miserable Dancer knoweth not that so many Paces as he maketh at a Ball, by so many leaps he draweth nearer to Hell.* They sin in their Ornaments in five respects; first, in being proud. In the second place, when they inveigle the hearts of those which look upon them in lust. In the third place, when they shame others which have not such Ornaments, giving them occasion to covet the like. Fourthly, when they make Women importunate in asking such Ornaments of their Husbands. In the fifth place, when not obtaining them of their Husbands, they procure them by other sinfull ways.

They sin in Singing and Playing on Instruments; for their Songs charm and make drunk the hearts of those which hear them with temporal joy, forgetting God, and uttering nothing in their Songs but lyes and follies. Yea the very Gestures themselves which are made in Dancing, bear witness of evil.

Men ought to know that Balls are the Procession of the Devil, and that who so entreth into the Ball entreth into his Procession; the Devil is the Leader, the Middle, and the End, and many there are who enter good and wise into the Ball, which come out corrupted and wicked. *Sarah* that holy Woman was none of these.

que non sia mensura & nombra. Dont Augustin disia. Lo miser non sap que tanti pas quanti el fay al Bal, tanti saut s'approcha en l'infern. Illi peccan en l'ornament en cinq manieras. La prima car sensuperbisson. La seconda car abrason li cor de li regardant a luxuria. La terça car fan vergongna a las autras personnas que non an aitals ornaments, donnant a lor causa de cubitar li semeillant. La quarta car fan lor esser demandosas, & greos a lor maris. La quinta si ellas non lo pon aver de li lor mari, ollas procuran d'aver li d'autra part per pecca.

Illi peccan en cantan, & en sonnar: car li cant de lor rompon & enubrian li cor de li auvent de goy temporal, & enaima enabria dementigan Dio & la lor pensa, & dison en li lor cant mesognias & folias. Dont mescime lo mouvament que se fay en Balar dona testimoni del mal.

E sapion que lo Bal es la procesion del Diavol, & qui intra al Bal intra en la soa procesion. Del Bal lo Diavol es la guia, lo mez & la fin. Et tala intra al Bal bona & savia, que sen sal corrotta & cattiva. Daitals non era aquella Sancta senna Sara.

ARTICLE XI.

After what manner Men ought to converse with those without.

Not to love the World.
To shun bad Company.
If it be possible, to have peace with all.

Non amar lo mond.
Fugir la mala consortia.
Si es possible aver paz cum tuit.

Non contendre en judici.
Non veniar si meseime.
Amar li ennemic.
Voler sostenir trabails, calomnias, menaças, riprovançs, vergognas, enjurias, & totas generations de torments per la verita.
Possesir las amas en patientia.
Non amenar joug cum li non fidel.

Non communicar a las malas obras, & totalment a las sabent idolatria, & del servici sentent zo meseime, & euaimi de las autras.

Not to sue at the Law.
Not to avenge ones self.
To love ones Enemies.
To be willing to undergo travels, calumnies, threatnings, rejection, shame, injuries, and all sorts of torments for the Truth.
To possess their Souls in patience.
Not to yoke themselves with Infidels.

Not to communicate at all with wicked works, and more especially with those which favour of Idolatry, or the service belonging to it, and so of other things.

After what manner the Faithfull ought to govern their Bodies.

Non servir a li desirier mortal de la carn.
Gardar li lor membres quilli non sian armas d' iniquitas.
Regir li lor sentiment.
Sotmettre lo corps a l' esprit.
Mortificar li membres.
Fugir la ocioseta.
Gardar sobrieta & mesura en maniar, & en beaure, & en parolas, & en las curas de la mond.
Far obras de misericordia.
Viore per se & per vita moral.

Combattre contra li desirier.
Mortificar las obras de la carn.
Istar an temp debit a Religion.

Ensemp recordar la divina volunta.

Examinar diligentament la conscientia.
Mundir & esmendar, & pacificar l' esprit.

Not to serve the carnal desires of the flesh.
To keep their Members that they be not weapons of iniquity.
To govern their thoughts.
To subject the Body to the Soul.
To mortifie their members.
To shun idleness.
To keep sobriety and moderation in eating and drinking, in speeches, and in the troubles of the world.
To work works of mercy.
To live by faith, and lead a moral life.
To fight against Lusts.
To mortifie the works of the flesh.
To observe times which are due to Exercises of Religion.
To confer together touching the will of God.
To examine diligently the Conscience.
To purifie, amend and quiet the spirit.

F I N.

The End.

CHAP.

CHAP. VI.

Extracts of feveral very authentick and rare Treatifes, compofed by the ancient Inhabitants of the Valleys of *Piemont*, a great part whereof were written about four hundred and twenty, others above five hundred and fifty Years ago, and the reft in all probability are of a far more ancient date.

The true Originals of all which were collected with no little pains and induftry, by the Authour of this Hiftory, during his abode in thofe parts, and at his Return, by him prefented to the publick Library of the famous Univerfity of *Cambridg.*

IT would now, without all queftion, be both naufeous, and injurious to ingenious Readers, for the Authour to prefume to intermingle his own private Gloffes or reflections upon the fubject of the foregoing Chapters. It is fufficiently evident what a Conformity both the Doctrine and Difcipline of the ancient Inhabitants of thefe Valleys, bear to the Doctrine and Difcipline of all the Reformed Churches at this very day. I muft needs confefs, this is a point, wherein I chiefly laboured from the firft beginning, to be clearly and fully informed of, partly for mine own private fatisfaction, and partly to anfwer the earneft defire of that Pillar of Learning, and Pattern of Piety, the late Lord Primate of *Ireland,* who fome few days before my fetting out for *Savoy,* fent for me on purpofe to his Chamber, and there gave me a very ferious and ftrict charge, to ufe my utmoft diligence, in the inquiry after, and to fpare no coft in the purchafe of all thofe Manufcripts and authentick Pieces which might give any light into the ancient Doctrine and Difcipline of thofe
Churches;

Churches; adding, that there was nothing in the World he was more curious and impatient to know, as being a Point of exceeding great weight and moment for stopping the Mouths of our Popish Adversaries, and discovering the foot-steps of our Religion in those dark Intervalls of the eighth, ninth, and tenth Centuries. This serious Injunction of that Reverend and worthy Man, together with mine own real Inclinations, caused me to leave no stone unturned, nor to lose any opportunity during my abode in those parts, for the real effecting this thing; and though the Popes Emissaries had already gathered the more choice Clusters and first ripe Fruits, yet I met at least with the Grape-gleanings of the Vintage, I mean, divers Pieces of Antiquity, some whereof had been a long time buried under Dust and Rubbish, others had been scattered about in the Valleys, some here, some there, in desert and obscure places, and without a singular providence had never come to light. Now to insert them all at length, would make the Work in hand swell into too great a Volume, therefore I have onely thought fit to insert a bare Catalogue of the whole, and out of that to pick some few, to present the Reader with, that so he may the better judg of the rest.

A Catalogue of divers Manuscripts, written by the ancient Inhabitants of the Valleys (the greatest part of them in their own Language) collected by the Authour of this History during his abode in those parts; the true Originals of all which are to be seen in the publick Library of the famous University of *Cambridg*.

The Volume marked with the Letter *A.* contains in it the following Treatises.

1. The History of the Creation and Deluge, written in their own Language.
2. An excellent Treatise of sundry profitable Instructions which a man ought to learn from the nature of divers Animals.
3. *Lo tratta de li pecca*, or a Treatise of Sin, which is an allegorical and moral Explanation of the *Beast* described, *Rev.* 13.
4. A Treatise of the Word of God, and the power and efficacy thereof; as also how it ought to be received; at the end whereof there is affixed the Date, either of the Work, or at least of the Copy of it, *viz. Anno Domini* 1230.
5. Several *Latin* Pieces, which are certain Rhapsodies concerning Priests and Friers.
6. A Treatise against *Tramettament*, or Traditions and Ordinances of Men, as not consonant to the holy Scriptures.   7. An

7. An Exhortation to *Herman*, to convert himself to God, and not to the Creatures.

8. Concerning Pharisaical Plantations which the Father hath not planted, *viz.* the Orders and Sects, of *Monks, Franciscan Friers, Dominicans*, and the like, which are not ordained by God.

9. A *Latin* Treatise *De Officiis Conjugum, Viri & Uxoris*.

10. A *Latin* Treatise *De Symbolo Apostolico*.

11. A *Latin* Treatise *De Ædificatione Urbium, Idololatriæ ortu & progressu, ejusque eversione per Evangelii predicationem*.

12. A *Latin* Treatise, *Quibus Modis peccatum fiat*.

13. A *Latin* Treatise *De verâ peccati purgatione*.

14. A *Latin* Treatise intituled, *Uni Deo placere studeamus*.

15. A *Latine* Treatise intituled, *Tres veritates* 1. *Doctrinæ*. 2. *Justitiæ*. 3. *Vitæ*.

16. A *Latin* Treatise intituled, *Solâ Dei Lege scriptâ definiri Fidei Controversias*.

In the Volume marked with the Letter *B*. are contained the following Treatises, all written in that which is called the *Waldensian* Language, in Parchment, and that in a very ancient, but excellent Character.

1. *Glosa Pater*, or the Explication of the Lords Prayer.

2. *Trecenas*, or divers passages of the Evangelists and Epistles.

3. *Doctor*, that is, divers Sentences and Testimonies of the Fathers touching Repentance.

4. *Penas*, or a Treatise concerning the punishment of sin.

5. *Li Goy de Paradis*, a Treatise concerning the Joys of Paradise.

6. An Epistle to all the Faithfull.

7. A Poeme intituled, *Novel Confort*.

8. A Poeme intituled, *Novel Sermon*, containing many wholesome Instructions to the People.

9. A Poeme intituled, *La Noble Leyçon*.

10. A Poeme intituled, *Pair eternal*.

11. A Poeme intituled, *Barca*, concerning the misery and shortness of mans life, and his arriving at the Haven of Salvation.

12. An Explanation of the ten Commandments.

13. An Explanation of the Articles of the Apostles Creed.

14. A Treatise concerning Vice, and Mortal Sins.

15. A Treatise concerning the seven Gifts of the Spirit, *Isai* 11.

16. A Treatise concerning the three Theological, and the four Cardinal Virtues.

17. A Treatise concerning the Goods of Fortune, Nature, and Grace.

18. A

18. A Treatife concerning the fix honorable things in this World.
19. Several Sermons upon feveral Texts of Scripture; Namely,
    1. A Sermon upon the fecond of *Matthew* touching idle words.
    2. A Sermon upon *Ephef.*4. touching the putting on of the New Man.
    3. A Sermon *Del Fantin Jefus*, or concerning the little Childe *Jefus*, during his abode in *Jerufalem*, *Luke* 2.
    4. A Sermon touching *Chrift's* being tempted in the Defert, *Matth.*4. & *Luke* 4.
    5. A Sermon upon *Matth.*8.25. *Save us, or elfe we perifh.*
    6. A Sermon touching the Rich Man, *Luke* 16.
    7. A Sermon upon the fixth of *John*.
    8. A Sermon upon the Parable of the Sower, *Matth.*13.

In the Volume marked with the Letter *C.* are contained the following Treatifes.

    1. An Exhortation to confefs our Sins one unto another, and unto God.
    2. A Sermon touching the Fear of the Lord.
    3. A Sermon touching the Accufation of Sinners before God, in Judgment.
    4. A Treatife touching Tribulations.
    5. A Treatife touching the Martyrdom of the *Macabees*, and others.
    6. A Treatife concerning the Sufferings and Conftancy of *Job*.
    7. An Extract of the Hiftory of *Tobias*,

In the Volume *D.* are many excellent and heavenly Meditations, touching the Miferies, Tribulations, and Shortnefs of this Life; as likewife of Repentance, Good Works, and the like; written in the Language of the ancient Inhabitants of the Valleys, in Parchment, but the Letter almoft worn out with age, which according to many probable circumftances of the place and manner of its prefervation, is judged to have been written at leaft fix or feven hundred years ago.

In

In the Volume marked *E*. are contained.

1. A *Latin Grammar* of the ancient *Barbes* or *Ministers*.
2. The Proverbs of *Solomon* and *Ecclesiastes*.
3. A pious Piece of Poesie in the Language of the ancient Inhabitants of the Valleys.
4. A Treatise concerning the Love and Fear of God, and the manner of Life which *Christians* ought to live.
5. A Treatise of Morals in *Latin*.
6. A Treatise of Arithmetick.

In the Volume *F*. are collected and written in Parchment, in that which is called the *Waldensian* Language, of a very ancient, but fair and distinct Character.

The Gospel of *Matthew*.
The first Chapter of *Luke*.
The Gospel of *John*.
The Acts of the Apostles.
The first Epistle to the *Corinthians*.
The Epistle to the *Galatians*.
The Epistle to the *Ephesians*.
The Epistle to the *Philippians*.
The first Epistle to the *Thessalonians*.
The second Epistle to *Timothy*.
The Epistle to *Titus*.
The eleventh Chapter of the Epistle to the *Hebrews*.
The first and second Epistle to *Peter*, but imperfect.

The

The noble Leſſon written in the Language of the ancient Inhabitants of the Valleys, in the Year 1100. Extracted out of a moſt authentick Manuſcript, the true Original whereof is to be ſeen in the publick Library of the famous Univerſity of *Cambridg.*

O frayre entendé una nobla Leyçon.

Sovent deven velhar e iſtar en ore-ſon.	O Brethren, give ear to a noble Leſſon.

Sovent deven velhar e iſtar en ore-ſon.

We ought always to watch and pray,

C. nos veen aqueſt mont eſſer preſdel chavon.

For we ſee the World nigh to a concluſion.

Mot curios deorian eſſer de bonas o-bras far.

We ought to ſtrive to do good works,

C. nos veen aqueſt mont de la fin apro-piar.

Seeing that the end of this World approacheth.

Ben ha mil e cent an compli entiera-ment.

There are already *a thouſand and one hundred years fully accompliſhed,*

Que ſo ſcripta lora, C. ſon al derier temp.

Since it was written thus, *For we are in the laſt time.*

Poc deorian cubitar; C. ſen al rema-nent.

We ought to covet little, for we are at what remains, *viz.* at the later end.

Totiorn veen las enſeignas venir à compliment.

We ſee daily the Signs to be accompliſhed,

En acreyſament de mal e en amerma-ment de ben.

And that in the increaſe of evil, and decreaſe of good.

Ayço ſon li perilli que l' eſcriptura di.

Theſe are the perils which the Scripture mentioneth,

L' Avangeli ho recoynta e Sant Paul aeſti.

In the Goſpels and St. *Paul*'s Writings:

Que neun home que viva non po ſa-ber la fin.

As alſo, that no man living can know the end.

Enperço deven mays temer; C. nos non ſen certan.

And therefore we ought the more to fear, as not being certain,

Si la mort nos penré enehoy o deman.

Whether we ſhall die to day or to morrow.

Ma cant venré al jorn del jujament.

But when the Day of Judgment ſhall come,

Un çaſcun recebre per entier payament.

Every one ſhall receive their full Reward.

Aquilli qu' auren fayt mal e aquilli qu' auren fayt ben.

Thoſe that ſhall have done either well or ill.

Ma l' eſcriptura di e nos creyre ho de-ven.

Now the Scripture ſaith, and we ought to believe it,

That

That all men shall pass two ways.

The good to glory, and the wicked to torment.

But he that shall not believe this Departure,

Let him search the Scripture from the very beginning,

Since *Adam* was formed untill this present time,

There he shall finde, if he hath understanding,

That *few are the saved* in comparison of the rest.

Wherefore every one that will do good works,

The honour of God the Father ought to be his first moving Principle.

He ought likewise to implore the aid of his glorious Son, the dear Son of the Virgin *Mary*,

And the Holy Ghost which lightens us in the true way.

These three (the holy Trinity) as being but one God, ought to be called upon,

Full of all power, wisedom, and goodness.

This we ought often to beg and pray for,

That he would enable us to encounter our Enemies,

And overcome them before our end,

Which are the World, the Devil, and the Flesh:

And that he would give us wisedom accompanied with goodness,

That we may know the way of life,

And keep pure that Soul which God hath given us,

Yea both Soul and Body in way of Charity,

So as we love the holy Trinity,

And our Neighbour, for God hath commanded it.

Que tuit li home del mont per dui chamin tenren.

Li bon yren en gloria, li fellon en torment.

Ma aquel que non creyré en aquel departiment.

Regarde l' escriptura del fin commençament.

Dos que Adam fo formà entro en aquest temp present.

Aqui poyré trobar si el aure entendement.

Que poc son li salva aver lo remanent.

M. çascuna persona que vol ben obrar.

Lonor de Dio lo payre deo esser al mençar.

E apelar en aina lo sio glorios filli car filli de Santa Maria.

E lo Sanct Sprit que nos don bona via.

Aquisti 3. la Sancta Trenità, enayma un Dio, devon esser aurà.

Plen de tota poysença, e de tota sapiença e de tota bontà.

Aquest deven sovent aurar e requerir.

Que nos don fortaleça encontra li enemic.

Que nos li poysian vencer devant la nostra fin.

ço es lo mont, e lo Diauol e la carn.

E nos done sapiença acompagnà au bontà.

Que nos poysian conoysser la via de verità.

E gardar pura l' arma que Dio nos a donà.

L' arma e lo cors en via de càrità.

En aysy que nos aman la Santa Trinità.

E lo proyme, car Dio ha ha comanda.

Non

Non solament aquilli que nos fan ben,
ma neys aquilli que nos fan mal.

E haver ferma esperança al Rey celestial.

Que à la 'fin nos alberge al sia glorios ostal.

M. aquel que non farè ço que se conten en aquesta leyçon.

Non intraré en la Santa Mayson.

M. aiço es de greo tenir à la caytiva gent.

Que aman l' or e l' argent.

E las empromesion de Dio han en despreçiament.

Illi non gardan la ley ni li commandament,

Ni li lay san gardar à alcuna bona gent,

M. segont lor poysança by fan empachement.

Perque es aquest mal entre l' umana gent?

Perço que Adam peque del fin commençament,

C el manié del pom otra defendement,

E à li autré germené lo gran del mal semenç,

El aquisté à si mort e à li autre ensegador;

Ben poen dire que aqui hac mal bocon;

M. Christ ha remps li bon per la soa passion.

M. nos troben en aquesta leyçon,

Que Adam fo mescresent de Dio lo sio Creator,

D. ayçi poen ver que ara son fayt pejor

Aquilli que habandonan Dio lo payre onipotent,

E creon à las ydolas al lor destruiment.

ço que defent la ley que fo del commençament,

Ley natural sapella cumuna à tota gent,

Lacal Dio pausé al cor del sio premier forma.

Not onely those which do us good, but those also which harm us.

Having hope in the King of Heaven,

That at the end he may receive us into his glorious habitation.

Now he who shall not do what is contained in this Lesson,

Shall never enter into this house.

Though it be never so hard to be received by the wicked,

Which love Gold and Silver,

Which have the promises of God in contempt,

Who neither keep his Law and Commandments,

Nor suffer those who would to keep them,

But rather hinder them to the utmost of their power.

How came this evil to enter into mankinde?

Because *Adam* sinned at the first beginning,

By eating of the forbidden Apple.

And thus the Grain of the evil Seed taking Root in others,

He brought Death to himself and all his Posterity;

Well may we say, this was an evil Morsel;

Howsoever *Christ* hath redeemed the Good by his Death and Passion.

But alas, we finde in this Lesson,

That *Adam* believed not God his Creatour,

Yea and we may see likewise, that now adays

Men forsake God the Father Almighty,

And believe in Idols to their own Destruction.

That which the Law forbids, which was from the beginning,

Called the Law of Nature, common to all sorts,

Which God put into the heart of that man whom he first formed.

Giving

Giving him a power of doing good or evil,

But commanding him to do the good, and efchew the evil.

And this you may fee was ill obferved,

For that we have left the good, and done the evil,

As did *Cain* the eldeft Son of *Adam*, who killed his Brother *Abel* without any caufe,

Save onely for that he was good, And had his hope in the Lord, and not in any creature.

Here we may take an Example of the Law of Nature,

Which we have broken and tranfgreffed,

We have finned againft the Creatour, and offended the Creature.

It was a noble Law that was given us by God,

And written in the heart of every man,

That he might there reade it and keep, and teach Righteoufnefs,

And love God in his heart above every Creature,

And that he might fear and ferve him without any Referve,

There being none to be found in the holy Scriptures.

That he might likewife keep firm the Mariage-tie, that noble accord or contract,

And have peace with his Brethren, and love all other perfons.

That he might hate Pride, and love Humility,

And do to others as he would be done by,

And if he did the contrary, that he fhould be punifhed.

Now few they were which kept well this Law,

And more were they who broke it, Who forfook the Lord, not honouring him,

De poer far ben o mal li doné franquetà,

Lo mal li a defendu, lo ben li ha commandá.

Ayço poes vos ben veer ques eyfu mal gardá,

Que haven lay fa lo ben e lo mal haven obrà,

En ayma fey Cayn lo premier filli d'Adam, que ucis lo fio frayre Abel fença neuna cayçon,

Mas car el era bon,

E havia fa fè al Segnor e non en autra creatura.

Ayçi poen penre eyfemple de la ley la natura,

Lacal haven corrota, pafsà haven de mefura,

Pecca haven al Creator, e offendu à la creatura.

Nobla ley era aquela lacal Dio nos doné,

El cor dun çafcun home fcrita la pausé,

Quel legés e gardés, e enfegneffa dreytura,

Amés Dio al fio cor fobre tota creatura,

Templés e fervés e non hy paufés mefura,

C non es atroba en la fanta Scriptura.

E gardés ferm lo matremoni aquel noble covenent,

E agues paç au li frayre, e amés tota autra gent:

Ayres argolli e amés humilità,

E façes à li autres en ayma el volia que fos fay à li,

E fi el façes per lo contrari quel en fofa puni.

Poc foron aquilli que aquela ley ben garderon,

Moti foron aquilli que la trapafferon,

E lo Segnor abandoneron non donant à lui honor,

M. Creferon

M. Creseron al demoni e à la soa temptacion,

Trop ameron lo mont e poc paradis,

E serviron al cors majorment que à l' esprit.

Enperço nos troben que moti en son peri.

Ayçi se po repenre tot home que di,

Que Dio non se la gent per laysar li perir.

M. gardese un çascun quel non li endevenga en aysi cant edevenc à lor.

C. ley duluvi venc e destrus li fellon,

M. Dio fey far una archa enque el enclaus li bon.

Tant fo cregu lo mal e lo ben amerma,

Que en tot le mont non ac masque oyt salva,

Eysemple poen penre en aquela sentencia,

Gardar nos de mal e tuit façam penedença.

C. Yesu Christ o a dit, e en Sant Luces Script,

Que trastuit periren aquilli que le non la faren.

Ma aquilli que scamperon, Dio lor sey empromession.

Que jamays en ayga non perire lo mont ;

Aquilli cregron e foron multiplica.

Del ben que Dio lor fey poc se foron recorda.

M. agron tant poc de fe e tant grant la temor,

Quilli non creseron ben al dit del Segnor.

M. temian que las ayga neesan encara lo mont,

E disseron de far torre per reduyre se aqui,

E ben la commençeron segont çoques script,

But believed the Devil and his temptation,

Who loved too much the World, and too little the things of Heaven,

And served the Body more than the Spirit.

Wherefore we finde that many have perished.

Here every one may be reprehended that saith,

That God created not Man to suffer him to perish,

But let every one take heed, that it happeneth to him, as it did to them.

For the Deluge came and destroyed the wicked,

But God caused an Ark to be made, in which he saved the good.

So were the bad increased, and the good diminished,

That in all the World there were saved but eight persons.

We may be instructed hereby

To keep our selves from evil, and that all ought to repent.

For *Jesus Christ* hath said it, and in St. *Luke* it is written,

That all those shall perish that shall not so do.

Now to those which escaped, God made a Promise,

That the World should never more perish by Water ;

And they believing it were multiplied.

But that good which God did them they soon forgat,

Being men of little faith, and so great fear,

That they did not throughly believe the Words of the Lord.

But they believed that the Waters should again trouble the World,

And thought of building a Tower to retire into,

Yea and they began it (as it is written)

Intending

Intending to make it fo large, fo high, and fo great,

That the top thereof might reach to Heaven, but alas they could not accomplifh their Defign.

For they difpleafed God thereby, the which alfo he then demonftrated.

This great City was called *Babylon*,

And now it is called *Confufion*, by reafon of its ruinous condition.

There was then but one onely Language amongft men,

But that they might not underftand each other, God made a divifion

That fo they might not finifh what they had begun.

The which Languages then fpread through all the World.

After this they finned grievoufly, renouncing the Law, *viz.* that of Nature.

For the Scripture faith, and it may be evidently proved,

That five Cities perifhed which did evil,

Being fentenced by God, to Fire and Brimftone.

He deftroyed the wicked, and the good he delivered,

Viz. Lot and his Family, which the Angel brought out,

They were four, but one was condemned,

For the Woman looked back, breaking the Command.

Here's now an Example for all Mankinde,

That they ought to take heed of that which God forbids.

In thofe days lived *Abraham* a Man well-pleafing God,

Who begat a Patriarch of whom came the *Jews*,

And thefe were a noble People in the fear of the Lord,

Who lived in *Egypt*, amongft other wicked People,

E diçian de farla larga, e tant hauta, e tant grant,

Quilli avengués entro al cel, ma illi non pogron far tant.

C. lo defplac à Dio e fey lor ofemblant,

Babelonia havia nom aquela grant ciptà,

E ara es dita confufion per la foa mal veftà.

Adon era un lengage entre tota la gent,

M. quilli non fentendefan hy fey Dio departimen,

Quilli non façefan quilli havian commençà.

Foron feli lengaje per tot lo mont fcampà.

Poi pequeron greoment abandonant la ley (çoes ley de natura)

C. l' Efcriptura di e ben fe po provar,

Que cinc fciptas periron lafcal façian lo mal,

En fuoc e en folpre Dio li condampné.

El deftrus li fellon e li bon delioré,

ço fo Loth e aquilli de fon oftal que l' Angel engiré,

Catre foron per nombre, ma l' un fe condampné,

ço fo la mollire pur, C. fe regarde otra defendement.

Ayçi ha grant eyfemple a tota hùmana gent,

Quilli fe devan gardar de ço que Dio defent.

En aquel temp fo Abram baron plaçent à Dio,

E engenré un Patriarcha dont foron li Jufio,

Nobla gent foron aquilli en la temor de Dio,

En Agit heiteron entre autra mala gent,

Lay

Lay foron apermu e coſtreyt per lonc temp,

E crideron al Segnor e el lor trames Moyſent,

E deliore ſon poble e deſtrus lautra gent.

Per lo mar ros paſſeron coma per bel eyſuyt,

M. li enemic de lor lical li perſequian, y periron traſtuit,

Motas autras enſegna Dio al ſio poble ſey ;

El li paç 40. an al deſert e lor doné la ley.

En doas taulas peyrienças la trames per Moyſent,

Troberon la ſcripta e ordena noblament.

Un Segnor demonſtrava eſſer à tota gent,

Aquel degueſan creyre, e amar de tot lo cor, e temer e ſervir entro al dia de la fin,

E un çaſcun amés lo ſio proyme enayma ſi:

Conſelleſan las vevas, e li orfe ſuſtenir,

Albergueſan li paure, e li nu reveſtir,

Pagueſan li fameiant, e li anant edreyceſan ;

E la ley de lui mot degueſan gardar,

A li gardant empromes lo regne celeſtial ;

Lo ſerviment de las ydolas mes en deſenſion,

Domecide, avoteri, e tota fornigaçion,

Mentir & perjurar e falſa garentia,

Uſura, e rapina, e mala cubiticia,

En apres avaritia, e tota felonia,

A li bon epromé vita e li mal auçia ;

Adéra viſtian en la ſoa ſegnoria :

C.aquilli que peccavan ni façian malament

Where they were oppreſſed and ſtraitened a long time,

And but crying to the Lord he ſent unto them *Moſes*,

And delivered his People, and deſtroyed the other Nations.

They paſſed through the Red Sea, as through a dry and pleaſant place,

But their Enemies who perſecuted them, periſhed all in the waters,

Many other Signs did God then give to his People ;

Feeding them fourty years in the Wilderneſs, and giving them the Law,

In two Tables of Stone, which he ſent by *Moſes*,

Which they found written, and nobly ordained.

This demonſtrated that there was a Lord of all men,

Whom they ought to believe, and love with all their heart, as likewiſe to fear and ſerve him to the end,

And that every one ſhould love his Neighbour as himſelf :

That they ſhould give counſel to Widows, and defend the fatherleſs,

That they ſhould receive the Poor into their houſes, & clothe the naked,

That they ſhould feed the hungry, and conduct the Traveller ;

And in ſum keep carefully this his Law,

Promiſing to thoſe that kept it, the heavenly Kingdom.

He forbad ſervice unto Idols,

Homicide, Adultery, and all ſorts of Whoredom,

Lying, Perjury, and falſe Witneſs, Uſury, Rapine, and evil Coveting,

As alſo Avarice, and all wickedneſs,

To the good he promiſed Life, but threatned Death to the wicked ;

Then were they clothed in their Principality :

But thoſe which ſinned and did wickedly

They

They died and were deftroyed without remiffion:

For the Scripture fays, and it is manifeft enough,

That thirty thoufand were left in the Wildernefs,

Thirty thoufand and more (as the Law faith)

Died by the Sword, by Fire, and Serpents;

And many others were deftroyed in another manner,

The Earth opening, and Hell receiving them.

And here we may have matter of reproving our felves very feafonably,

But thofe which did the will of the Lord, inherited the Land of Promife;

Now there were in thofe days many Worthies,

As *David*, and *Solomon* the King, *Ifaiah*, *Jeremy*, and many others,

Which fought for the Faith, and defended the fame.

There was one only People chofen by God out of all the World.

The Enemies were in great number round about which perfecuted them:

We have many things worth our learning and imitation in this Leffon:

When they kept the Law and the Commandments,

God fought for them againft the other Nations;

But when they finned and did wickedly,

They died, were deftroyed, and taken Captives by thofe other Nations.

But fo enlarged were thefe People, and fo abounding in Riches,

That they kicked againft the Lord,

Wherefore we finde in this Leffon,

That the King of *Babylon* put them into Prifon,

Illi eran mort e deftruit fença perdonament:

M. l' efcriptura di e mot es manifeft,

Que trenta milia foron li remas al defert,

Trenta milia e prus fegon que la ley di

Illi foron mort de glay de fuoc e de Serpent;

E moti autre periron del deftermenament,

La terra fe partic e receop li l' enfern.

Ayçi nos nos poen repenre del noftre grant fopere,

M. aquilli que feron ben lo plaer del Segnor ereteron la terra de l' emprome-fion;

Mot fo de nobla gent en aquela façon,

En ayma fo Davi, e lo Rey Salamon, Yfaya e Jeremia e moti autre Baron, Que per la ley combatian e façian defenfion.

Un poble era à Dio eyleyt de tot lo mont.

Li enemic eran moti dentora lical li perfequian:

Grant eyfemplen poen penre en aquifta leyçon:

Cant illi gardivan la ley e li commandament,

Dio combatia per lor encontra l' autra gent;

M. cant illi peccavan ni façian malament,

Illi eran mort e deftruit e pres de lautra gent.

Tant fo alargà lo poble e plen de grant ricor,

Quel vay trayre li cauç en contra fon Segnor,

Enperço nos troben en aquefta Leyçon,

Que lo Rey de Babelonia li més en fa preyfon,

Lay

Lay foron apermu e coſtreyt per lonc temp.

E crideron al Segnor au lo cor repentent ;

Adera li retorné en Jeruſalem poc foron li obedient que gardeſan la ley,

Ni que agueſan temor d' offendre lo lor Rey.

M. jac alcuna gent plen de tant grant falſetà,

ço eran li fariſio e li autre Scriptura,

Que illi gardeſan la ley motera demoſtrà,

Que la gent ovegueſſan per eſſer prus honorà.

M. poc val aquel honor que toſt ven a chavon.

Perſequeran li Sant e li juſt e li bon ;

Au plor e au gayment auravam lo Segnor,

Quel deyſendés en terra per ſalvar aqueſt mont :

C. tot l'uman lignaie anava à perdición.

Adonca Dio trames l' Angel anan nobla ponçela de lignaje de Rey,

Doçament la ſalute, C. ſepartenia à ley,

En apres li vay dire, no temer Maria,

C. lo Sant Sprit ſerè en ta compagnia;

De tu nayſſeré filli que apellares Yeſhu,

El ſalvaré ſon poble de ço quel ha ofendu.

Neo mes lo porte al ſio ventre la Vergena glorioſa,

M. quilli non fos repreſa ſo de Joſeph ſpoſa ;

Pura era noſtra dona e Joſeph atreſi,

M. ayço deven creyre, C. l' Avangeli o di,

Where they were oppreſſed and ſtraitened a long time ;

Then they cried to the Lord with a repentant heart ;

And he reſtored them to *Jeruſalem* , but few there were that were obedient and kept the Law,

And that feared to offend their King.

Yea ſome there were, men full of deceit and falſhood,

viz. the Phariſes and others who were verſed in Scripture,

Theſe kept the Law, (as plainly appears)

Onely that the World might ſee it, and to be the more honoured.

But little worth is this honour which ſoon vaniſheth.

Then were the Saints perſecuted, and thoſe that were juſt and good ;

Then they prayed unto the Lord with cries and tears,

That he would come down on earth and ſave this World :

For all mankinde was in the way of perdition.

Then ſent God the Angel to the noble Virgin of royal Deſcent,

Who ſweetly ſaluted her according to the command of him that ſent him,

And after ſaid unto her, Fear not *Marie,*

For the Holy Ghoſt ſhall overſhadow thee ;

Thou ſhalt bear a Son whom thou ſhalt call *Jeſus,*

He ſhall ſave his People from their ſins.

Nine Moneths the glorious Virgin bare him in her womb,

But that ſhe might not be made a publick Example, ſhe was eſpouſed by *Joſeph ;*

Pure was this Virgin and *Joſeph* alſo.

But this we ought to believe, for the Scripture ſaith it,

That

That they put the Infant in the Manger when it was born,
They wrapt him in fwadling cloaths, and lodg'd him but very meanly.

Here may be reprehended thofe covetous and avaricious men,
Which never ceafe to heap up Riches together.

Now there were many Miracles wrought when the Lord was born:
God fent the Angel to reveal this Myftery to the Shepherds:
In the Eaft appeared a Star to the three Wife Men.
Glory was given to God on high, and on Earth Peace to the good.

Afterwards the little Childe fuffered Perfecution,
But the Infant increafed in Grace and Age,
And in Divine Wifedom, in which he was inftructed,
And called the twelve Apoftles, which were rightly fo named,
And would change the Law which he gave before;
He changed it not, that it fhould be abandoned,
But renewed it that it might be better kept;
He received Baptifm for to give Salvation,
And commanded the Apoftles to baptife the Nations,
(For then began the Renewing)
The ancient Law forbad Fornication and Adultery,
But the new reprehends looking and lufting after a Woman;
The old Law had power to make null Mariage, and that Bills of Divorcement might be given,
But the new faith, Thou fhalt not marry her that is put away,
And what God hath joyned let no man feparate.
The old Law curfed the barren womb,

Que en la crepia lo pauferon cant fo
nà lo fantin,
Dé panc l' enveloperon, paurament fo
alberga.
Ayço fe pon repenre li cubit e li avar,

Que damafar aver non fe volon cofar.

Moti miracle foron cant fo nà lo
Segnor:
Que Dio trames l' Angel anunciar à li
paftor:
En Orient aparec una ftella à li trei
baron.
Gloria fo donà à Dio al cel, en terra
paç a li bon.
M. en apres un petit fufurc perfequecion,
M. lo fantin creyfia per gracia e per
età,
E en fapiença devina en lacal el era
enfegna,
E apelle xii. Apoftol lical fon ben nominà,
E volc mudar la ley què avant avia
donà;
El non la mude pas quilli fos abandonà,
M. la renovelle quilli fos prus fort
gardà;
El receop lo Baptifm per donar falvament,
E a li Apoftol vay dire que bapteifan la gent,
C. adonca commençava lo renovellament
Ben defent la ley vellia fornigar e
avoutrar,
M. la novella repren vefer e cubitar;

La ley antenia di partir lo matrimoni,
e carta de refufe deguefan donar,

M. la novella di non penré la layfà,

E nenguen non departa ço que Dio ha
aioftà.
La ley vellia maudi lo ventre que fruc
non aporta,
M. la

M. la novella cofellia gardar verge-
netà,
La ley vellia defent folament per-
jurar ;
M. la uovella di al poftot non jurar ;
E prus de fi o de non non fia lo tio par-
lar.
La ley vella comanda combater con-
tra li enemic e rendre mal per mal,

M. la novella di non te vollias ven-
gier,
M. layfa la vangiança al Rey cele-
ftial,
E layfa viore en paç aquilli que te
faren mal,
E trobarés pardon del Rey celeftial.

La ley vellia dy, amarés lo tio amic,
e aures en odi lo tio enemic,
M. la novella di non farés prus en
ayfi,
M. amà li voftre enemic, e façé ben
aquilli que ayreron vos,
Aurà per li perfequent, e per li acay-
fonantà vos,
Que vos fia filli del voftre payre local
es en li cel.
La ley vellia comanda punir li mal-
façent,
M. la novella di pardona à tota gent ;

E trobarés pardon del payre ..onipo-
tent,
C. fi tu non perdonarés tu non troba-
rés falvament.
Nengun non deo aucire ni ayrar nen-
guna gent,
Manc ui fimple ni paure non deven
fcarnir,
Ni tenir vil leftrang que ven d' au-
truy pays.
C. en aqueft mont nos fen tuit pelle-
grin.
C. nos tuit fon frayre deven à Dio
fervir.
çoes la novella ley que Yefbu Xrift a
dit que nos deven tenir.

But the new counfelleth to keep
virginity,
The old Law forbiddeth onely to
forfwear ;
But the new faith, *Swear not at all*,
And that thy fpeech be no more
than *Yea* and *Nay*.
The old Law biddeth to fight a-
gainft Enemies, and render evil for
evil,
But the new one faith, *Avenge not*
thy felf,
But leave thy vengeance to thy
heavenly King,
And let thofe live in peace which
do thee hurt,
And then fhalt thou finde pardon
with the heavenly King.
The old Law faith, Thou fhalt love
thy Friend, and hate thine Enemy,
But the new one faith, Thou fhalt
do no more fo,
But ye fhall love your Enemies,
and do good to them that hate you,
And pray for them that perfecute
you, and feek for occafion againft you,
That ye may be the Children of
your Father which is in Heaven.
The old Law faith, Punifh Male-
factours,
But the new faith, Pardon all forts
of People,
And thou fhalt finde pardon with
the Father Almighty,
For if thou doft not pardon, thou
fhalt not be faved.
None ought to kill or hate any
perfon,
Much lefs ought we to mock either fimple or poor men,
Nor defpife the ftranger which
cometh from far.
For in this World we are all Pilgrims.
Thus all we that are Brethren
ought to ferve God.
And this is the new Law which *Je-*
fus Chrift faith we ought to keep.

And

And he called the Apostles and commanded them

To go through the World, and teach all Nations,

To preach to *Jews* and *Greeks*, and all mankinde,

And he gave them power over Serpents,

To drive away Devils, and heal the sick,

To raise the Dead, and cleanse the Lepers,

And to do to others as he had done to them ;

To possess neither Gold nor Silver,

But to be content with Food and Raiment.

To love one another, and to be at peace.

Then he promised them the heavenly Kingdom,

And to those which were spiritually poor:

But he that should know who they are, would quickly number those,

That would be poor of their own accord ;

Then he told them what should happen,

How he ought to die, and afterward rise again.

And he told them the Signs and Wonders

Which ought to happen before the end.

Many excellent Parables he spoke to them and the People,

Which were written in the *New Testament.*

But if we will love *Christ* , and know his Doctrine,

We ought to watch, and reade the Scripture,

Where we may finde when we shall reade,

That onely for doing well, *Christ* was persecuted ;

E apellé sio Apostol e fey lor commandament

Que anisan per lo mont e ensegnesan la gent ;

Jusios e Grees prediquesan e tota humana gent,

E doné à lor poestà de sobre li serpent,

Gitesan li demoni e sanesan li enferm,

Resucitesan li mort e mondesan li lebros,

E façesan à li autre enayma el havia fayt à lor,

D' or ni d' argent non fossan possessent,

M. au vita e au vestiment a se tenguesan content.

E amesan se entre lor e aguesan bona paç.

Adera lor empromés lo regne celestial,

E aquilli que tenren pauretà spiritual .

M. qui sabrian cal son, illi sarian tost nombra ,

Que vollian esser pauro per propria voluntà ;

De ço que era avenir el lor vay anonciar ,

Cosi el devia murir e poys resucitar .

E lor dis las ensegnas e li demonstrament

Lical devian venir devant lo feniment.

Mot as bellas semblanças dis à lor e à la gent,

Las cals foron scriptas al novel testament.

M. se Xrist volen amar e saber sa dottrina ,

Nos coventa velliar e legir l' escriptura .

Aqui poyren trobar cant nos auren legi ,

Que solament per far ben Xrist fo persegu ;

El

El refu citava li mort per divina ver-
tu,

El façia vefer li cec que unca non ha-
vian viſt,

El mondava li lebros e li ſor façia
auvir,

E gitava li demoni , façent motus
vertus ;

E cant mays façia de ben, mays era
perſegu.

ço eran li fariſio lical lo perſeguian ;

E aquilli del Rey Herode e lautra gent
clerçia :

C. illi havian envidia, C. la gent lo
feguian ;

E car illi creyan en lui e en li fio com-
mandament,

Penferon lui aucire e far moti tor-
ment,

E parleron à Juda e feron li cove-
nent,

Que cel lo lor liorés, el agra 30. ar-
gent.

E Juda fo cubit e fey lo tradiment,

E lioré fon fegnor entre la mala gent,

Li Jufio foron aquilli que lo crucifi-
queron,

Li pè e las mans forment li claveleron,

E corona de ſpinas en teſta li pauſe-
ron,

Diçent li moti repropi illi lo blaſte-
meron ;

El dis quel havia fé, fel e açi liabeo-
reron.

Tant foron li torment amar e doloy-
ros,

Que larma partic del cors per falvar
li peccador.

Lo cors remas aqui pendu lobre en la
croç

El mey de dui laron 4. plagas li van
far fença li autre batement.

He raiſed the Dead by Divine
Power,

He made the blinde to fee, which
never had feen,

He cleanfed the Lepers, and made
the Deaf to hear,

He caſt out Devils, working many
Miracles ;

And by how much the more he did
good, fo much the more was he perfecuted.

The Pharifes were they which perfecuted him ;

And the People of *Herod,* and the
others, *viz.* them of the Clergy :

For they envied him , becaufe he
was followed by the People ;

Becaufe they believed in him and
his Commandments,

They fought how they might torment him and put him to death,

And for this reafon fpoke to *Judas*
and made an agreement with him,

To deliver him for thirty Pieces of
Silver.

Now *Judas* being covetous
wrought the Treafon,

And betrayed his Lord to thofe
wicked men,

The *Jews* were they which crucified him,

Nailing faſt his Feet and his Hands,

And putting a Crown of Thorns
on his Head,

And ſpeaking many Reproaches,
they blafphemed him ;

And when he faid, he was thirſty,
they likewife gave him Gall and Vine-
ger to drink.

The Torments were fo bitter and
painfull,

That the Soul parted from the Body to fave Sinners.

The Body having fuffered this,
hung there upon the Crofs

In the midſt of two Thieves ;
they gave him four Wounds, befides
other Blows.

And

And after that, the fifth, to accomplish the matter ;

For, one of the Souldiers came and opened his Side,

And immediately there issued out Water and Bloud mixed together,

Whereupon all the Apostles fled, but one returned,

And was there with two Women near unto the Cross,

All were very sorry, chiefly his Mother,

When she saw her Son dead and naked, fastened upon the Cross,

He was buried by the good, and watched by the wicked.

He rose out of the Grave the third Day,

And appeared to his Disciples, as he had said unto them ;

Then were they possessed with great joy, when they saw the Lord,

And were confirmed, for before they feared greatly ;

And he conversed with them untill the Day of the Ascension ;

Then our Saviour ascended into Glory,

And said to his Disciples and other Followers,

That to the End of the World he would be with them.

But at the Feast of *Pentecost* he remembred them,

And sent them the Holy Ghost, which is the Comforter,

And taught the Apostles by Divine Doctrine,

And they understood the Languages and the holy Scripture,

And then they remembered what he had said.

They spoke without fear, of the Doctrine of *Christ*,

They preached to *Jews* and *Greeks*, working many Miracles ;

And baptized those who believed in the Name of *Jesus Christ*.

Poys li feron la cinquena per far lo compliment ;

C. un de Cavalier venc e li ubere la costa,

Adonc y fic sanc e ayga ensemp mescla,

Tuit li Apostol fugiron, ma l' un i retorné,

E era aqui au doas monas istant josta la croç,

Grant dolor havian tuit----dena,

Cant illi veya son filli mort e nu e naf asus en la croç,

De li bon so sebeli e gardá de li fellon.

El tray li sio d' enfern e resucité alterç jorn,

E aparec à li sio enayma el havia dit à lor ;

Adonca agron grant goy cant vigron lo Segnor,

E foron conforta que anant havian grant paor ;

E conversé cun lor entro al dia de l' acension ;

Ad. monte en gloria lo nostre Salvador,

E dis à la sio Apostol e à li autre ensegador,

Que entro à la fin del seglen fora tavia au lor.

Mas cant à Pandecosta se recorde de lor,

Et lor tramés lo Sant Sprit local es consolador,

E ensegné li Apostol per divina dotrina,

E saupron li lengaje e la santa Scriptura,

Adonc lor sovenc de ço quel havia dit.

Sença temor parlavan la dotrina de Xrist,

Jusios e Grees predicavan façent motas vertus ;

E li cresent baptejavan al nom de Yeshu Xrist.

Ad.

Ad. ſo fayt vn poble de novel con-
verti ;
Creſtian foron nominà, C. illi creȷan
en Xriſt.

M. ço troben que l' Eſcriptura di,

Mot fort li perſeguian Juſios e Sara-
çins.
M. tant foron fort li Apoſtol en la te-
mor del Segnor,
E li home e las fenas lical eran cun
lor.
Que per lor non layſavan ni lor fayt
ni lor dit,
Tant que moti nauciſſeron enayma illi
havian Yeſhu Criſt.
Grant foron li torment ſegont ques
ſcript,
Solament, C. Monſtravan la via de
Jeſhu Xriſt.
M. aquilli que li perſeguian non era
tant a mal tenir ;
C. illi non havian la fé del noſtre
Segnor Jeſhu Xriſt,
Coma d' aquilli que queron ara cayſon
e que perſegon tant ;
Que Creſtian devon eſſer, ma mal o-
fan ſemblant.
M. enço ſepon repenre aquilli lical
perſegon e confortar li bon ;

C. non ſe troba en neguna leyçon,
Que li ſant perſegueſan nēun ne meſe-
ſan en preſon.
M. en apres li Apoſtol foron li doctor
alcun,
La via de Yeſhu Xriſt monſtravan lo
noſtre Salvador.
M. encara ſe troba alcun en aqueſt
temp preſent,
Lical ſon manifeſt à mot poc de gent,

La via de Yeſhu Xriſt mot fort volri-
an moſtrar,
M. tant ſon perſegu que poc o poyon
far,
Tant ſon li fals e Creſtian enceca per
erro,

Then was there a People new converted ;
They were called *Chriſtians*, for
they believed in *Chriſt*.
But we finde here that the Scripture ſaith,
That the *Jews* and *Saracins* perſe-
cuted them grievouſly.
But the Apoſtles were ſo fortified
in the fear of the Lord,
And the Men and Women which
were with them,
That for all that, they left neither
ſpeaking nor doing,
Whatſoever ſhould come of it, ſo
that they might have *Jeſus Chriſt*.
The Torments were great, accord-
ing to what is written,
Onely becauſe they taught the
way of *Jeſus Chriſt*.
But as for the Perſecutours we need
not ſo much wonder,
For, they had not the Faith of our
Lord *Jeſus Chriſt*,
Like thoſe who now ſeek occaſion
to perſecute the Saints ;
Which men ought to be *Chriſtians*,
but appear not to be ſuch.
And in this they are to be blamed,
for that they perſecute and impriſon
the good ;
For, it is not found any where,
That the Saints perſecuted or im-
priſoned any.
Now after the Apoſtles, were cer-
tain Teachers,
Who taught the way of *Jeſus*
Chriſt our Saviour.
And theſe are found even at this
preſent Day,
But they are known to very few,

Who have a great deſire to teach
the way of *Jeſus Chriſt*,
But they are ſo perſecuted, that
they are able to do but little,
So much are the falſe *Chriſtians*
blinded with Errour,

And

And more than the reft they that are Paftours,

For they perfecute and hate thofe who are better than themfelves,

And let thofe liye quietly who are falfe Deceivers.

But by this we may know that they are not good Paftours,

For they love not the Sheep, but onely for their Fleeces.

The Scripture faith, and it is evident,

That if any man love thofe who are good, he muft needs love God, and *Jefus Chrift.*

Such an one will neither curfe, fwear, nor lye,

He will neither commit Adultery, nor kill; he will neither defraud his Neighbour,

Nor avenge himfelf of his Enemies.

Now fuch an one is termed a *Waldenfian,* and worthy to be punifhed,

And they finde occafion by Lyes and by Deceit,

To take from him that which he has gotten by his juft labour.

However, he that's thus perfecuted for the fear of the Lord, ftrengthens himfelf greatly,

By this confideration, that the Kingdom of Heaven fhall be given him at the end of the World.

Then he fhall have a weight of glory in recompence for all fuch difhonour.

But herein is clearly manifeft the malice of thofe men,

That they which will curfe, lye, and fwear,

He that will frequently put his Money to Ufury, kill, and whore,

And avenge himfelf on thofe which hurt him;

This they fay is a good man, and to be accounted faithfull.

But let him take heed he be not deceived at the end,

E majorment que li autre autre aquilli que fon Paftor,

Que illi perfegon e aucion aquilli que fon mellior,

E layfon viore en paç aquilli que fon fals enganador.

M. *enço fe po conoyffer quilli non fon bon Paftor,*

C. *non fon aman las feas fi non per la toyfon.*

M. *l' Efcriptura di e nos o poen veyr,*

Que fel ama alcun bon quel vollia amar Dio e temer Yefhu Xrift.

Que non vollia maudire ni jurar ni mentir,

Ni avoutrar ni aucire ni penre delautruy,

Ni veniarfe de li fio enemic.

Illi diçon quel es vaudés e degne de punir,

Ban cayfon mençonias en engan,

Cufi illi li poyfan toler ço quel ha de fon juft a fan.

M. *forment fe conforte aquel ques perfegu per la temor del Segnor,*

C. *lo regne de li cel li feré aparellia à lifir d' aqueft mont.*

Ad. *auré grant gloria fel aure agu defonor.*

M. *en ço es mot manifefta la malicia de lor,*

Que aquel que vol maudire e mentir e jurar,

E forment preftar à ufura, e aucire, e avoutrar,

E veniarfe d' aquilli que li fan mal;

Illi diçon que es prodome e leal home recoynta.

M. *à la fin gardefe quel non fia engana,*

Cant

*Cant ven lo mal mortal, la mort lo
cofteng e à pena po parlar,*

E demanda lo prevere fe vol confeffar:

*M. fegont l' Efcriptura el ha trop tarcà
lacal commanda e di,*

*Sane vio te confeffa, non attendra à la
fin ;*
*Lo preverli demanda fi el ha nengun
peccà,*
*Dui mot o tre li refpont e ha toft ena-
vança ;*
*Ben li di lo prever que el non po effer
afot,*
*Sel non rent tot lautruy e efmende ben
fio tort :*
*M. cant el au ayço el ha grant penfa-
ment,*
E penfa entre fi fiel rent entierament,

*Que remanre à fio eyfant, ni que di-
ren la gent ?*
*A fio eyfant commanda quilli eymen
don fio tort,*
*E fay pat a lo prever quel poyffa effer
afot ;*
*Si el ha cent lioras d' autrui e encara
ben dui,*
Car lo prever lo quita per cent foç,

*E tal volta permens cant el non po
haver prus,*
*E fay li amones tanças e li promet
pardon,*
*Quel faça dire mefa per fi e per li fio
payron ;*
*E lor empromet pardon fia à juft o fia
à fellon,*
Ad. fi paufa la man fus la tefta,
*Cant el li layfa prus li mena prus
grant fefta,*
*E fay li entendement quel fia mot ben
afot.*
*M. mal fon eymenda aquilli de qui el
ha agu li tort,*

When he has received the ftroke of
Death, and when Death feizes on
him, and he becomes almoft fpeech-
lefs,
Then he defires the Prieft to confefs him :
But according to the Scriptures he
has delayed too long, for that commands us
To repent while we have time, and
not to put it off till the laft:
The Prieft asketh him if he hath
any fin,
He anfwers two or three words,
and foon has done ;
The Prieft tells him he cannot be
forgiven,
If he do not reftore, and examine
well his Faults :
When he hears this, he's very much
troubled,
And thinks with himfelf, if he reftore intirely,
What fhall he leave his Children,
and what will the World fay ?
Then he commandeth his Children to examine their Faults,
And buyeth of the Prieft his Ab-
folution ;
Though he hath a thoufand Livers
of another and a better Penny, yet
The Prieft acquits him for a hundred Pence,
And fometimes for lefs when he
can get no more,
Telling him a large Story, and promifing him Pardon,
That he'l fay Mafs for him, and for
his Anceftours ;
And thus he pardons them be they
righteous or wicked,
Laying his Hand upon their Heads,
(But when he leaves them, he ma-
keth the better chear)
And telling him that he is very well
abfolved.
But alas they are but fadly confef-
fed who are thus faulty,

And

And will certainly be deceived in fuch an Abfolution,

And he that maketh him believe it finneth mortally.

For, I dare fay, and it is very true,

That all the Popes which have been from *Silvefter* to this prefent,

And all *Cardinals, Bifhops, Abbots,* and the like,

Have no power to abfolve or pardon,

Any creature fo much as one mortal fin;

'Tis God alone who pardons, and no other.

But this ought they to do who are Paftours,

They ought to preach to the People, and pray with them,

And feed them often with divine Doctrine;

And chaftife the Sinners with Difcipline,

Viz. by declaring that they ought to repent.

Firft, that they confefs their fins freely and fully,

And that they repent in this prefent life,

That they faft and gives Alms, and pray with a fervent heart,

For, by thefe things the Soul findes Salvation:

Wherefore we *Chriftians* which have finned

And forfaken the Law of *Jefus Chrift,*

Having neither Fear, Faith, nor Love,

We muft confefs our fins without any delay,

We muft amend with weeping and repentance,

The offences which we have committed, & for thofe three mortal fins,

To wit, for the Luft of the Eye, the Lufts of the Flefh, and the Pride of Life, through which we have done evil;

M. el feré engana en aytal afolvement,

E aquel que o fay creyre y pecca mortalment,

M. yo aufo dire, C. fe troba en ver,

Que tuit li papa que foron de Salveftre en tro en aqueft,

E tuit li Cardinal, e tuit li Vefque, e tuit li Aba, tuit aquefti enfemp,

Non han tant de poeftà de dever afolvar quilli poyfan perdonar

A nenguna creatura pur un pecca mortal;

Solament Dio perdona que autre non o pofar.

M. ayço devon far aquilli que fon Paftor,

Predicar devon lo poble e iftar en orefon,

E payffer lo fovent de divina dotrina;

E caftigar li peccant donant à lor deciplina.

ços uraya amoneftança quilli hayan peniment.

Prumierament fe confeffon fença neun mancament,

E quilli façan penedonça en la vita. prefent.

Junare far almofnas e aurar aucor bullient,

C. per aqueftas cofas troba larma falvament :

D. nos creftianaytios creftians lical haven peccà,

La ley de Yefhu Xrift haven abandona,

C. non haven temor ni fé ni carità,

Confeffar nos coventa non y deven tarcar,

Au plor e au pentiment nos coven fmendar,

L' ofenfa que haven fayta per 3. pecca mortal,

Per cubiticia dolli e per de leyt de carn e per fuperbia de vita, perque haven fayt lo mal;

Aquefta

Aquefta via nos convent tenir.
Si nos volen amar ni fegre Yefhu
Xrift,
Paureta fpiritual de cor dcvcn tenir,

E amar la cafeta, Dio humilment
fervir,
Adonca enfegrian la via de Yefhu
Xrift,
E nayfi vcnccrian li noftre enemic.

Brcoment es recoynta en aquefta léy-
con
De las 3. leys que Dio doné al mont ;

La primiera ley demoftra qui a fen ni
raçon,
çoes à conoyffer Dio e onrar lo fio
Creator.
C. aquel que ha entendement po ben
penfar entre fi,
Que el non fes pas formà ni li autre
at refi :
D. ayçi po conoyffer aqucl que ha fen
ni raçon,
C. lo es un Segnor Dio qué ha formà
tot la mont,
E conoyfent lui mot lo deven hono-
rar ;
C. aqillilli foron dampnà que non o
volgron far.
M. la 2. ley que Dio doné à Moyfent,

Nos enfegna à temor Dio e à fervir
lui forment.
C. el condampnà e punis tot aquel
home que ofent.
Ma la 3. ley lacal es ara al temp pre-
fent,
Nos enfegna amar Dio del cor e fer-
vir purament :
C. atent lo peccador eli dona alonga-
ment,
Quel poyfa far penedenca en la vita
prefent.
L'autra ley dequienant prus non
deven haver,

We muft keep this way.
If we will love and follow *Jefus*
Chrift,
We muft have fpiritual poverty of
heart,
And love Chaftity, and ferve God
humbly,
For, fo we may follow the way of
Jefus Chrift,
And thus we may overcome our
Enemies.
There is a brief Rehearfal in this
Leffon,
Of three Laws which God gave to
the World ;
The firft Law directeth men who
have judgment and reafon,
Viz. to know God, and to pray to
his Creatour.
For he that hath judgment, may
well think with himfelf,
That he formed not himfelf, nor
any thing elfe :
Then here he who hath judg-
ment and reafon may know,
That there's one Lord God who
created all the World,
And knowing him, he ought much
to honour him ;
For, they were damned that would
not do it.
The fecond Law which God gave
to *Mofes,*
Teacheth us to fear God, and to
ferve him with all our ftrength ;
For he condemneth and punifheth
every one that offends.
But the third Law which is at this
prefent time,
Teacheth us to love God, and ferve
him purely :
For he waiteth for the Sinner, and
giveth him time,
That he may repent in this prefent
life.
As for any other Law to come after
we fhall have none.

Save

Save onely to imitate *Jesus Christ,* and to do his will,

And keep faft that which he commands us,

And to be well forewarned when *Antichrist* fhall come.

That we may believe neither to his words nor to his works,

Now according to the Scripture, there are already many *Antichrists.*

For, all thofe which are contrary to *Chrift,* are *Antichrists.*

Many Signs and great Wonders Shall be from this time forward untill the Day of Judgment,

The Heaven and the Earth fhall burn, and all the Living die.

After which all fhall arife to everlafting Life,

And all Buildings fhall be laid flat.

Then fhall be the laft Judgment,

When God fhall feparate his People, according as its written,

To the wicked he fhall fay, *Depart ye from me into Hell Fire, which never fhall be quenched;*

With grievous Punifhments there to be ftraitened;

By multitude of Pains, and fharp torment:

For you fhall be damned without remedy.

From which God deliver us, if it be his blefled will,

And give us to hear that which he fhall fay to his Elect without delay;

Come hither ye blefled of my Father,

Inherit the Kingdom prepared for you from the beginning of the World,

Where you fhall have Pleafure, Riches and Honour.

May it pleafe the Lord which formed the World,

That we may be of the number of his Elect to dwell in his Court for ever.

Praifed be God. *Amen.*

M. enfegro Yefhu Xrift e far li fio plaçer,

E gardar fermament ço quel ha commandà,

E efler mot avisà cant venré lente Xrift.

Que nos non crean à fon fayt ni à fon dit,

M. fegont l' Efcriptura ara fon moto Ante Xrift.

C. Ante Xrift fon tuit aquilli que contrarian à Xrift.

Motas enfegnas e grant demonftrament Saren dos aqueft temp entro al dia del jujament,

Lo cel e la terra ardren e murren tuit li vivent.

Poys refucitaren tuit en vita permanent,

E feren aplana tuit li hodificament,

Ad. feré fayt lo derier jujament,

Dio pardre lo fio poble fegont que es fcript,

Ali mal diré departé vos demi,

Ana el fuoc enfernal que mays non auré fin;

Per 3. greos condicions feré coftreyt aqui;

Per moteça de renas e per afpre torment:

E car feré dapnà fença defalhiment.

D' aqui nos garde Dio per lo fio placement,

E nos done auvir ço quel dire à la foa gent e nant quel tarçe gayre,

Cant el diré venevofen au mi beneyt del mio payre,

E poffefire lo regne local es aparellia à vos del commançament del mont,

Al cal luoc auré deleyt e riqueças e honor.

Praça aquel Segnor que formé lo mont,

Que nos fian de fi eyleyt per iftar en fa cort.

Dio gracias. Amen.

A Trea-

A Treatise concerning the fear of the Lord.

De la temor del Segnor.

LA temor del Segnor degieta li pecca. *Per la temor del Segnor naysson moti ben. Dont di Salomon, la temor del Segnor es commençament de sapiencia. E dereço di, l' ome es benaura local es totavia temeros. Car per la temor del Segnor las armas son deilioras de las penas d' enfern. E per la temor del Segnor son atroba li goy de paradis. Car l' amor de Dio & del proyme es carita. E aquel qu' a carita el a Dio. E aquel local ha Dio el se depart de las cosas mondanas, e aquel qu' ama Dio el tem las penas d' enfern, e desira li goy de paradis, en lieals el espera de pervenir, en licals el espera de permanir. En lical non es temor de la mort, ni temor de li enemic. A qui es vita sença mort. Donca per l' amor de Dio & del proyme es aquista vita eterna. E S. Paul di, l' amor de Dio & del proyme non hobra mal. E aquel que fare aquestas cosas non di trecorare en pecca. Ma aquel que s' enclina a las cosas temporals el se delogna de l' amor de Dio. Car las riqueças non pon esser aquistas sença peca en aquest mont. Car se l' un non pert, l' autre non po gagnar, & aquel local gagna s' a legra, e aquel local pert se contrista. Ma moti son lical esperan de far almosna de la sudor de li autre. E despollian l' un, e vierton l' autre. Ma l' amosna faita con enequita es desprecia derant Dio. Dont di Sant Au-*

Of the Fear of the Lord.

THe fear of the Lord drives away sin. By the fear of the Lord is procured much good. As *Solomon* saith, *The fear of the Lord is the beginning of wisdom.* And again, *Happy is the man that always thus fears.* For by the fear of the Lord his Soul is delivered from the pains of Hell, and by the fear of the Lord he findes the joys of Heaven. The Love of God and of our Neighbour, is Charity; and he that has Charity, is of God; and he that is of God, is weaned from the things of this World: and he which loves God, fears the Pains of Hell, and thirsts after the Joys of Heaven, of which he hopes to have the fruition, and wherein he hopes to live, where there is no fear of Death, or of Enemies, and where there is Life without Death; wherefore through the Love of God, and of our Neighbour is obtained eternal Life. And St. *Paul* saith, that the Love of God and of our Neighbour, works no evil. And he that shall do those things, shall never fall. Whereas he that lets his heart run after temporal things, departs from the Love of God. For Riches cannot be heaped up in this world without sin, because what one gaineth another loseth; and where the Gainer rejoyceth, the Loser is made sad. Now there are many who hope to give Alms out of the Sweat of other mens Brows, stripping one to cloath another, but such Alms-deeds are not at all acceptable before God, according-

ing

ing to that of St. *Auguſtin*, *Thoſe Alms are well-pleaſing to God, which are given out of a mans own ſubſtance, and are not the Fruits of Rapine and Uſury:* For, that Charity which proceeds from Rapine and Uſury, is not a Work of Mercy, but a fomenting and cheriſhing of ſin. O Brethren, what ſhall we ſay of theſe rich men that *heap up Riches, and know not for whom they have gathered them?* While they compaſs earthly things, they loſe the heavenly: and in gaining the World, loſe their own Souls. How many are there who think they are in the Light, and yet are compaſſed about with Darkneſs? O blinde Covetouſneſs, which divides the Soul from *Chriſt*, and joyns it to the Devil! juſt as that Rich man, who *fared deliciouſly every day!* O miſerable Rich men, why are ye not afraid and diſmayed? ye that covet ſublunary, and loſe celeſtial Treaſures? according to that of St. *James*, *Go to now ye Rich men! weep and howl for the Miſeries that are coming upon you!* Wo be to ſuch! for a Lover of Wealth ſhall finde no Mercy, and the covetous man who never ſays it is enough, is like unto Hell it ſelf, which look how much the more it hath ſo much the more it ſtill deſires; Now wo be to them who ſhall thus be ſwallowed up by the infernal Pit! who while they have time and opportunity, will not repent and amend their Lives; therefore when Death ſhall come and ſeize on them, they ſhall leave all their Power and Riches behinde them in this World; and onely their miſerable Souls ſhall depart into Hell Torments. Even as our Saviour ſays in the Goſpel, that *It is* (not onely hard, but) *impoſsible for him that truſts in his Riches, to enter into the Kingdom of God.* And the Apoſtle ſaith, that *Covetouſneſs* (or the Love of Money) *is the Root of all evil.* It was a Saying of St. *Gregory*,

guſtin, *aqueſta almoſna play à Dio lacal es faita de la propria ſoſtancia, e non de rapina, ni d'uſura. Car far almoſna de rapina ho d' uſura non es hobra de miſericordia. Ma es nutriment de peca. O frayre cal coſa diren nos da quilli ric lical traſorrion, e meſconoyſon a qui illi o aquiſtan, illi aquiſtan las coſas terrenals, e perdon las celeſtials, illi aquiſtan las riqueças, e perdon las lors armas. Car moti ſon lical penſan eſſer en lumena, e ſon en tenebras. O ceca cubiticia lacal departes las armas de Chriſt, e las aioſtas al diavol. En ayma aquel ric local maniava per caſcun dia reſplandiamment, ho miſerios rics perque non vos eſpavanta vos, lical cubitan las coſas terrenals, e perdon las celeſtials. Dont di Sant Jaco, ho ric faça ara plora udola las voſtras miſerias las cals ſeren faitas a vos. Malaventura a quilli tal. Car l' avar non a miſericordia. E lo cubitos es ſemblant à l' enfern. Car l' enfern entant cant el devora plus entant el cubita plus: en ayſi l' avar non es unca ſavia. E malaventura à quilli tal lical l' enfern tranglutire, lical demeſtre qu' illi an temp, e ſon en la lor poyſança illi non volun far penitença, e non ſe volon eymendar. Ma cant la mort venre adonca la lor poyſança, e las lors riqueças remanren al mont. E la ſola arma miſererioſa anare a las penas d' enfern. En ayma di lo Segnor en l' avangeli, lo es greo coſa, e non poderoſa li permanent en las riqueças intrar al regne de Dio. E l' Apoſtol di, cubiticia es reis de tuit li mal. Dont di Sant Gregory, lo ſuperbios,*

e l' avar

e l' avar non pon esser atroba sença su-
perbia. Car alcuna cosa non val non
aver las riqueças, si la volontà es de
posesir. Donca nos non deven desirar
las cosas terrenals. Car aquelas cosas
que son vistas perison, & aquellas que
son desobre permanon en eterna. Car lo
miserios pecador ha vergogna de confessar sio peca, e non tem de rendre raçon
denant la eternal juje al jorn del general giudici. Car adonca non sere
solament en cerca de li greo peca. Ma
neys de las cogitacions, e de las parollas
auciosas. E adonca non sere luoc al cal
li peccador se poysan rescondre. Adonca
li peccador diren à las montagnas chaje
sobre nos. Emperço nos nos deven gardar de la cubiticia, e de l' avaricia,
e non tresoruar en aquest mont. En ayma
di lo Segnor en Sant Mathio, non volhi
tresoruar à vos trasor en terra al cal luoc
ruilli, e camolas lo degastan. E dereço
es dit, cal cosa profeita a l' ome si el
gagna tot lo mont, e sufre destruyment
à la soa arma. E Sant Jerome di, que
si tuit li parent d' alcun home, local fo
danna, donesan totas las cosas las cals
son al mont illi non poyrian deiliorar
luy. Car en enfern non a alcuna reden-
sion. E Sant Johan di, non vollia amar
lo mont, ni aquellas cosas lascals son del
mont, si alcun ama lo mont la carità
del paire non es en luy. Car tot ço qu' es
al mont es cubiticia de olli, e cubiticia de
carn, e soperbia de vita, lacal non es
del paire, ma es del mont. Emperço
regarden nos meseyme, e pensen en cal
luoc son li Rey, en cal luoc son li Princy,
en cal luoc son li Poderos. Anc illi vengron de tánta poysança, e alegreça en

that *the covetous and proud man were
never found without pride and covetousness.* The truth is, it matters not at
all that a man is poor, if so be that his
minde be carried out with a desire to
possess. Wherefore we ought not so
much as to desire worldly things, since
*those things which are seen, are but tem-
poral, and those things which are not
seen, are eternal.* The miserable Sinner
is ashamed to confess his sin, but is not
afraid of giving an account before the
eternal Judg at the great Day of Judgment, where they must not onely give
an account of their more crying sins,
but also of their *very thoughts, and idle
words:* and then there will be no place
found for Sinners where to hide themselves! *Then shall they say to the Mountains, Fall on us.* For this reason we
ought to beware of Covetousness
and Avarice, and of *heaping up to our
selves Treasures in this World*; It is our
Saviour's counsel in the Gospel of St.
*Matthew, Lay not up for your selves
Treasures upon Earth, where the Moth
and the Rust corrupt.* And again he
saith, *What will it profit a man to gain
the whole World, and lose his own Soul?*
And St. *Jerome* saith, that *if all the
friends or kinred of a damned Soul should
give all that they have in the World, they
could not possibly redeem his Soul.* For in
the infernal Pit there is no Redemption. And therefore St. *John* counselleth
us *not to love the World, nor the things of
the World,* and saith, that *if any man do
love the World, the Love of the Father
is not in him:* for, *whatsoever is in the
World consists either in the Lust of the
Eye, the Lust of the Flesh, or the Pride
of Life, which is not of the Father, but
of the World.* This should cause us to
consider our selves, and to consider
where the Kings, Princes, and Potentates of the Earth now are, how they
have miserably fallen from so great a
heigth of Power and jollity into such

an

an extremity of misery and anguish, from so great riches to so great poverty, from such fulness to so much want, from so sweet pleasures to such a degree of sadness, from so short a life to so long a death, from so little a measure of health to so continued a sickness, from so little enjoyment of light to so long a night of darkness and obscurity: thus all those who are acquainted with *the Riches of this world, fall into temptations, and the snares of the Devil, into many vain and hurtfull Lusts,* which draw the Soul unto destruction and perdition. And St. *Augustin* says, that *the Lust or Concupiscence of a Man cannot be satisfied, and that it hath no bounds nor measure*; wherefore it is said, O thou covetous man, thou hast no spiritual eye to see Heaven, nor hast thou any heart to know God. And *by the hardness of thy heart thou treasurest up wrath unto the day of judgment,* (or *wrath.*) Wherefore let us not covet after earthly, but after heavenly things, and let us set our Love upon *Christ.* For the Love of Man bringeth Sorrow, but the Love of *Christ* quencheth the Fire of Hell, and expells the Love of the World. Let us not then do our own will, but the will of him who came down from Heaven, and said, *I am not come to do mine own will, but the will of him that sent me.* And again, *Thy will be done.* But there are many who are apt to say, I am yet young, and cannot break or bridle my will, but when I am older, then I will repent. Alas, this is to speak like a Fool, for the miserable wretch knows not whether he shall live till the morrow, and yet he thinks to live many years, yea till he reach old age. But what if the young man be constrained to depart this Life, for this Life is short, and this shortness is uncertain? When we rise in the Morning, we know not whether ever we

tanta *miseria,* e *angustia, de tantas riqueças en tanta pauretà, de tanta faciota en tant grant fam, de tanti daleit en tant longa tristicia, de tant poc de vita tant longa mort, de tant poc de fanità tant longa enfermetà, de tant poc de lume tant longas tenebras. Emperço tuit li ome lioal conoyson las riqueças d'aquest mont chayon en las tentations, e en li las del diavol, en moti desirier non profeytivol, ma noysivol, lical tiran las armas à destruyment, e à perdicion. E Sant Augustin di, que la cubiticia de l'ome non po esser façia, e non a alcuna mesura. Emperço es dit, O avar tu non as olli spiritual à veir lo cel, ni non as lo cor à conoiser Dio. E segont la dureça del tio cor tu trasoruares à tu l'ira de Dio al jorn del judici. Emperço non cubitan las cofas terrenals, ma desiren las celestials, e pausan la nostra amor à Christ. Car l'amor de l'ome amena à dolor, ma l'amor de Christ amorta lo fuoc de l'enfern, e degieta l'amor terrenal. Donca non vollian far la nostra volunta, ma la volunta d'aquel que descende del cel. E dis, yo non vine far la mia volunta, ma la volunta de luy local trames my. E dereço di, la toa volunta sia faita. Ma moti son lical difon, yo foy encara jove, e non pois rompre la mia volunta, ma cant serey velli adonca farey penedença. Anc aquest es un fol parlar. Car lo paure miserios mesconois si el viore entro à landeman, e pensa si viore moti ans, e pensa si viore entro à la vellieça. Fasia ço que lo jove sia costreyt de isir d'aquesta vita. Car aquesta vita es breo, e aquella brevetà es non certana. Car cant nos leven de matin nos mesconoisen*

si

*fi nos perveren entro al vefpre. E de-
reço autre fon lical dicon li noftre vifqueron, e non feron penitencia, bafta
a nos fi nos façen en ayma illi feron.
Jo volli vifitar las mias cofas dementre
que yo vivo. Car dura cofa es à my de
departir las mias cofas à i paure. O
home fol local diçes aqueftas cofas,
perque non regardas tu, Car li tio pairon lical vifqueron ya non fon. E cal
cofa profcita à lor las riqueças lafcals
illi agron, o qual profeit fereon à la
lors armas aquelas cofas qu' illi garderon à li lor aretiers. E fi tu regardas
aquelas cofas lafcals tu laifas, perque
non regardas tu aquelas cofas lafcals
tu perdes. Car cal cofa es à tu plus
d' aver la toa arma, o lo tio filli, local
fere à tu eftrag en apres la mort. Anc
aquel vio malament local fe depart de
la mifericordia de Dio, ya fia ço que el
mefeyme fia piatos, e patient, e mifericordios, e efpera que nos nos fmen-
dan. Car el non dona folament lo perdon ey repentent, Ma neys empromet à
lor lo guiardon, e ey perfeveran el dona
la corona. Nos aven eyfemple al leiron
local fo converti à la cros, e a qui aque-
fte d' anvir, yo dic verament à tu. Car
tu feres en coy cun my en paradis. Emperço aquel es benaura local es totavia
aparellia. Car lo Segnor venre en l' ora
lacal nos mefconoifen. Donca auren dementre que nos aven temp. E non nos
vollian deleitar en aqueft mont qu' es
plen d' enequità, al cal la noftra vita
es plena de tentacions. Donca dementre
que nos aven temp façan penedença.
Car la noftra vita es breo. E fugen
l' enemic non vefible, e coren à la fo-*

fhall live to fee the Evening. Again, there be others who-fay, Our fore-fathers have lived and never repented, it is fufficient to do as they have done before us. For my part I am refolved to enjoy what I have, as long as I live, for 'tis too hard for me to part with my Goods, and give them to the Poor. O foolifh man that thou art, who pleadeft thus! Wherefore doft thou not better confider? Thy Fathers indeed have lived, but now they are no more; and what do thofe Riches profit them which they fo greedily heaped up together? or what doth all their Subftance which they left to their Children, now avail them? And if thou haft regard to thofe things which thou leaveft behinde thee, why doft thou not regard thofe things which thou lofeft? Which hadft thou rather preferve, thy Soul or thy Son, who will become a ftranger to thee after Death? So then, he leads a wicked Life, who thus departs from Gods Mercy, although he be in his own perfon never fo meek, patient, and mercifull, and hopes to repent and amend: for, God doth not onely pardon thofe who repent, but alfo promifeth them to be their Guardian; and to thofe who perfevere, and hold on to the end, a Crown of Life. We have an Example in the *Thief*, who became converted even when he was *upon the Crofs*, and had his Petition granted him, with a *Verily I fay unto thee, This day fhalt thou be with me in Paradife.* Wherefore happy is he that is always in readinefs, for *the Lord will come in an hour that we are not aware of.* Let us pray while we have time, and not delight our felves in this World which is full of iniquity, and wherein our Life is full of temptations. I fay, Let us repent while we have time, for as much as our Life is but fhort; as likewife let us fhun our vifible Enemies, and
have

have recourfe to the fovereign City of God which ought to be our Sanctuary. He it is *who hath redeemed us by his own Bloud,* and whom we ought therefore to love above all things, and to keep his Commandments. But this thing ought not to be neglected by us, which the Lord *Jefus* hath fhewed by the holy Scriptures. For, the End of this World draws nigh and I truft the coming of the Lord is at hand, when he fhall come to judg all the World with Fire, and all things that are here before our Eys. For, we know that at the laft Day, when the fins of men are come to their full height, then fhall *Fire go forth from the Lord* and burn up all things which are found in the World; and then all the glory of this World fhall vanifh and turn to nothing by reafon of the fin of man. Then our Lord *Jefus Chrift,* and all the Angels of Heaven with him fhall come to Judgment in the *Valley of Jehofaphat*; and all Nations fhall be affembled before him, and they fhall be feparated the one from the other, as the Shepherd feparates the Sheep from the Goats. Wherefore it is faid in the *Revelation,* that *the days fhall come, when the wicked fhall call and cry for death, and fhall defire to die and fhall not be able, for, death fhall fly from them.* And that golden mouth'd St. *John* fays, that *the Lord has prepared a Kingdom for thofe* who fhall refift fin, and attain unto Grace, but for thofe which fhall not repent, are prepared the Pains & Fire of Hell.

beyrana città de *Dio,* local deo effer lo noftre refugery. Car el rens nos del fio propi fanc. E nos lo deven amar fobre totas cofas, e deven gardar li commandament de luy. Ma aquefta cofa non deo effer refconduo de nos, lacal lo noftre Segnor *Jefu Chrift* a demoftra per las fayntas Scripturas. Car la fin d'aqueft mont s'apropia, e yo fpero que l'avenament del Segnor fia pres, qu'el vegna jujar tot lo mot per fuoc, e totas las cofas que fon al regardament de li olli. Car nos faben que un dereiran jorn cant li pecca de li ome feren compli; Adonca fuoc ifire del Segnor, e ardre totas las cofas que fon al mont. E la gloria d'aqueft mont retornare à nient per li pecca de li home. E adonca lo noftre Segnor *Jefu Chrift* al judici en la val de *Jufafat,* e tuit li Angeli de Paradis cun luy, e totas las gent feren aiofta denant luy, e departire lor l'un de l'autre en ayma lo paftor depart las feas de li bouc. Dont lo es dit en l'*Apocalis,* qu'un jorn venre al cal li peccador apelaren la mort. Car illi volrian murir, ma illi non poiren, car la mort fugire de lor. E Sant *Johan* boca d'or di, que lo Segnor a aparellia lo fio regne à qu'illi que contrafteron à li pecca, e monteron à las virtus: ma à qu'illi que non volgron far penedença es aparellia la pena, e lo fuoc de l'enfern.

A Treatife

A Treatife of Tribulations.

De las Tribulacions.

MOtas *fon las tribulations de li juft. Ma lo Segnor deyliorare lor de totas. E Sant Paul di, per motas tribulacions coventa nos intrar al regne de Dio, e qui non aure part a las tribulacions non aure part à las confolacions. E lo Segnor di l' avangeli, ama li voftre enemic , e façe ben aquilli lical eyreron vos. E Auguftinus di, entant cant lo tio enemic te noyre entant plus deves luy amar. C. per aytal amor tu poyres aver vita eterna. C. fi lo mal home te volre noyre denant qu' el te aya fait lo mal el fere nafra al fio cor, e tot lo mal local el vollia far à tu retornare fobre luy. E fi lo fellon te tol ton aver per la foa felonia, e al pert plus tu local perdes lo tio aver, O luy local pert la foa arma. Aquilli que veon cun li olli del cor conoyfon la danacion de l' arma. Moti fon lical an li olli à conoyfer l' or, e l' argent. Ma illi non an olli à conoyfa la danacion de la lor arma. Lo Segnor conforta li bon home diçent ; Non vollia temer aquilli lical aucion lo cors. Ma non pon aùcir l' arma. Tuit aquilli lical contraftan à vos, forfeuan, C. illi non veon ni fe conoyfon , Ma fan en ayma fi alcun forfena tenia lo glay en la man , e talliava la gonella de l' autre, e en apres fe feria*

Of Tribulations.

MAny *are the Afflictions of the Righteous, but the Lord will deliver them out of all*; and St. *Paul* faith, that *through many Tribulations we muft enter into the Kingdom of God*; and whofoever has not his fhare of Perfecutions, fhall not be Partaker of the Confolations. Our blefled Saviour faith in the Gofpel, *Love your Enemies, and do good to them that hate you*; and St. *Auguftin* faith, *The more thine Enemy hurts thee, the more thou oughteft to love him, for, in fo doing thou fhalt inherit eternal Life.* For, the wicked even when he feeks to do thee harm, his Confcience accufes him before the Action, fo that all the evil and mifchief he devifeth againft thee, returns upon his own head. And if a Thief robs thee, and takes away thy Eftate from thee, he hath the greater lofs of the two, for, alas, he lofeth his own Soul. Thofe which fee with the Eys of the heart, they both know and fear the Damnation of their Souls. There are many men who are quick fighted enough to difcern Gold and Silver, but have no Eys to difcern the Damnation of their own Souls. The Lord comforts the Righteous when he bids them, *not to fear thofe who can kill the Body onely, but cannot hurt the Soul.* Our Adverfaries are doubtlefs bereaved of fenfe, who neither fee nor know themfelves, but do juft like a mad man, who having a naked Sword in his hand, firft cuts off the Lap of his Neighbours Garment, and then

fheaths

sheaths it in his own bowels. For as the Coat is the Vesture of the Body, so is the Body properly the Vesture of the Soul. And if a just man endure Persecution in this World for the Love of God, his Reward shall be eternal in that which is to come. Consider what the Lord suffered for thee, and how loth thou wouldst be to suffer (wert thou able) for his sake, what he has sustained for thee. Thou wouldest be loth to hang on such a Cross, as that on which the Lord was hung and crucified for thy sins. Think not that thine Enemy has any power over thee, but what God gives him; do not therefore so much minde what power God gives to wicked men, as what Reward he has promised to give thee. *O Beloved, we now see that we are the Children of God, although it doth not yet appear what we shall be hereafter: we know that when he shall appear, we shall be like unto him, for, we shall behold him as he is.* Christ is our Life, strive then to imitate *Christ*. *Christ* came into the World to suffer Martyrdom, and was afterwards exalted. *Christ* suffered Death for us, and rose again, as thou expectest to do; and if the work frighten thee, look upon the Recompence which God promises to give thee. How dost thou think to obtain the Joys of Heaven without labour and travel, seeing thou canst not have any earthly joy without some pain? *All that will live godly in* Jesus Christ *must suffer Persecution,* and shall be both despised and vilified, as if they were mad men, or fools. That Man or Woman hath no desire to be a Member of *Christ*'s Body, that is not willing to suffer that which God himself hath endured. He that will not bear the Yoke in this World, shall never come where God is. Pray not then onely for thine Enemy who persecutes thee, but even

al ventre. C. *en ayma la gonella es vistimenta del cors en ayssi lo cors es vistimenta de l' arma.* E *si l' ome just sufrire alcuna cosa de mal en aquest segle per l' amor de Dio lo sio guiardon durare sença fin. Regarda li mal lical lo Segnor a sostenga per tu. Tu non sufririas ya tanti mal per l' amor de Dio canti lo Segnor a sostenga per ta. Tu non sere ya pausa en eytal croç coma so pausa lo Segnor. Non vollias creyre que lo tio enemic aya posta sobre tu, sinon aquela lacal Dio autreya.* D. *non pensar la posta que Dio autreya à li mal home. Ma pensa lo guiardon que Dio promet à tu. Auvas cal cosa di l' Escriptura cal es lo guiardon local Dio promet à tu. O carissime nos sen ara filli de Dio encara non apares à nos cal cosa seren, nos saben que cum el apparessire nos seren semblant à luy.* C. *nos veyren luy en ayma el es.* Christ *es la nostra vita.* D. *sforçate de far en ayma fey* Christ. Christ *vene en aquest mont sofrir martiry, e en apres so eysqueta.* Christ *so pasiona per nos, e resucite en ayma tu deves far.* E *si l' obra t' espavanta regarda la macy que Dio te promet. En cal maniera pensas aver li goy del paradis sença lavor.* C. *tu non poç aver lo goy d' aquest mont sença pena. Tuit aquilli que volren viore bonament en* Jesus Christ *sufriren persegecion, e seren despreçia, e vil tengu en ayma forsena, e sença sen. Aquel non vol esser membre del cors de* Christ *local non vole sostenir ço que Dio sostene. Aquel que non vol sufrir lo di d' aquest mont non anare lay ont es Dio. Non pregar tant solament per tio enemic local te fay mal. Ma per tuit aquilli que aman lo mont.* C. *em-*

perço

perço fon mal. *C.* illi aman lo mont, e aqui ont illi penfan que fia lor vita es lor mort. E aqui ont illi fe penfan que fia lor falu es lor perdicion. Emperço las obras de li bon fon reprefas que ellas fian provas. *C.* fi tu fias repres de las toas bonas obras la toa marcy non es amerma. Ma creis. Ma fi tu laifas las toas bonas obras cant tu fies repres femblant es que tu las comencies per la laufor del fegle. Aquel que comença bonas obras per la laufor d' aqueft fegle las layfa viaçament cant el es repres. En cal maniera pos tu tenir li commandament de Dio fi tu non as enemic. *C.* lo Segnor di en l' avangeli, ama li voftra enemic. Ayçi fe po entendre que la coventa que li mal fian cun li bon. *C.* en ayma lo fuoc prova l' or en ayfi li mal provan li bon. Ly bon home fon en ayma l' or, e li mal home en ayma la pallia. Si tu feres mal tu feres mes al fuoc en ayma la pallia, e feres fum. Dont di lo propheta fuoc ardre las compagnias de li peccador. E Sant Paul di yo non penfo que las pafsions d' aqueft temps non fian enfemp dignas à la gloria avenadoira lacal es à revelar à nos. E Sant Auguftinus di, cal es aquefta gloria lacal fere revela à nos fi non que li juft fon filli de Dio, e fon eygal à li Angel. *D.* lo mont fermiffa ara, lo mont forfene ara, e detraya cun la lenga, ara perfega nos cun glay, ara dia à nos tot

for all thofe which love the World, for, therefore are they wicked, becaufe they love the World, and think to finde Life and Profperity, whereas on the contrary Death and Deftruction waits for them. Therefore are the Works of the Righteous reprehended; to the end they may be approved of, for, if thou fuffereft for thy good Works, thy Reward is not at all thereby leffened, but rather augmented. But if when thou art rebuked for doing good, thou doft thereupon defift, thou thereby makeft it appear that thy doing good was meerly to have praife of the World. He that begins to do well that fo he may get praife of the World, quickly gives it over when once Perfecution comes. How canft thou keep Gods Commandments, if thou haft no Enemies, for, the Lord faith in the Gofpel, *Love 'your Enemies.* By this it may be underftood, that it is neceffary there fhould be fome wicked perfons among the Righteous, for, as Fire is a means to try and refineGold from the Drofs, fo likewife wicked men ferve to try and prove the Righteous. Good Men are compared to pure Gold, and the Wicked to Stubble: therefore if thou art wicked, thou fhalt furely be burnt like the Stubble, and fhalt become as Smoak: as the Prophet fpeaks, *The fire fhall devour the bands of wicked men.* St. Paul tells us that *he accounts not all the fufferings of this prefent world, worthy to be compared with the glory which is to come, and which fhall be revealed in us.* And St. *Auguftin* fpeaking of this glory which fhall be revealed, fays, that *the Righteous are the Children of God, and fhall be like unto the Angels in glory.* Therefore let now the World be never fo mad, and never fo enraged againft us, and defame us with their tongues, let the ungodly now purfue us with naked Swords in
their

their hands ; let them now breath out all the evil they can against us, since that all the hurt they can do us, is but little in comparison of the Reward which God has laid up for us. He that kills thy Body, is not able to kill thy Soul, but rather serves as an Instrument to greaten thy Reward : Pray therefore for him, that so thy Reward be not the less. We ought for the Love of God to despise whatsoever seems to delight us most, yea not onely that which affords us delight, but likewise that which may terrifie and affright us, as prison, bonds, poverty, hunger, cold, sword, and even death it self. Thou must (I say) despise and lightly esteem all these ; and if thou art able to overcome all, then thou hast God to be thy Reward. Think how great would be thy fear, wert thou shut up close in Prison. Why then livest thou wickedly, knowing that for so doing thou must be one day a close Prisoner in Hell ? He that can kill thy Body cannot kill thy Soul, but thou mayst soon kill thine own Soul with thy Tongue, for the Tongue that speaks Lyes is said to kill the Soul. Let us consider then what things we ought, and what things we ought not to fear. He's worthy to be counted a Mad man that fears a Prison in this World, which soon hath an end, and in the mean time dreads not to go to Hell, where he must suffer perpetual Imprisonment. That man's void of Reason, that fears the Kings, Princes, and Prelates of this World, and yet dreads not to fall into the clutches of the Devils in Hell. I say, he's a very Mad man who fears the Death of this World, which is but transitory, and does not tremble at the very thoughts of Death infernal, which lasteth for ever ; who would ever purchase so long a Death for so short a Life ? so long a Mourning for so short a Mirth ?

lo mal local el po dire per parolla. C. tot lo mal local el po far à nos es petit à comparacion dal guiardon local Dio promet à nos. Aquel que auçi lo tio cors non po aucir la toa arma, Ma acoyta lo tio guiardon, e tu prega per luy que lo tio guiardon non defallia. Nos deven despreçiar per l' amor de Dio tot ço que nos deleyta en aquest segle. E non solament ço que deleita. Ma encara ço que nos spavanta. En ayma es carcer, liam paureta, fam, frit, glay, mort. Tu deves despreçiar, e tenir vil totas aquestas cosas. E si tu poç vençer totas aquestas cosas tu as atroba Dio. Pensa cant grant paur tu aurias qui metria tu en una grant preison. D. perque vives malament que tu sies mes en la preison de l' enfern ? Aquel que auci lo tio cors non po aucir la toa arma, e tu poç aucir la toa arma cun la toa lenga. C. la boca que ment auci l' arma. D. pensan cal cosa nos deven temir, e cal cosa non. Fol es aquel que tem la carcer d' aquest segle, lacal trapassa viaçament, e non tem la carcer d' enfern lacal durare eternalment. Fol es aquel que tem la carcer d' aquest segle lacal trapassa viaçament e non tem la carcer d'enfern, lacal durare eternalment. Fol es aquel que tem li rey, e li princi, e li prelat d'aquest mont, e non tem li demoni de l' enfern. Fol es aquel que tem la mort d' aquest segle lacal trapassare viaçament. e non tem la mort enfernal lacal permanre perpetualment. Per tant petita vita tant longa mort, per tant petit joy tant longa iristicia, per tant petit lume,

*tant grant tenebras, per tant petit ris
tant grant plor , e tant amaras lagri-
mas lafcals li peccador fufriren en
l' autre fegle, de lafcals di lo Segnor.
Malaventura à vos lical rye . C. vos
plorare , e plagnire , per tant petita
beleça tant grant. foçura, per tant petita fortaleça tant grant frevoleça, per
tant petita fegurita tant grant paur,
de lacal di Sant Auguftinus., vana
paur es temer perdre las cofas temporals, e non temer perdre las celeftials.
Vana paur es qui tem perdre la compagnia del paire, e de la maire, e non
tem perdre la compagnia de Dio, e de
la vergena Maria . Vana paur es qui
tem perdre la compagnia de li fraire,
e de las ferors, e non tem perdre la
fraireça de li Angle. De lacal di Sant
Fohan en l' Apocalis cant el volia aurar luy. Veias non fares. C. yo foy lo
tio eygal ferf, e de li tio fraire lical
an lo teftimoni de Fefus, aura Dio. Tu
local temes la toa mort, ama la toa vita, la toa vita es lo Sant Sperit, fi tu
peccas tu non plaçes à Dio . L' ome
juft es franc tant folament non l' autre.
L' eyfant cant el nays derant plora
qu' el non ry, las lacrimas las cals el
gieta portant teftimoni à luy qu' el ven
en la miferia d' aqueft mont. En ayfy
l' eyfant es propheta de li fio lavor. Si
l' ome juft viore el fufrire perfeguecion.
Car li mal home perfegon li bon, non
totavia cun ferre, ni cun peiras ni cun
bafton . Ma cun la lor mala vita, e
cun lor malas obras. Emperço Sant
Peyre lauve la vita de Loth. C. el avia*

fo long and fo great a Darknefs, for
fo fmall and fhort a Light? for fo fhort
a Laughter, fuch bitter weepings and
wailings as the wicked fhall fuffer in
the World to come, (of which our Saviour fpeaks, when he fayeth, *Wo unto
you that laugh, for ye fhall weep and lament*) fuch ugly filthinefs, for fo poor
and mean beauty? fuch great weaknefs
and infirmities, for fo fmall a ftrength?
fuch terrours and dreadfull affright-
ments, for fo little fecurity as the
world affords ? St. *Auftin* fays, it is
but a vain fear to be afraid to lofe
temporal things, and not to fear to
lofe the heavenly ; to be afraid to lofe
the company of Father and Mother,
and not to fear lofing the bleffed prefence of God the Father, and of *Jefus Chrift* ; to be fearfull to lofe the
company of Brothers and Sifters, and
not to fear lofing the bleffed Fraternity of Angels; of which Brotherhood,
St. *John* fpeaks in the *Revelations*,
when he would have worfhipped the
Angel, who forbad him, faying, *Take
heed thou do it not, for, I am thy fellow
Servant, and of thy Brethren alfo which
have the teftimony of* Jefus Chrift,
worfhip God. Therefore thou that fear-
eft Death, love thy Life, the Holy Spirit is thy Life. If thou finneft, thou
canft not pleafe God. None but the
righteous alone can be faid to do fo,
not the wicked. A childe, when he is
born into the world, weeps before he
laughs, the tears that come from him,
bearing witnefs that he enters into
mifery as foon as he begins to breathe;
fo that the childe may well be faid to
be a Prophet of his own mifery.
While a good man lives, he muft fuffer Perfecution, for, the wicked do always perfecute the juft, if not always
with the fword, ftones, or other weapons, yet they do it with their bad
Lives and wicked works. Wherefore
St. *Peter* praifeth *Lot's* converfation,
be-

becaufe he *fuffered tribulation among wicked men:* or, as St. *Paul* calls it, *Perils among falfe Brethren.* All other afflictions and perfecutions in this world may poffibly ceafe, but that wherewith the ungodly do perfecute the Righteous will never ceafe, and if thou doft not believ this to be a truth, do but once begin to do well, and thou fhalt quickly fee how the wicked will perfecute thee. The *Wife man* tells us, that the Friends of God ought to have three forts of patience; the firft whereof confifts in fuffering patiently all the evils that are both done, and faid againft them. The fecond, in the patient bearing their own infirmities, and what ever tribulations pleafes God to inflict on them in this world. And the third in refifting the Devil, who always ftrives to turn them afide from doing good works. Now no man muft expect to receive a Crown that hath not fought faithfully for it, and where the greateft Combate is, there's the greateft Reward, and the moft noble Crown (as the *Wife man* fpeaks) I fpeak to you according to the patience of God. For he that is moft patient in adverfities and under the perfecutions of wicked men, fhal have the greater Recompence; as thofe Grapes yield the moft Wine, which are the moft preffed and bruifed; or as the Olive, when 'tis moft fqueezed, the skins all flip afide and the Oyl remains pure and clear; or, as the Wheat when 'tis well threfht and beaten, is thereby feparated from the Chaff. Therefore if thou wouldft be good, whileft thou liveft in this world, patiently fuffer the wicked to converfe with thee. And *Solomon* fays, *The true patient man hopes to converfe with the Angels.* The true patient man is never in wrath. It is moft certain, that God loves them that hate the world for his fake; therefore ought

fufert tribulacion entre li mal home. E Sant Paul di, perilli en fals frayre. Totas las autras tribulacions, e perfeguecions pon defalliir. Ma la perfeguecion que li mal perfegan li bon non defalliire. E fi tu non o cres comença de ben viore, e veyres en cal maniera li mal home te perfegren. Lo fauy di, Tres paciencias devon aver li amic de Dio. La premiera es en tuit li mal lical fon fait, o dit à lor. La fegonda es en las lors enfermetas, e en tuit li traballi lical Dio autreia venir à lor en aqueft fegle. La terça paciencia es contra lo diavol local s'efforça de tranftornar los de lors bonas obras. Ma alcun non fere corona fi el non combatre lealment. E aqui ont a major batallia, a major fallu, e plus nobla corona. Dont di lo fauy, Jo dic à vos fegont la patiencia de Dio. C. aquel local es pacient en li flagel, e en las perfeguecions de li mal home aure major reguiardonança. En ayma lo raçin cant el es plus premu rent plus de vin. En ayma l'oliva cant illi es plus premua la morca vay d'una part, e l'oli reman clar. En ayma lo froment cant el es plus atrifa la pallia vay d'una part, e lo gran de l'autra. Ma fi tu voles effer bon dementre que tu fias en aquefta vita, fufre li mal home jofta tu en patiencia. E lo fauy di, lo veray patient fpera de aver la fraternita de li Angel. Lo veray patient non s'eyra. C. lo es cofa certana que Dio ama aquilli lical eyran lo mont per l'amor de luy.

Lo bon home fe deo alegrar en la pena, e al fio lavor, e en la foa paureta. C. *Dio promet à lui vita eterna. E l' ome fellon deo plorar al fio goy, e al fio daleit, e en las foas riqueças.* C. *per eytal goy, e per eytal deleit, e per eytal riqueças Dio autreia à luy pena eterna. Aquel apaga Dio local porta en patiencia tuit li mal lical fon fait à luy. E Sant Sift di, Non te aucias, ma fi alcun te aucire non te difplaça. E fi l' ome fellon noyre à tu recorde te que Dio es cun tu. E Sant Johan boca d' or di, fi Chrift es cun mi, cal temercy yo, fi totas las undas dal mar venian à my, e tuit li Princi d' aqueft fegle contraftava à mi, totas aqueftas cofas fon coma arena, e plus frevol d' arena, yo non dic ayço que yo aya fiança en my ni en las mias forças. Ma me confido al noftre Segnor Jefus Chrift e en li fio commandament lical yo aya al mio cor, e en las mias mans, ço es en las mias obras, lafcals fan mi fort. Si totas las undas dal mar venian à mi, e tuit li Princi d' aqueft fegle eran contra mi, tuit non pon vencer ni noire à my. Tuit aqnilli que fon al mar, e en terra non pon noyre al bon home, fi el mefeyme non fe noy. Li amic de Dio foron aflagely, e anguftia en plus fors manieras. Alcuns foron mort à glay. Enayma fo Sant Johan Batifta local fo degola en la carcer del Rey Erode.* C. *el reprenia lo peca de lufuria. Sant Laurenç fo rufti. Sant Jaco de çebedio perdè lo cap en Jopia.*

the righteous man to rejoyce in his pains, labours, poverty, and fufferings, of what kinde foever they be, knowing that God has promifed to give him eternal Life. But on the contrary, the wicked ought to weep and mourn, even in the midft of all his jollity, delights, and riches, as knowing that for all the joys, pleafures and wealth which he enjoys here below, God hath referved for him the wrath to come. That man or woman appeafeth God's anger, who bears with patience all the wrongs that are done unto them. St. *Sixtus* fays, Thou oughteft not to lay hands upon thine own Life, but if another feeks to kill thee, be not difpleafed at it, and if the wicked annoy thee, remember that God is with thee; and golden mouth'd St. *John* faith, *If Chrift be with me, who fhall be againft me?* Although all the waves of the Sea fhould rife, and all the Princes of this World were bent againft me, they are but as the Sand, and weaker than the Duft. I do not fay this, as having confidence in mine own ftrength; but I truft in our Lord *Jefus Chrift*, and in his Commandments, which I bear in my heart, and in my hands, that is to fay, in my works, the which make me ftrong. Suppofe all the waves of the Sea fhould rife up againft me, and all the Princes of the World were bent to ruine me, they were not all of them able to hurt or fubdue me. Whatfoever is found on the Earth, or in the Sea, cannot hurt a good man, if he himfelf become not his own Executioner. God's Friends have fometime been beaten and oppreft in feveral kindes; fome of them have died by the Sword, as St. *John* the *Baptift*, who was beheaded in a Prifon by King *Herod*, becaufe he reprehended him for the fin of Luxury. St. *Laurence* was rofted alive. St. *James* the Son of *Zebede* was beheaded in *Joppa*.

Joppa. St. *James* the Son of *Alpheus* as he was preaching in *Jerusalem*, the Son of a Bishop knockt him down dead with a Pole. St. *Bartholomew* was beaten with Rods, and was afterwards fleyed alive. St. *Peter* was crucified, his head downwards, and his feet upwards. St. *Andrew* was crucified on a Cross. St. *Matthew* was shot to death with Arrows. St. *Paul* was taken and cruelly beaten, and afterwards lost his head. Our blessed Saviour humbled himself so far for mans sake as to come down from Heaven, and enter into the Virgins womb ; he who was God blessed for ever, and King over the Angels, became a mortal man for our sakes, was *put into a Manger,* and *wrapt in swadling cloaths,* he was *carried away into* Egypt *for fear of* Herod *that sought to kill him* ; he was wearied and tired with travelling, *tempted of the Devil,* suffered *hunger* & *thirst* for our sakes : he was called *a mad man,* and *one possessed with the Devil* by the *Jews,* and *the Son of a Carpenter,* he suffered for our sakes all that a man could possibly, sin onely excepted ; and finally, he was *betrayed* by one of his Disciples, *as a Murtherer,* and an excommunicated person ; he was by them sold for our sakes, he was *condemned, buffetted,* and *despised,* he was *crowned with Thorns,* and *thrust through with a Spear in his side* ; and this he did to redeem us from Death by the effusion of his own Bloud, even he himself who was holy, pure, and without sin, was delivered, not by force, but of his own will and consent. St. *Stephen* was stoned to death, *Isaiah* the Prophet was sawn asunder, *Jeremy* was stoned to death, *Daniel* was cast into the Lions Den; the three Children *Shadrach, Meshech,* and *Abednego,* were thrown into the burning fiery Fornace ; several other men and women lost their limbs, and obtained the victory, re-

Sant *Jaco Alfio* cum el fos en *Jerusalem,* e prediques , lo filli d' un vesco done à lui d' una pertia sobre lo cap, e cagic mort. Sant *Bartholome* fo batu cun vergas , e en apres fo scortiga. Sant *Peyre* fo pausa en la croç li pe de sobre, e lo cap de sot. Sant *Andrio* liy fo mes de travers. Sant *Matio* fo sagieta. Sant *Paul* fo pres, e lia, e batu, e en apres perde lo cap. Lo nostre Segnor *Jesus Christ* se humilie tant il per ome qu' el degne deysendre dal cel al ventre de la vergena. El meseyme local era Dio, e Rey de li Angel so ome mortal per nos. E so pausa en la crepia , e envelopa de panç . El fo traporta de *Judea* en *Egit* per *Erode* qu' el non fos mort de luy. El fo fatiga dal viage, e fo tenta del diavol. El famege per nos, e setege. El fo apela de li *Judio* endemonia, e filli de faure. El sostene per nos totas las cosas lascals home po sostenir stier qu' el non fey pecca. E à la fin el fo liora d' un sio deciple en ayma homecidier, e scuminiga. Per lor fo liora per nos, condana, e scarni, e fait vil, e corona d' espinas, e trafora cun la lança al layrier, e deliore nos de mort per lo decorament de sio sanc . El meseyme local era sant, e mont , e sença peca fo liora non constreitament, Ma de gra, e de la soa volunta. Sant *Steve* fo lapida. *Isaya* fo resca. *Jeremia* fo lapida. *Daniel* fo pausa al lac de li leon. Li trey fantin *Sydrac* , e *Misac* , e *Abdenago* foron mes en la fornais del fuoc ardent. E motos autres homes , e senas perderon li lor membres, e agron vitoria de la *batallia, e receopron la marci de li lor lavor, e son corona al cel. E lo savi di, Regarden la vita de li sant martre, de li ome, e de las senas lical se layseron aucire, e liorar la lor carn à mort, e à martiri. Ma non pense en van qu'illi se laysesan aucir, e liorar la lor carn à mort, e à martiri s'illi non saupesan fermament que d'aquesta vita trapasivol venguesan à la perpetual. E Sant Augustinus di en las festivetas de li sant, nos non deven pregar Dio per lor. Ma per nos, que Dio done à nos segre las vias las cals illi an segu, e aver carita enayma illi an agu, e qu'el nos done seser al regne de li cel en ayma illi seon. Emperço las vitas de li sant son scritas que nos liy prenan eysemple.*

ceiving the reward of their Travels, and are now crowned in Heaven. And as the *Wise man* says, Let us look upon the Life of those holy Martyrs both Men and Women, which yielded themselves to be put to Death, giving up their Bodies to be martyred : and let's not think they would thus have suffered their Bodies to be put to death, and torments, if they had not been truly perswaded that from this momentany life, they were to pass to a life which is eternal. St. *Austin* says, that *in celebrating the joyfull remembrance of the Saints, we ought not to pray to God for them, but rather for our selves, to the end he would grant unto us, that we may follow the same paths which they traced out to us, and that we may sit in the Kingdom of Heaven as they do.* Therefore are the Lives of the Saints written, to the end that we may take example by them, and imitate the same.

Glosa Pater noster.

O *Tu lo nostre Payre local sies en li cel. Nos deven saber que entre totas las obras lascals pon esser faytas en aquesta vita, neuna obra non es prus honorivol, ni prus profeytivol, ni prus legiera que aurar Dio : Illi es prus honorivol, car grant honor es parlar sovendierament e familiarment au lo Rey terrenal, ma mot major honor es parlar familiarment au lo Rey celestial e eternal au local nos parlen aurent; dont dis Isidori, Aquel que vol esser sovendierament au Dio aure e legissa sovendierament; car cant nos aurèn nos parlen au Dio, ma cant nos legen Dio parla au nos. Dreco profeytivol cosa es aurar, car*

A Gloss upon *Our Father*.

O *Thou our Father which art in Heaven.* We ought to know that amongst all the Works which may be done in this Life, none is more honourable, profitable, or easie, than to pray to God; it's most honourable, for, if it be a great honour to speak often and familiarly with an earthly King, it's then certainly a much greater honour to talk familiarly with the heavenly and eternal King, with whom we discourse in Prayer; therefore *Isidorus* faith, *He that will be often with God, let him pray and reade,* for when we pray we talk with God, and when we reade, God talketh unto us. Again, it's a profitable thing to pray,
for

for as the Lord faith, *Verily I fay unto you, whatfoever you fhall ask in Prayer, believe that ye fhall receive it, and it fhall be given unto you.* It's the eafieft thing in the World to pray, for a man may pray in all places, and at all times. Neither is it neceffary to bring any thing of a mans felf, feeing that to think onely and defire well, is to pray. Therefore *David* faith, *The Lord heareth the defire of the Poor,* (*i.e.* the humble;) now the poor are thofe infirm creatures who cannot fpeak or do any thing fave onely pray with defire, and God is ready t > hear the Prayer of their defire; fo alfo faith *David, The Lord heareth the defire of the poor.* Again, feeing that Prayer is a work fo honourable, fo profitable, and fo eafie, and alfo feeing it is faid in the Gofpel, the Apoftles asked of *Chrift* (as good Difciples of a good Mafter) *that he would teach them to pray,* (for they knew that they could not learn a better Leffon) and *faid unto him, O Lord teach us to pray,* who anfwering faid, *When you pray, do not fpeak much, but pray thus, O thou our Father which art in Heaven.* In this Prayer he teacheth us, firft, to get the good will of God, and to ask for our felves all things which are needfull; when he faith, *O thou our Father which art in Heaven,* it is as if he had faid, Thou art our Father by Creation; To the fame purpofe alfo fpeaks *Mofes* in *Deuteronomy, Is not he thy Father which hath poffeffed thee, made thee, and created thee?* But thou art our Father by Redemption, for thou haft *ranfomed us with thine own Bloud,* which thing is the greateft fign of love that any father can fhew towards his children; therefore it's faid in the *Revelation, Which loved us, and wafhed us from our fins in his own Bloud.* Again, *Thou art our Father,* in refpect of nourifhment, government, and inheritance, and therefore the Lord faid

enayma di lo Segnor; *Jo diç nominament à vos, cal que cal cofa orant demander é en oraifon, crefe que vos la recebré e feré fayta à vos:* Illi es prus legiera, car loma po aurar en tot luoc e en tot temp, ni non conventa querre alcuna cofa de fi, car folament ben penfar e ben defirar es aurar. Dont dis David, lo Segnor e fauciç lo defirier de li paure, ços de li humil; oli paure fon li enferm lical non pon parlar ni far alcuna cofa, ma tant folament pon aurar au defirier, e Dio es aparellia à efauçar l' oraifon dal lor defirier, en ayma dis David lo Segnor efauciç lo defirier de li paure, don car aurar es obra tant honorivol, tant profeytivol & tant legiera. En perço en ayma es dit en l' A-vangeli, Apoftol demanderon de Chrift en ayma bon Deciple de bon Meyftre quel enfegneffa lor aurar; car illi fabian que illi non poyan enpenre mellior leyçon, e differon à luy: O Segnor enfegna nos aurar; local refpondent dis; cant vos aura, non vollia mot parlar, ma vos aurare en ayfi. O tu lo noftre payre, local fies en licel; en aquefta oraifon enfegna nos premierament aqueftar la benevolença de Dio e demandar de lui meyme totas las cofas befognivols à nos, cant el di, ô tu lo noftre payre local fies en licel; quafi diça, tu fies lo noftre payre per creation; en ayma dis Moyfent Deuteronomi el meyme; non es lo tio payre, local pofefir, e fé, e creé tu? O tu fies lo noftre payre per redempcion; car tu reymiés nos del tio propi fanc: lacal cofa fo major fegnal d' amor que alcun payre poyfa demonftrar à li fio filli; dont es dit en l' Apocalice, local amé nos, e lavé nos de li noftre pecca al fio fanc. Dereço tu fies lo noftre payre per nutriment e per gouvernament e per eretà: en perço lo Segnor diçia à li fio deciple; non
vollia

vollia apellar à vos payre sobra la terra; car unes lo vostre payre local es en li cel: Dereço el di ô tu lo nostre payre, quasi diça tu non deves refuda la nostra auracion, ma deves donar à nos aquelas cosas lascals nos demanden à tu: e tu sies lo nostre payre local creyés e remp sies nos e local paysses, e nos regisses e promesies la toa eretà: ma en ço que sensec, local sies en li cel; lo Segnor ensegna nos esser tals que nos sian degne esser apellà cels: car enayma lo Segnor heita en li cel material, en aysi en li cel spiritual, çoes en li sant per istament de gracia, dont dis Ysidorus, local es à mi seti, del cal seti dis Salamon: l'arma del just es à mi seti. Dereço, si nos sen cel spiritual, çoes alumenà dentre per veraya fé, e de fora per honesta conversacion. Dereço estendu e larc per carità à Dio e per pietà al proyme, e per misericordia à li enemic. Dereço aut e exlevà de la terra per contemplacion de las cosas celestials e per des pressi de las terrenals, en aysi que nos poysan dire au l'Apostol, la nostra conversacion es en li cel: en aquela via lo Segnor reconoysse la vouç de la nostra oraison cant nos dicen, ô tu lo nostre payre local sies en li cel. Aquesta es la premiera partia de l'oraison del Segnor, en lacal ensegna nos aquestar premierament la benevolença de Dio e demandar de luy meyme totas las cosas besognivols à nos; ma loes à saber que d'aquest luoc entro à la fin de loreson del Segnor se contenon sept requerenças breoson parolas: ma geos e longas en sentancias. Dereço que aquesta oreson à pena po esser exponua compliament per tuit li Meystre lical son al mont. En aquestat set requerenças son demandas totas las cosas lascals son besognivols à nos en la pre-

to his Disciples, *Call no man father on earth, for there is one your Father, which is in Heaven.* Again, he saith, *O thou our Father;* as if he had said, Thou shouldest not refuse our Prayer, but give us these things which we ask of thee, and thou art *our Father* which hast created, redeemed, fed, and governed us; and hast promised us thine inheritance. But as for that which followeth, *Which art in Heaven;* the Lord teacheth us to be such, that we may be worthy to be called heavenly; for, as the Lord dwelleth in material Heaven, so he dwells in spiritual Heaven, (*i.e.* in the Saints by the habitation of grace;) therefore saith *Isidorus, The Heaven is my Throne;* of the which Throne saith *Solomon, The Soul of the Righteous is my Throne.* Again, if we be Heaven, *i.e.* we are enlightened within by true Faith, and without by honest Conversation. Again, it is extended and enlarged by Love towards God, and by Charity towards our Neighbour, and Mercy towards our Enemy. Again, it is high and elevated above the Earth, through contemplation of heavenly things and despising of earthly, so that we may say with the Apostle, *Our conversation is in Heaven;* in this way the Lord acknowledgeth our Prayer when we say, *O thou our Father which art in Heaven.* This is the first part of our Lords Prayer in which he teacheth us to get first the good will of God, and then to ask of him all things which are necessary for us. But this is to be observed, that from this place to the end of the Lords Prayer are contained seven Petitions, brief in words, but weighty and large in their sense and meaning. Again, that this Prayer can scarce be sufficiently expounded by all the Doctours in the World. In these seven Petitions or Requests, are contained all things necessary for this present

present Life, or that which is to come. But let us take at present for our edification a plain and down-right Exposition.

The first Petition.

The first Request is *Hallowed be thy Name*. In this Request we desire the Sin of Lust may be removed, and that the Virtue of Chastity may be given us, for, we bear the Name of *Christ*, and are called *Christians*, which is nothing else but to be Disciples, Servants, and Children of *Christ*: but thy name is polluted, vilified, and blasphemed in us, when we live in pollution and luxury : and on the contrary, it is sanctified and purified when we abstain from all pollutions of heart, mouth, and body; and wash and purifie our sins past by true Repentance : for, so those *Christians* which do indeed bear the Name of *Christ*, are purified, that is, are made Saints; now a Saint is such a one, who is without stain, but the sin of Lust is rightly termed a stain, because as a stain taketh from cloath or wooll the natural colour, so the sin of Lust taketh from the Soul the benefit of Baptism, and all Graces. Again, as a stain passeth through the cloath, within and without, so Lust defileth a man within and without, and it first of all defileth a man at the heart by base and vile thoughts, and consenting to pleasures; as likewise the eys by unchaste looks, the ears with filthy words that heat and inflame unto sin ; the nose by the unsavoury smels of ointments, which serve for allurements unto whoredom, with which some women being possessed by the Devil, paint themselves to please their lovers ; the mouth by unchaste words, kisses, and superfluous dainties, whereby Lust is nourish-

sent vita e en la venedoyra ; ma pernan al present à la nostra edificacion una ruda e grosa exposicion.

La premiera Requerença.

La premiera Requerença es lo tio nom sia sanctifica. En aquesta requerença nos demanden esser ostà de nos lo pecà de luxuria, e esser dona à nos la vertu de castità ; car nos porten lo nom de Christ, e nos sen apella Chrestian, lacal cosa non es alcuna autra cosa sinon que esser deciple e serf, e filli de Christ : ma aquel nom es soçà & fayt vil e blastem en nos, cant nos viven soçament e luxuriosament, ma el es sanctificà e mondà cant nos nos stenen de totas las soççuras del cor e de la bocca, e del cors, e laven e purifiquen li pecca trapassa por uraya penedença, car en ayma li Crestian lical portan lo nom de Christ son purificà, çoes son fayt sant, car sant es dit sensa tentura ; ma lo pecca de luxuria es apella tentura ; car en ayma la tentura osta al drap ô à la lana la color natural, en aysi lo pecca de luxuria osta a larma la non noysença del Baptisme e totas las vertus, en ayma la tentura trapassa lo drap dedinç e de fora, en aysi la luxuria soça tot lome dedinç e de fora. E illi soça lome premierament al cor per la soça e per la non munda cogitacion e deleytacion e consentiment. En apres li olli per lo regardament non cast, e en apres las aurellias per las parolas cuiosas e enflammans à pecca, en apres las nariç per li soç odorament de li onguent meretricienç de li cal las senas dyablanças se pegnon à placer à li lor amador. En apres la bocca per las parolas non castas, e per li baysament, e per li delicà e soperchivol maniar per li cal la luxuria es nuria e embrasà.

Dereço

Dereço las mans per li toccament non caſt. E derieramant tot lo cors per li ſcuminiguivol repaus per lical lo Dyavol amena li miſſerios peccador duy e duy à l' enfern. Dereço loes entendement lo tio nom ſia ſanctifica, çoes ô Segnor dona à nos gracia que nos lical haven lo tio nom e ſen nomina de tu creſtian, que nos ſian ſant, çoes ſenſa tentura e ſoçura de carnal pecca, ô Segnor tu farés aqueſtas coſas ſi tu donarés à nos vertu e gracia de contenença que nos nos garden del pecca de luxuria. Daqueſta ſantification di l' Apoſtol, monden nos de tot ſoçament de carn e deſprit, perfacer la ſantification en la temor del Segnor. E dreço l' Apoſtol, aqueſta es la volonta de Dio la voſtra ſantification, que vos vos ſtegne de fornicacion; mar car nos non poen far ayço ſinon per l' ajutori de Dio, & en ayma dis Salamon; alcun non po eſſer contenent ſinon que Dio lio done, e aqueſta era ſobeyrana ſapiença ſabè del cal fos aqueſt don. En perço nos haven beſogna cridar per çaſcun dia al Segnor, ô tu lo noſtre payre local ſies en li cel, lo tio nom ſia ſantificà.

La ſeconda reqaerença.

Ara ſenſec la ſeconda requerença; lo tio regne venga. En aqueſta requerença nos demanden del payre celeſtial eſſer oſta de nos lo pecca d' avaricia, e eſſer dona à nos la vertu de pauretà ſpiritual, e de pieta e de miſericordia: car lo regne di cel es denega à li avar e à li ric d' aqueſt mont: dont dis l' Apoſtol, li avar non poſſeſsiè ren lo regne de Dio: & lo Segnor dis en l' Avangeli, lo ric entraré greoment al regne de li cel, car

ed and made much of; the hands by unchaſte touches; and finally, all the body by the deteſtable act of uncleanneſs, by which means the Devil leades the miſerable Sinners, two by two, to Hell. Again, the ſenſe of *Hallowed be thy Name*, is as much as to ſay, O Lord do us the favour, that we which bear thy Name and are called *Chriſtians*, may be holy; that is, without ſpot or defilement of carnality and ſin: O Lord thou wilt do theſe things for us, if thou pleaſe to give us the virtue and grace of continency, ſo that we may keep our ſelves from the ſin of luſt; of this ſanctification ſpeaketh the Apoſtle, *Let us cleanſe our ſelves from all filthineſs of fleſh and ſpirit, perfecting holineſs in the fear of the Lord*. And again the Apoſtle, *This is the will of God, even your ſanctification, that ye abſtain from whoredom*. But as for that, we cannot do it without the aſſiſtance of God; according to that which *Solomon* ſaith, *None can be continent except God enable him*. And this is the chief wiſdom, to know from what fountain this gift cometh; for this cauſe we have need to cry daily to the Lord, *Our Father which art in Heaven, Hallowed be thy Name*.

The ſecond Petition.

Now followeth the ſecond Petition or Requeſt, *Thy Kingdom come*. In this Requeſt we beg of our heavenly Father, that the ſin of Covetouſneſs may be removed, and that the grace of ſpiritual poverty, pity, and mercy, may be beſtowed upon us; for, the Kingdom of Heaven is denied to the covetous and rich men of this world; therfore the Apoſtle ſaith, *The covetous ſhall not inherit the Kingdom of God.* And the Lord ſaith in the Goſpel, *The rich ſhall hardly enter into the Kingdom* of *Heaven* ; *and it is easier for a Camel to go through the eye of a needle, than for a rich man to enter into the Kingdom of Heaven.* And again he faith, *Wo unto you rich men , which have your consolation in this life .* But on the contrary, the Kingdom of Heaven is given to the poor ; therefore the Lord faith, *Blessed are the poor in spirit, for theirs is the Kingdom of Heaven.* They are fitly called *Poor in spirit,* that is , voluntarily, not constrained or from any necessity in this life , which is also conformable to what St. *Bernard* faith, that *there are three sorts of poverty , viz. feigned, constrained, and voluntary.* Again, we ought to shun the feigned poverty of which *David* speaketh ; they will be poor in such fort that they notwithstanding suffer no necessity ; we ought to endure patiently the *constrained* poverty, and embrace the *voluntary* with all the heart, and so we shall become *poor in spirit.* Of this poverty St. *James* speaketh , *Hath not God chosen the poor of this world, rich in faith, and inheritors of the Kingdom which God hath promised to them that love him.* And *Augustin* faith in the person of *Christ, I have to sell, but what ? The Kingdom of God, Heaven, the Kingdom of Heaven . After what fashion is it to be bought ? by poverty ; for labour and travel is to be purchased rest, and life, by death ; and thus the Kingdom of Heaven belongs to the poor.* Again, it must be gotten by poverty, for, such were the holy Apostles, and their Disciples that followed their steps, *viz.* those religious men, who forsaking all temporal things followed *Christ* in poverty , so that he is bought by the poor by works of mercy done to the poor, as *Zacheus* did, who gave the half of his goods to the poor, and if he had done wrong to any man he restored fourfold ; so also

prus legiera cofa es tr apaffar lo camel per lo pertus de lagullia que lo ric intrar al regne de li cel. E dreço di malaventura à vos rics lical avé ayçi la voftra confolacion ; ma per lo contrari lo regne de li cel es dona à li paure ; dont dis lo Segnor, li paure per fprit fon benayra, car lo regne de li cel es de lor meyme. Ben di paure per fprit, çoes de volunta non força ni de befogna en la vita ; & en ayma dis Sant Barnart, lo es paureta de trei manieras, çoes à faber enfegnayriç, befognivol, e voluntariç. Dreço nos deven fugir l' enfegnariç ; de laca dis David, Illi volon effer paure praytal pat qu' illi non fufran alcuna befogna, Nos deven foftenir pacientement la befognivol e embraçar voluntayriç de tot lo cor en ayfi farian fayt paure per fprit. Daquefta paureta dis San Jacob, Dereço Dio non eylegic li paure en aquest mont ric en fe, heretier del regne, local Dio ha empromes à li amant fi. Et Sant Auguftin dis en perfona de Chrift, Yo hay à vendre, yo hay à vendre ; e que ? lo regne de Dio, li cel, lo regne de li cel. En cal maniera es compra ? per paureta, lo repau per lo lavor ; la vita per la mort ; lo regne de li cel es de li paure. Dreço conventa luy effer aquefta per paureta, en ayma foron li fant Apoftol e li enfegador de lor, çoes tuit li baron religios lical layfan totas las cofas temporals & fegon Chrift per paureta ; fi may que nos conventa luy effer compra de luy paure per las obras de mifericordia donas à li paure ; en ayma fe Jaquio, local doné à li paure la meyta de li fio ben, e fi el havia frauda alcun, el ho rendia à dobles ; e enayma fan

tuit

tuit li bon ric à lical seré dit al dia del judici ; vené beneyt del mio payre posfesé lo regne local es aparellia à vos del commençament del mont , ma nengun non se po scusar dal comprament d' aquest regne ; car en ayma di Gregori, lo regne de Dio valc tant cant tu lias, e el valc à li sant Apostol la nao à li reç e valc à Jaquio la meyta de li sio ben, e valc à una veva doas porysas lascals illi pausé en lautar de Dio, e valc à un autre un calici dayga froyda. En ayma dis Gregori ; Dreço alcuna cosa non es plus vil cant illi es compra, ni plus cara cant illi es possesia ; ma si tu dices que tu non poç hav er un calici dayga freyda à donar à li paure ; encara non te poç scusar del comprament del regne celestial, car tu si non has altra cosa la bona voluntà basta à tu lacal Dio recoynta à tu per fayt. Car en ayma di l' Apostol, la volunta es receopua segont ço quilli ha & non segont ço quilli non ha. E Gregori dis, la man non es unca voyda del don si larca del cor es plena de bona voluntà. Dreço lo es entendement, lo tio regne venga ; çoes ô Segnor dona à nos pauretà voluntayriç per lacal cose ven al tio regne e doan à nos pieta e misericordia, per lascals lo tio regne es compra de li paure e osta de nos cubiticia e avaricia, car lo regne de li cel seré teot de li avar e de li cubit.

do all the rich which are good , to whom it shall be said at the Day of Judgment, *Come ye blessed of my Father, inherit the Kingdom prepared for you from the beginning of the world.* But none may excuse themselves from buying this Kingdom ; for as *Gregory* saith , *The Kingdom of God costeth as much of goods as thou hast.* It cost the holy Apostles the Ship and the Nets ; it cost *Zacheus* the half of his goods ; it cost one Widow two Mites, which she put into Gods Treasury ; it cost another a Cup of cold Water, (so saith *Gregory.*) And again, *Nothing is more cheap to be bought, and nothing more dear, when one hath bought it.* Thou mayst perhaps say, that thou canst not get a Cup of cold Water to give to the poor, but yet thou canst never excuse thy self from the purchase of the heavenly Kingdom, for although thou hast nothing else, yet a good will sufficeth, which God accounteth for the deed ; for, as the Apostle saith , the will is accepted according to that a man hath, and not according to that which he hath not. And *Gregory* saith, *The hand is never empty of a gift, if the chest of the heart be full of good will.* Again, the sense of these words, *Thy Kingdom come,* is, O Lord, give us voluntary poverty, by which we may come to thy Kingdom, and give us bowels of that compassion and mercy through which thy Kingdom is purchased by the poor, and root out of our hearts concupiscence and avarice ; for, the Kingdom of God shall be taken away from the avaricious and covetous.

La terça requerença.

Ara sensec la terça requerença, La toa volunta sia fayta. En aquesta requerença nos demanden esser osta de nos

The third Petition.

Now followeth the third Petition, *Thy will be done.* In this Petition we request, that the sin of negligence

may

may be taken from us, wch is an enemy to all goodnefs, for, it begetteth luft, feeds the belly, foweth detractions, and caufeth trouble for that which is good, that is, when we are troubled to do any thing, or to fee others do well; or if we do any thing which is good, we do it idlely, coldly, and unfavourily; and fo inftead of obtaining a blefling we get a curfe, as *Jeremiah* faith, *Curfed is he that doth the work of God negligently:* wherefore heedlefnefs or idlenefs is, when we do not finifh the good which we have begun; and therefore we receive not the wages; for it is the end that crowns & not the battel; Idlenefs is directly oppofite to the Command of the Law, in which it was enjoyned to offer up all the Sacrifice, *(the head with the tail.)* The Sacrifice is every good work which we fanctifie to God, as doing the fame for his honour; the *head* is the beginning of the work, and the *tail* is the end. To God we offer the Sacrifice, *(the head with the tail)* when perfevering, we continue good works to the end. Now the negligent and idle would fain not do any thing, but be always idle, which thing is exceeding dangerous both for body and foul. And fo it is faid in the Book of *Wifedom, Idlenefs begetteth much evil, for, the belly of man can fcarce be idle; for, when it is not imployed in good, it is imployed in evil.* And St. *Bernard* faith, that *Idlenefs is the the hold or ftorehoufe of all evils.* The Hold is the loweft place in the Ship, and there are eafily bred Serpents and creeping things; alfo it is often feen, that in the idle foul are bred evil thoughts, confentings to and delighting in fin. And *Gregory* faith, *The reafon why the heart of* Solomon *forfook the wifdom of God fo foon was, for that no Difcipline outward kept him in.* Again, it is neceffary for a man to be very watchfull

lo pecca d' acidia, lacal cofa, çoes encreyfament de ben; car aquefta aperturis la luxuria, nuris la gola, femena detracions, fcomumtençons, çoes encreyfament de ben, çoes à faber cant lo nos nos encreyfen far ben, o nos encreys vefer li autre befaçent: ô fi nos facen alcuna cofa de ben, nos la façen pigrament e tebiament e defprecivolment, e enayfi dont nos deven aqueftar benedicion, nos aqueften maledicion; en ayma dis Jeremia, Aquel es maudit local fay lobra de Dio pare çofament. En perço accidia es cant nos non amenin à fin li ben lical nos commencen; Enperço nos non confeguen lo guiardor, car la fin corona, non la batallia: & li pareços fan encontra lo commendament de la ley, en lacal es commanda ufrir tota l'oftia, lo cap au la coa. Loftia es una çafcuna bona obra lacal nos fanctifiguen à Dio, lacal nos facen per l' honor de Dio; lo cap es lo commençament de lobra; ma la coa es la fin. A Dio nos ufren loftia, lo cap au la coa cant perfeverant amenen la bona obra à la fin. Et li accidios e li pareços non volrian far alcuna cofa, ma effer totavia occios: lacal cofa es grant perilli al cors e à larma; & en ayma es dit en fapiença loççiofita enfegna moti mal; car la penfa de lome à pena po effer oççiofa: car enço quilli non es empa cha en ben, illi es empacha en mal. Et San Bernart dis que loççiofita es fentina de tuit li mal, La fentina es lo luoc prus bas en la nao, & nayfon legierament aqui ferpent & raptilias. En ayma fen deven fovendierament que en larma oççiofa nayfon malas cogitacions, confentiment, deleytacions. E Gregori dis, Lo cor de Salomon abandone al poftot la fapiença de Dio, enperço calcuna dieciplina non gardé lui de fora. Dreço la conventa lome velliar ence que
la

over himſelf, and to look carefully unto the Caſtle of the Body and Soul,
and to imploy himſelf ever in ſome
good thought, word, or work ; as
Hierom ſaith, *Be always doing ſome good
thing, that ſo the Devil may finde thee
imployed.* Again, we pray that this
dangerous ſin of Idleneſs may be taken from us, when we ſay *Thy will be
done.* And we requeſt that the Grace
of Devotion may be given to us, and
of true love and good works, for, devout men, and ſuch as are inflamed
with divine love, will never be idle,
but ſtudy always to occupy themſelves
in doing the will of God on earth, as
the Saints in Heaven did, and do it.
But for that we cannot do this without divine Grace, we ought to pray
*Thy will be done in Earth as it is in Hea-
ven.* For, the will of God is done in
Heaven without intermiſſion, ſorrow,
murmuring, or contradiction ; and
thus all good *Chriſtians* labour to do
it. Alſo *Gregory* ſaith, *The approbation
of the work is the accompliſhment of
love, and the love of God is never idle ;
for, it doth great things, if it be active,
but if it refuſe to work, it is not love.*
And St. *Bernard* ſaith, *O bleſſed* Jeſus, *thy Love is never idle ; thoſe
which love thee never cool ; to ſpeak of
thee is perfect conſolation ; to think of
thee is full ſatisfaction ; to draw near to
thee is eternal Life ; to depart from thee
is eternal Death. O bleſſed* Jeſus, *thou
art Honey in the Mouth, a ſweet Song to
the Ear, and Joy to the Heart.* So then,
in this third Petition, *Thy will be done,*
we pray, that the ſin of Idleneſs may
be taken from us, and the Grace of
Devotion and of good Works be beſtowed upon us.

*la garda de ſi, e gardar curioſament lo
caſtel del cors e de larma, e empacharſe
totavia en alcuna bona cogitacion, o parlament, o obra ; en ayma dis Jeromi, ſay
totavia alcuna coſa de ben que lo dyavol
te trobe empacha. Dreço nos demanden
eſſer oſta de nos aqueſt mot perillios pecca
dacidia, cant nos diçen la toa volunta
ſia fayta. E demanden ayçi eſſer dona la
vertu de devocion e de uraya amor e de
bona obra ; ma li ome devot e enflama de
la divina amor non volon unca eſſer :
ma ſeſtudian totavia empacarſe enſar la
volunta de Dio en la terra; en ayma feron
e fan li ſant lical ſon en li cel ; ma car
nos non poen far ayço ſença la devina
gracia, enperço deven demandar la toa
volunta ſia fayta, en ayma illi es fayta al
cel ſia fayta en la terra ; car la volunta
de Dio es fayta al cel ſença entrelayſa-
ment, ſença triſticia, ſença murmura-
cion, e contradicement : en ayſi s'eſtudian
de far en terra tuit li bon Creſtian ; en
ayma dis Gregori, Lo provament de lobra es compliment de lamor ; & lamor
de Dio non es unca oççioſa, car illi obra
grant coſas ſilli es ; ma ſilli refuda do-
brar non es amor. E San Bernart dis,
ô bon Jeſu la toa amor non es unca oççioſa; aquilli lical aman tu non ſempegreciſ-
ſon ; parlar de tu es parfeyta conſolaci-
on, parlar de tu es plen reſaçiament ;
acoſtarſe à tu es vita eterna, departirſe
de tu es mort perpetual : ô bon Jeſu tu
ſies mel en la boca, douç cant en lau-
rellia, alegreça al cor. Dreço aqueſta
es la terça requerença ; la toa volunta
ſia fayta, en lacal nos demanden eſſer
oſta de nos lo pecca dacidia, e eſſer dona à
nos la vertu de devocion e de bona obra.*

Theſe Gloſſes are continued throughout the ſeveral Branches
of the *Lord's Prayer,* after which likewiſe follows an Expoſition
upon the *Ten Commandments, &c.* But that the Work may not
seem

seem over tedious, I rather chuse to break off abruptly, and refer the Reader to the very original Manuscripts in the University Library of *Cambridg* for the perusal of all those Pieces which are not here inserted ; assuring him, that I have no other Design, by the exclusion (or rather omission) of these, than to make place for some others of no less moment and consequence.

CHAP. VII.

An Extract of those famous Treatises which were written by the ancient Inhabitants of the Valleys, concerning Antichrist, Purgatory, Invocation *of* Saints, *and the* Sacraments.

ARTICLE I.

Of Antichrist.

This Book concerning the *Antichrist* is extant in an old Manuscript which containeth many Sermons of the *Bardes*, collected in the Year 1120. and therefore written before *Waldo*, and about the time of *Peter de Bruis*, who taught in *Languedoc*, where he was burnt, namely, at St. *Giles*, before *Waldo* came forth out of *Lions*, and since that time this Treatise hath been preserved among the *Waldenses* of the *Alpes*, of whom Mr. *Paul Perrin* procured the same, together with many other.

Antichrist is a Falshood worthy of eternal Damnation, covered over with a shew of Truth, and of the Righteousness of

Antichrist es falsetà de damnation eterna cuberta de specia de la verita, & de la justitia de Christ, & de la soa Sposa : contrapansa

*panfa a mefcime la via de verita, de Fu-
ftitia, de Fe, d' Efperanza, de Carita,
& a la vita moral, & a la verita minifterial de la Gleifa meniftra per li fals
Apoftols , & defendua opiniofament de
l' un & de l' autre bras : o es engan re-
fcondu de la verita de falu de cofas fub-
ftantials, & minifterials : o es fraudu-
lenta contraricta de Chrift & de la foa
Spofa , & a un chafcun membre fidel.
Et enaymi non es alcuna fpecial perfona
ordena en alcun gra, o uffici, o meneftier, & aizo regardant univerfalment.
Ma mefeima la falfeta panfa a contra a
la verita quilli fe cuebre & fe orna de
belleza, & de pietà, de fora de la Gleifa de Chrift, enaima de nom de officis,
de Scripturas & de Sacramens, & de
motas autras cofas. La iniquita d' a-
quefta maniera com li feo Meniftre ma-
jors & menors , com li feguent ley de
maluas cor & cec, aital congregation enfemp prefa es apella Antichrift, Babylonia, o quarta beftia, o mcretrix, o home
de pecca, filli de perdition.*

*Li feos Miniftres fon apella fals Pro-
phetas, maiftres mefongers, Miniftres de
tenebras. Sperit de error, mcretrix Apocalyptica, maire de fornication, niolas
fenza aguia, arbres automnals morts &
auranc as per doas vez, undas del crudel
mar. Stellas errans, Balaamitiens, Gif-
fiptiens.*

*El es dit Antichrift, emperço ca cu-
bert & orna fot fpecia de Chrift, & de la
Gleifa, & de li feo fidel membre, contraria a la falu faita per Chrift, & amini-
ftra verament en la Gleifa de Chrift ; &
participa de la fidel per Fe, per Efperança, & per Charita : en liqual modo*

Chrift, and his Spoufe, contrary to the
way of Truth, Righteoufnefs, Faith,
Hope, and Charity, as likewife to moral Life, and to the minifterial Truth
of the Church , adminiftred by the
falfe Apoftles, and refolutely upheld
by the one and the other Arm of Secular and Ecclefiaftical Power ; or elfe
we may fay, *Antichrift* is a Deceit
which hides the Truth of Salvation in
fubftantial and minifterial matters ; or,
that it is a difguifed contrariety to
Chrift and his Spoufe, and every faithfull member thereof. And fo it is not
any one particular perfon, ordained to
fuch a Degree, Office, or Miniftery, it
being confidered univerfally ; but it is
Falfhood it felf, in oppofition to the
Truth, covering and adorning it felf
with a pretence of Beauty and Piety,
not futable to the Church of *Chrift,*
as by the Names, and Offices, the
Scriptures, the Sacraments, and many
other things may appear. Iniquity
thus qualified with all the Minifters
thereof great and fmall, together with
all them that follow them, with an
evil heart, and blindfold; fuch a Congregation comprifed together, is that
which is called *Antichrift,* or *Babylon,*
or the *fourth Beaft,* or the *Whore,* or
the *Man of Sin,* the *Son of perdition.*

His *Minifters* are called *falfe Prophets,
Lying Teachers , Minifters of Darknefs,
a Spirit of Errour,* the *Whore* in the *Revelation,* the *Mother of Fornications,
Clouds without Water, withered Trees
twice dead and plucked up by the Roots,
Waves of the raging Sea, wandring Pla-
nets,* Balaamites, *and* Egyptians.

He is called *Antichrift,* becaufe being
decked and garnifhed with a fhew of
Chrift, and of his Church, and faithfull
Members, he doth oppofe himfelf to
that Salvation which was wrought by
Chrift , and truly adminiftred in the
Church of *Chrift,* whereof the Faithful
do partake by Faith, Hope, & Charity;
Thus

Thus he opposeth himself, by the wisdom of the World, by false Religious, &by a counterfeit Piety, by Ecclesiastical Power, by Secular Tyranny, by Riches, Honours, & Dignities, & by the delights and pleasures of the World.

And therefore let every one take notice hereof, that *Antichrist* could not come in any wise, but all these forementioned things must needs meet together, to make up a complete hypocrisie and falshood, *viz.* the worldly wise men, the Religious Orders, the Pharisees, Ministers, Doctours, the Secular Power, with the worldly people joyntly together. And thus all of them together make up the Man of sin and errour compleatly ; for, although that *Antichrist* was conceived already in the Apostles time, yet being but in his infancy as it were, he wanted his inward and outward members ; and therefore he might then have been more easily known, destroyed, and excommunicated, as being then more raw and rude, and as yet wanting utterance. For he was then destitute of rational, defensive, definitive, decretive, (or determinative) wisdom, he wanted yet those hypocritical Ministers, and humane Ordinances, and the outward shew of those Religious Orders. And therefore though fallen away into that sin and errour, yet he had then wherewithall to cover his villany, or the shame of his errours, or of that sin, having none of those riches yet, nor of those endowments whereby to allure unto himself any Minister for his service, or to be enabled to multiply, preserve and defend his adherents : for he wanted the secular strength and power, and could not force nor compell any from the truth unto falshood. And because he wanted many things yet, therefore he could not defile or scandalize any by his deceits, and thus,

el contraria per sapientia del mond, per falsas Religions, & per enseinta bonta, per poesta spiritual, per tyrannita secular, per riguessas, honors de degnetas, per delicancas & per deleit del mond, & contraria per aquesti modi.

Per aizo sia manifest a un chascun que per neun modo l' Antechrist non po esser complir ni venir sinon quant aquestas cosas nommas foron conjointas ensemp per far perfecta hypocrita & falseta, zo es cum li sani del mondi, Religios, Pharisios, Ministres, Doctors, la potesta secular cum lo poble del mond foron ensemp conjoint. Adonca feron l' home de pecca ensemp & d' error entier. Car al temp de li Apostol ja sia zo que l' Antechrist era ja conceopu, ma car essent enfant mancava de li debit membre interiors & exteriors. Emperzo el se conossia & se destruia, & se excommunicava plus legierament enaima rostic & grossier, el era fait mut : car el manqué de sapientia rational, scusativa, definitiva, sententiativa. Et car el manqué de li sols Menistres senza verita, & de li statut humans, manqué de li Religios de fora. Emperzo el era vengu en l' error & al pecca, ma non hac cum liqual el pogues cubrir la sozura o vergongna de las errors o del pecca, cum el manque de riquecas & de dotations, non poc conduire alcun Ministre per si, ni non poc multiplicar, conservar, defendre lor : & car el manqué de poissanza o poesta secular, el non poc forçar o costreigner neun de la verita a la falseta. Et car el manqué de mot, el non poc scozar ni escandalizar neun per li seo soleniament. Et enaimi essent trop tenre & frevol

non

non poc obtenir Inoc en la Gleisa, total-
ment en tota Gleisa. Ma creissent en li
seo membres, zo es en li Menistre cec &
hypocrit, & de li sojet del mond & el
meseime creisec entro a Baron parfait en
en pleneta daita zo es cum li spirituals &
seculars, & li amadors del mond, cec en
la fe, son multiplica en la Gleisa com
tota poesta essent mals. Volent esser or a
& honra en la cosas spirituals, & cubrir
la soa propria magesta, malicia & pec-
cas, & a huza desains & Pharisios, a
aizo enaima esdit de sobre : Car maxi-
ma iniquita es cubrir & ornar la iniqui-
ta digna de excommunication, & voler
esser per aizo que non es dona a l' home,
ma conven al sol Dio & a Jesus Christ
tanta coma Mediator. Ostar aquestas co-
sas a Dio fraudulentament per rapina,
& traportar sobre si & las soas obras, es
vist esser maxima felonia, enaimi rege-
nerar, perdonnar li pecca, distribuir las
gracias del Sanct Esperit, confeitar
Christ, & enaimi de las autras. Et cu-
brir se en totas aquestas cosas de mantel
d' authorita, & de forma de parolas, &
enganar per aquestas cosas lo poble rostic
seguent lo mond. En aquestas cosas que
son del mond, & de partir de Dio & de
la vera Fe, & de la reformation del
Sanct Esperit, departir de la vera Peni-
tentia, de la vertuosa operation, de la
perseveranza al ben, departir de la Ca-
rita, de la patientia, de la paureta, de la
humilita, & zo ques plus peissime de
tot, departir de la vera Speranza, &
pansar ley en tot mal, & en la vana Spe-
ranza del mond, servir a tuit li menesti-

being so weak and tender, he could obtain no place in the Church. But growing up in his Members, that is to say, in his blinde and dissembling Ministers, and in worldly Subjects, he at length became a complete man, grew up to his full age, to wit, then when the lovers of the world in Church and State, blinde in faith, did multiply in the Church, and get all the power into their hands. And so it came to that pass, that as evil as they were, they would be sought unto, and honoured in spiritual matters, covering their authority, malice, & sins, for which end they made use of the worldly wise, and of the Pharisees, in manner abovesaid. For, it is a great wickedness to cover & colour iniquity worthy excommunication, and to go about establishing ones self by such a means as cannot be attributed to man, but belongs to God alone, and to *Jesus Christ* as Mediatour. And for man to deprive God of such and such things by fraud &usurpation, &to arrogate the same unto themselvs & their works appears to be the greatest Felony; as when one doth attribute unto himself the power of regeneration, of pardoning sins, of dispensing the Gifts of the Holy Ghost, &to represent *Christ*, and such like matters. And in all these things to cover themselves with the cloak of authority and of the Word, thereby deceiving silly people, that follow the world, in such things as are of the world, separating themselves from God and the true Faith, and from the Reformation of the Holy Spirit, withdrawing themselves from true Repentance, pious practice, and perseverance in goodness, and turning their backs upon Charity, patience, poverty, humility, and that which is worst of all, they forsake the true Hope, and rely on all evil, and on the vain hope of the world, serving all those Ceremonies instrumental hereunto,

unto, and deceitfully caufing the people to commit Idolatry with all the Idols of the World under the Name of Saints and Relicks and their worfhip; in fo much that the people pernicioufly erring from the way of truth, and being perfwaded they ferve God, and do well, are ftirred up to hate and to be enraged againft thofe that love the truth, even to murder fo many of them, fo that according to the Apoftle we may truly fay, This is that man of fin complete, that lifts up himfelf againft all that is called God, or worfhipped, and that fetteth himfelf in oppofition againft all truth, fitting down in the Temple of God, that is, in his Church, and fhewing forth himfelf as if he were God, being come with all manner of deceivablenefs for thofe that perifh. And fince he is truly come, he muft no longer be looked for; for he is grown old already by God's permiffion; nay, he begins even to decay, and his power and authority is abated: for the Lord doth already kill this wicked one by the fpirit of his mouth; by divers perfons of good difpofitions, fending abroad a power contrary to his, and thofe that love him, and which difturbeth his place, and his poffeffions, and puts divifion into that City of *Babylon*, wherein the whole generation of Iniquity doth prevail and reign.

What are the Works of *Antichrift*?

The firft Work of *Antichrift* is, to take away the Truth, and to change it into Falfhood, Errour, and Herefie. The fecond Work of *Antichrift* is to cover Falfhood over with a femblance of Truth, and to affert and maintain Lyes by the name of Faith and Graces, and to difpenfe Falfhood

er a aquestas cofas, far idolatrar lo poble, fervir fraudulentament a las idolas de tot lo mond fot li Sanct, & a las reliquas & a li menestier de lor, enaimi que lo poble errant peissament de la via de verita pense si fervir a Dio & far ben, escommou a quel poble a odi, & a ira, & a malicia contra li fidel, & en contra li amant la verita, & fay moti homecedi, & enaimi l' Apostol dis verita. Quel es home de pecca compli & que el se esleva fobre tot zo ques dit Dio, o zo ques collu e quel contraria a tota verita, & quel fee al temple de Dio, zo es en la Gleifa, demonstrant fe enaima el fossa Dio, & quel ven en tota feduction a aquilli que perisson, & si aquel felon ja venc perfectament, & non es de querre, car el es fait de Dio ja veil, & que el descreis ja: car la foa potesta & authorita es amerma, & que lo Segnor Jefus occi aquest felon per lo Sperit de la foa bocca, en moti home de bona volunta, & tramet potesta contraria a fi & a li feo amador, & decipa li feo luoc & poffeffions, & depart aquesta cita de Babylonia e laqual tota generacion hac vigor de malicia.

Quas fon las obras de l' Antechrist?

La prima obra de l' Antechrist es toller la verita & cambiar ley en falfeta & en error & en heregia. La feconda obra de l' Antechrist es cubrir la falfeta de la verita, & de las errors, & provar & confermar ley per la fe & per las vertus, & de intremenar la falfeta en las

fpi-

spirituals al poble soget o sia en li Meni-stre o sia en li menestier, o sia en tota la Gleisa. Et aquestas doas obras contenon perfecta et complia malicia laqual non pogron far neun tyran, neun poissant del commençament del mond entro en li temp de l' Antechrist. Ma Christ non hac alcuna vez aital enemic devant aquest que pogues enaima pervertir la via de verita non sensiblament, & con-vertir aquella meseima verita en falseta, & la falseta en verita, non semeillanta-ment lo cootivador de l' un & de l' autre, de la verita & de la falseta. Enaimi que la Sancta Mayre Gleisa cum li seo veray fil li es tota squalqueia en las veri-tas, specialment en las ministerials de li veray ministre en verita, & de li mene-steri, & de li menesteri, & de l' usar de lor, et de li filli participant, illi plora plorilvoment per lo parlar, et per lo plaint de Jeremia disent. En qual ma-niera se sola la cita del poble Pagan et non circoncis? illi es faita veufua zo es de verita del seo Spos. La dona de las gens per subjection de las errors, de li pecca, Princessa de las Provincias per departiment del mond, et daquellas co-sas que son al mond. Plora et veias plus enant, et atrobares ara totas cosas com-plias per lo temp: car la Sancta Gleisa se sia et es tengua per Synagoga. Et la Synagoga de li malignant, es predica per maire ben cresent en la Ley. La fal-seta es predica per la verita, la enequeta per la eygaleza, la non justitia es predica et tengua per la justitia, la error per la fe, lo pecca per la vertu, la messognia per la verita.

intermingled with spiritual things un-to the People under his Subjection, ei-ther by means of his Ministers, or by the Ministry, or any otherwise in rela-tion to the Church. Now it is certain that these two ways of proceeding do contain so perfect and complete a wickedness, the like no Tyrant and no Power in the World was ever able to compass since the Creation, until the time of *Antichrist.* And *Christ* had ne-ver any Enemy yet like this, so able to pervert the way of Truth into Falf-hood, and of Falshood into Truth, and who in like manner did pervert the Professours of the one or the other, viz. of Truth and of Falshood, in so much that the holy Mother the Church with her true Children, is al-together troden under foot, especially in the Truth, and in what concerneth the true worship in the Truth, and the Ministry, and the exercise thereof, and the Children partaking thereof; which causeth her to weep bitterly, in the language and complaints of *Jere-my,* saying, *Ah how desolate art thou, O City of the heathen people and uncir-cumcised? she is become a Widow*; namely, being destitute of the Truth of her Bridegroom, Lady of People, by reason of the subjection to Errours and to sin; Princess of Provinces, by partaking with the World, and the things that are in the World; Weep and look but abroad a little, and thou shalt finde those things now accom-plished at this time: for, the holy Church is accounted a Synagogue of Miscreants, and the Congregation of the Wicked is esteemed the Mother of them, that rightly believe in the Word. Falshood is preached up for Truth, Iniquity for Righteousness, Injustice passeth for Justice, Errour for Faith, Sin for Virtue, and Lyes for Verity.

What are the Works that proceed from thefe firft Works?

Anfw. Thefe, the firft is, that it perverts the fervice of *Latreia*, that is, the worfhip properly due to God alone, by giving it to *Antichrift* himfelf and to his Works, to the poor creature, reafonable or unreafonable, fenfible or fenflefs; to the reafonable, as to man, male or female Saints deceafed, and unto Images, Carkaffes, or Relicks. His Works are the Sacraments, efpecially the Sacrament of the Eucharift, which he adoreth as God, and as *Jefus Chrift*, together with the things bleffed and confecrated by him, and prohibites the worfhipping of God alone.

The fecond Work of the *Antichrift* is, that he robs and bereaves *Chrift* of his Merits, together with all the fufficiency of Grace, of Juftification, of Regeneration, Remiffion of Sins, Sanctification, Confirmation, and fpiritual Nourifhment, and imputes and attributes the fame to his own authority, to a form of words, to his own Works; unto Saints and their Interceffion, and unto the Fire of the Purgatory; and feparates the People from *Chrift*, and leads them away to the things aforefaid, that they may not feek thofe of *Chrift*, nor by *Chrift*; but onely in the works of their own hands, and not by a lively Faith in God, nor in *Jefus Chrift*, nor in the Holy Spirit, but by the will and pleafure, and by the works of *Antichrift*, according as he preacheth, that all Salvation confifts in his Works.

The third Work of *Antichrift* confifts in this, that he attributes the Regeneration of the Holy Spirit unto the dead outward work, baptizing Children in that Faith, and teaching,

Quals obras procedon de las premieras obras?

Refpond. Aqueftas. La premiera obra es que el convertis lo cootivament de Latria, propiament propi al fol Dio, a fi, et a li feo fait, a la paura creatura rational et non rational, fenfible o non fenfible. Rational enaima li home, Sanct o Sanctas trapaffas d' aquest mond, et a las imagenas de lor, galas, reliquias. Li fait de luy fon li Sacrament, fpecialment lo Sacrament de la Euchariftia que el col per Dio et per Jefu Chrift fimellantament, col las cofas benitas et confacras, e proibis adora lo fol Dio.

La feconda obra de l' Antechrift es quel ofte et tol deChrift lo merit de Chrift con tota la fufficientia de la gratia, de la juftitia, de la regeneration, remifsion de li pecca, de la fanctification, de la confirmation et de l' Efperitual nuriment, et lo deputa et lo tribuis a la foa authorita, a la forma de las parolas, a las foas obras, et a li Sanct, et a la lor enterceffion, et al fuoc en Purgatori, et depart lo poble de Chrift, et amena lo poble a aqueftas cofas ja dictas, que el non quera aquellas de Chrift, ni per Chrift: ma folament en las obras de las lors mans, et non per la fe viva en Dio ni en Jefu Chrift, & el Sanct Sperit, ma per volunta e obras de l' Antechrift, enaimi que el predica tota la falu conftar en las foas obras.

La terza obra de l' Antechrift es que el attribuis la reformation del Sanct Sperit a la fe morta de fora, et bapteia li enfant en aquella fe, et enfeignant effer a *confegre*

confegre per ley lo Baptifme et la regeneration, et prefta et dona en lei mefeima li orden, et li autre Sacrament, et fonda en ley tota la Chriftianita, que es contra lo Sanct Efperit.

La quarta obra de l' Antechrift es la qual enfemp baftic, et edifique tota Religion et fanctita del poble en la foa Meffa, et enfemp ha teiffut varias ceremonias en un Fudaicas et de li Gentil, et de li Chriftian. A laqual conducent la congregation et lo poble a auvir ley, lo priva de l' efpiritual et Sacramental maniament, et lo depart de la vera Religion, et de li Commandament de Dio, et fe ofta de las obras de mifericordia per li feo offertori, et per aital Meffa alogué lo poble en vana fperanza.

La quinta obra de l' Antechrift es quel fai totas las foas obras que el fia vift, et que el obre la foa non fazivol avaritia, enaimi quel aya totas cofas vendablas, et non faza alcuna cofa fenza fymonia.

La fexta obra de l' Antechrift es, quel dona luoc a li pecca manifeft, fenfa fententia Ecclefiaftica, et non excommunica li non penitent.

La feptima obra de l' Antechrift es quel non regis ni defend la foa unita per lo Sanct Sperit, ma per potefta fecular, et enfemp pren lei en adjutori de las fpirituals cofas.

La octava obra de l' Antechrift es, que el eyra, et perfec, et acaifonna, roba et mortifica li membre de Chrift.

Aqueftas cofas fon quafi la plus principals de las obras de luy, lafqual el fai contra la verita, lafquals per neun modo non pon totas effer numbras ni fcriptas. Ma bafte al prefent d' aver deita d' a-

that thereby Baptifm and Regeneration muft be had, and therein he confers and beftows Orders and other Sacraments, and groundeth therein all his Chriftianity, which is againft the Holy Spirit.

The fourth Work of *Antichrift* is, that he hath conftituted and put all Religion and holinefs of the People in going to Mafs, and hath patcht together all manner of Ceremonies, fome *Jewifh*, fome heathenifh, and fome *Chriftian*: and leading the Congregations thereunto, and the People to hear the fame, doth thereby deprive them of the fpiritual and facramental manducation, and feduceth them from the true Religion, and from the Commandments of God, and withdraws them from the works of compaffion; by his offerings; and by fuch a Mafs hath he lodged the People in vain hopes.

The fifth Work of the *Antichrift* is, that he doth all his Works fo that he may be feen, that he may glut himfelf with his infatiable avarice, that he may fet all things to fale, and do nothing without Symony.

The fixth Work of the *Antichrift* is, that he allows of manifeft Sins, without any Ecclefiaftical Cenfure, and doth not excommunicate the Impenitent.

The feventh Work of *Antichrift* is, that he doth not govern nor maintain his Unity by the Holy Spirit, but by Secular Power, and maketh ufe thereof to effect fpiritual matters.

The eighth Work of the *Antichrift* is, that he hates, and perfecutes, and fearcheth after, difpoils and deftroys the Members of *Chrift*.

Thefe things are in a manner the principal Works which he commits againft the Truth, they being otherwife numberlefs, and paft writing down. It fufficeth for the prefent, to

have

have obſerved the moſt general, and thoſe whereby this iniquity lies moſt covered and concealed.

Firſt and chiefly, he makes uſe of an outward Confeſſion of the Faith; and it is that whereof the Apoſtle ſpeaketh, *For, they confeſs in words, that they have known God, but by their deeds they deny him.*

Secondly, he covers his Iniquity by the length or ſucceſſion of time, and allegeth, that he is maintained by certain wiſe and learned men, and by religious Orders of certain Votaries of ſingle Life, Men and Women, Virgins and Widows: and beſides, by a numberleſs People, of whom it is ſaid in the *Revelation, That power is given him over every Tribe, Language, and Nation, and all that dwell on Earth, ſhall worſhip him.*

In the third place, he covers his Iniquity by the ſpiritual authority of the Apoſtles, againſt which the Apoſtle ſpeaketh expreſly, *We are able to do nothing againſt the Truth, and there is no power given us for deſtruction.*

Fourthly, by many Miracles here and there, whereas the Apoſtle ſaith, The coming of them is according to the Work (or, operation) of Satan, by all manner of Miracles, and Signs, and Wonders of Lyes, and by all kinde of deceitfull Iniquity.

Fifthly, by an outward Holineſs, by Prayers, Faſtings, Watchings, and Alms-deeds, againſt which the Apoſtle teſtifies, ſaying, Having a ſhew of Godlineſs, but having denied the power thereof.

Sixthly, he covers his Iniquity by certain Sayings of *Chriſt*, and by the Writings of the Ancients, and by Councils, which they obſerve ſo far forth onely as they do not deſtroy (or, overthrow) their wicked Life and Pleaſures.

Seventhly, by the Adminiſtration

queſtas qnaſi comma plus generals, per laſquals coſas es cuberta aqueſta eneque-ta.

Premierament et maximament per la confeſsion de fora de la fe. De laqual coſa di l' Apoſtol: car illi confeſſan lor aver conegu Dio per parolas, ma illi lo denegan per fait.

Secondiariament per la longueza de temp, et per manteza de li ſavi, de li Religios, de li vergeno, et vergenas de las veſuas, et de las honeſtas, etc. Et lo poble non numbrivol de loqual es dit en l' Apocalyps. Et poeſta fo dona a lei en tot trib, et lenga, et gent, et tuit aquilli que habitan en la terra adoraren lei.

Terzament, per authorita ſpiritual de li Apoſtol, contra liqual di. Nos non poen alcuna coſa contra la verita, et poeſta non dona en deſtruiment.

Quartament per moti miracli fait da-qui entro aqui, de laqual coſa di l' Apoſtol. L' advenament del qual es ſecond lobra de Sathanas, en tota vertu et enſeignas, et merevillas meſſongieras, et en tot engan d' enequita.

Quintament per Sanctita de fora, et orations, et dejunis, vigilias et almonas: contra aizo di l' Apoſtol. Havent la ſemblanza de pieta, ma denegant la vertu de ley.

Sextament per alcunas parolas de Chriſt, et per li eſcrit de li Antic, et per li Concili, loſquals illi gardan entant quant non deſtruon la mala vita et volupta de lor.

Septimament, per l' adminiſtration de

de l Sacrament, per liqual illi vomen la universita de las errors.

Octavament, per correptions, et predications verbals de li vici : car illi dion et non fan.

Nonament, de liqual alcuns fan enfeintament, et alcuns verayament et maximament per vita vertuofa. Car li efleit de Dio ben vollent et ben fazent, detengu aqui enaima en Babylonia, fon enaima or per loqual lo felon Antechrift cuebre la foa vanita, loqual non fuffre far lo veray cootivament al fol Dio, ni tenir la fperanza al fol Chrift, ni entendre a la veraia Religion.

Aqueftas cofas et motas otras fon enaimi mantel et veftiment de l' Antechrift con lafquals el cuebre la foa mefongiera malicia, quel non fia reprova tant coma Pagan, et en lafqual el po proceder defhoneftament, & a las meretrix. Si lo Chriftian es entengu per commandament departir fe de l' Antechrift, lo es dit, & es prova del Veilli & de Novel Teftament : car lo Segnor dis , Efaia cinquautadous. Departé vous, Departé vous, ifsi d' aqui, non voilla tocar lo foza, iffe del mez del, vous liqual porta li veiffel del Seignor fia munda : car vous non ifsire en la rumor, ni non vous appropiare a la fuga, &c. Et Jeremia cinquanta. Fugé del mez de Babylonia, faille de la terra de li Caldei, & fia enaima cabri devant lo grez. Et vevos yo amen arei grand congregation de gent de la terra d' Aquilon en Babylonia, & feren appareilla en contra & d' aquienant fere prefa. Numbre 16. Departié vous del mez de la congregation azo que yo deftrua & perda aquifti viazament. Et dereço. Departés vos del tabernacle de l;

of the Sacraments, in which they lay open the univerfality of their Errours.

Eigthly, by Corrections (or, Difcipline) and meer verbal Preachings againft Vices; for, they fay, and do not.

Ninthly, by the virtuous Lives of fome that live feignedly fo, but efpecially, of fuch as live fo indeed among them. For, the Elect of God, that defire and do that which is good, are detained there, as in *Babylon*; and are like unto Gold, wherewith the wicked *Antichrift* doth cover his Vanity, not fuffering them to ferve God alone, nor to put all their hope in *Chrift* alone, nor to embrace the true Religion.

Thefe things & many others, are as it were a Cloak and Garment, wherewith *Antichrift* doth cover his lying wickednefs, that he may not be rejected as a Pagan, (or, Infidel) and under which he can go on to act his villanies boldly, and like a Whore. Now it is evident, as well in the *old*, as in the *New Teftament*, that a *Chriftian* ftands bound, by exprefs Command given him, to feparate himfelf from *Antichrift*. For, the Lord faith, *Ifai 52.* Withdraw, withdraw your felves, go forth thence, touch no unclean thing, go forth from the midft of her;cleanfe your felves, ye that bear the Veffels of the Lord : for ye fhall not go forth in hafte,&march not flying,&c.And *Jer. ch.50.* Flee out of *Babylon*, and come away out of the Land of the *Chaldeans*, and be like to the he-goats that go before the flock : for behold, I go to raife up againft *Babylon* an Affembly of great Nations, from the North, who fhall range themfelves in battailaray againft her, that fhe fhall be taken. In the 16. Chapter of *Numbers*, Separate your felves from amidft this Affembly, and I will confume them in a moment. And again, withdraw from the Tabernacle of the wicked,

and

and touch nothing of what belongs unto them, left you be involved in their fin. In *Leviticus*, I am the Lord your God, that have feparated you from the reft of the Nations; and therefore fhall ye feparate the clean beaft from the unclean, and fhall not defile your fouls in beafts, nor in fowls, nor in any things that move themfelves on the earth, and which I fhewed you that they are unclean. Again, in *Exodus, chap.* 34. Take heed you make no friendfhip (or, alliance) with the Inhabitants of that City, for, that would be thy ruine. And a little further, Make no agreement with the men of that Countrey, left they having gone a whoring after other gods, and worfhipped their Idols, they call thee and invite thee to eat things confecrated unto them. Nor fhalt thou take thee a Wife from among their Daughters, left they having plaid the harlot, that is to fay, committed Idolatry, they caufe thy children to go a whoring likewife after their gods, *Leviticus* 15. And therefore ye fhall teach your children, and bid them beware of their uncleanneffes, and that they may not die in them, having polluted my Sanctuary, *Ezech.* 2. But the heart that walks on offending, and in its offences, I will render their way upon their head, faith the Lord, *Deut.* 20. When thou fhalt have entred into the Land, which the Lord thy God fhall give thee, take heed thou do not according to the abominations of thofe people: for the Lord abhorreth all thofe things: and by reafon of fuch fins, he will blot them out, when thou fhalt enter their Land, thou fhalt be clean and without fpot with thy God. Thofe people whofe Land thou goeft to poffefs, hearken to the Soothfayer, and Diviner; but thy God hath difpofed otherwife in thy behalf. Now it is manifeft in the *New*

felon, & non voilla tocar aquillas cofas que apartenon a lor, que vos non fia enveloppa en li pecca de lor. Levitico *Yo foi lo voftre Seignor Dio loqual departic vos de li autre poble. Donc & vos departire dereço lo jument mund del non mund, & loiffel mund del non mund, & non fozare la voftras armas en las beftias en li oiffel, & en totas aquellas cofas que fon moguas en terra, & lafquals yo moftrei a vos fozas.* Item Exodi 34. *Garda que un qua non conjongnas amicitia cum li habitador d' aquella Cita, laqual fia a tu en ruina. Et dedines non far pact cum li home d' aquella Region, que cum illi auren forniga cum li lor Dios, et auren adora las fimulacras de lor, alcun apelle tu que tu manges de las cofas fanctificas a lor. Ni non penres moiller de las fillas de lor a li teo filli que en apres cum ellas auren forniga zo es idolatra, non fazan fornigar li teo filli en li Dio de lor.* Levit. 15. *Donc vous enfeignaré li filli difent que illi fquivon las non mundicias, & non moran en las lor fozuras que illi auren foza lo mio tabercle.* Ezechiel 2. *Ma lo cor loqual vay per offendament & per las foas offenfions, yo paufarey la via d' aquifti a lor cap dis lo Seignor.* Deut. 20. *Quand tu fere intra en la terra laqual lo teo Seignor Dio donare a tu, garda que tu non volhes refimeillar las abominations d' aquellas gens: car lo Seignor ha totas aqueftas cofas en abomination. Et per li pecca d' aquefta maniera el sfacare lor al teo intrament. Tu feres perfeit & fenza macula cum lo teo Dio. Aqueftas gens de lafquals tu poffefsires las terras auvon li Argariador et li Devin, ma tu fies ordena autrament del teo Dio. Ma del No-*

vel

vel Teſtament es manifeſt. Joan. 12. *Que lo Seignor venc et ſo paſsiona per zo quel aioſtes en un li filli de Dio. Et car per aqueſta verita de unita, et depart, et commandé eſſer departia dizen. Matth.* 10. *Car yo venc departir l' home encontra lo ſio paire, la filla encontra la ſoa maire, et la nora contra la ſoa ſacra, et li domeſtic de l' home ſon ennemic de luy. Et commandé eſſer departi dizent. Si alcun non laiſſare lo ſio paire et la maire, etc. Item, Garda vos de li fals Prophetas liqual venon a vos en veſtimenta de feas, etc. Item, Garda vos del levam de li Phariſio. Item, Garda vos que alcun non vos engane: car moti venren al mio nom enganaren moti. Et adonca ſi alcun dire a vos. Venos Chriſt es aizi o aylai non o voilla creire, non voilla anar en apres lor. Et en l' Apocalyps: admoneſta per propia vouz et commanda lo ſio poble iſsir de Babylonia dizent. Et auvi vouz del cel dizent a mi. O lo mio poble iſsi de lei et non ſia parzonnier de li pecca de lei, et non receba de las plagas de ley. Car li pecca de lei pervengron entro al cel, et lo Segnor ſe recorde de las enequitas de ley. Co meſeime di l' Apoſtol. Non voilla amenar jouc cum li non fidel. Car qual participation es de la juſtitia cum l' iniquita, o qual compagnia de la luz cum las tenebras, ma qual convention de Chriſt al Diavol, o qual part et de li fidel cum li non fidel, o qual conſentiment del temple de Dio cum las idolas? Et dedines. Per la qual coſa iſſe del mez de lor, et ſia departi diſ lo Seignor, et non tocare lo non mund et yo recelarey vos et ſerey a vos en paire, et vos ſere a mi en fillis et en fillas diſ lo Seignor tot poderos. Item,*

Teſtament, John 12. That the Lord is come and ſuffered death, that he might gather together the Children of God; and by reaſon of this Truth of Unity, and ſeparation from others it is, that he ſaith in St. *Matthew, chap.* 10. For I am come to ſeparate a Man from his Father, and ſet the Daughter againſt her Mother, and the Daughter in Law againſt her Mother in Law, and they of a mans Houſhold ſhall be his Enemies. And he hath commanded this Separation, ſaying, *Whoſoever doth not forſake his Father and his Mother, etc.* And again, *Beware of falſe Prophets, which come unto you in Sheeps cloathing.* Again, *Beware of the Leven of the Phariſees:* and *Take heed leſt any ſeduce you; for, many ſhall come in my Name, and ſeduce many.* And then, *If any tell you, Behold,* Chriſt *is here or there, believe him not, and walk not after them.* And in the *Revelation* he warneth by his own voice, and chargeth his, to *go out of Babylon,* ſaying, *And I heard a voice from Heaven, ſaying, O my people come forth out of her, and be not partakers of her ſins, that ye receive none of her plagues: for, her ſins are come up into Heaven, and the Lord remembereth her iniquities.* The Apoſtle ſaith the ſame, *Join not your ſelves under one yoak with the unbelievers, for what participation hath Righteouſneſs with Iniquity, or what fellowſhip is there between Light and Darkneſs, and what communion hath* Chriſt *with the Devil, or what part hath the Faithfull with the Infidel, or what agreement is there of the Temple of God with Idols? And therefore go forth from among the midſt of them, and ſeparate your ſelves, ſaith the Lord, and touch no unclean thing, and I will reſcue you, and will be inſtead of a Father to you, and you ſhall be as Sons and Daughters* to me, *saith the Lord the Almighty.* Again, *Ephes* 5. *Do not partake with them; for ye were in the way of darkness, but now ye are in the light of the Lord.* Again, 1 *Cor.*10. *I would not have you become the companions of the Devil. Ye cannot participate of the Lords Table and of the Table of Devils.* So 2 *Thess.*3. *O Brethren, we declare unto you in the Name of our Lord* Jesus Christ, *that you beware of every Brother walking dishonestly, and not according to the customes, which ye received from us. For, ye know after what manner ye ought to be followers of us.* And again a little after he saith, *If there be any that obeys not our word, set down in this Epistle, have ye nothing to do with him, that he may be ashamed.* Again, *Ephes.* 5. *Have no communion with the works of Darkness, which are unfruitfull.* And 2 *Tim.* 3. *Be it known unto you, that in the later times, there will be troublesome times.* And afterwards, *Having a shew of piety, but having denied the power thereof, turn thy self away from such.* By what hath been said hitherto it appears clearly, what is the wickedness of *Antichrist* and his perversness. Also the Lord commands our separating from him, and joyning our selves with the holy City of *Jerusalem*: therefore knowing such things, the Lord having revealed them unto us by his Servants, and believing this Revelation according to the holy Scriptures, and being admonished by the Commandments of the Lord, we do both inwardly and outwardly depart from *Antichrist*, because we know him to be the same; and we keep company and unity one with another, freely and uprightly, having no other intent and purpose but purely and singly to please the Lord, and to be saved: and by the Lords help, we joyn our selves to the Truth of *Christ*

*Ephes.*5. *Non voilla esser fait parzonier de lor, car vos eras a la via de tenebras: ma ara sé luz al Seignor.* Item, 1 *Corinth.*10. *Yo non voil vos esser fait compagnons del Demoni. Vos non poe esser fait parzonier de la taula del Seignor & de la taula de li Demoni.* Item, 2 *Thess.*3. *O fraires nos anuncien a vos al nom de nostre Seignor* Jesus Christ *que vos garde de tot fraire anant deshonestament, & non second las costumas lasquals vos receopes de nos. Ca vos meseimes sabe en qual maniera convent a resimeillar nos. Et dedins. Si alcun non obedirè a la nostra parola nota per aquest Evescoa, & non sia ensemp mescla cum luy que el sia confondu.* Item *Ephes.*5. *Nos voilla vos accompagnar a las obras non fructuosas de tenebras.* Item 2 *Tim.* 3. *Ma sapia aizo. Ca per illos temps istaren en li derreiran dia. Et dedins. A certa havent la semblança de pieta: ma denegant la vertu de ley, squiva aquisti. De las cosas notas desobre se demonstra manifestament la malitia de l'Antichrist, & la soa perverseta, &c. Et car lo es commanda del Seignor departir se de luy meseime dedins & defora. Et conjoingner se a* Hierusalem *sancta Cita. Donc nos conoissent aquestas cosas, lo Seignor revelant per li seo serf & cresent aquesta revelation iosta las sanctas Scripturas, & nos ensemp admonesta de li Commandament del Seignor, nos fazen departiment exterior & interior de luy, loqual nos cresen* Antechrist, *& aven uni compagnia, & unita de bona volunta, et de dreita entention, de pur & simple perpausament de plaser al Seignor, & asser salva: lo Seignor ajudant, & la verita la* Christ *& de la soa Sposa enaima pechi-*

nita de l' intellect po sostenir. Donc *nos ordonnen notar quals sian las cosas del nostre departiment, & encara de la nostra congregation, afin que si lo Seignor aure dona aver aquesta meseima verita: Porte ensemp cum nos l' amor en lei meseima. Et si peraventura non sossa ben enlumena, recepia ajutori per aquest menestier, lo Seignor arrosant. Et si lo es dona plus a alcun, & plus autament; & nos desiren esser enseigna plus humilment, & saber meilli de luy, & esser corrigi en li nostre deffect. Donc aquestas cosas que ensegon son causa del nostre departiment.*

Sia manifest a tuit et a sengles la causa del nostre departiment esser ista, aital per la verita essential de la fe, & menesterial la verita essential de la fe, es la interior conoissenza d' un verai Dio, & unita de Essentia en tres personas, laqual non dona carn ni sang. Coottivament convenivol al sol Dio, l' amor de luy meseime sobre totas cosas, la sanctification & l' honoration de luy sobre totas cosas et sobre tuit li nom: speranza viva per Christ en Dio, la regeneration et renovation interior per Fe, per Esperança, et per Charita; lo merit de Jesu Christ cum tota sufficientia de gratia et justitia: la participation o la communion de tuit li esleit: la remission de li pecca: la sancta conversation, et lo fidel compliment de tuit li Commandament en la fe de Christ: la vera penitentia, et la final perseveranza, et vita eterna.

Las veritas ministerials son aquestas. La congregation exterior de li Ministres, cum lo poble suject, en luoc, et en temp,

and his Spouse, how small soever she appear, as far forth as our understanding is able to comprehend. And therefore we thought good to set down here for what causes we departed, and what kinde of Congregation we have, to the end that if the Lord be pleased to impart the knowledg of the same truth unto others, those that receive it, may love it together with us. And if peradventure they be not sufficiently enlightened, they may receive help by this Ministery, and be sprinkled by the Lord. If some one have more abundantly received, and in an higher measure, we desire the more humbly to be taught, and to learn better of him, and to amend our defects. Now then the causes of our Separation are these ensuing.

Be it known unto every one in general and in particular, that the cause of our Separation is this, namely, for the real Truths sake of the Faith, and by reason of our inward knowledg of the onely true God, and the Unity of the Divine Essence in three Persons, which knowledg Flesh and Bloud doth not afford; and for the befitting Service, due to that onely God; for the love of him above all things, for Sanctification, and for his Honour above all things, and above every Name: for the living hope through *Christ* in God; for Regeneration, and the inward renewing by Faith, Hope, and Charity: for the Merit of *Jesus Christ*, with all the sufficiency of his Grace and Righteousness: for the Communion of Saints; for the Remission of Sins; for an holy Conversation, and for the faithfull accomplishment of all the Commandments in the Faith of *Christ:* for true Repentance, for final perseverance, and Life everlasting.

The Ministerial Truths are these, the outward congregating of the Pastours with the People in convenient place

place and time to inſtruct them in the
Truth by theMiniſtry,&leading,eſta-
bliſhing,& maintaining the Church in
the Truth aforeſaid. The ſaid good
Miniſters preſs Faith and good Life,
and are exemplary for manners and
obedience, and watchfully follow the
Example and Work of the Lord, toward the Flock.

The things which the Miniſters are
obliged to do for the Service of the
People are theſe, the preaching of the
Word of the Goſpel: the Sacraments
joyned to the Word, which do certifie, what the intent and meaning
thereof is, and confirm the hope in
Chriſt unto the faithfull; the Miniſterial Communion hath all things by
the eſſential Truth. And all other
Miniſterial things may be reduced to
the foreſaid. But as to the particular
Truths ſome of them are eſſentially
neceſſary to Mans Salvation, other
ſome conditionally. They are contained in the twelve Articles of the
Chriſtian Faith, and in divers paſſages
of the Apoſtles. As for *Antichriſt* he
hath reigned a good while already in
the Church by Gods permiſſion.

The Errours and Impurities of *Antichriſt* forbidden by the Lord are
theſe, *viz.* a various and endleſs Idolatry, againſt the expreſs Command
of God and *Chriſt*. Divine Worſhip
offered, not to the Creatour, but to
the Creature, viſible and inviſible,
corporal and ſpiritual, rational and
ſenſible, natural and artificial, under
the name of *Chriſt* or Saints, Male or
Female, and of Relicks, and Authorities; unto which Creatures they offer
the Service or Worſhip of Faith and
Hope, Works, Prayers, Pilgrimages,
Alms, Oblations, and Sacrifices of
great price. And thoſe Creatures they
ſerve, honour, and adore ſeveral ways,
by Songs, and Hymns, Speeches, Solemnities, and Celebrations of Maſſes,

*en la verita, per las miniſterials, en la
verita toca deſobre, amenant, eſtablent,
et conſervant per fidella et ſovendiera
compagnia; li bon Meniſtre perſen de la
ſe et de vita, eſſent en coſtuma et obedientia, et perfaçent eſueillament la pra-
tiqua et uzança del Seignor ſobre lo
grecs.*

*Las coſas laſquals li Meniſtre ſon en-
tengu ſervir al poble ſon aqueſtas. La
parola Evangelica, et la parola de re-
conciliation, o la ley de gratia al ſen o
entention de Chriſt. Ca el deo notificar
la parola Evangelica: lo Sacrament
ajoinct a la parola certifica lo ſeo ſen et
entendament, et conferman l'eſperança
en Chriſt et en lo fidel. La communion
miniſterial a totas coſas per la verita
eſſential. Et ſi alcunas autras coſas ſian
miniſterials totas ſe pon ja conclurre en
aqueſt dit. Ma d'aqueſtas ſingulars veritas, alcunas ſon neceſſarias eſſential-
ment a la ſalu humana, alcunas conditi-
onalment ſe contenon en 12. Articles, en
l'aioſtament de pluſiors parolas de li
Apoſtol. Ma car l'Antechriſt per lo
paſſa ja regnant en la Gleiſa per la permiſſion Divina, etc.*

*Las errors et las non munditias entre-
ditas per lo Seignor de l'Antechriſt ſon
aqueſtas, varia et non nombrivol, idola-
es contra lo Commandament de Dio et de
Chriſt, dona a la creatura, et non al
Creator, veſibla et non veſibla, corporal
o ſpiritual, entendivol, et ſenſibla natural o fabrica, per qual ſe ſia art ſot qual-
que qual nom de Chriſt, o de li Sanct o de
las Sanctas, et de las reliquias & de las
authoritas, a laſquals creaturas es ſervi
per ſe, per ſperanza, per effect, per orations, per peregrinations, per alimoſnas,
per offertas, per ſacrificis de grand de-
ſpenſas. Laqual creatura illi colon, ado-
ran, honran per pluſors manieras. Per
canzons, proimis, per ſolemnizations, et
celebrations de Meſſas, de Veſpras, de*
                                    Com-

Complet as a lor mefeime, per horas, per vigilias, per feftivitas, per aquiflament de gratia, loqual de gratia ifta al fol Dio effentialment, et en Jefu Chrift meritoriament, et es aquifta per la fola fe, per lo Sanct Sperit.

Car la es non alcuna autra caufa de idolatria finon falfa opinion de gratia, de verita, de authorita, d' envocation, d' entrepellation, laqual el mefeime Antechrift departic de Dio et en li meneftier, et en las authoritas, et en las obras de las foas mans, et a li Sanct, et al Purgatori. Et aquefta enequita de Antechrift es dreitament contra lo premier article de la fe, et contra lo premier Commandament de la Lei.

Semeillament lo defordena amor del mond, de l' Antechrift, es del qual germenan tuit li mal et li pecca en la Gleifa, de li guiador, de li regidor, de li officier; liqual pecca iftan fença correction, illi fon contra la verita de la fe, et contra la conoiffença de Dio lo Paire. Teftimoniant Joan. loqual dis. Aquel que pecca non conois ni non ve Dio. Car fi alcun ama lo mond, lo Charita del Paire non es en luy. La feconda eniquita de l' Antechrift es d' efperanza de perdon, et de gratia, et de juflitia, et de verita, et de vita eterna, non repofta en Chrift, ni en Dio per Chrift, ma en li home vio et mort et en authoritas, et en meneftier Ecclefiaftic, en benedictions, en facrifications, en orations, et enaimi de las autras fobre nombras, ni per vera fe laqual obra penitentia per charita, et per departiment del mal et per aioflament al ben. Iftablament et principalment l' Antechrift enfeigna non fperar en aiço, la regeneration, la confermation, la fpiritual refection, o communion, la

Vefpers, fitted unto the fame, by certain Hours, Vigils, Feaft-days, thereby to obtain Grace, which is effentially in God alone, and meritorioufly in *Chrift*, and is to be obtained by Faith alone, through the Holy Spirit.

And indeed, there is nothing elfe that caufeth Idolatry, but the falfe opinion of Grace, Truth, Authority, Invocation, Interceffion, which this *Antichrift* hath deprived God of, to attribute the fame to thefe Ceremonies, Authorities, the Works of a mans own hands, to Saints and to Purgatory. And this Iniquity of *Antichrift* is directly againft the firft Article of Faith, and againft the firft Commandment of the Law.

So alfo, the exceffive Love of the World, that is in *Antichrift*, is that whence fprings fuch a World of Sin and Mifchief in the Church, as well in them that govern, as in them that officiate in the fame; who fin without controul; they are againft the Truth of Faith, and againft the knowledg of God the Father. Witnefs St. *John* faying, *He that finneth knoweth not, nor feeth God: for, if any love the World the Love of the Father is not in him.* The fecond Iniquity of *Antichrift*, lieth in the hope which he gives, of Pardon, Grace, Juftification, Truth and Life everlafting, as things not to be fought and had in *Chrift*, nor in God by *Chrift*, but in men either living or already deceafed, in humane Authorities, in Ecclefiaftical Ceremonies, in Benedictions, Sacrifices, Prayers, and fuch other things, as were before mentioned, not by a true and lively Faith, which worketh Repentance by Love, and caufeth one to depart from evil, and give himfelf up to God. Again, *Antichrift* teacheth not to fettle a firm hope in thofe things, *viz.* Regeneration, fpiritual Confirmation, or Communion,

munion, Remiſſion of Sins, Sanctification of eternal Life; but to hope, through the Sacraments, or, by means of his wretched Simony, whereby the People are greatly abuſed; in ſo much that putting all things to ſale, he invented a number of Ordinances, old and new, to get moneys; giving way, that if any do but ſuch and ſuch a thing, he ſhall get Grace and Life. And this twofold Iniquity is properly called in the Scriptures Adultery and Fornication. And therefore ſuch Miniſters, as lead the ſimple People into thoſe Errors, are called the Whore of the Revelation. And this Iniquity is againſt the ſecond Article, and again, againſt the ſecond and third Commandment of the Law.

The third Iniquity of *Antichriſt* conſiſts in this, that he hath invented, beſides the matters aforeſaid, certain falſe Religious Orders, and Rules, of Monaſteries, putting men in hope of acquiring Grace by building certain Churches, as alſo becauſe they do therein often and devoutly hear Maſs, receive the Sacraments, make confeſſion to the Prieſt (though ſeldom with Contrition) obſerve his Faſts, and empty the Purſe for him, and be a profeſſed Member of the Church of *Rome*, or if one have dedicated or vowed himſelf to be of ſuch an Order, Cap or Frock; all which he doth preſs as Duties, contrary to all Truth. And this Iniquity of *Antichriſt* is directly againſt the eighth Article of the Creed, *I believe in the Holy Ghoſt*.

The fourth Iniquity of *Antichriſt* is, that notwithſtanding his being the *fourth Beaſt* formerly deſcribed by *Daniel*, and the *Whore of the Revelation*, he nevertheleſs adorns himſelf with the Authority, Power, Dignity, Miniſtry, Offices, and the Scriptures, and makes himſelf equal with the true and holy Mother the Church, where–

remiſſion de li pecca, la ſanctification de vita eterna: ma per li Sacrament, et per la ſoa ſimonica, pravita per laqual lo poble es ſcarni, et avent totas coſas vendablas, atrobe varias ordonnanzas anticas et novas ſot obtennement de pecunias, permettent ſi alcun auré fait aizo o autre, dit o autre fait, vol qu' aital a-quiſtare gratia et vita. Et aqueſta dobla eniquita es appella propriament en las Scripturas, avorteri et fornication. Emperzo aitals Miniſtres regent lo poble beſtial, en aquellas errors ſon appella meretrix Apocalyptica. Et aqueſta eniquita es contra lo ſecond Article, et dereço contra lo ſecond et lo ters Commandament de la Ley.

La terza eniquita de l' Antechriſt es quel atroba autrament que es dict, falſas Religions, et reglas, et Monaſtiers, en Gleiſas per aquiſtament d' eſperanza. Enaimi quaſi alcun ſovendeiant auvire devotament Meſſas, et autre uſa de li Sacrament, o ſere confes, (ma rarament contrit,) et ſatisfazent per dejunis et deſpoillament de borſa, o ſi ſere iſta, o ſere membre en Gleiſa Romana, o ſi el ſere dona, o liora a la regla o a la cappa, illi af-ferman contra tota verita dever. Et aqueſta eniquita de l' Antechriſt es dreitament contra loyten article del Symbolo. Yo creo al Sanct Sperit.

La quarta eniquita de l' Antechriſt es car el meſcime eſſent la quarta beſtia devant ſcripta per Daniel, et meretrix Apocalyptica, ſe orna de nom de authorita, de poteſta, dignetas, de meneſtiers. d' officis, de ſcripturas, et ſe aigala et comara a la vera et ſancta Maire Gleiſa,

en

en taqual menefterialment es falu, et non autrament, en laqual es la verita de la vita, et de la doctrina, et de li Sacrament, et de li fojeĉt. Car finon quilli fe cubres enaimi, e li feo Meniftre erronic, et manifeft peccadors, conoiffua feria abandonna de tuit. Car li Emperador, & li Rey, & li Princi eftimant ley effer femblant de la Sancta Maire Gleifa, ameron ley mefeima, & la doteron contra lo Commandament de Dio. Et aquefta eniquita, de li Meniftre, de li fojeĉt, de li ordennä en error & en pecca, es dreitament contra lo noven. Yo creo la Sancta Gleifa. Aqueftas fon de la prima part.

Secondament, car li participant a las folas cofas defora en las coftumas, ordenas & atrobas humanament, creon o efperan lor participar a la verita de li offici paftoral, & de la cura, cum fi quilli fian tondu enaimi aquel, & fian oinct a modo de las pares, & fian benaizi tocant lo libre & lo calici com la man, confeffan la lor effer ordena dreitament Sacerdots. Semeillantament (enaima es dit de fobre) lo poble fojeĉt, communicant per parolas, per fegnals, per exercitations defora, & per li lor fouvent divers fait penfan ja lor participar a la verita traita d'aqui mefeime. Et aizo es contra l'autra part del noven Article. Yo creo la Communion de li Sanĉt. Lo es de ifsir de la pefsima communion de li Monach, a la participation de laqual amenant li home carnal, pois fan lor fperar en cofas de nient per l'avaritia, fian quals fe fian o luxurios o avars, folament quilli donan a lor mefeimes, dizon lor participar a la lor paureta & caftita.

in Salvation is to be had minifterially, and no where elfe ; wherein is found the Truth of Life, and Doctrine, and of the Sacraments, and Subjects. For if he fhould not cover himfelf in this manner, his Minifters being fuch notorious Sinners, he would foon be abandoned by all : for Kings and Princes fuppofing him to be like or equal to the true and holy Mother the Church, they loved him, and endued him againft the Commandment of God. And this Iniquity of the Minifters, Subjects, and ordained perfons given up to Errour and Sin, is directly againft the ninth Article, *I believe an holy Church.* Thus much for the firft part.

In the fecond place, thofe that being partakers of the outward Ceremonies onely, inftituted by humane Inventions, do believe and hope to partake of the reality of paftoral Cures and Offices, if they be but fhaved or fhorn likeLambs, & anointed or daubed like Walls, and made holy by touching the (Mafs-) Book, and the Chalice into their hand, they proclaim and publifh, that they are ordained lawfull Priefts to all intents. In like manner alfo the People (as is faid before) fubject unto them, communicating with them, by words, figns, and other outward exercifes, they conceive they partake of the Truth thereon depending. And this is againft the other part of the ninth Article, *I believe the Communion of Saints.* But it behoves us to depart from the wicked Communion of the Monks, by whom carnal men are eafily drawn away, they through covetoufnefs making them to truft in things of nought, be they never fo riotous and wretched, provided onely they give liberally unto them, and then they fay, Such men are made partakers of their poverty and chaftity.

The

The fifth Iniquity of *Antichrist* consists in this, that he doth feign and promise Pardon and Remission of Sins unto Sinners, not the truly contrite, but such as are wilfully persevering in their evil practises: in the first place he doth promise them Forgiveness of their Sins, for their auricular Confessions sake, and humane Absolution, and for their Pilgrimages, and this he doth out of Covetousness. And this Iniquity is against the eleventh Article of the Faith, *I believe the Remission of Sins.* For the same is in God authoritatively, and in *Christ* ministerially, through Faith, Repentance, Charity, and Obedience to the Word, and in Man by participation.

The sixth Iniquity lies herein, that to the very end of their Lives they go on hoping and trusting thus in the fore-mentioned Iniquities and coverings, especially till they come to the *last Unction,* and their invented *Purgatory;* in so much that the ignorant and rude Multitude do persevere in their Errour, they being taught and made to believe, that they are absolved of their Sins, though they never freely depart from them, for to hope Forgiveness of Sins and Life everlasting. And this Iniquity is directly against the eleventh and twelfth Articles of the Faith.

La quinta eniquita de l' Antechrist es quel promet enseintament perdonnanza & remifsion de li pecca a li peccador non contrit verament, & non cessant iftablament de las malas obras: ma premierament remifsion de li pecca en la confefsion auricular, & en l' absolution humana, en las pelegrinations per avaricia. Et aquefta eniquita es contra lonzen Article de la Fe. To creo la remifsion de li pecca. Car illi es en Dio authoritativament, & en Chrift minifterialment, per Fe, per Speranza, per Penitentia, per Carita, per obedientia de parola, en l' home participativament.

La fexta eniquita es, ca illi fervon a fperança entro a la fin de la vita per las devant ditas cubertas enequitas, per li manifeft peccador, & fpecialment per la extrema onction, & lo Purgatori foima, enaima que li home ruftic de la verita perfeveron en error, & font abfout de li pecca de liqual unqua non fe departiron per libra volunta que illi fpereffan la remifsion avenador, & vita eterna. Et aquefta eniquita es dreitament contra lonzen & lo dozen Article de la Fe.

ARTICLE II.

Of the Purgatory Dream.

The Purgatory Dream which many Priests and Monks hold forth and teach as an Article of Faith, with many Lyes, afferting is this; that after

Lo Purgatori foima, loqual moti Preires & Fras promovon & enfeignan coma Articl de Fe, & com motas meffongnias difent. Quen apres aquefta vita, en apres

apres lo montament de Chriſt al cel, las armas ſpecialment d' aquilli que devon eſſer ſalva, non ſatisfaçent en aqueſta vita per li lor pecca iſſen del corps, ſoſtenren penas ſenſiblas, & ſon purga en aquel ſobre dit Purgatori en apres aqueſta vita, & ſaillon de luy en apres la purgation, alcunas premieras, alcunas en apres, alcunas al dia del judici, & alcunas ara devant lo dia del judici : per laſquals armas un chaſcun fidel devon & poon adjudar en apres aqueſta vita per ligam de Charita, con orations, & Dejunis, et con almonas, & con Meſſas. Sobre loqual Purgatori per compliment de la lor avaritia moti en enſeint motas coſas en enſeignant & predicant coſas non certas, diſent que aitals armas ſian tormentas al ſobre dit Purgatori, alcunas entro al col, autras entro a la çentura, la autras lo de, & diçor que alcunas vez, ſeen et manian en tàula, & ſan convilli, & ſpecialment quan es la feſta de totas las armas, quand la gent uſſron a li Preyre largament ſobre las ſepulturas de lor. Et diſon que alcunas vez coillon las briſas ſot las taulas de li ric. Totas aqueſtas coſas et motas autras meſoingnas, l' avaricia & ſimonia es creiſua & alarga encerquaizo, & las clauſtras ſon haulças, & li temple ſumptuos ſon edifica, & alarga, & an multiplica autars outra modo, & non nombrivol monteça de Moynis, et de Canoinis, & an d' intremena autras coſas laſquals an donna caiſon dalargament & deligament, & donna la parola de Dio en deſprezi. Et lo poble es mot deceopu & engana en las armas; et en la ſubſtantia liqual ſan lor eſperar en coſas non certas, et li fidel ſon reſcondu : et quand illi

this Life, ſince the Aſcenſion of *Chriſt* into Heaven, the Souls, eſpecially of ſuch as are to be ſaved, not having ſatisfied in this Life for their Sins, departing their Bodies, muſt endure very ſenſible Pains, and be throughly purged after this Life in Purgatory, and that being purged, they come forth thence, ſome ſooner, ſome later, and other ſome not till Doomes Day, and others readily and long before it; in commiſeration of which Souls, every faithfull man may and ought to help them, even after this Life, by the Bond of Charity, through Prayers, Faſts, Alms, Maſſes. And in this Purgatories behalf, many have, to glut their Avarice, invented abundance of uncertain things, which they taught and preached, ſaying, That thoſe Souls are tormented in the ſaid Purgatory, ſome up to the very Neck, others to their Middle, others by the Finger; and that ſometimes they ſit and eat together at Table, and make good Chear, eſpecially on the Day of *All Souls*, when the People do offer largely unto the Prieſts upon their Sepulchers. And ſometime, ſay they, they are picking up Crums under the rich mens Tables. By means of all which & many other Lyes, their Avarice and Symony is grown and multiplied to a great height. There are Cloiſters raiſed, Temples coſtly built and endowed, Altars reared up and multiplied above meaſure, and a world of Monks and Canons, who have invented many things more, whereby to relieve and releaſe thoſe poor Souls, making a meer Mockery of the Word of God. And the People are grievouſly cheated and abuſed about the matter of their Souls, and their ſubſtance, they being made to put their truſt in ſuch uncertain things, whiles the Faithfull muſt heal themſelves; for, if once they refuſe to teach

teach the faid Purgatory as an Article of Faith, they are forthwith moft cruelly condemned to death and martyred.

And therefore we ftand engaged to fpeak of this Purgatory, and to hold forth what we conceive of it.

Firft then, we fay, that the Souls of thofe which are to be faved, muft finally be purged of all their uncleannefs, according to Gods Ordinance, declared *Revel.* 21. No unclean thing giving up it felf to abomination and Lying, fhall enter into Heaven. Now we do hold, that Faith and the Scriptures do promife us many and fundry ways of purging or cleanfing thofe that are in this prefent Life of all their Sins. But St. *Peter* fhews *Acts* 15. that the Hearts are purged by Faith, and that Faith is fufficient to cleanfe evil, without any other outward means. As it is made plain by the Thiefs cafe on the right hand of *Chrift*, who believing, and fincerely acknowledging his Sins, became worthy of Paradife. The other way of purging the Spoufe of *Chrift*, is, by Repentance, fpoken of *Ifai* 1. the Lord commanding there, *Wafh your felves, cleanfe your felves, remove the evil out of your thoughts from before mine eys, defift doing perverfe things.* And afterwards, *Though your fins were like Scarlet, they fhall be made as white as Snow; though they were as Crimfon, they fhall be as white Wooll.* In which place the Lord prefents himfelf unto the truly penitent in manner aforefaid, and thofe that were guilty of fin, fhall be made as white as Snow. There is another way yet of purging Sin, mentioned by St. *Matthew, ch.* 3. where it is faid, *He hath his Fan in his hand, and will purge his threfhing floor clean, and gather his Grain into his Barn.* Which paffage *Chryfoftom* applies to the Church prefent in this

non volon enfeignar aquel dit Purgatori per fe, fon condamna a mort crudelment et martureia.

Donc nos fen a parlar d' aqueft Purgatori, & notificar encerca lui lo noftre femblant.

Nos difen premierament, que las armas de li devent effer falva, fon finalment de dever effer purgas de totas las lor non munditias fecond l' ordennament de Dio, enaimi es manifeft en l' Apocalyps 21. Alcuna cofa foza facent abomination in mefongna non intraré en lei. Nos fot porren que la fe & l' efcritura fpon a nos moti & divers modi de purgar per liqual fon purga li habitant en la vita prefent de tuit li lor pecca, &c. Ma Sanct Peire demonftra. Act. 15. que li cor fon purifica per fe, & que la fe es fufficient a purgar li mal fença antre aioflament de fora. Enaima es manifeft del lairon iftant de la deftra, loqual crefent, & reconiffent li feo pecca viazament, fo degne de Paradis. Autre modo de purgar l' Efpofa de Chrift per penitentia, es toca en Efaia, alqual luoc lo Seignor dis. Lavavos eftas munda, ofta lo mal de las voftras cogitations, de li meo oilli repanfa vos de far perverfament. Et fenfec. Li voftre pecca feren enaima vermeillon, illi feren emblanquezi enaima neo, feren enaima verniz illi feren enaima lana blanca. Alqual luoc lo Seignor demoftra fi mefeime a li veray penitent, fegond lo modo fpoft, aquilli liqual auren pecca feran emblanquezi coma neo. Autre modo de purgar li pecca, es toca en Sanct Matth. 3. Alqual luoc di. Lo ventailli loqual en es la foa man, el mundare la foa aira, & aioftaré lo froment al feo granier. Laqual parola Chryfoftome fpon de laira de la Gleifa prefent, & del fuoc

fuoc de la tribulation. Et non folament lo Seignor munda la foa aira per las tribulations, ma munda per fi mefeime la foa Spofa, aizi en aquefta vita. Enaimi dis Sanct Paul. Chrift amé la Gleifa, et lioré fi mefeime per lei, quel fanctefiques lei mundant lei cum lavament daiga en parola de vita, que el mefeime donnes a fi gloriofa Gleifa, non avent macula ni ruga ni alcuna cofa d' aquefta maniera, ma quilli fia fancta & non foza. Dont l' Apoftol demoftra que Chrift amé tant grandament la Gleifa quel non vuolé mundar la con autre lavament, finon con lo feo propi fang, & non enaima non fufficient que la remagna alcuna immnndicia: ma donc lei a fi enaimi gloriofa quilli non aya mailla ni ruga, ni alcuna cofa d' aquefta maniera, ma quilli fia fancta & non foza. Et aqueft teftimoni non folament refonna en terra del fufficient mundament de l' Efpofa de Chrift al fang de luy: ma acer es teftimoni al cel d' aquilli liqual an confegu ley mefeima zo es aquella mundicia actualment, de liqual es dit en l' Apocalyps. Aquifti fon liqual vengron de la grand tribulation, & laveron las lor veftimentas, & las emblanzixeron al fang de l' Agnel, emperzo fon devan lo feti de l' Agnel & forvon a luy. Vevos quanti modi fon cuilli de la fe de l' Efcritura; per li qual li fazent viage en aquefta vita fon purga al prefent de li lor pecca.

Nos fupponen terzament, que lo es cofa fegurifsima que un chafcun viva enaima en la vita prefent, quel non befongne en apres d' alcuna purgation. Car lo es meilli far ben en la vita prefent, que fperar en apres non certan ajutori. Et vita plus fegura es que lo ben loqual alcun

Life, and the Tribulations thereof. And not onely by Tribulations, but by himfelf alfo doth the Lord here in this Life cleanfe his Spoufe and threfhing floor, as St. *Paul* faith, Chrift *loved the Church, and gave up himfelf for it, to hallow it, cleanfing it by the wafhing of Water, by the Word of Life, to make unto himfelf a glorious Church, having neither fpot nor wrinkle, nor any fuch thing, but to be holy and unblameable.* Where the Apoftle fhews, that *Chrift* fo loved his Church, that he would not cleanfe it by any other Wafhing, but by his own Bloud; and that doubtlefs not fo, as that it fhould be any ways infufficient, but effectually, in fuch fort, that there remains no uncleannefs at all; he having fo glorified her, that fhe hath no fpot nor wrinkle, nor any fuch thing remaining upon her, but is made holy, and undefiled. And this Teftimony of the Wafhing of the Spoufe of *Chrift* in his Bloud is not onely rendered here on Earth, but Teftimony is given alfo from Heaven by thofe which obtained this effectual Wafhing, it being faid of them in the *Revelation, Thefe are they, that came out of great Tribulation, and wafhed their Garments, and whitened them in the Bloud of the Lamb, and therefore they are before the Seat of the Lamb, and ferve him.* And thus ye fee, how many ways may be taken forth by Faith out of the Scriptures, to fhew that thofe that fojourn in this Life, are purged of their Sins here before they leave it.

We hold in the third place, that it would be far fafer for every one fo to live in this prefent Life, that he fhould not need any Purging afterwards. For, it is much better to do well in this Life, than to hope for uncertain help after it. And it is the far furer way, inftead of what good
others

others will do us after our death, to do the same our selves while we are yet alive, it being a happier thing for a man to depart hence in a free condition, than to seek for liberty after he shall be fettered.

Besides what hath been said, we maintain, that it cannot be made out by any express passage of the holy Scriptures of the Law of God, nor any holy Teachers grounded upon the said Scriptures, without wresting them, that it hath been held by common consent, that the Faithfull ought to believe of necessity, and publickly to profess as an Article of Faith, that there should be such a place as Purgatory, after this Life to be entered into for sins after the Ascension of *Christ*, by such Souls especially, as being otherwise to be saved shall not have made satisfaction in this Life for their sins committed, where they should endure most sensible Pains, being once departed their Bodies, and to be cleansed, and that thence some should come forth again sooner, and some later, some at Dooms Day, and others before. And as to the first part, *viz.* Scripture proofs, there is none at all to be found throughout the *Bible* for it; let us peruse the whole Law of God, we shall not meet with any one passage obliging or binding a *Christian* necessarily to believe, as an Article of Faith, that after this Life there should be such a place as Purgatory, as some aver. There is not one place in all the holy Scriptures, to shew it, neither can there be any evidence produced that ever there entered any one Soul in such a Purgatory, and came out again from thence.

And therefore it is a thing not to be credited, nor believed : for proof whereof St. *Augustin* in the Book which he entituled *Mille verba*, writes thus, We believe by Faith universal,

spera esser fait per li autre en apres la soa mort, quel lo faça per si meseime aizi dementre quel vio, cum la sia plus beneura cosa saillir libre qu' en apres li ligam cercar liberta.

Aquestas eosas devant pausas nos dizen, que la non se troba spressament per las sanctas Scripturas de la Ley de Dio ny de li sanct Doctor fondant en illa meseima, & non squivolment, que la non es vist amenar concordivol sententia, que li fidel dean esser costreit de necesita creyre ni tenir, ni confessar publicament coma per Article de Fe que la sia aital luoc de Purgatori en apres aquesta vita per li pecca, al qual en apres lo montament de Christ al cel, las armas, specialment d' aquilli liqual devon esse salva, non satisfacent en aquesta vita per li pecca, & sostenent penas sensiblas eisent del corps, & sian purgas, del qual alcunas saillon premieras, alcunas en apres, & alcunas al dia del judici, & alcunas ara devant lo dia del judici. En quant a la premiera part, zo es de l' Escriptura, que non sia deducivol cosa segond ley meseima; daiso appareis manifestament, car transcorrent tota la Ley obligant li Christian, non es vist esser alcuna spressa Scriptura de la Ley per la qual a li fidel sia de necesita creyre coma Article de la Fe, que en apres aquesta vita sia aital luoc de Purgatori, enaima alcuns dison. Ni a luy meseime non es dona la premiera signification d' alcuna part de la sancta Scriptura, ni non se po far se d' alcuna arma que sia intra en aquel dit Purgatori & sia sailli de luy.

Donc non es de creire ni de tenir per fe. A confermation daizo, Augustin al libre loqual s' appella Mil Parlament, scri enaima. Car nos cresen per Fe Catholica,

tholica, & per Divina Authorita lo regne de li cel esser lo premier luoc alquel lo Baptisme es receopu. Lo segond la pena a laqual li scomminga strang de la Fe de Christ soostenren eternal torment. Lo ters nos mesconoissen al postot, ni acer trobe lui en la sancta Scriptura.

Aquel meseime sobre aquella meseima parola. Non possesiren lo regne de Dio scri enaimi. O fraires alcun non s' engane: car la son dui luoc, & lo ters non es al postot. Car aquel que non merita de regnar cum Christ, perire cum al Diavol senza alcuna dubitation. A consideration d' aquestas cosas di Chrysostome sobre Matth.20. Lo regne de li cel es semblant al home paire de familla: sobre laqual parola di. L' home Paire de familla es Christ, alqual lo cel & la terra es quasi coma una maison. Ma las famillas son li celestial & li terrenal, loqual edifique maison de tres cambras. Co es l' enfern, lo cel, & la terra. Li combatent habitan sobre la terra, en l' enfern li venzu, al cel li venzedor. Que nos pausa al mez non voillan descendre a aquilli que son en l' enfern, mas montar a aquilli que son al cel desobre.

Ve vos aquestas authoritas sonan aizo, que la son tant solament dui cert luoc en apres lo montament de Christ al cel, en apres aquesta vita de las armas sallias del corps, & lo ters non es al postot, ni se troba quel sia en las Scripturas, &c.

Donc com en alcun luoc en la Ley non faza alcuna spreza mention d' aital luoc de Purgatori, ni li Apostol an laissa a

and by Divine Authority, that the Kingdom of Heaven is the firſt place; whereinto Baptiſm is received. The ſecond, is that where the Excommunicated and Stranger from the Faith of *Chriſt*, ſhall ſuffer everlaſting Torments. As for a third, we know none ſuch at all, and finde nothing certified of it in the holy Scriptures.

Again, in the ſame Book upon this paſſage, [*Shall not enter into the Kingdom of God*] he writes thus, O Brethren, let none deceive himſelf, for there are but two places, the third is not at all: for he that is not found worthy to reign with *Chriſt*, doubtleſs muſt periſh with Satan. To this purpoſe St. *Chryſoſtom* on the twentieth Chapter of St. *Matthew*, where it is ſaid, *That the Kingdom of Heaven is like unto a Houſekeeper* : ſpeaks in this manner, This Houſekeeper is *Chriſt*, to whom Heaven and Earth is an Houſe, as it were, and the Families are the Celeſtial and the Terreſtrial Creatures : in this Houſe he hath built three Chambers, Hell, Heaven, and Earth. The Militant or combating party are theſe which inhabit the Earth ; thoſe that are overcome go down to Hell ; but they that have overcome, enter Heaven. Let us take heed (ſaith he) we that are in the middle Region, that we deſcend not after them which are in Hell, but rather that we may mount up to them which are above in Heaven.

Is it not plain by theſe Authorities, that there are but two certain places, after *Chriſt*'s Aſcenſion into Heaven, whither the Souls do go, departing from their Bodies, and that there is no third place at all, and none to be found any where in the holy Scriptures.

And therefore no expreſs mention at all being made throughout the Law of God, of any ſuch place as Purgatory;

tory, and the Apostles having not left us any instruction about the same; and the Primitive Church also, governed according to the Gospel, and by the Apostles themselves, having not left any Ordinance or Commandment behinde about it: and seeing Pope *Pelagius* first five hundred and eight years after *Christ*, began to make this Institution, that Rememberance should be made of the Dead in the Mass; it follows, there being no one express proof for it in the Law of God, that it is needless to believe the said Purgatory as an Article of Faith, and that there should be such a thing after this Life.

But whence is it then (one might wonder) that People now a days are so much taken with this opinion of assisting the Dead? seeing that in all the Scriptures there is nothing expresly taught concerning it, unless it be in the Book of *Maccabees*, which doth not belong to the *Old Testament*, nor is Canonical, and that neither *Christ*, nor any of his Apostles, nor any of the Saints, next succeeding and living after them, ever taught any to pray for the Dead; but were all of them very carefull to teach that the People that lived unblameably, should be holy: therefore answering his Quære, we say, that the first cause hereof is, the Deceit and Craft of the Priests, proceeding from their greedy Avarice, who did not teach and instruct the People as the Prophets and Apostles of *Christ*, well to live, but onely to offer roundly, and to put their trust and hope of Deliverance and Salvation upon Purgatory.

nos alcun spres enseignament. Ni la Gleisa primitiva conversant second l' Evangeli de laqual li Apostols eran regidors, non an liora a nos alcuna cosa per ordenament ni per commandament: ma Pelagi Papa en apres li an del Seignor cinq cens & cinquanta huit, se legis luy aver ordena: que en la Messa se aya recordanza de li mort. La resta que de l' Escritura amena spressament de la Ley de Dio, que la non es de necessita creire enaima Article de Fe, esser aital luoc de Purgatori en apres aquesta vita, &c.

Ma la corre dobi per que li home modern ayan tant d' afect a li adjutori de li mort, com en tota la sacra Scriptura lo Seignor non enseigne aizo spressament, estier lo libre de li Machabei, loqual non es del Veilli Testament, ni acer Canonico. Ni Christ, ni li Propheta com li seo Apostol, ni Sanct, prochan ensegador de lor, non euseigneron orar per li mort: ma enseigneron mot curiosament que lo poble vivent sença crim fora Sanct. Donc respondent al dubi d' avant dit sot jong; que la prima causa es lo decebament & engan de li Preire, procedent d' avaricia, liqual non enseigneron lo poble al modo de li Propheta de Christ, & de li Apostol curiosament a ben viore: ma enseigneron uffrir mot, mettent a lor sperança de liberation & beatification del Purgatori.

AR-

ARTICLE III.

Of the Invocation of Saints.

Ara es a dire de l' envocation de li Sanct, laqual acer li Maistre com li aiostant se a lor predican & promonon con grand diligentia publican coma per Article de Fe, disent que li Sanct existent en la patria celestial son desser prega de nos viant en aquel modo loqual solon usar communament li Preyre, & li autre popular per lo lor amostrament enjoignent a lor meseimes, & autras cosas per ajutori d' envocation. Per laqual envocation, autorisation, & magnification, lo poble es vist sentir d' aizo carnalment & arrivolment : cresent que enaima se say devant lo Rey terrenal essent ira, li autre non enaymi ira intercedon per alcun mitigant la soa ira devant luy meseime, enaimi lo poble estima esser fait devant Dio, que li Sanct eirant se al peccador mitigon l' ira de lei.

Et aizo non es vist esser de creyre, com enaimi non seria vist esser vera conformita de la volonta de li Sanct com la volonta de Dio : car a aquel alqual Dio sendegnaria non seria vist que illi meseime seire san a Ley.

Secondament per aquesta magnification & envocation de li Sanct, lo poble encorre en idolatria, confidant se plus à alcun de li Sanct que a Dio, & servent a luy plus affectuosament que al sol Dio. Et demostrant aizo persait, & per ornament d' autars plus precios, & per sons

Now we shall speak also something of the Invocation of Saints, concerning which, some of our Masters and their Adherents preach and keep a stir, to publish it as an Article of Faith, saying, that the Saints departed, and being possest of the heavenly Countrey, ought to be prayed unto by us, in such a manner as the Priests use to do, and other People by their Instruction, enjoying them many other things to further and facilitate their Invocation; by which Invocation, authorizing and magnifying of it, the People believe carnally and erre greatly; conceiving, that as it is practised in the Courts of earthly Kings, being provoked or wroth, that some about them, which are not in the like passion, do intercede for others, and mitigate their displeasure; so it must needs be also with God himself; that is to say, that the Saints deceased must asswage God's anger, when it is kindled against a Sinner.

But we ought to believe no such matter; for, if that were true, there would be no true conformity, between the will of the Saints, and that of God. For, it would have an appearance, as if the Saints were not moved with indignation against him, that provokes God to indignation.

And secondly, by this magnifying of, and praying to the Saints, the People falls away into Idolatry, putting more trust in the Saints, than in God himself, and serving them with more affection than the onely God; which they do effectually make appear by the adorning of their Altars

most

moſt precioufly, their lowdeſt Peals (of Ringing and Singing) the multi-plicity of Lights and Candles, and other Solemnities about them; by all which the fimple People conceives no otherwife of them, than that the Saints are more mercifull than God himſelf, as being able to deliver from Damnation, by their Interceſſion to God, thoſe whom God had already condemned. Befides to maintain this the better, the filly People are taught, that the faid Saints love to have Gifts and Prefents offered them, and that they are delighted to hear their Praifes, and that they intercede moſt for thofe that offer, and praife, and honor them moſt;all which are things to be carefully ſhunned, and had in a-bomination.

This fort of Invocation it is, that we are now to treat of, and to make known what we do hold concerning this Invocation of Saints. And firſt and foremoſt we will fay, what Invo-cation is, Invocation is an earneſt De-fire of all the Minde and Soul, addreſt to the onely God, by Voice, in Pray-ing. Secondly, we hold, that *Chriſt* Man is Mediatour between God and Man, and our Advocate towards God the Father, having paid for our Sins, 1 *Tim.*2.4 approaching unto God of himſelf, ever-living to intercede for us: *No man comes to the Father, but by him.* And, *Whatſoever* (faith he him-felf) *ye ſhall ask of the Father in my Name, I will do it.* Who giveth abundantly to all that ask him, and upbraideth no man. He is our Advo-cate towards God the Father, and he forgives our Sins. The Truth is, he preſents himſelf in fome fort unto us, before we ftir our felves. He ftandeth at the Gate, and knocketh, that we ſhould open to him; and to obftruct all means and occafions of Idolatry, he fitteth at the right hand of the

plus reſplandent, & multiplications de candelas, & per autras folemnitas. Per lafquals cofas appareis a li ſimples que illi meſeime fian plus miferidios que Dio, & que aquel loqual el meſeime aure con-damna illi meſeime deſlioran encara de la damnation per orations. Per laqual cofa, outra d' aizo li ſimple aprenon que li Sanct defiran dons uffertas & propias laufors, & qu' illi entercedon majorment aquilli liqual donaren a lor encens, uffer-tas, & autras laufors & honors, lafquals cofas fon totas d' eſquivar & abominar con grand diligentia.

Donca nos fen a parlar d' aqueſta en-vocation de li Sanct, & notificar encer-qua Ley la noſtra entention. Premicra-ment & devant totas cofas nos fotponen qual fia lo nom d' aquella envocation. Envocar es meſeime, lo defier de tota la ment & de tota l' arma manda la vouz en la oration al fol Dio. Nos fotponen fe-condament que l' home Chriſt es megen-cier de Dio de li home, & Advocat en apres lo Paire, & a pagador per li noſtre pecca. Appropiant a Dio per ſi meſeime vivent totavia prega per nos. Alcun non ven al Paire finon per luy. Et qual-quequal cofa nos demandare al Paire al meo nom yo fareyaiço. Loqual dona a tnit abondivolment & non la repropria. Et el es Advocat en apres lo Paire, & perdonador per li noſtre pecca. Acer el fa prefenta el alcuna maniera a nos de-vant que nos nos movan. El iſta a l'hus, & buta que la li fia hubent, loqual vo-lent claure la via de tota idolatria exi-ſtent al cel en la dextra del Paire, vol

que

que tuit fidel aya luy en la ment, & atenda a Ley mefeime : cum la cura de li fidel deo effer a Chrift per cogitation & per affection, & refimillament en entendre a aquel qu' es defobre. Iofta zo qu'es dit. Si vos enfemp refufcites cum Chrift queré aquellas cofas lafquals fon defobre, al qual luoc Chrift es, fe fent en la dextra de Dio. El es l' hus per loqual fi alcun intrare fere falva. Alcun non ven al Paire finon per mi. Nos fotponen terçament que li Sanct non fon laifa a nos a cottivament, ma a refimillament. Sanct Paul dis. O fraires fia refimillador de mi enaimi yo de Chrift, & garda a aquilli que van enaimi, vos avé la noftra forma. Sanct Peire non laiffe fi adorar a Corneilli, ni l' Angel de Johan l' Evangelifta. Et per aizo Auguftin fcrivent enaimi de la vera Religion. O Religios lo cootiva de li home mort non fia a vos : car filli vifqueron fanctament, illi non fe an enaimi quilli queran tal honor ma volon luy effer colu de nos, per loqual enlumena fategion nos effer confort con lor. Donc illi fon deffer honra per refimillament non deffer adora per Religion. Aqueftas cofas fobre paufas, nos dizen que alcun home ifsi del corps autre que Chrift non es deffer adora, ni non es cert ni veray Advocat ni meiencier de Dio & de li home, ni entrepellador per li peccador en apres lo Paire ni es neceffari quilli fian invoca per aquella entrepellation de li viant. Loqual jurant receop lo proverage en aiço que demande & auré per l' humana generation, laqual el re-

Father in Heaven, and wills that every faithfull Soul fhall minde him onely, and have an eye and recourfe to him alone : for all the care and thought of the Faithfull fhould be bent to *Chrift*, with all the heart & affections, imitating him that is above. In which regard it is faid, *If ye be rifen with* Chrift, *then feek the things that are above, where* Chrift *is, fitting at the right hand of God.* He is the *Gate, whofoever enters by him fhall be faved. No man comes to the Father* (faith he) *but by me.* In the third place, we hold, that the Saints are not fet before us to adore them, but to imitate their practice, as St. *Paul* faith, *Be ye followers of me, as I am of* Chrift, *and take heed to them that walk, as ye have us for an Example.* St. *Peter* would not fuffer himfelf to be worfhipped by *Cornelius,* nor the Angel by St. *John* the Evangelift. And therefore doth Saint *Auguftin* write thus in his Book of true Religion. Do not (faith he there) O religious People, give your felves to worfhip the Dead, for if they lived holily, they were not fuch, as ufed to feek or defire thofe honours, to be worfhipped by us; by him, that illuminates them, they rejoyce, that we are made partakers with them. And therefore we fhould honour them by imitation, not worfhip them by Religion. All this being fet down for our Foundation, we fay, That no man bodily born, whofoever, but *Chrift,* ought to be adored,& none other is the certain and true Advocate or Mediator between God and Man, nor Interceffour for our Sins, towards God the Father, but he alone, and there is no need at all that any fuch religious Addrefs fhould be made unto the Saints deceafed by the Living. He *(viz. Chrift)* alone hath that Prerogative, to obtain whatfoever he requefts in behalf of Mankinde,

kinde, whom he hath reconciled by his Death. He is the onely and fole Mediatour between God and Man, the Advocate and Intercessour towards God the Father for Sinners, and so sufficient that the Father denies nothing to any one, which he prays and sues for in his Name; but for his sake he heareth them still that pray unto and ask in his Name. For being near unto God, and living of himself, he prayeth continually for us. For it became us to have such an High Priest, as was holy, guiltless, blameless, separated from Sinners, and exalted above the Heavens, the firstborn, who being above all men should have Power and Authority to sanctifie others, and to pray and intercede for them. St. *Austin* writes concerning *Christ* on *Psal.* 64. saying, Thou art the Sacrificer, thou art the Sacrifice, thou art he that offers, and the Offering it self. *Jesus* entred not into places made with hands, which were Figures of the true ones, but he is entred into Heaven, to appear there in our behalf, before the face of God.

And it is of him that St. *John* faith, We have an Advocate with the Father, *viz.* *Jesus Christ* the Righteous. And St. *Paul* faith, That *Jesus* who died for us, did also rise for us, and fitteth at the right hand of God, praying for us.

Therefore it were but a foolish part to seek for any other Intercessour; for *Christ* is always living and maketh continual Intercession for us to God the Father, and is ever ready to succour them that love him. And therefore keeping close to what he said, and is said of him, to what purpose should we address our selves to any other Saint for Mediator? seeing he is himself far more loving and far more ready to succour and relieve us, than any of them: confidering with-

conciliè per la soa mort. Et es unial & sol megencier de Dio & de li home, & Advocat & Entrepellador al cel en apres lo Paire per li peccador, enaimi sufficient que lo Paire non refuda alcun loqual demande al seo nom, ma per la soa reverentia exaucis luy de zo per que el demanda & aura. Car apropiant a Dio, per si meseime vivent prega tota via per nos. Car aital vescovo convent ava que fos a nos Sanct, non noisent, non soza departi de li peccador fait plus haut de li cel, filli premier, engendra del Paire, loqual unial de tuit li home en issiment, a potesta et authorita de sanctificar li autre, et orar et entrepellar per lor. Augustin scris al 64. Psalmo de Christ. Tu sies Preire, tu sies Sacrifici, tu sies l' offrmour, tu sies l' ufferta, etc. Jesus non vint è en las cosas faitas de man, exemplaria de las appareisent et veraias, ma emmeseime lo cel quel appareisa ara al voult de Dio per nos, etc.

Del dis Johan. Nos aven Advocat en apres lo Paire Jesu Christ lo just, entro per tuit aquilli del mond. Et Sanct Paul di, Jesu Christ loqual moric per nos acer resuscité, loqual es a la dextra de Dio, loqual acer prega per nos, etc.

Donc aquel seria sol loqual requerria autre intercessor. Car Christ es sempre vivent en apres lo Paire, et prega per nos, et es mot apparailla et alarga en la ment d' un chascun viador loqual ame luy. Donc a penre lo seo parlament, non besongna demandar autre Sanct per meienzier, com el sia plus benigne & plus prompt d' ajudar que alcun autre de lor. Et ostaria que la ment de li viant *fia difperfa per la manteza de li Sanct liqual el aura, con l'affection fe deſlongna de Chriſt, & per confequent illi fe remet com illi fia enaimi fparfa en plufors. Et es viſt a moti que quand l' oration fos fingularment a un endreyza, a aquella perfona mezana per adjutori ſpiritnal. Adonca la Gleiſa profiteria et creiſſeria plus quilli non fay ara quand lo fen arrobas motas intercefsions. Donc lo feria viſt eſſer grand folia abandonnar la fontana plus appareilla, & apropiar fe al rio trebol & plus lognan. Donc aqueſtas cofas fon declairas, que alcuna cofa non es ni fe po impetrar de Dio finon per Chriſt mecengier. 2. Que la feria plus fpedient adorar Chriſt entre li home fimplament: car el es optime & benigniſsime Mediator & Interceſſor, en quant a l' una & a l' autra extremita. 3. Que a penre lo parlament de luy non befongna entremezar li autre Sanct, com el fia plus prompt de ajudar que alcun autre Sanct, loqual es ordena de Dio a aizo, que la entrepellation o intercefson per luy loqual es plus mifericordios que liautre: car el fapper liqual fia juſta cofa de pregar per lor car el fcampé lo feo fang per lor, del qual el non fe dementiga unqua, avent lor fcrit en las foas mans & al feo peict. 4. Que aquel feria fol qui requerria autre interceſſor. 5. Qu' en la primitiva Gleiſa l' oration fo fingularment endreyça en aquella per fonna mezana per adjutori ſpiritual. 6. Que adonca la Gleiſa profeité & creiſſé plus que non fay ara atrobas motas intercefsions, liqual fon enaimi nivolas fenza aiga fcurzent*

all, that the Spirit of him that prayeth muſt needs be diſtracted and ſtraying, through the multitude of Saints to be prayed unto, fo that the affection muſt needs abate and grow remiſs towards *Chriſt*, it being divided among ſo many. And there are many that think the addreſſing of ones Prayer to one alone, making him his fole Interceſſour, proves more beneficial in ſpiritual matters; yet doubtleſs the Church would advance and improve much more, if ſhe acknowledged no ſuch multitude of Interceſſours newly invented. It were great folly indeed to abandon the Fountain of Living Water, and go to the Rivolets that are nothing nigh fo clear and ready at hand. Thus then it is evident, that there is nothing obtainable at God's hand, but by *Chriſt* the Mediatour. 2. That it were far more expedient to adore *Chriſt* alone of all men, he being abſolutely the beſt and kindeſt Mediatour and Interceſſour, in all kinde of extremities. 3. That keeping to his Word, we need not make our Addreſs to any other Saints for Interceſſours, for as much as he is much more ready to help us, than any other Saint, as being ordained by God for that very purpoſe, *viz.* that our Addreſs and Interceſſion ſhould be made by him, that is more mercifull than any of the reſt; for he knows for whom it is fitteſt to intercede, he having ſhed his Bloud for them, which he can never forget; they are written on his hands and on his breaſt. 4. That it would be folly to feek for another Interceſſour. 5. That in the Primitive Church men addreſt their Prayers to this fingular perſon, as Mediatour for ſpiritual help. 6. That the Church then did profit and increaſe more than now ſhe doth, ſince they found fo many Interceſſours, which are but as fo many Clouds without

without Water, obfcuring *Chrift* the Sun of Righteoufnefs, who is the true Interceffour: for many waiting for fpiritual aid, found themfelves forfaken, through their vain hope. For as God is juft, and we unjuft, and infufficient for our felves, he it is that pardons our fins, as well paft as prefent: for he hath given himfelf for our Redemption, that is to fay, he was the Oblation, whereby our Pardon was procured: God fent his Son to be the Forgiver of our Sins; he is the Remedy againft Sin, to keep us from falling into Defpair. We muft have recourfe to *Chrift* the Advocate, who perpetually pleads our Caufe, interceding to the Father in our behalf, being not onely our Advocate, but our Judg alfo: for the Father hath given up all Judgment unto the Son; and therefore the penitent have great hope, being fure to have him for their Judg, that is, their Advocate. This Faith is grounded in *Chrift*, as upon a Corner-ftone, whereon the Saints always fafely repofed, and which was held always fufficient, untill the Man of Sin got power to introduce this new Interceffion of Saints: which Faith all the Saints had, whiles they were here, and they confefs to this day, that they are not faved by the Oblation or Interceffion of any other God, and that they arrived to the heavenly Kingdom, according to that of the *Revelation, chap.* 5. 9, &c. O Lord, thou art worthy to receive the Book, and to undo the Seal thereof, and to open the fame. Thou that haft been flain, and haft redeemed us to God by thine own Bloud, out of all Tribes and Languages, and haft made us Kings & Priefts unto our God. Lo, how their humility and their acknowledgment refounds on earth ftill, they leaving fuch record behinde them, that they entred where now they are,

lo *Soleil de juftitia Chrift, loqual es veray Interceffor. Car plufors fpeitant l'adjutori fpiritual fon abandonna per vana fperanza. Car com Dio fia juft, & nos fian non juft & non fufficient per nos, el mefeime es perdonador per li noftre pecca, tant paffas coma prefent. Car el done fi mefeime per la noftra redemption, zo es, fo oftia per laqual la perdonnanza es faita: Dio trames lo feo Filli perdonador per li noftre pecca, & es enaimi remedi encontra lo pecca, que nos non caian en defperation. Lo es de fugir a Chrift patron, loqual garda continuament la noftra caifon, demandant al Paire per nos, loqual non folament aven luy per Advocat: ma per Juge. Car lo Paire doné tot lo judici al filli, & per confequent a li pentent es grand efperança que lo noftre Advocat fia fait lo noftre Juge. Aquefta Fe es fonda en Chrift enaima ferma peira, en laqual la compagnia de li Sanct ifté totavia ferma, & dreita, entro que l'home de pecca receop poefta laqual d'intremené las novas intercefsions de li Sanct: laqual Fe tuit li Sanct ifsi del corps attengu iftant aizi, & entro encoi confeffan quilli non fon falva per las uffertas, ni per las entrepellations d'autre Dio, & lor mefeime fon falva & pervengu al regne celeftial, fegond zo qu'es dit en l'Apocalyps 5. O Seignor tu fies digne de recebre lo libre, & defliar li fagel de luy & nbrir luy, loqual fies ifta aucis & rempfies del teo fang propi a Dio, de tuit li trib & lengas, & fezies nos Regnes & Preires al noftre Dio. Vevos la humilita & la lor agradivoleza refonna encara en terra, quant illi reconoiffen effer intra aqui al fang del mefei-*

mt, et confeffan aver agu per luy tot lo ben loqual illi an, et tenon de tuit li iftament aizi. Quilli non recebon alcun ben finon per lo bon Meiencier et Interceffor Jefus Chrift.

by no other means, but his Bloud, and confefs to have received by him all their weal and welfare there, and whatfoever they enjoyed during their abode here. In a word, that they received no kinde of good at any time, but by our good Mediatour and Interceffour *Jefus Chrift.*

ARTICLE IV.

Of Baptifm and the reft of the Sacraments in the Church of *Rome.*

Fora lo neceffari encerca l' adminiftration del Baptifme, fon li exorcifmi, lo fofflor, lo feng de la cros al peit et al front, lo mettre lo fal en la bocca, l'ognament de la faliva en las aureillas et al nas, l'ognament al peit, le fcapupchin, l'ognament de la chrefma vertis, et las femblant cofas confacras per lo Vefco, lo donar li ciri en las mans, l'empanfament de la veftimenta blanca, lo benaiffir l'aiga, lo poufar tres ves, lo requirament de li Pairin. Totas aqueftas cofas encerco l'adminiftration d'aqueft Sacramen fon fora befogna, aizo es non de necefsita, ni de fubftantia requift al Sacrament del Baptifme, de lafquals moti prenon occafion majorment d'error, et de fobreftition que edification de falu, et fecond alcuns Doctors non fon d'alcuna vertu ni profeit.

That which is of no neceffity in the Adminiftration of Baptifm, is the Exorcifm, the Breathing on, the Sign of the Crofs upon the Infants Breaft and Fore-head, the Salt which they put into his Mouth, the Spittle put to his Ears and Nofe, the Anointing of his Breaft, the Capuchin, the Unction on the Crown of the Head, and all the reft of thofe things confecrated by the Bifhop, putting Wax in their Hands, arraying them in white, bleffing the Water, plunging the Infant three times, feeking for God-fathers: all thefe things commonly practifed about the Adminiftration of this Sacrament are needlefs, as being not at all of the fubftance of, nor requifite in the Sacrament of Baptifm; thefe things giving but occafion to many that they rather fall into Errour and Superftition, than that they fhould be edified by them to Salvation; which made fome Doctors profefs, that there was no virtue, nor benefit to be had by them.

Del Sacrament de la Sancta Cena.

Lo maniar del Pan Sacramental es maniar lo corps de Chrift en figura,

Of the Sacrament of the *Lords Supper.*

The Manducation (or Eating) of the Sacramental Bread is the eating of *Chrift's*

Chrift's Body figuratively, *Chrift* having faid, Whenfoever ye do this, do it in remembrance of me : for if it had not been a figurative Eating, *Chrift* had hereby obliged himfelf, to be eaten continually ; for we ftand in a manner always in need of feeding on him fpiritually, according as *Auftin* faith, He truly eateth *Chrift*, that believeth in him. And *Chrift* faith, that to eat him is to abide in him. In the Adminiftration of this Sacrament, thefe things are profitable, Prayer, Charity, the Preaching of the holy Scriptures in a known Tongue, for Edification, and whatfoever elfe is inftituted as tending thereunto, according to the Law of the Gofpel, for the increafe of Peace and Charity among the People : but as for other things, befides the Confecration of the Euchariſt, fuch as are thofe which the Priefts act in the Mafs, or the Clergy chants in the Quire, from the beginning to the end, and the Ornaments of the Priefts, fuch as the *Roman* Church and her Adherents now makes ufe of, they are not of neceffity to this holy Supper.

Of Mariages and Orders.

Concerning Mariage, it is behooffull to make ufe of Prayer, of Fafting, and due Admonitions, Inftructions, and warnings about it ; but the Coupling of the Hands, and Tying of the Robe, and fuch other Ceremonies as are in common ufe about it, and of humane cuftome, befides the exprefs Scripture, are not of the fubftance of, nor at all requifite to Mariage.

As touching Orders, we ought to hold, that Order is called the Power which God gives to man, duely to adminifter or difpenfe unto the Church the Word and the Sacraments. But

dizent Chrift. Per quanta via vos fare aizo, fafe lo en la mia recordanza : car fi aizo foſſa maniar non en figura, Chrift fe ferie obliga en aizo continuament : car lo fpiritual es quafi befongnivol chel fia fait continuament : coma di Auguftin. Aquel mania Chrift en verita loqual cre en luy. Et Chrift di que maniar luy, es permaner en luy. Encerca la celebrita d' aqueſt Sacrament es profeitivol : l' oration, l' amour, la predication de las fanctas Scripturas en volgar & edificatorias : & autras quals que quals cofas fon ordenas a aizo, fecond la ley Evangelica, que paz & charita creiſſe al poble. Ma las autras cofas itier la confecration de la Euchariſtia, coma la cofas que fan li Preire en la Meſſa, o lo Clerc canta al coro, de l' introito entro a la fin : & li ornament de li Preire en aifi coma fe ufa al prefent de la Gleifa Romana com li adherent, a fi non fon de neceffita pertinent a la Sancta Cena.

Del Mariage & de li orden.

Encerca la celebration del matrimoni es profeitivol l' oration, lo dejuni, & la debita admoneftanza, enfeignament & avizament encerca aizo. Ma lo compaufament de las mans, & l' encerque ligament de l' eftola, & las autras cofas que fe obfervon encerca aizo communament, per coftuma humana otra l' efpreſſa Scriptura non es de fubftantia, ni de neceſſita requiſt al Matrimoni.

De l' orde fe deo tenir, que orde es appella poiſſança dono de Dio a l' home per aminiſtrar debitament a la Gleifa la parola & li Sacrament. Ma la non fe a
per

per *se d' Escritura ma per costuma de la Gleisa de li tal Sacrament. Et las lettras testimonials, l' ognament de las mans, lo donament de la centura, & de l' ampola en las mans, & las autras cosas que se observan encerca aizo communament fora l' expressa Scrittura non es de substantia ni necesita requist al' Orde.*

we have nothing in the Scriptures touching such Orders as they pretend, but onely the Custome of the Church. And all those Testimonial Letters, the Anointing of the Hands, the giving of the Girdle, and putting the Lamp into the Hand, and the rest usually observed in this case, besides the express Scripture, is not of the substance of, nor any necessary requisite unto Order.

De la Cresima, o Confirmation.

Of the Chrisme, or Confirmation.

Ara es de desir de la Cresima, laqual al present es appella Sacrament de Confirmation, mancant de fondament d' Escritura en aizo ; quel sia premierament consacra del Vesco, & confeita d' oli d' olivas, & do balsamo, viant a l' home bapteia, al front, & figura de croz en aquesta forma de parolas. Yo segno tu del seng de la croz, & confermo tu per seng de salu: In nomine Patris, & Filii, & Spiritus Sancti : loqual es fait com al pisation de mans, & encerca ligament de vestiment blanc al cap: loqual appellan ara Sacramen de Confermation, non est vist esser ordena de Christ, ni de li seo Apostol. Car Christ exemplari de tota la Gleisa non fo en sa persona talament conferma, ni non requis a seo Bateime Chresima d' aqhesta maniera, ma algu singular. Donc aital Sacrament non es vist esser de necesita de salu alqual lo se blesterma en Dio, & sia d' entremena per movament Diabolic, afin que lo poble sia scarni en la fe de la Gleisa, & sia plus cresa a la salennita, o necesita de li Evesques.

Now to speak of the Chrisme, which they also call a Sacrament, having no ground at all in Scripture, to this purpose; that first, it must be consecrated by a Bishop, and compounded of Oyl-Olive, and of Balm to be applied to the person baptized, upon the Fore-head with the Sign of the Cross, and with these words; [I sign thee with the Sign of the Cross, and confirm thee by the Sign of Salvation, in the Name of the Father, of the Son, and of the Holy Ghost.] Which is performed by imposing of Hands, and with a white Attire fastened to the Head. This is that which they call the Sacrament of Confirmation, which we finde not instituted by either *Christ* or his Apostles. For *Christ* the Patern of all his Church, was not confirmed in his person, and he doth not require, that there should be any such Unction in Baptism, but onely pure Water. And therefore such a Sacrament is not found needfull for Salvation, whereby God is blasphemed, and which was introduced by the Devils instigation, to seduce the People, and to deprive them of the Faith of the Church, and that by such means they might be drawn the more to believe the Ceremonies and the necessity of the Bishops.   Of

Of the Extreme Unction.

The seventh Sacrament of the Church of *Rome* is the Extreme Unction of the Sick, which they go about to prove by the saying of the Apostle St. *James*. There is no ground to shew, that *Christ* or his Apostles did institute any such thing. For, if this bodily Unction were a Sacrament, as they would make us believe, *Christ* or his Apostles would not have past over in silence the evidence of putting the same in ure: upon the deliberate consideration whereof, we dare not presume to hold or profess it as an Article of Faith, that this Sacrament was instituted by *Christ* or any of his Apostles.

Of Fasting.

It follows now to say something also of Fasting, which is twofold, *viz.* the bodily & the spiritual. The spiritual is, to abstain from sin; the bodily is, to abstain from meat. But the *Christian* is at liberty to eat at all times, as also to fast at any time, provided he do not observe the Fast superstitiously, as by a virtue of abstinence.

And observe, that there are some Fasts which ought not to be kept nor commended by the Faithfull, but rather to be abhorred and eschewed: such as are the Fasts of the Scribes and of the Pharisees, and those instituted by *Antichrist*, favouring of Idolatry; the Fasts of Hereticks and superstitious People, observed by Enchanters, Sorcerers, and Necromancers, and the Fasts dedicated unto Creatures, and not to the Creatour, which have no ground in the Law of God. Those Fasts are inordinate which are kept by feeding onely on rarer, costlier, and

De l' extrema Onction.

Lo septen Sacrament de la Gleisa Romana es l' extrema Onction de li enferm, laqual perforcan se fondar lei al dit de Sanct Jaco Apostol. Non es vist esser ordenna de Christ ni de li Apostol de luy. Car si aquesta Onction corporal fossa Sacrament, en aizi coma se feing; Christ o li Apostols non taisiria la debita manifestation de l' execution de lei. Li pensant ben aquestas cosas non deven ausar, tenir, ni confessar en aizi coma article de fe, aquest Sacrament esser ordenna de Christ & de li Apostol.

Del Jejuni.

Ara s' ensec del Dejuni, loqual es doble, aizo es spiritual & corporal. Lo spiritual es stenir se de li pecca, lo corporal es stenir se de li maniar. Ma liberta es al Christian de maniar en tot temp, com tuit li jorn sian act de dejunar, non observant sobresticiosament coma per vertu de continenza.

Nota que lo son alcuns Dejunis, liquals non son de tenir, ni de laudar a li fidel, ma majorment son de scommingar, & de fugir. Enaima son li Dejuni de li Scrib, Pharisio, & que son ordena de l' Antichrist sabent idolatria. Li Dejuni de li hereges & sobresticios liqual observan li encantador & feituriers, & nigromant, & li Dejuni limitas a las creaturas non al Creator, non fonda en la Ley de Dio. Li Dejuni desordena en maniars specialment plus rars, plus precios, & de-

lica ; enaimi coma fon beftias marinas, figas, paffas, uvas, amandolas, de liqual li paures fon defponilla, & li ric engorzela, & l' almona esfoftrata al paure, al qual lude filli dejuneffon en maniars plus legers & communs, illi poirian miniftrar plus legerament & plus facilament a la lor familla, & a li autres paures. Com la non es dejunar de neun maniar corporals, quafi coma mals o non mond: Car tot as cofas fon mondas a li mond, & alcuna cofa non es de refudar laqual fi a receopna con fazament de gratias : car es fanctifica per la parola de Dio, & per l' oration. Tuit aquilli determina Dejunis, fon excommingas, & non promogu de li fidel. De lafquals cofas non deorian effer repres ni encolpa.

choicer Meats, fuch as all manner of Sea Fifh, Figs, Raifins, and Almonds, of which the Poor are deprived, and with which the Rich abound, whiles Alms are withdrawn from the Poor; whereas if they fafted fo, as to eat afterwards more common and lefs chargeable Meat, they would be able to provide the better both for their own Families, and for the Poor. So then, it being plain, that Fafting confifts not in the abftaining from any bodily Meat, as unclean, becaufe all things are clean to them that are clean ; and nothing is to be refufed, being taken with thankfgiving, or fanctified by the Word of God, and by Prayer. It followeth, that all thefe Fafts aforefaid are to be detefted and rejected by the Faithfull ; and of fuch things they ought to be guiltlefs, and remain unfpotted.

CHAP.

CHAP. VIII.

A particular Discourse concerning the Barbes *or ancient Pastors of the Evangelical Churches of the Valleys of* Piemont.

Whereto is added a Catalogue of the Names
of all those who have been renowned
amongst them, within the compass of
500. Years and upwards, so far as
they have come to the Au-
thours knowledg.

HAving treated so largely in the foregoing Chapters concerning the ancient Doctrine and Discipline of the *Evangelical Churches* in the Valleys of *Piemont,* and presented to the Reader many rare Pieces of Antiquity, in order thereunto, it will not be amiss, now in the close of this Book to give him a brief account of the Authours and Pen-men of these, and the like Treatises, who were then known by the name of *Barbes,* that is to say, their Pastours or Ministers.

Rainer. de formâ hæret. f.8.
The Monk *Rainerius* in a Treatise of his, doth indeed give a strange Description of the Office and Customes of those *Barbes,* namely, that they had a *Chief Bishop* amongst them, who had always two attending him, the one whereof he called his Eldest, and the other his Youngest Son ; and besides these two, he had also a third that followed him in the quality of a *Deacon* ; he adds likewise, that this Bishop laid his hands on others, with a soveraign Authority, and sent them about, hither and thither, as he pleased, and that in as imperious a manner as the Pope himself.

Book 1.Ch.5.
Art.2,
With these and the like fictitious Notions or *Chimera's Rainerius* would fain possess the mindes of men, but all in vain, for, it is manifest by what has been already inserted in the fifth Chapter of this Book, that both the Calling of those Ministers, and the Administration of their Office, was quite of another nature and strain ; there we shall see, that those who were to be received as Pastours among them, were

so

to intreat the People to receive them, and to pray to God for them, that they might be made worthy of so great a Charge ; and this principally, to give a proof or evidence of their humility. Again, there we shall finde that *none of those Pastours were impowered to act the least matter without the consent and advice of their Brethren and Associates in the Ministry.*

In the third place we shall there finde, that *they had no other Food or Raiment, than what was bestowed on them by the free charity of the good People whom they instructed.* All which are very far from being any Arguments to prove that absolute sovereignty, and worldly pomp, which the above-named *Rainerius* would willingly father upon those poor Shepherds of the little Flock of *Christ*, not so much (it may be) out of a Principle of Malice, as to make the World believe that those poor People were Lovers and Admirers of the *Romish* Ceremonies and Superstitions ; however he intended, yet sure I am, that all the Histories, Records, and Works which they have left behinde them, speak them to be quite otherwise, namely, a Generation of humble, holy and harmless men, of a meek, peaceable, and quiet spirit ; exceeding painfull in their Calling, and carefully watching over the Flocks committed to their Charge ; labouring faithfully in the Lords Vineyard, and imploying their whole time and Talents for turning many Souls unto Righteousness ; and this they did by much *Labour* and *Travel*, by *Watchings* and *Fastings*, by suffering many *buffetings*, *stripes*, and *Imprisonments*, yea and many times even Death it self, they being for the most part constrained to seal the Truths they preached to others, with the last Drop of their own Bloud, and by suffering the most exquisite Torments, their bloudy Persecutours could possibly devise. In sum, these were men mortified to all the Pomp, Glory, and Riches, to all the Pleasures, Honours, and Preferments that this World could afford them ; having their Conversation as *Strangers*, *Pilgrims*, and *Sojourners* here below ; whose *Hope* was not *in this Life*, but who expected another *City*, to wit, *the heavenly* Jerusalem, *and a House not made with Hands, eternal in the Heavens* ; that so, having *fought the good Fight*, and *finished their course, they might inherit the Crown which God has laid up for all those who love him and his appearing.* Now as for that which concerns the suffering part of their Life, I shall refer the Reader to the following Book ; but if he desire further satisfaction, as to the Point of their Life, and to know with what zeal and holy affection they laboured to draw their People to Repentance, and to instruct them in the Faith, I shall recommend to him for brevities sake one onely Epistle of one of those ancient *Barbes*, written in their own Language to the Church of *Pragela,* whereby he may the better judg of their spirits and Principles.

An

An Epiſtle of the *Barbe Bartholemi Tertian,* written to the Evangelical Churches of *Pragela.*

Jeſus be with us.

To all our faithfull and beloved Bre-thren in *Jeſus Chriſt.* I ſalute you all. *Amen.*

This Epiſtle is to advertize your Fraternity, acquitting my ſelf of that truſt which is committed to me by God, concerning you, in order to the Salvation of your Souls, according to that Light of Truth which is given us by the Moſt High, that you would pleaſe, every one of you to maintain, increaſe, and cheriſh, to your utmoſt, and by no means weaken or diminiſh thoſe good Principles, Forms, and Cuſtomes, which have been left us by our Anceſtours, and of which we were unworthy. For it would be but a very ſmall and poor advantage for us to have been renewed by the fa-therly Perſwaſions of God himſelf, and that Light which he hath given us, if we ſhould now give our ſelves up to a worldly, diabolical, and fleſhly Converſation, forſaking the principal Good (which is God) and the Salva-tion of our own Souls, for a ſhort and temporal Life. For the Lord has ſaid in the Goſpel, *What will it profit a man to gain the whole World, and loſe his own Soul?* And, *It were better ne-ver to have known the way of Righte-ouſneſs, than having once known it, to walk contrary to it.* Yea, we ſhall be *altogether inexcuſable,* and our Con-demnation will be more ſevere, for as much as there will be greater Puniſh-

Jeſus ſia con nos.

A tuit li noſtres fidels & ama tant cant coma fraires en Jeſus Chriſt. Salva ſia a tuit vos. Amen.

La preſent es per advertir la voſtra fraternita, pagant lo meo debit de mi a vos de la part de Dio, maximament ſobre la cura de la ſalu de las voſtras armas en lo lume de verita, departi a nos de l' al-tiſsime, que la plaza a un chaſcun de lo mantenir, accreiſſer & favorir ſegond poſsibilita, & non venir a ments de tot bon principi, huzanças & coſtumas donas de li noſtras anteceſſors, & a nos non degnes. Car poc profeitaria a nos eſſer muda de l' inſtantia paternal, & dal lume dona de Dio a nos, per donar nos a la mundana, & diabolica, & carnal con-verſation, abandonant lo principal que es Dio, & la ſalu de las armas, per la breo vita temporal. Car lo Seignor di en l' Evangeli. Qual coſa profeita a l'home ſi el gagna tot lo mond, & ſuffre deſtrui-ment alla ſoa arma. Car meil ſeria a nos non aver conoiſſu la via de juſtitia que avent la conoiſſua far lo contrari. Car al judici de Dio nos ſaren non eſcuſe-vols, & damna plus profondament. Car plus fort torment ſere donna, a li plus

fort,

fort, *& a li plus conoiſſent per laqual coſa yo prego vos per la carita de Dio, non voilla diminuir, ma accreiſſer la carita, la temor, & l' obedientia degua a Dio, & a vos entre vos, & totas bonas coſtumas apartenent & auccias & entenduas de la part de Dio, & noſtra & oſtra, & purgar d' entre vos tot deffeēt & Mancament conturbant la paz, l' amor & la concordia ; & tota cauſa de vos oſtar la liberta del ſervici de Dio, & la voſtra ſalu, & de l' adminiſtration de la verita, ſi vos deſira que Dio vos proſpere en li ben temporals & ſpirituals. Car vos non poe far alcuna coſa ſenza luy. Et ſi vos cubita eſſer heritiers de la ſoa gloria faca ço qu' el di. Si tu voles entrar a vita, garda li meo commandament. Item fazé que entre vos non ſe nuriſſa juoc ni gormanderias, ni ribauderias, ni bal, ni autras deſordonnanças, ni queſtions, ni l' engan, ni barat, ni uſura, ni malvolenças, ni diſcordias : ni voilla ſuportar entre vos, ni ſoſtenir perſonas de mala vita,ni que done ſcandol & mal exemple entre vos. Mas carita & fidelita regne entre vos&tot bon exemple,traētant l'un l' autre enaima un chaſcun volera eſſer faiēt per ſi meſeime. Car autrament non es poſsible alcun poer eſſer ſalva, ni haver la gratia di Dio, ni de home en aqueſt mond, ni en l' autre la gloria. Et tot aiço ſapparten principalmens mantenir & favorir a li Regidors & Gouvernadors. Car quant li cap ſon enferm tuit li membres en ſemp ſe dolon. Pertant ſi*

ments inflicted upon thoſe that have had the greateſt meaſure of knowledg. Wherefore I beſeech you for the Love of God, not to diminiſh but increaſe that Love, Fear, and Obedience which is due unto him, and to one another, as alſo to keep the good Cuſtomes which you have ſeen and heard of God, by our means. And that ye will take away and purge out from among you all thoſe Faults and Failings which interrupt your Peace, Love, and Concord, with whatſoever obſtructs your Liberty in the Service of God, and your own Salvation, and the Adminiſtration of Truth ; and all this, in caſe you deſire that God ſhould be propitious to you, in regard either of your ſpiritual or temporal Eſtate, conſidering that you cannot do any thing without him. If then you deſire to be Heirs of his Glory, do as he commands you: and *if you would enter into Life, keep my Commandments* Moreover, beware that you entertain among you no vain Sports, Gluttony, Whoredom, Balls, or other Debaucheries, as likewiſe no Queſtions, Frauds, Uſury, Envies, or Diſcords. And laſtly, take heed of ſupporting or upholding in the midſt of you, any perſons of an ill Life, who may become a Scandal, or an evil Example to others. But on the contrary, let Love, and Faithfulneſs, and all manner of good Examples reign amongſt you, *doing one to another as every one would that it ſhould be done to him* ; for otherwiſe it is not poſsible that any can be ſaved, or finde grace and favour with God and Man in this World, or Glory in that which is to come. And it is neceſſary that the Leaders, and thoſe who govern and bear Rule amongſt you, ſee to the putting of theſe things into execution ; for when the Head is ſick, all the Members are diſtempered : wherefore

if

if ye hope and defire to inherit eternal Life, and to be in good efteem and credit, and to profper in the World, both as to Temporal and Spiritual good things; Cleanfe your felves from every diforderly way among you, fo that God may be always with you, *Who never forfakes thofe, who put their truft in him.* But know for certain, that God does not dwell with Sinners, neither does he in his Soul cleave to evil doing, or to the Man that is a Slave fold under fin. Wherefore let every one rectifie the way of his own Heart, and fhun Dangers, if he will not perifh in them. I fhall not add more for the prefent, but onely this, that ye fee to the performance of thefe things, and *the God of Peace be with you all,* and accompany us, according to our truly devout and humble Prayers for, and Salutation of all the faithfull and beloved of *Chrift. Amen.*

I am wholly, yours *Bartholomeus Tertianus,* ready to ferve you in all things in our power according to the will of God.

vos fpera & defira poffefsir vita eterna,& bona voouz,& bona fama,& bon credit, & profperar en aqueft mond; en li ben fpiritual & temporal: purga vos de tota vita defordonna entre vos, afin que Dio fia totavia con vos, loqual non abandonna unqua fi fperant en fi. Mas fapia aiço per cert que Dio non exaucis ni habita con li peccador, ni en l' arma malvolent, ni a l' home fotmes a li pecca. Pertant un chafcun paufe lo feo cor fobre la foa via, & fugia li peril, fi el non vol perir en lor. Non autre per lo prefent, finon que vos meta en effeEt aqueftas cofas, & Dio de paz fia con tuit vos, & nos accompagne a las urayas, devotas & humils orations, en faludant tuit li fidel & ama de Chrift. Amen.

Totus vefter, Bartholomeus Tertianus, ad omnia fecundum Deum pofsibilia paratus.

True

True it is, that as to the particular circumstances of the form of Discipline amongst those *Barbes* in those times, as namely their *Consistories* and *Synodical* Constitutions, those Remainders of their Antiquities which the *Popes* Emissaries have left us (or rather which have been miraculously preserved from the flames) are something dark, and imperfect; However what has come to my hands concerning this matter, I shall faithfully impart unto the Christian Reader. As to their *Synodical* Constitutions, the above-specified Manuscripts tell us, that the *Barbes* (or Pastors) assembled once a year, to treat of their affairs in a General Council; And the Italian Manuscript (the Original whereof is to be seen with the rest in the University Library of *Cambridge*, bearing date 1587.) tells us, that this Council was constantly held in the Month of *September*, and that some hundreds of years ago, there were seen assembled together in one *Synod* held at *Valone del Laufo* in *Val Clufone*, no less then an hundred and forty *Barbes*. The same Manuscript adds, that they had always their *Consistories*, and a form of Discipline amongst themselves, except it were in the time of Persecution, and then the *Barbes* had their *Consistories* in secret, and did also preach to their Congregations, during the Winter season, in their own private houses, and in the Summer time, upon the tops of Mountains, as the people were there feeding their flocks.

Of these *Barbes* some were married, to manifest thereby their approbation of the state of Matrimony; Others kept themselves single, for convenience sake, forasmuch as they were oft-times obliged to remove and shift their habitations and abodes, and (as occasion required) to undertake long and tedious voyages for the propagating of the *Gospel* in remote Countries, with whom they then had a particular and constant correspondence, after the year 1160, namely, in *Bohemia, Germany, Gafcogny, Provence, Dauphine, England, Calabria,* and *Lombardy,* whither the abovesaid *Barbes* went by turns, as Itineraries, to visit their Brethren there, and to preach the Gospel of *Christ* amongst them. Those *Barbes* who remained at home in the *Valleys*, (besides their officiating and labouring in the work of the Ministry) took upon them the disciplining and instructing of the youth (especially those who were appointed for the Ministry) in Grammer, Logick, Moral Philosophy, and Divinity. Moreover the greatest part of them gave themselves to the study and practise of Physick, and Chirurgery; and herein they excelled (as their Histories tell us) to admiration, thereby rendring themselves most able and skilfull Physicians both of soul and body. Others of them likewise dealt in divers Mechanick Arts, in imitation of St. *Paul*, who was a *Tent-maker*, and *Christ* himself, who untill the time of his manifestation wrought with his *putative* father *Joseph*, as *Juftin Martyr* reports in a certain Dialogue of his with *Triph. contra Jud.*

Here I suppose it will not be unacceptable to insert the Names of all those *Barbes* or *Paftors* of the *Evangelical* Churches of *Piemont*, which are found scattered here and there, in their Writings, not knowing of what use it may be to any future discoveries of their Antiquities,

at

[margin notes:]

The Synodical Assemblies of the *Barbes*, or ancient Paftours of the Evangelical Churches of Piemont. *Lib.1. c.5. Art.4. Historia breve de l' affari de i Valdefi delli Valli.* 1587. 140. Barbes feen together at a General Council in *Val. Clufone. pag.15.*

pag.16. pag.17.

pag.17.

pag.16. Juftin Mart. Dial. Triph. contr. Jud.

at leaſt they may ſerve to let us ſee that God has never wholly removed his *Candleſticks,* nor his *burning and ſhining Lights,* out of theſe remote and dark Corners.

A *Catalogue of the Names of all thoſe* Barbes *or ancient Paſtors of or belonging to the* Evangelical *Churches of the Valleys of* Piemont, *who have been eminent within the compaſs of* 500 *years laſt paſt, and upwards ; ſo far as they have come to the Authours hands.*

Mr. *Arnoldo,* who taught about the year 1150. from whom his Diſciples were called *Arnoldiſts.*

Mr. *Eſperone,* who taught about the year 1156. from whom his followers were named *Eſperoniſts.*

Mr. *Joſepho,* who taught about the ſame time, and thoſe who embraced his Doctrine, were in mockery called after his name *Joſephiſts.*

Pietro Valdo, who began to teach the people, who were called after him *Waldenſes,* in the year 1160.

Pietro Bruis, from whom his hearers were called *Bruſiens.*

Mr. *Henrico,* who together with *Pietro Bruis* taught in the Biſhopricks of *Arles, Ambrun, Die,* and *Gap,* whither they were driven, and received at *Thoulouze.*

Bartholomew of *Carcaſſone,* who taught and was eminent in *Hungaria, Dalmatia,* &c. Inſomuch that he was nick-named (by *Mattheus Paris*) their *Pope* and *Biſhop,* alledging likewiſe to this purpoſe a Letter, which a certain Biſhop (the *Popes* Legat in thoſe parts *)* wrote to the Archbiſhop of *Roüan* to demand ayd and aſſiſtance againſt them, until at laſt they were conſtrained to retire *into the Deſert,* according to that Rev. 12. 5, 15. Propheſie in the Revelation, That *the woman that brought forth the man-child,* and is the true Church of God, ſhould be ſo cruelly perſecuted by *the Dragon ,* which ſhould *caſt water as a River out of his Mouth, to devour it,* that ſhe ſhould be conſtrained *to flye into the Deſert, where ſhe ſhould be nouriſhed a time, and times, and half a time,* or for the ſpace of forty two Months, or twelve hundred and ſixty days.

Belazinanza, of *Veronne.*

Giovanni, of *Lugro.*

Theſe two were very famous (as *Raineriuſ* obſerves) about the year of our Lord, 1250.

Arnoldo Ilot, a famous *Barbe,* who held the grand diſpute at *Mont Real.*

Lollardo, who was in great Reputation amongſt the *Evangelical* Churches of *Piemont,* by reaſon of a Commentary that he made upon the *Revelation :* As alſo for having conveyed the knowledge of their Doctrine into *England,* where his Diſciples were known by the name of *Lollards.*

Paolo Gignoſo, of *Bobio.*

Pietro, of *Piemont.*

M. Antonio, of the Valley of *Suſa.*

Giovanni Martino, of the Valley of *S. Martino.*

Mattheo,

Matheo, of *Bobio.*

Philippo, of the Valley of *Lucerna.*

Georgio, of *Piemont.*

Stephano Laurenzo, of the Valley of *S. Martino.*

Martino, of *Meana.*

Giovanni, of the Valley of *Lucerna,* who for a certain default, was suspended from his Office by the other *Barbes* for the space of seven years, during which time he resided at *Genoa,* where the *Barbes* had a house, as they likewise had another house very large and beautifull at *Florence.*

Giovanni Girardo of *Meana,* who afterwards went to *Geneva,* and was their Printer.

Barba Bartholomeo Terxiano, of *Meana,* who lived about 230 years ago. This *Barbe* was surnamed *della-groffa-mano,* becaufe of his great Hand and brawny Arm.

Tomafsino Baftia, of *Angrognia,* who died in *Puglia.*

Baftiano Baftia, of *Angrognia,* who died in *Calabria.*

Giacomino Bellonato, of *Angrognia.*

Giacobo Germano, of the Valley of *Perofa.*

M. Benedetto Goivanno.

Giovanni Romagnolo, of *Sifena* in *Italy.*

Francefchino, of *Fraifciniera.*

Michael Porta, of the Valley *Puta,* which is called at prefent *Loifa.*

Peiron Flotto, of *Pragela.*

M. Angelino, della Cofta.

Daniele, of *Valenza.*

Giovanni, of *Molines.*

Thefe two were fent by the other *Barbes* into *Bohemia,* to preach to the *Waldenfian* Churches that were gathered together in that Kingdom; but thefe men moft fhamefully betraying their truft, and thofe Churches, difcovered to the Enemy whatfoever they knew of their flocks, which afterwards occafioned a very heavy and fore perfecution; whereupon the Churches of *Bohemia* wrote Letters to the *Evangelical* Churches of the *Alpes,* to entreat them never to fend any for the future in fuch imployments, but thofe of whofe fidelity they had had long experience and good affurance.

M. Pietro Maffone of *Borgognia,* and *Georgio Morello,* of *Fraifciniera,* were fent into *Germany* in the year 1530, to treat with the chief Minifters of *Germany* (*viz.*) *Oecolampade, Bucer,* and others, touching the Reformation of their Churches. But *Pietro Maffone* was taken prifoner at *Dijon.*

Stephano Negrano, and *Ludovico Pafchale,* were fent into *Calabria* in the year 1560 to the Churches of *Montald, Sainct Xift,* and other neighbouring places: but *Stephano Negrino* was carried to *Cofence,* where he was ftarved to death in prifon. And *Ludovico Pafchale* was carried to *Rome* where he was burned alive, in the prefence of *Pope Pius* the fourth and his Cardinals, whom he then, even as he was in the midft of the flames, moft couragioufly fummoned to appear before

the

the Throne of the Lamb to give an account of their barbarous cruelties.

Giovanni of *Mus*, in *Provence*, who being sent to *Calabria*, died by the way, near to *Luca* in *Italy*, being taken prisoner in *Provence* upon the account of Religion, and afterwards delivered by a singular providence.

Tomaso Bermondo, of *Pragela*.

Pietro Bevilacqua, of the Valley of S. *Martino*.

Barba Gioannetto, of *Fraisciniera*.

Barba Paolo Bermondo, of *Pragela*.

Pietro Borrelo, of *Vilareto*, in the Valley of *Clusone*, who was detained prisoner in a certain place called *Poccapaglia* as he was going to *Calabria*; but was delivered, paying his ransom.

Mattheo Gautiero, of *Faeto*, in the Valley of *Clusone*.

Antonio Grenone, of *Angrognia*.

Martino Gonino of *Angrognia*, who suffered Martyrdom at *Grenoble*, as he was returning home from *Germany*.

Martino Arnollo, of *Angrognia*.

Laurenzo Pignatelo, in *Fenestrelle*.

M. *Francesco Vallo della Comba*, of the Valley of *Lucerna*.

M. *Gilio de Gili*, of the Valley of *Perosa*.

M. *Francesco Laurenzo*, of the Valley of S. *Martino*.

A Catalogue of the Names of some of the Disciples and kinred of those ancient Barbes, *who lived about the Year* 1587. *And imployed their talents in the work of the Ministry.*

M. *Stephano Peroto di Usseo*, in the Valley of *Clusone*.

M. *Philippo Pastore*, of *Pragela*.

M. *Ugho Pastore*, of *Pragela*.

M. *Pietro Bernardello*, of *Pragela*.

M. *Daniele Bermondo*, of *Pragela*.

M. *Andrea Riperta*, of *Fraisciniera*.

M. *Giovanni Nicoleto del Villaro*, of *Bobio*.

Besides the above-named there were several others who exercised in the Ministry in the Valleys at the same time, whose Names are as followeth.

M. *Melchior di dio della Torre*, in the Valley of *Lucerna*.

M. *Paolo Garnero* of *Dobio*.

M. *Daniele Chanforano* of *Angrognia*.

M. *Antonio Bongiorno* of *Bobio*.

M. *Henrico Rostagno*, of *Val. Peroso*.

M. *Pietro Giordano*, of the Valley of *Clusone*.

M. *Daniele Monino*, of *Villaro* in *Lucerna*.

M. *Stephano Laurentio*, of the Valley of S. *Martino*.

M. Pie-

M. Pietro Gilio, of the Valley of *Perofa.*
M. Michaele Appla, of St. *Giovanni,* in *Lucerna.*

Thefe are the Names of the principal and moft eminent of thofe *Barbes* which I could meet with in their Records ; And though it's rationally to be fuppofed that they are but a very fmall number in comparifon of thofe of whom there is no mention there made, yet thefe are abundantly fufficient to manifeft that the Lord has had always *Labourers in that his Vine-yard,* maugre all the malicious practifes of wicked men utterly to extirpate the memory of them from off the face of the earth ; Which is the fubject of the following Book, and to which I humbly refer the Reader for a more ample and fatisfactory account.

The End of the Firft Book.

THE
SECOND BOOK
OF THE
HISTORY
OF THE
EVANGELICAL CHURCHES
OF
The Valleys of *PIEMONT.*

CHAP. I.

The several Troubles and Perfecutions of the E-
vangelical Churches in the Valleys of Piemont
from time to time, becaufe of their Religion.

ARTICLE I.

He *Evangelical* Churches of the *Valleys* of *Piemont,* as well as thofe of *Dauphine,* have indeed been forely perfecuted, from the very beginning, by the *Ecclefiaflicks,* that is to fay, ever fince the A-poftacy of the *Roman* Church hath taken place in the World ; and all becaufe they would by no means comply with their belief and cuftomes. *Rai-* nerius in his Treatife *de Valdenfibus* tells us, that *among all thofe that have*

Rain. de Val-denfibus.

have rebelled againſt the Church of Rome, there have been none ſo perni-
cious as the Waldenſes. And truly, we may ſay on the other ſide, with as
much juſtice and truth, that of all the Enemies that have oppoſed the
true *Evangelical* Doctrine, and worſhip of thoſe poor *Chriſtians,* there
have been none ſo cruel, and malicious, as the *Popes* of *Rome* and their
Emiſſaries be, for no other reaſon then this, That thoſe poor people
did, upon all occaſions openly bear witneſs againſt the luxury, avarice,
and errours of the ſaid *Popes,* and their adherents, who had ſo ſubtilly
and ſerpent-like wound and inſinuated themſelves (firſt the head, and
then the whole body) into the true Church of Chriſt ; And becauſe

Rainer. cap. de
ſtudio perver-
tendi alios, &
modo docendi,
fol. 98.

they taught and maintained (as *Rainerius* himſelf confeſſes) that
thoſe were the true Succeſſors of the Apoſtles, who imitated their life ; and
that the Pope, the Biſhops, and that crue of other Clergy-men, who hun-
ted after, and got into their poſſeſsion the riches and treaſures of this world,
were not the true Shepheards, neither was it ever Chriſts intention, to com-
mit the charge of his chaſte, and dearly beloved Spouſe to thoſe, who
ſhould ſo ſhamefully proſtitute her by evil examples and wicked works. The
very truth is, This *little flock* of *Chriſt* in the Valleys of *Piemont,* by
reaſon of the remoteneſs and obſcurity of their Country, and habitations (adding thereto the natural *genius* of thoſe plain and ſimple people, which was not at all to effect high things) did for many *Centuries*
together, peaceably enjoy, or at leaſt preſerve amongſt them the purity of that Doctrine which was left them by *Chriſt* and his *Apoſtles ;*
and therefore when once the *ſeaven horn'd beaſt riſing out of the bottom-*
leſs pit, began to ſhew it ſelf in the world, and corruption to be foiſted
into the Church by the *Roman* Clergy, thoſe *true Nathaniels,* could by
no means drink down ſuch abominations, but did with all their might
reſiſt and oppoſe the ſame, and that oft times, even unto bloud ; and
upon this account, and this alone, was it, that they became firſt the
objects of their enemies hatred, and afterwards the ſubjects of their
Antichriſtian fury.

The firſt means they uſed, to exterminate and extirpate them, were
their thunderbolts, and *Anathema's ;* their *Canons, Conſtitutions,* and
Decrees, with whatſoever might render them odious to the Kings,
Princes, and people of the earth, prohibiting them all manner of
communion, and ſociety with any of their own tribe, ſentencing them
as men unworthy, and uncapable of the leaſt charge, honour, profit, or
inheritance ; (nay not ſo much as a burying place amongſt other
Chriſtians !) confiſcating their goods, diſ-inheriting their children,
and razing their houſes down to the ground : And theſe very ſenten-
ces are at this day to be ſeen, together with ſeveral Letters of *Pope A-*

Pope Alexan-
der the third
his endeavours
to extirpate
the Waldenſes

lexander the third, and many others after him, with the formal inſtructions which were given by them to thoſe Inſtruments whom they
then imployed for the effecting of that work ; as alſo the ſtrict commands they laid upon Kings, Princes, Magiſtrates, Conſuls, and
People, to make an exact *Inquiſition,* to ſhut the Gates of their Cities,
to lay violent hands upon, and to ſlay without mercy thoſe poor innocent Lambs ; giving their Accuſers a third or thereabouts of their
goods

Goods, and laying some Punishments upon all those, whoever they were, who should attempt to conceal any one of them.

But now in process of time, when as these means were judged too mild and gentle, for the effecting a business of so high a nature, and that notwithstanding all their industry, those People began to multiply exceedingly, and that their Ministers did not at all cease to teach and preach to their respective Congregations, that the *Pope* was *Antichrist*, the *Mass* an Abomination, the *Host* an Idol, and *Purgatory* a Fable; *Innocent* who succeeded Pope *Celestin* by name, about the Year 1198. took a more speedy and effectual course for the Extirpation of them, by giving some Inquisitours, appointed purposely for that Work, a plenipotentiary power, first to form their Processes, as they should see good, and then to deliver them to the Magistrate, and thence to hasten them to the Stake, or Gibbet; by which means, in a few years, they had filled the greatest part of *Christendom* with most formidable and lamentable Spectacles of their barbarous and *unchristian* Cruelties.

Now that this power of these Inquisitours was unlimited, and unbounded, is plain by their constant practises. For, they had power to assemble the People when ever they pleased, at the Sound of a Bell! they had power to proceed against the Bishops themselves, if they found occasion, and to make their Process themselves! Yea, they had power to imprison whom they would, and whom they would to release! All manner of accusation was valid with them! A Sorcerer, or a Whore, was a sufficient Witness to take away the Life of any *Waldensian* Heretick! And what was more, there was no necessity of confronting Parties with Parties, or examining the Business, but it was sufficient to exhibit a Bill before the Inquisitour, without either Witness or Law whatsoever! If any man were rich, his wealth was a sufficient proof, either to convict him of Heresie, or at least to be a Favourer of the same. No Advocate durst plead their Cause, nor any Notary receive any Act in their behalf: when any was caught in this Net of the Inquisition, he was sure never to escape; if happily he was let out, it was but in Mockery, to bring him in again, (as a Cat plays sometimes with a Mouse a while, and then crushes the Bones of it between her Teeth) and as if it were too small a Punishment to take away their Lives, there are yet to be seen many Sentences of those bloudy Inquisitours against the very Bones of those poor *Waldenses*, to dig them up after they had been buried at the least thirty Years, and then to burn them in the open Streets, and other publick places. The Children of such Parents as were thus proceeded against, durst not inherit their Lands and Possessions, for fear of being condemned, as inherititing together with such Possessions their pretended Heresies.

And to keep the People more in aw, those holy Fathers were wont to lead about in triumph their Prisoners and Captives as oft as they went in Procession, forcing some to whip and lash themselves as they marched along in the Streets, and others to wear red Cassocks with yellow Crosses, under the Name of *Benedictin Converts*, to signifie thereby, that

[marginal note:] The unlimited power of the Inquisitors for the prosecution of the Waldenses.

[marginal note:] The bones of some Waldenses dug up, and 30. years after they had been buried.

that they were convicted of fome notorious Errours, and that the next Fault they fhould commit, they fhould be condemned as Herericks, without Remiffion. Others they made to follow them in their Shirts, bare-footed and bare-head with a green With about their Necks, and a Wifp of Straw in their Hands, and in this miferable equipage did they force perfons of all quality and fexes to go up and down publick-ly (to the great grief and terrour of all the Beholders) prohibiting them to enter into their Churches, during the time of their Service, or fo much as to caft their Eys upon the *Hoft* when the Prieft lifted up the fame : and which is not much inferiour to any of the reft for cruelty, many were enjoyned by way of Penance, to take Voyages as far as the *Holy Land,* or other remote Corners of the World, (at their own Ex-pence and Charges) for a fet term of time, and that without once daring to make the leaft inquiry at their Return, either what was be-come of their Eftates, or what familiarity thofe holy Fathers had with their Wives in their abfence, leaft thereby they fhould incur the Cen-fure of relapfed and impenitent Perfons, and confequently render themfelves uncapable of ever being pardoned.

Befides all thefe practifes, they had a certain Form of cunning De-vices, and fubtil Stratagems, whereby they ufually regulated all their Proceffes againft thofe poor *Waldenfes*; as may be feen in the follow-ing Maxims, or Rules of Caution, which Providence hath fuffered to come to Light, how clofely foever they were contrived by thofe Sons of Darknefs, in fecret Corners as were the reft of their Defigns.

An Extract of certain Rules of Caution, whereby the In-quifitours formerly regulated their Profecution of the *Waldenfes*.

1. *It is not expedient to difpute concerning Matters of Faith before Laymen.*

2. *None ought to be reputed as true Repentants, but fuch as difcover all thofe whom they knew to be of the fame principles and profeffion with them-felves.*

3. *He that accufes and difcovers not thofe of the fame profeffion with himfelf, ought to be cut off from the Church as a rotten and putrified Member, left he fhould corrupt and infect the reft.*

4. *After any is delivered over to the Secular power, he muft not be at all permitted to excufe himfelf, or to declare his innocence before the people; for, if fuch a one be put to death, it fcandalizes the Lay-men; and if he efcape, it becomes a prejudice to our Religion.*

5. *There muft be great caution had of promifing life to any man who is condemned, before the people; becaufe there's no Heretick would ever be burnt, if he could efcape by virtue of a promife. And in cafe he fhould promife Repentance before the people, and then be put to death, that would neceffarily fcandalize the people, and make them believe that fuch were wrongfully put to death.*   6. *The*

6. *The Inquisitour ought always to presuppose the Fact, and (waving that) onely to inquire concerning the Circumstances of the Fact, after this manner. How many times hast thou confest thy self to Hereticks ? In what Chamber of thy House did they lie ? And such like Questions.*

7. *The Inquisitour must hold some Book before the accused Party, during the Examination, as if he had there written the whole Life of him whom he examines.*

8. *He must threaten him with Death, in case he will not confess, and tell him that he is a dead man, that he ought to think upon his Soul, and wholly renounce his Heresie, since that he must die, he ought to take patiently whatever befalls him. And if he answer, Since I must die, I had rather die in this my Faith, than in that of the* Roman *Church, Then be sure there's no hope at all of such a one, and therefore he must be delivered forthwith to Justice.*

9. *There is no hope at all of convincing Hereticks by the knowledg of the Scriptures, and Learning, for as much as oft times it falls out, that very learned men are confounded by them, and by that means, the Hereticks fortifie themselves, when they thus finde that even learned men themselves are deceived by them.*

10. *Hereticks must never be suffered to answer directly to any thing. And when they are pressed by frequent Interrogatives, they have a Custome to make answer, that they are poor ignorant men, and not able to answer. And if they perceive that the Standers by are any whit moved with compassion towards them, as being poor harmless men, and wrongfully accused, then they take courage, and seem to cry and take on, like poor miserable Wretches, and so flattering and smoothing the Judg, endeavour to escape the Inquisition ; saying, Sir, if I have offended in any thing, I shall willingly do Penance, but I beseech you assist and deliver me from this Infamy, which has been cast upon me by pure malice and envy, and altogether undeservedly But then must the couragious Inquisitour not at all bend, or be moved by these Flatteries, nor give the least ear or credence to any such Fables.*

11. *Lastly, the Inquisitour must prevent them, by assuring them, that they shall gain nothing by Swearing falsly, for as much as they have sufficient Proofs to convict them otherwise ; and therefore that they should not at all think to escape the Sentence of Death thereby. But withall, he must promise them, that if they confess freely their Errour, they shall finde Mercy. For, in such a perplexity as this, there are many that will confess their Errour, in hopes to escape.*

These were the inhumane Practises of these Sons of Violence from the Year of our Lord 1206. to the Year 1228. during which time, there were so great a number of the *Waldenses* apprehended through out most of the parts of *Europe,* that the Arch-bishops of *Aix, Arles,* and *Narbonne,* being assembled at *Navignon,* in the said Year 1228. had compassion on so great a Multitude of miserable Wretches, and told the Inquisitours, that they had apprehended so many of the *Waldenses,* that it was not possible to get a sufficient quantity of Lime and Stone to build Prisons for them ; and therefore desired them to forbear

bear the imprifoning of them, till they heard further from the Pope. The truth is, we need no better poof for this, than what then came even from the Mouths of thofe Inquifitours themfelves ; for it being put to the Queftion among them, whether thofe that received the Sacrament with the *Waldenfes* were excufable, or might pretend ignorance, that they knew not that they were *Waldenfes* ? It was anfwered, *That there had been fo vigorous and open a Perfecution of all Qualities and Sexes of the* Waldenfes, *fo many of them put to Death, and fo many conftantly ftanding in a moft forlorn condition before the Doors of their Chapels and Churches, that it was not pofsible that any Man could pretend ignorance in fuch a cafe.*

Vignaux in his *Memoires des Vaudois.* Paul *Perrin* *Hiftoire des Vaudois lib. 2. cap. 3.* Pierre *Gilles* *Hiftoire Ecclefiaft. c. 4.*

If I fhould here undertake to fpeak at large of all the Perfecutions that ever befell thofe poor People, I fhould certainly too much ftraiten my felf in the Relation of what is yet behinde ; therefore I fhall content my felf to begin onely with the Year of our Lord 1400. wherein the Inhabitants of the Valley of *Pragela* were fet upon by their Popifh Neighbours about the time called *Chriftmafs,* and that in fo violent and furious a manner, that thofe poor Creatures were forced to fly in all hafte with their Wives and little one in their arms, to one of the higheft Mountains thereabouts, (which has been ever fince called the *Albergean,* from the *Italian* word *Albergo,* becaufe the poor People made it their Place of Refuge) In this their flight, a very great number of them were overtaken by their Purfuers, whofe *Feet were fwifter to fhed Bloud,* than the Feet of the others to fly, and fo were moft barbaroufly murdered. The refidue being overtaken by the Night, wandered up & down in the Snow, till fuch time as their Joints were frozen and become ftiff by the extremity of cold, in fo much that there were found the next Morning, lying on the Snow, no lefs than fourfcore fmall Children, and moft of their Mothers by them, all frozen to Death, a moft miferable Spectacle to behold.

At this time, and for many years after, the Arch-bifhop and the Inquifitours of *Turin* imployed all their ftrength and power againft the *Waldenfes* of *Piemont,* yea they compelled fome of thofe, who were fallen into their hands, to promife them, that they would change their Religion ; but thofe their new Converts not being able to continue fo with a good confcience ; and on the other fide, fearing to fall again into the Paws of the Lion and the Bear, quickly fet in order their Affairs as well as the Circumftances of that Conjuncture would permit, and retired themfelves, fome into *Provence,* and the reft into *Calabria,* and the adjacent places . Now when this was known to *Jean Compefio,* Arch-bifhop of *Turin,* and to *Andrew d'Aqua-pendente* (Inquifitour) there were fet forth feveral Bulls againft them upon the 28. of *November* 1475. By virtue whereof, (though the moft part of thofe poor Wretches found a way to efcape, yet neverthelefs many fuffered Martyrdom in a moft cruel and bloudy manner, and that in moft Towns and Cities of *Piemont* : *Jordan Tertian* was burnt at *Sufe* ! *Hippolite Roufsier* at *Turin* ; *Hugo Chiamp de Feneftrelles* having been brought to *Turin,* they pulled his Guts

out

out of his Belly, and fo he died in a fad and wofull condition.

A while after, the Pope feeing that his Perfecutions upon particular Men, had not effects according to his Minde, he refolved to come to a general violence,and to that effect,having appointed *Albertus de Capitaneis* Arch-deacon of *Cremone*,to be his Legate and CommiffionerGeneral for that Affair,he fent him with Bulls and Patents to all the Lords & Princes,in whofe Dominions there were found any *Waldenfes*, to incite them to affift the faid Legate with fufficient Forces, to exterminate all the *Waldenfes* or poor People of *Lyons*,who inhabited in their Dominions. And that the World may be fatisfied concerning the Contents, I have here inferted a true Copy of that famous Bull of Pope*Innocent*, given to the faid *Albertus de Capitaneis*, in the Year 1487. referring all that are curious in Matters of this Nature, to the Univerfity Library of *Cambridg*, where they may fee and compare it with the very Original.

Albertus de Capitaneis fent with Bulls from Pope Innocens againft the Waldenfes, 1487.

AR-

ARTICLE II.

The Bull of Pope *Innocent* for the Extirpation of the *Waldenfes*, given to *Albertus de Capitaneis* his Legate and Commiffioner General for that Imployment in the Year 1487.

The true Original whereof is to be feen, together with the reft, in the publick Library of the famous Univerfity of
CAMBRIDG.

ALbertus de Capitaneis *Juris u-triufque Doctor , Archidiaco-nus Ecclefiæ Cremonenfis , & Blaxius de Bena, Ordinis Prædicatorum, Sacræ Theologiæ Profeffor, hæreticæ pra-vitatis Inquifitor, & in hac parte Nuncii & Commiffarii a Sanctifsimo in Chrifto Patre Domino noftro, Domino Innocentio Divinâ Providentiâ, Papa octavo fpecia-liter Deputati, &c. Univerfis & fingulis Dominis, Abbatibus, Prioribus, Præpofi-tis, Plebanis , Vice-plebanis , Decanis, Archidiaconis, Scholafticis, Cantoribus, Cuftodibus, Thefaurariis, Sacriftis, tam Cathedralium quam Collegiatarum, Ca-nonicis , Parochaliúmque Ecclefiarum Rectoribus feu horum locatorum Curatis, & non Curatis, Vicariis perpetuis, Alta-riftis, cæterifque Presbyteris , Clericis, Notariis, & Tabellionibus publicis ac fe-cum Refidentibus & Miniftralibus Gra-dualibus , & quarumcunque Curiarum, tam fpiritualium quam temporalium, Judiciis Juratis per Civitates & Dio-cefes Ebrodunenfem, Lugdunenfem, Vi-ennenfem, aut alias ubilibet conftitutis, & eorum cuilibet in folidum, illíque vel* ... *ad quem vel ad quos noftra præ-*

ALbertus de Capitaneis Doctour of both Laws, Arch-deacon of the Church of *Cremona,* and *Blaxius de Bena* of the Order Pre-dicants, Profeffour of Divinity, In-quifitour againft the perverfnefs of Hereticks, and for this end Meffen-gers and Commiffioners in a fpecial manner deputed by our moft holy Fa-ther in *Chrift* our Lord, *the Lord* In-nocent *the eighth* by Divine Provi-dence *Pope, &c.* To all and every one the Lords, Abbots, Priors, Over-feers of the Vulgar, *&c.* their Vice-gerents, Deans, Arch-deacons, Scho-lars, Singers, Keepers, Treafurers, Sacrifts, Canons, as well of Cathe-dral as Collegiate Churches, and Re-ctors of Parochial, or their confti-tuted Curates, and Parochial Vicars without Cure, Altarifts, and all other Priefts, Clerks, Notaries, and Publick Regifters, and Refidents with them, and Minifterial Graduates, and fworn Judges of all Courts as well Spiritual as Temporal throughout the Cities and Diocefes of *Eureux, Lions, Vien-na,* and others conftituted in any other place ; each of them entirely, and to him or them, to whom feverally or
jointly

jointly thefe our prefents (or in truth rather Apoftolical'Letters) fhall come or be prefented, greeting in the Lord. Our faid Commiffioner being ftraitly commanded to obey thefe our (or rather truly Apoftolical)commands, hath fignified to us with due Reverence as became him, that he had received Letters or Apoftolical Bulls, figned duly with a Leaden Seal hanging by a Hempen String, after the manner of the *Romans*, as Bulls are ufually made valid and entire, nor fufpected of any falfification in any part thereof, but wholly free from all fault and fufpition, according to the tenour and form following;

Innocentius Bifhop, a Servant of the Servants of God, to our beloved Son *Albertus de Capitaneis*, Arch-deacon of the Church of *Cremona*, Nuntio of the See Apoftolick, and our Commiffioner for the Dominions of our beloved Son, that noble perfon, *Charls* Duke of *Savoy*, on this and on the other fide of the Mountains through the City and Diocefe of *Delphinate*, *Vienna*, and *Sedun*, and the places near adjoyning thereunto, greeting and Apoftolical Benediction. Our hearty Defires chieflytend to this, that as touching thofe for the gaining of whom to the Church the fupreme Maker of all things was pleafed himfelf to undergo human infirmities, we, to whom he hath committed the Care and Government of his Flock may with all watchfull Induftry endeavour to withdraw them from the *precipices* of Errours, that providing for their Salvation, as it fhall pleafe God to favour us with Grace, we may continually labour, that the Catholick Faith may in our times be propagated, and the evil of Herefie be rooted out from the borders of the Faithfull.

We have heard, and it is come to our knowledg, not without much dif-

fentes, imò verius Apoftolicæ literæ pervenerint, aut præfentatæ fuerint falutem in Domino. Et noftris hujufmodi, imo verius Apoftolicis, firmiter obedire mandatis, literas feu bullas Commifsionis noftræ Apoftolicas debitè figillo plumbeo cum cordulâ cannabis in pendente more Romanæ Curiæ bullatas fanas & integras, nec in aliqua earum parte de vitio falfitatis fufpectas fed omni prorfus vitio & fufpicione carentes, Nos cum ea qua decuit reverentia monentes recepiffe hujufmodi fub tenore;

Innocentius Epifcopus Servus Servorum Dei, dilecto filio Alberto de Capitaneis, Archidiacono Ecclefiæ Cremonenfis, ad Dominia dilecti filii Nobilis viri Caroli Ducis Sabaudiæ citra & ultra montes per Delphinatum Viennenfem & Sedunenfem Civitatem & Diocefim ac illis adjacentia loca noftro & Apoftolicæ Sedis Nuncio & Commiffario falutem & Apoftolicam benedictionem.

Id noftri cordis vota præcipue depofcunt ut pro quibus fuper eorum afcribendis cœtui ipfe omnium fummus rerum opifex humanos languores perpeti voluit; Nos quibus gregis fui curam regimenque commifit, illos ab errorum præcipitiis vigilanti curemus eripere ftudio, ut eorum faluti divina nobis propiciante gratia jugiter intendamus ad noftrum, qui defideranter in votis gerimus ut Fides Catholica noftris profperetur temporibus, & pravitas hæretica de finibus fidelium extirpetur.

Non fine difplicentia grandi pervenit auditúmque quod nonnulli iniquitatis

fi i

filii, Incolæ Provinciæ Elredumensis, sectatores illius perniciosissimæ & abominabilis sectæ hominum malignorum pauperum de Lugduno, seu Valdensium nuncupatorum, quæ dudum in partibus Pedemontanis, & aliis circumvicinis, procurante satore malorum operum, per studiosa diverticula & præcipitia latebrosa, oves Deo dicatas illaqueare, & demum ad perditionem animarum perducere, mortifera sagacitate conatur, damnabiliter insurrexit, sub quadam simulata sanctitatis specie in reprobum sensum ducti a via veritatis vehementer abhorreat & superstitiosas ac hereticas ceremonias sectantes, quam plurima orthodoxæ fidei contraria & oculos Divinæ Majestatis offendentia, ac gravissimum in se animarum periculum continentia dicunt, faciunt & committunt. Et cum dilectus filius Blasius de Monte regali ordinis prædicatorum & Theologiæ professor, Inquisitor generalis in partibus illis, per olim Generalem Magistrum dicti ordinis, & deinde per dilectum filium nostrum Dominicum ū Sancti Clementis presbyterum Cardinalem, in partibus illis Apostolicæ sedis Legatum, & demum per fælicis recordationis Sixtum Papam IIII. immediatum prædecessorum nostrum ad hujusmodi & alios quoscunque errores extirpandos destinatus, ad Provinciam ipsam se contulisset, ut eos ad abjurandum errores prædictos, & veram Christi fidem profitendam induceret, more duri aspidis aures suas obturantes, nedum pessimos & perversos errores suos deposuerunt, maxima mala malis addentes, illas publicè prædicare, & prædicationibus alios Christi fideles

pleafure, that certain fons of iniquity, inhabitants of the Province of *Eureux*, followers of that abominable and pernicious Sect of malignant men, who are called the poor people of *Lyons*, or the *Waldenfes*, who have long ago endeavoured in *Piemont*, and other neighbouring parts, by the procurement of him who is the fower of evil works, through by-ways, purposely fought out, and hidden precipices, to infnare the fheep belonging unto God, and at laft to bring them to the perdition of their fouls by deadly cunning, are damnably rifen up under a feigned pretence of Holinefs, being led into a reprobate fenfe, and do greatly erre from the way of truth; and following fuperftitious and heretical Ceremonies, do fay, act and commit very many things contrary to the Orthodox Faith, offenfive to the eyes of the Divine Majefty, and which do occafion a very great hazard of fouls. And whereas our beloved Son *Blafius de Monte regali*, of the Preachers Order, and Profeffour of Divinity, and General Inquifitor in thofe parts, was appointed heretofore by the General Mafter of the faid Order, and afterward by our Beloved Son *Dominicus* ū Prieft of *St. Clement*, and Cardinal, and Legat of the Apoftolical See in thofe parts; and laftly by our immediate Predeceffor of bleffed memory *Sixtus* the IIII. *Pope*, to extirpate fuch like and all other Errours whatfoever, having tranfported himfelf unto that Province, that he might induce them to abjure the Errours aforefaid, and to make profeffion of the true Chriftian Faith, they were fo far from leaving their moft wicked and perverfe Errours, that ftopping their ears like the deaf Adder, adding greatly evil to evil, they did preach publiquely thofe Errours, and by their preaching did draw other Chriftian believers

believers thereinto ; defpifing the Excommunications, and prohibitions, and other Cenfures of the fame Inquifitor, overthrowing the houfe of his habitation, and the things that were therein, as alfo fpoiling and robbing with the goods of fome others, true believers, killing the fervant of the fame Inquifitor, and waging a War in a hoftile manner refifting their temporal Lords, and making fpoil of their goods, forcing them and their Families to fly from their Parifhes, burning and demolifhing their houfes, depriving them of all their Revenues, and doing them all the harm they could ; together with an infinite number of other deteftable and horrible acts, which they were not afraid to commit.

We therefore having determined to ufe all our endeavours, and to imploy all our care, as we are bound by the duty of our Paftoral charge, to root up and extirpate fuch a deteftable Sect, and the forefaid execrable Errors, that they may not fpread further, and that the hearts of believers may not be damnably perverted from the *Catholick* Church ; and to reprefs fuch rafh undertakings; & having fpecial confidence in the Lord concerning your Learning, your ripenefs in counfel, your zeal in the faith, and your experience in the management of affairs ; and in like manner hoping that you will truly and faithfully execute the things which we fhall think good to commit unto you for the extirpating of fuch errours ; we have thought good to conftitute you at this time, for this Caufe of God and the Faith, the Nuntio Comiffioner of us, and of the Apoftolical See, within the Dominions of our beloved Son *Charls* Duke of *Savoy*, and the *Delphinat*, and the Cities and Diocefs of *Vienna*, and *Sedun*, and the adjacent

in eofdem errores protrahere , ejufdem Inquifitoris excommunicationes & interdicta, aliafque cenfuras vilipendere, domum habitationis ejufdem fubvertere, & quæ in ea erant nonnullorumque aliorum fidelium bona diripere & derrebare, ejufdemque Inquifitoris famulum interficere, certamen hoftili more inire; illorum Dominis temporalibus refiftere, & illorum bona deprædari, ipfófque & eorum familias a fuis Parochiis præfugos facere, domus incendere feu evertere, & a redditibus privatos tenere, & quæ potuerint eis damna inferre, infinita quoque alia deteftabilia ac abhorrenda facinora perpetrare veriti non fuerunt.

Nos igitur hujufmodi fectam deteftabilem & premiffos ipfius execrandos errores ne propagentur ulterius, neve per eos corda fidelium damnabiliter corrumpantur ab Ecclefia catholica, prout ex debito Paftoralis officii tenemur evellere, & radicitus extirpare , ac hujufmodi temerarios aufus reprimere cupientes omnes conatus noftros adhibére, omnemque folicitudinem impendere decrevimus, ac fumentes de tuis Literarum fcientia, confilii maturitate , fidei zelo, & in agendis experientia in Domino fiduciam fpecialem, pariter & fperantes quod ea quæ tibi pro hujufmodi extirpandis erroribus committenda duxerimus probè & laudabiliter exequeris, te noftrum & Apoftolicæ fedis Nuncium & Commiffarium, ad Dominia dilecti filii Caroli Sabaudiæ Ducis ac Delphinatum , Viennen civitatem & Diocefem Sedunenfem , & illis adjacentia

Provincias

Provincias, civitates,terras & loca quæ-cunque, pro hac Dei & fidei caufa im-prefentiarum duximus deftinandum, ut eundem Inquifitorem ad fui officii li-berum exercitium recipi & admitti fa-cias, & corundem nefandiffimos Wal-denfium fectæ fectatores,& alios hæreticæ pravitatis cujuflibet labe pollutos ad ab-jurandum eorum errores, & parendum mandatis Inquifitoris ejufdem & tuis, opportunis remediis inducas; & ut id tanto facilius efficere valeas, quanto major fuerit tibi per nos data facultas, & autoritas attributa tibi, per te vel alium feu alios movendi & inflantiffimé requirendi Univerfos Archiepifcopos & Epifcopos in Ducatu, Delphinatu, & adjacentibus locis prædictis conflitutos, quos in partem folicitudinis nobifcum evocavit altiffimus, eifque in virtute fanctæ obedientiæ mandandi ut unà cum venerabilibus fratribus noftris locorum Ordinariis vel eorum Vicariis, feu offi-cialibus generalibus in quorum civita-tibus & Diocefibus duxeris ad præmiffa procedendum & injunctum tibi offici-um exequendum, & cum Inquifitore præfato viro, utique literarnm fcientia prædito, & fervore fidei & zelo falutis animarum accenfo, fe tibi in præmiffis affiftere & unà tecum ad eorum exequu-tionem procedere potuerint vel voluerint adverfus Valdenfes prædictos & alios quofcunque hæreticos armis infurgant, eofque veluti afpides venenofos commu-nicatis invicem proceffibus conculcent; & ut populi eorum curæ crediti in con-feffione veræ fidei perfiftant & robo-rentur, diligenter procurent, & ad eo-rundem hæreticorum tam fanctam tam-que pernecceffarium exterminationem

Provinces, Cities, Lands and places whatfoever, to the end you fhould caufe the fame Inquifitor to be recei-ved and admitted to the free exercife of his Office, and that you fhould in-duce the followers of the moft wicked Sect of the *Waldenfes*, and all others polluted with any other Heretical pra-vity whatfoever, to abjure their Er-rours, and to obey the Command-ments of the fame Inquifitor, and give way to your feafonable remedies: And that you may do this fo much the more eafily, by how much the greater Power and Authority is given you by us, to wit, a Power, that by your felf, or by fome other perfon or perfons, you may admonifh and re-quire moft inftantly all Archbifhops and Bifhops feated in the *Dutchy, Del-phinat*, and other the forenamed ad-jacent places, whom the moft High hath called to fhare with us in our cares, and command them by vertue of Holy obedience, that together with our Venerable Brethren the *Ordinaries* of the places, or their Vicars, or Ge-neral Officials, in whofe Cities and Diocefes you fhall think fit to proceed in the premifes, and to execute the Office which is injoyned you with the forenamed Inquifitor, a man no doubt endued with Learning and fervent Zeal for the falvation of fouls, they do affift you in the premifes; and to-gether with you be able and willing to *proceed to the execution thereof againft the forenamed Waldenfes, and all other Hereticks whatfoever, to rife up in Arms againft them, and by a joynt communi-cation of proceffes, to tread them under foot, as venemous Adders,* and to pro-cure diligently that the people com-mitted to their charge do perfift in the confeffion of the true Faith, and be confirmed therein; and that they do with a ready mind, as they are bound, bend all their endeavours, and beftow

all

all their care towards so holy and so necessary an extermination and dissipation of the same Hereticks : And they are to be required to omit nothing which may contribute thereunto.

Moreover, that *Charls* our most beloved Son in Christ the illustrious King of *France*, and our beloved Sons the Noble *Charls* of *Savoy* and of the adjacent forenamed places , and the Dukes, Princes, Earls, and temporal Lords of the Cities, Territories; and Universities of places, and the Confederates of *High Germany* , and all others of those parts who are believers in Christ, do take up the Shield of the Orthodox Faith which they did profess when they were Baptized, and of the cause of our Lord *Jesus Christ*, by whom Kings Reign, and Lords bear Rule, and give assistance to the same Archbishops, Bishops , and to you and the foresaid Vicars and General Officials, and to the Inquisitor, with seasonable favours, and their secular power, as they shall see it expedient for the execution of this most necessary and wholsome Inquisition ; and ardently oppose themselves against *those most detestable Hereticks,* for the defence of the Faith, for the safety of their native Countrey, and for the preservation of themselves, and of all that belong unto them, *by procuring that they may be exterminated and destroyed.* And if you shall think it expedient, to cause, exhort, and induce all the faithful in those parts, by fit Preachers of Gods word, preaching the Cross or the Croisado, to fight manfully against the same Hereticks, having taken the saving sign of the Cross upon their hearts and garments : And to grant, that such as are signed with the Cross, and fight against the said Hereticks, or such as contribute thereunto, may obtain according to

& dissipationem adhibeant omnes conatus, omnemque solicitudinem impendant promptis animis ut tenentur, nilque ex his quæ ad id conferre possint obmittant requirendi.

Insuper tam carissimum in Christo filium nostrum Carolum Francorum Regem illustrem, & dilectos filios nobiles viros Carolum Sabaudiæ, & locorum adjacentium prædictorum Duces, Principes, Comites & temporales Dominos civitatum, terrarum & locorum Universitates, & superioris Alemaniæ confederatos, & alios quoscunque Christo fideles illorum partium, ut clypeum defensionis orthodoxæ fidei quam in susceptione sacri Baptismatis professi sunt, & causæ Domini nostri Jesu Christi per quam Reges regnant & Domini dominantur, assumant ; & eisdem Archiepiscopis, Episcopis, & tibi ac Vicariis seu officialibus generalibus prædictis ac Inquisitori, opportunis favoribus & seculari brachio eorum, prout expedire cognoverint, in exequatione tam pernecessariæ & salutaris Inquisitionis officii hujusmodi assistant , & adversus eosdem nefandissimos hæreticos pro defensione fidei, pro salute patriæ, pro tuitione propria & suorum omnium se ardenter opponant, & illos exterminare & delere procurent: Et, si expedire putaveris universos, fideles illarum partium, ut contra eosdem hæreticos, salutiferæ crucis signo in cordibus & vestibus assumpto, viriliter pugnent per idoneos verbi Dei prædicatores crucem sive cruciatam prædicantes exhortari & induci faciendi, ac cruce signatis ac contra eosdem hæreticos pugnantibus vel ad id contribuentibus, ut plenariam omnium peccatorum suorum indulgentiam & remissionem juxta tuam desuper

per ordinationem femel in vita, & etiam in mortis articulo affequantur concedendi ; præcipiendi quoque in virtute
fanctæ obedientiæ & fub excommunicationis latæ fententiæ pœnas quibufcunq;
idoneis verbi Dei prædicatoribus fecula-
ribus & cujufcunq; ordinis etiam men-
dicantium exempti & non exempti regu-
laribus, ut eofdem fideles excitare &
inflammare debeant ad hujufmodi labem
vi & armis de medio exterminandam, &
ut fuis viribus & facultatibus occurrant
ad commune periculum repellendum mandandi. Abfolvendi infuper fic crucem
affumentes, pugnantes, vel contribuentes
& confentientes, ab omnibus & fingulis
Ecclefiafticis fententiis, cenfuris & pœnis
quibus forfan qualitercunq; ligati forent, præterquam ab hodie fpecialiter la-
tis, a quibus ligatos prævia fatisfactione
vel parte confentiente duntaxat abfolvendi. Nec non cum eis difpenfandi fuper irregularitate divinis fe immifcendi,
vel ex Apoflafia qualibet contracta &
fuper occulte vel male perceptis, ac bonis
indebite acquifitis incertis, in expug-
natio nem hæreticorum duntaxat con-
vertendi, concordandi & componendi ;
quæcunque etiam cum juramento peregri-
nationis & abflinentia ac alia emiffa
vota, caflitatis & ingreffus Religionis,
ac ultra marino & vifitationis liminum
Apoflolicorum, ac Ecclefiæ Sancti Jacobi
in Compoflella votis duntaxat exceptis,
in defenfionem Catholice fidei contra
hæreticos, venientibus & pugnantibus
feu ad id contribuentibus vel tantum
dantibus quantum verifimiliter expofi-

your appointment, once in their life,
and alfo at the point of death, a ple-
nary Indulgence and remiffion of all
their fins ; and alfo to command by
vertue of Holy obedience, and under
the penalty of the fentence of Excommunication, already given to all fit
Preachers of Gods word, Seculars,
and Regulars, of what Order foever
alfo of the Mendicants, exempted and
not exempted, that they ftir up and inflame the fame believers, to root out
this kind of Peft by force of Arms,
and to fet themfelves againft the common danger with their beft ftrength
and faculties. And moreover, to abfolve fuch as thus take up the Crofs,
fighting, or contributing and con-
fenting thereunto, from all and every
Ecclefiaftical Sentences, Cenfures, and
Penalties, wherewith happily they
may in any wife be bound up ; except
from fuch as this day in a fpecial manner are denounced, from which they
that are bound therewith are to be
abfolved by a previous fatisfaction,
or alone by the confent of the party.
And alfo to difpenfe with them, concerning the irregularity contracted by
intrufion into holy things, or by reafon of any kind of Apoftacy ; or concerning goods fecretly and evilly gotten, or uncertain goods unduly purchafed, to agree and compound that
they may be converted onely to the
war againft Hereticks. Alfo to exchange all vows made with an Oath of
Pilgrimage and Abftinency, and other
the like Vows, except onely thofe of
Chaftity, and of entring into Religious Orders, and going beyond the
Seas, and of vifiting the threfholds of
the Apoftles, and the Church of *St.
James* in *Compoflella*, to them that go
to fight for the defence of the Catholick Faith againft the Hereticks, or to
fuch as contribute thereunto, or do
give fo much as in all likelihood they
would

would expend in paffing to the due places, or as the due qualities of places and perfons being confidered, it fhall feem good to you, or to fit Confeffors by you to be deputed. In the mean time to chufe, depute and confirm one or more fit Generals of War, and Captains for the gathering of the *Croifado* Army, in our name, and in the name of the Church of *Rome*, and command them that they take this burthen upon them, and execute it faithfully for the praife and defence of the Faith; and that all others do endeavour joyntly to obey him or them: And to injoyn that all the moveable and immoveable goods of the Hereticks may be lawfully feized and given away by any body whatfoever; and to make a booty of all goods which the Hereticks bring, or caufe to be brought unto the Territories of the Catholicks, or carry, or caufe to be carried out of the fame; and to command, that all who are in the fervice of the fame Hereticks any where, fhall depart within the time by you prefixed unto them, under fuch penalties as you fhall fee good; and to admonifh and require them, and all Ecclefiaftical and Secular perfons, of what Dignity, Age, Sex, or Order foever they may be, to yeeld obedience, and give attendance with reverence to the Apoftolical commands, under the penalties of Excommunication, Sufpenfion or Interdiction; and that they abftain from all commerce with the forefaid Hereticks: And to Declare, that neither they nor any others, who by any contract or otherwife are in any fort bound unto them to perform or pay any thing, are henceforth at all obliged, or by the fame authority can be compelled thereunto: And to deprive all perfons, whoever are not obedient to your admonitions and commands, of what Dignity, State,

turi effent in tranfitu ad loca debita, vel aliis debitis, penfatis locorum & perfonarum qualitatibus, prout tibi feu per te ad hoc deputandis confefforibus idoneis videbitur in hoc ipfum commutandi. Interea fuper ipfa cruciata & congregando exercitu in Ducem belli & Capitaneum unum vel plures, idoneos noftro & Ecclefiæ Romanæ nomine eligendi, deputandi & confirmandi, & ut onus hoc ad laudem & defenfionem fidei fufcipere, & fideliter gerere, & ut reliqui omnes ei vel eis obediant pariter & intendant, injungendi & mandandi, bona quæcunque mobilia & immobilia hæreticorum quibufcunque licite occupandi & concedendi, ac ea quæ hæretici ad terras Catholicorum vel e contra ex terris Catholicorum ducerent aut duci facerent in prædam dandi; omnibus quoque in fervitiis hæreticorum eorundem exiftentibus ubicunque ut intra terminum per te eis præfigendum difcedant fub pœnis de quibus tibi videbitur mandandi; illofque ac Ecclefiafticos & Seculares quofcunque, cujufcunque dignitatis, ætatis, fexus vel ordinis exiftant, fub excommunicationis, fufpenfionis & interdicti pœnis monendi & requirendi ut mandatis Apoftolicis reverenter obediant & intendant; ac ab omni commercio hæreticorum prædictorum abftineant: Ac eos & alios quofcunque qui eis ex quovis contractu vel aliter qualitercunque tenerentur vel obligarentur ad aliqua illis ftatuenda & folvenda nullatenus deinceps obligari & ad id poffe compelli eadem autoritate declarandi, ac quofcunque tuis monitionibus & mandatis non parentescujufcunque dignitatis, flatus,

ftatus, gradus, ordinis vel præeminen-
tiæ fuerint Ecclefiafticos, dignitatibus,
officiis & beneficiis, feculares vero ho-
noribus, titulis, feudis, & privilegiis
fuis, exigente eorum inobedientia & re-
bellione, privandi, & beneficia aliis ido-
neis de quibus tibi videbitur, etiam quæ-
cunque, quotcunque & qualiacunque
beneficia Ecclefiaftica obtinentibus &
expectantibus conferendi, ac privatos
hujufmodi ad fimilia & alia impofterum
obtinendi, inhabiles perpetuò & infames
decernendi, nec non cenfuras quafcunque
Fuftitia, Rebellione vel inobedientia
exigente, prout tibi videbitur fulminan-
di, & interdictum ponendi, ac pofitum
ex bonis caufis & refpectibus, ficut expe-
diat vel utile aut necefarium cognoveris,
tollendi vel perpetuò feu ad tempus fuf-
pendendi, præcipue vero per eos dies in
quibus forfan publicandæ effent indul-
gentiæ aut cruciata prædicta, nec non
contra victum omnis generis, arma &
alia prohibita eifdem hæreticis, & com-
plicibus fuis afferentes, aliofve auxilia-
tores, fautores & confultores ac recepta-
tores eorum publicos vel occultos, & quo-
vis modo impedientes feu perturbantes
tam falutaris negotii exequutionem, fim-
pliciter & de plano, fine ftrepitu & figu-
râ judicii folâ veritate infpectâ proceden-
di, & omnes & fingulos tranfgreffores,
cenfuras & pænas tam fpirituales quam
temporales in talia facientes a jure in-
flictos incurriffe, etiam declarandi ; pæ-
nitentes & reverti volentes ad gremium
Ecclefiæ, fi id humiliter petierint in
forma Ecclefiæ confueta, etiam fi jura-

State, Degree, Order, or pre-eminency foever they be, the Ecclefiaftical perfons of their Dignities, Offices,
and Benefices, and the Seculars of
their Honours, Titles, Fewds, and
priviledges, according to the nature
of their difobedience and Rebellion;
and to confer the Benefices upon
other fit perfons, as it fhall feem good
to you, alfo to fuch as have obtained,
or are in expectation of any or any
kind of Ecclefiaftical Benefices whatfoever ; and to decree thofe men who
are deprived thereof, to be thenceforth incapable to obtain the like or
others, and to be for ever infamous;
and alfo to thunder out any kind of
Cenfures, according as Juftice, Rebellion, or difobedience fhall feem to
you to require it ; and to eftablifh
and interdict, or to take it off, or to
fufpend it for ever, ot for a feafon,
as you fhall think it expedient, ufefull, or neceffary for good caufes and
refpects, but chiefly upon thofe days
in which perhaps Indulgences are to
be publifhed, or the forefaid *Croifado*; and alfo againft thofe that bring
to the faid Hereticks or their Complices, victuals of all forts, Arms,
and other things prohibited, or others
their helpers, favourers, and coun-
fellors and receivers of them, publickly or fecretly, or any that in any
kind fhall hinder or trouble the execution of fo wholefome a bufinefs;
to proceed againft them fimply and
plainly, without noife and form of
Judicature, onely upon evidence of
the truth, and to declare that all and
every fuch tranfgreffors have incurred
the Cenfures and Penalties, as well
fpiritual as temporal, which the Law
inflicts upon thofe that do fuch things;
and to abfolve the penitents, and fuch
as will return to the bofome of the
Church, if they humbly petition it
in the ufual form of the Church, although

though they fhould have bound themfelves by Oath to favour the Hereticks, and had ferved them in the War, and had furnifhed them with Arms and Victuals, and other things neceffary for livelihood, and other prohibited matters, upon condition that by taking another Oath they promife, or otherwife give fit caution, that thenceforth they will yield obedience to our Commands, to the Churches, and to yours, whether they be Corporations, Univerfities and particular perfons of what ftate, order, or pre-eminency foever they may be, and what dignities foever they may be eminent for, whether Ecclefiaftical or worldly; and to make them capable, and to reftore and re-eftablifh them into their Honours, Dignities, Offices, Benefices, Fewds, Goods, and all their Rights, as in former time; and alfo to grant, difpofe, exercife, do, conftitute, order, command and execute all other matters, and every thing which fhall any ways be neceffary or feafonable for this wholfome bufinefs, although they fhould be fuch things which require a fpecial Command, and fall not under the general Commiffion; and to reftrain all gainfayers whatfoever by Ecclefiaftical Cenfures, or other remedies of Law, not regarding any appeal; and if need be, to implore the Secular powers help. And by the tenor of thefe prefents we grant and give a full and free power, licence and authority; And we make void and of no effect, all priviledges, exemptions, Letters and *Apoftolical* Indulgences whatfoever, general or particular, granted by us, or according to the forenamed, under any form of words and expreffions, all which fo far as they obftruct the effect of thefe prefents, or can retard the fame, our will is that they be as Letters not gi-

mentum præftitiffent de favendo hæreticis, & ad eorum ftipendia militaffent, ac arma, commeatum, & res ad victum neceffarias, & alia prohibita hæreticis eifdem fubminiftraffent, dummodo per præftationem alterius juramenti promittant aut alias idoneè caveant, quod deinceps mandatis noftris & Ecclefiæ, ac tuis parebunt, etiam fi communitates & univerfitates, ac particulares perfonæ fuerint, & cujufcunque ftatus, ordinis, vel præeminentiæ fuerint, & quacunque, Ecclefiaftica vel mundana præfulgiant dignitate, abfolvendi & habilitandi, ac ad honores, dignitates, officia, beneficia, feuda, bona, & jura fua omnia aliafque in priftinum ftatum reftituendi & reponendi; necnon omnia alia & fingula ad hoc falutare negocium neceffaria feu quomodolibet opportuna, etiam fi talia effent, quæ mandatum exigerent fpeciale & in generali Commiffione non caderent concedendi, difponendi, exercendi, faciendi, ftatuendi, ordinandi, mandandi & exequendi, ac contradictores quofcunque per cenfuras Ecclefiafticas & alia oportuna juris remedia appellatione poftpofita compefcendi, & fi opus fuerit auxilium brachii fecularis invocandi. Plenam & liberam tenore præfentium facultatem, licentiam & autoritatem concedimus, & impartimus privilegiis, exemptionibus, literis & indultis Apoftolicis quibufcunque in genere vel in fpecie, per nos, vel fecundum præfatum fub quavis verborum forma & expreffione conceffis, quæ omnia in quantum effectui præfentium obviare, vel retardare illum poffent pro infectis & non conceffis literis volumus &

viribus evacuamus. Cæterifque contrariis quibufcunque, aut fi aliquibus communiter vel divifim, a prædicta fit fede indultum, quod interdici, fufpendi, vel excommunicari, aut fuis dignitatibus & beneficiis privari feu alia quavis pœna multari non poffint, per literas Apoftolicas non facientes plenam & expreffam ac de verbo ad verbum de indulto hujufmodi mentionem.

Tu igitur dilecte fili onus tam meritorii negotii devota mente fufcipiens, te in illius exequutione fic folicitum ac verbo & opere ftudiofum & diligentem exhibeas, quod ex tuis laboribus divina tibi favente gratia fructus fperati adveniant, tuque per folicitudinem tuam, eam quæ pias caufas gerentibus pro retributione impenditur palmam gloriæ, non folum confequi merearis, verum etiam apud nos & fedem prædictam non immeritò valeas de exactiffima diligentia & fideli integritate uberius commendari. Et quia difficile effet præfentes literas ad fingula ubi illæ effent neceffariæ loca tranfmittere, volumus & Apoftolica autoritate decrevimus quod earum tranfumpto manu alicujus publici notarii fubfcripto & alicujus prælati Ecclefiaftici munito, plena fides adhibeatur & illi ftetur firmiter ficuti originalibus ftaretur literis fi forent exhibitæ vel oftenfæ. Datum Romæ apud Sanctum Petrum, anno incarnationis Dominicæ Millefimo quadringentefimo octuagefimo feptimo, Quinto Kal. Maii ; Pontificatus noftri anno tertio.

Hic Balbianus poft quarum quidem literarum five bullarum Apoftolicarum præfentationem & receptionem vifas & per nos ut præmittitur factas, quia pro

ven nor granted. And in like manner all others that are contrary ; or if it hath been granted by the See aforefaid unto any, joyntly or feverally, that they may not be interdicted, fufpended, or excommunicated, or be deprived of their Dignities and Benefices, or be punifhed by any other penalty by Apoftolical Letters, which make not a full and exprefs mention of this Indulgence word by word.

Thou therefore, beloved Son, taking upon thee with a devout minde the burthen of fo meritorious a work, fhew thy felf in the execution thereof fo carefull, in word and deed, and fo ftudious and diligent, that the hoped for fruits by Gods grace may redound unto thee from thy labours ; and that thou mayeft by thy carefulnefs not onely obtain the Crown of Glory, which is given for a retribution to thofe that profecute Godly caufes, but alfo mayeft be defervedly further commended by us and the *Apoftolical* See, for thy moft exact diligence and faithfull integrity. And becaufe it would be difficult to tranfmit thefe prefent Letters to all the particular places where they might be neceffary, We will, and by *Apoftolical* authority have decreed, That a tranfcript thereof fubfcribed with the hand of a publick Notary, and confirmed by fome Ecclefiaftical Prelate, fhall be fully credited, and that the fame fhall be of force as firmly as if the Original Letters themfelves were exhibited and fhewed. Given at *Rome* at *St. Peters*, in the year of our Lords incarnation One thoufand four hundred eighty feven, the Twenty feventh of *April*, and in the Third year of our *Popedome*.

Here *Balbianus*, after the prefentation and receiving of thefe Letters and *Apoftolical Bulls*, by us feen and made as aforefaid ; becaufe on the behalf

half of the moſt Reverend Father in Chriſt, and Lord, the Lord Archbiſhop of *Evreux*, and of the Proćtor of his Exchequer, it hath been made known to us, That the forenamed moſt Reverend Archbiſhop of *Evreux* hath manfully proceeded againſt ſome who are in his Dioceſs (to be named at the end of theſe preſents) ſuſpećted to have communion with the Heretical pravity, and cauſed them to be cited before him to anſwer concerning their faith, under the ſentence of Excommunication, and other cenſures and penalties, who nevertheleſs have with contumacy neglećted to appear and anſwer before him, and have by contumacy incurred the penalties and cenſures, and therefore were bound up with the bonds of the ſentence of Excommunication by the ſame Lord Archbiſhop of *Evreux* : And becauſe nevertheleſs a certain Reverend Lord *Thomas Capitis Niga*, the pretended Judge of the pretended Primacy of *Vienna*, pretending that he hath a ſuperiority and power to abſolve thoſe ſuſpećted in their Faith againſt whom the ſaid Lord Archbiſhop hath proceeded, at the inſtance of the ſaid ſuſpećted in the Faith, and of the Inquiſitors, is ſaid to have cauſed an inhibition to be made unto the ſaid Lord Archbiſhop, & that he ſhould not proceed further againſt them, and to proceed in the cauſe of the Appeal aſſerted on the behalf of the ſame ſuſpećted perſons in general, by the ſame Lord Archbiſhop, interpoſing before the ſame on the xxviii day of this moneth, the ſaid Lord Judge of the Primacy of *Vienna* hath (as is ſaid) commanded the worthy *Proćtor* of the Treaſury of the forenamed moſt Reverend Lord Archbiſhop of *Evreux*, to be cited, that he might ſee the benefit of abſolution to be beſtowed upon the ſuſpećted perſons

parte reverendiſſimi in Chriſto Patris & Domini, Domini Archiepiſcopi Ebredunenſis, & ejus Procuratoris fiſcalis nobis extitit expoſitum, Qui prælibatus reverendiſſimus Archiepiſcopus Ebredunenſis contra nonnullos de communione hæreticæ pravitatis ſuſpećtos in ejus Dioceſi exiſtentes, & in pede præſentium nominandos viriliter proceſſit ; & de fide reſponſuros coram eo vocari fecit ſub ſententia excommunicationis, & aliis cenſuris & pænis, qui tamen contumaciter coram eo comparere & reſpondere neglexerunt, pænas & cenſuras ipſos contumaciter incurrerunt, propter quod ab eodem Domino Archiepiſcopo Ebredunenſi fuerunt vinculis ſententiæ Excommunicationis & cenſurarum Eccleſiaſticarum invadati : Et quia nihilominus quidam reverendus Dominus Thomas Capitis Niga, prætenſus Judex prætenſæ primatiæ Viennenſis, prætendens ſe habere ſuperioritatem & poteſtatem tales ſic de fide ſuſpećtos contra quos per dićtum Dominum Archiepiſcopum extitit proceſſum abſolvendi ad inſtantiam prædićtorum ſuſpećtorum de fide, & inquiſitorum eidem Domino Archiepiſcopo inhibere feciſſe dicitur, ne contra eoſdem ad ulteriora procederet, & ad procedendum in cauſa aſſertæ appellationis parte eorundem ſuſpećtorum in genere ab eodem Domino Archiepiſcopo interponente coram eodem ad diem xxviii. menſis hujus, idem Dominus aſſertus Judex primatiæ Viennenſis citari mandaſſe dicitur egregium Procuratorem fiſcalem prælibati reverendiſſimi Domini Archiepiſcopi Ebredunenſis ad videndum dićtis ſuſpećtis beneficium

abſolu-

absolutionis impendi; & alias sic vel aliter prout in dictis assertis literis de-super confectis & processu apparere dicitur, ad quas quatenus expediat pro sufficienti in eis contentorum narratione, citra tamen illarum approbationem nisi in concernentibus favorem fidei, debita habeatur collatio dicitur contineri. Et quoniam prædicta tangunt & concernunt officium Commissionis nostræ prædictæ, idcirco autoritate Apostolica qua vigore præinsertæ Commissionis nostræ fungimur in hac parte & nobis commissa, causam & causas prædictam, & prædictas cum dependentiis emergentibus, & quorumvis, de, & pro ac ex eisdem universim & toto principali negotio ad nos advocantes, vos omnes & singulos supradictos quibus præsentes nostræ imo verius Apostolicæ literæ diriguntur tenore præsentium requirimus & monemus primo, secundò, tertiò & peremptoriè ; vobisque & vestrum cuilibet in solidum in virtute sanctæ Dei obedientiæ & sub excommunicationis sententiæ pœna quam in vos & vestrum quemlibet trina & canonica monitione præmissa sedentes pro tribunali ferimus in his scriptis, nisi feceritis quæ vobis in hac parte præcipimus & committimus, districtè, præcipimus committimus & mandamus, quatenus infra trium dierum spatium post præsentationem seu notificationem præsentium vobis aut alteri vestrum fiendam, & postquam pro parte præfati Procuratoris fiscalis prælibati Domini Archi-

aforesaid, and so thus or otherwise, as it is said to be contained in the foresaid Letters made concerning this, and in the Proces is said to appear, unto which, so far as is expedient for a sufficient narrative of the contents, nevertheless without any approbation thereof, except in things concerning the favour of the Faith, a due conference be had. And because the aforesaid particulars do touch and concern the duty of our Commission before-named, therefore by the Apostolical authority, which by vertue of our before-inserted Commission we exercise in this behalf, and which is committed to us, taking into our own cognizance the cause and causes aforesaid, with the dependencies emergent, and relating to any persons whatsoever, concerning, for, and because of the same causes universally, and the whole principal business, We by the Tenor of these presents do a first, second, and third time, and peremptorily require and and admonish you all and every one in particular before mentioned, to whom our present or rather Apostolical Letters are directed ; and we strictly enjoyn, order, and command you and every one of you, by vertue of the holy obedience of God, and under penalty of the sentence of Excomunication, which we sitting before his Tribunal, do in these presents pronounce againft you and every one of you, in case, after Canonical admonition three times pre-declared, ye shall not do what we command and enjoyn you in this particular, that is to say, within three days time after the presentation or notification of these presents shall be made unto you, or either of you, and after that on the behalf of the forenamed Proctor of the Exchequer of the afore-

said

said Lord Archbishop of *Evereux*, you or either of you shall by vertue of these presents, upon occasion of this business, be required immediatly to follow; and of those three days we assign one for the first, one for the second, and the remainder for the third and peremptory day, by Letters and *Canonical* admonition; yet so, that in the execution thereof, one of you should not wait for another, nor one excuse himself by another : That the forenamed suspected of their faith, to be named at the foot of these presents, and every other person intervening, or willing to intervene and defend, and all and every other who shall think themselves in common or severally concerned, be peremptorily cited, or caused to be cited in their own proper persons, if conveniently they can be apprehended, or otherwise in their dwelling places, if you can safely have access thereunto, or in the Parochial Church or Churches where their abode is, or in the Cathedral of the forenamed City of *Evereux*, or in the foresaid Parochial Church or Churches, or other Churches and publick places whatsoever, wheresoever, whensoever, and so oft as shall be expedient, at the time of *Mass*, or other solemnities of Divine service, while the multitude of the people is met and gathered together to hear Divine service, or otherwise, on our behalf, or rather on the behalf of the *Apostolical* See, with a loud and intelligible voice publickly; yet so, that such a citation may come to the knowledge of those that are cited, or in likelihood may come to their knowledge, that they may not be able to pretend any ignorance, or alledge any thing touching the premised or subjoyned writings; whom we also, and every one of them, by

episcopi Ebredunensis vigore præsentium super hoc fueritis requisiti, seu alter vestrum fuerit requisitus immediate subsequentes; & quorum trium dierum unum pro primo, unum pro secundo, & reliquum pro tertio & peremptorio literis ac monitione canonica assignamus; ita tamen quod in his exequendis, unus vestrum alterum non expectet nec alius pro alio se excuset, præfatos de fide suspectos in pede præsentium nominandos, & quamcunque aliam personam intervenientem seu intervenire & defendere volentem, ac omnes & singulos alios sua communiter vel divisim interesse putantes in eorum proprias personas, si commode apprehendi poterint, alias autem in hospitiis habitationum suarum si ad eam vel ad eas vobis pateat tutus accessus, vel in parochialibus Ecclesiis sub qua vel quibus degunt & morantur, sive in Cathedrali præfata civitatis Ebredunensis aut dictis parochiali seu parochialibus Ecclesiis aliisve Ecclesiis & locis publicis quibuscunque, ubi, quando & quoties expediens fuerit intra missarum & aliarum divinarum horarum solemnia, dum ibidem populi multitudo ad divina audiendum convenerit, seu aliàs congregata fuerit ex parte nostra, imo verius Apostolica, publicè, alta & intelligibili voce peremptoriè citetur & citare curetur; ita tamen quod citatio hujusmodi ad ipsorum citandorum notitiam indubitatam perveniat seu verisimiliter valeat pervenire; Ne de præmissis seu infra scriptis ignorantiam aliquam prætendere valeant seu quodlibet allegare; Quos nos etiam & eorum *quemlibet tenore præfentium fic citamus, quatenus die poft harum exequutionem, nifi fexta etiam hora vicefima horologii in conventu Sancti Laurentii, extra muros Pinerolii, ordinis humiliatorum Thaurinenfis Diocefeos coram nobis legitimè compareant per fe vel Procuratorem feu Procuratores fuos idoneos ad caufam & caufas hujufmodi fufficienter inftructos, cum omnibus & fingulis actis, actitatis, literis, fcripturis, privilegiis, inftrumentis, monumentis & juribus caufam feu caufas hujufmodi tangentes, feu quomodolibet concernentes; & quicquid contra dictas Bullas commiffionis nobis factæ, nofque & perfonam noftram dicere, opponere, feu allegare valuerint, dicturos, oppofituros & allegaturos, & in dicta appellationis caufa feu caufis hujufmodi, ad omnefque & fingulos actus earundem neceffarios ufque ad definitivam fententiam inclufivè, gradatim, & fucceffivè debitis & confuetis terminis procedendi ut moris eft proceffuros & procedi vifuros; aliafque dicturos, oppofituros, allegaturos, recepturos, audituros & facturos id quod juftitia fuadebit & ordo dictaverit rationis: Certificantes nihilominus eofdem fic citandos qui five citationis termino, ut præmiffum eft, comparuerint five non, nos nihilominus ad partis comparentis & caufam feu caufas hujufmodi profequi curantis inftantiam ad præmiffa omnia & fingula & alios prout juftum fuerit procedemus; dictorum citatorum abfentia feu contumacia in aliquo non obftante, caufante difficultate & longitudine itineris & attenta natura caufæ & perfonarum; paratos nos efferentes in caufa & caufis hujufmodi reverendos Dominos dictorum*

the tenor of thefe prefents do thus cite, That on the ____ day after the execution of thefe, if they appear not on the fixth, and alfo the twentieth hour of the Clock, in the Covent of *St. Laurence*, without the Walls of *Pignerol*, of the Order of *the Humbled*, in the Diocefs of *Thurin*, before us legally, by themfelves, or by their Atturney or Atturneys, fitted and fufficiently inftructed for fuch caufe and caufes, with all and every the Acts and agitations, Letters, Writings, Priviledges, Inftruments, Monuments, and Rights which in any wife touch or concern this caufe or caufes, and whatfoever they fhall be willing to fay, oppofe, or alledge againft the faid *Bulls* of our Commiffion, and againft our perfon, to fay, oppofe, and alledge, and to proceed and fee the proceeding in the forefaid caufe of Appeilation, or caufes of that kind, and to all and every of the Acts neceffary thereunto, till the definitive fentence be given, inclufively, gradually, and fucceffively proceeding in the due and ufual terms, as the cuftome is; and otherwife to fay, oppofe, alledge, receive, hear, and do what Juftice fhall induce unto, and the order of Reafon fhall dictate: Certifying neverthelefs thofe thus to be cited, whether they appear or appear not at the term of the citation premifed, that we fhall proceed neverthelefs to all and every one of the premifes, at the inftance of the party appearing, who doth procure the profecuting of fuch kind of caufe or caufes, notwithftanding the abfence or contumacy of thofe that are cited as aforefaid, the difficulty or length of a journey which caufeth it, and nature of the caufe and of the perfons being confidered; fhewing our felves ready to admit in fuch caufe and caufes the Reverend Lords the *Ordinaries*

of

of the forefaid places, and their Vicars in fpiritual offices who are not fufpected in the premifes, if they think themfelves concerned, and if they will be prefent, and alfo attending while the caufe or caufes fo depending before us are undecided.

Therefore we charge and command all and every one of you, to whom thefe ours, or rather the *Apoftolical* Letters are directed, by the forenamed authority, and under the penalty of the forefaid fentence of Excommunication, denounced by a three-fold and Canonical admonition, That after the legal execution of the forefaid citation, to the forefaid Lord *Thomas Capitis Niga,* the pretended Judge of the pretended Primacy of *Vienna*; and to the Ordinaries of certain places, and to each of them, and to their Vicars and Officials in fpirituals and temporals, and to all and every Officials, Judges, ordinary and extraordinary Executioners and Commiffioners, and to all others whoever they be, and what authority foever they adminifter in the faid Cities and Diocefes of *Evereux,* *Lyons,* and *Vienna,* or elfewhere, in any place conftituted, and to the faid perfons who are to be named at the foot of thefe prefents, and to all others whom it doth concern, or whom in any wife hereafter it may concern, with what names foever they are called, and with what dignity foever they are eminent, that of the things whereof you or either of you fhall be required on the behalf of the faid *Proctor* of the Exchequer of the forementioned Lord Archbifhop of *Evereux,* by vertue of thefe prefents, on our behalf, or rather on the behalf of the forefaid *Apoftolical* Authority, that you joyntly and feverally inhibit, to whom alfo we

locorum Ordinarios, & eorum in fpiritualibus Vicarios,in præmiffis tamen non fufpectos, admittere, fi fua intereffe pu taverint, & intereffe voluerint, & infuper attendentes quod caufa feu caufis hujufmodi fic coram nobis indecefis pendentibus.

Idcirco vobis omnibus & fingulis fupradictis quibus prefentes noftræ, imo verius Apoftolicæ literæ diriguntur, præfata autoritate Apoftolica committimus, & mandamus & fub præfatæ excommunicationis latæ fententiæ pæna trina & canonica monitione, Quatenus poft legitimam dictæ citationis exequutionem, prælibatis Domino Thomæ Capitis Niga, pretenfo Judici præenfæ primatiæ Viennenfis, ac quorundam locorum Ordinariis & eorum cuilibet,ipforumque in fpiritualibus & temporalibus Vicariis & Officialibus, ac univerfis & fingulis Officialibus, Judicibus, ordinariis & extraordinariis Exequutoribus & Commiffariis, & aliis quibufcunque, quacunque autoritate fungentibus per dictas Civitates & Diocefes Ebredunenfem, Lugdunenfem, & Viennenfem, aut alias ubilibet conftitutis dictifque, in pede præfentium nominandis, cæterifque aliis quorum intereft intererit aut intereffe poterit quomodolibet in futurum quibufcunque nominibus cenfeantur, & quacunque præfulgeant dignitate, de quibus pro parte dicti Procuratoris fifcalis prælibati Domini Archiepifcopi Ebredunenfis fuper hoc vigore præfentium fueritis requifiti, feu alter veftrum fuerit requifitus ex parte noftra, imo verius Apoftolica prædicta autoritate, conjunctim & divifim, inhibeatis, quibus & nos etiam tenore pra-

fentium

sentium inhibemus sub præfata Excom-
municationis latæ sententiæ pœna, trina
& canonica monitione præmissa ut su-
pra; Ne ipsi seu alter ipsorum in vili-
pendium litispendentiæ & jurisdictionis
nostræ, imo verius Apostolicæ sedis con-
temptum, dictorumque Dominorum Ar-
chiepiscopi Ebredunensis, & ejus Pro-
curatoris siscalis, & jurium suorum
præmonitorum in causa & causis hu-
jusmodi coram nobis indecisis pendenti-
bus, quicquam per se vel alium seu alios,
publicè vel occultè, directè vel indi-
rectè, quovis quæsiti colore attentare vel
innovare præsumant seu præsumat:
Quod si secus factum fuerit id totum
revocare, & in pristinum statum re-
ducere curabimus, ad dictamque Ex-
communicationis sententiam publicato-
riam, & alia Juris remedia fortiora
procedemus Justicia mediante. Diem
vero seu dies citationis & inhibitionis
hujusmodi, adque formam & quicquid
in præmissis feceritis, seu alter vestrum
fecerit nobis per vestras patentes literas,
aut instrumentum publicum in pede
præsentium describendum, remissis præ-
sentibus quam citius fideliter insinuare
curetis. Absolutionem vero omnium &
singulorum qui dictam nostram Excom-
municationis sententiam incurrerunt seu
incurrent quovis modo nobis vel superio-
ri nostro tantummodo reservamus. In
quorum omnium & singulorum fidem, &
testimonium præmissorum, præsentes li-
teras seu præsens publicum Instrumen-
tum hujusmodi nostras Avocationis,
Citationis, & Inhibitionis in se conti-
nentes seu continens exinde fieri &
per Notarium nostrum publicum, &
hujusmodi causæ coram nobis Scribam

by the tenor of these presents do inhibit, under the penalty of the foresaid sentence of Excommunication
denounced, a three-fold and Canonical admonition being premised, as
above mentioned; that neither they
nor either of them do presume to attempt or innovate, by themselves or
others, publickly or secretly, directly or indirectly, under any pretence
whatsoever, any thing tending to
the disparagement of the undecided
process, and of our Jurisdiction, or
rather to the contempt of the Apostolical See, and of the said Lords
the Archbishop of *Evereux*, and of
the *Proctor* of his Exchequer, and of
his forementioned Rights in any cause
or causes of this kind depending before us undecided: If any thing be
done to the contrary, we shall cause
it wholly to be revoked and reduced
to the former state, and we shall proceed to the foresaid publication of the
sentence of Excommunication, and
to other stronger Remedies of Law,
according to Justice. As concerning
the day or days of this way of citation and inhibition, and the form thereof, whatever you or either of you shall
do therein, cause the same to be intimated to us with speed and faithfully, by your Letters Patents, or a
publick Instrument to be written at
the foot of these sent back again.
And we reserve the Absolution of all
and every of them who have incurred
or shall incur our said sentence of
Excommunication in any wise, onely
to our self or our superiour. In witness of, and to give credit to all and
every of these premises, we have
commanded these presents our Letters, or present publick Instrument,
containing this kind of Avocation,
Citation, and Inhibition to be made,
by our publick Notary, and to be
subscribed by our Scribe of such Causes

fes before us underwritten; and have caufed and commanded them to be confirmed with the impreffion of our Seals.   Given and Acted in the forefaid Covent of *St. Laurence*, without the Walls of *Pignerole*, in the year from the Nativity of our Lord, *One thoufand four hundred eighty and feven*, on the fifth Indiction, and on the Six and twentieth day of the moneth of *June*, and in the Third year of the *Popedome* of the forenamed our moft Holy Lord *Pope Innocent*, there being in the fame place prefent the eminent men, *Heuftanus Nomelli* of *Otzapio*, *Bonifacius Bellini* of *Briceyrapio*, Treafurers of the Diocefs of *Ambelis*, the Notaries, as Witneffes to the premifes, being called, defired and joyned to affift, to the end that nothing fhould be innovated by any body.

infra fcriptum fubfcribi mandavimus, noftrorumque figillorum fecimus & juffimus impreffione communiri. Datum & Actum in dicto conventu Sancti Laurentii extra muros Pinerolii fub Anno a Nativitate Domini Milleffimo quadringenteffimo octuageffimo feptimo, Indictione quinta, & die Vigefima fexta menfis Junii, Pontificatus prælibati fanctiffimi Domini noftri Papæ Innocentii Anno tertio, præfentibus ibidem Egregiis viris Heuftano Nomelli de Otzapio, Bonifacio Bellini de Briceyrapio, Thefaurariis Diocefeos Ambelis Notariis teftibus ad præmiffa affentire vocatis, rogatis & adhibitis, nihil fit per quempiam innovandum.

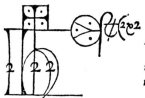

Heufta-   *nus Por-*   *porati of*   *Velmaria*, dwelling at *Pignerol*, Treafurer of the Diocefs, Publick Notary by Imperial appointment of *Savoy*, and of the two moft Reverend *Apoftolical* Commiffioners, and of the forenamed Caufe on this behalf Scribe, becaufe I was prefent at the premifed Avocation, Citation, Inhibition, and other things above-written, and received the forefaid Inftrument; therefore according to the General Licence given unto me concerning this, by the forenamed moft Illuftrious Lord, our Lord the Duke of *Savoy*, I have caufed it to be drawn in this form by another faithfull Publick

Heuftanus Porporati de Velmariahabitator Pinarolii, *Thefaurarius Diocefeos, publicus Imperiali ordinat. Sabaud. auctor. Notarius & prælibatorum Reverendiffimorum duorum Commiffariorum Apoftolicorum, & caufæ prædictæ in hac parte Scriba, quia præmiffis Avocationi, Citationi, Inhibitioni, & aliis fuprafcriptis præfens fui, & Inftrumentum dictum recepi, ideo in hanc formam publicam licentia generali mihi fuper hoc per prælibatum Illuftriffimum Dom. Dom. noftrum Sabaudiæ Ducem conceffa levari feci per alium fidelem Notarium*

publicum

Publicum meum Coadjutorem, nuncque ſubſcripſi manu mea propria , & ſignum meum tabellionatus conſuetum appoſui in teſtimonium veritatis.	Notary, my Coadjutor, and no w have with my own hand ſubſcribed it ; and to teſtifie the truth, I have put my ordinary Seal of my Notaries Office thereunto.

Tranſcript

Tranflate of a *Latin* Manufcript, intituled, *Origo Valden-
fium, &c.* The Original of the *Waldenfes*, and the
Procefs againft them.

The true Original whereof is to be feen, together with
the reft, in the Publick Library of the famous
Univerfity of *Cambridg.*

Vobis Reverendiffimo in Chrifto Patre, & Domino, Domino Ro-
ftagno Ebredunenfi Archi-epifcopo, Vobifque Reverendis Pa-
tribus & Dominis, Fratri Laurentio Ciftavicenfi Epifcopo, &
Thomæ Pafchali, &c.

To you the Right Reverend Father in Chrift, *and Lord, the Lord* Ro-
ftagnus *Arch-bifhop of* Evereux, *and to you Reverend Fathers and Lords,
Brother* Laurence, *Bifhop of* Ciftow, *and* Thomas Pafchal, *Official of*
Orleance, *the Apoftolical Commiffary, under the Authority of the King,
and the Daulphinate, fendeth greeting. As concerning the Caufe of
thofe poor Men of* Lyons, *commonly called* Waldenfes, *from* Waldo, *Citizen of the faid chief City of* Lyons, *depending in the Town* Val-grant,
know that the faid Waldo *being rich, and the Prince of Herefie, was according to Writers, the firft Authour of the Herefie of the Sect of the*
Waldenfes, *who renouncing temporal Goods, began with his Complices to
lead an Apoftolick life, with the Crofs, and poverty, and defpifing Ecclefiaftical Men, affociated many Difciples to himfelf, who thereupon were called
poor Men of* Lyons, *and pretending to live under Apoftolical obedience,
(yet feparating themfelves from it) did ftubbornly anfwer, when reproved,
that they ought rather to obey God than Man; for which they were at laft,
(and defervedly) condemned by the Church militant. But not being fully
extirpated, flying from* Lyons, *they betook themfelves to the utmoft parts of*
Dauphine, *in the Diocefes of* Evereux *and* Turin, *among the* Alpes, *and
in the Caves of the Mountains, (places exceeding difficult to approach)
where more than fifty thoufand of them did inhabit. In thefe places
through the great diligence of the* Sower of Tares, *they became fo numerous in a fhort fpace of time, that they fent out thence their Colonies into* Li-
guria, Italy, *and beyond* Rome, *into* Puglia. *And as* Chrift *our Redeemer
fent his Difciples by two and two, to preach, fo was the Mafter of that curfed
and beaftly Sect, wont to fend other inferiour Paftours, created and approved by himfelf, (whom commonly we call* Barbes) *by two and two, to
preach and teach the abovefaid Doctrine. Now thefe Barbes were wont to
be created by their great Mafter (or Chair-man) in the City of* Aquila, *in
the*

the Kingdom of Naples, *and in the creation of them there was wont to be great solemnity ; they had their Names changed, when they were admitted to this Office, in derision to the Bishop of* Rome, *to whose Doctrine and Worship the Followers of this most damnable Heresie, namely, the Men and Women of the Valley of* Cluſone, *in the Dioceſs of* Turin, *with all the Males and Females of the Valley of* Fraiſſimere, Argenteria, *and* Loyſia, *in the Dioceſs of* Evereux, *have time out minde, been contrary (as more than an hundred of them have confeſſed, and that of their own accord) in the following Articles which are contrary to the Faith which they confeſs to have held, and which they inviolably obſerve. And that this may be evident and more clearly appear, the* Procurator *of the place and places thereabouts in the parts of* Brianſon *and* Evereux, *for the maintenance of the* Chriſtian *Faith, and for the exalting of his native Countries honour, againſt all and every one of the ſaid Valley of* Fraiſſimere, *gives in and exhibiteth the following Articles, which he deſires may be admitted for proof (to avoid the burden of ſuperfluous proof, to which he intends not to tie himſelf ;) in reference whereunto, by way of Charge, he ſolemnly proteſts againſt them all, and each particular perſon.*

Inprimis, ponit & dicit, & probare intendit, quod ipſi homines Vallis Fraxininieræ fuerint a centum annis, citra & ultra, ac, &c.

Inprimis, *he allegeth, and ſaith, and intends to prove, that the ſaid men of the Valley of* Fraiſſimere, *have been there this hundred years, or thereabouts, for the ſaid term, and beyond that, even time out of minde, have been, and for the preſent are, Hereticks, and have held, and do hold the following Points of Doctrine, contrary to the Catholick Faith. And this is a Truth, notorious, publick, and manifeſt.*

2. Item, *that at the preſent they are commonly held, eſteemed, and reputed for Hereticks and* Waldenſes, *and that by all who have knowledg of them, their Life, Manners, or Converſation. This alſo hath been, and is a Truth notorious, publick, and manifeſt.*

3. Item, *that this hath been, and is the common voice and fame, not onely among their Neighbours, but even among thoſe that are more diſtant from the ſaid Valley, for the ſpace of an hundred Leagues round about, and upwards. This alſo is true, notorious, publick, and manifeſt.*

4. Item, *that they have been, and at preſent are infamous throughout the whole World, for the Hereſie, and moſt damnable Sect of the* Waldenſes, *contrary to the* Chriſtian *Faith. And this hath been, and is true, notorious, and manifeſt.*

5. Item, *that for this cauſe their Neighbours of the adjacent parts, (though true Catholicks, and faithfull* Chriſtians) *are every where ſlandered for this their Fault, yea and they (ſuffer ſometimes great Loſſes, and are barred from many Honours and Profits, meerly from a ſuſpition and jealouſie of their being tainted with the Hereſie of the Men of* Fraiſſimere. *And this hath been and is true, notorious, publick, and manifeſt.*

6. Item, *that the ſaid Hereticks of* Fraiſſimere *are called, and appear to be*

be wicked, obstinate, corrupt, perverse, and contrary to the Catholick Faith; *and are accounted, esteemed, and reputed, to hold the following Particulars in opposition to the* Christian *Faith. And this is true, notorious, publick, and manifest.*

Their Accusations comprised in the following Particulars.

First, for that they call the Church of Rome, *a Church of Malignants, defaming and reproaching the same; and this is their damnable Belief, contrary to the Catholick Faith. This also is true, publick, notorious, and manifest.*

2. Item, *for that they believe, and have believed, that the Church of God is constituted in those onely, who live in poverty, believing in their Creed, the holy Church without spot or wrinkle. And this is true.*

3. Item, *for that they have damnably believed, and do believe, that their Masters the* Barbes *have power of Binding and Loosing, and that accordingly sins are to be confessed to them, and not to the Priests of the* Roman *Church, which is contrary to the Faith. This also is true.*

4. Item, *for that they have believed, and do believe, that it neither hath been, nor is lawfull for the Prelates of the* Roman *Church, to have Patrimony or temporal Jurisdiction in this World, and that since St.* Sylvester, *there hath not been a true* Pope. *And this is true.*

5. Item, *for that they have believed, and do believe that none has a greater degree of Power and Authority in the Church, than he hath of Holiness, contrary to the Faith. And this is true.*

6. Item, *for that they have believed, and do believe, that the Sacraments administred by the Priests of the* Roman *Church, are of no efficacy or virtue, contrary to the Faith. And this is true.*

7. Item, *for that they have believed, and do believe, that Tithes are not to be paid to the said Priests of the* Roman *Church, neither are Offerings to be given them, contrary to the Faith. And this is true.*

8. Item, *for that they have believed, and do believe, that the Censures and Penances inflicted by the Prelates of the* Roman *Church, are to be slighted; for that they do not urge or binde for want of holiness, because they walk not in the footsteps of* Christ, *which is contrary to the Faith. And this is true.*

9. Item, *for that they have believed, and do believe, that the* Roman *Church is an House of Confusion,* Babylon, *the* Whore, *and the Synagogue of the Devil, contrary to the Faith. And this is true.*

10. Item, *for that they have believed, and do believe, that none ought to yield obedience to the said* Roman *Church, or the Prelates of the same; and that all that obey them are damned, contrary to the Faith. And this is true.*

11. Item, *for that they have believed, and do believe, that there's no Purgatory in another World, but that the Living are purged in this onely; and that when a Man dies, he either presently mounts up into Heaven, or is cast down into Hell: affirming that the* Roman *Church were moved by a*
Principle

Principle of *Covetoufnefs* to invent *Purgatory* ; *and that upon this account, the Dead are not to be prayed for, which is contrary to the Faith. And this is true.*

12. Item, *for that they have believed, and do believe, that it is not lawfull to fwear any thing, be it true, or be it falfe, contrary to the Faith. And this is true.*

13. Item, *for that they have believed, and do believe, that it is lawfull wantonly to meet, and accompany together, and that for any perfons though joyned in never fo near a degree of Confanguinity and Affinity, (provided they be all of one and the fame Sect) during the time of their Preachings, and fo likewife afterwards, when the Lights are put out, contrary to the Faith. And this is true.*

14. Item, *for that they have believed, and do believe it to be as profitable to pray to God in a Stable, as in a Church, which is againft the Faith. And this is true.*

15. Item, *for that they have believed, &c. that onely God is to be prayed to, and not the Virgin* Mary, *nor the Saints, becaufe being at fo great a diftance from us, they cannot hear our Prayers, which is contrary to the Faith. And this is true.*

16. Item, *for that they believe, and have believed, that Rain-water has as great a virtue as the Holy Water, which is in the Church, becaufe all Waters were bleffed by God, which is contrary to the Faith. And this is true.*

17. Item, *for that they have believed, and do believe, that temporal Lords are not to be obeyed, except they be fuch as are of their own Sect, contrary to the Faith. And this is true.*

18. Item, *for that they have believed, and do believe it to be an irremiffible fin, for any man to detect another of the faid Sect, contrary to the Faith. And this is true.*

19. Item, *for that they have believed, &c. that out of their Sect no man fhall be faved, and that thofe of their own Sect are the true Saints, contrary to the Faith. And this is true.*

20. Item, *for that they have believed, &c. that no man ought to obferve the Feftival Days of Saints, which were brought in by the* Roman *Church; and that it is lawfull to do any fervile work upon every of the fix Days, contrary to the Faith. And this is true.*

21. Item, *for that they have believed, &c. that it's lawfull to eat Flefh every where, and at all times; and that the Fafts brought in by the* Roman *Church, are not to be kept, who begin their* Lent *on the fecond Day after the firft Lords Day in* Lent, *contrary to the Faith. And this is true.*

22. Item, *for that they have believed, and do believe, that it is not lawfull for the Hereticks of their Sect to be given in Matrimony with Catholicks, and many other enormous and wicked things they have held, believed, and preached, according to their own Confeffions, and contrary to the Faith. And this is true.*

The

The Endeavours used to extirpate the *Waldenses.*

1. Item, *that for that cause both the most reverend Bishops and Prelates* of Evereux, *and the Inquisitours of heretical pravity, have heretofore taken great pains for the rooting out of those parts the said heretical Sect, even to the Days of the Right Reverend Father in* Chrift, *and Lord, the Lord* John *Arch-bishop of* Evereux, *lately deceafed. And this is true.*

2. Item, *that the forefaid moft reverend Lord* John *Arch-bishop of* Evereux *prefently after his Affumption, and from the Year of our Lord* 1461. *(left their Bloud might be one day required at his hands) ufed his utmoft Endeavours for the correcting of their Extravagancies, and the rooting out of that heretical Sect, beginning firft with frequent Admonitions, Exhortations, and Threats ; but through intervening Impediments, he could not effect his Defires. And this is true.*

3. Item, *for that caufe, from the Year of our Lord* 1473. *Frier* John Veyllet *of the Order of the* Minorits, *Doctour of Divinity, and Inquifitour, deputed by Apoftolical Authority to proceed againft thofe of the Valleys of* Fraiffimere, Argenteria, *and* Loyfia, *formed a Procefs, by which he hath detected the said heretical Sect, they confefsing themfelves to believe the above-mentioned Articles. And this is true.*

4. Item, *that the forenamed the Right Reverend Lord* John, *late Arch-bishop, from the Year of our Lord* 1483. *(affifted by true Catholicks, and others who were of their Complices,) of that Sect, took to the number of ninety and nine Informations, from all which it appears that all thofe of the Valley of* Fraiffimere, *and many of the Valley of* Loyfia, *and* Argenteria, *are moft infamous and fufpected, for the said heretical Sect. And this is true.*

5. Item, *for that caufe the forefaid moft Reverend Lord* John, *Arch-Bifhop, from the Year of our Lord* 1486. *and the eighteenth and nine and twentieth Days of* June, *in the fame Year, and the third and ninth of* July, *caufed them to be admonifhed generally within a certain term prefixed in the Letters, and by Letters Patents duly executed, the which they neglected to obey. And this is true.*

6. Item, *that for that caufe both fuccefsively, and from the Moneth of* Auguft, *the Right Reverend Lord* John, *fometimes Arch-bishop, commanded all thofe that were fufpected, to be cited by Name, to make anfwer concerning the Faith, offering them favour, if they would return into the bofom of the Church, but they contumacioufly neglected to appear. And this is true.*

7. Item, *that fuccefsively from the said Year, and the nineteenth Day of* September, *the said Right Reverend Lord* John, *fometimes Arch-bishop, publifhed his Letters Patents, and Excommunications alfo againft them for their perfidious and obftinate contumacy, the feventeenth of the said* September, *and this Excommunication they underwent even to the fixth Day of* February, *in the Year of our Lord* 1487. *and long beyond that time have they lain under Excommunication, amongft whom was named* Angelinus

gelinus Palloni, *who at this very day labours so earnestly to palliate the Truth by his Impostures. And this is true.*

8. Item, *and that successively, the Reverend Father* Albertus de Capitaneis, *Arch-deacon of* Cremona, *a Man not meanly learned in both Faculties, being deputed by Apostolical Authority, proceeded against them, and took Informations, from the Year* 1488. *and the sixth Day of* February, *and informed himself by four of their Complices, agreeing in effect with others whom the foresaid Right Reverend the late Lord* John, *Arch-bishop, examined upon these Matters; hereupon Process being made, he was moved by certain Reasons to obtain from the Apostolical See to proceed without calling the Ordinary; by virtue whereof he at length commanded them to be cited by Name, to answer concerning the Matters of Faith, offering grace and favour to such as would return to the unity of the Church. Now to these Citations those obstinate Hereticks refused to appear; since when on the eleventh of* February *successively, he caused them to be cited the second time by Letters duly published: but they again contumaciously neglecting to appear, he deservedly sent out Excommunicatory Letters against them, which likewise were duly published; but they always sustained the Excommunication, and made the aggravation the greater by their obstinacy; whereupon they were cited to come to certain places, where they might happily have been put under an Ecclesiastical Interdiction, but still they refused to appear. And this is true.*

9. Item, *and that successively, the foresaid Commissary sent often to them many persons fearing God, and seeking the good of the Souls of those Hereticks, to reduce them (if possible) to the way of Light and Grace; but they then were not in any wise to be perswaded, being obstinate as to the point of begging any Pardon. And this is true.*

10. Item, *and that successively, for this cause, the said Commissary commanded them to be cited by Name, that they might appear before him to hear his definitive Sentence, which was to be recorded, and that by Letters duly published the second day of* March *in the said Year; but they always most stubbornly and contumaciously neglected to appear; whereupon the said Lord Commissary, seeing their heart to be hardened, and no signs of Repentance to appear, nor any good effects of the counsels and admonitions of those experient men, whom he had sent to them, all things aforesaid being now duly published and seen, he proceeded to his definitive Sentence, whereby he delivered them up as stubborn and rebellious Hereticks to the Secular Power. And this is true.*

11. Item, *that therefore by Commission of the last Parliament of* Dauphine, *for the Secular Power there was imployed the valiant Souldier the Lord* Hugo de Palide, *Count of* Vavax, *and Lieutenant of* Dauphine, *and that magnificent Doctour of the Laws, and Counsellour of* Dauphine, John Raboli, *who observing what ought to be observed, proceeded against them, they leaving their Houses, betook themselves to the Holes and secret places of the Mountains, and the Clefts of the Rocks for their Fortresses. A while after, the said Apostolical Commissioners again offered them Grace, and the Bosom of the Church, provided they would return with a pure heart, and Faith unfeigned. Whereupon they all in a manner descended*
from

from the *Rocks* of their own accord, *not forced or questioned, and those of them that would come (both Men and Women) were bountifully received to Grace by the said Apostolical Commissioner, who likewise confessed themselves freely, and without fear of Torture, to have been and to be* Waldenses, *or poor Men of* Lyons, *and to have held the Heresie or Sect abovementioned, and to have believed the Articles thereof before specified; amongst the rest there was one* Angelinus Palloni *who pursues the business to this present, witnessing and justifying the Process in approved form. And this is true.*

12. Item, *that either twelve or fifteen in number being in the company of those that were content with Grace and Pardon, being possessed with a Diabolical Spirit, fled from the rest, and as Men out of measure obstinate, were outlawed. And this is true, notorious, and manifest.*

13 Item, *they that were admitted to* Grace, *confessing of their own accord, did after Sermon solemnly abjure the said most damned Sect of the* Waldenses, *and all those heretical Tenents above mentioned, in which their Abjurations they did expresly promise, amongst other things, never to receive or conceal the foresaid Outlaws, but to repell them when they came, revealing the same to the Church, as likewise efficaciously to fulfill all satisfactory Decrees, injoyned them in a constant order, for their sins, under the penalty of Relapse contained in the Process. And this is true.*

14. Item, *for their Penance it was especially injoyned them, after the aforesaid Abjuration, that such Men as had defended themselves in the Holes of the Rocks for five years, others for two, should wear two Crosses in their upper Garment sewed on before and behinde, the which was strictly and in a more especial manner injoyned them to wear as oft as they came before the Doors of the great Church at* Evereux. *And this is true.*

15. Item, *and that successively, the said abjured persons, not long after their Abjurations, did obstinately refuse to obey the Commands, Admonitions, and Abjurations of the Church, or keep the Promises which they had so solemnly made: and therefore they were cited by Name, to see the Witnesses examined and swear against them, which were to be produced by the Procuratours of the Faith; who not appearing, and the Witnesses of their contumacy being examined, they were again cited to see the Attestations published, but they notwithstanding refused to appear. From the Depositions of those Witnesses, as well Priests as other good Catholicks, worthy of credit, being clearer than the noon-light, it appeared that the said Inhabitants of* Fraissimere *have been, and are relapsed, and but feignedly converted, for as much as they have harboured Hereticks, and have not fulfilled the Penances injoyned them, yea, being called they refused to come, and not onely so, but they also immediately received the* Barbes, *and Masters of the* Waldenses, *and after their wonted manner and fashion were confessed by them. And this is true.*

16. Item, *and that successively, Frier* Francis Plirery *of the Order of the* Minorits, *Professour of Divinity, was deputed as Inquisitour in the said Valleys, who from the Year of our Lord* 1489. *and the first day of* January, *understanding that they of* Fraissimere *were defamed, as Men relapsed; and being signally informed by the Curats of the place, and many others of* Fraissimere

Fraiſſimere, *true Catholicks, yea and by ſeveral of their own Complices, to the number of threeſcore and ſix, by whoſe Sayings it appeared that the aforeſaid Inhabitants of* Fraiſſimere *had not fulfilled the Penance impoſed on them, neither had worn Croſſes in their upper Garments, but on the contrary had received the outlawed Hereticks, not revealing them to the Church, contrary to their former Abjurations, (amongſt whom was* Angelinus Paloni, *who now proſecutes the buſineſs, found noted) proceeded with the Ordinary (becauſe he could not alone) and iſſued out Letters Patents, commanding them all to be cited by Name, to anſwer concerning Matters of Faith, and for their Relapſe ; but they refuſing to appear, there were other Letters duly publiſhed, whereby they were cited the ſecond time in the ſame Year, upon the eight and twentieth day of* May, *however they neglected to appear, (two onely excepted) and therefore were the third time cited by Letters of the ſeventh of* June, *duly publiſhed, and not appearing, were excommunicated and aggravated by reaſon of their contumacy, which daily increaſed, which Sentence they underwent with an obſtinate hard heart, (yea and even to this very day do they bear it) wherefore by other Letters iſſued out in the uſual manner upon the* 28. *day of* June *in the ſame Year, they were once more cited to hear and ſee themſelves (as pertinacious and relapſed Hereticks) ſentenced to be delivered over to the Secular Power, and their Goods to be declared confiſcate from the Day of the Crime committed. Moreover they were again cited the ſame Year upon the fifth day of* July, *and after that upon the ſixth day of* September *to hear the Sentence pronounced againſt them: after all this, they were yet as obſtinate as ever, utterly refuſing to appear. Now when as there was no hopes, they were juſtly and equitably condemned, and are not now at all further to be heard, being excommunicate, and interdicted perſons, and declared for pertinacious Hereticks, and that by Sentences paſſed into Act, and to be ſuſpended by no Appellation, and againſt which they are not to be admitted to ſpeak any thing, except firſt impowered by the Admonitions, Judgments, Mandates, and Solutions of the Church. For all which the aforeſaid Precuratour, as upon a fore-judged Article requeſteth Judgment to be pronounced, and that by humbly imploring your Juſtice and the Execution of your Office.*

Debaud *pubick* Notary.

This Popiſh Commiſſary being aſſiſted by the Forces of thoſe Princes and Potentates, whoſe help he deſired, did not a little miſchief to the *Waldenſes* in all Nations and Countries, but above all to thoſe of *Piemont*, who without doubt were recommended unto him in a more eſpecial manner, as being within the Bounds of *Italy :* he went againſt them with an Army of eighteen thouſand men, beſides a great multitude of Voluntiers of *Piemont*, who willingly joyned with them, to obtain thereby the Pardons offered by the Pope, and alſo to have a ſhare of the plundered Goods of the poor *Waldenſes*. This Army being divided into ſeveral Squadrons, that ſo they might the better aſſault them in ſeveral places, was contrary to all mens expectations, ſtrangely

ſtrangely ſhattered and broken in pieces, and Divine Providence did ſo aſſiſt his People in every place, that the Remainder of that Army having wandered up and down, in and about the Valleys, for the ſpace of almoſt a year, to the great prejudice of the whole Countrey, *Philippe* 7. Duke of *Savoy*, and Prince of *Piemont*, put an end to that War, which he perceived to be ſo diſadvantageous to all his Subjects ; yea the Story tells us, that it pleaſed God ſo to touch his heart with compaſſion for that poor People, that he ſpoke it openly, that for as much as he had always found them to be moſt faithfull and obedient Subjects, he would not ſuffer them to be ſo dealt with by force of Arms for the future ; onely for what was paſt, he ordered for formality ſake, that twelve of them ſhould come to *Pignerol,* where he then was, there to beg his Pardon for having taken up Arms in their own Defence, the which they accordingly did, and his Highneſs receiving them courteouſly, forgave them freely all that had paſſed during the time of the War, giving them to underſtand, that he had been miſinformed, both as to their perſons, and their Principles ; and withall he deſired to ſee ſome of their little ones, becauſe there were ſome who had made him believe, that they were ſtrange and monſtrous Creatures, having but one Eye in their Fore-head, with four Sets of black Teeth, with many other ſuch like Fictions ; whereupon ſome were brought before him, and he finding them on the contrary, handſomly ſhapen and well favoured, did openly profeſs, how ill ſatisfied he was with the Calumnies and Slanders of their malicious Adverſaries, and thereupon did not onely confirm their Privileges and Liberties, but withall made them a gracious Promiſe, to ſettle and eſtabliſh the ſame for the time to come. And this was undoubtedly the real intention and reſolution of that Prince at that time, however afterwards wrought upon (or at leaſt deluded) by the ſubtil Devices of the Inquiſitours, who took the boldneſs, notwithſtanding all the gracious Promiſes of their Prince, to continue to proſecute thoſe poor *Waldenſes,* laying violent hands on them, and delivering them up to the Secular Powers, who alſo in moſt places were not at all backward to lend them their helping hands.

*Phil.*7. Duke of *Savoy* and Prince of *Piemont.*

Amongſt others *Marguerite de Foix,* Lady *Marquize* of *Saluces,* at the ſolicitation and requeſt of the *Roman* Clergy, did moſt cruelly perſecute the faithfull *Waldenſes* of *Pravilleſia,* who were all forced to abandon their own & Countrey, to retire into *Val Lucerna,*where after they had petitioned during the ſpace of five years the reſtitution of their Eſtates uſurped by their Popiſh Enemies, and found that all their Intreaties were fruitleſs, they reſolved at length to take courage in the Lord, and by that means regained their Lands by Force of Arms ; which they accordingly enjoyed for the ſpace of an hundred years after.

In the Year 1534. *Charls* Duke of *Savoy* was ſo importuned by the Arch-biſhop, and by the Inquiſitour of *Turin,* to perſecute his Proteſtant Subjects, and to deliver them over to the Secular Power, that he appointed a certain Gentleman, by name *Sieur Pantaleon Berſour* of

Roc-

Roccapiata near *Pignerolio* as his Commiffioner for the Execution of that Defign. This Gentleman very zealous to acquit himfelf honourably of fo great a Truft repofed in him, fo ordered his Affairs, and laid his Defigns, that the year following he fecretly conveyed into the Valleys, about five hundred Men, Horfe and Foot, and there fpoiled, plundered, and deftroyed all that came in his way; and the truth is, the News of this fuddain and furious Onfet did at the firft not a little furprize thofe poor People, but when they had fomewhat recollected their fpirits, they took courage, and every Man leaving his Plough and all other work, went in hafte to ftop the Enemy in their Retreat, and with Slings and other Weapons which came next to hand, plied them fo clofe, that they were forced to fly, leaving their Booty behinde them, befides many of their Men dead upon the place.

When his Highnefs faw that one Skin of a Proteftant was like to coft him a dozen of his other Subjects, he would not fuffer them to be molefted any longer thus openly by force of Arms, but thought fit rather to wafte and confume them by little and little, in a more fecret and obfcure manner, and to this purpofe he fet certain Souldiers to lay in Ambufh for them as they came down from the Mountains into *Piemont*, (two or three in a company) about their ordinary occafions. And although it's true that thofe whom they thus intrapped, feldom or never efcaped with their Lives, yet notwithftanding, this did not at all hinder them from perfevering in the Faith, both in Life and Death, witnefs *Catelan Girard* of *St. Giovanni* in *Lucerna*, who being condemned to be burnt at *Revel*, as he was upon the Pile of Wood, called for two Pebble-ftones, and holding them in his hands, told his Perfecutours, You think (fays he) to abolifh and bring to nought our Churches by thefe your Perfecutions; but it will be no more poffible for you to do it than for me to crufh into Powder thefe ftones with my hands, or elfe to fwallow down and digeft the fame. And indeed, notwithftanding fo many Perfecutions in general, and particular, againft the *Waldenfes*, *George Morel* in his *Memoires* written in the year 1530. confeffes, that *at that very time there were above eight hundred thoufand perfons profefsing the Religion of the* Waldenfes.

G. *Morel* his *Memoires* written 1550.

In the Year 1536. *Francis* the firft, King of *France,* having conquered *Piemont*, Pope *Paul* the third, intreated and perfwaded the Parliament of *Turin*, to proceed againft the *Waldenfes*, as being moft pernicious Hereticks; accordingly that Parliament burnt many of thofe poor People, imitating therein the other Parliaments of *France*; hereupon the poor People having made their humble Addreffes to the King by way of Petition, their condition grew much worfe, for the King injoyned them to live after the Laws of the *Roman* Church, giving them to underftand that otherwife he would have them to be punifht as Hereticks, adding that *he did not burn the* Lutherans *in all parts of* France, *to fuffer a Referve of Hereticks in the* Alpes. The Parliament alfo commanded them upon pain of Death to fend away their Minifters, and to receive in their rooms certain Priefts to fing Maffes, whereunto the *Waldenfes* anfwered, that they could by no means obey
any

any Commands that were contrary to the Laws of God, to whom they had much rather be obedient in every thing that concerns his Service, than to follow the mindes and fancies of Men.

The King having at this time many Irons in the Fire, the Parliament did onely purfue them by the Inquifition, committing to the Fire fuch as were delivered them by the Monks. Amongft others they burnt one *Bartlemy Hector,* a Book-feller, which poor man died (as it is recorded) very conftant, and much to the edification of the Beholders, from whofe Eys he drew many Tears, and compaffionate Expreffions from their Mouths ; and this was done at *Turin,* the 20. of *June* 1555. in the place of the Caftle.

However, not long after, this very fame Parliament fent a certain Prefident called *De St. Julien,* with a *Collateral,* termed *De Ecclefia,* with power and inftructions to exterminate the *Waldenfes :* in profecution whereof they went to *Perofa,* and there caufed Proclamation to be made in the Kings name, whereby the Inhabitants were commanded to go to Mafs, upon pain of Death; afterwards they went to *Pignerol,* where many were fummoned to appear before them , amongft whom there came a poor Plough-man, whom the Prefident commanded to have his Childe rebaptized; the poor Man begged firft fome little time to feek God in Prayer, and having made an end of Prayer, he told the Prefident, that he was contented to have his Childe rebaptized, provided that the Prefident would difcharge him, by a Note under his Hand, of the fin he fhould commit in fo doing, by taking it upon Himfelf and his Pofterity to anfwer for the fame another day before God, and likewife to fuffer all fuch Pains and Punifhments, as fhould be inflicted for the fame. The Prefident hearing this, thought he had fins enough of his own to anfwer for, without taking upon him other mens, and fo fent him away with injurious words, without urging the poor Man any further.

This Prefident, having made many Proceffes againft feveral perfons inhabiting the faid Valleys, and finding not the Fruits of his Labours anfwerable to his Expectations, thought to have allured them by the Preaching of the Monks, whom he brought along with him into the Valley of *Angrognia* for that purpofe, but finding this means alfo as little effectual as the former, he returned to *Turin,* where he made his Report of the great Danger there was in attempting to reduce that People to Extremities, adding, that it was an Enterprize, fitter for the King, in whofe power alone it was to exterminate them, and that the beft expedient was to fend his Majefty all the Informations and Writings, and fo wholly to remit to his prudence and pleafure the management of fo dangerous and difficult an Enterprize.

Now for as much as ufually all Courts advance but flowly in weighty Affairs, it was a whole Year and upwards, before the poor People received their Allarm, however at length there came from the Court, an exprefs Order, by the Hands of the abovefaid Prefident, who coming to *Angrognia,* commanded them in the Kings name, to go to Mafs, upon pain of Confifcation of Body and Goods. To this it was
                                        anfwered,

anfwered, by the Deputies and Elders of thofe Evangelical Churches, that they were not bound to obey fuch Commands, for as much as they proceeded from Man, and not from God; and that it fhould be confidered, that they worfhipped all one and the fame God and Saviour *Jefus Chrift*, and had the fame Law, and the fame Hopes with them, and that feeing the *Jews* and *Mahometans* who are Blafphemers, and Enemies to the Name of *Chrift*, were notwithftanding permitted to live amongft them in peace, and in the quiet enjoyment each of their own Religion apart, it was much more reafonable that thofe who worfhip the trueGod in*Chrift*,fhould be fuffred to live in peace amongft their Hills and Mountains, efpecially confidering that they were ready to embrace any thing, that fhould be proved to be fuitable to the Word and Will of God, as likewife to yield all due obedience to their Superiours and fovereign Magiftrates, protefting they would live and dy in this Refolution.

This Anfwer did fo incenfe the Parliament of *Turin* againft them, that they burnt as many of them, as they could catch in *Piemont*, and upon the Frontiers of the Valleys, amongft others Mr. *Jefferey Vavaille* Minifter of *Angrognia* was burnt in the Year 1557. whofe Death was of much edification to the Beholders: he was executed in the place of the Caftle, there being a great number of People who faw him perfevere in calling on the Name of God, to the very laft gafp. *Nicholas Sartoris* of *Quiers* in *Piemont*, a Student in Divinity, and entertained by the Lords of *Berne*, was burnt for the fame Caufe at *Val d' Ofte*, the fourth of *May*, 1557. having valiantly overcome all the Temptations which they could devife to lay before him.

During thefe Troubles, Duke *Philibert Emanuel* was again reftored to his Eftate by the general Peace of 1559. and perfwaded by the Monks of *Pignerol* to condemn all the *Waldenfes* of the Valleys to the Fire and Fagot, as likewife to beftow the Plunder of them upon the Neighbour Garifons. But the *Waldenfes*, to avoid this Storm, made their Addreffes to their Prince, as follows.

An

An Extract of the humble Supplication of the poor *Waldenses*.

To the moſt Serene and moſt High Prince *Philibert Emanuel,* Duke of *Savoy,* Prince of *Piemont,* our moſt gracious Lord.

FEſtus *Governour of* Judea, *being required by the chief Prieſts and Elders of the People, to put to Death the Apoſtle* Paul, *anſwered no leſs wiſely than juſtly, that* the *Romans* were not wont to put any to Death, before they had brought his Accuſers face to face, and given him time to anſwer for himſelf. *We are not ignorant,* Moſt Gracious Prince, *that many Accuſations are laid againſt us, and that many Calumnies are caſt upon us, to make us ſtink in the Noſtrils of all the Princes and Monarchs in the* Chriſtian *World. But if the* Roman *People (though Pagans) were ſo equitable, as not to condemn any man before they had known and underſtood his Reaſons, and if* the Law *condemns no man (as it is teſtified by* Nicodemus, John 7.) *before he hath been heard, and before it is known what he hath done, the matter now in queſtion being of ſo great concernment, (namely, the Glory of the moſt high God, and the Salvation of ſo many Souls) we do implore your clemency (moſt Gracious Prince) that you will be pleaſed to lend a willing ear to your poor Subjects, in ſo juſt and righteous a Cauſe.*

Firſt, we do proteſt before the Almighty, and All-juſt God, before whoſe Tribunal we muſt all one day appear, that we intend to live and die in the holy Faith, Piety, and Religion of our Lord Jeſus Chriſt, *and that we do abhor all Hereſies that have been and are condemned by the Word of God.*

We do embrace the moſt holy Doctrine of the Prophets and Apoſtles, as likewiſe the Nicene *and* Athanaſian *Creed; we ſubſcribe to the four Councils, and to all the ancient Fathers, in all ſuch things as are not repugnant to the Analogy of Faith.*

We do moſt willingly yield obedience to our Superiours; we ever endeavoured to live peaceably with our Neighbours, we have wronged no man; though provoked, neither do we fear that any can, with reaſon, complain againſt us.

Finally, we never were obſtinate in our opinions, but rather tractable and always ready to receive all holy and pious Admonitions, as appears by our Confeſsion of Faith.

And we are ſo far from refuſing a Diſpute, or rather a free Council,
                                                                    where-

wherein all things may be established by the Word of God, that we rather desire the same with all our hearts, &c.

We likewise beseech your Highnes to consider, that this Religion we profess, is not onely ours, nor hath it been invented by Men of late years, as it is falsly reported, but it is the Religion of our Fathers, Grand-fathers, and Great-grand-fathers, and other yet more ancient Predecessours of ours, *and of the blessed* Martyrs, Confessours, Prophets, *and* Apostles, *and if any can prove the contrary, we are ready to subscribe and yield thereunto, &c.* The Word of God shall not perish, but remain for ever; *wherefore, if our Religion be the true Word of God, (as we are perswaded) and not the Invention of Men, no humane force shall be able to extinguish the same, &c.*

Your Highnes knows, that this very same Religion hath for many Ages past been most grievously persecuted in all places, but so far from being abolished or rooted out thereby, that it hath rather increased daily, which is a certain Argument, that this Work and Counsel is not the Work and Counsel of Men, but of God, and therefore cannot be destroyed by any violence. Besides, it is not a small sin to fight against God; witnes all those who have untill now persecuted the People of God and his holy Word. Therefore we beseech your most Serene Highnes (most Illustrious Prince) to consider what it is to undertake any thing against God, that so you may not imbrue your Hands in innocent Bloud! Jesus *is our Saviour, we will religiously obey all your Highnes Edicts, as far as Conscience will permit; but when Conscience says Nay, your Highnes knows we must rather obey God than Man. We unfeignedly confes, that we ought to give* Cæsar *that which belongs unto* Cæsar, *provided we give also to God what is due to him.*

There want not those (it may be) who will endeavour to incite the generous minde and courage of your Highnes, to persecute our Religion by force of Arms. But, O magnanimous Prince! you may easily conjecture to what end they do it, that it is not out of zeal to Gods glory, but rather to preserve their own worldly Dignities, Pomp, and Riches; wherefore we beseech your Highnes not to regard or countenance their Sayings.

The Turks, Jews, Saracens, *and other Nations, though never so barbarous, are suffered to enjoy their own Religion, and are constrained by no Man to change their manner of Living or Worship; and we who serve and worship in Faith the true and Almighty God, and our true and onely Soverign, the Lord* Jesus Christ, *confessing one God, and one Baptism, shall not we be suffered to enjoy the same Privileges?*

We humbly implore your Highnes goodnes, and that for our onely Lord and Saviour Jesus Christ *his sake, to allow unto us (your most humble Subjects) the most holy Gospel of the Lord our God, in its purity, and that we may not be forced to do things against our Consciences, for which we shall with all our hearts beseech our Almighty and All-good God, to preserve your Highnes in prosperity.*

In the mean time the Souldiers of the neighbouring Garisons, to the number of four hundred, advancing by night, surprized the Village

lage of *St. Germano,* whereupon many of the poor People receiving the Allarm, recovered the Mountain, amongſt theſe there were about five and twenty, who after they had ſought God in Prayer, aſſaulted the Enemy ſo couragiouſly, that their hearts began to fail them, above all, for that they had obſerved them to fall down upon their Knees before they came to fight, yea this their Fear grew to ſuch an height, that many as they were flying for fear, were drowned in a ſmall Brook which they were to paſs over in their Retreat.

Soon after, the Duke ſent againſt them a complete Army under the Command of the Lord *de la Trinité,* who ſeeing his Men diſcouraged, and beaten in ſeveral Encounters, began to flatter the poor *Waldenſes* wih ſmooth words, and having perſwaded them to lay down their Arms, and to ſend away their Miniſters, they ſecretly gariſoned many places, and afterwards dealt moſt unmercifully with them : however this barbarous and ſhamefull Cruelty did not ſo much aſtoniſh the People, ſo as to cauſe their hearts to fail, but on the contrary it did ſo much the more increaſe their Conſtancy, and made them reſolve to take Arms again, in hope of new Victories, as may be ſeen in a following Letter written by a certain Miniſter of the Valleys named *Scipio Lentulus, Anno Domini* 1561.

AR-

ARTICLE III.

Copy of a Letter of *Scipio Lentulus*, a *Neapolitan*; Containing a brief Relation touching the Faithfull Profeffors in the Valley of *Angrogne*.

An Authentick Tranfcript of the Original whereof, is to be feen in the publick Library of the famous Univerfity of *C A M B R I D G*.

Cum mihi fignificaveris te cupere, quæ apud nos in Pedemontio *contigerunt noffe, ut commodius hac in re tibi morem gererem, volui Epiſtola potius, quam Sermone ea referre : Id quod,* &c.

MOST HONOURED SIR,

" SEeing you have given me to underftand, that it is your defire to
" know what things have faln out among us in *Piemont*, to the end
" that I might the more conveniently anfwer your expeftation in this
" particular, I have determined to give an Account of thofe things
" by Letter, rather then by word of mouth : Forafmuch as it will be
" of fome ufe alfo to ferve the purpofe of thofe men who defire to
" have the fame things committed to writing, and are able to fet them
" forth much more exaftly.
   " There is a certain Valley in the Country of *Piemont* within five
" or fix miles of Mount *Vefulo*, which from the Town *Lucerna*, is
" called the Valley of *Lucerna* ; And in it there is a little Valley, which
" from *Angrogna*, a fmall River running through it, is called the Val-
" ley of *Angrogna*. Next adjoyning to this there are two other Val-
" leys, that is to fay, the Valley of *Perofa*, fo called from the Town
" of that name, and the Valley of S. *Martino*. In thefe there lie divers
" little Towns and Villages, whofe Inhabitants, affifted by the Mini-
" fters of Gods Word, do make open profeffion of the Gofpel.
   " Moreover, I fuppofe that there are near eight thoufand faithfull
" fouls (as I may call them) inhabiting in this place. But among the
" men, who are bred up to endure labour, feeing they have from their
" childhood been inured to Husbandry, you will finde very few that
" know how to engage in combate with any. From hence it comes to
                                                              " paffe,

" paffe, that very few of them are ready, upon any urgent occafion, to
" defend themfelves againft publick injuries. Yea and the Valleys
" themfelves lie fo remote from each other, that they cannot help one
" another till it be too late. And although thefe Towns and Villages
" have their Counts or Lords (as they call them) yet the Duke of *Sa-*
" *voy* is Lord over them all.

" This Duke before he came from *Nice* into *Piemont,*diligently took
" order with thofe Counts and Lords of Places that they fhould admo-
" nifh the Inhabitants of the Valleys to fubmit to him and the Pope ;
" that is, that cafting off their Minifters, they fhould admit Popifh
" Preachers, and the abominable Mafs. Whereupon, our people fent
" a certain Meffenger to *Nice,* together with the Confeffion of Faith,
" and Petitions unto the Prince, befeeching him that he would take it
" in good part, if they were refolved rather to die than lofe the true
" Religion of Jefus Chrift, forafmuch as they had received it, through
" a very ancient Tract of Time, as it were by hand from their Ance-
"ftors ; and that he would not doubt but they fhall be ready to amend
"their errors, if any were, in cafe it could be manifefted to them out
"of the word of God,to which alone they are to fubmit in this bufinefs;
" And as to what concerneth them in matters of behaviour,&Tributes,
" and other things due both to him and to their other Lords, that
" he would fend perfons to make diligent enquiry whether they have
" at any time committed any offence, that fo due punifhment may be
" inflicted on them, becaufe he fhould affuredly know they will endea-
" vour, that he may underftand they are willing to approve themfelves,
" with due reverence, moft obedient to him in all thefe things.

" Thefe Petitions came to the hand of the Prince, but availed no-
" thing with him, who was become a fworn Enemy with Antichrift a-
" gainft Chrift. Thereupon, he fent forth Edicts, declaring that thofe
" who fhould be prefent at the Sermons of the Minifters of the Valleys,
" if but once, they fhould be fined at one hundred Crowns, and if a
" fecond time, then they fhould be condemned to the Galleys for ever.
" Order alfo was given to a certain Judge, to ride circuit up and down
" to put the penalties in execution, and to binde Chriftians and impri-
" fon them. The Lords alfo and Magiftrates of Places had the fame
" power given them, and at length the godly were by this moft im-
" pious Prince utterly given up to be plundered by all forts of Villains,
"and afflicted with moft grievous calamities.

" He fent alfo a certain Collateral Judge of his own, firft to *Ca-*
" *rignan,* there to act inhumane Butchery upon the Faithfull ones of
" Chrift ; whereupon he caufed one *Marcellinus* and *Joan* his Wife, he
" being a Frenchman, but fhe a woman of *Carignan,* to be burnt alive
" with fire four days after they had been apprehended. But in this wo-
" man God was pleafed to manifeft an admirable example of conftan-
" cy: For, as fhe was led to execution, fhe exhorted her husband, fay-
" ing, *Well done my Brother, be of good courage, this day doubtlefs we fhall*
" *enter together into the joys of Heaven.* Some few days after this, there
" was apprehended alfo one *John Carthignan,* an honeft plain man and
                                                        " truly

" truly Religious, who after three days imprifonment, endured the
" torments of fire with very great conftancy. Who is able to reckon
" up the feveral Incurfions, Slaughters, Plunders, and innumerable
" miferies wherewith this moft favage generation of men did daily af-
" flict all pious men, becaufe being exhorted by their Minifters to pa-
" tience, they took no courfe to defend themfelves againft injuries.
" Not long after alfo they apprehended one *John*, a Frenchman and a
" Minifter, at a Town called *St. Germano*, and carrying him to a certain
" Abbey near *Pignerol*, they burnt him alive, who left behinde him a
" notable example of Chriftian conftancy. The like was done alfo to
" the Minifter of the Town of *Meane*, who was put to death at *Sufa*
" by a flow fire, while he in the mean time ftood as it were immove-
" able, and not being touched with any fence of fo incredible a cruelty,
" having his eyes fixed upon heaven, he breathed out his happy
" foul.

" Therefore when things were come to this pafs, and thefe miferies
" were encreafed every day more and more, and feeing that the pati-
" ence and extream mifery of our people, could not in any meafure
" allay the fury and rage of thefe moft mercilefs Brutes, they at length
" refolved by force, as well as they could, to free themfelves and their
" Wives and Children from that barbarous ufage. And although fome
" of our Minifters declared it was not well done, yet no admonitions
" could keep the people from refolving to defend themfelves by Arms.
" Hereupon it came to pafs, that feveral encounters falling out, within
" few days, there fell about fixty of the Plunderers. When news here-
" of was brought to the Tyrant, he commanded his men to forbear,
" and fent two of his Noblemen, principal perfons, to wit the Lord *Ra-*
" *conyfi*, and the Lord *de la Trinitie* (whom I fhall for difcourfe fake
" more aptly call the Lord *de la Tyrannitie*) that fo they might bring
" matters to an accommodation with our people : But when it was
" perceived, that all their drift was, that our Minifters might be caft
" out and the Pope received, the people would by no means yeild to it ;
" and fo they departed *re infect â*.

" Wherefore when the Prince came into *Piemont*, and refided at *Ver-*
" *fello*, about the Kalends of *November*, in the year 1540 ; with intent
" to deftroy all in the Valleys by Fire and Sword, he fent an Army
" of above Four thoufand Foot and Two hundred Horfe, under the
" command of the Duke *de la Tyrannitie*. And the next day in the
" morning they fall into *Angrogna*, which lay firft in their way. But
" there being in a fteep place of a Mountain fome men of ours which
" kept Guard there (who were not above fifty in number) they with
" flings, wherewith moft of them were armed, fuftained the firft af-
" fault made by One thoufand two hundred men : But afterwards, o-
" thers coming in feveral ways to the affiftance of ours (though the
" whole number hardly amounted to Two hundred) they not onely
" put the Enemy to flight, but flew feventy of them, with the lofs of
" no more but Three of our own : And the next day, when they at-
" tempted to come up to us out of another part of the Valley hard by
" *Villaro*

" *Villaro* and *Taillaretto*, a small number of ours put a very great Body
" of the Enemies to flight, and slew of them about Thirty. For these
" causes then, that most crafty Fox, the Lord *de la Tyrannitie*, under-
" standeth that to be a very difficult businefs, which he conceived o-
" therwise moft eafie, forafmuch as our men, who, he fuppofed, would
" have been frighted with the bare name of an Army, fought ftoutly
" and moft valiantly, although they were but ill armed, a fmall num-
" ber, and without experience of Military affairs ; Wherefore he
" thought it requifite to have recourfe (as his manner is) unto de-
" ceitfull practifes. To this end, he employed perfons to give hopes
" of Peace, if they would lay down Arms ; whereupon certain falfe
" Brethren, in defigne to ferve their own private ends (as experience
" hath made manifeft) perfwaded the people, though almoft all the Mi-
" nifters cried out againft it, that too eafily giving credit to the moft
" falfe promifes of their Enemies, laying down Arms, and fending De-
" puties to the Prince to promife obedience, and beg pardon in the
" name of all the people, they might for 16000 Crowns redeem both
" themfelves and their Religion. As foon as all thefe things were yield-
" ed to,& promifed by the too credulous people(with whom fome men
" confented that ought not to have done it)through a vain hope of ob-
" taining Peace & Religion,and when our Deputies arrived at *Verfello*,
" they were from thence carried by theLord *de la Tyrannitie* to a certain
" Cloyfter,there to abide for twoMonths fpace(to the end there might
" be time for collecting the moneys) and at length cafting themfelves
" down at the feet of the Prince, and of the Pope's Legat (who were
" both there, attended by a great number of the Nobility and men of
" inferiour Rank) they were conftrained to fupplicate the Prince
" firft, then the Pope's Legat, that they would take pitty on the people
" from whom they were fent,and to promife them by an Oath,thatthey
" would be ready to do all things that fhould be commanded by them.
  " The Prince therefore growing confident upon this folemn pro-
" mife, immediately fent perfons to command our people to re-
" ceive and imbrace that horrid Idol of the Mafs : Whereupon confi-
" dering the inconftancy of their Deputies, and the deceit, or rather
" extream perfidioufnefs of the Tyrants being difcovered, they plain-
" ly refufed to yield that thofe things fhould be ratified which their
" Deputies had unadvifedly tranfacted, through their own levity, not
" with the confent of the people ; for, they had been fent upon fuch
" terms, that they fhould do all thofe things in the name of the whole
" people, which might conduce to Peace, with the fafety of Religion.
" Then the Tyrant, as foon as he came to underftand this, was much
" more inflamed than ever before with anger, or rather outragious
" fury againft our people ; and recollecting a rabble of an Army, he
" gave command to the Lord *De la Tyrannitie* to wafte and deftroy all
" by fire and Sword, without any regard either of Sex or Age.
" Hereupon houfes were every where fet on fire, goods plundered,nor
" is there any kind of mifchief fo great which was not acted by thofe
" moft wretched Villains : By which means they forced our people
                                                              " with|

" with their Wives and Children, to have recourfe to the more craggy
" places of the Mountains: A thing indeed very lamentable to be
" feen! For, at the very firft affault they were in a manner aftonifhed,
" becaufe being fpoiled both of their Arms and Goods, living in ex-
" tream want of all things, they did not fee by what means they might
" be able to undergo fo great and troublefome a War.

" But at length taking heart, and trufting in the mercy and help of
" God, and the goodnefs of their Caufe, and being confident becaufe
" of the impiety and treachery of their Adverfaries, they refolved
" once again to defend themfelves. To this end they appointed their
" Guards and Garifons, fortified feveral places, blocked up paffages,
" and were wholly refolute upon this point, to die, rather than they
" would in any meafure obey a perfidious and wicked Prince in fo
" abominable a matter. But what need many words? Things were
" come to fuch a pafs, that in feveral Fights above 900 of the Ene-
" mies were flain, whereas on our fide hardly Fifteen were wanting.

" But I muft not omit alfo to inform you, that at that time there
" fell Eight of thofe Leaders whom the Prince held in higheft efteem,
" becaufe of their extraordinary Valour and skill in Military Affairs,
" whereof he had had experience, chiefly in his War againft the King
" of *France*. Of that number was *Charls Truffet*, Lord of a certain
" Town called *Runclaret*, a man of great ftrength, moft daring, and
" not onely exercifed in Arms from his very Childhood, but one
" generally reputed moft ftout in Action. This man leading two Re-
" giments, confifting of about Six hundred men, on that fide where
" ours little imagined any Enemy would come, advanced with his
" men to the top of a Mountain, where he over-looked our Party:
" Which as foon as ours beheld, then pouring out prayers before the
" Lord (for they always have a Minifter with them) although they
" were fcarce Thirty in number, they couragioufly proceeded againft
" the Enemy; who being very jocund, as if they had already gained
" the Victory, came down. They were no fooner engaged, but fix
" Slingers of ours, by a paffage unknown to the Enemy, immediately
" poffeffed themfelves of the top of the Mountain, which the other
" fearing nothing had quitted; and crying out aloud from thence, *Let*
" *Jefus Chrift be glorified*, they iffued down upon them with fo great
" a force, that the Enemy utterly failed both in ftrength and courage,
" while ours in the mean time became the more active and couragi-
" ous. And as foon as the Enemies perceived about Eighty men
" advancing from the next Town for the fuccour of our friends, they
" all prefently betook themfelves to their heels: Whereupon the fnow
" being then above a Cubit deep, and thofe that fled finding the
" paffages very ftraight and cumberfome, they part of them threw
" themfelves headlong from broken Rocks, and part were flaughtered
" at pleafure by the purfuers. As for *Truffet*, he being led betwixt
" two Souldiers (becaufe his Leg had been broken by a blow with a
" ftone) was with his own Sword moft miferably flain by a certain
" plough-boy, after he had levelled another ftone at his Back from a
" Sling

" Sling with fuch a force, that being left by the Souldiers, he fell
" down upon the ground half-dead: And in that Fight there fell
" about Two hundred of the Enemies, without any lofs of our own,
" Many more fuch paffages might be related of feveral Encounters,
" wherein a few of our friends have always worfted a great number of
" the Enemies ; of the truth whereof this is a very ample evidence,
" that fo great ftore of Arms came to the hands of ours, that they
" were not at all troubled for the lofs of their own formerly through
" treachery, feeing a return made of them in fo great abundance.
   " Thefe are the Occurrences which at this time I could communi-
" cate to you concerning this bufinefs ; and if fo be that you think
" them too few, I promife you I will very diligently take care that
" within thefe few days you may receive a more large account: For,
" I am every day in expectation of a perfon who was not onely pre-
" fent, but a principal man alfo in all thefe actions. In the mean
" time, you will (I hope) entertain thefe which I have by fnatches
" rudely written, to the end that I might (how meanly foever) teftifie
" my fingular love and refpect towards you, who are fo worthy a per-
" fon. *Farewel.*

Signed,   *Tui ftudiofiffimus,*
          Scipio Lentulus, Neapolitanus.

Or,
Yours moft affectionately devoted,
Scipio Lentulus, *Native of* Naples.

The fame Prince (as it is reported by *D' Aubigné* in his Univerfal
Hiftory) borrowed of the King one *Maugiron*, a Commander, with
ten Companies of Foot, and Monfieur *La Mothegondrin* with fome
Trained Bands.

D' Aubigné, 2 Book, 9 Chapt.

But the *Waldenfes* not wanting courage when there was occafion,
did before the very face of the *French* befiege the Fortrefs of *Villaro*,
which had been built againft them, which after eight days was accordingly yielded up to them upon Articles of Compofition..

The next day Mr. *De la Trinité* was ftopt from morning to night
with his whole Army, by thofe Peafants. Afterwards the *Pré de la
Torre* was affaulted by 7000 men four days together, but with the lofs
of 400 Souldiers, fome whereof were Colonels, and fome Captains,
whereupon *Mr. de la Trinité* fent for fome Artillery, and for feveral
Spanifh Troops to affift him ; but all in vain, for thofe poor Shepheards fell fo hot upon the Army, that they wholly put them to the
rout, killing many upon the place; and not content with that, fell
afterwards upon the Rear, and purfued the Victory as far as *Angrogna*.

Thefe wonderfull fucceffes, together with the Dutchefs interceffion for that poor people (whofe Doctrine fhe was fufpected to favour)
moved the *Duke* to come to a Treaty. Their Deputies being arrived
                                                            at

at *Turin*, one *Chaffincourt*, who was then Gentleman-Ufher to the *Dutchefs* (as *D' Aubigné* relates it) began to queſtion them, *How they ever durſt be ſo impudent (poor wretches as they were) to appear before their Soveraign Prince, to treat with him, after they had made War againſt him ; and with what confidence they durſt contradict him as touching that Religion which was countenanced by the whole world, or conteſt againſt ſo great a Prince, who had the counſel of ſo many Doctors, whereas they were but poor ſhepheards, and ignorant of all things.* In ſum he told them, that *ſince they were ſo ill adviſed, they could expect no other fruit of all their fooleries and ſottiſhnes, then to come to the Gallows.* To this one of the aboveſaid Deputies made him anſwer thus ; *Sir, That which gives us the boldneſs to appear before our Prince, is, becauſe his goodneſs encourages and calls us thereunto : Our defending our ſelves has been juſt, becauſe we have been forced ſo to do, and God has juſtified it by his wonders : As for our goods, we have ſuffered the loſs of them without reſiſtance ; but when we ſaw that the deſign was to oppreſs our Conſciences, and utterly to aboliſh the true ſervice and worſhip of God amongſt us ; and when we ſaw our Prince unwillingly executing (as we charitably believe) the Popes commands, and acting by the will of others, contrary to his own natural inclination, and therefore exerciſing the power of Judicature,not as a Soveraign, but as an inferiour Lord, who hath another Soveraign over himſelf, we thought, that to defend our ſelves, was onely to oppoſe that Supream power and tyranny, which the enemies of God have uſurped over our Soveraign Lord and Saviour Jeſus Chriſt. This is the Supream Power that ought to be preferred before all the Powers of the world ; and being once engaged to him by an Oath, we are thereby diſobliged from all other that are contrary to it. As to that ſimplicity you are pleaſed to upbraid us with, God himſelf hath bleſſed it, to ſhew thereby, that he needs not the greatneſs of the world to act great things ; the moſt abject and vile inſtruments have been often the moſt pleaſing to him. As for counſels, thoſe we receive from his Spirit are wiſe enough, and thoſe hearts are ſufficiently couragious whom he animates, thoſe Arms alſo that are ſtrengthened by him cannot want any ſtrength : We are ignorant, 'tis true, and aim at no other Eloquence, then to pray in faith. As to death, wherewith we are threatned, the Word and Honour of our Prince is a thing more precious then our Lives ; however, even death it ſelf is not in the leaſt able to diſmay thoſe who have the fear of God deeply ingraven in their hearts.*

These and the like expreſſions did ſo nearly touch the heart of *Chaffincourt*, that it made him turn Proteſtant: As alſo theſe and the like expreſſions and comportments of theſe Deputies of thoſe poor people, obtained the following Edict, in the year 1561.

Article 4.

ARTICLE IV

An Edict of the Duke of *Savoy*, bearing Date the 5th. of *June*, 1561. in favour of the Evangelical Churches of the Valleys of *Piemont*.

An Authentique Copy of the true Original whereof is to be seen in the publick Library of the famous University of *Cambridge*.

Al nome di Dio.

Si fpediranno Lettere Patente di fua Altezza, per lequali coftara qualmente S. A. fa remiffione a gli huomini della Valle d' Angrogna, Bobio, Villaro, Valguicchiardo, *&c.*

In the Name of God.

His Highneſs iſſueth out his Letters Patents, by which it may appear, in what manner his Highneſs grants an Indemnity to the people of the *Valleys of* Angrognia, Bobio, Villaro, Valguicchiardo, Rora, Tagliaretto, and La Rica di Boneti at the end of La Torre, S. Martino, Peroſa, Roccapiatta, and S. Bartholemo, and every of theſe, as alſo to all ſuch as ſhall be found to have aſſiſted them, for all offences by them committed, whether they be damages, deaths, ruines, or fines ; as well in particular, as in general, either againſt his Highneſs, their mediate Lords, or other particular perſons within his Highneſs Dominions, reſtoring them into his favour as if they had never acted any thing againſt his Highneſs ; and upon this account, receiving them into his ſafeguard and protection.

1. Sara permeſſi a quelli d' Angrogna, Bobio, Villaro, *&c.*

1. *It ſhall be permitted to thoſe of* Angrogna, Bobio, Villaro, Valguicchiardo, *and* Rora, *being members of the Valley of* Lucerna, *and likewiſe to thoſe of* Pralibece, Roderet, Maſel, Maneglia, *and* Salea, *Members of the Valley of* S. Martino, *to have preaching Aſſemblies, and other Miniſterial Offices, according to their Religion, in their wonted places.*

2. Sara

2. Sara permeſſo al Villaro membro della Valle di Lucerna, *&c,*

2 *It ſhall be permitted them to have the ſame at* Villaro, *which is a member of the Valley of* Lucerna ; *And this ſhall be until ſuch time as his Highneſs ſhall make a Fort in the ſaid place ; for after that ſuch a Fort is erected, it ſhall not be permitted to the people of the ſaid place to have preaching, or Congregations within the bounds of the ſaid place : But it ſhall be lawfull for them to erect a place convenient for ſuch like ſervices, in ſome adjacent place towards* Bobio, *as they ſhall find moſt convenient. Neverthelefs it ſhall be permitted to the Miniſters to come within the ſaid bounds, to viſit the ſick, and perform other neceſſary duties of their Religion, provided that they neither preach, nor gather together any ſuſpected Congregation. At* Togliaretto *and* Rua de Boneti, *which are the Confines of their Lands, it ſhall be permitted them to have preaching, and Congregations in the wonted places ; provided, that they do not enter into the other confines of their Lands, to do the like.*

3. Non ſara permeſſo a quello prementionati delle, *&c.*

3. *It ſhall not be permitted to the above mentioned members of the Valley of* Lucerna, *and* S. Martino *above-ſaid, to come within the other bounds of the ſaid Valley, or the reſt of his Highneſs Dominions, paſſing the bounds of their preſcribed limits there, to have preaching Congregations, or Diſputations, having onely permiſſion to do this within their own bounds. And if by chance they ſhall be demanded any thing as touching their faith, it ſhall be lawfull for them to make anſwer, without incurring thereby any puniſhment, either real, or perſonal.*

4. Sara permeſſo a quelli della Parochia di, *&c.*

4. *It ſhall be permitted to thoſe of the Pariſh which is on the other ſide of* Peroſa, *who are at preſent Fugitives for the ſake of the ſaid Religion, and were wont to have preaching, and Congregations, as alſo other Miniſterial Offices, according to their ſaid Religion, onely in the place nominated, and not in any other place within the bounds of the ſaid Pariſh.*

5. Sara permeſſo a quelli della Parochia di Pinachia, *&c.*

5. *It ſhall be permitted to thoſe of the Pariſh of* Pinachia, *in the Valley of* Peroſa, *and to thoſe of* Roccapiatto, *who are at preſent Fugitives for the cauſe of their ſaid Religion, and do adhere to it, to have one Miniſter onely, which ſhall have liberty one day to adminiſter and preach in the place of* S. Germano *called* Adurmiglioſo, *and the other day at* Roccapiatta, *onely in the place of the ſaid* Goadini, *and not in any part elſe of the ſaid place, to perform all other Offices of their Religion,*

6. Sara permeſſo a tutti quelli di tutte le terre di, *&c.*

6. It ſhall be permitted to all perſons of the Lands of the ſaid Valley, who are at preſent Fugitives, and do adhere to their ſaid Religion (not-withſtanding any promiſe or abjuration made againſt their Religion before this War) to return and live in their houſes with their families, according to their Religion; and to go to, and return from the Sermons and Congregati-ons which ſhall be made in the ſaid places, and other adminiſtrations of their Religion ; provided, that they obſerve all which the above-mentioned promiſe to obſerve. And foraſmuch as many of the aboveſaid will be found in the Lands of the ſaid Valley at a great diſtance from ſuch places, and will thereby neceſſarily ſtand in need of viſitations, and other Miniſterial functions, according to their Religion ; it ſhall be permitted to their Mi-niſters (ſuch as dwell within their limits, without any prejudice to ſuch limits) to viſit and perform other Miniſterial duties, according as they ſhall have occaſion ; onely they ſhall not have publick preaching, or ſuch as may give the leaſt ſuſpicion.

7. A tutti li predetti delle dette Valli, & a tutti, *&c.*

7. To all the Inhabitants of the ſaid Valleys abovementioned, and to all the forenamed Fugitives, and thoſe who perſiſt in their Religion, as well thoſe of the Territories of the ſaid Valleys, as thoſe of Roccapiatta, *S.* Bartelomeo, *and* Miana, *their goods that have been confiſcate ſhall be reſtored to them ; provided, they be not confiſcate for any other cauſe then that of Religion, and the preſent or paſt War.*

8. Sara permeſſo a tutti i predetti poter per via, *&c.*

8. It ſhall be permitted to all the forenamed, to recover by courſe of Juſtice, their moveables and their cattel, whereof they have been robbed, and which ſhall be found to have been ſold by their neighbours, provided they be not Souldiers ; and the like is permitted to their neighbours againſt the abovementioned.

9. Saranno alli predetti confermate tutte le, *&c.*

9. All the Freedomes, Immunities, and Priviledges, (as well general as particular) which have been granted either by his Highneſs moſt Il-luſtrious Predeceſſors, his Highneſs himſelf, or other mediate Lords, ſhall be confirmed to the forenamed ; provided, they evidence the truth thereof by Authentick Acts, and Inſtruments.

10. Saranno li predetti di dette Valli tenuti, *&c.*

10. Thoſe of the ſaid Valleys ſhall be obliged to write down the names
and

and firnames of all fuch as belong to the Territories of the forefaid Valleys, who are fled by reafon of the perfecution of their Religion, as well fuch as have abjured, as others who have remained with their goods and families, that fo they may enjoy the favours and benefits that their Prince and Lord fhall pleafe to beftow upon them. .

11. Perche fi fa, ch'il Principe ne li fuoi paefi, &c.

11. *Becaufe it is lawfull for a Prince in his own Countrey to caufe Forts to be made, according to his pleafure, without being controlled or oppofed by any of his Vaffals, or Subjects, To remove any caufe of fufpicion which might be entertained in the minds of the forenamed of the faid Valleys, it is declared, That from this time forward within fome few days, his Highnefs may peradventure caufe a Fort to be made in the place of* Villaro ; *neverthelefs it fhall be without any coft of thofe of the Valley, except in what it fhall feem good to them to contribute lovingly to their Prince : Which being done, by Gods permiffion, it fhall be provided with a Governour, and a Captain, fuch as fhall attend onely for the fervice of his Highnefs : Neverthelefs, this fhall be without the leaft prejudice to any mans Confcience, or his Goods.*

12. Sara lecito a predetti, prima che, &c.

12. *It fhall be lawfull for the forenamed, before the Minifters be difmiffed (whom it fhall pleafe his Highnefs to order to be fent away) to have others in their places ; provided, they do not retain Mafter* Martino of Pragella ; *nor may they change or fhift their abodes from one place to another of the faid Valleys, otherwife then it fhall be permitted to them.*

13. In tutte le parocchie di dette Valli, dove, &c.

13. *In the Parifhes of the faid Valleys, where preaching is ufed, and Congregations are inftituted, or the Minifteries of the faid Valley exercifed,* Mafs *fhall be celebrated, and other offices according to the cuftome of* Rome ; *but the forenamed fhall not be conftrained to go thereunto, or to give any help or affiftance to any that officiate in that kind ; and if any fhall be pleafed to go thither, no difturbance fhall be given him by the forenamed.*

14. Sara da S. A. a i predetti, fatto dono, e remiffione, &c.

14. *His Highnefs fhall make a free gift, and irrevocable remiffion of all the expences which he hath been at in this War, and of the* 8000 *Crowns which the forenamed did owe unto his Highnefs, upon account of* 16000 *Crowns accorded in the former War, commanding that they be as non-fubfcribed in reference to this Accompt.*

15. Saranno rimeſſi tutti li prigioni, che ſi truoveranno, &c.

15. *All the priſoners which are found in the Souldiers hands, ſhall be reſtored and ſet at liberty, provided they pay a reaſonable tax, according to their faculties, leaving the judgement and tax to diſcretion of the Lord* de Raconiſi, *and to the Lord* della Trinite : *And all thoſe whom the ſaid Lords ſhall judge to be no lawfull priſoners, ſhall be releaſed without any tax, cauſing in like manner to be releaſed without any payment, all thoſe of the ſaid Valleys who ſhall be found in the Galleys for cauſe of their Religion, and not for any other offence.*

16. Finalmente tutti li predetti di dette Valli, &c.

16. *Finally, His Highneſs ſhall permit all the foreſaid of the ſaid Valleys, and the aforeſaid of* Miana, Roccapiatta, *and* S. Bartelmeo, *of what ſtate and condition ſoever they be (provided they be not Miniſters) to be included in the common ſociety and converſation with his other ſubjects, to ſtay, go, and come, in all places and Countreys of his Highneſs Territories ; as likewiſe to buy, ſell, and traffique in all ſorts of Merchandizes, provided they refrain from preaching, from drawing together Aſſemblies, or to raiſe diſputings, as is aboveſaid : And thoſe that are in the limits, who have not a ſetled reſidence without their own limits, nor any within the Territory of the ſaid Valleys, without their own Territory, and the confines thereof, and thoſe of* Miana, Roccapiatta, S. Bartelmeo, *ſhall not uſurp beyond their own confines : And theſe things being punctually obſerved on their parts, no diſturbance or moleſtation (whether real, or perſonal) ſhall be offered unto them, but they ſhall remain under the protection and ſafeguard of his Highneſs.*

17. Oltra di queſto ſi mandaranno fuori ordini, &c.

17. *Moreover, Orders ſhall be iſſued out by his Highneſs, wherein there ſhall be ſufficient proviſions made againſt all diſturbances, inconveniences, or plots of malignant ſpirits, to the end that the abovenamed may peaceably and quietly enjoy their own Religion.*

18. Per oſſervanza di tutte le predette coſe, &c.

18. *For the obſervance of all the premiſſes, and that no inconvenience may ariſe about the performance and execution of the abovewritten Articles,* Georgio Moneſtieri *of* Angrogna, *ſent by the ſaid Valleys, and Sindicus of* S. Conſtance, *and of* Ateſzani ; *and* Rambaudo *Sindicus of* Bobio ; Michele Remondett, *ſent by the Communalty of* Tagliaret, *and a* Rua di Bonetti *unto* La Torre ; Giovanni Mala-notte, *ſent particularly by thoſe of* S. Jovanni ; Pietro Paſquale, *ſent by the Communalty of the Valley of* S. Martino ; Thomaſſo Romano, *of* S.Germano, *ſent*

fent by the faid Commonalty, and by the whole Valley of Perofa, *do pro-mife for their Commonalties refpectively, that the contents of the above-faid Articles fhall be inviolably obferved ; and in cafe of non-obfervance, they do fubmit to fuch punifhment as it fhall pleafe his Highnefs to inflict on them ; promifing in like manner to caufe this their Engagement to be appro-ved and confirmed* (per capita Domorum) *by their faid Commonalties.*

L' Illuftriff. Monfig. di Raconigi, promette, &c.

The moft Illuftrious Lord of Raconigi *doth promife that his Highnefs fhall ratifie and approve the abovewritten Articles to the underwritten, in particular, and in general, granted by the interceffion of the moft ferene* Madama, *as a pure act of her fpecial grace : In witnefs whereof the fore-faid Lord hath fubfcribed thefe prefents with his own hand ; and the Mi-niflers, in the name of all the aforefaid Commonalties, have underwritten their names* in quor. fid. *this Fifth of* June, 1561.

Phillippo di Savoya.

Francifco Valle, *Minifter of* Villaro *in* Lucerna.
Claudius Bergio, *Minifter of* Tagliaretto.
Georgio Moneftierii *of* Angrogna.
Michele Raymondetti *of* Tagliaretto.

But in the year **1565.** another Edict, bearing date the Tenth of *June*, was publifhed, at the importunate requeft of the *Popifh* party, whereby all men who lived within the *Duke* of *Savoy's* Dominions, and would not conform to the *Romifh* Religion, were enjoyned to come and declare the fame to the refpective Magiftrates of their feveral habitati-ons, within ten days after the publication thereof, and two moneths af-ter to leave the Countrey, having one years time given them to difpofe of their goods moveable and unmoveable ; during which time they fhould enjoy the revenue thereof: And as for the Magiftrates, they were commanded to watch and obferve diligently, who they were that were ftubborn and refractory, and having fo done, to fend up their informa-tions to his Highnefs, that fo they might be proceeded againft accord-ing to his will and pleafure.

Now the news and tidings of this cruelty fo wrought upon the hearts of the Proteftant Princes of *Germany*, that they fent an Embaffie to his Highnefs of *Savoy*, to intercede in their behalf. Among whom, the Prince Elector Palatine was exceeding zealous ; and, at the return of one *John Junius*, one of his ancient Councellours of State, and a per-fon of fingular worth, whom he had fent in the quality of his Ambaffa-dor to the Duke of *Savoy* meerly upon that account, having heard the faid *Junius* his report of the moft unworthy and unhandfome dealings of that Court, and finding, notwithftanding all their fair and golden promifes which they had made to his Ambaffador, that they did not at all ceafe to perfecute and moleft the poor people, he wrote a very fmart and fignificant Letter to the faid Duke, which indeed is fit to be com-municated to pofterity.   Article 5.

ARTICLE V.

A Copy of a Notable Letter, Written by the *Prince
Elector Palatine* to the Duke of *Savoy,* in favour
of the *Evangelical* Churches of the Valleys of *Piemont.* 1566.

I Received with great contentment and satisfaction, (*my most dear Cousin*) the report which my Junius had made me of your good affection towards me, and your great civility towards him, which you had likewise
given an ample testimony of, by your promise to deliver and set at large for
my sake, and the sake of the other Protestant Princes, those that were imprisoned, and in the Galleys, upon the account of their Religion. But this
my contentment has been somewhat intermingled with grief and trouble, by
that Act of the Senate of Savoy, who have taken the boldness to diminish
that benefit, which you had granted to me and to the other Protestant Princes, by condemning to perpetual exile those nine poor innocent souls, who
were detained prisoners at Cambery, as guilty of Sedition, and Treason :
For, I my self am not such a one, as had I once granted Y. H. any kindness,
would ever have permitted any of mine to have made the least diminution of
my Liberality, but would much rather have inlarged the same (as is both
usual and ought to be in the Acts of Princes.) But now I do not onely esteem
the above-mentioned persons to be altogether innocent of the crimes laid to
their charge, but its a thing whereof I am fully perswaded. For, by the Letters signed by Y. H. own hands, and the hands of your Chancellour and Secretary, and sealed with the Seals both of the one and the other, I perceive that it is undoubtedly so. For by the said Letters, they are so far from
being accus'd, that they are excused, and justified from having in the least
conspired against your Highness, That if they would but have received those
Letters, they had long since been set at liberty. But they could not consent
thereto with a good conscience, forasmuch as your Highness required of them
such conditions as would have obliged them to have followed for the
time to come, the Customes, and Superstitions of the Church of Rome,
which truly is a matter no less grievous either to them, or any other of Gods
faithfull ones, then if you should press them to renounce Jesus Christ himself ! Whereupon I easily judge, that it is by the perswasion of the Pope and
his Counsellors, that your Highness accuses them of Sedition, having sufficient ground to believe that they are so transported with hatred, and furious passion against Our Religion, that they invent and search out all occasions imaginable, right or wrong, to add affliction to the Misery of those
poor creatures, who notwithstanding desire nothing more, then to yeeld all
manner of obedience and fidelity to your Highness, provided, they be not
constrained in matters of Religion, to make a breach upon their consciences.
And this I easily perceived (though to my great trouble) by your Highness
last

last Letters, which, the very truth is, I could not read without sadness, and I profess to you seriously and sincerely, that this manner of proceeding against those poor creatures, doth exceedingly grieve me. For, to whom is it (I beseech you) that they should have delivered up those Fortresses which your Highness writes they would have betrayed? was it to the King of France? He's your Kinsman and Ally, who would never have undertaken any such enterprize against your Highness, but on the contrary severely chastized the Authors of such a suggestion. I dare affirm the like of Spain. To whom was it then they should have delivered them? was it to them of Geneva? I cannot perswade my self that they ever had such a thought or imagination. Would they have kept it for themselves? every man sees that a meer impossibility. Wherefore if your Highness consider and weigh well this matter, you will easily see, that these are impudent calumnies forged by their adversaries. And I easily see whither the designs of your Highness Councellors and Officers tend, namely, to drag those poor people to prison, and there to constrain them by torments to confess some treason, that so they may have at least a colour and pretext to destroy all the Churches of the Valleys as seditious, and to condemn them as disturbers of the publick Peace. But let your Highness know, that there is a God in Heaven, who not onely beholds and sees the actions, but also tries the hearts and the reins of men, and to whom all things are naked and open. Let your Highness beware of a wilfull fighting against God, and of persecuting Christ in his members; for although he may bear it for a while, to try the patience of his Saints, he will notwithstanding in the end chastise the Persecutors of his Church and People with horrible punishments. Let not your Highness suffer your self to be abused by the perswasions of the Papists, who possibly may promise you the Kingdome of Heaven, and eternal life, as a reward, in case you banish, imprison, and exterminate those Hugonots (so they stile the good Christians) be it by what means or instruments soever. For certainly, cruelties, inhumane actions, and calumnies are not the High-way to the Kingdome of Heaven; no, there must some other way be found out : Nay, your Highness may easily see what success the last Forty years of Persecution have had! You may see what the fires, swords, gibbets, prisons, tortures, and banishments have advantaged those who call themselves Catholiques, either in Germany, England, France, or Scotland! No, there's no need in matters of Religion, of the power, or authority, or severity of Men, as the Histories both of the Jews and Primitive Church, sufficiently witness; where we find that those who have afflicted, banished, and delivered up to death the Christians, have been so far from having gained any thing thereby, that on the contrary, they have encreased their number, insomuch that it hath begotten a Proverb among the Christians, that The ashes of the Martyrs are the seed of the Christian Church. The Church resembles in this the Palm-tree, which raiseth it self up the more it is depressed; which your Highness may easily observe, if you please but to open your eys; yea, I intreat you to understand, and consider, that Christian Religion may be perswaded, but not forced. And that it is a real truth, that Religion is no other then a firm, and setled perswasion of God, and of his will, revealed in his word, and imprinted in the spirits

of

of men by the Holy Spirit, which having once taken root, cannot easily be loosened or plucked up by any torments, or tortures ; and such men will sooner endure the worst that can befal them, then receive or embrace any thing, which they apprehend contrary to Religion and Godliness.   Wherefore it were very good and wholsome counsel, that every one would endeavour to deliver that Religion, which they call Ancient (but indeed is but of yesterday, in comparison of that of Christ and his Apostles) from so much Idolatry, abuse, and superstitions introduced and foisted into the Church, by the ambition, avarice, and negligence of the Roman Bishops and Clergy ; As likewise to lend their helping hand, for the restoring of Religion to its primitive estate and lustre, rather then to persecute with fire and sword, with tortures and banishments, those who will not defile themselves with such Idolatries and superstitions ; and to grant the liberty of serving God in truth, according to his word, and to call upon his name in sincerity, rather then constrain men to observe humane Inventions and Decrees, obtruding the same upon their fancies, instead of the true word and worship of God.   For, by the grace of God, the Evangelical truth is now in such splendour, that the errours and deceits of the Bishop of Rome, and all his Clergy, are sufficiently known in a manner by all men ; neither must the Pope think henceforth to abuse the world, as he hath done in former Ages.   Wherefore I intreat your Highness, whom I understand to be of a sweet and gentle nature and disposition, that you would consider and lay to heart these things, and not further molest those poor people for the sake of their Religion, nor refuse them the free exercise thereof, but rather that you would please to grant them the liberty of assembling in publick for the service and worship of God, whereby you will easily discover the falsity of their Enemies Accusations, and have an evident proof of their loyalty and obedience.   And this will be the true way and means to establish the peace and tranquillity of your Highness Dominions.   Peradventure your Highness fears to draw upon your self some damage or inconvenience thereby, but you must also have a due regard to a greater and more considerable danger, which now hangs over your head, and rather apply the remedy to the present evil, then purpose to apply preventing Physick against future Distempers ; for those are uncertain, and in the hands of God, but these are certain, and near at the door.   Your Highness hath seen and known, what evils and mischiefs have been brought upon France, through those their violences, banishments, and cruel persecutions, what combustions and flames, which have in a manner consumed the whole Kingdome, and what ruines have followed thereupon, which notwithstanding have all been appeased by one onely Edict, granting Liberty of Conscience, and that now they live in peace and tranquillity amongst themselves, although they profess divers Religions.   And out of that singular love which we have for your Highness, we are afraid on your behalf, lest the like evils and mischiefs should befal your Dominions.   And the plain truth is, if your Highness out of compliance with the Bishop of Rome, the Cardinals, the Prelates, and others who are interessed in the Roman Religion, be resolved still to continue to persecute those poor people, there is no question, but you must find and feel the same evils and mischiefs which other Nations
have

have found and felt, to their great damage, and difadvantage. For, no violent thing is of long continuance, *and* we muft not always follow the Wolf into the Wood ; *and its juftly to be feared, left Patience being fo oft vexed and provoked, become Fury, and that the evil and mifchief thereof redound to the Publick.* Poverty and Hunger are no fmall torments, nor is't an eafie thing to lead fo long and miferable a life in exile, being rob'd of all our Goods and Eftates. 'Tis the higheft of injuftice and mifery, to be conftrained to fubmit to the yoke and tyranny of the Bifhop of *Rome,* and be prohibited from worfhipping God according to his Word. Yea, 'tis altogether infupportable for good and faithfull Subjects, to be accufed as Rebels and feditious perfons.

Your Highnefs ought much rather to confider thefe things, than lend an ear to thofe who are byaffed by their paffions, and who are fworn enemies of the truth, and true Evangelical *doctrine, compaffing their own ends under the pretext and covert of the* Roman *Religion : Neither ought your Highnefs to confent to thofe paffions and furies which are fo implacably bent againft the Gofpel-worfhip.*

Now for the better applying a fpeedy remedy to all thefe evils, your Highnefs cannot think ever to find out one more proper (without offering vi.lence to your own natural clemency and gentlenefs) than to promife your poor Subjects (which is the onely thing they requeft at your hands) the free exercife of their Religion, forafmuch as this is efteemed the onely true way to avoid thofe dangers and miferits which have befallen France, *and other parts, upon this account, and may well befall your Countrey, if they proceed as they have begun, forafmuch as this is the true means to retain your Subjects in their due obedience, and ready execution of your commands.*

But it may be your Highnefs will tell me, That there's no enduring two Religions under the fame Prince, *and in the fame Countrey, objecting to me that common Proverb,* One Law, one Faith, one King. *This truly were a thing very defirable, but fince that the true Religion and Faith is the gift of God, infufed and engraven in the hearts of men, which (as I have already faid) no man can extinguifh but God alone, thofe men are extreamly inconfiderate, who think it a bufinefs of necefity, that every individual of a Country (or that the whole* Chriftian *world) fhould be brought to be of the fame Religion, by force of Arms, or perfecutions : Poffibly it might be fo, if Religion were founded upon the Authority and good will of men ; yet that would not be a Religion, but rather Hypocrifie and diffimulation: For the true Religion having God for its Author, it cannot be effected by any force or reafon, that thofe who have received this perfwafion of God, fhould ever fuffer themfelves in the leaft to be drawn afide from it.* Nay, it hath neven been feen fince the beginning of the world, that all were of the fame Religion, exactly agreeing in their Cuftomes and Ceremonies, as it appears in the Family of our Firft Father. And fo before the coming of* Chrift, in the Kingdomes of the* Egyptians, Affyrians, Chaldeans, Medes, and Perfians, *in the adminiftrations whereof, thofe Kings and Lords were conftrained to countenance the* Jews *in their Kingdomes, with the exercife of their Religion, although they abominated the fame in*

their

their hearts. After the coming of Chrift, *the* Roman *Emperours, after they had in divers manners perfecuted the* Chriftians, *and charged them with all forts of Calumnies, neverthelefs feeing that their number always increafed, and that they could not finde Hangmen enough to torment them, were fain to permit them in the Empire (as Hiftories bear witnefs) granting them the free exercife of their Religion, and (which was more) allowing them their Temples, as is reported of* Alexander Severus, *who permitted the fame at* Rome ; *yea, and the fame was done by divers others, who prohibited their Subjects to injure or calumniate the* Chriftians, *although they did in no wife approve their Religion, but detefted from their very hearts the Name of* Chrift. *In like manner, among the Pagans, how great muft needs be the diverfity of their Religion, in that fome knew not the Names of the Gods of others? Was not the* Roman Empire *thereby troubled and divided? Are there not at this day under the* Turks Dominions Jews, Perfians, Mahometans, *and* Chriftians, *which are all of divers Religions, and exceeding contrary one to another? and yet notwithftanding we fee how it is grown up and increafed. Now if Diverfity of Religion be the Caufe of Seditions and Tumults, furely the Empire of the* Turks *would not be fo much greatned , to the mifchief and detriment of the* Chriftian *World. Your Highnefs fees the Eftate of* Germany, France, Polonia, Scotland, Switzerland, *and other Countreys, where are found both the one and the other Religion, yet notwithftanding they live in fweet peace and tranquillity. Wherefore your Highnefs ought not to fear, that the fuffering or permitting the Profeffion of the Reformed Religion in your Countrey will beget Seditions and Tumults. Nay, you ought rather to fear the event of a contrary proceeding! And this I fay, as one that is defirous your Highnefs fhould follow good counfel, and who fhould be very forry that any Inconvenience fhould befall you upon this account. But I intreat your Highnefs not to refift God, who hath decreed to plant his Gofpel in your Countrey, and that you would pleafe to fet before your Eys the Examples of thofe who ftrove to hinder the courfe of the Gofpel in its infancie, and the Evils they brought upon their Heads thereby, and to follow the counfel of* Gamaliel. *Let your Highnefs fee and confider what has been done for the Faithfull and thofe that fear God,* for if this Counfel were of Men, it would not ftand, it would certainly have been diffolved of it felf, and been extinguifht long ago : but God being the Authour, it cannot be abolifhed or diffolved by any Torments or Perfecutions whatfoever. Let not your Highnefs think it a fit thing to refift or fight againft God, for, he will be Conquerour, however it be. Let me intreat this one thing of your Highnefs, (for as much as your Magiftrates cannot diffemble, or hide the hatred they bear to the Faithfull, upon the account of their Religion, in oppreffing thofe poor People by all ways imaginable, loading them with Crimes of Rebellion, and Sedition, meerly for affembling themfelves with no other intention than to pray to God in fincerity, and to hear or read his Word, or if they hear Sermons out of your Highnefs Territories , and fo provoke your Highnefs againft them) *that you would not permit them to take cognizance of matters of Religion, but referve the fame rather to your felf alone. For,*

by

by this means you would eafily know, that thofe men are not fuch as they are reprefented to your Highnefs. For, this is a perpetual occafion of all Tumults, (if we confider well both facred and profane Hiftories) when the Governours of Provinces, and their Officers give themfelves Libertie (though contrary to the Decrees of Princes) to handle poor People at their pleafure, meerly to fatisfie private mens pafsions, to the great prejudice of the publick peace and tranquillitie. Let it then pleafe your Highnefs to reprefs the pafsions and perverfe zeal of fuch kinde of people.

As to what remains, I underftand, (and not without grief) that there is in a manner nothing obferved, that your Highnefs promifed my Junius with your own Mouth, and that thofe poor Wretches, who were kept in the Galleys, upon the account of their Religion, (whofe Names he had delivered into your Highnefs) are yet detained, which makes me eafily fee, that thefe are the actions of your Highnefs Counfellours, who are tranfported with a deadly hatred againft our Religion; which I have not onely by hear-fay, but have experienced the fame in the Example of two, who have been driven away by Banifhment. But this feverity *(to fay no more)* is well pleafing neither to God nor Man, neither is it the way to bring Men to the true knowledg of God, but it muft be done by Perfwafions and Scripture-proofs, not by Perfecutions. Your Highnefs will (it may be) reply, that our Religion hath been a long time condemned; but by whom? and how? by him who hath violated and corrupted all as well divine as humane Rights, making himfelf both Party and Judg, and hath lately confirmed at the Council of *Trent* all his Idolatries, Superftitions, and Abufes introduced into the Church. But let your Highnefs reade and examine the holy Scriptures, and fearch the Truth, and you fhall find it to be fo. Never fuffer your felf to be deluded by thofe Deceivers, which do not uphold their Idolatries and Superftitions upon any other account, than to ferve their Bellies, and that they may lead the Lives of Epicures. Let your Highnefs confider, that you muft one day appear befor the Tribunal of *Chrift*, to give an account of the Souls of your Subjects, where, I thought fo, or I efteemed it to be fo, will not ferve the turn. For, God hath revealed his will in his Word, and willeth that we follow the fame without turning either to the right hand or to the left. Now the Word of God is clear and plain; let but your Highnefs hear and embrace it, and you will eafily finde out the whole Truth. I fay all this, as one defirous of the good of your Highnefs Soul, to whom I heartily wifh as well as to mine own felf, and beg of the Lord inceffantly, that he will pleafe to enlighten your underftanding, and to call you home to his true Light, that you may difcern Truth from Falfhood; and fo having a knowledg of the horrible Abufes of the Church of *Rome*, you may ferve God in truth and fincerity. *Wherefore I pray your Highnefs, that you will give us a Token and Evidence of that Efteem which you have for us, by delivering thofe poor People who are now in the Galleys, and by recalling thofe who have been lately banifhed by the Senate of Savoy, as you promifed my Junius, and my felf, by your Letters. Have compafsion upon fo many poor wandring Exiles, deprived of all their Goods and Eftates! Call them*

home

home, and restore them to their Houses and Habitations, and grant both them and the other Inhabitants of your Highness Countreys the publick exercise of their Religion, which they account to be more necessary *than their daily* Food ! *Absolve those poor People of the Valleys falsly accused, that so all of them may live in peace and tranquillity under your Highness Government ! Make such Articles of Peace with them, as may be conserved without alteration ! Preserve them in peace and quiet in the exercise of that Religion which you have permitted unto them, and be their Defence, bridling and restraining the bitter hatred, which their Governour* Castroca- ro *exerciseth against them, warning him to molest them no more for the future, as he hath done hitherto, and enjoyning him to refrain from imposing on them false Crimes and Accusations, whereby he pretends to colour his Tyrannie, for, such things are not at all convenient for a Magistrate and Governour, who ought to be a Father unto those who are committed to his Charge.* If your Highness please to grant me those things which I now desire of you with so much affection and earnestness, I doubt not but you will experimentally finde the favour and blessing of God, and you shall have us ready to oblige you in all things; if not, you will both provoke God to lift up his Hand against you, and also estrange from you the affection and courage of all those who desire to do you pleasure and service. Let then your Highness more esteem the favour of God, and the good will of Princes, than the Promises of the Pope and his Creatures. Do not render your self as an Instrument of their insatiable Desires, to spill the Bloud of *Christians* ! Countenance not their Cruelty and Inhumanity against those who are in no wise perverse, but real *Christians*; who desire nothing more than to serve God purely and sincerely under your Highness Government, and to pay all manner of obedience and fidelity which is due unto you, and to imploy and lay out themselves wholly (their Goods, Bodies, and Lives, if need require) for your service. Let it please you then to have compassion on them, and you will always finde them the more faithfull and obedient; and in so doing you will do that which will be most acceptable to God, and oblige to your self for ever those poor Creatures, and finde us always more ready, with all that we have to do you any pleasure upon all occasions. Wherefore I intreat your Highness, that you would please to lend an Ear to these our Requests, and in the end you will abundantly know, that we have sought after nothing so much as your own advantage, and the tranquillity of your Dominions. *The great and All-powerfull God, guide and govern by his Holy Spirit your Highness, and keep and defend you long in health and safetie.*

Dated and signed thus in the Original,

Augustæ Vindelicorum 1566. V. D. Consanguineus Palatinus Elector.

A R-

ARTICLE VI.

Now for a more particular knowledg of the Reason why the *Elector Palatine* made such heavy Complaints in this his Letter, as touching the *non*-observance of what his Ambassadour had been promised, it is to be observed, that *Castrocaro* being extremely troubled that the said Ambassadour had obtained several Promises at Court, for the poor Peoples advantage, did immediately after his Departure cause to be published throughout the Valley of *Lucerna* two Ordinances, one of which bare Date the one and twentieth of *April*, 1566. whereby he commanded all the Inhabitants throughout his Government that were not Natives, to depart within a Day after the publication thereof, upon pain of Death, and Confiscation of their Goods. By the other Ordinance, he prohibited upon the same penalty those of the Reformed Religion, inhabiting *Lucerna, Bubbiana, Campiglione,* and *Fenile,* to hear Sermons at *St. Giovanni.* And for as much as the poor People, having been permitted to have their publick Meetings there, by a formal Capitulation with his Highness in the Year 1561. were not thereby discouraged from continuing their wonted Exercises, *Castrocaro* imprisoned and tormented a great number of them in the Castle of *La Torre;* hereupon the poor People made their Address to the Dutchess, who had pity on them, and wrote a Letter to the said *Castrocaro* in their behalf, commanding him in the Duke's Name, to *set at Liberty the Imprisoned, and to cease to molest them in the enjoyment of their ancient Habitations and Privileges.*

This Letter of the Dutchess did indeed for that time put a Bridle to the Fury of that *Castrocaro,* though it was far from working any change in his spirit or Principles, as is too evident by his after-actions and rude behaviour towards them, especially in the Year 1571. at which time he did so incense the Governour of *Bobio* against the poor Inhabitants of the Valley, that he did not onely grievously molest them upon all occasions as they came under his Clutches, but likewise wrote bitter Letters to his Highness against them, and improved the best of his parts and power to ruine & extirpate them. And certainly *Castrocaro* had brought his Designs to their desired Issue, had not the Dutchess then upon the joint Supplications and Requests of all the Evangelical Churches, very effectually interposed for them, and procured the continuation of their just and undoubted Rights and Privileges.

Here, by the way the *Christian* Reader may be pleased to take notice of the great Blessing from Heaven upon that sweet Harmony and Unity that was at that time amongst those Evangelical Churches, which always (but now more especially) appeared by their constant fellow feeling of one anothers Miseries and Sufferings, and their marvellous readiness to minister to each others Necessities, even to the hazard oft times of both their Estates and Lives. The truth is, besides many

Leagues

Leagues of Amity and *Chriftian* Unity, which had been before this time eftablifhed, and punctually obferved amongft thofe People, they did upon occafion of this Recourfe to the Duke, in a more formal way and manner, ftrike a League amongft themfelves, figning an Agreement, the fubftance whereof is contained in the following Articles.

An

An Extract of a League or Agreement made between the Evangelical Churches of the Valleys of *Piemont*, in the Year 1571. for the mutual affiftance of each other in Times of Trouble and Perfecution.

1. *We promife by an Oath, to perfift inviolably in that ancient Union, that hath been continued from Father to Son, amongft the Faithfull of the Evangelical Churches of the Valleys, unto our Times; and not to depart from it upon any condition whatfoever, according to the following Conditions and Promifes.*

2. *To continue all in the Profefsion of the true* Chriftian *Reformed Religion, which we have to this day embraced, which Religion confifteth in the believing in, and worfhipping one onely true God, and one onely Head of the Church, and Mediatour between God and Man,* Chrift Jefus; *and in the onely Rule of believing and living well, which is contained in the Canonical Books of the* Old *and* New Teftament, *together with the two Sacraments inftituted by our Lord and Saviour* Jefus Chrift, *namely,* Baptifm *and the Lords Supper. Promifing according to the Word, to yield obedience to all exteriour Order and Difcipline, already eftablifhed, and heretofore obferved among us. And detefting all Herefies, and falfe Doctrines which are contrary to this Word of God contained in the Books of the* Old *and* New Teftament.

3. *Item, we promife to be faithfull and obedient to his S. Highnefs, and to thofe Magiftrates, who fhall by him be conftituted to govern, and bear rule over us, in all that either humane or divine Laws fhall oblige us to, according to the Word of God.*

4. *Item, for as much as there is always fome or other who, contrary to the Capitulations and Concefsions granted them by the clemency of his Highnefs through the Intercefsion of Madam the Dutchefs, endeavour to trouble the Peace of their Churches, and the Members thereof, and to infringe their Concefsions, we all promife to ufe our utmoft power and intereft upon all occafions, as it fhall be judged neceffary, for the maintaining all the faid Churches in general, and each Member in particular, in the enjoyment of the faid Concefsions, as well by having conftant recourfe to his Highnefs for fo long a time as fhall be thought requifite; as by all other lawfull ways and means, juftifiable by the Word of God upon fuch occafions, and all the Churches in general fhall undertake all the lawfull Protection and Defence (fo far as it may concern them) of each Church, and every particular perfon and member of the fame, who fhall be molefted for the Caufe of Religion, by contributing their counfel, goods, and perfons, if there be occafion.*

5. Item,

5. Item, *that as in thofe Requefts which are made in matters of Religion and their Dependencies, or may be made by the Churches in general, all the faid Churches fhall unanimoufly anfwer, and give Confent as it were with one Mouth ; fo, if any Church in particular chance to be molefted concerning any matter of Religion, or their Concefsions, no particular Church fhall undertake to give any Anfwer, without having taken a fufficient term of time to communicate with all the reft of the Churches, and Members of this Union, to take counfel as concerning a common Intereft, to anfwer and act by common confent and advice, with all modefty, candour, and fincerity, fuitable to good* Chriftians, *according to the Dictates of a good confcience, and for mutual edification.*

6. *Finally, we do all and every one voluntarily fubmit, in cafe any one come to fail in any one of thefe premifes (which God forbid) againft the Declaration of this Union, to a Cenfure, nay Correction and Ecclefiaftical Difcipline, and to be accounted by the reft of the Body of the Union for Schifmaticks, and perjured perfons, if the Fault require fo fevere a Punifhment, and that without any exception of perfons ; and fo we all promife with our Hands lifted up to the Almighty God, Father, Son, and Holy Spirit.*

Made and ratified the 11. *day of* Novemb.1571.

In this very Year many of the poor Proteftants of the Valleys were grievoufly molefted, under pretext, that in the former War of *France* againft thofe of the Religion, they joyned themfelves to the Proteftant Troops. But *Charls* the ninth being moved with compaffion towards them, wrote a Letter to the Duke of *Savoy* in their behalf, as followeth.

A Letter of *Charls* the ninth to the Duke of *Savoy*, in the behalf of the poor Proteftants, *Anno Dom.* 1571.

Mon Oncle, Je m' affeure que la feverite dont vous avez ufe, &c.

My Uncle,

I affure my felf, the feverity you have ufed towards your Subjects, who are of the Reformed Religion, and have followed thofe People of mine, who (as was pretended) took up Arms againft me, during the late Troubles, was onely through the regret and difpleafure you had, to fee them undertake a thing, which you judged offenfive to me, and not at all any offence they had committed againft you ; wherein I cannot but commend your good Intentions on my behalf, but fince that you know that I have on my part cleared my felf of all manner of difcontent, and accommodated their affairs one a-
mongft

mongſt another, and eſtabliſhed every one in his Right, whereof he might
have been deprived upon the occaſion of thoſe Troubles, (during the which,
paſsion did as much diſtemper the Patient as the Diſeaſe it ſelf) I ſhall now
make one Requeſt to you, not an ordinary one, but one as affectionate as
I am able to make you, which is, that as out of love to me, you have treated
your Subjects in an extraordinary manner upon this occaſion, you would alſo
upon my account, entreaty, and eſpecial recommendation, receive them with
gentleneſs into your grace and favour, and re-eſtabliſh them in their
Eſtates, which have been confiſcated upon this occaſion ; and give me this
contentment, that I may let mine own Subjects underſtand, that I ſhall not
onely accompliſh and obſerve what I have promiſed and ſworn to them in an
Edict of mine, but alſo out of the ſame love wherewith I have embraced
them, I deſire to do for thoſe which have been the occaſion of affliction to
my Friends on their behalf, that ſo they may reſent that favour, grace, and
protection which I ſhall ſhew unto them. This Cauſe is ſo juſt in it ſelf,
and ſo full of affection on my part, that from the aſſurance you will willing-
ly grant the effects, I ſhall not make more preſsing inſtances, but pray God,
my Uncle, that he would have you in his protection.

Given at Blois *the* 28. *of* Septemb. 1572.

Your good Nephew
CHARLS.

    The ſubject and expreſſions of this Letter were not onely ſatisfa-
ctory to thoſe, for whom it interceded, but alſo to all other faithfull
ones of the Valleys, and neighbouring parts, out of the great hopes
they had of a future tranquillity ; but this dured no longer than till
their Enemies had an opportunity of moleſting them, which they very
greedily embraced, upon the News of the horrible Maſſacres in
France ; for *Caſtrocaro* did thereupon ſo threaten the poor Proteſtants,
under his Juriſdiction, that they retired themſelves, with their Families and Moveables to the tops of the neighbouring Mountains, and
all other places where they hoped to be moſt ſecure. But the Duke of
Savoy ſeeming not at all to approve of the Cruelties exerciſed againſt
the Proteſtants in *France*, ſent to thoſe his Subjects who were thus
withdrawn, to command them to return to their Houſes and Habitations, reſting upon his word, that they ſhould ſuffer no prejudice, or
incur the leaſt Danger thereby : neither indeed were their Sufferings
very great from that time forward, ſo long as Madam the Dutcheſs was
living, (whom all Hiſtorians have recommended to poſterity, for one
of the moſt prudent, moderate, and charitable Princeſſes of her Age)
for as much as ſhe was always the Sanctuary and Refuge of thoſe poor
Evangelical Churches, when ever they found themſelves oppreſſed by
their Adverſaries.

    After the Death of this Princeſs (which happened the nineteenth of
October, 1574.) the Popiſh party came forth like Lions out of their
Dens, and were not wanting in their Endeavours to devour and de-
ſtroy

ftroy the poor People upon all occafions, but the goodnefs of God was fo great towards them that they conftantly found very confiderable Friends to ftand in the Gap, and to incline the heart of the Duke who then reigned, to much gentlenefs and moderation. However, after the Death of *Philibert Emanuel,* which happened upon the thirtieth of *Auguft,* 1580. *Charls Emanuel* his Son having invaded the Marquifate of *Salufes,* and *Monfieur de l' Efdiguieres* feifed by way of Retaliation, upon the Valleys of *Piemont,* the *French* Army was no fooner gone home, but there was a great Rumour fpread throughout the Valleys, that the Duke was refolved to take this occafion to extirpate all the Proteftants Churches, becaufe they had taken an Oath of Fidelity to the King of *France* ; neither was it altogether without ground, for the thing was really propofed in the Dukes Councel, but it pleafed God fo to order Affairs, that the chief leading Men amongft them did not at all approve the Bufinefs, yea, the Duke himfelf did extremely diflike it, and after he had retaken *Mirebouc,* did not a little revive the fpirits of the Reprefentatives of the Proteftants of *Lucerna,* who met him at *Villaro,* on purpofe to affure his Highnefs of their Loyalty and Fidelity, and to beg the continuance of his Grace and Favour ; (and that in the prefence of a great number of Lords and Courtiers) in the following terms, *Be but faithfull to me, and I fhall be fure to be a good Prince, nay a Father unto you ; and as to the Liberty of your Confciences and the Exercifes of your Religion, I fhall be fo far from innovating any thing againft thofe Liberties in which you have lived unto this prefent, that if any offer to moleft you, have your recourfe to me, and I fhall effectually relieve and protect you.*

Thefe words being fpoken in the prefence of fo many confiderable perfons, and in fo obliging a manner, were exceeding advantageous to the poor Peoples Intereft, not onely for the prefent, but alfo for fome time after, they often ferving to counterbalance the Threats of their fierceft Enemies. However, neither did their rememberance of this laft always, for, there were thofe among the Popifh party there, who thought it an unpardonable fin, to fuffer them to have one years refpit, and on the contrary a confiderable fervice, to difturb and moleft them, fometimes by fecret ftratagems, other times by open force and violence.

This was now the condition of thefe poor People from the Year **1595.** to the Year **1602.** at which time all the Mafters of Families in the Valley of *Lucerna,* profeffing the Proteftant Religion, were cited to appear before the *Seigneur Comte Charles de Lucerna,* the Governour *Ponte,* the Arch-bifhop *Broglia,* and feveral others, and by them commanded in the Dukes Name, either to go to Mafs, or to quit *Lucerna,* and all their pretenfions there, without the leaft hopes in the world of ever obtaining leave to return, as likewife (in cafe of difobedience to the faid Order) to prepare themfelves for inevitable Mifchiefs and Calamities. And thefe their Threats were by them preffed fo home, that it caufed many of the poor Creatures to fubmit to (at leaft) a feeming change of their Religion, though many others of them did rather take

the

the deeper rooting by being thus ſhaken. From *Lucerna*, the Lords above mentioned, ſoon after removed their Seat to *Bubiana*, where they found the Reformed ſo ſtiff in their Principles, that they were not able to move them an hairs breadth, wherefore they cauſed the chief of them to be ſummoned to appear at *Turin* before his Highneſs, thinking that the Dukes preſence might better prevail upon them than all their threatning Speeches. Thoſe who were thus ſummoned were Mr. *Valantine*, and *Matthew Boules* his Brother, with one *Pietro Mareſc*, and *Samuel Falc*, who were brought in diſtinctly, one after another before his Highneſs; the firſt was Mr. *Valantine*, to whom the Duke ſpake after this manner, *That his deſire being to ſee all his Subjects profeſs the ſame Religion with him, and knowing alſo how much the ſaid* Valantine *was able to contribute thereunto, becauſe of his great reputation amongſt thoſe of his party, he had ſent for him to exhort him to embrace the Catholick and Apoſtolick* Roman *Religion, which he (who was his Prince) did follow, and afterwards to induce his Proteſtant Neighbours by his Exhortations and Example, to do the ſame; and in ſo doing, beſides the ſpiritual profit he ſhould reap thereby, he ſhould alſo receive ſuch Rewards, that he ſhould know and perceive he had done his Prince no ſmall or inconſiderable ſervice.* To this Mr. *Valantine* anſwered, *That he did intreat his Highneſs to aſſure himſelf, that next to the Service of God, he had no greater deſire than to obey and pleaſe his Highneſs, in whoſe ſervice he would willingly imploy and venture his perſon and his Goods (according to his duty) when ever there ſhould be any occaſion. But as for his Religion, which he knew to be true, and eſtabliſhed by the Word of God himſelf, he could not abandon it, without diſobeying God, and wounding his Conſcience in ſuch ſort, that he could never enjoy any comfort in his ſoul afterwards. And therefore he humbly intreated his Highneſs to be ſatisfied with ſuch things as he could do with a good Conſcience, and ſo leave him in the libertie of his Religion, which he did value above his own Life.* Whereupon the Duke replied, *That he alſo was carefull for his own Soul, and that he was likewiſe perſwaded, that his Religion was the true Religion, otherwiſe he would neither follow it, nor induce any other to embrace the ſame.* And withall he added this, *that he would indeed ſhew them, who ſhould embrace it, that they had much gratified him in ſo doing, but would notwithſtanding force the Conſcience of no man,* and thereupon gave him leave to depart, but he was not ſuffered to ſpeak, or have any diſcourſe with the other three, leſt he ſhould ſpoil the Deſign, yea and to colour the Buſineſs the better, it was given out, that the ſaid *Valantine Boule* had engaged to turn Papiſt, which was altogether untrue.

During the Reign of *Charls* Emperour, there paſſed not one year wherein the Monks attempted not, both ſecretly and openly, to undermine the Proteſtant Religion in the Valleys. And although the ſaid Prince, together with *Victor Amedeo* his Son, did always give ſmooth and promiſing words to the Deputies of the Valleys, aſſuring them that they ſhould be maintained in their ancient Privileges and Conceſſions, yet notwithſtanding the Church-men, being ſet on by the Pope, never gave them reſt, but employed all along, both force and

and cunning to ruine and deſtroy them ; and certainly it can be interpreted no other than a ſingular and a wonderfull providence that has
always preſerved thoſe poor and tender Lambs, in the midſt of ſo many ravenous Wolves and Beaſts of Prey. I leave it to the thought and
judgment of the courteous and *Chriſtian* Reader, if any Deſign could
be more bloudy, or uſage more barbarous, than the late Maſſacre ;
and yet God ſuffered not thoſe Wretches altogether to obtain their
ends, but hath to this very day continued a Remnant that call upon
his Name, as ſhall be ſhewn more at large in the ſequel of this Diſcourſe, after I have given him a brief Account of ſome of the moſt
remarkable Troubles that have befallen the poor *Waldenſes* in the Mar-
quiſate of *Saluces,* upon the account of their Religion, which is not at
all beſide our purpoſe.

CHAP.

CHAP. II.

A Description of the Marquisate of Saluces, *with its several Troubles and Perfe-cutions.*

WHat and how great the miseries of the poor *Protestants* have been, not onely in the Valley of *Piemont* proper-ly so called, but also in all the Dominions of the Duke of *Savoy,* where there were any of that profession, We need look no further for a lively proof, then in the neighbouring Country called the *Marquisate of Saluces* ; who so soon as ever they were under the *Dukes* Jurisdiction, had nothing but the *bread of sor-row* given them to eat, and *the Waters of affliction* to drink. True it is, they were divers times molested under the King of *France,* which lasted until the year 1588, but never in the manner as afterwards, and they found by wofull experience that the first did onely *chastise them with whips,* but the last, *with scorpions.*

The Situation of the Marquisate of *Saluces*
The Valley of *Po.*

The *Marquisate* of *Saluces,* is on the South side of the Valleys of *Piemont,* containing in it several Cities, and confiderable Valleys, and plain Countries, extreme fertill in all forts of fruits: Its most Nor-thern Valley is that of *Po* (so called because that famous River *Po* hath its rise and source from thence) one onely Mountain separating it from the Valley of *Lucerna,* on the North side. In this Valley of *Po,* were those ancient Churches of the *Waldenses,* namely *Pravillelm, Biolets,* and *Bietoné,* who there retained the purity of the Christian Religion for several hundreds of years, and lived in great union and Commu-nion with their neighbouring Churches of the fame Profession: The truth is, the Reformed Religion was received in divers parts of this *Marquisate* of *Saluces,* so soon as the same was published and tolerated in other Countries. As for example ; In the year 1561. the Church of *Dronier,* which was always one of the most flourishing, understanding that the publick exercise of the *Reformed Religion* was permitted in *France,* by an Edict of January, Obtained Letters of the Kings Coun-cil to *Sieur Lovis* of *Birague,* Governour of that Country, in the ab-sence of the Duke of *Nevers,* whereby he was ordered to provide for the Petitioners a convenient place for the publick Exercises of their Religion ; But not long after, their Adverfaries by their importunity prevailed so far, that the said Letters were revoked. Whereupon they sent

The Churches of *Pravillelm, Biolets,* and *Bietone.*

The Church of *Dronier.*

sent Deputy into *France*, *Sieur Francois Galatée*, one of their Ministers, together with some others, to recover (if possible) their former Priviledges; But this voyage being made in the time of the first troubles of *France*, (although they had procured the favourable mediations of divers persons of high rank and quality) all that they were able to obtain, was onely bare promises: In the mean time, they received not a few exhortatory and consolatory Letters from many of the chief Ministers of the Churches of *France*, among others from those of *Grenoble* and *Lions*, by name Mr. *Viret* of *Nismes*, and others, who endeavoured by all means to perswade them to patience and perseverance in that truth which they had embraced; The which also the Lord enabled them to do, notwithstanding all the malice and subtilty of their adversaries, who procured the reiteration of former Edicts. And thus their Churches were continued and upheld, therebeing convenient order had for the preaching of the Word, the Administration of the Sacraments, and the exercise of their Discipline, with other sacred Offices; Onely there wanted in several places a liberty of having General Assemblies and publick Sermons.

Now for the better safety and security of their Ministers in the places that were most dangerous, one *Pastor* had the charge of the faithfull in several Cities and Communalties, which rendred their Residence, and their exercises, less visible to their adversaries, Which also appears by the Acts of their *Synodes*, which they held at *Pravillelm*, the second of *June* 1567; and at *Dronier* in the Palace of the Lords of *Montauraux* the 14 of *October* in the year abovesaid. The aforesaid *Sieur Galatée* was Pastour of the faithful of *Saluces*, *Savillan*, *Carmagnole*, *Levaldis*, and *Villefalet*; *Monsieur Second Masseran*, of those of *Verzol*, *Alpeafe*, and *Coftilloles*; *Monsieur Francois Truchi*, Pastour of the Church of *Drodier*; *André Lancianois* of those of *Sainct Damian*, *Palliar*, and *Cartignan*; *Peter Gelido* of *Aceil*; Sieur *Jaques Iloard*, of *St. Michel*, *Pras*, and *Chanues*; Sieur *Francis Soulf*, of *Pravillelm*; Mr. *Bertrand Jordan*, of *Biolets*, and *Bietoné*; and *N. N.* Pastour of the Churches of *Demont*, and *Fefteone*.

Now the Gospel at this time made a very considerable progress, at *Dronier*, *Verzo*, and some other places that were of more note, and a great part of the others likewise had embraced the Religion. The Church of *Aceil*, the highest of the *Val de Mairi*, was extraordinarily peopled, and enjoyed more liberty then the others, by reason of the scituation of the place; But notwithstanding, *Sathan* the Enemy of the Church, and Kingdom of *Jesus*, perceiving such a growth and increase of the Reformed Religion in those places, did not cease to employ all his force and subtilty, to hinder the same: He made use of two instruments especially, namely a number of *Anticodemites*, the Ringleader whereof was *Baronius*, who always bestowed himself at *Valgrane*, and thereabouts, accommodating himself to the time, so that when ever the Church had but the least ease, then he set himself to write strange things, and cry out against the abuse of *Popery*, But in time of persecution, then he usually plaid the hypocrite, and laboured to perswade

Sieur Francis Galatee.

Synods held at *Pravillelm* and at *Dronier* 1567.
Sieur Galatee his charge.
M. *Second* his charge.
M. *Fr.Truchi* his charge.
Andrew Lancianois his charge.
Peter Gelido, *Sieur Jaques Iloard*, & Mr. *Bertrand* their several charges.

The progress of the Gospel at *Dronier*, and other places. The Church of *Aceil*.

The *Anticodemite Baronius*, and his Proselytes, in those places.

swade and draw others to do the same, by which means he had a multitude of followers ; amongst others, a certain Lord of *Valgrane* and *Cervignale*, called *Maximilian de Saluces*, who lent his name to *Baronius* to add more lustre to his Writings against the Ministers, reproaching them and casting in their teeth, that because they would not give way to any dissimulation in their Disciples, they exposed them thereby to great extremities, and to this purpose cited the dissipation of the neighbouring Church of *Caraill*. This Lord had some kind of learning and knowledge of the truth, but to avoid the *bearing of the Cross*, he thought it convenient (with *Baronius*) to play the Hypocrite, and condemn those who any ways gain-sayed the Papists. However the *Sieur Gelido*, Minister of *Aceil*, opposed them both very learnedly, and in lively termes, by several Letters that he wrote unto them ; as likewise did the Sieur *Truchi*, Minister of the Church of *Dronier*, together with other Pastors of the neighbouring places, demonstrating by testimony of the Holy Scriptures, and by the doctrine and practise of the *Primitive* Church, That they ought to do what they did, and had done but what every faithfull soul ought to do ; and that consequently the opinion of *Baronius*, and his Disciples, was very pernicious to the Church in the time of Persecution.

The other instruments which that Arch-enemy of souls made use of in those days, to hinder the progress of the Church of *Christ* in this place, were the *Roman* Clergy, with their cholerick and passionate Proselytes, which would fain have done to these people (if it had been in their power) as their *Brethren in iniquity* had done to their Neighbours in the Dominions of the Duke of *Savoy* ; That is to say, banish, imprison, put them to death, and confiscate the goods of the Protestants ; Forasmuch as the *King* by his Edicts, confirmed to those his Subjects of *Saluces* professing the *Reformed* Religion, a peaceable habitation, without being molested for Conscience or Religion-sake, or questioned for any thing that they did in their private houses ; (provided that they abstained from the publick exercise of their Religion) by which means the Ministers had their opportunities of assembling in small Companies, their Baptizing, Marrying, comforting the sick, and instructing every one in particular ; which was the reason why their adversaries bent their designes chiefly against the Ministers, thinking if they could finde any means to extirpate them, they should easily prevail upon the ignorant people, especially when they should have none to animate or instruct them.

Accordingly they caused to be published an Edict the 19 of *October* 1567, in the name of the Duke of *Nevers*, Lieutenant General of the *King* on this side of the Mountains, by which it was enjoyned to all of the Religion there inhabiting, or otherwise abiding within his Jurisdiction (that were not the Kings natural Subjects) to depart together with their families, three days after the publication of the said Edict, and never to return thither to inhabit, pass, or otherwise to abide, without special safe conduct, upon pain of life and confiscation of goods.

But

The Lord of Valgrane a favourer of Baronius.

The 2. sort of Instruments the Devil used to hinder the progress of the Gospel in the Marquisate of Saluces.

Their designs were chiefly against the Ministry.

Their edict of the 19. Octob. 1567.

But now, forasmuch as the greatest part of the above-named Ministers were not natural Subjects of the *King*, and consequently it was necessary that either they should quit the Marquisate according to the Edict, or else obtain a safe Conduct, or in the last place forfeit the penalty specified as abovesaid, they found themselves in an unhappy *præmunire*; for on the one side they could by no means obtain a safe conduct, because of their Charge, and on the other side they thought themselves obliged in conscience not to abandon their People and Congregations; wherefore striving to abide in their Charges, two of them were imprisoned, namely Sieur *Francois Truchi*, native of *Cental*, and Sieur *Francois Soulf* native of *Cuni*, and were detained in prison at *Salutres* for the space of four years, four months, and some odd days; the poor people not being able by any means to procure their deliverance, notwithstanding their continual solicitations of the Sieur *Ludovic de Birague* their Governour, and others who had undertaken the management of these affairs. However, the Lord always manifested his fatherly care towards these his faithfull Servants, not permitting their Enemies to touch the life of any of them (a thing which was much pressed by their passionate and engaged enemies!) yea by little and little there was obtained for them a more spacious and convenient Prison, than that to which they were at first confined.

Sieur *Francis Truchi* and Sir *Fr. Soulf* imprisoned four years and four months, and odd days.

At length, to procure their full and absolute deliverance, the Churches of the *Marquisate* sent their supplications to the *King*, by the hands of the above-named Minister *Galatée*, with another to accompany him. Who set out the 27 of *July* 1571. and went as far as *Rochel*, to implore the Intercession of the Queen of *Navarre*, as also to intreat the assistance of divers others in several places. Moreover the Great Patrons of the Reformed Religion disputed their cause before the King, And in the end they obtained Letters signed by his own hand, and the hands of his Secretaries *Neufville*, and *Lomenie*, by which was granted to the abovesaid Prisoners their enlargement the 14 of *October* 1571. But the Chancellour *René Birago*, Cousin to the Governour of the *Marquisate*, made such difficulty to signe the same, that they were forced to stay several Months before they could have their expedition, the Chancellour alledging always for a pretext, that before the business could be signed, it was necessary to have a verbal conference with the King, who had then made a Voyage into *Bretagne*; Although the Admiral never ceased solliciting, and assisting continually the said Sieur *Galatée* by his Secretary, or some other of his domestiques. Also, perceiving that he was fain to trot up and down on foot, and so spend and wast himself, he gave him 50 Franks to accommodate himself in his journeys.

At length, the *King* being returned from *Bretagne*, the Chancellour spake with him, and afterwards signed the said Letters, and would needs send them himself to the *Marquisate*, to his Cousin *Birague*, who by vertue of the same, caused the said Prisoners at last to be enlarged and delivered.

A little after the Sieur *Galatée* arrived, being over-joyed, aswell for the

the prosperous succefs, and iffue of his Negotiations and Voyage (although otherwife very long and tedious) as for the great hopes that he promifed himfelf of a profound peace, founded upon the fmooth words and treatments of his Majefty, and upon the Alliance which he had made by the Marriage of his fifter with the King of *Navar,* profeffing the Reformed Religion, touching the particulars whereof he made an ample difcourfe. But this joy for the Peace, and Marriage, dured not in the Valleys, and *Marquifate,* any longer then from the Month of *May* 1572. to the beginning of *September,* at which time there arrived the horrible and lamentable news of I know not how many great perfonages, and others of the Reformed Religion, that were cruelly maffacred in divers places of *France,* to the great aftonifhment of all the faithfull in thofe parts.

The Maffacre in *France,* 1572.

At the fame time there arrived Letters from the *King* to the Governour *Birague,* by which he was ordered to have an eye, that at the arrival of the news of what had happened at *Paris,* thofe of the Reformed Religion fhould make no combuftion ; remitting the reft of his pleafure, to thofe Inftructions which he had fent him by the Bearer thereof ; the contents whereof were, that he was to put to death all the chief of the *Proteftants,* within the limits of his jurifdiction, whofe names he fhould finde in the Role that fhould be prefented him.

This *Birague* having received this command, together with the faid Role or Catalogue, was not a little troubled, and immediatly called his Council together, whom he acquainted with the Kings Orders. Whereupon fome were of opinion that they ought to be executed without any delay ; But others, among whom was the Arch Deacon of *Salutres,* forafmuch as the King in His late Patents, not many Months before, had enlarged the Minifters who were imprifoned, and had likewife Ordered that thofe of the *Reformed* Religion fhould not any ways be molefted for their Confcience fake, but treated as his other Subjects ; as likewife, upon confideration that there had nothing occurred fince that time worthy of fuch a change, and that it was probable that the ground of all this was occafioned by fome falfe report, were of the judgement that it would be fufficient onely to fecure the perfons of fuch as were enrolled, and defer the execution for a while ; And in the mean time to inform the King, That they were perfons of honour, faithfull to His Majefty, living peaceably with their Neighbours, and in fum, fuch as (except the matter of their Religion) were altogether without reproach or blemifh ; Adding this, that in cafe His Majefty were refolved to have them put to death, there would be yet time enough to execute his pleafure and commandment.

This advice was therefore approved of by *Birague,* and accordingly fome were apprehended, and others efcaped, and retired themfelvs under Covert ; And in the mean time he difpatched a Meffenger to the *King,* to inform him as abovefaid, and to know his pleafure concerning the fame : This Meffenger met another at *Lions,* whom the *King* had fent to *Birague* to advertize him, That in cafe his former Order were not already put into execution, he fhould wholly defift from

the

the same, and onely have a special care, that those of the *Religion*, did not make any insurrection within his Government, nor presume to have any publick exercises or meetings.

In the mean time those of the *Reformed* Religion, were not a little terrified, throughout the whole *Marquisate*, having understood how cruelly their Brethren had been massacred in *France*, without distinction of Age, Sex, or quality, whatsoever. Insomuch, that divers of them fled, many Papists likewise had secretly caused to retire the families of their kinred, and neighbours of the *Reformed* Religion, until such time as *Birague* had published the Kings pleasure; after which notwithstanding they returned by little and little : And although their publick exercises were prohibited, yet they very much prized the assurance of their lives, and their goods, besides that they had the liberty of exercising in their private families, as before that time they were often wont to do.

This was now the condition of the *Protestant* Churches of the *Marquisate* of *Saluces*, during the time that it was under the Dominions of the *King* of *France*, which continued until the Year 1588. as abovesaid, at which time His Highness of *Savoy* took the possession, who for a certain season suffered them to enjoy their priviledges in general, But in particular, a certain number of the chief Members of the Church of *Dronier* (one of the most considerable Churches of the whole Province) being cited to *Turin*, were so smoothed by subtil artifices, that one part of them promised to go to *Mass*. And the truth is, this gave a considerable blow to the said Church, which notwithstanding lost not its courage in general, although the great failing of the first abovementioned, occasioned and encouraged their Adversaries the more to attempt them in the same manner, as well by words, as by Letters, among which the following was the most remarkable.

1588.

The Duke of *Savoy's* Letter to the said People, Translated out of the *Italian*.

Turin 27. *March.* **1597.**

Well-beloved Friends, *&c.*

IT being our desire that all our Subjects in the Marquisate *of* Saluces *should live under the obedience of our Mother the Catholique Apostolique Roman Church; And knowing how much our Exhortations have prevailed upon others, and hoping that they will have the same effect upon you, and that you are willing to adhere to the truth; We thought fit upon these grounds to write you this Letter, to the end that laying aside that Heretical obstinacy, you may embrace the true Religion, both out of respect to Gods glory, and love to your own selves; In which Religion we for our parts are resolved to*
live

live and die ; which action of yours will, upon the account of so good an example, undoubtedly lead you to eternal life. Dispose your selves onely to do this, and we shall conserve the memory thereof for your advantage, As the Lord de la Mente *will more particularly certifie you on Our part, to whom We refer our selves in this regard, praying the Lord to assist you by his Holy grace.*

Carolo Emmanuel

RIPPA.

The Churches of the *Marquisate* having received this Letter, returned an Answer to the *Duke,* in a large Letter in form of a Request, which contained two branches ;

In the first, they returned His Highness thanks, for that he had until then suffered them peaceably to enjoy their Religion ; and that in the same manner as he had found them in the Year 1588, *when he took possession of the* Marquisate.

In the second place, they most humbly entreated him, to continue to them the said benefit, as also to grant them his Protection, forasmuch as they knew that their Religion was founded upon the Holy Scriptures, According to which they did order their life and conversation, in such a manner that none could have any just occasion to be offended at them. And considering that the very Jews, *and other enemies of Christ, were suffered to live in peace, and the enjoyment of their Religion, they had that confidence, that those who were found Christians, and faithfull to God and their Prince, should not be denied the same priviledge.*

After this their Answer, they were left a while in quiet, in the mean time happened an occasion for the *Dukes* taking a voyage into *France,* which was followed with a War in *Savoy,* during which time they continued as before : But after that the Exchange of the *Marquisate* was established, together with *la Bress,* the smooth and soft Letters were turned into sharp Edicts, commanding expresly all those of the Religion of the said *Marquisate,*

A sharp and severe Edict against all those of the Marquisate in July 1601.

That they should every one go and declare to his ordinary Magistrate, within 15 *days following, whether he would renounce his Religion, and go to Mass, or no ; in which case they were promised not onely to be suffered to abide and remain peaceably in their houses, but likewise favoured many other ways : But if on the other side, they were resolved to persist in their Religion, they were enjoyned to retire, and depart out of His Highness Dominions within the space of two months, after the publication of this Edict, and never to return without express permission ; And that upon pain of death, and confiscation of all their goods : the which goods of theirs they were notwithstanding permitted within the said term of two months, to transport as they should think meet, provided that they transgressed not the limits of the said obedience, but upon no other terms.*

This unexpected Edict being published throughout the *Marquisate,* in the end of the Month of *July* 1601, much troubled those of the
Reformed

Reformed Religion in that Country, who immediatly fent Deputies toHis Highnefs to obtain either a Revocation(or at leaft a Moderation) of the fame : And of this they had fo much hopes given them by divers perfons of quality, that many of the poor people refting upon this broken Reed, let flip a great part of the faid prefixed time, without fetting their Affairs in order for their departure, whereby they were fo much the more furprifed and amazed, when they underftood not many days before the time was expired, that all hope of remedy was now wholly taken away. However, the greateft part of them difpofed themfelves for their departure, fome recommending their goods to their kinred and friends, who remained in the Country, others leaving all they had at random, except what they could carry along with them, to ferve for their prefent neceffities.

But now during thefe two Months, thofe who were refolved to depart, (in cafe there were no other remedy) were perpetually fet upon by their friends and kinsfolk,by all perfwafions and motives imaginable, to divert them (if poffible) from this their refolution, efpecially then when they prefented themfelves before the Magiftrate to give in their Anfwer in writing : To this purpofe they were obliged to make it in a certain Pew in publick view, where the Magiftrates had either the Monks, or other *Roman* Ecclefiafticks, and men of note, who ceafed not to propound and urge all that they could poffibly imagine probable to fhake the faith and conftancy of thefe poor people. Amongft others, a certain *Capucin* Frier, by name *Philip Ribot,* who a little before had exercifed his gifts in the very fame manner in the Valley of *Perofa,*being now imployed in the *Marquifate,* was very diligent therein, running up and down from place to place, to make as many Profelytes as he could poffibly, ufing all the fubtilties imaginable, efpecially among thofe whom either the feeblenefs of age, the weaknefs of fexe, or the want of eftates and riches, might in any probability render them more ductile, and eafie to be wrought upon ; befides all this, they caufed them to be brought before the Magiftrate one by one, to the end that the conftancy of fome might not encourage others. Yea very hardly were the husbands permitted to declare for their Wives or Children, and they did fo fift the tender ones, That it was very hard to efcape without making fhipwrack of their Faith and Religion; And further, to accomplifh their defignes, they prohibited all upon pain of death, any ways to diffwade any one from revolting.

However, it pleafed the Lord fo to fortifie thofe people, that a great number of them departed unfhaken, who *went forth* as Providence guided them, *not knowing whither they went* : Some fteered their courfe beyond the *Alpes,* to *France, Geneva,* and other places ; Others retired themfelves into the Valleys of *Piemont,* where yet was continued the liberty of the reformed Religion, and where they remained without trouble, notwithftanding the Edict imported,that they fhould depart out of the Dominions of His Highnefs.

Now in the beginning of this General perfecution, their Adverfaries

ries fearing fome bold and refolute union of thefe poor perfecuted people, to prevent any combuftion or difturbance, gave it out among the Churches of the mountains, that though the terms of the Edi& were general, yet the intention thereof was onely to unlodge all thofe who inhabited in the lower plain, and in the great villages, and other publick places; And that all thofe who inhabited among the Mountains might be aſſured of living in peace and quiet.

This Cautelous dealing caufed, That at the firſt, there was not fuch an univerfal union of thofe of the Reformed Religion in all the quarters deftined for flaughter,as they could have defired. However in the end, the difcovery of their fraud occafioned a more clofe union among them; For the truth is, at laft they fpared thofe of the Mountains, no more then thofe of the Plains, except that they made no ſhew of inquiry after the Church of *Pravillelm,* and the quarters thereabouts, which the people of thofe places perceiving, as likewife trufting to the Anci-entnefs of their poffeffions, never troubled themfelves to make any de-claration before the Magiftrate, or to prepare themfelves at all for their departure, as if the Edi& had not at all concerned them. Neither in-deed were they at all difturbed,until all the reft who perfevered in their Religion, were departed out of the Province, and fcattered abroad here and there in feveral places. At length, they were given ferioufly to un-derftand,that forafmuch as they had not yeilded obedience to the Edi&, they were thereby become obnoxious to the punifhment therein con-tained and fpecified. Whereupon there were fome who warned them to have a care of themfelves,both in general and particular; Infomuch that when they had bethought themfelves, they as members of the Communalty befought the Syndicks, of the faid communalty, to in-tercede for them, alledging the reafons for which they conceived them-felves not to have been comprized in the Edi&, and by confequence that they had not offended out of any malicious intention.

Thefe Syndicks accordingly (whether ferioufly or perfun&orily,the Lord knowes) made many journeys about this bufinefs, but always returned with fad and uncomfortable meſſages, and fuch orders, that they found themfelves forced in the end to follow. One part of them (the men having given Order to their Families which they left in their houfes) retired themfelves into the Weftern Mountains; Thofe who were capable to bear Arms(which were about two hundred in number) with their Arms, retired themfelves into the *Chaftellenie de Chafteau Dauphin,* which was not far diftant; But thofe of *Dauphinè,* and who were lefs difpofed, retired themfelves into their higheft Forrefts.

Now before their departure they had given their Neighbouring Pa-pifts to underftand, that being forced to retire themfelves by the threats which were made them for the caufe of their Religion, and not being able to take along with them their Families, they intreated them to have them in recommendation, promifing fuddenly to make a re-turn either of the good or evil that fhould be done to thofe their relati-ons either by them, or any ways by their permiffion: Upon this, the Papifts either out of fear, or for fome other reafons, did fo far follicite, that

Thofe of the church of Pra-villelm Perfe-cuted and Ba-nifhed.

that in the end, they obtained so far of their Superiours, that the others had Liberty of returning with assurance to their Ancient habitations, without being molested, and that for many years together.

During this persecution, the *Sieur Dominique Vigneaux* Pastor of the Church of *Villaro*, of the *Val Lucerna*, & one of the most ancient & grave persons that were in those days in the Churches of the Valleys, being likewise adorned with excellent qualities, wrote many Considerable Letters, both to their poor persecuted Brethren, to exhort them to perseverance and patience, by encouraging them with lively consolations, as also to certain Lords of quality, to entreat them to intercede in their behalf; as namely, to the Lord *De la Mente* Governour of the *Marquisate*, with whom he had some intimacy, and unto whom he most amply propounded the justice of the cause of the poor persecuted people, with many notable motives and reasons, thereby endeavouring to induce the said Lord, to undertake their protection.

Sieur Dominique Vigneaux a famous Minister of Villaro.

CHAP.

CHAP. III.

The cunning Artifices, and wicked Practifes both formerly and at prefent ufed, to confume and deftroy the remainder of the Faithfull in the Valleys of Piemont.

IN the foregoing Chapters, we have the Enemy of our falvation reprefented unto us, as a *Roaring Lion*; In this, as a *Cunning Serpent*, fubtilly intruding himfelf, and fecretly wounding the Faithfull. And indeed, though it be extreme difficult (as the wife man obferves) to find out *the way of a Serpent upon a Rock*, yet the poor *Evangelical* Churches, have from time to time had fufficient experience of, and tafted the wofull and bitter fruits of his deadly malice and hatred, wherein he has not onely improved the wickednefs of feveral private men, but found out a way alfo to make the publick Authority fubfervient thereunto, often transforming himfelf into an *Angel of Light*.

His inftruments that he made ufe of for the compaffing of his Defignes upon thofe poor people, were for the moft part the Priefts and Monks, who continually loaded them with black afperfions, thereby to render them odious and abominable in the fight of all men; nay, they did not onely reprefent them as Hereticks, but alfo as *Monftri Infernali* ('tis Prior *Rorenco's* own expreffion in the *Italian* language) that is, *Infernal Monfters,* or the moft curfed creatures, that Hell it felf affords.

The treacheries, lies and impoftures fuggefted by thofe, who were under-hand imployed by the *Popifh* Clergy-men, infenfibly to exterminate thofe poor people, are innumerable; yea there is nothing more fure then that they both had in thofe days, and at this very day have under pay feveral perfons, whofe bufinefs it is, to kindle ftrifes and quarrels amonft the *Proteftants*, and to engage them in fuits of Law one againft another; And when they fee them reduced to poverty and defpair, then they come and offer fecretly, to each of them feparately, all the favours imaginable, and an abfolute victory over their Enemies. Provided they will either openly revolt, or remain as fpies amongft their Brethren to betray them. And the better to prepare and difpofe them hereunto by degrees, they affure them, that in cafe they will imploy fome Church-men to recommend their affairs to the Judges, they may undoubtedly obtain their defires. But if they cannot perfwade either the one, or the other, to revolt or to betray their

own

own party, they then foment their quarrels, embittering and infla-
ming their spirits more and more by means of their usual and ordinary incendiaries (that is to say the Gentlemen, the Lawyers, the Atturneys and the *Popiſh* Notaries, the moſt part whereof receive Pen-
ſions from *Rome* for this very purpoſe, who at length endeavour to
make them fight it out, promiſing help to each, that ſo they may, under a pretence of friendſhip, bring all their perſons and eſtates to ruine ;
flattering ſtill both the one and the other by the aſſiſtance of ſome third
perſon, with a good opinion of their pretended right, and perſwading
them, that in caſe they ſhould come to a friendly agreement, (as they
are exhorted by their Miniſters) they ſhould do themſelves infinite
wrong and injury. And by this courſe they do oft times oppoſe and
hinder the good endeavours of the Miniſters and Elders, whoſe deſires
are, to preſerve peace and Chriſtian unity amongſt their Brethren.
Yea, thoſe kindlers of diſcord, diſguiſing, and making an ill con-
ſtruction, of the Miniſters exhortations taken out of the Word
of God, do what they can, to perſwade the Magiſtrates and Judges
themſelves, that it ſtrikes at their Authority, and ſpoils their
Practice. And which is more then all the reſt, the Prieſts and Friers do not ceaſe to enquire and wind themſelves more particularly
into all the diſcontents and diviſions that at any time happen or ariſe
between man, and wife ; maſter, and Servant ; father, and child ; and
having incenſed them what they can one againſt another, they endeavour to perſwade the weaker party to revolt ; and that he may be
in a better capacity to revenge himſelf, the ſaid Monks and their Aſ-
ſociates offer then all the aſſiſtance imaginable, from the Authority of
the *Popiſh* Magiſtrates, who in all publick employments are to that very end preferred before the *Proteſtants*, and made their Superiours in
power, that ſo they may ſway and over-rule them as they liſt.
The *Popiſh* Clergie-men likewiſe knowing (by experience) that
Young men are apt to be in Love, which uſually binds and Captivates
reaſon, do frequently propound unto them, by their Emiſſaries, to
match with ſome *Roman Catholick*, whoſe portion and other advantages they accordingly Amplifie by officious lies ; And ſo inveigle many innocent Souls, ſometimes unknown to their Parents and Friends,
and ſometimes by open force, and againſt their wills. And when
there is any ſo Wicked and Rebellious amongſt the ſaid *Proteſtants*, as
not to regard admonitions and exhortations, So that the Miniſters are
forced to proceed to more ſevere Cenſures, or Excommunications,
then theſe Monks and Prieſts ordinarily Cenſure the *Conſiſtories*, and
do what they can to perſwade the *Young man void of underſtanding*, to
abandon that party, by whom he is (as they pretend) ſo ill uſed, and
to embrace the *Popiſh* Religion, where he ſhall not onely finde a ſure
ſhelter againſt thoſe who purſue him for his crime, and offences, But
ſhall alſo be ſet over them in all politick offices, and employments,
that ſo by that means he may have power in his hands to be revenged
of them. This hath been certainly practiſed by the Monks in the
years 1640, 1641, 1642, *&c.* Even towards ſome who were manifeſtly
convinced

convinced of Witchcraft, who having revolted at the perswasion of the Monks, had their lives given them, and were set at liberty. And, (because the Monks could not deny but that those miserable creatures were actually Witches, especially in the valleys where they were known by the name of *Maschi*) whensoever they were upbraided with countenancing such Wretches, They answered in a jeering (and as they thought a Witty) manner, *Sapiamo dismascarli,* that is to say, *we have a device to make Witches, to become no Witches,* which was the secret of those men, whereof the Prophet *Isaiah* speaks, saying; *They call Darkness Light, and Evil Good, &c.* and even as *Bellarmin* boasts that the *Pope* hath power to make *de peccato non peccatum; That which is sin, to become no sin.* And thus those Sorcerers and Witches, have frequently injoyed the very same Exemption from all charges and accusations, which is granted by H. R. H. to all others that revolt, or change their Religion, and not onely so, but oft times also they have been rewarded for their Wickedness, by presents of Money, Merchandizes, and other things, according to their several capacities and occupations : And where any such Apostates were owners of Lands, they were exempted from all manner of Taxes, that so they might thereby enrich themselves, and to this purpose the Gentlemen and other rich Papists, are wont to make them counterfeit sales of their Farms and Tenements, and accordingly send them in their conveyances &Rent-Roles, and afterwards secretly and under hand part stakes with them for the profits arising from such emptions, from Taxes and other such like payments. And when the *Protestants* have complained thereof (as they had good reason, the burden laying just so much the heavier on their Shoulders, by how much the others were eased) His *Royal* Highness gave them indeed a favourable answer, by an Edict bearing Date the thirtieth of *June* 1649. but they could never obtain the putting thereof in execution.

The truth is, of all the ways and means, wherein the publick Authority, both Ecclesiastical, and Political, hath usually concurred for these last 60. years, for the rooting out, and utterly ruining the poor *Protestant* Churches in the Valleys of *Piemont,* there hath been none like unto that of the *Missionaries,* established by *Clement* the 8th. in the year 1596. as *Rorenco* mentioneth in His *Memoires,* Chapter 29. p. 135. and Chapter 30, and 31, *&c.* And indeed, the Monasteries of those Firebrands (as the said *Rorenco* observes page 142.) have always been as so many Citadels in the Valleys, wherein have been harboured many Legions of evil Spirits, who have never ceased to plot and contrive mischief, by their officious Lies, Calumnies, and false Reports, wherewith they have filled the Ears of their Magistrates and Princes, who also for the most part have given more credit to their Counterfeit protestations, then to the real and better grounds and Complaints of those of the poor *Reformed* Churches in their own just defence, and accordingly have either themselves made bloudy Edicts against them, or at least, have sub scribed unto such as were suggested & Contrived by the Priests, the *Missionary* Monks, or the Congregation

De

*Rorenco*Mem. c.29.p.135. & c.31,32,&c. *Rorenco* 142.

De extripandis hæreticis. And although the *Proteſtants* have reiterated their humble ſupplications, and laid the ſame at the feet of His R. H. yet the Innocency, and boldneſs of thoſe *Miſſionary* Beaſts hath from that time to this, ſo increaſed and is come to ſuch a heighth, that it is altogether inſufferable. And that which makes them more confident and inſolent, is, that they know they areare to be puniſhed by any Magiſtrate, whatſoever they ſay or do to the ſaid *Proteſtants :* No, not when they ſteal away their very Children! Whereas the *Proteſtants* are put to death by the Magiſtrates, if they ſpeak but the leaſt word againſt the *Miſſionary* Prieſts, or attempt to diſſwade ſo much as any of their own Domeſticks from turning Papiſts. As may be ſeen in the *Dukes* Edict (whereof *Rorenco* in His *Memoires* makes mention p. 136, and 137.) which doubtleſs was extorted by the ſaid *Miſſioners.* [Rorenco page 1636. 137.] For contrary to all right and equity : Yea, againſt the expreſs words of the Law of God, *Deut.* 19. 15. It is ſaid in that ſame Edict, *That one witneſs ſhall be ſufficient to prove any thing of that Nature againſt a Proteſtant :* And there is *a Reward of an hundred Crowns ordained for that man, who will come and witneſs againſt them.* Beſides, that ſuch an informer *is by no means to be diſcovered or made known.* And all this to encourage thoſe, who either out of Revenge, Envy, or Covetouſneſs, ſhould witneſs and report falſe things, as they ſhould be deſired and directed by the *Romiſh* Fryers, ſee the expreſs words of the very Edict as follows.

Per le preſenti, di noſtra certa ſcienza, ſuprema authorità, & aſſoluta poſſanza, prohibiamo, & eſpreſſamente inhibiamo à tutti gl' huomini, & habitatori reſpettivamente in dette Valli, di qual qualità, e conditione ſiano, che ſotto pena della vita, & confiſcatione de loro beni, non habbino ardire, ne preſumino di diſſuadere, &c. *andare alle Prediche delle Reverendi Padri Gieſuiti,* &c. *ne preſumino di fare alcuno inſulto, e offeſa in fatti, ne in parole, à detti Predicatori,* &c. *Nella qual pena dichiariamo incorrer quelle, che à relatione d' uno ò due, che ſi ſaranno ritrovati, alla contraventione ſudetta,* &c. *Promettendo a qual onque aviſarà ò denoncierà i traſgreſſori che ſarà tenuto ſecreto, è di più quadragnerà ſcudi cento,* &c. [Edict.]

By theſe Preſents, upon Our certain knowledge, by vertue of our ſupreme Authority, and abſolute Power, We do prohibit, and expreſly inhibit all perſons, inhabiting the ſaid Valleys reſpectively, of what quality or condition ſoever they be, that upon pain of death, and confiſcation of their goods, they do not preſume or dare to diſſwade, &c. *to go and hear the Sermons of the Reverend Fathers the Feſuits,* &c. *nor preſume to make any diſturbance, or otherwiſe injure the ſaid Preachers, either in word or deed upon this account,* &c. *Declaring that all thoſe who ſhall be found preſent at ſuch turbulent meetings, ſhall by the mouth of one, or two witneſſes incur the aboveſaid puniſhment,* &c. *promiſing, that whoſoever ſhall diſcover the Offenders, ſhall not onely have his name concealed, but likewiſe ſhall for his encouragement, receive a reward of an hundred Crowns,* &c.

By vertue of the aforeſaid Edict, the Monks being not a little zealous in the Devil their Maſters cauſe, made bold upon all occaſions, both

both in the streets, and publick places, yea in the very Temples (and that during Sermon-time) to assault the *Protestant* Ministers, with all the most base, vile, unworthy, and unsufferable speeches they could possibly devise to vomit out against them, knowing that no man durst censure their *Catholick* zeal, much less witness any thing against their *Fatherhoods*, in the behalf of the *Protestants*, for fear of incurring thereby Excommunication, and other Penalties, ordained against the Favourers of Hereticks: Nay, on the contrary, if by such bravadoes they could at any time draw any word, out of the Ministers, or any other mans Mouth, that did not please theit Worships, they had their Hired Witness in a readiness, to bring the poor Minister or other *Protestant* to the stake, and that without remission.

There can be no other reasonable interpretation made of that Edict, which they got cunningly of Mad. R. the 16. of *January* 1642. and had it Printed at *Turin*, by *John Sinibaldo*, Printer to the *Duke*, having made His R. H. believe, 'That the Papists were compelled to contribute towards the Maintenance of the *Protestant* Ministers, with some such other fictions and false tales, upon which they obtained an Order of His R. H. for the officers, called *Castellani*, to give the *Missioners* all the writings they should desire or demand of them. *Commandato alli castellani di dover spedir senza difficultà tutte le scritture che dalli Padri Missionari gli fossero richieste.* By means whereof, the *Missioners* usurping the supreme power of the Prince over the said *Castellani*, and consequently over the poor *Protestants*, compelled the said *Castellani* to make the most unjust ordinances that can be imagined against those poor people, and dictate unto them as many officious lies as they pleased, I leave it to others to consider, whether a Prince may justly lay his *Protestant* Subjects under the power of their profest Adversaries, to whom he gives Authority over the Magistrates themselves? And whether the *Protestants* are bound in Conscience to obey such Magistrates, as are onely the Notaries, or rather the Servants of those who are yet slaves to the *Pope*, and who are sold, to serve the desires of those *Missioners*, without any scruple in, or in the least manner questioning the justice of such proceedings, and by this means expose his poor harmless Subjects to all manner of Wrongs and Oppressions.

What actions so base and injurious to humane Society, may not private men invested with this power put into execution? But to speak more home to the *Missionary* Priests, it is too well known that they did frequently hereby hinder the Papists from bearing witness to the truth, when they came to attain any thing in the behalf of their *Protestant* neighbours, no though the matter were never so palpable, and evident on their sides. As for example, when the question is concerning their Habitation, The *Missioners* do perswade those that come to Witness the truth, that so to do were to favour the *Hereticks*, and so to fall irrevocably under the Penalty of Excommunication, whereas it is a meritorious work to bear Witness against them by such officious lies as are dictated unto them by the *Popish* Clergie-men: Nay, they will

will not give leave fo much as to the Judges, to profecute the *Caufe that is right, or to judg righteous Judgment,* when it reflects in the leaft upon the Catholick party ; neither are they fuffered at all to make any Executions upon fuch *Roture*-Lands as are given to the *Roman* Clergy, making thofe Lands free of Charges, and laying the fame upon the Necks of the poor Proteftants. And that they may have the better opportunity and pretext to negotiate with thofe of the Reformed Religion, all the Monks and Friers of the neighbouring Cloifters, ufually procure of his Royal Highnefs every year, the Affignations of Grain, and other Impofitions, all that they poffibly can, that fo thofe of the Reformed Religion, being obliged to make their Payments into the hands of thefe Publicans, they may have the better advantage of fhewing favour, and giving ample Rewards to fuch as will comply with their Idolatry and Superftitions, and lay heavie Loads upon the Backs of thofe who ftand faft to their Principles : by which means the one party grows great infenfibly, and the other is proportionably weakened and impoverifhed. And this has been their practice for many years together at *La Torre, St. Martino,* and divers other places.

I might here mention their frequent falling into the faid Valleys with Troops of Armed men, under pretence of quartering there, (as they did in the Years 1560,1561,1624,and 1655)thereby miferably to furprize, and make a prey of them. As likewife the crafty Wiles and cunning ftratagems which they have always ufed in their Treaties, which have been ftill as full of deceits and Jefuitical Equivocations, as of Lines and Sentences, (witnefs the laft unhappy Agreement made at *Pignerolio*) following therein the Maxime of *Rome* ; That is, *Never to keep Faith with Hereticks.*

To this I may add their diligent Search and ftrict Inquiry after all Proteftant Books and Writings, committing them with much devotion to the flames, left they fhould difcover the rottenefs of their Principles, and the wickednefs of their Actions to the World, and confequently thofe *Craftfmen's* Ware and Trade in danger to *be fet at nought, and the magnificence of their great Goddefs Diana defpifed,* and thofe *Demetrii* not have fo quick a vent for their *Silver Shrines.*

But I cannot here pafs over one of their moft notorious Stratagems to allure and induce to revolt fuch as regard their Bodies more than their Souls, and *love the world above God,* which indeed is nothing elfe, but in imitation of the Devil, when he tempted our bleffed Saviour ; for, as foon as they fee a Proteftant reduced to poverty, and very hungry, they immediately *carry and fet him upon the Pinacle of the Temple, and fhew him all the Riches, Glory, and Preferments of this world,* profering to give him *all thofe, in cafe he will but fall down and worfhip their Idol.* And to give the bufinefs a better luftre, as it was the Prince of this world that tempted our Saviour, fo are moft commonly proffers of this nature (through the great fubtilty of *Jefuitical* heads) made and publifhed in the Princes name, and under the notion of his bounty and benificence ; and to this purpofe dexteroufly wreft Orders out of
their

Rorenco Hist.
pag. 138.

their Princes hands, or at least force and counterfeit the same ; a lively proof whereof may be seen in the Dukes own Letter of the twentieth of *Feb.*1596.as it is related by *Rorenco* himself,138. As also by that Edict published *Jan.* the 16, 1642. where it is expresly said,

Extract of the
Edict publi-
shed 16.Jan.
1642.

Per dar animo à tutti li sudetti heretici di Catholizarci, vogliamo, & expressamente commandiamo,che tutti quelli che sono venuti nel passato anno, e che veranno à l'auvenire à la santa sede, godano dell' essentione, & immunità d'ogni & qualcunque carico reale, & personale da imporsi durante cinq' anni dal giorno di loro conversione ; Inhibendo alli, esattori & ad' ogni altro che Spettarà di molestargli per detti carichi sotto pena di scudi cento d'oro.

To encourage all the abovesaid Hereticks to turn Catholicks, it is our pleasure, and we do hereby command expresly, that all those who either did the last year, or shall for the future embrace the holy Faith, shall enjoy an Exemption and Immunity from all and every Tax,(whether real or personal) to be imposed on them, and this for the space of five years, commencing from the day of their Conversion. And we do hereby inhibit the Collectors, and all other Officers whom these presents shall concern, to molest them by virtue of their said Offices, upon pain of an hundred crowns in Gold.

Now it is remarkable, that notwithstanding by the Order abovesaid, his Royal Highness promises them Exemption but for the space of five years, yet he has upon occasion, redoubled and extended these five years to ten, nay some times to fifteen. Although the Mystery of all this is (as hath been above specified) that those Burdens which are taken off the Shoulders of the Revolters, should be laid upon the Backs of those who persevere in the true Religion, the better to break and destroy them.

But as if all this were too little to compass their ends upon the poor Protestants, they found out an admirable and complete Invention,for the more speedy effecting thereof, as may be gathered from *Belvedere*'s own relation, *pag.* 286. where he saith,

Belv.p.286.

S. A. R. determina ad intercessione di Monsignor Illustrissimo Gio. Battista Vercellino horo vescovo di Aosta, Prelato benemerito della nostra santa sede, e benignissimo alle missioni,instituire una Congregatione sopra gl'affari dell' erisie, sotto la Presidenza del serenissimo Prencipe Cardinal di Savoia, & in essenza di Monsignor Illustrissimo Arcivescovo, col l'intervento di Primi Presidenti, e Signori del stato, e di alcuni Ecclesiastici Teologi.

His Royal Highness hath determined at the Intercession of the most Illustrious Lord Gio. Battista Vercellino, now Bishop of Aosta, *a Prelate deserving much of the Holy Faith, and most favourable to the Missions, to institute a Congregation for the Affairs of Heresie, under the Presidency of the most serene Prince Cardinal* di Savoia, *and in his absence , of the most Illustrious Lord Arch-bishop, together with the chief Presidents, Lords of State, and some Ecclesiastical Divines.*

It

It was this fame Congregation *de extirpandis Hereticis,* which in the Year 1655. undertook to judg concerning the Rights of the Proteftants; their Meeting-place was in the Arch-bifhop's own Houfe, the Bifhop himfelf being Prefident, and with him the Confeffour of his Royal Higlnefs; the Abbat *de la Monta,* the Prior *Rorenco,* Marquefs *Pianeffa,* the great Chancellour, the chief Prefident of the Chamber, by name *Philippa Ferraris,*the chief Prefident of the Senate, together with the Prefidents *Beletis* and *Nomis,* every one of them hired by the Court of *Rome,* to undermine the Liberty of the Proteftant Churches, by robbing them of their ancient Privileges, under feveral Pretences, and upon falfe and wicked Informations, fometimes in one refpect, and fometimes in another: and the better to palliate and difguife thefe their Actions, they ufually furprize the Duke with heavy and grievous Accufations, and fo upon the fudden obtain feveral Edicts again ft the poor Proteftants, before they can be heard in their own Juftification, as you may fee in *Rorenco's* Book intituled, *Narratione dell' introduttione de gl' heretici nelle valli del Piemonte,* which was printed at *Turin,* in the Year 1632. where he exprefly fays, that *the intention of his Royal Highnefs is rather to reftrain, than to enlarge the Limits prefcribed to the Proteftants,* boldly charging his own Defign upon the Prince. It was to this Council likewife that were fent all thofe who might have any pretenfion of preferving their Goods, upon the account of revolting, in the Year 1650. as it plainly appears by thofe Orders, at that time publifhed again ft thofe, who pretended to inhabit out of their prefixed Limits, which Orders are in a manner the very fame with thofe of the Year 1655. For after the Narrative of the Declaration of the Confifcation of Goods, and out of fpleen to thofe who fhould not yield obedience thereto, there are thefe Expreffions,

Con Dichiaratione, che tal riduttione reftarà circonfcritta, e cofi di niffun pregjudicio, in quanto à quelli, che faranno fede inanzi l' Eccellentiffimo Configlio da S. A. R. erctto in Torino, per l' aumentatione, e confervatione della fede Catolica d' efferfi catolizati, &c. fra giorni quindeci.

That is, *That fuch a Reduction fhall reft circumfcribed, and fo become no prejudice at all to thofe who fhall engage the moft Excellent Council of his Royal Highnefs, erected in* Turin, *for the augmentation and confervation of the Catholick Faith, to turn Catholick, &c. within fifteen days.*

It was at the earneft Suit and Requeft of fuch like men as thefe, that *Emanuel Philibert* in the Year 1565. *June* the tenth, *commanded all fuch, as would not go to Mafs, to depart within two Moneths out of his Territories, and as for the Inhabitants of the Valley of* Barcelona, *t o depart within one Moneth,* as it is related by *Rorenco* in his *Hiftorical Memoires, pag.*74,76, *&* 107. But the faid Duke perceiving foon after, that the thing was very unjuft,he gave them leave to ftay,and to enjoy thofe their ancient Liberties, which he himfelf hath confirmed unto
them

Rorenco Narratione dell'Introduttione de gl' heretici nelle valli di Piemonte.

Ror. Hift. p. 74, 76, & 107. Belvedere.

them in the Year 1560. as the Adverfaries themfelves, namely, Priour *Rorenco*, and *Belvedere* the Frier, do mention in their Hiftorical Relations.

Edict againft
the Proteftants
of the Valleys
1602.

In the very fame Shop, and by the fame hands, were fabricated the
following Edicts, defcribed at large by the faid *Rorenco* in his *Narrative*, whereof one bare date in the Year 1602. *February* 25. wherein
they make *Charles Emanuel* fpeak and fay, that *he will utterly deftroy the
faid Religion* (pretended to be) *heretical*. And to that purpofe, *he en-
joyns the Proteftants, upon pain of Death, to banifh from amongft them, all
manner of Schools, either private or publick* (even as *Julian* the Apoftate

Amian.Marc.
l.22.p.259.

did formerly, to extirpate the *Chriftian* Religion; witnefs *Amianus
Marcell.* in his two and twentieth Book) *forbidding them alfo to receive
any ftrangers amongft them, that fhould be either Minifters or School-ma-*

Another Edict
of 18. Decemb.
1622.
Rorenc. p.233.

fters. And in another Edict of the eighteenth of *December* 1622.
*He forbids them all manner of fending their Youth into any foreign Schools
fufpected to be infected with the pretended Herefie*, witnefs *Rorenco, pag.*
233. whereby it manifeftly appears, that the Defign was indeed to
have deftroyed the Proteftant Religion.

In the forefaid Edict of *February* 25. 1602. *He debars* (for the fame
end) *all manner of Proteftants from publick Offices, either great or fmall*.
I fhall infert his own very words,

*Prohibiamo che alcuno eretico della detta pretenduta Religione, pofsi ha-
ver ufficii publici in alcuna communità, ò terra, ò luogo del dominio noftro,
e quelli che lihanno debbino lafciarli, ne effer ammefsi all' ufficio di noda-
ro, &c.*

And from this very caufe, proceed all other Edicts which have been
iffued againft the Proteftants of *Saluces*, whereby they are forced and

Rorenc. p.192,
193.

compelled to go to Mafs, whether they will or no, which thing P. *John
de Moncalier* Miffionary Monk, maintains to be lawfull, witnefs *Rorenco* in his fore-mentioned Book, *pag.* 192. & *193*. where we muft
obferve by the way, that both the faid Miffioner, together with Priour *Rorenco*, and all the Doctours of the *Romifh* Church, who have
perufed and approved the faid Book, have not well obferved in what
Epiftle *Paul* relates the Inftitution of the Holy Supper, faying, *Ego
enim accepi à Domino, quod & tradidi vobis, &c.* For the fame
Book fays in *pag.*194. that it is in the Epiftle to the *Hebrews*. It's a
pity thofe Seraphick Doctours are no better verfed in the Scriptures.

To the fame effect, that is to fay, to fmother and extinguifh the

Rorenc. p.152.

true Religion, came out an Edict in the Year 1601. whereby *all Proteftants were commanded, either to go to Mafs, or to depart the Land two
Moneths after the publication thereof*. And by another Edict of the
Year 1602. the fame is commanded, and but fifteen days time given
to depart: and in the very fame Year, *Monfieur Ponte*, Governour of
Pignerol, enjoyned in the name of his Royal Highnefs, the Proteftants
of *Lucerna, Fenile, Bubiana*, and *Campiglione, to quit their Habitations
and*

and Countrey within five days upon pain of death. The same order was given to those of *Val Perosa* some few days after. To this we may (not unfitly) joyn *Prefect Reffan*'s Order, given out the eighteenth of *November,* 1634. enjoyning the Protestants of *Campiglione,* to leave that place within four and twenty hours, upon pain of Death, which was executed without mercy. The same was done the last Year 1655. by *Gastaldo,* who gave no longer term than four and twenty hours for those of *Val St. Martino* and *Perosa,* to depart upon pain of Death, and three days to those who lived beyond *Pelice.*

Now there is nothing more clear, than that the Monks and Priests were the Framers of those Edicts against the Protestants, and that they suggested them to the Duke ; for his Royal Highness has many times revoked the same, perceiving that he had been abused by the said Informers, (as he himself declares in his Concessions of the twentieth of *June* 1620. saying, that he would have the same to be observed, *Nonostante ogni altro ordine in contrario,* i. e. *Notwithstanding any other Order to the contrary.* It will be again more than evident, if we consider, that before the publication of those Edicts, some Projects or Draughts thereof, have been seen in the Great Chancellour *Piscina*'s House, written by Priour *Rorenco* his own Hand ; the same is likewise clear by Duke *Charls Emanuel* his Letter, written the eighth of *March* 1602. to *Philippe Ribotti* Missioner and Jesuite, and registered in *Rorenco*'s *Memoires, pag.* 159. wherein his Sacred Highness speaks in the following terms, *Faremo li ordini particolari che V. P. ci accenna effer necessarii.* i. e. *We will make those particular Orders which your Fatherhood esteems to be necessary.* & *pag.* 180. *Padri Missionari ne diedero parte a S. A. la quale fece Editto come segue.* i. e. *The Missionary Fathers communicated to his Highness who made an Edict as follows.* We may see this also by the Edict of the said Prince of the three and twentieth of *December,* 1622. against the Protestants, the which (says he) were made according to the Popes Brief of the second of *July* in the same Year.

But now many times on the other side, when these Missionary Fathers saw that they could not possibly perswade his Royal Highness to an open Persecution against the generality of the Protestants, then they usually tormented them one by one, upon several calumnious pretences, whom they delivered up to the Inquisitours, who contrary to all Forms of Justice, forthwith condemn them, without so much as hearing, or letting them know their Accusers. They took (amongst others) one Mr. *Sebastian Basan,* in the Year 1622. and after the Inquisitours had cruelly tempted and tormented him for the space of fifteen Moneths, they burned him alive at *Turin,* in the *Palace yard* on the three and twentieth of *November,* 1623. where he died, singing the praises of God in the midst of the flames.

One of the most diabolical and unsufferable Cruelties committed by the Priests, and Missionary Monks, against the Protestants, is that of stealing away their Children, which was the Trade of *Bonaventure de Palazzolo,* and of Priour *Rorenco,* who doth not stick to boast of it

in

Rorenc. p. 153.

Rorenc. p. 260.

The Order of *Gastaldo.*

Concessions of 20. of *June* 1620.

Rorenc. p. 159.

p. 180.

An Edict of 23. *Dec.* 1622.

Seb. Basan first tormented, then burnt.

in his *Memoires, pag.*235. They stole away very many in the Year 1655. in the time of the Massacre, whom they would not afterwards restore, notwithstanding that his Highness had promised it by his Patent, and for to continue that Trade with licence, those wicked men have caused that Article of the Patent to run thus,

Non potra alcuno di detta Religione pret. Rifor. esser sforzato d' abbraci-ar la Religione Catholica Apostolica Romana, n'ei figliuoli potranno esser tolti alli loro parenti, mentre che sono in età minore, cioè li maschi di dodeci, & le femine di dieci anni.

That no person whatsoever of the said pretended Reformed Religion, be in any wise compelled (or forced) to embrace the Catholick, Apostolical, Roman Religion. Neither shall their Children be stollen or taken away from their Parents, during their minority, that is to say, the Males twelve years of age, and Female ten.

The truth is, this is the most execrable of all the *Turkish* Tyrannies, for the *Turks*, in some of their Provinces, do steal away the *Christians* Children, and infect those tender Infants with the Impieties of *Mahomet*, thereby to root out by degrees the *Christian* Religion; but there is this difference, namely, that the *Turks* do so to their own Subjects onely, whereas the Popes Ministers do it to those over whom they have no right at all.

In sum, the cunning Wiles and Stratagems to exterminate the poor *Waldenses*, are too numerous to be comprehended in a short Discourse; neither is it indeed at all needfull to dwell upon this point any longer, for as much as the sequel of this History consists of almost nothing else; and though the Court of *Savoy* will by no means acknowledg the matter of Religion to be the true fundamental cause of the late Troubles in those Valleys, yet the effects plainly shew it to be so, there being very few either of those that were slain, or those that were Prisoners, who were not tempted to the utmost to renounce their Religion. I shall only content my self to instance in two very sad Examples, where certainly (if ever) the subtil windings and insinuating Arguments of Jesuitical Spirits, with *all manner of deceivable-ness of unrighteousness,* sufficiently evidenced their great power and influence. I must needs confess, I should be very tender in bringing upon the Stage other mens Infirmities, but for as much as the following Declaration was by the parties themselves penned for that very end and purpose, besides that there are many Lessons therein contained, from which the *Christian* Reader cannot but reap much satisfaction and advantage, I have inserted the same in its native and original Expressions, as followeth.

*L*A

La Declaration repara-
tive que les Sieurs Pierre Gros, &
François Aguit cy devant Pasteurs
en la Vallée de *Luserne* en *Piemont*,
ont faite en pleine assembleé le 25.
& 29. du mois d' Aoult 1655. au
lieu de Plnache en la Vallée de *Pe-
rouse*, pour témoigner l' extreme
deplaisir qu' ilz ont eu de leur pre-
cedente revolte, à laquelle ils s' ê-
toient pottés par infirmité, durant
le temps qu' ils ont *été* detenus es
prisons *à* Thurin avec un abjuration du Papisme.

Messieurs & tres Honores
Peres & Freres au Seig-
neur,

*N*Ous eussions souhaité, qu'un suiet
moins fâcheux nous eût obligés
de parêtre en public, & qu' une occa-
sion plus favorable nous eut appellés à
nous faire conoitre au monde par quel-
que action signalée, dont la memoire
fut in benediction dans l' Eglise : Mais
puis qu' il faut que nôtre nom ne soit
rendu celebre que par les extremes
malheurs, qui nous ont accablés, &
par l' horrible scandale, que nous ve-
nons de donner à l' Eglise de Dieu
nous sortons des cachots de nôtre
confusion, & nous presentons de-
vant les hommes, pour faire parêtre
à tout le monde nôtre conversion & re-
pentance, & donner des preuves indu-
bitables du dêplaisir qui nous reste d' a-
voir été si lasches, que d' avoir a-
bandonné nôtre premiere profession.

A *Declaration reparative*
made in a full Congregation the 28
and 29 *of August* 1655 *at* Plnache *in*
the Valley of Peroule, *by* Mr. Peter
Gros, *and* Mr. Francis Aguit *for-*
merly Ministers, in the Valley of Lucerna, *in* Piemont ; *to testifie their*
extreme sorrow, for their defection
through infirmity, from the true Re-
ligion, during the time of their im-
prisonment at Turin, *together with*
their abjuration of Popery.

Most Honoured Fathers and
Brethren in the Lord.

WE could have wished that
a less sad Subject had caused
this our appearance in publick, and a more favourable occasion
had made us known to the World by
some notable action, the Memory
whereof might have been as a blessing
in the Church: But since our names
cannot be famous, but by the extream
misfortunes which have overwhelm-
med us, and by the horrible scandal which we have given to the
Church of God, we now come forth
out of the Dark Dungeons of our
own shame and confusion, and present our selves before men, to Testifie to all the World our Conversion and Repentance, and to give
indubitable proofs of our griefs, for
that we have been so base, as to forsake our former profession.

When

When we make reflexion upon thofe advantages, wherewith the Lord hath gratified us, above an infinite number of others, fuch as to have been born in his Church, to have fucked in piety together with our Milk, to have received the Grace of his faving knowledge, and been taught the true happinefs; And finally to have been called to the higheft imployment that men can have in this World, *viz,* to be the Heralds of Gods Juftice, and Preachers of his Truth, we cannot fpeak of our offence without horrour, and muft needs confefs, that it is a fin fo much the more odious, and that, having known our Mafters will, we have yet withdrawn our fhoulder from his Service, to go act quite contrary to his commandements.

It was in thefe laft Calamities which have over-run our Countrey, we thus made fhipwrack, after we had loft our liberty, with all our goods, when the Enemies of the truth, having refolved wholly to extirpate the Reformed Religion in the Valleys of *Piemont,* did exercife moft Barbarous cruelties upon our Countrey-men; And we being fallen into their hands, after they had fhewed us how far their Inhumanity could reach, to give us a proof of the utmoft degree thereof, they caufed us to be thrown into Prifon, where they proceeded againft us, and Sentenced us to Death, as guilty of Treafon, and Ring-leaders of Rebellion, and ceafed not to fet before our Eyes the torments and punifhments to which we were condemned, to render us more flexible to the inticements of the Jefuits who did inceffantly folicite us, to accept of a pardon which they fhould obtain for us, provided we could but

Quand nous faifons reflexion fur les avantages, dont le Seigneur nous avoit gratifiès, par deffus une infinité d' autres perfonnes, nous ayant fait naître dans fon Eglife, & fuccer la pieté avec le lait. Nous ayant encore honorés de fa falutaire conoiffance & enfeigné le chemin de la vraye felicité, & finalement nous ayant appellés à la plus haute des charges, dont il honore les hommes en ce monde, pour nous faire des Herauts de fa juftice & des Annunciateurs de fa verité, nous, ne pouvons parler qu' avec horreur de nôtre faute,& avoüer franchement que c' eft un peché d' autant plus enorme & deteftable, qu' ayant fceu la volonté de nôtre maître, nous avons tiré, lépaule arriere de fon fervice,pour faire tout le contraire de ce qu' il nous commande.

Céft en ces dernieres calamitiés qui ont Inondé nôtre paÿs, que nous fimes naufrage, apres avoir perdu la liberté, avec tous nos biens, lors que les ennemis de la verité,S'étant propofé d'exterminer entierement la *Religion Reformée* es *Vallées du* Piemont, exercerent leurs barbaries & cruautés fur nos compatriotes; eftant tombés entre leurs mains, a pres nous avoir fait experimenter júfques où peut aller leur inhumanité, pour nous en faire-tirer les dernieres preuves, ils nous firent traduire dans les prifons, où on nous a formé un procés, & fententiés à la mort comme *Criminels de leze Majefté &chefs de rebellion* & on n'à ceffé de nous propofer les tourmens & le fupplice aufquels on nous deftinoit, pour nous rendre d' autant plus ployables aux femonces des *Jefuites* & autres qui ne fe laffoient jamais de nous folliciter à recevoir la grace qu' ils promettoient, nous faire obtenir, moyennant que nous embraf-

faffions

fassions le Papisme en abjurant nôtre Religion.

Aux premieres attaques il sembloit que bien loin de succomber nous avoins assez de force & de vigueur, pour meprifer, tout ce que la superstition pouvoit mettre d'effroyable, devant nos yeux, & que ces ombres funestes de mort desquelles on nous menaçoit en n'avoient pas assez depouvoir pour éteindre cette lumiere celeste, qui rayonnoit dans nos ames. Mais nous avons appris à nôtre extreme regret quelle est la fragilité humaine, & reconnu combien fallacieuse est la prudence de la chair, qui pour nous faire joüir d'une vie Caduque & passagere, nous à fait renoncer aux biens innerrables, qui sont preparés aux enfans de Dieu, & à la joye Eternelle de la quelle sont participans ceux qui perseverent jusques à la fin. C'est elle qui par un desir de conserver cette maison d'argille & cet habitacle terrestre, & de nous souftraire d'une mort honteuse, & d'un supplice infame aux yeux du monde, nous à portes à une honteuse revolté, & a tourner le dos à celuy, qui est la source de vie, Nous avons presté l'oreille à cette trompeuse Dalila, & incore qu'il n'y ait eu aucan raisonnement si puissant qui ayt peu en quelque façon obscurcir la verité que nous professions, nous confessons librement, que la crainte de la mort, & l'horreur du supplice ont ébranlé nos courages & abbatu nos forces, & que nous sommes ecôulés, comme de léau, pour ne resister pas jusques au sang, ainsy que la profession non seulement de Chrétiens, mais qui plus est de Pasteurs de l'Eglise nous y obligeoit.

Persuadés par un raisonnement trompeur, que nôtre vie étoit meilleure

imbrace Popery, and abjure our Religion.

At their first onsets, we were confident, that being far from yeilding unto them, we had strength and constancy enough, to despise whatsoever Superstition could present as dreadfull or terrible before our eys, and that the dark and mournfull shadows of Death it self, wherewith they threatned us, were not powerfull enough to extinguish that Heavenly light which then shined in our Souls. But we have learned to our extreamest grief, how frail our nature is, and how deceitfull the Wisdome of the flesh, which for the injoyment of a frail and transitory life, made us forgo those inexpressible good things which God hath prepared for his Children, and that everlasting joy, whereof those that persevere to the end, are made partakers. It was this carnal wisdome, which out of a desire to preserve this House of Clay, and this earthly tabernacle, and to avoid a shamefull death, and a punishment ignominious in the eyes of the world, induced us to a shamefull falling away, and to a turning our backs upon him who is the fountain of life; We have lent our Ears to this deceitfull *Dalilah*, and although there were not offered us any reasons so strong as in the least measure to obscure the truth that we did profes, yet we freely confes, that the fear of death, and the horrour of torments, did shake our courage, and beat down our strength, and we have decayed, and dried up like water, not resisting to bloud, as the profession, not onely of *Christians*, but (what is more) of Ministers of the Church did oblige us to do.

Having been perswaded by deceitfull reasoning; *That life was better then*

then Death ; That we might be further
profitable to the Church, to our Country, and to our poor families, that there
was no glory to die as Rebels ; And that
one day we might get out of Captivity
to manifest unto the World, that if the
Confession had been wanting in our
mouths , yet the faith was not wanting in
our hearts.

Thus we accepted of pardon, under these miserable conditions, and
have not stuck to enter into the Temple of Idols, and give up our mouths
and tongues , to utter Blasphemies
against the Heavenly truth, in denying and abjuring of the same, and
our Sacrilegious hands likewise , to
subscribe the Acts and Events of this
infamous Apostasie , which have
drawn many others into the same perdition : Our light is become darknefs,and our salt hath lost its favor,we
have faln from Heaven to the Earth,
from the Spirit to the flesh, and from
life unto death ! We have been
made the Object of the curse of the
Lord, who pronounceth wo to those,
by whom Scandal cometh ; And having made light of the threatnings
of the Son of God against those,
who shall deny him before men, we
have deferved to be denied by him,
before his Heavenly Father ! Finally, we have rendred our selves unworthy of Divine favours and mercy, and have drawn upon our guilty heads, whatsoever is most dreadfull in the Wrath of God, and his
indignations ! and have deferved to
be rejected of the Church, as Stum-
bling blocks or stones of offence, and
that the Faithfull should even abhor
our company.

But as we have learned in the School
of the Prophets, that the mercies of
God are infinite, and that the Lord
taketh no pleasure in the Destruction of his poor Creatures , but cal-

que la mort, que nous pourrions encore
être utiles à l' Eglise, à la Patrie, à nos
pauvres familles , qu'il n'y avoit point
de gloire de mourir comme rebelles, &
qu'un jour nous pourrions sortir de cap-
tivité, pour faire parêtre a tout le monde, que si la confession nous manquoit à
la bouche, la foy ne defailloit pas dans le
cœur.

Nous avons accepté la grace sous ces
funestes conditions, & n'avons pas fait
difficulté de nous porter au Temple de
l'Idole & d'employer nôtre bouche &
nôtre langue pour prononcer des bla-
sphemes contre la verité celeste, en l'abjurant & renonçant, & nôtre main sa-
crilege pour signer les actes de cette infame apostasie, qui en à attiré plusieurs
en la mesme perdition, nôtre lumiere est
devenüe tenebres, & nôtre sel à perdu
sa Saveur, nous sommes tombés du ciel
en la terre, de l'esprit en la chair, & de
la vie en la mort ! nous avons été faits
l'object de la malediction du Seigneur
qui prononce malheur contre ceux par qui
scandale âvient , & ayant meprisé la
menace, que le filz de Dieu fait contre ceux qui le renieront devant les
hommes , avons merité d' être reniez
devant son pere celeste : En fin nous nous
sommes rendus indignes de la faveur divine, & avons attiré sur nos testes
criminelles, tout ce qu'il y à de plus
épouvantable dans la colere de l'Eternel & en ses indignations, & avans
merité que l' Eglise nous rejette comme
pierres d'achoppement & de scandale,
& que les fideles ayent horreur de nôtre
rencontre.

Mais comme nous avons apris en
l'école des Prophetes, que les misericor-
des de Dieu sont infinies, & que l'Eternel ne prend point de plaisir en la destruction de sa pauvre creature, ains ap-
pelle

pelle le pecheur a repentance pour luy don-
ner la vie, nous prenons la hardieffe, de
nous prefenter devant fa face, & de nous
humilier en fa faincte prefence, pour de-
plorer la grandeur de nôtre forfait, &
pour luy faire une libre confefsion de nô-
tre iniquité : pleüt à Dieu, que nôtre
tefte fe fondit en eaux d' amertume &
que nos yeux fuffent changés en vives
fontaines de pleurs pour reprefenter la
douleur, dont nos ames font angoiffées
Nôtre peché qui n' eft pas ordinaire et du
commun demande une repentance extra-
ordinaire, & comme nous le reconnoiffons
comme l' un des plus grands qui fe com-
mettent dans le monde, aufsy fouhaiteri-
ons nous que nôtre repentance pe ut at-
teindre le dernier degré d' humiliation,
afin que les actes de nôtre contrition fuf-
fen connus à toute la terre. Si David
pour de plus legeres fautes a voulu que fes
doleances, Et la profonde repentance fuf-
fent perpetuelles dans l' Eglife, nous n' au-
rons point de honte de publier aux hom-
mes l' inconfolable regret, qui nous refte
d' avoir offenfé Dieu, fcandalifé l' affem-
blée des Saincts & imprimé fur nôtre
front la marque d' un Eternel opprobre,
par une miferable revolte pour en faire
viure la memoire a perpetuité, fi feule-
ment nous pouvons faire confter de l' ex-
treme deplaifir que nous en avons conceu,
pour defavoüer tout ce que la crainte nous
a fait faire par force contre les fentimens
de nôtre confcience. Nous efperons que
celuy qui a pardonné à St. Pierre fes re-
niemens dans la Cour de Caiphe, nous fe-
ra les mefmes graces, puifque nous venons
luy en demander un tres humble pardon
la l' arme à l' oeil, la confeffion à la bouche,
& la contrition au coeur, & que comme il
y a joye au ciel pour un pecheur qui vient
a repentance il y aura aufsy joye en l' af-
femblée des fideles, quand ilz verront
nôtre converfion au Seigneur.

leth the Sinner to Repentance to give
him life, we are bold to appear before
his Face,& to humble our felves in his
holy prefence, to bewail the greatnefs of our Sin and make unto him
a free Confeffion of our Iniquity : O
that our heads might melt into waters of bitternefs, and our Eys were
turned into Fountains of Tears, to
exprefs the grief wherewith our Souls
are preffed down. Our Sin as it is not
ordinary, fo it requireth of us an extraordinary Repentance ; and as we
acknowledg it to be one of the greateft that may be committed, fo do we
wifh, that our Repentance may attain
to the higheft degree of Humiliation,
that fo the acts of our Contrition may
be known to the whole World. If
David, for lighter faults was willing,
that his Complaints,and his deep Sorrow, and Repentance fhould be left as
it were for a Memorial in the Church,
well may we not be afhamed to publifh amongft men the inconfolable regret which we have for having offended God, and given occafion of Scandal to the Affembly of the Saints, and
we deferve to have imprinted upon
our Foreheads the mark of a perpetual Infamy, by our miferable Fall, to
make the Memory thereof continue
for ever. And if we can make it appear, that the Sorrow it hath begotten
in us is extreme, and that we difclaim
now whatever fear formerly forced us
to do againft the Dictates of our Confciences ; we hope, that he who forgave *Peter* his Denying of *Chrift* in
Caiaphas his Court, will grant us the
fame Grace, fince we are come to beg
Pardon in all Humility with Tears in
our Eys, Confeffion in our Mouths,
and a Contrition in our Hearts ; and
that as there is Joy in Heaven for one
Sinner that repenteth, fo there may be
Joy in the Congregation of the Faithfull, when they fhall fee our Converfion to the Lord. Great

Great God! Almighty Father! dreadfull in thine anger, in whofe prefence no Sinner can fubfift a moment, we proftrate our felves at the feet of thy Greatnefs, as poor miferable Offenders, acknowledging, and confeffing, that we have juftly provoked thee to anger, by our Tranfgreffions and Iniquities, and drawn upon our felves thy righteous Judgments, in that we have forfaken thy heavenly Truth, and bowed the Knee before the Idol! But how fhall we now appear before thee, O thou Judg of the Quick and the Dead, fince we have by fo doing, deferved to feel not onely in this Life thy moft fevere Rod, and Punifhments, but that thou fhouldft alfo cut us off from the number of the Living, and caft us headlong into the Lake of Fire and Brimftone, where there is weeping and gnafhing of teeth. O God! rich in Compaffions, and infinite in Mercies! which thou multiplieft even in Judgment, do thou convert us, that we may be converted! be mercifull to us, forgive us our offence! blot out our Iniquity!&impute not unto us our fin! open unto us the Door of thy Grace, that we may be Partakers of thy Salvation! O Lord *Jefus*, Redeemer of our Souls, who cameft into the World for the fakes of poor penitent Sinners, look upon our affliction! receive us to mercy! and grant that our fins being wafhed away in thy moft precious Bloud, we may draw near the Throne of thy Grace, with confidence to obtain mercy : raife us up from our Fall! ftrengthen us in our weaknefs! and although Satan hath fought to fift us, fuffer not our Faith to fail! work in us effectually both to will and to do according to thy good pleafure. It is thou that haft ftretched out thine arm towards us! It is thy ftrong hand which hath helped us! Thou haft ta-

Grand Dieu & pere tout puiffant redoutable en ton ire, & devant qui nul pecheur ne peut fubfifter un moment, nous nous profternons aux pieds de ta grandeur, comme des pauures Criminels, reconnoiffans & confeffans que nous avons irrité ta jufte colere par nos iniquitez & tranfgrefsions, & attiré tes juftes jugemens fur nous, lors que nous avons abandonné ta verité celefte et ployé le genouil devant l' Idole, mais comment comparoitrons nous devant ta face irritée, Juge des vivans & des morts, puis que par cela nous avons merité non feulement d' experimenter en cette vie ce que tu exerces de plus horrible en tes verges & chatiments, mais mefmes que tu nous retranches du nombre des vivants, & nous precipites dans les abyfmes de mort & dans l'eftang de feu & de foulfre ou il y a pleur & grincement de dents? O Dieu tu abondes en compafsions, & es infiny en tes mifericordes, tu les muliplies à l' encontre du jugement, Converty nous afin que nous foyons convertys, fay nous mifericorde, pardonne nous nôtre peché, efface nôtre iniquité, ne nous impute point nôtre faute, ouure nous la porte de ta grace, afin que nous participions à ton falut. O Seigneur Jefus redempteur de nos ames, qui es venu au monde pour les pauures pecheurs repentans, regarde à nôtre douleur reçoy nous à mercy, & fay que nos pechésêtant lavés en ton precieux fang, nous nous puifsions approcher en confiance du throne de ta grace pour obtenir mifericorde, Releve nous de nôtre cheute, fortifie nous en nos foibleffes, & encore que Satan ait demandé à nous Cribler, ne permets point que nôtre foy vienne à defaillir, produis en nous avec efficace & le vouloir & le parfaire felon ton bon plaifir. C' eft toy qui nous as tendu le bras. C' eft ta main forte qui nous a fecourus, tu nous as tiré de capti-
vité

vité corporelle & spirituelle dans laquelle nous Croupissions pour nous mettre en liberté de te pouvoir invoquer, tu nous as exaucés des lieux profonds, & nous as donné nouvelle matiere de nous égayer en tes bontés,& benir ton sainct nom, Gloire Eternelle t' en soit rendü een tout temps, & en tout age. Ainsy soit il.

Ames fidelles qui voiés comme nous portons un coeur contrit et une ame brisée devant l' Eternel, pour nous humilier devant sa face. Ayez commiseration de nôtre lamentable Etat, Aprenés par nostre exemple à reconnoitre quelle est la foiblesse humaine & en quel precipice nous trébuchons, lors que Dieu retire sa grace arriere de nous. Considerés que comme ce nous a esté un malheur extrême d'estre tombés dans un si grand peché, vous avés matiere de vous éjovir en Dieu de la grace qu' il vous fait d'estre encore debout, Veillés & priés afin que vous n'entriez pas en tentation. Tenez ferme ce que vous avez; que nul ne vous ravisse vôtre Couronne. Soyez fidelles au Seigneur Jesus j' usques a la mort, pour obtenir la Couronne de vie, & soyés persuadés que hors de la profession de sa verité, dont vous possedés l' avantage exclusivement à toute autre religion,il ny a qu'ombre de mort, horreur & épouvantement. C' est dequoy nous vous pouvons asseurer par nôtre propre experience,puisque des le moment que nous eümes donné nôtre consentement à cette maheureuse Apostasie nôtre conscience ne nous a donné aucun repos, & par ses bourrellemens & continuelles agitations, ne nous a laissé jouir d' aucune des consolations, dont une ame Chretienne est participante en la tribulation j' usques à ce qu' il à pleu à Dieu de nous tirer du bourbier infame de Babylon, pour nous faire rentrer dans son Eglise.

ken us out of captivity both of Body and Soul,in which we lay languishing, to afford us the liberty to call upon thee! Thou hast heard our cries out of the deep, and hast given us new cause to rejoyce in thy goodness, and to bless thy holy Name, to whom be everlasting glory ascribed at all times, and in all Ages. *Amen.*

You faithfull Souls, who see how we bring a contrite heart, and a broken spirit before the Lord, to humble our selves in his presence, O commiserate our lamentable condition! Learn by our Example to know how great humane frailty is, and what a precipice we fall into, whensoever God with-draweth his grace from us! Consider, that as it hath been unto us an extreme unhappiness to have fallen into so great a sin, so have you an argument to rejoyce in God, in regard of that grace which he affordeth you as yet to stand! Watch and pray, that ye enter not into temptation! Hold fast what you have, that so no man take away your Crown from you! Be faithful to the Lord *Jesus* even unto death, that so ye may obtain the Crown of Life! and be assured, that out of the profession of his Truth, which you profess exclusively from all other sorts of Religion whatsoever, there is nothing but death, horrour, and astonishment. This is a thing which we are able to assure you by our own experience, seeing from the very first moment, that we gave our consent to this unhappy Apostacy, our Consciences have given us no rest at all, and through their continual combustions and agitations have they not suffered us to enjoy any other comfort whatsoever which a *Christian* Soul at any time enjoyeth in tribulation, untill it pleased God to draw us out of the filthy Quagmire of *Babylon*,and caused us to return into his Church. You
Christians

Chriſtians, who ſee us return into the boſom of the Church, lend us your helping hand, and let your arms be opened to embrace us, ſeeing we beg your pardon for the Scandal which we have given you. Do not think us unworthy of your holy Communion, although we have been an occaſion of offence! Suffer us to pour into your boſoms a torrent of tears, to deplore our condition, and to aſſure you in the anguiſh of our Souls, that our grief is greater than we can expreſs! Help us by your holy Prayers to the Lord, and publiſh our Repentance in all places where you conceive our ſin hath been, or ſhall be known, that ſo it may be evident to all the World, that from the very bottom of our Souls, we grieve & ſorrow for it, and that in the preſence of God, and of his holy Angels, and in the ſight of thoſe who are Witneſſes of our Converſion, that we do abjure, and deteſt the pretended Sacrifice of the Maſs, the Authority of the Pope, and in general, all ſorts of Beliefs, and Worſhips dependent upon them. We recant whatſoever we may have pronounced to the prejudice of the Evangelical Truth, and promiſe for the future, through the grace of God, to perſevere in the Profeſſion of the Reformed Religion, to the laſt moment of our Life, and rather to ſuffer Death and Torments, than to renounce that holy Doctrine which is taught in our Church, according to the Word of God, even as we ſwear and promiſe, with our bended Knees upon the Earth, and our Hands lifted up to the Eternal, our Almighty God and Father, Son, and Holy Spirit. As we deſire his Aſſiſtance to do this, even ſo help us God. *Amen.*

Chreſtiens qui nous voyés retourner au gyron de l' Egliſe tendés nous la main, et nous reçevés a bras ouverts, puis que nous vous demandons pardon du ſcandale que nous vous avons donné, Ne nous dedaignez pas en vôtre ſaincte Communion, en core que nous ayons êté en achoppement, Permettés nous de verſer dans vos ſeins un torrent de larmes, pour deplorer nôtre condition, & de vous dire dans la triſteſſe de nôtre ame, ce que nôtre douleur ne peut exprimer. Aydez nous par vos ſainctes prieres au Seigneur, & publiés nôtre repentance par tout, ou nôtre peché aura êté connu, afin qu' il ſoit notoire à tout le monde que nous en gemiſſons du plus profond de nôtre ame, & qu' en la preſence de Dieu & de ſes Saincts Anges, & à la veüe de ceux qui ſont têmoins de notre converſion, Nous abjurons & deteſtons le Sacrifice pretendu de la Meſſe, l' authorité du Pape, et generalement toutes les creances & les cultes qui en dependent, Nous nous retractons de tout ce que nous pouvons avoir prononcé au prejudice de la verité Evangelique, & promettons à l'avenir moyennant la grace de Dieu de perſeverer en la profeſſion de la Religion Reformée j' uſques au dernier ſoûpir de nôtre vie, & de vouloir plûtoſt ſouffrir la mort & le ſupplice, que d' abandonner cette ſaincte doctrine qui eſt enſeignée dans nôtre Egliſe ſelon la parole de Dieu, comme nous le jurons et promettons les genoux à terre et mains levées à l' Eternel nôtre Dieu tout puiſſant Pere, Fils et Sainct Eſprit, Ainſy nous faſſe t' il et ainſy nous ajoute. Amen.

CHAP.

CHAP. IV.

The Grounds or Motives of the late Perfecution, in the Year 1655. with the publication of that bloudy Order of Gaftaldo, and the Flight of the Proteftants in the midft of Winter.

I Have often mufed in my more retired thoughts (becaufe fuch an effect cannot be without its moving caufe) what might be the Ground or Reafon, why the Devil fhould be always fo extremely malicious againft the Sons and Daughters of Men, who are his poor fellow Creatures, and originally of an inferiour Rank and Degree, yea, who in all probability, were never in a capacity of giving him a proportionable provocation. And its poffible that the *Chriftian* Reader may be as curious and inquifitive in his private Reflections, what may be the Grounds or Motives that fhould provoke the Court of *Savoy*, to perfecute and profecute with fuch rancour and violence, their own poor Natives and Countrymen, and that of the meaneft Rank and Quality amongft them, whofe poverty and indigency could never give occafion for Envy, nor their Parts and Education, in any Age, threaten very deep Defigns, and who (in a word) have never been otherwife guilty of difquieting their Popifh adverfaries, than the Lamb in the Fable of troubling the Waters, where the Wolf was drinking.

The Naturalifts obferve of the Monkey, that when he once begins to gnaw and feed upon his Tail, it is a certain fign, not onely, that he is diftempered, but that his Difeafe is incurable. And truly for my part, I could never yet learn any fatisfactory Reafon, why fome particular Jefuitical fpirits of that Court, whom I may (without ftraining the Metaphor) fitly ftile the Popes Monkeys, fhould thus continually gnaw and devour their own flefh (I mean their Proteftant Brethren and Countreymen) yea, and that they fhould chufe the leaneft and the pooreft part thereof, befides that incurable difeafe of Malice and Envy, wherewith the Devil hath infected them. However, what the opinion of others is upon this fubject, who are more intimately acquainted with their affairs, I fhall here faithfully relate in their own expreffions, (the Originals whereof I have in my cuftody) and fo leave the probability or improbability thereof to the judicious Reader. Now according to their defcriptions and reprefentations of this matter, the Reafons are of two forts, the firft more general, and the other more particular.

The general Grounds are :

The first general ground why the Court of Savoy persecutes the poor Protestants.

1 Their pretended Zeal for the Religion of the Church of *Rome*; for these Men believing that to be the true Church, and consequently that which we profess to be a most detestable Heresie, they look upon themselves as obliged in Conscience to use all Endeavours for the extirpation of the same. As *Christ* himself forewarneth his Disciples, *John* 16. 2. *The time cometh,that whosoever killeth you, will think he doth God service.*

2. General Ground.

2 The belief which they have, that in matters of Heresie, all Princes ought to conform themselves to the judgement of the Pope and the Clergy; although in the mean while they well know, that the *Reformed* Churches, accuse the *Pope* himself of many notorious Heresies, Idolatries, and Impieties. And the Question is,whether the *Pope* should herein be his own Judg, or whether any Prince ought so far to lean upon, or comply with anothers conscience, as to condemn his Subjects thereupon; yea, and that before he be assured whether it be good or evil,for which he condemns them, especially when the condemned parties offer to make good both their principles and practises.

The particular Motives of the late Persecution in the year 1655.

But to come more closely to our purpose; the more particular Grounds which (say the Authors of them) do move and incline some of the chief Officers and Gentry of *Savoy*, to endeavour to extirpate the Reformed party, are,

1 Particular Motive.

1 To the end that by evil treating the *Reformed Churches*, they may conserve the *Papal* Authority, of which they have oft times so much need, namely, to cover and cloak their incestuous Mariages,contracted by Dispensations from the *Pope.* And thus they become engaged to defend and maintain Popery, for fear of being declared guilty of Incest, although for ought I know, the first may be the worst of the two.

2 Motive.

2 By persecuting the Reformed party, those Courtiers receive (as a *Reward of Iniquity*) divers Prebendaries, Bishopricks, Abbeys, and Priories, especially those who are Members of the Council, *De propaganda fide & extirpandis hæreticis.*

3 Motive.

3 Under this pretext, the poor people of the Valleys, become a continual prey to the abovesaid Courtiers, who daily rob and spoil them, by extorting from them the best part of their Livelihood, by all sorts of stratagems and subtil devices.

4 Motive.

4 The Gentry of *Lucerna,* (being otherwise very poor) do what they can, to promote this work, by perpetual calumnies against the Reformed party, either in general or particular, rendering themselves by such good offices, capable of meriting and receiving those Pensions, which are assigned them by the Court of *Rome,* for the same purpose.

5 Motive.

5 Upon this account of late years, (that they might leave no means unattempted for the absolute ruining and extirpation of those Protestant Churches) they have made the Gentlemen of the respective
Valleys

Valleys fubordinate to the Monks and Mafs-priefts, who ufually pre-fcribe them what they ought to do, that is to fay, as to the bearing falfe witnefs againft their Brethren, the fowing difcord amongft them, the murdering of fome or other of them, the procuring of Affaffi-nates, the affifting in ftealing and carrying away their Children, or any fuch like ill offices ; without the ready performance whereof, they refufe to pay them their annual Penfions.

6. But in the fixth and laft place, the chief and main Ground of all why the Court of *Savoy* do fo much ftrive to extirpate thofe poor People, is the Defign that they have to wreft *Pignerolio* out of the hands of the King of *France*, to which the Habitation and Liberty of thofe People is a very great Obftacle. For becaufe they inhabit in the neighbouring parts of *Pignerolio*, both in the Plain and in the Mountains, and cannot upon the account of their Confciences, be brought to tamper in any fort, or make any agreement with the *Spanifh* party, for the affaulting and furprizing of that place ; I fay, therefore it is, that the Court of *Savoy* feeketh all manner of occafions and pretexts poffible, to root them out, efpecially thofe of *Lucerne, Fenile, Bobio, Campiglione, Bri-cheras,* and *St. Secondo,* which are near *Pignerolio.* And for this very Reafon was that Citadel of *La Torre* formerly built in the very centre of the Valleys of *Lucerna* and *Angrogna,* near the confluence of the two great Rivers, by that means the better to block up *Pignerolio* on that fide, and to deprive it of all manner of Commodities which it receiveth from that Valley, which alone does ufually furnifh it with more than all the neighbouring Valleys belonging to the Duke. Now the Court of *Savoy,* by exterminating the faid People, and putting in their places, men forward to execute their Defigns, might very eafily feize on *Malange* a narrow paffage above *Pignerolio,* on that fide which looks towards *France,* where a very few perfons would be able to hinder the *French* Army from relieving *Pignerolio.* And upon this account many fober perfons believe, that *France* is on the contrary very much concerned to preferve the Intereft of thofe poor People in all the places of their ancient Habitations in the Valleys, for, fay they, *(marginal note: The Intereft of France in preferving the Intereft of the poor Proteftants.)*

1. The Inhabitants of the Valleys, being a good part of them native *French* men, which came thither, about five hundred years ago, have a natural obligation upon them to be faithfull to the Crown of *France,* and are certainly much fitter in that regard, to inhabit there, than thofe of the *Spanifh* Faction, which would undoubtedly fupply the others room in cafe they were extirpated. *(marginal note: The firft Reafon why France is thus concerned to preferve the Intereft of the poor Proteftants.)*

2. The Valleys being naturally very ftrong, it would be almoft impoffible ever to remove the Enemy when once got into poffeffion. *(marginal note: 2. Reafon.)*

3. The places of the Valleys being poffeffed by perfons well affected to the Intereft of *France,* do not onely ferve as Centinels and Bulwarks, (which coft nothing) to guard it on that fide, but alfo conftantly furnifh the fame with Victuals, Hay, Oats, and Wood. *(marginal note: 3. Reafon.)*

4. Again, this is a moft convenient paffage for the *French* into *Italy,* it being the very fame which *Hannibal* heretofore made ufe of, *(marginal note: 4. Reafon.)*

of, and fince that time, divers Kings of *France*, efpecially *Charls* 8.

5. The Duke of *Savoy* having remitted all into the hands of the King of *France*, and indeed the King of *France* being bound thereunto by a formal Treaty, made *Anno Domini* 1535. it is to be prefumed, that his Moft *Chriftian* Majefty, will look upon himfelf as interefled and obliged to make good the Acts and Edicts of his Predeceffours, taking into his confideration, that the Promifes of Kings and Princes are facred things, and ought to be as inviolable as the Laws of the *Medes* and *Perfians*.

Upon thefe and the like Grounds (fay many knowing perfons) the Court of *Savoy*, and their Creatures, have from time to time fought the deftruction of thofe poor Proteftant Churches, although it's true that in all the Perfecutions which they have raifed againft them, (and more efpecially in this laft of 1655.) thofe *ravening Wolves* have always approacht in *Sheeps cloathing*, the better to difguife their bloudy actions, and to fall upon thofe *innocent Lambs* at unawares. It is evident, that the Evangelical Churches of the Valleys had now long before this fatal Year of Five and fifty cleared themfelves of thofe Calumnies which the Council *De extirpandis hereticis*, (an Affembly made up of the Penfioners of *Rome*) to the end that they might enjoy their promifed Penfions, had endeavoured to afperfe them with; and thereby to render them odious in the eys of their fovereign Prince; yea, his Royal Highnefs had now given an ample teftimony of his being fully fatisfied in this point, having accorded unto them by an authentick Decree, printed and publifhed in the Year 1649. the confirmation of their Conceffions; the which were alfo again confirmed and enlarged by his Royal Highnefs the fecond and fourth of *June*, and the nine and twentieth of *December* 1653. eftablifhing them in the enjoyment of the Conceffions, granted them in 1603. and 1620. without either addition or diminution, amplification or reftriction, as may be feen by the following Copies of their Requefts, and the Decrees of his Royal Highnefs thereupon, an authentick Copy of the true Original whereof is to be feen in the publick Library of the famous Univerfity of *Cambridg*.

R.H.

R. A.

Li fideliſſimi & humillimi ſudditi di V. A. R. profeſſanti la Religione Riformata nella Valli di Lucerna, Peroſa, Martino, Roccapiatta, S. Bartolomeo, Praruſtino, & luoghi aneſſi, proſtrati alli piedi di quella, &c.

THe moſt faithfull and moſt humble ſubjects of your Royal Highneſs, profeſſors of the Reformed Religion in the Valley of Lucerna, Peroſa, S. Martino, Roccapiatta, S. Bartholomeo, Paroſtino, *and the annexed places, being proſtrate at your feet, do in all humility make their obeiſance to you, beſeeching his Divine Majeſty to give you a happy and proſperous Reign, under which we deſire quietly and peaceably to live, and to render you all manner of obedience, due from true Subjects unto their lawfull and natural Prince, as they have always done under the happy Dominions of your moſt ſerene Predeceſſors, of famous memory. And now renewing our addreſs to your Royal Highneſs, we moſt humbly requeſt, that according to your wonted bountie and clemencie, you would be pleaſed to grant unto us the following Articles: And we ſhall continue to pray to God, for the proſperitie of your Royal Highneſs, and your whole Royal Family, and for the increaſe and enlargement of your Dominions.*

The Firſt Article.

Si compiaccia confirmar luoro le gratie & privilegii a luoro conceſſi, & piu volte confirmati & interinati da ſereniſſimi ſuoi Predeceſſori di glorioſa memoria, &c.

That you will be pleaſed to confirm unto us, the Immunities and priviledges, before granted, and often confirmed and interinated by your moſt ſerene Predeceſſors of glorious memory, and more particularly thoſe of the late deceaſed moſt ſerene Duke, Charls Emanuel, *your Grandfather, bearing Date the 9th. of* April, 14 May, *and 29* September, 1603. *interinated the 20* June, 1620. *and confirmed by your Royal Highneſs, by your anſwers made in the* Memorial *to the ſeven* Articles, June *the 30th.* 1649. *that ſo they may peaceably reap the fruits of the ſame, together with all the Priviledges, which the reſt of your ſubjects do enjoy indifferently, according as they have done under the happy Reign of your moſt ſerene Predeceſſors above ſaid, without let, or moleſtation of any kind whatſoever, and this notwithſtanding any Orders made, or to be made to the contrary.*

The Dukes Anſwer to the Second Article.

S. A. R. confirma tutti li privileggii gratioſamente conceſſi alli
ſuppe-

ſuppeti, ſecondo luoro forma & tenore ſi e come ſono interinati &
ſono ſenza abuſo, in uſo del beneficio de quali, e mente ſua, che
goldino ſenza, *&c.*

His Royal Highneſs gracioufly confirms to the Petitioners, all their Pri-
viledges, according to the form and tenor of them, and as they are interi-
nated, and that without the leaſt alteration: And for the benefit of the
Petitioners, his meaning is, that they ſhall enjoy the ſame without any di-
ſturbance, upon the conditions therein contained and comprehended: And
withal, that they ſhall not make uſe of any Foreign Miniſters, nor accept
of any ſtrangers of the Reformed *Religion to dwell, or ſo much as ſojourn*
amongſt them, for the ſpace of above ten daies together, without the ſpecial
leave of his ſaid Royal Highneſs; as likewiſe that they ſhall not exerciſe
any manner of Functions relating to the exerciſe of their Religion, be it
Preaching, or of any other kind, without the limits gracioufly tolerated unto
them: Neither ſhall they hinder, or any way difquiet the M. R. Fathers
Miſſioners, *in their Functions, nor give them or their attendants the*
leaſt diſturbance, either in their Churches, Miſſions, *or elſewhere; And*
above all, that they punctually obſerve the contents of the Tolerations gra-
ciouſly indulged to them, as well by his ſaid Royal Highneſs, as by his moſt
famous Predeceſſors; which, or any of which Conditions being broken or
violated on their part, all ſuch Grants, Graces, and Tolerations are decla-
red to be void, and of no effect.

The Second Article.

Che fiano ameſſi ad ogni forte d' officii publice, in dette tre Valli
indifferentamente, come gl' altri fuoi Judditi, *&c.*

That we may be admitted indifferently with the reſt of your Sujects to all
ſorts of publick Offices or Employments in the three Valleys aboveſaid, as
was granted in the abovementioned Priviledges of the year 1603. Art.4.

The Dukes Anſwer to the Second Article.

S. A. R. tolera, che nelli luoghi exiſtenti fra li limiti gratioſamente
tolarati, dove fono tutti della Religione pret. Rif. poſſino li fuppeti
deputare Sindici Confegn. *&c.*

His Royal Highneſs grants, that in the places within the limits graci-
ouſly tolerated, where all the Inhabitants are of the pretended Reformed
Religion, the Petitioners may depute Syndicks, Councellors, Procurators,
and other Comiſſioners, of the ſame pretended reformed Religion, as hath
been tolerated by the moſt ſerene Predeceſſors of his Royal Highneſs, in their
gracious

gracious Grants. And as touching Notaries, they shall be tolerated onely in the forefaid places of the pretended Religion ; provided they abstain from receiving any Instruments, Acts, or Writings, of what sort soever, in the which is either directly or indirectly contained matter prejudicial and contrary to the Precepts, Rules, Institutions, or Rights of the Catholick, Apostolick, and Roman Church, or against the sense of the Edicts of the most serene Predecessors of his Royal Highness. And they shall be bound to come hither to obtain their Patents in their due form ; his Royal Highness strictly prohibiting and forbidding them to preach, or have Lectures, upon pain of incurring the punishments contained in the said Edicts, and particularly in that of 25 Febr. 1602.

The Third Article.

Liberarli dalle pene, nelle quali potrebbano effer incorfi, fi in generale che in particolare, per contravenire a glordini di V. A. R. concernenti fatto di Riligione, *&c.*

To free us of all penalties, the which we may have incurred, as well in general, as in particular, for not observing, or yielding obedience to the Orders of your Royal Highness, in matters relating to our Religion, as also of all other transgressions and excesses made and committed in that case, as the taking up of Arms, with all Acts that followed thereupon ; and in a word, all molestations, either real or personal ; and likewise to have leave to till our grounds, and to use Traffick,&c. according to the Concessions.

The Dukes Anfwer to the Third Article.

S. A. R. aboliffe le proceffure e condanne fi corporali che pecuniarie & confifche fequite in odio de fuppeti per contravenire in fatto di Religione, *&c.*

His Royal Highness abolisheth all Processes and Judgements, against either bodie or goods, all Sequestrations procured out of hatred against the Petitioners, for not yielding obedience in matters of Religion ; and particularly those that follow, which were made against the Commonaltie and Parishioners of Bobbio, *for demolishing a meeting place, set out and appointed for a Church in the said place, by Order of his Royal Highness, signified and published by his Auditor* Gaftaldo ; *or against the Parishioners of* Angrogna, *and* Villaro, *for the demolishing and plundering of the Church and Houfe of the F.* Miffioners. *Yet however it is alwaies to be underftood, that in this Grant we in no wife include the afternamed Minifters,* A. Leggiero, Gatino, Mangietto, *and his Wife, with the five particular Delinquents who had a hand in the firing and fack-*
ing

ing of the Church of Villaro, *to wit,* John Baylo *of* Pragela, Gugliel-
mino Peyrinello *of* Gigleftra, *Inhabitants of* Villaro, Giacomo d'Ufi-
no, Pietro, Ricca, *and* Giovanni Viglino, *all of the faid place of* Villaro, *concerning whom the Commons of* Villaro *are to ufe all diligence,*
that they may be apprehended and punifhed according to the fubmiffion figan-
ed the 26 April, *of this prefent year, fubfcribed by* Conte Todefco, *the*
Prior Marco Antonio Rorenco , Conte Chriftophero di Lucerna.
And the Petitioners fhall be bound, not to occafion the leaft trouble or mo-
leftation to the right reverend F. F. Miffioners, *in their Houfes and*
Churches, which either at prefent are, or for the future fhall be built in the
places of fuch as have been demolifhed. And as to the houfe of Angrogna,
the R. F. F. Miffioners *fhall not be hindered in the practife and proceedings*
already made by them, nor in any other that fhall hereafter be made, in cafe
of a new election ; And all this with a Declaration, that if the Petitio-
ners incur any delicts of difobediencie againft the Edicts of his Royal High-
nefs, and his moft ferene Predeceffors in fuch cafe, all the Graces at this
prefent granted to them, fhall be void, null, and of none effect. Further-
more, it is permitted them, and they fhall be fuffered to pafs through any
part of the Countrey as they fhall have occafion, in order to their tillage
and harveft, and they fhall have the libertie and freedome to converfe and
traffick, provided it be but by way of intercourfe, without contracting for
dwelling places, and in cafe they abftain from teaching or preaching, and
in all other particulars obferve our Orders.

The Fourth Article.

Che attefta la eftrema miferia & poverta alla quale fono ridotti li
fuppeti, fi degni mandar gli fiano li fudetti cappi conceffi, confirmati
& interinati gratis, &c.

That confidering the extream miferie and povertie to which the Petitio-
ners are reduced, your Royal Highnefs will vouchfafe to command that the
abovefaid Article may be granted, confirmed and interinated them gratis,
with leave to print them, and that fuch printed Copies may be accounted
as valid as the very Original it felf.

The Dukes Anfwer to the Fourth Article.

S. A. R. manda al Senato & Camera d'interinare le prefenti rifpofte & conceffioni fenza veruna difficolta ne limitatione & dechiara
alla Copia ftampata, &c.

His Royal Highnefs gives Order to the Senate *and* Chamber, *to have*
the prefent Anfwers and Conceffions interinated, without the leaft diffi-
cultie

cultie or limitation, and Declareth, that the printed Copies shall have the same credit and validitie as the Original it self. Given at Turin, *the* 2d. *of* Jan. 1653.

Signed,

Carolo Emanuel.
Va. Morozzo.
Va. Trabucho per il Presidente d' Ordine di S. A.

Contrasignatura.
Morozzo.
Ferrari.
Filippa.
Fauzzone.
Pe. Binelli.

Sottote Menyeri.
Attesto quod solverint alibi arbitranti pensiones & emolumenta ad libras ducentum.

Morosius.
St. Cancellaria t. 82.
Vaudagna.
Per l' Arbergo t. 40.
Ferraris.

St. Libras 200.
Vaudagna.
Regiftratto
lib.3. fol.252.
Gratia per il Q.
Filippa.

Royal H.

Li fedeliffimi & obedientiffimi fudditi di V. A. R. profeffanti la Relig. riformata nelle Valli di Lucerna, Perofa, S. Martino, Roccapiatta, S. Bartholomeo, Praruftino, & luoghi anneffi, proftrati a piedi,*&c.*

The most faithfull and most obedient Subjects of your Royal Highness, professing the reformed Religion, in the Valley of Lucerna, Perofa, St. Martino, Roccapiatta, St. Bartholomeo, Praruftino, *and the places annexed, being proftrate at your feet, return you their most humble thanks, for the favourable Anfwers, which it hath pleafed you to give to their Me-morial and Articles of the fecond of* June *laft paft, fomewhat amplified, and declared the fourth of the fame. But forafmuch as there are certain conditions, never before inferted in their Conceffions, the which if prepofteroufly interpreted by thofe that are difaffected to us , might occafion ftrange troubles to your Petitioners, to the prejudice of their Confciences, and againft the true meaning and intention of your Royal Highnefs ; and forafmuch as we defire nothing more than that we may live quietly under your happie Dominions, and render you all that obedience and fidelitie which is due from true and faithfull Subjects, to their lawfull and natural Prince. Upon this ground we renew our addrefs to you.*

Humilmente

Humilmente fupplicano verti fervita confirmargli le gratie et privi-
le gg1 luoro conceffi da fereniffimi Predeceffori di *V.A.R*, &c.

*Humbly requesting, that it may please your Royal Highness, to confirm
to us the Graces and Priviledges granted us by Your most Serene Predeceffors; especially those of the Most Serene Duke Charles Emanuel, of famous memory, Apr.9. May 14. and Septemb.29. 1603. interinated
June 20. 1620. which were confirmed by your Royal Highness, June 30.
1649. without any restriction or alteration, notwithstanding any other Order whatfoever made, or to be made to the contrarie.*

At the bottome of the Petition is written as followeth.

Dichiara S.A.R. non effer di mente fua, che per le rifpofte date
al Memoriale a Capi delli 2 Giugno 1653. S'intendino ampliate, *&c*

*His Royal Highness declares, That it is not his intent, that by the An-
fwer made to the Memorial and Articles of the fecond of June, 1653. it
fhould be at all underftood, that the Conceffions, being duly expedited,
which the Petitioners formerly obtained of the deceafed Duke Charls Emanuel his Grandfather, and of others his moft ferene Predeceffors, fhould
fuffer the leaft addition or diminution.*

Torino, 29 Dec. 1653.

Upon the leaf annexed to the Petition with the feal, was written.

Carlo Emanuel per gratia di Dio, Duca di Savoya, Principe di Piemont, Re di Cypro veduta nelle udienze noftre l'alligata fupplica,
el fuo tenore confiderato, *&c*.

*Charls Emanuel by the Grace of God, Duke of Savoy, Prince of Pie-
mont, King of Cyprus; having viewed the annexed Petition, and confidered the contents thereof, and underftood the whole cafe: We do by thefe
prefents, from our certain Knowledge, and by our full Power, abfolute Authoritie, and with the advice of our Council, declare, That it is not our
meaning, that by our Anfwers given to the Memorial of the fecond of June
laft paft, the Conceffions which the Petitioners have obtained of the deceafed Duke Ch. Emanuel my Grandfather of Glorious Memory, and others
our moft famous Predeceffors, fhould admit of the leaft addition or diminution. For fo is our will and pleafure. Given at Turin, Decemb.29.1653.*

Signed,
Ch. Emanuel, Moroffo, *di* St. Thomas, Chirollo Ultino Vaudagna.

Underneath
Chriftiene *of* France, Moroffo, Vaudagna, Binelli.
Under-

Underneath the Seal was written,

Per li profeffanti la Religione riformata nelle valli di Lucerna, Perofa, S. Martino, Roccapiatta, S. Bartholomeo, Praruftina, & luoghi an-neffi V. A. R. dichiara non effer di mente, &c.

His Royal Highnefs declares, That as for the Profeffors of the reformed Religion in the Valley of Lucerna, Perofa, St.Martino, Roccapiatta, St. Bartholomeo, Praruftino, *and the places annexed, it is not his intent, that by his Anfwers given to their* Memorial *of the fecond of* June *laft paft, it fhould be underftood, that the Conceffions, which they have obtained of the deceafed Duke* Ch. Emanuel, *Grandfather of his Royal Highnefs, and of other his moft ferene Predeceffors are diminifhed or augmented.*

Royal H.

Li Deputati delle Valli di Lucerna, Perofa, S. Martino, & altri ve-nuti per retirare le Conceffioni che benignamente ha compiaciuto a V. A. R. di confirmare, &c.

The Commiffioners of the Valley of Lucerna, Perofa, St. Martino, *and others, being come to take out thofe Grants which your Royal Highnefs hath been gracioufly pleafed to confirm, find, that over and above the charge there given them, of not following Innovations contrary to the ancient Conceffions, there are fome additions made, and other paffages which may admit of a double conftruction, fome whereof we have here fpecified; humbly requefting that your Royal Highnefs will be pleafed, for our future peace and tranquillitie, to make the following alteration.*

Firft Particular.

Si compiacia levare le parole che in cafo d' inobedienza reftino nulle le conceffioni, &c.

That it will pleafe you to ftrike out the words, In cafe of Difobedience, all the Grants fhall become null and of no effect: *And to declare,That it fhall onely reach fuch particular perfons onely as fhall offend, and that others fhall not be obliged further,then to affift Juftice, as is contained in the Conceffions of* 1603. 29 Sept. Article 3.

The Dukes Anfwer to the Firft Particular.

S. A. R. dichiara effer di mente fua che la pena e la privatione del beneficio delle conceffione e toleranze, &c.

His)

His Royal Highne(s declareth, that it is his mind that the penaltie, and pri-
vation of the benefit of the said Conce(sions and Tolerations, shall not be in-
flicted or extended upon such persons and places as are not partakers or guil-
tie of the offence ; provided, that such as are not guiltie, do put the Delin-
quents in the hands of Justice. And when it happens not to be in their pow-
er, then, that they do lend their helping hand, and be assisting to the Offi-
cers of Justice of his Royal Highne(s, that so the place or places, and parti-
cular Delinquents may be punished, and the offence purged.

The Second Particular.

Nel medeffimo capo ove viene prohibito di fare fontioni fuori delli
limiti, *&c.*

In the same Article where Ministerial Functions are prohibited without
the Limits, that it would please your Royal Highne(s to declare, that this is
not to be understood so as thereby to hinder the visiting of the sick, and the
like ; as is specified in the Grant of 1561.Art.8. *and confirmed* 1628.Art.5.

The Dukes Anfwer to the Second Particular.

Quando il cafo porti che nelle Valli di S. Martino, Perofa, & Lucerna, fi ritrovaffe alcuno della pretefa Religione riformata che foffe
infermo fuori de luoghi & limiti tolerati, *&c.*

When it so falls out, that in the Valleys of St. Martino, Perofa, *and*
Lucerna, *any of the pretended reformed Religion fall sick, without the said*
places and Limits which are tolerated, which by the present Conce(sions must
not be thought any wise enlarged; upon this account, his Royal Highne(s is
willing (in cafe of inftant danger of death, through some sharp fit of sick-
nefs) that a Minifter, accompanied with another that is not a Minifter,
may repair to the place where the sick partie is, to visit and comfort him :
Provided, that he make no longer abode in any such place without the Limits
than one day, or two at the moft ; as also that he do not catechize, or use
any other Function (either publick or private) relating to the pretended
reformed Religion; but that he confine himself to, and intend the said visit
onely.

The Third Particular.

Che V. A. R. li concedi l' effercitio de gl' officii publici in de tre
Valli indifferentemente, *&c.*

That your Royal Highne(s will be pleafed to permit the exercise of publick
Offices in the said three Valleys, without diftinction, as it is specified in the
Conce(sions of the 9th. *of* April, 1603. Article 4. *and confirmed in the*
year 1620.

The

The Dukes Anfwer to the Third Particular.

S. A. R. dechiara che nonoftante la rifpofta datta al capo fecondo del Memoriale delli due Giugno, fara permeffo, *&c.*

His Royal Highnefs declareth, that notwithftanding the Anfwer made to the fecond Article of the Memorial *of* June 2. *it fhall be permitted to Notaries (lawfully created) of the pretended* Reformed *Religion, and dwellers in the places tolerated, to receive Inftruments of Agreement, and Acts indifferently between the Inhabitants living within the three Valleys : Provided, they do obferve in the faid Inftrument, the form and ftile of Catholick Notaries, and that they receive no Wills, or other fort of Teftament, of any* Catholick. *Given in* Rivoli, June 4. 1653.

Under-written.

Charls Emanuel.

Morozzo.

Fabruco; *and for the 52 Prefident by Order of his R. H.*

paid Twelve pound.

Moroffus.

Anfwers to the *Memorial*, and its feveral Articles, prefented to your Royal Highnefs by the Commiffioners of the Valleys of *Lucerna, Perofa,* and *St. Martino.*

R. 30. fol. 252.

paid Twelve pound.

Vaudagna.

Morozzo.

Ferraris.

Prefident Binelli.

Now as the poor people fought for an *Interination* of the fame, His *Royal Highnefs* knowing right well that the delay thereof proceeded not from any fault or negligence on their part, but was rather occafioned by the multitude of Troops that were then quartered upon them, by which means they could not poffibly have the convenience of affembling, *&c.* out of his great goodnefs towards them, declared by an Edict, printed and publifhed *May* 19, 1654. That his intention was, that they fhould enjoy the Conceffions effectually as if they had been again confirmed and *interinated,* upon condition they did procure the *Interination* thereof within three moneths following : The tenor of which Edict is as followeth.

Having

HAving accorded by the Confeffions of the fecond and fourth of
June, and the 29 *December,* 1653. to
the Inhabitants of the Valleys of *Lucerna, Perofa,* and *St. Martino, Roccapiatta*, *St. Bartholomeo, Peruftin*,
and the places annexed, profeffing the pretended Reformed Religion, the continuation of the
fame Priviledges and Conceffions
which they had obtained of the late
deceafed Dukes, *Charls Emanuel,* and
Victor Amedea, my Grandfather and
Father of glorious memory, which
they could not to this prefent obtain
the Interination of, becaufe of the
French Troops which were quartered
in the faid Valleys, and the neigbou-
ring places, during the laft Winter,
and do yet continue there, as likewife by reafon of the ruine and damages which they have made: And
forafmuch as it is our intention that
they fhould hence forward entirely
enjoy the fame, and that without
any trouble or moleftation (provided
that they caufe the fame to be interinated within three months following.) We do by thefe prefents
from our certain knowledge, and
by our abfolute Authority, with the
advice of our Council, command and
order, That the faid Conceffions be
obferved in all things and throughout, according to their form and tenour. And for the due obfervation
of the fame, we permit thofe of the
faid Reformed Religion, to make
their harveft and threfh their Gorn
in the other places of our Dominions,
as alfo to have free exercife of commerce and traffick as paffengers (yet

*HAvendo noi per Conceffioni delli 2,
è 4 di Giugno, & 29 Decembre,*
1653. *accordato à gl' habitanti nelle
valli di Lucerna, Perofa, S. Martino
Roccapiatta, S. Bartholomeo, Praruftino, & luoghi anneffi profeffanti la preteza Religion riformata, la continuatio-
ne de medeffimi Privileggi, e Conceffioni, che dalli furono Duchi Carlo Emanuel, & Vittorio Amedeo mei Avo &
Padre di gloriofa memoria havevano ot-
tenuto, che per caufa de gl' allogiamenti
della Soldatesca Francefe fequiti in dette
Valli, & luoghi nell' hor fcorfo inverno,
i quali per anco continuano al prefente,
& delle ruine, e danni apportatigli, non
hanno ancora potuto far interinare. E
volendo pure che di effi habbino agioire
intieramente, e fenza verun impedimen-
to fin d' adeffo mentre, che quelli faccino
interinare, fia trè mefi. Per le prefenti
di noftra certa fcienza, affoluta authorità, & col parer del noftro Configlio
mandiamo, & ordiniamo doverfi obfer-
var le foura defignate Conceffioni in
tutto, e pèr tutto fecondo loro forma, e
tenore, & in loro offervanza permettia-
mo alli detti huomini della preteza Religione riformata di poter andar à meffo-
nare, e far ayrature nel rimanerite delli
ftati noftri, & infieme di poter commerci-
are è trafficare per modo però di paffagio,*

e fen-

e senza 'che vi possino contrahere habi-tatione e domicilio, il tutto senza mo-lestia alcuna per fatto di Religione ; con-che però s' astenghino di dogmatizare, ne diano causa di scandale, & nel resto observino gl' ordini nostri, & de serenis-simi nostri Antecessori. Dichiarando la publicatione delle presenti da farsi per voce di crida, & afficione di copia all; luoghi soliti tanto valer, come se a cias-cune fossero personalmente, intimate & alla copia stampata dal stampatore nostro, e Camerale Sinibaldo darsi tanta fede come al proprio Originale, che tal e no-stra mente. Dat' in Torino li diecenove di Maggio, 1654.

C. Emanuel

V. Morozzo.

In Torino, per Gio Sinibaldo, Stam-patore di S. A. R. & Illustrissima Camera. 1654.

not establishing there any habitati-ons or dwelling place) and all this without receiving the least trouble for the cause of their Religion ; provided that they abstain from Preaching, and give no occasion of scandal, and in all other particulars observe Our Ordi-nances, together with those made by our Predecessors. Declaring the publi-cation of these presents,which shal(be-ing read by the publick Crier, and af-fixed in the places accustomed) be as authentick as if they were notified to every one in particular. And they are to give as much credence to the Copy Printed by *Sinibaldo*, Printer to Us, and to the Chamber, as to the proper and very Original, forasmuch as this is our intention. Given at *Turin*, the 19 of *May*, 1654.

C. Emanuel.

V. Morozzo.

At *Turin*, by *John Sinibaldo*, Printer to His Royal Highness, and the most Illustrious Chamber. 1654.

So that until this time,namely *May* 19.1654.no man can fay that thofe
of the Reformed Religion,had committed any thing whereby to be deprived of the benefit of their conceffions.It is not here worth the while,
to mention fome Monks and Fryers, or the Childifh toys of fome
Young Children of *La Torre*, partly *Papifts*, and partly *Proteftants*,con-
cerning which fome of their Adverfaries endeavored to form an accufation, forafmuch as it was foon afterwards fufficiently known to be a bufinefs fo impertinent,falfe and Malignantly wrefted to the difadvantage
of thofe poor people,That the faid Legat*Gaftaldo*,having at their requeft
taken particular cognizance thereof, declared plainly and openly, that it
was a thing not worth the taking notice of, and that he would neither fpeak, nor hear any more concerning it.   And the truth is, neither
he nor the *Marquefs Pianaffa*, in all their Orders, and Letters, wherein
they notwithftanding fcraped together whatfoever they could any way
imagine prejudical to them, thereby to render them odious, and fo
have fome colourable pretext for the late maffacre, did never make the
leaft mention of thofe Childifh ftories. Wherefore all that *Gaftaldo*,
and the faid *Marquefs* accufed thofe poor *Proteftants* of, being things
whereof they had before cleared themfelves,and which had been terminated a long time before the faid confirmation in the Year 1654. And
the principal point,namely their habitation, being an undoubted Right
which they had injoyed time out of mind. I fay, all this plainly ar-
gues, that there was nothing happened on the *Proteftants* part, which
could alter the intention and good pleafure of His Royal Highnefs, or
hinder and retarde the interination of their conceffions : Yea, befides
all this, the poor people (notwithftanding the great expences of that
affair) did not ceafe to folicit the Court, with all poffible diligence and
inftances, reprefenting the Original of the faid decrees. They agreed
to pay all the Emoluments or *Regales*(they call it)to 80~~ livers,referring
it to the good pleafure of the *Chamber*, and in one word, they fatisfied all their demands whatfoever. Alfo, the faid *Chamber* diftributed the papers, and remitted the decrees to the *Advocate Patrimonial*,
who ought to have fignified the Conclufions, and from day to day
have reported them to the Chamber for the perfecting of the fame.
But the adverfe party,who think they do agreat fervice in contradicting
and controlling whatfoever concerns the intereft of thofe poor people,
fuggefted, that they could not be interinated becaufe they had never
been paffed in the *Chamber*, nor in the *Senat*, and by confequence
they could not give credence to them. But the very truth is,they really
thought that the *Proteftants*, had abfolutely loft the Originals of the
Interination, made 1620. and that the Copies which they had at that
prefent, were not authentique ; and therefore faid, if thofe of the *Re-*
formed Religion could produce the fame, there fhould remain no further
difficulty. The poor people yet furmounted this difficulty alfo,and produced their Authentique papers. But yet notwithftanding,after all this,
having been a long time amufed with vain hopes, and almoft confumed
with expences, contrary to all expectation, fome days after, namely 25
of *Jan.*1655.the following Order was publifhed,which I have fet down
word for word in its Original language.   Here

Here follows the famous Order of GASTALDO.

Andrea Gaſtaldo Dottor di Leggi conſigliere, Maeſtro Auditore Ordinario, ſedente nell' Illuſtriſſima Camera de Conti di S. A. R. & Conſervatore Generale della Santa Fede, per oſſervanza de gli' Ordini contro la preteſa Religione Riformata della Valle di *Luſerna, Peroſa, S. Martino,* publicati, & in queſta parte ſpecialmente da detta S. A. R. Delegato.

INſeguendo noi *l'autorità che da S. A. R. teniamo, delli tredici del corrente in debita forma ſpedita, ſigillata & ſottoſcritta* Violetta, & *l'inſtruttione à parte dataci con l' inſtanza fattaci da M.*Bartholomeo Gaſtaldo *interveniente per il Fiſco Regio, committiamo & mandiamo al primo meſſo di Corte giurato di far comandamento & ingiuntione, come con queſta ſi comanda & ingiunge ad ogni capo di caſa particolare della preteſa Religione Riformata, di qual ſi voglia ſtato, grado & conditione, niuna eccettuato habitanti & poſſidenti beni nelli luoghi & finaggi di* Luſerna, Luſernetta, *S.* Giovanni, *la* Torre, Bubbiana, & Fenile, Campiglione, Bricheraſſio, & San Secondo, *di dover fra giorni trepoſsimi doppo la publicatione & eſſecutione di queſte, ritararſi, abbandonare, & eſſerſi con le famiglie loro ritirati da detti luoghi, & portati nelli luoghi & limiti di S. A. R. & ſino à ſuo beneplacito tolerati, che ſono* Bobbio, Villaro, Angrogna, Rorata, & *contrada de Bo-*

Andrew Gaſtaldo, *Doctor of the Civil Law, Maſter Auditor Ordinary, ſitting in the moſt Illuſtrious Chamber of Accompts of His Royal Highneſs, and Conſervator General of the Holy Faith, for the obſervation of the Orders publiſhed againſt the pretended Reformed Religion, of the Valley of* Lucerna, *and* S. Martino, *and upon this Account particularly deputed by his ſaid Royal Highneſs.*

WE, by vertue of the Authority which we hold of His Royal Highneſs, of the 13th. inſtant, iſſued out in due form and manner, ſealed, and ſubſcribed *Violetta*, the Inſtructions given to us apart, together with the addreſs made unto us by Mr. *Bartholomeo Gaſtaldo* appearing for the Royal Treaſury, do command and charge the chief ſworn Meſſengers of the Court, to give commandment and injunction, even as by theſe preſents we command and enjoyn every head of a family with its Members of the pretended Reformed Religion, of what rank, degree, or condition ſoever, none excepted, inhabiting and poſſeſſing eſtates, in the places of *Lucerna, Lucernetta, S. Giovanni, La Torre, Bubbiana,* and *Fenile, Campiglione, Bricheraſsio,* and *S. Secondo,* within 3. days after the publication and execution of theſe preſents, to withdraw and depart, and to be with their families withdrawn out of the ſaid places, and tranſported into the places and limits tolerated by his royal Highneſs, during his good pleaſure, as namely, *Bobbio, Villaro, Angrogna, Rorata,* and the Country of *Bonetti*

netti, under pain of death and confifcation of houfes and goods, fituated or being out of the faid limits ; *Provided always, in cafe they d, not make it appear to us within twenty dayes following, that they are become Catholicks, or that they have fold their goods to the Catholicks.* His R. H. declaring, that it never was (much lefs is) either his own, or his Anceftors mind, by any Act whatfoever, either made, or to be made, to confent, much lefs actually to intend, to enlarge the faid limits. But on the contrary, he has commanded us to declare, as we do declare by thefe prefents, That the faid Acts are meer ufurpations, contrary to the intention as well of his Orders, as of his Magiftrates, publifhed to fuch an end, as is clearly manifeft, and therefore the tranfgreffours have incurred the punifhments therein contained. Furthermore, in the abovefaid places favourably tolerated, His R. H. intends, and willeth, that in every one of them fhall be celebrated the Holy Mafs, inhibiting thofe of the faid pretended Reformed Religion, any wayes to moleft, either in deed, or word, the Miffionary Fathers, and thofe that attend them, much lefs divert or diffwade any whoever he bee of the faid Religion, that would turn Catholick, under the fame pain of death, giving it in charge particularly to the Minifters of the faid pretended Religion, inviolably to obferve the abovefaid, upon pain of anfwering the fame in their proper names. Declaring the execution of thefe Prefents, which fhall be made by Copies fixed in the ufual places, to be as valid, as if they were executed, or intimated to every one in particular. Given in *Lucerna,* the 25 *Jan.* 1655.

ANDREA GASTALDO,
Auditor and Deputy.

netti, fotto pena della vita, & confifca di loro cafe & beni efsiftenti fuori di efsi limiti, qualunque volta che fra giornivinti indi feguenti non faccino conftar avanti noi defferfi Catollizati, ò venduto loro beni à Cattolici. Dichiarando S. A. R. non efferfi mai ftata, meno effer fua mente, ne de Reali fuoi antecefsori, che per qualunque atto fatto, & da farfi, non haver voluto meno efferfi intefo ampliar detti limiti. Anzi ei ha ordinato di dichiarare, come per le prefenti dichiaramo effer ftati detti atti mere ufurpationi contra la difpofitione fi delli ordini fuoi, che de Magiftrati in tal fatto publicati, come chiaramente ne confta. Perco li tranfgrefsori effer incorfi nelle pene in efsi contenute. In oltre nelli predetti luoghi che vengono benignamente tolerati da S. A. R. intende & vuole che in caduno di efsi fi celebri il facrificio della Santa Mefsa, inhibendo alli fudetti della pretefa Religione di far alcuna forte di moleftia tanto in fatti che in parole à Padri Mifsionari & lore fervienti, meno divertire ne diverfare chi fii di tal pretefa Religione fi volefse Cattolizare fotto la fuddetta pena della vita, Incaricando particolarmente li Miniftri di detta pretefa Religione di farne inviolabilmente obfervare quanto fopra à pena d' effer rifponfali del proprio. Dichiarando l' efecutione delle prefenti di farfi per affifione di copia valere come fe adog'n'un fofse perfonalmente effeguita. Dato in Luferne *li* 25. *Gennaro Mille fei cento cinquanto cinque.*

ANDREA GASTOLDO,
Auditore & Delegato.

It is eafie for every man to conjecture the great Evils and inconveniences in the midst of a flight in the midst of Winter, especially to such a People, a great part whereof were aged and decrepit, a great part sick and diseased, besides a multitude of Women big with Child, or newly brought to Bed, together with a number of tender infants; And yet all forced to fly, none being in a capacity to succour or assist another.

This is the reason why our Saviour *Jesus Chrift* taught his Disciples to pray, that their flight might not be in the Winter, *Matth.* 24. that so, in that general Calamity, they might at least have the benefit of a favourable season, thus teaching them to pray for a moderation of so violent a persecution. But the counsel *de Propaganda fide*, moved by a principle quite contrary and repugnant to that Spirit of meeknefs, and sweetnefs in *Jesus Chrift*, have thereby manifested to the World the inhumanity of this persecution in choosing on set purpofe, and out of design, the most violent and rigorous Winter season to chase and drive out of their houses, all on a sudden, those poor People, who had scarce cloaths to cover their nakednefs, much less provided to resist the extremities of cold and hunger, thinking by this means, either to force them to change their Religion, or elfe to caufe them to perish and die among the craggy Rocks and snowy Mountains. Yea they were so malicioufly subtil, or rather so subtilly malicious, as to choose those very days, and that very nick of time, when by reason of the multitude of violent Waters in the plain, and of Snow upon the Mountains, they judged it absolutely impoffible for those poor silly sheep, ever to escape.

Now the poor people confidering with themselves that the Apostafie which was propounded unto them by their Enemies, on the other side, was a precipice which would lead them to eternal damnation, chose rather to follow *Jesus Chrifts, bearing his Crofs*, though in a way never so full of *thorns and briers*, and to hazard their temporary lives, then to lose their souls for ever. Yet neverthelefs, to the end that they might leave no lawful and juft means unattempted for the avoiding the sad effects of this cruelty, immediately after the iffuing forth of the barbarous Edict, they sent their Deputies to the Deputy, to reprefent to him, what a ftrange command this was, to force them, with their whole Families, to abandon their habitations, As alfo that it was absolutely impoffible for so many Souls as they were in number to subfift in the said places, where they were confined by the Edict, they being hardly sufficient to supply in any sort those that already inhabited the same. As likewife that this command was exprefly contrary to all their Conceffions, upon which account, they made their *Proteftations*, and appeal to *His Royal Highnefs*, their Soveraign Prince. But the said Delegat, or Deputy, knowing well the intention and design of the Councel, *de Extirpandis hæreticis* would by no means admit either the one, or the other. Hereupon, the poor People, feeing they could obtain nothing which they fought, for (though never so juft and equitable) intreated him to grant them

at

at the leaft fome fpace of time, to have recourfe to *His Royal Highnefs,* by humble fupplications. But even this was alfo refufed them, unlefs they would confent to draw up their petition after fuch a model as fhould be prefcribed them, which was prejudicial both to their juft rights, and confciences (neither of which they thought it their duty by any means to confent unto!) I fay thefe poor people, feeing that they could really obtain nothing, to the end that they might remove all manner of pretext for accufing them of Rebellion, under fuch a covert to ruine and deftroy them, hoping likewife that in the end they might find fome means or other to convey their griefs to the feet of *His Royal Highnefs,* and that his clemency and juftice would in the end re-eftablifh them in the juft poffeffion of their goods and habitations, out of which the faid Delegat had driven them, they chofe rather to fuffer this violence, and therefore recalling their Proteftation, thereby to teftifie their moft profound refpect to their Prince, quitting their houfes and goods, they retired with their Families, their Wives, and Children, great and fmall, Young and Old, whole and fick, yea, in many places, the Halt, the Lame, and the Blind, together with feveral Innocents, dragging all thofe that were infirm either by ficknefs, or age, through the Rain, Snow, Ice, and a thoufand difficulties.

Here I leave all compaffionate Souls, that are any way *touched with the afflictions of Jofeph,* to imagine the bitter tears, and wringing of hands, the fmitings upon the Breaft, the Mournings, Sighs, and lamentations in the Families of thofe miferable and diftreffed Creatures, who were now reduced to the greateft extremity, that is well imaginable. Before them, though not a Red Sea, yet a multitude of violent and Roaring Waters, on either fide moft barbarous and Snowy Mountains! Behind them, men feven-fold worfe then the Ægyptians, to butcher and deftroy them! Yet neverthelefs, recommending themfelves, their Souls, Bodies and all to the protection of the *God of their Souls and lives,* they were refolved to undergo the worft of temporarie miferies, rather then by quitting their Religion, to incur the pains of eternal fire.

This conftancy and refolution of thefe poor Saints, was no fmall confolation to the other Churches, and on the other fide a matter of great aftonifhment to their Perfecutors; And that fo much the more, confidering the great advantages which are to be purchafed in thofe parts, by quitting the *Reformed Religion,* and embracing the other, as namely if they be criminals, they have their pardons (as has been already fpecified) if Prifoners they have their liberty, exemption from Taxes and impofts, as alfo of all charges real, and perfonal, for the fpace of 5. years after the day of their abjuration, according to the Order of *Madame Royal* Guardian of *His Royal Highnefs,* bearing Date the 26. of *January* 1642. which in the execution, extended even to the Lands, which were made over to them by falfe and counterfeit contracts, and by fuch artifices the poor people who remained conftant in their profeffion of the true Religion, were laden with the Burdens which

which they took off from the backs of others, infomuch that they were even quite ruined and undone by it.

In fum, they were no fooner departed out of their houfes, but a very great number of Theeves and Robbers (the Lord knows by whofe inftigation) entred their Houfes, fpoiling and pillaging what ever thofe poor Wretches had left behind them (a far worfe condition then that of the Ifraelites, who inftead of lofing any thing at their departure, rather fpoiled the Ægyptians) pulling down their Houfes, cutting down all their Trees, and turning the places of their ancient habitations into a confufed and defolate Wildernefs. And all this, wiihout the leaft prohibition or Order to hinder this violence, from the faid Delegat, who on the contrary, kept the faid goods under the protection of *His Royal Highnefs*, which plainly fhews the defign of their Adverfaries in this enterprize.

Yea, upon the complaints which the poor people made of this violence, the anfwer given them from *His Royal Highnefs*, was onely this, That they muft name the particular Authors of thefe actions, which any man may at the firft view perceive to have been impoffible for thofe poor people, which were thus driven from their habitations at 2, 3, or 4. leagues diftance.

Now upon this Anfwer, the poor people at leaft conjectured that the intention of *His Royal Highnefs* was not, that they fhould be driven from their Houfes, but on the contrary that they fhould remain there, till fuch time as their caufe might be heard and judged. And in this confidence they fometimes returned to their Houfes by little and little, to guard them from thefe Robbers, and cultivate their Lands, to the end that they might have wherewith to pay their Taxes. And for this, they were branded with Rebellion, although they had not given the leaft caufe of fufpicion by their actions, having neither taken up arms, not exercifed any act of hoftility, every one living in his Houfe peaceably without giving the leaft offence to any.

CHAP.

CHAP. V.

The most humble, and earnest supplications of the Evangelical Churches, *in the Valleys of* Piemont, *to their* Prince, *for justice against the inhumanity of the* Order *of* Gastaldo.

G*astaldo* having thus driven those poor people out of their ancient Inheritances, without either citing them in a formal and legal way, or hearing them plead in their own defence (and which is more) without admitting the least time to provide themselves for so sad a voyage, their last refuge was, to have their recourse to the *Lord,* by fervent prayers, and to their *Prince,* by humble supplications; Wherein, as well those which the said *Gastaldo* had driven out of their Houses, as the rest of the *Reformed Religion* (the cause being common to them all) joyned together, and drew up their Addresses, and Requests, in the following terms.

The humble supplication of the poor *Evangelical Churches* of the Valleys of *Piemont,* to His Royal Highness.

An Authentick Transcript of the true Original whereof, is to be seen in the publick Library of the famous University of *Cambridge.*

Altezza Reale,

Esponeno li fideliffimi et obedientiffimi fudditi di V. A. R. profeffanti la Religione Riformate nelle Valli di Luferna, Perofa, Saint Martino, Rocapiatta, San. Bartholomeo, Paruftino & luoghi anneffi, *&c.*

May

May it pleafe your Royal Highnefs,

THe *moſt faithfull and obedient Subjects of your* Royal Highnefs, *profeſſing the* Reformed *Religion, in the Valleys of* Lucerna, Perofa, S. Martino, Roccapiatta, S. Bartholomeo, Paruſtino, *and the places thereunto annexed, declare, That in the very inſtant, that they thought to have obtained the* Interination *of their Ancient Conceſſions, confirmed unto them by your* Royal Highnefs, *they were ſummon. ned unexpectedly (that is to ſay, thoſe of* Lucerna, S. Giovanni, Fenile, Bubbiana, S. Secundo, Torre, Bricheraggio, *and the Confines, unto the Country of* Bonetti) *by an Order publiſhed by the direction of the moſt Illuſtrious Lord* Auditor, Maſter *of the* Chamber *and Deputy of your* Royal Highnefs, Andrew Gaftaldo, *to quit houſes and eſtates within three days, upon pain of Death, in caſe they did not make it appear that they were become Catholicks within twenty days: So that being all diſlodged, without prejudice notwithſtanding to the ſaid Conceſſions, and upon this account only, that ſo they might not have the leaſt failing, or default laid to their charge: There now remain ſeveral hundreds of Families, miſerably reduced to the extremities of hunger and cold, among the Mountains and Snow, where they find no manner of ſhelter, or ſuccour, which, after ſo many ruines, both at preſent and heretofore ſuffered, forceth them almoſt to a total deſperation, which things they cannot poſſibly beleive to proceed from your* Royal Highnefs *natural inclination or intention, but rather from ſome ſiniſter Information ; And therefore, being proſtrate at your feet, do moſt humbly beſeech you to be pleaſed, to grant unto them the underwritten Articles, and they ſhall continue to pray God for the proſperity of your* Royal Highnefs *with all your* Royal *Family, and for the enlargement of your Dominions.*

1. *That you will be pleaſed to recal, as well the aboveſaid Order, as every other Order whatſoever, either made, or to be made, whereby the Petitioners have been moleſted upon the account of their Religion, together with all manner of Confiſcations, Proceſſes, or declarations of puniſhments thereupon, reſtoring all things to their ancient and peacable ſtate.*

2. *To give commandment to thoſe of the moſt Illuſtrious* Chamber of Accompts , *to make an* Interination *of their ſaid Ancient Conceſſions (which indeed were formerly* Interinated *the* 17. *of* Auguſt, 1620. *and your* Royal Highnefs *confirmed them likewiſe on the* 29. *of* September, 1653. *with an expreſs Declaration, not to adde to, or take from the ſame) that ſo they may peaceably enjoy the Fruits thereof, according as they did enjoy them in the happy Raign of his High-neſs* Charles Emanuel, *Your* Royal Highnefs *Uncle, of Glorious memory, who made a formal promiſe to the underwritten Deputies, in the name of the Natives, and Inhabitants, of the reſpective Valleys, and Communalties, and confirmed the ſame unto them, without any innovation, or alteration whatſoever.*

3. *That upon the account of their ſtrange Deſolations paſt and preſent, your* Royal Highnefs *would be pleaſed ſo far to have compaſſion on them, as to grant them the* Interination *of theſe their requeſts,* gratis.

Thus

Thus did thofe poor diftreffed Churches ufe all the lawful means imaginable, for their prefervation, having recourfe to their Sove-raign Prince, who certainly ought to have fhown himfelf their *Nurfing-father*, in this their great mifery and oppreffion, and to have preferved them under his Wings, *from the blaft of the terri-ble ones, which was now as a ftorm againft the wall.* But alas, they found both his, and all mens Ears ftopt to their wofull cries, and no poffibility of fo much as entring into his *Royal Highnefs* pre-fence.

Amongft many other devices, and fubtil Artifices of their mali-cious Adverfaries to this purpofe, Five days after the publication of the Order of *Gaftaldo*, bearing Date the 30. of *January* 1655. the more to exafperate and embitter the fpirits both of his *Royal High-nefs* and the *Dutchefs* his mother, againft their poor *Proteftant* Sub-jects, and confequently to difguft them from giving ear to their Re-quefts, *Jean Ange Reffan*, Prefident of the Province of *Pignerolio*, (a moft peftilent perfecutor of the *Proteftants*, and a Penfioner of *Rome*) found out a ftratagem, not unlike that which *Nero* of old ufed againft the *Chriftians*, to render them odious in the fight of all men, and to deftroy them from off the face of the earth. For, as that wicked *Nero* caufed firft the City of *Rome* to be fet on fire, and then a report to run, that the *Chriftians* were the Authors thereof ; juft fo this wicked *Ref-fan*, having for many years together, born a moft deadly fpleen againft the Prieft of *Fenile*, (as was well known to all the neighbours round about) took this opportunity to *kill two Birds at a fhot*, caufing one that he had hired for that purpofe, to affaffinate the Prieft ; and his Secretary at the fame time, to fpread the report all the Country over, both by Letters, and by word of mouth, that the *Proteftants* (who about five days before that time had been driven out of *Fenile*) were the Authors of that murther. This report (though nothing more falfe) coming from the mouth and pen of the *Roman* Catholicks, was received with fo general an applaufe among the *Papifts* dwelling in the remoter parts, that it was reputed to be as authentick as the *Sybils O-racles*, and foon after, it was reprefented to the world through the *magnifying* and *multiplying Glaffes* of the *Parifian Gazette*. But how-ever, upon the place, the *Caufa caufati* or chief Author of this affaffi-nation and murther, was fo well known, that whatfoever reports were raifed about it, they were not able to faften any belief in the mindes of the dead Priefts friends and kindred, nor hinder them from apprehending both the Secretary and his Mafter : By which means, the innocency of the *Reformed* party was made manifeft to the world, in-fomuch that the *Marquefs* of *Pioneffa* in thofe very Letters, wherein he fought all pretexts that he could poffibly devife, to lay fomething to their charge, was too politick to mention this in the leaft, for fear of marring and blemifhing the credit of all the reft.

After this it happened, that one *Berru* moft inhumanely affaffina-ted *Pietro Revoir*, Conful of *Mean*, (which adjoyns to *La Capella*, belonging to the *King*) and afterwards fled to *Pignerolio*, where he
was

was met with by this *Reiſſan*, who was now returned from *Turin,* where he had been a long time detained priſoner, and had his liberty no otherwiſe then upon a very good ſecurity, foraſmuch as the ſaid *Berru*, and others, had not long before taken their Oathes againſt his Secretary *D' Agot*, and himſelf, as guilty of the aboveſaid aſſaſſination. But after ſome private meetings and diſcourſes had together, *Reiſſan* ſo wrought upon the miſerable wretch *Berru*, with gifts and promiſes, that in fine, he perſwaded him to return back with him to *Turin*, and there, not onely to retract and recant his former depoſition, but alſo to ſwear that he had been ſolicited thereto by the two Paſtors, *Leger*, and *Michelin*, as alſo by *Antonio* and *Franciſo Danna*, chief Elders of the Church of *S. Giovanni*: In ſum, by the means of this *Diabolical* Retractation and calumny, both *Reiſſan* and his Secretary were diſcharged and cleared in the moneth of *July*, 1655, which was in the very heat of the War between the *Catholicks* and the *Proteſtants*; ſo that they had liberty of forging what impoſtures they pleaſed againſt the *Proteſtants*, both at *Lucerna*, and *Turin*, without the leaſt contradiction; which accordingly they did to purpoſe. For, at *Lucerna*, were publiſhed at the ſame time, two perſonal Citations againſt the ſaid *Leger*, *Michelin*, and *Danna*: And as for *Berru*, he was likewiſe at the ſame time (as a recompence for his perjury procured for him by *Reiſſan*) diſcharged and ſet at liberty, notwithſtanding he had been convicted of two aſſaſſinations, the one whereof we have already mentioned, and the other at *S. Giovanni*, where he murthered one *Giovanni Bertot*, a *Proteſtant*. After this trayterous and baſe action, he came (like *Sinon* to the *Trojans* in *Virgils Æneads*) to the ſaid *Leger*, and a great number of the Paſtors, and chief of the Valleys, and leaning upon his ſtaff, and bemoaning his condition, he proteſted, *That he was hardly able to ſtand upright, by reaſon of the many blows and knocks that he had received by the Papiſts, to make him forſwear himſelf againſt the ſaid* Leger *and the reſt; but that, as he could not in Conſcience do ſo wicked a thing, ſo he had withſtood them to the utmoſt, telling plainly thoſe that ſo urged him, that he would rather endure to be torn in pieces with wilde horſes; who thereupon ſeeing his conſtancy, had beaten him moſt unmercifully, and then caſt him out into the midſt of the open ſtreet, where he had miſerably died, had not a certain Jew had compaſſion on him, and took him up as he was groveling on the ground, and ready to give up the ghoſt.* In the mean time, the *Treaty of Peace* being finiſhed at *Pigneroglio*, namely, in the moneth of *Auguſt*, 1655. Mr. *Leger* and the reſt, againſt whom the proceſs had been made, as againſt Criminals, (a thing that they never in the leaſt dreamt of !) making ſome abode at *Pigneroglio*, came to hear the news thereof; and immediately addreſſing themſelves to the *Prefect Reiſſan*, who was the chief Miniſter of Juſtice (or rather Injuſtice) in that Province, earneſtly intreated him to tell them, if it were true that *Berru* had thus accuſed them; who made them anſwer in ſuch dubious terms, that they began to have a very great jealouſie of the thing, inſomuch that they thought it high time to have immediate recourſe to the *Senator*

Prerrofhino, who had been a little before deputed by his Royal Highnefs, to give him an Information concerning the affaffination of the
Prieft, befeeching him with all poffible importunity, to declare unto
them the truth of the whole matter, and to appoint them a fet time
and place for to make their Juftification.   Whereupon, this Senator
told them plainly, that *Berru* had really accufed them of fuborning
him to fwear falfly againft *D'Agot* and his Mafter, and therewithal
fhewed them a Copy of the Citation againft the faid *Leger*, and the
reft of his Complices ; the fum and fubftance whereof was, *To banifh
them out of his Royal Highnefs Dominions, in cafe they did not appear perfonally at* Turin, *to anfwer to fuch Interrogatories as fhould be made to
them about that bufinefs.*   Upon this the *Sieur Leger*, by the affiftance
of *David Leger* Minifter, handled the matter fo, that they immediately after caufed *Berru* to be apprehended in the plain of *Angrognia*,
where he was newly arrived, and lurking in the Highways, where the
faid *Leger* was wont to pafs to and fro, on fet purpofe, and with full
defign to affaffinate him with the very firft opportunity. This wretch,
finding himfelf thus furprized, ufed all the devices he could poffibly,
to get out of their hands, although they affured him, that they intended nothing more againft him, then to make him verifie what he had
formerly confeffed before a full Affembly of their Minifters and others.
Now when the *Sieur Leger* was affured that *Berru* was apprehended
and in faft hold and cuftody, he went and declared openly the whole
ftory to the *Senator Perrichini*, to the *Referendano Tarquine*, yea and
to *Reiffan* himfelf, who was on the fudden not a little furprized at it.
And after that, to the *French Ambaffador,* and the Ambaffadors of the
Evangelical Cantons; and in the end (though with much difficulty)
he got leave to bring the perjured perfon to *Pigneroglio*, whither he hoped to obtain leave of coming face to face aginft him in open Juftice,
and to that end extreamly folicited, as well all the Minifters of his
Royal Highnefs, as the *French*, and *Switzar Ambaffadors* for their Interceffion ; the laft whereof openly protefted, that in cafe of a refufal,
they would complain *De denegatâ juftitiâ,* &c. But the plain truth is,
all the fatisfaction that the perfons injured then received, was onely
this, that *there fhould be a Letter written to* Turin *about it,* annd a while
after, *that the Anfwer from* Turin *was, that there could be nothing done
in it.* And fo the faid *Leger* was conftrained to content himfelf with
the honour of apprehending a perjured perfon, and to be declared (as
indeed they were, both he and the others who had been accufed by
His Royal Minifters, in the prefence of the *Ambaffadors*, and all the
Deputies of the *Valleys*) by the mouth of *Monfieur Balcet* Notary of
Pragela, as *perfons altogether innocent, and clearly and throughly juftified
from the accufation which* Berru *had made againft them :* But as for any
other formal nulling thereof, they were made to believe, that the third
Citation having not yet been publifhed, the Accufation of *Berru* was not
at all valid, and therefore they ought to fit down and be quiet. After
this, *Berru* was brought to *Turin*, from whence he was faid to be fent
to the *Venetian Galleys*, although he had been convicted (as hath been
already

already noted) to have been the very man who aſſaſſinated the Prieſt
in the company of *Daniel* the ſon of *Bartholomeo Belin*, a young man
newly turned Papiſt. And in effect, there needs no better proof for it
than *Reiſſan*'s own Atteſtation, who did divers times give it to *Mr.*
Leger, and the others, yea, and which is more, he wrote to one *Bar-*
tholemo Genolat, Syndick of *S. Giovanni*, a diſtinct Narrative of the
whole Tranſaction in the following terms; namely, that *a certain*
young man by name Giovanni, *ſon to the deceaſed* Laurentio Benech *of*
Fenile, *Brother in Law of* Berru, *had ſuffered himſelf to be prevailed up-*
on, and perſwaded to ſtand Centinel, whileſt Berru *and* Belin *committed*
the Murther before-mentioned; and moreover, that he had intreated the
ſaid Genolat *to order the matter ſo, that the ſaid* Benech *might appear*
before the open Juſtice, according to the uſual form, to make an Authen-
tick Depoſition, aſſuring him, that upon the account of his Non-age, as
alſo that he had been deceived by his Brother in Law, he could ſuffer no pre-
judice in the world: Yet notwithſtanding all this, through the great
diſtruſt and fear that ſeized upon the ſpirit of this young man, they
were not able with all their Rhetorick to perſwade him to it; onely ſo
far they wrought upon him, as to appear before the Sieurs *Leger*, and
Genolat, in the preſence of *Sr. Jacopo Baſtie*, and *Giovanni Prin* his
Kinſman, to whom he confeſſed and affirmed, *That it was really true*
that Berru *and* Belin *had committed this aſſaſſination, and that they had,*
unwittingly, and before he was aware, engaged him to ſtand Centinel.
And indeed, the young man repreſented all the circumſtances thereof ſo nakedly and plainly, that he left not the leaſt doubt or ſcruple in their minds about the truth of them. Beſides all this, the
Mother in Law and Wife of this *Berru* aſſured them, that the matter
was juſt ſo as it was repreſented. And certainly, though it be a matter of no ſmall difficulty to penetrate into the Depths of *Satan*, yet
this buſineſs looks with a very ſuſpicious countenance; for if *Berru*
had depoſed juſtly and righteouſly againſt thoſe Miniſters, why ſhould
he have refuſed to be confronted with them, and ſo have brought
thoſe Impoſtors and ſuborners to Juſtice? And on the contrary, if the
Miniſters were innocent, why ſhould a man charged with no leſs then
two aſſaſſinations, and as many perjuries, be ſuffered to eſcape? No,
though there had been no more preſſing arguments than thoſe ſad
complaints, and thoſe bitter tears alone, which that poor Widow of
Mean poured out at *Pigueroglio*, demanding Juſtice of *Monſ. de Ser-*
vient, in terms that were ſufficient (one would have thought) to have
moved the very ſtones in the Walls to have pity and compaſſion on
her. To conclude, it's too too evident, that ſome more mighty and
potent adverſary of the *Reformed party*, lying in *Ambuſh*, was the con-
triver of this murther, to have the better pretext for all their cruel dealings, however perhaps it might be immediatly acted by inferiour hands;
who certainly, in caſe they had not been protected by ſuch means, had
received no better a reward for their pains, than *Giovanni Odin* of *An-*
grognia did not long before; who for a fact of the very ſame nature
was baniſhed the Dominions of *His Royal Highneſs*, and ſo cloſely

purfued by Juftice, that he looked not upon himfelf to be fecure, no not within the Territories of *France* it felf, until fuch time as he had renounced his Religion.

Upon thefe and the like frivolous and feigned Accufations, were the Deputies of thofe poor Creatures, and their Supplications unhappily and miferably rejected by the Court of *Savoy* : For, having been at *Turin* to prefent this their Requeft, as alfo inftantly to befeech the chief Minifters of State to favour them with admittance into His Royal Highnefs prefence, there to caft themfelves at his feet ; the Council *De propaganda fide & extirpandis hæreticis*, (which was compofed of the Archbifhop of *Turin*, His *Royal Highnefs* Confeffor, the *Abbey* of *La Montà*, the *Prior Rorenco*, the Lords of *Lucerna*, together with the *Marquefs* of *Pioneffe*, the great *Chancellor*, The chief *Prefident* of the *Chamber*, the chief of the Senate *Ferrais*, and the other Prefidents, *Beletis* and *Nomis*) hindred the faid Deputies from having audience of their prince, and contrary to all juftice and equity, ufurped the cognizance of this Affair, which no way belonged to them, being of the adverfe party. And thus were they conftrained to feek Juftice of their Oppreffours ! And although poffibly fomething might have been done even with that Council, if they could but have obtained audience of them, (it being not impoffible, nor altogether improbable, that fome of their Confciences might have rebuked them, and that mifery with importunity might have wrought upon them) yet neither was this granted to the poor Deputies, no not fo much as to come perfonally before the faid Council *De extirpandis Hæreticis*, but they were forced to fend in their *Procurator Gibellino* a Papift ; who knowing right well, that Excommunication was the certain punifhment of all thofe who any ways favoured the *Heretical Proteftant* party, durft not fpeak a word, before he had fallen down upon his knees, and begg'd leave of the *Archbifhop*, who was Prefident of the faid Council. And the Conclufion was, *That thofe of the Valleys were commanded to make no more requefts to His* Royal Highnefs *touching this bufinefs, unlefs they would fend Deputies with Procuration, and power to accept and promife* (a poor recompence for fo long a delay) *all that which fhould be ordered them.* This Anfwer made the poor people almoft for ever defpair of ever making another Addrefs : However, like the *importunate Widow* in the *Gofpel*, they fent again their Deputies to *Turin* with their Requeft, and with Order to endeavour to get audience of *His Royal Highnefs.* And to this end, befides other Interceffions, they inftantly requefted *Madam Royal* to have pitty on them, and to procure the fame for them , writing Her a Letter, as followeth.

A

A Supplicatory Letter of the poor *Evangelical Churches* of theV alleys of *Piemont,* to *Madame Royale.*

An Authentick Copy of the true Original whereof is to be seen in the publick Library of the famous University of Cambridge.

Dal 1638. si compiaque l'equita & clemenza di V. A. R. confirmare l'antiche Concessioni del fu Signor Duca Carolo Emanuel suocero di Gloriosa Memoria, e Serenissimi Predecessori, & hacci di gratia speciale, tutto il tempo della sua felice regenza conservati nel pacifico & quieto goldimento, *&c.*

*I*N *the year* 1638. *your Royal Highness was pleased, according to your Justice and Clemencie, to confirm those Ancient Grants of the deceased Lord,* Duke Ch. Emanuel, *your Father in Law, of glorious memory, and your most serene Predecessors: And by your especial grace you have kept us, all the time of your most happie Reign, without the least innovation or alteration, in a peaceable condition, and quiet enjoyment of the same ; for the which we render you our most humble acknowledgements.* Now, *may it please your Royal Highness, our most gracious Princess and Ladie, notwithstanding the same confirmation made unto us of the said grants, by the sinister and malicious Information of such as bear us hatred and ill will, as if we had transgressed the bounds allotted us by those Concessions, and our most ancient Customes (the quite contrary whereof we both have and shall sufficiently make appear in due time and place) the Auditor* Gastaldo *hath published an Order the* 25 *of* January *past, by which all the Inhabitants of* Lucerna, Lucernette, Fenile, Bubiana, Campiglione, S. Giovanni, La Torre, Bricherasio, *and* S. Secundo, *who would not turn Catholicks, were commanded to forsake their Houses and Estates within three days, upon pain of death ; and not onely so, but constrained to betake themselves, some to the tops of the Mountains amidst the Snow and Ice, and many into Caves for want of shelter. And when they sought for a redress, with most humble Requests to your* H. R. *they were rejected by their Excellencies, the principal and chief Ministers of State, by whom they were appointed to depute Commissioners with sufficient Procuration and Authoritie to make and accept of new Propositions and Conditions, without which we were never to return, or appear in their presence more. But we, not able to undergo such Conditions, for several considerable Reasons, which the experience of past evils hath taught us, and judging them not at all necessary, because we demand nothing but a confirmation of those Grants that have been alreadie confirmed in the year* 1620. *by* Your Royal Highness, *and to enjoy the same as we have done for many Ages, and time out of mind, under the happie Reign of your most famous Predecessors ; and refusing to act against our Consciences, according to the true intent and purpose of our Concessions, though in all things else we have constantly behaved our selves as becometh faithfull Servants and most obedient*

dient *Subjects of your Royal Highness, are now, upon this very account, reduced to great exigencies and desolations ; and therefore it is, that we have recourse to the Clemencie, and the exemplary Pitty of your* Royal Highness, *most earnestly beseeching you, to extend the bowels of your compassions towards so many hundreds of poor Families, Women and small innocent Babes, who being ready to perish with hunger and cold, do with Rivers of bloudie tears implore your mercifull assistance, and to vouchsafe, in imitation of so many most serene Princesses of* your Royal *Family, of famous memorie, to become an instrument of our Tranquillity with his* Royal Highness : *That so being restored to our former peaceable condition, and all Orders to the contrary being revoked, we may continue both in life and death that faithfull obedience which we ow to your Royal Highness. And we will pray,* &c.

From the Valleys, Febr. 20. 1655.

They wrote also other Letters to several of the Princes of the bloud, touching the same subject, in the following terms : An Authentick Transcript of the true Original whereof is to be seen in the publick Library of the famous University of *Cambridge.*

Serenissimo Signore,

Il Signor Duca Emanuel Filiberto Avo di V. A. Serenissima per accordio a capi del 1561. havendoci stabiliti certi limiti per gl' essercitii publici di nostra Religione limito parimente l' habitatore all' luoghi & terre delle Valli di Lucerna, Perosa, S. Martino, fuori delli quali ci fu interdetto, salvo, &c.

Most Serene Lord,

EManuel Philibert, *Duke, and Grandfather to your most* serene Highness, *having by an agreement to several Articles in the year* 1561. *established certain bounds for the exercise of our Religion, did confine also our habitations within the places and Lands of the Valleys of* Lucerna, Perosa, *and* S. Martino, *which we were forbidden to exceed (such onely excepted as were expresly nominated) And the benefit of these Articles we have still peaceably enjoyed until the end of the year 1602. at which time an Order was surreptitiously obtained by such as hated us, from the most serene Duke* Ch. Emanuel, *Father to your most serene Highness of glorious memorie ; by vertue whereof, those of* Fenile, Bubiana, Bourgh, *and* Lucerna, *came to be molested: Although upon better Information of the truth of those Affairs, His* most serene Highness *of his Clemencie expresly commanded, by a Grant of the* 9 Apr. *and another of the* 14 May, 1603. *that they should be restored to their ancient possessions ; which was*
likewise

likewise confirmed by a third Edict, in the year 1620. *the same being duely interinated.* Yea, *His Royal Highness, who by the grace of God at this day reigns, after a long and chargeable debate, hath confirmed unto us the very same Concessions, with a formal Declaration, not to adde to, or diminish the same, as appears by his Decree of the* 29 *of* December, 1653. *But yet notwithstanding all this, having without intermission solicited for the Interination thereof, and satisfied all the demands of the most Illustrious* Chamber of Accompts *in order thereunto* ; *at the very instant and nick of time, when according to the intention of the abovesaid Acts we hoped to obtain those our Requests, came the* Auditor Gastaldo *with Orders to constrain us to quit our habitations in* Fenile, Bubiana, S. Secundo, Lucerna, Lucernetta, Bricherasio, S. Giovanni, *and* La Torre, *where, by vertue of the abovesaid Concessions, and long before, time out of mind, we have peaceably remained: By which means, more than a thousand Families, and those very numerous, who never committed any thing contrarie to the Orders of your* Royal Highness, *being alreadie ruinated by various calamities which they have undergone, must now perish in a sad and miserable manner among the snowie Mountains, where they have onely the Canopie of Heaven for their shelter and covert. Now being thus pressed with so many calamities, and all from a pure hatred to that Religion which we profess, we had resolved to address our most humble Supplications, and to flie for refuge to the Clemencie of his Royal Highness, our most serene Prince and Lord, had we not been rejected by their Excellencies the chief and principal Ministers, and by them threatned never to admit of one more Petition for the future, in case we did not first submit to certain conditions which were never before practised under the happie Reign of your most* serene Predecessors; *and particularly, in case we did not forthwith send Commissioners with a plenipotentiarie power to conclude and accept of new Conditions, which we are in no sort able to perform, forasmuch as we demand nothing, save onely, that his* Royal Highness *will be pleased, according to his gracious promises often made us, to suffer us to enjoy the aforesaid Concessions, as we before enjoyed the same under the reign of his most* serene Predecessors, *and especially seeing there hath not happened since the decease of the father of your most serene Highness, any change or alteration, excepting onely what hath been to our prejudice. In these Exigencies and Calamities, being destitute of all other Counsel in the world, but such as Despair usually suggests to Men driven from their homes and habitations* ; *and seeing themselves in the mean while plundered by their malicious neighbours, whose aim is, by that means to induce them to some act of revenge, to the end his* Royal Highness *may have an occasion to be yet more exasperated against them (who has indeed alreadie been too falsly informed against us, to the advance and promoting of our final banishment :) And having no freedome of access to his Royal Highness, we cast our selves at the feet of your most* serene Highness, *to whom, as to a Sanctuarie, we have our recourse, humbly beseeching, that you would suffer your self to be moved with compassion towards so many hundreds of small and innocent* Christian *Babes, according to that influence which your interposition and endeavours cannot but have upon the heart of His* Royal Highness, *and his most excellent*

cellent

cellent *Minifters of State* ; *And that you will be pleafed to procure us the revoking of fuch fevere Orders, to the end that we may enjoy the ufe of the forementioned Conceffions onely, which we have formerly enjoyed under the happie Government of the moft* ferene *Predeceffors of his* Royal Highnefs. *Thefe graces and favours we hope for at the hands of your moft* ferene Highnefs, *in the mean while moft humbly intreating you to vouchfafe to pardon that boldnefs and importunitie which neceffitie puts us upon : And we fhall continue to pray to God for the profperitie of his* Royal Highnefs, *and all the* Royal *Family* ; *and in particular of your moft ferene Highnefs, remaining*

Your moft Serene Highnefs

In *Angrogna,*   moft humble and obedient
Febr.20. 1655.   Servants, the men profeffing
                        the Reformed Religion in the
                             Valleys of *Lucerna,* *Pero·*
                             fa, and *St. Martino.*

Befides all this, they reiterated their fupplicatory Letters to the *Great Chancellor,* and to the Marquefs of *Pioneffa* ; but all in vain: For neither the *Princes,* nor the *Great Chancellor* vouchfafed to anfwer them a word. But *Madame Royale* fhe fent them to the *Marquefs of Pioneffa,* and the *Marquefs of Pioneffa* he fent them to make good the Procuration which the Council *De extirpandis Hæreticis* had formerly enjoyned them, without which he refufed to give them any Audience; which indeed was a fecret and fubtil Defign of his, to tempt the poor people by this means obliquely to yeeld up the Right of their former Conceffions, and purely fubmit to *His Royal Highnefs* pleafure : In which cafe, the Council *De extirpandis Hæreticis* would have undoubtedly taken the advantage of perfwading *His Royal Highnefs,* that fince they had foregone their Conceffions, *His Royal Highnefs* was altogether difingaged of all former promifes and Conceffions, and ought to exterminate them out of his Dominions. Which ftratagem the poor people perceiving, wrote another fupplicatory Letter to *Madame Royale,* as likewife one of the fame nature to the *Marquefs Pioneffa,* as follows.

A

A Supplicatory Letter of the *Evangelical Churches* of the Valleys of *Piemont*.

An Authentick Tranſcript of the true Original whereof is to be ſeen in the publick Library of the famous Univerſity of Cambridge.

Altezza Reale,

Dalla ſingolar gratia & benigno favore, che moſſe ultimamente la clementia di V. A. R. a far Riſponder quella che s'inardiſſimo preſentarle ſotto li 20 Feb. ſperiamo, come humiliſſimamente la ſupplichiamo, che ſi degnara porger l'orechio alla preſente replica che a ſuoi piedi proſtratti, *&c.*

Royal Highneſs,

*F*Rom *the experience of that ſingular Grace, and bountifull Favour which lately moved your Royal Highneſs clemencie, to cauſe anſwer to be made to one of our Letters (bearing Date the 20th. of* Febr. *) which we took the boldneſs to preſent you*; *we hope (as with all humilitie we requeſt) that you will vouchſafe to give ear to the preſent Replie which we your poor ſubjects, being proſtrate at your feet, do here humbly tender unto you, with no other intent then to inform your Royal Highneſs touching ſome Articles, whereby it will manifeſtly appear, that your Royal Highneſs hath been greatly miſ-informed. As for example. Firſt, whereas it is alledged,* That the places prohibited in the Order publiſhed by the *Auditor Gaſtaldo,* have always been oppoſed and excepted, *it cannot be proved as to the places of* S. Giovanni, La Torre, S. Secondo, *and the others : And much leſs, that any of the moſt ſerene Predeceſſors of your Royal Highneſs had ever any intention to limit our dwellings to thoſe four Places which are now deſigned for their preciſe bounds*; *but on the contrarie, they have alwaies granted and permitted us that libertie in all the wonted places of the three Valleys*; *and onely* Roccapiatta, S. Bartholomeo, *and* Praruſtino *are nominated as Towns not appertaining to the three* Valleys, *as in the firſt* Article *of that Grant which bears Date the* 14th. *of* May, 1603. *may be plainly ſeen. And although by that of* 1602. Fenile, Bubiana, *and* Lucerna

came

came to be *difquieted, His Royal Highnefs* Charls Emanuel *of glorious memorie, did yet by another Grant, bearing Date the 9th. of* Apr. 1605. *in the third and fixth Articles, permit them to re-inhabite thofe places. Yea, and in another of the 29th. of* Septemb. *in the fame year, it is exprefled in formal terms, in the very firft Article, That* fuch as had Goods without the prefcribed Limits (that is to fay, the Limits apointed for Preaching, according to the Grants of 1561.) fhould be permitted to return to their dwellings. *In the which faid Grants, the Limits of* Preaching *are often found to differ from thofe of* habitation ; *which* Limits of habitation *are extended to all the Towns and places appertaining to the three Valleys, with their places adjacent, as is to be feen in the eighth, ninth, eleventh, and twentieth Articles, which to avoid tedioufnefs we fhall not here repeat. Thefe things being reprefented unto his faid Royal Highnefs* (Charls Emanuel *of glorious memorie*) *made him incline to revoke the Orders publifhed againft thofe of* Fenile, Lucerna, Bubbiana, *and to reftore all to a peaceable condition, and to confirm the fame with an irrevocable Edict, bearing Date* Aug. the 17th. 1602. *upon which Account they paid* 6000. Ducatons, *as appears by the Decree made and interinated at that time by the moft Illuftrious* Chamber, *and moft ferene* Senate. *By all which it is evident, that we are fo far from having juftly deferved the imputation of tranfgreffing the Limits, or abufively ufurping the leaft Priviledge, that on the contrarie, we have ftrictly kept our felves within our juft meafure and compafs, as the* Cataftri *of the Commonalties may fufficiently witnefs for us. In the fecond place, we are accufed of many extravagancies and exceffes ; but we are not confcious to the leaft (after the clearing up that of* Villaro, *at the coming of* Conte Todefco) *fave onely, that forged one of* La Torre, *fo ridiculoufly invented and interpreted, that the Auditor* Gaftaldo *himfelf having difcovered the abfurditie thereof, promifed no more words fhould be made of it. Yea, put the cafe any Crime had been involved in it, it could not be any ways imputed to thofe of* Lucerna, Fenile, Bubbiana, Campiglione, Bricheraffio, S. Secundo, *and the reft, forafmuch as by the Grant of the 29th. of* Septemb. 1603. Art. 3. *as alfo by that of his Royal Highnefs, by the Grace of God now reigning, bearing Date the 4th. of* June, 1653. *it is plainly declared,* That the innocent are not to fuffer with the guilty, but that Juftice fhall be upheld with a ftrong hand for the fuppreffion of the refractory. *As to the efcape of* Berruto, *we might with truth alledge, that having upon the firft demand of* Mr. Collateral Perrachione, *caufed him to be fecured in that very place where we were required, we ought not to be queftioned, or demanded any further account of him, as being no waies acceffary to his efcaping, efpecially feeing that immediately after that accident happened, we fpared no endeavours to retake him ; and it manifeftly appears by divers and fundrie Examinations, That he broke Prifon for no other caufe then to efcape the great inconveniencies and tortures which in fome manner he was threatned with ; the great noife and rumour whereof, together with the imprifonment of* Berruto, *might well be the caufe why others would fay little, as not daring to bear witnefs to the Truth, for fear of the like danger. By all thefe paffages, your* Royal Highnefs *may eafily*
                                                                    fee,

see, how the Truth is prejudiced and sophisticated, and how just the Title is which we claim of dwelling in those places which are at present so much disquieted and molested, and consequently the innocencie of us poor Fugitives, who upon these grounds of truth and uprightness, are imboldned to cast themselves once more at your Royal Highness *feet, humbly begging, that they may, out of your great clemencie, be re-established, being turned over to the Council* De propaganda Fide, *which is expresly erected against us, who next after God, acknowledge no other Patron but His* Royal Highness, *and their Excellencies his Ministers of State, (as we believe that we ought in Conscience to do:) And that the most faithfull and most obedient Subjects of the Crown may not be forced to wander and stray into other Countries, since that all the other places of the Valleys scarce suffice to contain their own native Inhabitants. This is the singular Grace and Favour that we hope from the Clemency and Compassions of your Royal Highness, that His* Royal Highness *would vouchsafe to behold and grant these our most humble Requests. And in the mean time, we shall not cease to continue our most ardent prayers to Almighty God, for the prosperity of your Royal Highness, with the peace and enlargement of His* Royal Highness *Dominions, as being*

Your Royal Highnefs

In *Angrogna,*
March 16.
1655.

moſt humble and moſt obedient
Servants, the Commiſſioners of
the Valleys of *Lucerna, Perofa,*
S. Martino, for the places adjacent, and for themſelves.

A

A fupplicatory Letter of the poor diftreffed Churches of the Valleys of *Piemont,* to the Marquefs of *Pioneffa,* 16. *March* 1655.

Excellentifsimo Segnor,

La benegnita & patienza con laquale V. Eccellenza fi e degnata rifponder alle lettere che s: inardiffimo addrizzarle fotto li.8. cadutto Feb. ci fa fperare che anche adochiera la prefente replica, che con la debita riverenza veniamo a prefentarle, &c.

*T*He benignity and patience wherewith your Excellency vouchfafed to *anfwer the Letters, which we were emboldened to write to you, bearing date the eighth of* February *laft, gives us fome ground to hope, that you will accordingly caft your Eys upon this prefent Reply,which with all due reverence we prefent unto you, to the end onely, that we may better inform you,touching certain Heads or Articles;humbly begging your pardon for this our flownefs, which the diftance of places, and the difficulty in affembling our People, hath againft our wills, occafioned. Firft, your Excellency accufeth us, as guilty of* many exceffes and exorbitances committed, and that we have given juft caufe, for the publication of the Order, publifhed by the Auditour *Gaftaldo. Although after the clearing our felves of the Fact at* Villaro, *(which was fufficiently done at the coming of* Conte Todefco) *we have not heard of the leaft Mifcarriage laid to our charge, unlefs your Excellency would urge againft us that foolifh bufinefs of* La Torre, *which was acted by a company of Youths, (a great part whereof were the Children of* Catholicks) *not at all reflecting upon the Catholick Church, or having the leaft appearance of any affront either to the Mafs, or thofe that faid it, as the Auditour* Gaftaldo *was very well informed, and to that end made us a promife, that nothing more fhould be fpoke of it, (though fhould there have been any Delinquents, who had had a hand in fuch a bufinefs, yet his Royal Highnefs declares in the firft Article of that Act of* June *the fourth* 1633. *in order to the Explanation of the Conceffions of the nine and twentieth of* September 1603. *in the third Article,* That it is not at all his meaning, that the innocent fhould be punifhed with the guilty, provided always, that we make fevere Inquifition after the later, *which we have never refufed to do) And whereas, touching the Limits of Habitation, your Excellency is informed,* That we pretend this ground for our defence, namely, that they were fet out, after the Conceffions made by *Raconigi* ; which not being true, our dwelling places remain ufurped and abufive. *We intreat your Excellency with all humility, and for the love of God, to vouchfafe to believe that our Reafons do manifeft quite another thing ; as alfo, that on the contrary, we alleged our Limits in fome places have been ftraitened. We will not fay, by reafon of their banifhment out of the Marquifate of* Saluzzo, Praviglielmo, Fefteone, *and many other Cities and Towns of* Piemont, *which are not fpecified*

or

or expreſſed in the ſaid Grants (however, that even all thoſe places have in times paſt been tolerated) but particularly upon the account of the Valley of Meane in them expreſſed, together alſo with Campiglione and Borgo of Bubiana, which were comprehended in them, as under the Towns of the three Valleys, which were at that time uſually tolerated, in which the reverend Raconigi after the Wars, d d again ſettle us ; as alſo his Royal Highneſs by his Grants 1603. confirmed the ſame, cauſing it to be interinated in the Year 1620. And it's evident, that in the Anſwers to the third and ſixth Articles of the firſt Memorial, of the ninth of April 1603. given to thoſe of Fenile, Bubiana, and Lucerna, whoſe dwelling onely found oppoſition, and none others till that time, it was permitted them to be re-eſtabliſhed, becauſe that thoſe Towns and places were common and tolerated in the three Valleys appointed for the Limits of Habitation. And in the firſt Article of the Grant of the nine and twentieth of September, in the year aboveſaid, it may be clearly ſeen, that without any Reſerve, in the ſaid three Valleys, all ſuch might return to their reſpective Habitations, who had their Eſtates without the Limits for Preaching, which was confirmed the ſeventeenth of Auguſt 1620. and interinated 1620. with an expreſs Act for the Payment of ſix thouſand Ducatoons upon that very Account. And ſo was the Habitation of thoſe beyond Pelice rendred peaceable, firm, and perpetual ; although not altogether free from divers Vexations that were brought upon them, by their ill-affected Neighbours. To this may be added, that Roccapiatta, St. Bartholomeo, Praruſtino, were not named diſtinctly and apart, in the third Article of the Conceſsions of the fourteenth of May 1603. and the firſt Article of thoſe of 1620. for any other reaſon, than this, namely, becauſe thoſe Towns did not belong to the three Valleys, as may be there found ; which is a manifeſt proof, that touching our Dwelling or Habitation, no Town belonging to the three Valleys frequented and tolerated before, ſuffered the leaſt oppoſition : beſides all this, the Agreement made by the Lord Raconigi which onely doth eſtabliſh the Limits of Preaching, the ſame which now are appointed for Habitation, doth permit alſo their Habitation without and beyond the bounds of Preaching, in all the other Towns of the three Valleys and their adjacent parts. When the great and the ſerious Affairs of your Excellency ſhall permit you to reade the 8, 9, 10, 11, 12, 13, 14, 20, and 21. Articles, (which we do not here ſpecifice, to avoid trouble and tediouſneſs) we are fully perſwaded, that the Limits for Preaching, having been ſo often diſtinguiſhed from the other of Habitation, which have no other bounds, but thoſe of the three Valleys and their adjacent parts, your Excellency will not blame us for endeavouring, to make good the juſt Title of our Habitations, againſt any ſophiſtical Interpretations and Diſtinctions. For, really, ſo far are we from being our own Judges in the Interpretation of ſuch Grants, (which belongs onely to the Sovereign himſelf, who makes them) that we wholly refer our ſelves to the Intentions of the ſame Sovereigns, who granted thoſe Acts, with the expreſs terms of ſuch their Conceſsions, as likewiſe to the uſe, practiſe, and obſervation of the ſame under their happy Government. Nor can it be objected to us with truth, That we have any ways in after-times encroached, or enlarged our ſaid Limits. For, on the contrary, they have been every way

way leſſened, and contraƈted. And if any of the Reformed Churches have at any time bought any Lands of Catholicks (as is notwithſtanding permitted by the twentieth Article of the Conceſsions of 1561.) your Excellency may aſſure your ſelf, that they have alſo ſold four for one, to the very ſame Catholicks. All which being really true, we intreat your Excellency, to improve your Intereſt, for the re-eſtabliſhment of ſuch poor diſtreſſed People,and the annulling of all Orders whatſoever to the contrary,to the end, that ſo many faithfull Subjeƈts of his R.H. be not deprived of the graces and favours granted to and enjoyed by them, under ſo many of his Predeceſſours, and by him, (as alſo by his moſt ſerene Grand-father, of glorious memory) ſo often confirmed, with ſo ſtriƈt a Charge, and by ſo expreſs Aƈts. And that they may not be forced to quit and abandon their Eſtates, (as otherways they muſt be forced to do) eſpecially conſidering, that all the other Towns of the Valleys, have not wherewithall to imploy and maintain their own inbred Inhabitants. All which we hope to obtain by means of the powerfull Influence and Authority of your Excellency, who is ſo full of Pity, Clemency, and Juſtice; which ſhall cauſe us to continue to offer up our Prayers to God, for the increaſe of his Royal Highneſs Dominions, and the proſperity of his Perſon, and Royal Family, and in particular of your Excellency, as being

In Angrogna   *Your Excellencies*

16. March,   *Moſt humble and moſt obedient Servants, the Comiſsioners*
1655.   *for the Valleys of* Lucerna, Peroſa, St. Martin,
                 and the places adjacent, and for themſelves.

    Theſe and ſuch like were the reiterated Supplications of the Deputies of thoſe poor diſtreſſed Churches, who notwithſtanding did all the while but *Surdo canere*, for they could not poſſibly obtain Audience of the Dukes Court, unleſs they would yield to give their Deputies a plenipotentiary power as aboveſaid; which to do without any limitation, and according as the Marqueſs had preſcribed them, they knew right well could have no other effeƈt or iſſue than this, namely, to yield tacitly to the quitting and renouncing their former Conceſſions, and other Privileges. In ſum, when they ſaw themſelves conſtrained to it, they choſe their Deputies, and gave them Inſtructions as ample as they could poſſibly, which were ſigned by all the Paſtours and Deputies of their Churches, who were likewiſe authorized by the power of *Lucerna*. The ſubſtance of thoſe Inſtructions, after their due Proteſtation of fidelity and obedience, was, that they *ſent thoſe their Deputies to* Turin, *to accept of, and promiſe all that it ſhould pleaſe his Royal Highneſs to appoint them, according to their ancient Conceſsions, and the Rules of a good Conſcience. But as there's no charming a Lion that is greedy of his Prey*, ſo were all the Intreaties and Solicitations in the world to little purpoſe, as to the ſoftening of *Pioneſſa's* ſtony heart, who thirſted ſo violently after the Bloud of thoſe poor Creatures. And accordingly he ſlighted this laſt Supplication of
theirs

theirs with as much difdain as he had the former: however, that he might not too openly difcover the black Defign of the Council, *De propaganda fide & extirpandis Hæreticis,* before the hour of its Execution, he ftrove to difguife all his Anfwers to the poor People, in fuch ænigmatical terms, (not unlike the Devil heretofore in the Oracles) that though he gave them but cold comfort, yet he left them not without fome glimmering hopes at leaft of a Day of Audience, for the hearing of their Grievances and Complaints, that fo during this paufe and intervall of time, all things might be in a better readinefs for the Day of Slaughter; which is the fubject of the following Chapter.

CHAP.

CHAP. VI.

A brief and most authentick Narrative of some part of those extraordinary Cruelties which were exercised against the poor Protestants of the Valleys of Piemont *, during the heat of the late Massacre , in the Year of our Lord* 1655. *in the Moneth of* April.

Every particular Circumstance whereof was abundantly verified to the Authour, during his abode in those parts, both by Word of Mouth, and by the formal Attestations and Subscriptions of those very persons who were both Eye and Ear Witnesses of those inhumane Cruelties, the true Originals of some whereof he hath exposed to publick view in the Library of the University of *Cambridg*, and for several weighty Reasons hath reserved the rest in his own custody, ready to give any ingenuous person full and clear satisfaction.

IN the former Chapter the *Christian* Reader hath had a large Account of the Popish Design upon the poor Evangelical Churches of the Valleys, this gives him a distinct and faithfull Narrative of the Execution thereof; which verily was as adequate to the contrivance, (as to matter of Cruelty) as an Impression to the Seal.

Upon *Saturday* the seventeenth of *April* 1655. while the poor Deputies of the Protestants were, by the artifice of *Pionessa,* detained at *Turin* for an Answer to their Requests, (where the fifth and last Chapter leaves them) there arrived a great Army at *St. Giovanni,* which was now, together with *La Torre,* and all the lower parts, disinhabited, and in a most desolate and lamentable condition. This Army encamped, for the space of some hours together, in a place called *St. Georgio,* and in the Dusk of the Evening, fell into the Burgh of *La Torre,* where they met with not so much as one soul of the Protestants,

save

save onely a little company of eight or ten persons, who not at all thinking that the Enemy was there, were seeking up and down for something to satisfie their hunger: but so soon as ever they approached the Covent, they were immediately descried by the Monks, and the Troopers who had lien there concealed several days before, for that very purpose, who, to shew the kindness they had for them, saluted them with a great Volley of Shot, whereby they slew upon the place one *Giovanni Combe* of *Villaro*, and hurt *Pietro Rostain* of *La Torre*; thereupon the rest, who saw themselves thus encompassed on every side, immediately fled for their Lives.

Upon the Lords Day following, which was the eighteenth of the same Moneth, the Enemy ranged up and down throughout the Communalties of *La Torre*, and *St. Giovanni*, plundering and pillaging at pleasure. And upon the nineteenth (being now, like a Snowball, become the bigger by rowling, and their number increased to about fifteen thousand) they set upon the Protestants in several Quarters among the little Hills of *St. Giovanni*, and *La Torre*, but the poor People having for a long time foreseen their Design, and being prompted, by the Law of Nature to self-preservation, took courage, and stood upon their own defence, and the Enemy was vigorously opposed on every side; in one place, by Captain *Jahier*, and in other places, by the Officers of *St. Giovanni*, *Angrognia*, *Roccapiatta*, and their Troops. The next day, which was *Tuesday*, the Popish Army made three several Attempts to take away the Bell of *St. Giovanni*, and to burn the Church, (although situated in the Confines of *Angrognia*, to which the Marquess of *Pionessa* had always assured his Protection, as being a place excepted in the Order of *Gastaldo* for that purpose, and named for the Retreat of the rest that he banished and drave out of their Habitations) nevertheless for a diversion, they set upon those of *St. Giovanni*, who had their Rendezvouz about a Mile off, in a certain place called *Castelus*, on the side of the Mountain of *Briqueras*, as also at *La Torre*, towards *Taliaret*: but those of the poor People, who were then in Arms, did so couragiously resist them, that they were constrained to a shamefull Retreat, with the loss of about fifty of their Men, and had not their Cavalry defended the Plain, they had been utterly defeated. In the mean while, there were none of the Protestants slain, except one of *Roccapiatta*, (upon whose dead Carkase they sufficiently revenged themselves) and another, *viz. Giovanni Brocher* of *St. Giovanni*. Upon the one and twentieth of the same Moneth, which was the terrible fatal day to the poor Protestants, the Marquess of *Pionessa*, by a hellish Stratagem held in Parley the Deputies of the Valley of *Lucerna* till Noon, and then treated them with a large Dinner, after which, they went their ways with much satisfaction and chearfulness, their mindes being as well filled with good hopes, as their bellies with meat; for indeed, the Marquess of *Pionessa* by his smooth language and solemn asseveration had fully perswaded them, that there should not be the least hurt done to any, except those of *St. Giovanni* and *La Torre*, as being the places specified in the Order of *Gastaldo* to

be

be prohibited to those of the Reformed party ; but as for all the rest, in case they should but receive and quarter some few Troops, as a token of their obedience, and that but for a short time, they might set their hearts at rest without fear or jealousie of the least inconvenience. Hereupon, the Agents of *Angrogna* went up to the head of those who it was pretended should onely go and quarter in those places, and there bestirred themselves with all the Perswasions imaginable, to keep the Men of their own party from making the least resistance ; the same did those of *Villaro* and *Bobio,* never dreaming the sad consequence of so great unadvisedness ; but the Enemies Men had no sooner entred in, but they found (when it was too late) how far the Catholicks keep Faith with those that they call Hereticks : for having used all possible artifices to draw the rest within their reach, they presently clapt to their Nets, and divided the Prey, putting all to Fire and Sword, slaying all they met with, that had but the likeness of Mankinde, and that in the most barbarous manner they could possibly devise ; for a general description whereof, I shall refer the Reader to an Extract of one of their own Letters, before I come to a more particular description of those horrid and unheard of Cruelties.

A faith-

A
FAITHFUL TRANSLATE

O F

A fad, and mournful Letter, written (as is
fuppofed) by fome of the poor diftreffed Proteftants of the Valleys of *P I E M O N T.*

C O N T A I N I N G,

A Summary, or brief Narrative of thofe horrible Cruelties, which were exercifed againft them,
in the late Mafsacre, in *April*
1655.

Peres & Freres,

*Nos l' armés n' ont plus d' eau, mais de fang, qui n' offufquent pas feu-
lement,* &c.

Brethren and Fathers,

"OUr tears are no more tears of water, but of bloud, which do
" not onely drown and obfcure our fight, but even opprefs our
" very hearts! Our pen is guided by a trembling hand! our brains
" are made dry by the many knocks we have received! and our minde
" fo exceedingly troubled by fuch unexpected and fuddain alarms,
" that we are not able to form a Letter, anfwerable to the intent of our
" mindes, or to the ftrangenefs of our defolations. Wherefore we en-
" treat your pardon herein, and that you would be pleafed among
" fo many clods of bloud, to gather up, and pick out the fenfe of
" our conceptions, and what we would (at leaft) impart unto you
" Whatfoever reports have been fpread abroad of our ftubbornefs in
" refufing to have recourfe to his Royal Highnefs, for the redref-
" fing of thofe our heavy grievances and moleftations, you cannot
" but know that we have never at all defifted, from writing fuppli-
" catory Letters, or prefenting our humble Requefts, by the hands
" of our Deputies, and that, they were fent, and referred, fometimes
" to the Council *de propaganda fide,* other times to the *Marquefs of*
" *Pioneffa.* And the laft 3. times they were plainly rejected, and denied
" fo much as an audience, under pretext that they had no Credenti-
" als,

"als, or Inftructions fufficient to empower them, to promife and ac-
"cept, in the name, and on the behalf of their refpective Churches,
"whatfoever it fhould pleafe his Royal Highnefs to grant to, or be-
"ftow upon them. And by the inftigation, and contrivance of the
"*Roman* Clergy, there was fecretly let in ambufh an Army of fix
"Thoufand men, who upon a fuddain (being animated and encou-
"raged thereto by the prefence and utmoft activity of the *Marquefs*
"*of Pioneffa*) fell moft violently upon thofe of *S. Giovanni* and *La*
"*Torre.*

"This Army being once entred, and having gotten footing, was
"foon encreafed, and became exceeding numerous by the addition
"of a multitude of the neighbouring Inhabitants throughout all *Pie-*
"*mont*, who hearing that we were given for a prey to the Plunderers,
"fell upon the poor people with an impetuous fury. To thefe were
"added a numberlefs number of Out-laws, prifoners, and other Of-
"fendours, who thought hereby to have both faved their fouls, and
"filled their purfes. And for the better opportunity to put their de-
"figne in execution,they were forced to receive five or fix Regiments
"of the *French* Army, befides fome *Irifh*, to whom (as it is repor-
"ted.) our Country was promifed, and feveral other Troops of
"Highway men, and Vagabond perfons, under pretext of coming
"into the Valleys for a *Rinfrefco* (as they term it) or frefh Quarter.

"This great multitude, by vertue of a Licenfe from the *Marquefs*
"of *Pioneffa*, being animated by the Monks, and conducted and en-
"ticed to the work by our wicked and unnatural neighbours, fell up-
"on us with fuch violence on every fide, and in fo horridly treache-
"rous a manner, (efpecially in *Angrognia*, *Villaro*, and *Bobio*, to whom
"the Marquefs had engaged himfelf, that in cafe they would but con-
"defcend to the lodging and quartering of one onely Regiment in
"each place, or Communalty, they fhould be fecured from all harm
"or violence) that in one moment of time all was turned into a con-
"fufed heap, and the Inhabitants conftrained, after fome skirmifhes,
"which they endured in their way for their own defence, to fly for
"their lives, together with their wives and little children; and that
"not onely thofe of the Plain, who had betaken themfelves to the
"Mountains, but likewife thofe of the Mountains themfelves, who
"had otherwife been certainly betrayed, and furprifed. However, all
"the diligence they could poffibly ufe for their prefervation, was not
"fufficient to prevent the deftruction of a very confiderable number
"of them: For in many places, (as in *Villaro*, and *Bobio*) they were fo
"hem'd in on every fide, the Enemy having feized on the Fort of
"*Mireburg*, and by that means ftopt the paffage, that there was no
"way left to flye or fave themfelves, but were moft fearfully maffacred
"and put to death. In one place they cruelly tormented no lefs then
"an hundred and fifty women and fmall children, and afterwards
"chopt off the heads of fome, and dafht the brains of others againft
"the Rocks. As for a great part of the Prifoners which they took,
"from fifteen years of age and upwards, who refufed to go to *Mafs*,
"they

" they hanged fome, and nailed the feet of others to trees, with their
" heads hanging towards the ground, all which they endured conftant-
" ly. It's reported that they carried fome of note, prifoners to *Turin*,
" as namely our poor Brother Mr. *Gros* Paftour, and fome part of his
" family. In fum, there's neither Cattle nor any other provifion left
" in the Valley of *Lucerna* ; what was faved was inconfiderable, and all
" the reft our Enemies carried and fold to feveral Towns in *Piemont*.
" 'Tis too evident, that all is loft, fince there are fome whole Com-
" munalties, efpecially S. *Giovanni*, and *La Torre*, where the bufinefs
" of fetting fire to our Houfes and Churches, was fo dexteroufly ma-
" naged by a *Francifcan Frier* and a certain *Prieft*, that they left not
" fo much as one of either unburnt. In thefe defolations the Mother
" has been bereft of her fweet Childe ! the Husband of his dear Wife!
" Thofe who were the richeft among us, are forced to beg their bread,
" yea which is worfe, they are weltring in their own bloud, and depri-
" ved of all the comforts of this life. And whereas there were fome
" Churches in S. *Martino* and other places, who have always been
" heretofore as a Sanctuary to the perfecuted, they have now them-
" felves been fummoned to quit their dwellings, and to depart every
" foul of them, and that upon a fuddain, without the leaft refpit, un-
" der pain of life. Neither is there any mercy for any of them, who
" are found within his Royal Highnefs Dominions. The pretext of
" thefe ftrange Maffacres, are, that we are Rebels to the Orders of his
" Royal Highnefs, for not having brought the whole City of *Geneva*
" within the Walls of *Mary Magdalene* Church ; or in plainer terms,
" for not having performed a pure impoffibility, in departing in a mo-
" ment from our houfes and habitations in *Bubbiana, Lucerna, Fenile,*
" *Bricheras, La Torre,* S. *Giovanni,* and S. *Secondo* ; And alfo, for ha-
" ving had our recourfe to his Royal Highnefs by unceffant fupplicati-
" ons to take pity on us ; who on the one fide, told us, that he would
" make no innovation ; and on the other fide, refufed to give us leave
" to depart out his Dominions peaceably, as we oft times befeeched
" him, in cafe he would not fuffer us to abide and enjoy the liberty of
" our confciences, as had always done his Predeceffours. True it is,
" that the Marquefs of *Pioneffa*, did produce us another excufe, by the
" hand of our *Procurator,* (and we have in our hands the very original !)
" which was, that it was his Royal Highnefs pleafure to abafe and take
" down our pride, for endeavouring to fhroud our felves and take
" Sanctuary under the protection of Foreign Princes and States.
" To conclude, our beautifull and flourifhing Churches are utterly
" loft, and that without remedy, unlefs God Almighty work mira-
" cles for us ! Their time is come, and our meafure is full ! *O have*
" *pity upon the defolations of Jerufalem* ! and , *Be grieved for the af-*
" *flictions of poor Jofeph* ! Shew the real effects of your compaffions!
" and let your bowels yearn upon fo many thoufands of poor
" fouls who are reduced to a morfel of bread , for *following the*
" *Lamb whither ever he goes*. We recommend our poor Shepherds,
                                               " together

" together with their fcattered and difperfed flocks, to your fervent
" Chriftian prayers, and reft in hafte

27. *April,* 1655.   *Your moft humble, and moft obliged*
                                      Servants and Brethren in
                                          the LORD.

I prefume the Chriftian Reader is now fomewhat prepared, by what
has been already hinted, with the greater conftancy, to behold thofe
dolefu l fpectacles which he fhall have here prefented before his eys.
The truth is, the cruelties which are here related, would abundantly
exceed the belief of any man (fave onely the Authors and Actors of
them) were they not accompanied with fuch Authentick proofs, that
he who denies the truth of them, muft, at the fame time deny his own
reafon and underftanding : For if the formal Atteftations of thofe that
were eye witneffes and by-ftanders, may be of any force with us ; if
the ftrong and wofull cries of fo many defolate and poor wretches,who
have been miferably rob'd and bereft of their relations, houfes, lands,
and all other comforts, may in any manner gain our belief; In a word,
if the formall depofition of one of the chief Commanders of that very
Army who were the Actors of thofe cruelties, figned with his own
hand, and that in the prefence of two fufficient Witneffes, may perfwade us to give any credit to fuch a Relation ; Or (which is yet one
degree nearer)if the voluntary confeffion of one of the Souldiers themfelves, and one who had his own hands embrewed in the bloud
of thofe poor creatures, to fome of his Comrades, in a boafting way,
that he had many times during the heat of the *Maffacre,* furfetted
with eating the boyled Brains of thofe † *Barbets* (or *Proteftants*) I
fay, if the Voluntary confeffion of fuch *Canibals* as thefe, may be accepted as Authentick proofs, then I doubt not but to give ample fatisfaction to all, as well to thofe that fain would not, as thofe that as
yet cannot eafily believe fuch Monftrous cruelties, having inferted
here, as followes, the true Copies of the faid Depofitions and Atteftations, (which are indeed worthy of being communicated to pofterity)
and prefented the very Original Subfcriptions to the publike Library
of the famous Univerfity of *Cambridge.*

Note here
that in *Pie-
mont* they call
Barbets thofe
whom they
in *France* call
Hugonots.

The

The Declaration of M. *du Petit Bourg*, firſt Captain of the Regiment of *Grancey*, touching the Cruelties that were exerciſed upon perſons of all ages and ſexes, among the poor *Proteſtants* of the *Valleys* of *Piemont*, ſubſcribed with his own hand at *Pignerol.* 27. *Novemb.* 1655. in the preſence of two other Commanders.

The true Original whereof is to be ſeen, together with the reſt, in the Publick Library of the famous Univerſity of *Cambridg.*

JE *Sieur du* Petit Bourg, *premier Capitaine au Regiment de* Grancey, *le commandant, & ayant eu ordre de Monſieur le* Prince Thomas *d' aller joindre le Marquis de* Pianeſſe, *& prendre ordre de luy,* (lequel Marquis *eſtoit à la* Tour;) *ſur mon depart je fus envoyé querir par Monſieur.* L' *Ambaſſadeur, lequel me pria de parler à Monſieur de* Pianeſſe, *& m' employer à accommoder les troubles qui eſtoyent arrivez parmi ceux de la Religion des Vallées de* Piemont, *en ſuite dequoy, je me ſuis addreſſé au dit Marquis, le priant avec beaucoup, d' inſtance qu' il aggreaſt, que j' entreprinſe le dit accommodement, & que je me promettois d' en venir à bout, ce qu' il me refuſa à diverſes fois, qu' inſtance que j' en aye ſçeu faire; & au lieu*

I Sieur *du Petit Bourg,* firſt Captain of the Regiment of *Grancey,* who alſo commanded the ſame, having received direction from *Prince Thomas* to go and joyn with the Marqueſs of *Pioneſſe,* and to receive his Orders, (which Marqueſs was then at *La Torre*) when I was juſt upon my Departure, the Ambaſſadour ſent for me, and deſired me to ſpeak to *Monſ. de Pioneſſe,* and to uſe my endeavour to accommodate the Troubles which were happened amongſt thoſe of the Religion in the Valleys of *Piemont:* in order whereunto I then addreſſed my ſelf to the ſaid *Marqueſs,* intreating him with much earneſtneſs, that he would give way, that I might undertake the ſaid Accommodation, which I ſuppoſed I might have been able to effect: But he refuſed this my Requeſt, and that divers times, notwithſtanding all the Endeavours I could poſſibly uſe to perſwade him thereunto. And inſtead of the leaſt mitigation

mitigation of Affairs, that this or any other consideration which I could lay before him, did then produce, on the contrary, I was witness to many great Violences and extreme Cruelties exercised by the *Bandets* and Souldiers of *Piemont*, upon all sorts of every age, sex, and condition whatsoever, whom my self saw massacred, dismembred, hanged up, burned, and ravished, together with many horrid confusions. And so far is it from truth, that the whole was done by virtue of those Orders which were given out by me (as is falsly alleged in a certain Relation printed in *French* and *Italian*) that I beheld the same with horrour and regret. And whereas it is said in the same Relation, that the Marquess of *Pianessa* commanded me to treat them peaceably, without hostility, and in the best manner I could possibly, the event clearly demonstrated, that the Orders he gave were altogether contrary, for as much as it is most certain, that without any distinction of those who resisted, from those who made no resistance, they were used with all sort of inhumanity, their houses burnt, their goods plundered, and when Prisoners were brought before the Marquess of *Pianesse*, I saw him give order to give them no quarter at all, because (said he) his Highness is resolved to have none of the *Religion* in any of his Dominions.

And as for what he protests in the same *Delaration*, as namely, that there was no hurt done to any, except during the Fight, nor the least Outrage committed upon any persons not fit to bear Arms. I do assert and will maintain, that it is not so, as having seen with my eys several men kill'd in cold bloud; as also women, aged persons, and young children, miserably murdered.

que cela ni aucune autre considération que je luy aye donnée, aye en rien adouci les affaires, au contraire j' ay esté tesmoin de plusieurs grandes violences & extremes cruautés exercées par les Bandits du Piemont, & Soldats, sur toute sorte d' aage, de sexe, & condition, que j' ay veu Massacrer, desmembrer, pendre, brusler & violer, & de plusieurs effroyables incendies. Tant s' en faut, comme porte faussement une certaine relation imprimée en François & Italien, que le tout à esté fait en suite des ordres que j' aye donnez, que je l' ay veu avec regret & horreur. Est aussi faux ce que porte la dite Declaration que le Marquis de Pianesse, m' ait commandé de les traitter paisiblement, sans hostilité, & le mieux qu' il me seroit possible; & l' evenament a bien monstré que les ordres estoyent du tout contraires, veu qu' il est constant que sans distinction de ceux qui faisoyent resistance ou qui n' en faisoyent point, l' on les à traitté avec toute sorte d' inhumanité, bruslé leurs Maisons, & saccagé leurs biens: quand l' on amenoit des prisonniers au Marquis de Pianesse j' ay veu ordre qu' il falloit tout tuer, pource que S. A. ne vouloit point de gens de la Religion dans toutes ses terres.

Quant à tout ce qu' il proteste en la mesme Declaration qu' on n' a jamais touché à aucun sinon dans le combat, ni fait le moindre outrage aux personnes inhabiles aux armes, je soustiens que cela n' est point, puis que j' ay veu de mes yeux meutrir des hommes de sang froid, & tuer miserablement des femmes, des vieillards & petits enfants.

*Pour ce qui eſt de la forme, en laquel-
le ils ſe ſont mis en poſſeſſion de toute la
Vallée d'*Angrogne, *pour la piller &
bruſler entierement, ils n'ont pas eu
beaucoup de peine, car excepte ſix, on
ſept qui firent quelque mine de reſiſtance, voyant qu'il n'y avoit point de
mercy pour eux, il envoya tout le reſte
ſans aucune reſiſtance, car les payſans
penſoyent, pluſtoſt a fuir qu' a combattre,
tellement que je nie formellement & le
proteſte devant Dieu que rien des cru-
autez que deſſus, n'a eſté executé par
mon ordre, au contraire voyant, que je ne
pouvois y apporter de remede, je fus con-
trainct de me retirer & abandonner la
conduite du Regiment, de peur d' aſ-
ſiſter à de ſi mauvais es actions. Fait à
*Pinerol *ce* 27. *Novembre* 1655.

DU PETIT BOURG.

*Nous ſubſignez Capitaines aux Regi-
ments d' Infanterie de Sault, & d' Auvergne, atteſtons avoir veu faire la
preſente Declaration dans ceſte Ville
de* Pinerol, *au Sieur du* Petit Bourge,
Capitaine au Regiment d' Infanterie de
Grancey, *& là aſcrite & ſignée de ſa
propre main, en nôtre preſence, en foy
de quoy nous avons ſigné le preſent a Pinerol ce* 25. Novemb. 1655.

S. HILAIRE Capitaine
d' Auvergne.
Du FAURE Capitaine
du Sault.

As for the manner how they put
themſelves in poſſeſſion of all the
Valley of *Angrognia,* to pillage, and
burn the ſame entirely, they did it
with eaſe enough, for (excepting ſix
or ſeven, who ſeeing there would be
no Mercy ſhown them, made ſome
ſhew of oppoſition) he ſent them a-
way without the leaſt reſiſtance, the
Peaſants thinking rather how to flie,
then to fight the Enemy: In ſum, I
deny abſolutely, and proteſt, as in the
preſence of God, that none of thoſe
cruelties above mentioned, were executed by my Order, but on the contrary, ſeeing that I could not procure
a remedy, I was conſtrained to retire,
and quit the Conduct of the Regiment, for fear of being preſent at ſuch
wicked actions. Done at *Pignerol* the
27. *Novemb.* 1655.

Du PETIT BOURG.

We whoſe Names are here ſubſcribed, Captains of the Regiments of
the Infantery of *Sault* and *Averne,*
do atteſt that we have ſeen the preſent
Declaration made by the *Sieur du Petit Bourg,* Captain of the Regiment of
Infantery of *Grancey,* in the City of
Pignerol, and by him written, and ſigned with his own hand, in our preſence.
In witneſs whereof, we have ſigned
this preſent Atteſtation at *Pignerol,*
this 25 of *Novemb.* 1655.

S. HILAIRE *Captain
of Auvergne.*
Du FAURE *Captain.
of Saul.*

The

The Attestation of *Thomas Guiot* (Chirurgeon) and *Francis Pra,* touching the boiling and eating of the Brains of some of the poor protestants during the heat of the Massacre in the Year 1655. Made the 7. *Octob.* 1655.

The true Original whereof is to be seen, together with the rest, in the publick Library of the famous University of
CAMBRIDG.

VVE whose Names are underwritten do certifie, that we being at *Pignerol*, upon the three and twentieth of April, in the Year 1655. (it being a Feast day and the Fair of St. *George*) heard a certain young man of *Cumiane*, who was lately come from the Valley of *Lucerna*, and from the War that had been in those parts, (where he had al-

Nous soubsignez, certifions que nous estans trouvés à Pincrol, le vingtroizieme d' Auril, de l' année 1655, jour de la feste, & foire de St. George, nous avons ovy un jeune homme de Cumiane, n' agueres venu de la Vallée de Luzerne, & de la guerre qu' on y faisoit, qui mesme etoit un peu blessé à la

main

main ; se vantant qu' avec six autres ses compagnons, ilz avoient communement fait cuir la teste d' un barbet, & Mangé la cervelle, mais qu' elle luy faisoit mal au coeur, ce qu' il disoit à un autre Piemontois, qui vendoit des pales, & autres outilz de fer , & en la presence d' un Francois, qui neantmoins tous nous estoyent incognus, ce que nous asseurons en parole de verite comme l' ayant ovy de nos propres Oreilles, en testimognage dequoy nous avons icy apposé nos seings, ce septieme Octobre 1655.

   Thomas Guiot Chirurgien.
   François Pra.

so received a Wound in his Hand) boasting, that he, together with six other of his Comrades, had frequently boiled the Heads, and eaten the Brains of several *Barbets*, which (by the same token) had made him sick at heart. This he likewise related to an Ironmonger, where was present also a *French* man, who notwithstanding was unknown to any of us. All which we assure in words of truth, as having heard the same with our ears : in witness whereof we have hereto put our Marks the seventh of *October* 1655.

   Thomas Guiot, Chirurgeon.
   Francis Pra.

The

The Atteſtation of divers Perſons of known Honour and Integrity, who were for the moſt part both eye and ear Witneſses of the following barbarous and horrid Cruelties which were exerciſed againſt ſome particular Members of the Evangelical Churches in the Valleys of *Piemont,* during the heat of the late Maſsacre in the Year 1655.

The true original Subſcriptions whereof the Authour has in his cuſtody, ready to be produced, as occaſion ſhall require, for the better ſatisfaction of the *Chriſtian* and curious Reader.

Nous ſous ſignes atteſtons, que le contenu, &c.

WE whoſe Names are here underwritten, do atteſt and declare in words of truth and ſoberneſs, that the following Narrative or Relation of ſeveral horrid Cruelties exerciſed againſt the poor Proteſtants in the Valleys of *Piemont,* contains nothing but the pure and naked truth; having here omitted many Relations of divers other Cruelties, exerciſed againſt thoſe poor People, becauſe not ſo ſubſtantially and abundantly verified ; in faith whereof, we have here ſubſcribed.

Sara

Sara Raſtignole des Vignes.

S*Ara Raſtignole des Vignes,* about ſixty years of age, being overtaken in a certain place called *Eyrals,* by divers Souldiers, was by them commanded
to ſay her Prayers, which ſhe having done, they urged her to repeat *Jeſus Maria,*
but the poor Woman refuſing to do it, one of the Souldiers thruſt a Sickle into

the lower part of her Belly, and ript her up to the Navel, and afterwards dragg'd
the poor miſerable Creature upon the ground, being half dead, till another of
them came and ſevered her Head from her Body. The Daughter in Law to this
poor Woman, who was conſtrained to hide her ſelf in the Snow for the ſpace of
two days after, without any ſuccour or nouriſhment, was an Ey-witneſs of this
horrible Butchery.

Martha Constantine of St. Giovanni.

A certain Woman of *St. Giovanni*, whose name (as is credibly believed) was *Martha Constantin*, the Wife of *Jacopo Barral*, after she had seen several others before her most cruelly put to death, was her self first ravisht, and then had her Breasts cut off, and likewise part of her Privities, by some of the Souldiers, who also carried the same to *Macel* in *Piemont*, where they fried them, and set them before some other of their Comrades, whom they there met accidentally, making them believe that they were Tripes, but having eaten a good part thereof, they told them plainly, that they were no other than Womens Dugs, &c. This

was taken so extremely ill by those that had been thus beguiled, that immediately a Quarrel arose thereupon, and indeed not without sufficient reason; for, all those that had eaten thereof found it to be of so ill a digestion, and it lay so heavy in their Stomacks, that they straightway fell grievously sick upon it, and some of them died soon after. This is certified by one of *Dauphine*, a *Roman* Catholick, (whom it were easie to name, if need required) and he related the same to one *Andrea Javel* of *Pinachia*.

Jacopo

Jacopo Michalino of *Bobio* his Servant.

A certain man of *Trafsiniere*, fervant of *Jacopo Michalino* of *Bobio*, being taken prifoner the 8th. of *May*, received divers ftabs with a Dagger in the fole of his feet, and in his Ears, by the hands of one *Gulielmo Roche* a famous Maffacrer of *Lucerna*, and another called *Mandolin*, who afterwards cut off his privy Members, and then applied a burning candle to the wound, frying it with the flame thereof, that fo the bloud might be ftopt, and the torments of that mife-

rable creature prolonged ; This being done to their mindes, they tore off his Nayls with hot pincers, to try if they could by any means force him to renounce his Religion. But when nothing would do, they tied one of his Legs to the Marquefs of *Lucerna's* Mule, and fo dragg'd him along the ftreets, till fuch time as he had almoft ended his painfull life, and then binding his head about with a Cord, they ftrained and twifted the fame with a ftaff fo hard, that it made his Eys and Brains drop out of his Head ; In the end, when they had fufficiently fatiated their appetites with all the variety of cruelties they could well devife, they caft the dead Carkafs into the River, that fo both one and the other Element might be the better enabled one day to bear witnefs againft their barbarous and inhumane actions.

Pietro

Pietro Simond of *Angrogna*.

Pietro Simond of *Angrogna*, about fourscore years of age, was tied Neck and Heels together, and violently hurl'd down vast and formidable Precipices, but as he was falling down, he by the way met with a cragged branch of a Tree, and

there hung faft, in a moft languifhing condition for feveral dayes together (a moft lamentable fpectacle to behold !) not being able to help himfelf in the leaft, nor indeed capable of the help of any other, by reafon it was a Precipice altogether in-acceffible: I leave the Reader to make out the reft of this Tragedy, confeffing my felf not able to exprefs it.

Esaia Garcino of *Angrogna*,

and

Daniel Armands Wife of *La Torre*.

Esaia Garcino of *Angrogna*, an old man of ninety years of Age, had firft his body cut and hack'd in fmall pieces, and then his head chopt off: The like alfo was in a manner done to *Daniel Armands* Wife of *La Torre*, the gibblets and mammocks of whofe torn Carkafs were ftrawed along the High-way, and hung upon the Hedges.

Two

Two poor Women of La Torre.

Upon the 22th. of *April* 1655. in a certain place called *La Sarcena*, One Captain *Pola* of *Pancalier*, took two poor women of *La Torre*, and with a Fau-

chion ript up their Bellies, and left them groveling upon the Snow in this lamentable condition. And this was seen by Monſieur *Groſs* Miniſter of *Villaro*.

Four poor Women, one of Villaro, *and the other three of* La Torre, *with divers ſmall children.*

In the ſame place the Souldiers of *Bagnols* of *Pravillerm*, cut off firſt the Noſe, then the fingers, and laſt of all the hands of a very ancient and decrepit woman, then left her to languiſh and die in this deplorable condition, without having ſo much as a hand to guide a morſel of bread to her mouth. They

alſo took many ſmall children and tender Infants, and flung them down the Precipices, as the aboveſaid Captain *Pola* confeſſed to Monſieur *Aghuit*, and Monſieur *Groſs*, during the time of their impriſonment at *Turin*. Another woman of *La Torre*, by name *Magdelena*, Widow to *Giovanni Bertino*, being ſtript naked, had her Head tied between her Legs, and was thrown down a Precipice fearfull to behold. Another lame woman of *La Torre*, by name *Maria Reymondet*, Widow of the deceaſed *Jacopo Coing*, was found in a Cave, the fleſh all ſlic'd from off the bones, and chopt as ſmall as herbs to the pot; ſo that her body appeared no other then a meer Skeleton, or Anatomy. Another woman of *Villaro* whoſe name was *Magdelena*, Widow of the deceaſed *Pietro Pilot*, being exceeding decrepit, and blind with old age, was cut in pieces in a certain Cave near *Chaſtelus*.

Anna

Anna Daughter to Giovanni Charboniere

Anna, Daughter to *Giovanni Charboniere* of *La Torre*, had a long Stake thruſt into her Privities, by ſome of the Souldiers, who in a barbarous way carried her upon their ſhoulders in manner of an Enſign, till they had wearied them-

ſelves, each man in his turn, and then they ſtuck the other end down into the ground, and ſo left her hanging in the ayr upon the Stakes end, as a moſt formidable and horrid ſpectacle to all that paſſed by that way.

Giovanni

Giovanni Andrea Michialin.

Giovanni Andrea Michialin of *La Torre*, being taken prisoner, escaped miraculously, after he had beheld with his eyes three of his Children torn in pieces limb-meal, and the fourth that was not above six Weeks old, snatcht out of

the arms of the Mother, it's swadling clothes taken off, and stript naked, and then its brains dasht out against the Rocks.

Jacopo Perrin, and David his Brother, of Villaro.

Jacopo Perrin, an Elder of the Church of *Villaro,* and *David* his Brother, were taken prisoners in their Beds, in a certain Village called *La Baudine,* and carried from thence to *Lucerna,* where they were clapt up in the *Marquess* his prison, where they were most barbarously and inhumanely used ; amongst other things, the bloudy Butchers of that place stript off the skin off their Arms and Legs by long slices, in the form of Leathern points, till such time as they had left the flesh quite bare, and at length they were miserably starved to death in the same prison, where their Carkasses were likewise suffered to lye and putrifie.

Giovanni

Giovanni Pelanchion of Villaro.

Giovanni Pelanchion, a young man about 25. years of age, having been taken prisoner, and made his escape, was afterwards retaken by the souldiers, who

tied

tied one of his Legs to the tail of a Mule, and so dragg'd him violently through all the streets and corners of *Lucerna*; and because the poor wretch sometimes lifted up his head and hands through the great pain and anguish that he suffered by the grating of his body against the ragged flints in the streets, the hard-hearted Villains battered and bruised his Body with Stones and Brick-bats as he passed along, crying that he was possessed with a Devil which kept him from dying. After this they cut off his privy Members, and violently cramb'd them into the poor creatures mouth, and down his throat to stop his breath: At last they chopt off his head, and dragging him to the Rivers brink, there left him unburied. This cruelty hath been divers times verified in publike (with great regret) even by several of the Catholicks, as likewise by many of the poor Protestants themselves who were then prisoners, and were made to look on this dolefull spectacle.

Magdalena, Daughter of Pietro Fontano.

Magdalena, Daughter to *Pietro Fontano*, a beautifull and well-favoured Girl, about ten years of age, was taken by some of those Lecherous bruit beasts, and because her age and stature was uncapable of the ordinary course of

Nature, they forced her Body (I leave the Reader to make up the rest) in so inhumane manner, that she was found afterwards half dead, and wallowing in her own bloud.

A poor Woman of Villaro, with her young Infant.

Giovanni Tolaſano, a Mercer of *Villaro,* as he was paſſing by the Hill of S. *Juliano,* ſaw a poor woman flying from the ſouldiers with a Cradle upon her head, wherein was a young ſucking Childe, but ſeeing ſhe was like to be overtaken by them, ſhe left her Cradle in the middle of the way, as verily believing thoſe Butchers could not poſſibly have ſuch hearts of Adamant, as

to lay violent hands upon the poor innocent Babe, and ſo hid her ſelf not far from the place in the cleft of a Rock. But thoſe bloud-hounds having found the Infant in the Cradle, in a moſt Salvage manner took it out, and pull'd it into four pieces or quarters, and afterwards finding the Mother, raviſht her, then cut off her head, and left her dead body upon the ſnow.

The

The Daughter of *Moyſes Long*, of *Bobio*.

The Daughter of *Moyſes Long* of *Bobio*, about ten years of age, was taken by the Souldiers of *Piemont*, as ſhe was flying upon the Snow, who broaching her upon a Pike or Halberd, roaſted her alive upon a broad ſtone not far off from the place: when they had thus done, they cnt off a ſlice of

her fleſh, intending to have made a meals meat on her, but not finding it throughly roaſted, their ſtomacks would not ſerve them to eat it. This happened at *Villa Nova*, hard by *Mireboc*, and the Authors of this barbarous Act, were heard by divers to tell the ſtory to their Comerades, in a vaunting and boaſting manner.

Jacopo

Jacopo Michelino of Bobio.

Jacopo Michelino, one of the chief Elders of the Church of *Bobio*, being taken prisoner, had his two hands tied to his privy Members, and afterwards hung upon a certain Gate in a most ignominious posture; but alas the shame was nothing to the torments, for, the whole weight of his body hanging upon so tender a part, the pain was most exquisite and almost incredible. And all this they did to make him (if possible) renounce his Religion; but seeing they could not prevail, they caried him away, together with other prisoners, where,

after having with incredible constancy endured a world of other cruelties, he exchanged the sufferings of this miserable life, for the joys of a better. In like manner, *Pietro Gras*, during the time he was prisoner, saw two of the poor Protestants a little above *La Sarcena*, hanging in a most hideous manner meerly by their privy members, and their hands tied behinde them, till at last their very bowels were almost torn out, and thus they died with horrible pain and anguish.

Giovanni

Giovanni Rostagnol of *Bobio.*

Giovanni Rostagnol, being full fourscore years of age, had his Nose, his Ears, and other parts of his Body cut off, and left in this languishing and forlorn con-

dition upon the Snow, where having laid a long time, at last he gave up the ghost.

Daniel

Daniel Salvagiol, and his Wife, with *Giovanni, Ludovico,* and *Bartho-lemo Durant,* and *Daniel Revel,* all of *Roras,* and *Paolo Reynaud* of *Bobio.*

Daniel Salvagiol, with his Wife, as likewise *Giovanni Durant, Daniel Revel, Ludovico* and *Bartholemo Durant,* Brothers, all of *Roras,* and *Paolo Reynaud* of *Valguichiard* in *Bobio,* were taken by the Souldiers, who cramming Gun-powder

into their Mouths, and down their Throats, set Fire to the same, and so tore their Heads in flitters. I leave the *Christian* Reader to make what Reflections he please upon this devilish and prodigious usage of the poor Saints of *Jesus.*

Jacopo

Jacopo di Ronc.

Jacopo di Ronc, a School-mafter of *Roras*, being ftript ftark naked, after that they had tore off his Nails with Pincers, and made a thoufand Holes in his Hands with a Daggers point, was dragged by a Cord that was faftened about his Middle, through the Bourg of *Lucerna*, and every ftep as he marched along, one of the Souldiers on one fide cut off a Piece of his Flefh with a Fauchion, and another on the other fide gave him a great Blow with a Staff, crying in the following words *E ben Barbet andares tu à la Meffa?* that is, *Well! what fayeft thou now Barbet, wilt thou yet go to Mafs?* To which the poor Creature with an incredible conftancy, as long as he was able to fpeak, made anfwer, *Piu preft la Mort, que la*

Meffa! amaffeme preft per amour di Dio! that is, *Much rather Death, than the Mafs! Difpatch me quickly for the love of God!* By and by came one *Villelmin Roche*, a famous Perfecutour, who as foon as ever he faw him, cried out, *Lo, here's the Minifter of* Roras, giving him a deadly Blow athwart the Head with a Back-fword, after which he caufed him to be brought to the Bridg *L' ayal*, and cutting off his Head, threw him into the River of *Pelis*, which rolled the dead Body down as far as *Bubliana*, where it was found and buried.

Paolo

Paolo Garnier.

Paolo Garnier of *Roras* being taken by thofe Murderers, they firft violently pull'd out his Eys, and cut off his privy Members, thrufting his Yard into his Mouth: and in this pofture expofed him to publick view for feveral days toge-

ther. But being not content with this, they afterwards in a moft butcher-like manner ftript this poor Creature alive, and then cutting the Skin into four parts, hung the fame up, in four Windows of four of the principal Houfes of *Lucerna*.

Daniel

Daniel Cardon of *Roccapiatta.*

Daniel Cardon of *Roccapiatta,* being taken by ſome of the Souldiers a little above the Temple of *S. Giovanni,* they cut off his Head, and then took out his

Brains, and frying the ſame, eat them up, they alſo cut open his Stomack, and were taking out his Heart to fry that and eat it, but they were affrighted by ſome of the poor Peoples Troops that were coming that way.

Margarita

Margarita Revel of *La Cartere,* and *Maria de Pravillerm* in *S. Giovan-*
ni ; as likewife *Madona Lena* and *Jeanna Batzan* of *La Torre,*
the third eighty, the firft fourfcore and five, and the
other two ninety years of age, of whom the fecond and the third were blinde.

Margerita Revel of *La Cartere* of the age of fourfcore and five years, the Mother in Law of Captain *Paolo Genoulat,* and *Maria di Pravillerm* of the age of
ninety years and blinde, both of *S. Giovanni,* were taken, and in a moft barbarous manner burned alive in the place called *Les Vignes,* on the one fide of *An-*

grogna; which was feen and hath been attefted by *Judith Grand,* and by the
Wife of *Matthieu Jordan* of *La Torre,* as alfo by *Maria* Daughter of *Jacobo Da-*
vide. In like manner were handled *Madona Lena,* and *Jeanna Batzan,* both of
La Torre, the laft ninety, and the firft eighty years of age, and blinde.

The

The Widow of the deceased *Giovanni Ugon* of *La Torre*.

A certain Widow of the deceased *Giovanni Ugon* of *La Torre*, who had lain extreme sick for three years together, was taken by the Souldiers, and together with one of her Daughters, drawn upon a kinde of a Car, through the Streets of *La Torre*, where, as they passed along, some of those Sons of Bloud, stab'd their Bodies with Prongs, Pitch-forks, and other such like Instruments, others

bruised their Bodies with Flints, and afterwards flung them into the River of *Angrogna*, where they soon dispatcht them with Flints and Bats: the truth of which is attested by several of the Papists themselves, and that with an abhorrency of so abominable a Cruelty.

Paolo

Paolo Giles of *La Torre.*

Paolo Giles of *La Torre,* as he was flying from the Murderers, received a Shot on the Neck, in a certain place called *La Combe di Macanail,* after which they slit

all his Face through the Chin and Nose, and then having dispatcht him, left his Carkase to be eaten by the Dogs.

Eleven

Eleven Men forced to throw one another into the Fire.

Mr. *Groſs* Paſtour of *Villaro* in *Bobio*, told the Authour, during his abode at *Geneva*, that being at *Pignerolio*, he heard ſeveral perſons affirm in the preſence of *Monſieur de la Simone Major* of *Pignerolio*, that ſome of the Murderers having

taken eleven Men at *Garcigliana*, heated a great Oven or Furnace red hot, and cauſed thoſe poor Creatures to throw one another into the ſaid burning fiery Furnace ſucceſſively; and when it came to the laſt Man, they themſelves threw him in alſo.

It

It is a thing moſt certain likewiſe, that very frequently thoſe Bloud-hounds purſued and hunted out Multitudes of thoſe poor Proteſtants among the Rocks and Mountains, by the very traces of their bleeding Feet and Legs, which had

been ſorely cut and mangled by the Ice and Flints which they met with by the way, in their Flight.

The foregoing Relations are ſome choice Stories pick'd and cull'd out of the Heap, to preſent the Reader with in their lively Idea's. Theſe that follow, are a Meſs of Cruelties, which may very well ſerve for the ſecond Courſe, many of them being notoriouſly cruel and barbarous, and every ſyllable of them verified by moſt authentick Atteſtations, which the Authour reſerves by him for ſeveral weighty Reaſons, being ready to give any ingenious perſon all poſſible ſatisfaction therein.

In

In S. Giovanni.

Michel Gonet.

Michel Gonet of *Lucernetta,* a man of ninety years of age at the least, was burnt alive in a place called *Sarcena,* towards the Mountains of *Bobio,* where he had fled and hid himfelf.

Bartholomeo Frafche.

Bartholomeo Frafche, of *Fenile,* was taken by the Souldiers, who after they had all flafhed and fliced his Legs, thruft a poyfoned Knife through his heels, and in this wofull plight dragg'd him to the common prifon at *Turin,* where he died foon after.

Giovanni Baptifta Oudri.

Giovanni Baptifta Oudri, an old man of *S. Giovanni,* was cruelly murthered at a place called *La Sarcena,* after he had been very barbaroufly ufed.

Magdalena la Peine.

Magdalena la Peine, a woman of about thirty five years of age, being purfued clofe by the Enemies, and knowing what meafure fhe fhould receive from them, chofe rather to caft her felf down a Precipice very formidable to behold, then to fall into the hands of fuch bloudy Butchers.

Marguerita Revella.

Marguerita Revella, a woman of about fourfcore and five years of age, together with another woman of ninety, and blinde with very age, by name *Maria di Pravillerm,* were burnt to death.

Maria Davi.

Maria, the Daughter of *Jacopo Davi,* was murthered by the Souldiers.

Michele Bellino.

Michele Bellino, with one *Anna di Pol Bochiardino,* and *Giovanni Pietro Marguet,* their fervant, were beheaded by the hands of *Cattalino,* and *Francifco Lemna* of *Briqueras.*

Daniele Pellene.

Daniele Pellene was maffacred in *Angrognia.*

Michele

Michele Parife.
Michele Parife was beheaded at *Cavor.*

Giovanni Danna.
Giovanni Danna, was burnt alive in a Barn, at a certain place called *La Maria,* in *Angrognia.*

Daniele Gonin, and *David Chianforan.*
Daniele Gonin, and *David Chianforan,* of *La Piene* were cruelly maffacred.

Pietro Mallanots Daughter.
The Daughter of *Pietro Mallanot;* a Counfellor of S. *Giovanni,* was rolled from the top of a Precipice, to the bottome, with her Brother, a little infant of eight moneths old, in her Arms, and two days after they were found by their Father quite dead, upon the Snow, both the Girle, and the little infant her brother in her arms.

Giovanni, Son of Pol Parife.
Giovanni, Son of *Pol Parife,* with his Wife and childe, as alfo the Daughter of *Giovanni Prin,* were all fearfully murthered; efpecially the Wife of *Pol Parife,* who was hurled down a mighty Rock, with a little infant in her arms, and three days after, was found dead with the little childe alive, but faft clafped between the Arms of the dead Mother, which were cold and ftiff, infomuch that thofe that thus found them, had much ado to get the young childe out.

Paolo Chiariet's Wife.
The Wife of *Paolo Chiairet,* together with two fmall Infants, was inhumanely put to death.

Fofepho Chiairet, and *Paolo Garniero.*
Fofepho Chiairet, who had received a wound in the fight a little before, was flay'd at *Lucerna,* and had the Greafe taken out of his body. The fame likewife done to *Paolo Garniero.*

Maria Peul.
Maria Peul was maffacred.

Mattheo Turin.
Mattheo Turin being taken at *Angrognia,* was carried from thence and maffacred at *Lucernetta,* clofe by the Bridge of *Lucerna,* and his Carkafs was afterwards eaten by the Dogs.

Marguerita Saretta.
Marguerita Saretta, was ftoned to death, and her dead body caft into the River from off the Bridge of *Balfre* in *Angrognia.*

Fofhua

Joshua Albarino.

Joshua Albarino, was made Prisoner, and afterwards privily made away, so that he was never more to be found, nor was it at all known what became of him.

Laurentio Port.

Laurentio Pont, was murthered at *Bubbiana.*

Cypriano Baslia.

Cypriano Baslia was inhumanely starved to death at *Luserna,* and his dead body afterwards cast to the Dogs.

In Angrognia.

Jacopo Simond, and *Catharina Coissone.*

Catharina Coissone a poor lame woman, and fourscore years old, was dragged bare-foot, to a certain place called *Chiodet,* where they cut off her head, and left her body unburied upon the Snow. The like was also done to *Jacopo Simond.*

Isaiah Ricca, and *Catharina Simond.*

Isaiah Ricca, and *Catharina* the Wife of *Pietro Simond,* a decrepit old woman, were taken by the feet, and hurled down the Precipices of the ragged Rocks, in a manner dreadfull to behold. The last of these, *viz. Catharina,* had first her brains dasht out against the Rocks, before she was thus thrown down the Precipices.

Jeanna Praessuch.

Jeanna a poor innocent, the sister of *Antonio Praessuch,* had her head cut off in a certain place called *Gachet,* and her body cast into the cleft of a Rock, whence it was with very much difficulty taken out some days after.

Bartholomeo Odin.

Bartholomeo Odin, a poor man of at least fourscore years of age, was first thrown down some part of the Rocks; and it happening that he was not quite dead with the fall, he was afterwards in a barbarous manner dispatcht by the Souldiers, who left his dead body naked and unburied.

Davide Fenovil, and the two Daughters of *Stephano Chiauvia.*

Davide Fenovil, who had been lame for above twenty years before, as also the two Daughters of *Stephano Chiauvia,* had first their heads
chopt

chopt off, and afterwards their bodies thrown down the Precipices.

David Ricca.

David Ricca, was murthered in a Barn, and afterwards the Barn was thrown down upon his dead body (a better grave then the rest of his fellowes had.)

Laurentio Odino,
Pietro Coga,
Thomas Benech, } all cruelly murthered.
The Mother and a Sister of *Paolo*
Giouvio,

Antonio Bertino.

Antonio Bertino, flying for his life to the higher part of *Angrognia,* had first his Nose, Paps, and Privities cut off, and then his head cleft in twain.

Two Children of Giovanni Pont.

Two Children of *Giovanni Pont* were murthered, and then their bodies burnt and consumed to ashes.

Daniel Bonet a Reverend Elder,
and } massacred.
Davide Fraschia,

Giovanni Revel.

Giovanni Revel was first used in a horrible and barbarous manner, and then had his head cut off by *Gulielmo Roche,* for answering him upon his Interrogates, that he would live and dye in the *Protestant* Religion.

Jeanna Bonetta.

Jeanna Bonetta, above fourscore years of age, was cruelly put to death.

Maria Genolat.

Maria, the Wife of *Giovanni Genolat,* although a very aged woman, was first abused by the Souldiers, and then   to the ground.

Josepho Pont.

Josepho Pont, had first a wound in the Reins of the back, and then his body cut off in the middle, which was found in this lamentable condition a while after at *La Roche.Maneod* unburied, and not to be approached by reason of its noysom smell.

At

At La Torre.

Mattheo Peloux.

MAttheo Peloux, of *Pravillerm*, inhabiting formerly at *Chabriols*, was taken at *La Comba* of *Villaro*, and having received firft a wound in his body, by a Mufquet-fhot, was burnt alive in the Church of *De Combe*.

Daniele de Maria.

Daniele de Maria, being fled into a certain place called *Clotigat*, and lying there fick, after he had feen two of his own children murthered before his eyes, was himfelf barbaroufly difpatched in his bed.

Maria Remondet.

Maria Remondet, Widow of the deceafed *Jacopo Coing*, a lame woman, after fhe had lain five Weeks in a Cave, her body was found cut in pieces, and minced (as the Proverb is) *as fmall as herbs to the Pot.*

Juditha.

Juditha, Widow of the deceafed *Daniele de Roftagnol*, being four-fcore years old, was a long time dragg'd up and down upon the ground, and at length they cut off her head.

Magdalena Grand.

Magdalena Grand, the Wife of *Giovanni Grand*, as fhe was flying for her life, fell into a deep River, and was drowned.

Magdalena the Mother of *Daniele Reymond*,
Daniele Martino,
Mattheo Bertino, and *Marguerita* his Wife,
} maffacred.

Philippo Viton.

Philippo Viton was maffacred in a certain place called *Pertufel*.

Magdalena Armand.

Magdalena, Widow to the deceafed *Jacopo Armand*, was murthered at the mouth of a Cave at *La Sarcena*.

Three Infants of *Pietro Fine* were ftifled in the Snow.

Paolo Belin,together with his Mother and Daughter,were maffacred.

Giovanni Charboniere.

Giovanni Charboniere, Son of the deceafed *Antonio*, was maffacred, and his Daughter (who was an innocent) was firft ftript ftark naked and then had a long Stake driven through her belly,whereof fhe died.

Lucia

Lucia Beſſon.

Lucia the Wife of *Pietro Beſſon,* a woman very great with childe, and not far from the time of lying down, as ſhe was flying for her life, was ſo affrighted with the diſmal cries and ſcreetchings of ſome that were murthered not far from the place where ſhe was, that ſhe was brought a bed upon the Mountain *Julian,* where ſhe was afterwards found dead, with the Infant that was newly born, and two other ſucking children lying by her.

Franciſco Gros.

Franciſco, ſon of the deceaſed *Valerio Gros,* a Miniſter, was taken, and while he was yet alive, had his body cut in ſmall Gibblets, in the preſence of his own wife (to add to the miſery) and afterwards the ſame men took two of their ſmall children, and moſt cruelly murthered them.

Thomas Margher.

The Sieur *Thomas Margher,* an Elder of *La Torre,* being hunted from his Houſe and habitation to a place called *Mirobocas,* was there miſerably ſtarved to death with hunger and cold.

Three infants of *Stephano Millan,* maſſacred.

Juditha Revelin, with ſeven Children.

Juditha Revelin, and her ſeven Children, great and ſmall, were all barbarouſly murthered in their beds.

Joſepho Michialino, and his three Children.

Joſepho Michialino, was murthered, and three of his Children were ſtifled in the Snow.

Daniel Reveline, maſſacred.

Anna Armand.

Anna the Widow of *Daniel Armand,* a woman about 75. years old, was taken at a place called *Tagliaretto,* and there cut in pieces by the Souldiers of *Cavor.*

Anna Armand, Faci Magnet, Daniel Coin and his Mother, *Giovanni Cynard,* } all cruelly maſſacred, and moſt of them beheaded.

Anna Mallanot, an innocent, inhumanely butchered.

Magdalena Creſpin, cruelly beaten to death.

Giovanni Roſſet, together with his Wife, and three of his children, maſſacred.

Paolo Giaquino died in priſon at *La Torre,* through hard and cruel uſage.

Jacopo

Jacopo Pecols Wife and Son,
Marguerita Fontana,
Magdalena Ugon,
Laurentio Malanot's Wife,
Marguerita Bonets,

} were all thrown down the Rocks at *Tagliaretto,* and ſo died miſerably.

Gaſpar Fayol's Wife.

The Wife of *Gaſpar Fayol* was firſt taken Priſoner, and after they had forced her to labour hard for them about cutting of Corn, and other Harveſt work, at laſt came behinde her and cut off her Head as ſhe was thus labouring with much diligence.

Jacopo Roſſeno.

Jacopo Roſſeno refuſing to ſay *Jeſus Maria,* being firſt moſt cruelly beaten with Sticks and Clubs, and having received ſeveral Shots in his Body, had at laſt his Head cloven in two by the Souldiers.

Anna Giaymet.

Anna the Wife of *Giovanni Giaymet* of *La Torre,* had her Head cut off between *Bagnoli* and *Cavor,* and her Body expoſed to wilde Beaſts.

Three Children of *Giovanni Dominico,* and *Marguerita* his Wife.

Three Children of *Giovanni Dominico,* with one who belonged to him, by name *Filaſtre,* were burned alive together in a Houſe, at *Bruneto* in *Tagliaretto.*

Two Children of *Stephano Milano Franceſquino,* (both of them dumb Creatures) were moſt unmercifully and ſavagely murdered.

Bartholemi Bertinet.

Bartholemi Bertinet, the Son of *Jacopo Bertinet,* was murdered at *Famolaſe,* becauſe he would not put off his Hat, and worſhip a certain Temple in that place, as he was paſſing by it, and had his dead body expoſed to the wilde Beaſts.

Bartholemi Giamet.

Bartholemi Son of *Bartholemi Giamet,* as he was flying for his life, was ſmothered in the Snow at the Hill of *St. Juliano.*

Suſanna Giacquin.

Suſanna the Daughter of *Paolo Giacquin,* as ſhe was making reſiſtance againſt a certain Souldier that would have abuſed her, and by chance had puſht him down a Rock, was cut in pieces by ſome other Souldiers that came that way juſt at the ſame time.

Maria Bellin, and *Maria Paglias.*

Maria Widow of the before deceaſed *Jacopo Bellin,* and *Maria* Widow

dow of the before deceafed *Giovanni Paglias*, were both maffacred, and their dead Bodies afterwards devoured by wilde Beafts.

Marguerita Chialmis, and *Marguerita Bonetta* were both murdered.

Pietro Richiardon, together with the Wife of *Giovanni Allova, alias Ben,* and *Marguerita Copin,* were all maffacred.

Giovanni Pallias.

Giovanni Pallias, a poor Peafant of the Communalty of *La Torre,* being taken Prifoner by the Souldiers, after all manner of Reproaches and Scorns which thofe of the Convent and Town caft upon him, both in Words and Actions, was by fpecial Order of the Marquefs of *Pioneffa,* dragged by the Hangman to a certain place not far from the Convent, where the faid Marquefs was himfelf in perfon ; when he came thither, the Marquefs plaid the Under-Sheriff, (a worthy Imployment for a Gentleman of his quality) and commanded the Hangman to place the poor Peafant at the foot of a Ladder, which was fet up againft a Tree, and to prepare all things for Execution ; at which time the Monks and Mafs-priefts who had conducted the condemned Innocent from his Prifon to the Gallows, (and who indeed ought to have fhewn him the way up the Ladder alfo) did not ceafe to ufe all the Arguments which either the Devil, or their own Invention could poffibly furnifh them with, to fhake the Faith and the conftancy of this poor Creature : but all in vain ; for, fo far was he from being affrighted with the pale face or terrours of Death, that all his Expreffions or outward Geftures plainly demonftrated the inward Extafies and Joys of his Heart, to fee himfelf *accounted worthy to fuffer for the Crofs of Chrift :* and notwithftanding they often preffed him to remember the fad Eftate that he muft leave his Children and Family behinde him in, he always anfwered them, that it was his hearty Prayer to Almighty God, that his Children might follow their Fathers fteps, and die like himfelf : whereupon the Mafs Priefts feeing all their Perfwafions and Temptings were but as founding Brafs and tinckling Cymbals, they lent the Hangman their helping hands to end the poor man's miferable days ; and becaufe they could not fhake him from his Principles, they haftened to turn him off the Ladder.

Paolo Clement.

This Sieur *Paolo Clement,* an Elder of the Church of *Roffana,* not many days after the Execution of the abovefaid *Pallias,* was brought by the Monks and Mafs Priefts to the very fame place, where they fhewed him the dead Body of the other, thinking thereby to fcare him out of his Principles and Profeffion ; but the good man anfwered them with undaunted courage, that *they might be able to kill the Body, they could never be able to prejudice the Soul of a true Believer.* However, he affured them, that God would be the Avenger of all the innocent Bloud that they had fpilt, (*Iddio farà la Vendetta di tanto fangue innocente*

cente che si spande) and thereupon, having first used some spiritual Ejaculations, and prepared himself *to yield up his Soul to God that gave it,* he defired the Hangman to difpatch him. Now three or four days after the death of this holy and devout Man, the Marquefs of *Pioneſſa* happening to pafs that way, one of his Souldiers difcharged a Mufquet againft the dead Corps, whereupon there gufhed out a Stream of frefh coloured Bloud, which the faidMarquefs obferving, told fome that were near him, *Quefto fangue crida vendetta. i.e. This Bloud cries for vengeance.* After this, both their dead Bodies were hanged up, each of them by one foot, upon a Tree, near to the Gate of *La Torre*; and when any Prifoner of the Reformed party paſſed by that way, they were compelled to go and kifs thofe dead mens privy members, that fo they might put a like ignominy upon the Living and the Dead together. But by reaſon of the multitude of Bullets that were ſhot againft them by the Souldiers paffing that way, it was not long before they fell all in pieces.

Andrea Gillio, Son of *Pietro Gillio* Paftour of *La Torre,* and *Bartolemi Copin*, were both cruelly maffacred.

Magdalena Juliano.

Magdalena, the Wife of *Stephano Juliano*, was firft wounded with a Shot which ſhe had received, and then had her Body cut all in pieces.

In Villaro.

Daniele Rambaut.

DAniele Rambaut of *Villaro,* a Man charged with a numerous Family, was taken Prifoner and carried to *Payfana*, with feveral others his Neighbours, where after he had been a while imprifoned, and by no means to be wrought upon by the Monks & MafsPriefts to pronounce the words *Jefus Maria,* (although preffed to it with many Threats and Artifices) the Tormentours firft cut off his Fingers, one after another, and then his two Hands, and laft of all with a Shot in his Stomack gave him his deadly Wound: but (as their ufual cuftome was) not contenting themfelves without exercifing their malice upon the dead Bodies of the Proteftants, they dragged his Carkafe to the Rivers fide, where it was eaten up and devoured by Dogs and wilde Beafts.

Pietro Chabriolo.

Pietro Chabriolo the Son of *Jofepho Chabriolo* of *Villaro*, being taken by the Souldiers near the Houfe of one *Laurentio Durant,* they placed

a great

a great quantity of Gun-powder about his Body, and putting Fire to the fame, tore him to pieces.

Pietro Bertino Maghit.

Pietro Bertino Maghit, of *Villaro,* was maffacred in the Village of *Pertufel,*having been firft forely wounded with thofe many Slafhes and Cuts that he had received in moft parts of his Body.

Pietro Mondon.

Pietro Mondon of *Villaro,* (whither he had formerly fled for Refuge) was overtaken by the Enemies as he was flying from his own Houfe towards the Mountains of *Chiapelet,* and there was cruelly murdered by them.

Giuditha Roflagnol.

Giuditha the Widow of the afore deceafed *Daniele Roflagnol* of *Villaro,* had firft her Head chopt off in a certain Cave of *Chaftelus,* and afterwards her Body thrown down the Rocks.

David Geimet and his Mother.

David Geimet of *Villaro,* together with his Mother who was exceeding aged and decrepit, was barbaroufly murdered by the Souldiers among the Villages of *Mouffa.*

Daniele Fellipone.

Daniele Fellipone had his Head hackt off from his Body as he was lying in his Bed in the Houfe of one *Giovanni Fiantino,* at *Villaro.*

Antonio Calieris.

Antonio the Son of the afore deceafed *Samuele Calieris,* (a dumb and innocent Creature) was moft inhumanely butchered, as he was fitting by the fires fide, at a place called *Clotillart.*

Peiron Minan.

Peiron Minan was caught by the Souldiers as he was making his Efcape out of his own Houfe, and in a very cruel manner by them killed upon the place where they caught him.

Pietro Moninat.

Pietro Moninat and his Wife lying both of them extreme fick and weak, were butchered at the Alpe of *La Rouffa* by the Souldiers; who alfo finding in the fame Houfe one of their Children, being a poor Infant, lame and impotent, cut off its Legs, and fo left it in that miferable plight. There was alfo in the fame Houfe a poor Girl, another of their Children, who had been dumb from its Cradle, found by fome of the Neighbours not long after, ftarved to death for want of fuftenance.

Sufanna

Sufanna Fantino.

Sufanna, Widow of the afore deceafed *David Fantino,* was cruelly murdered in the Village of *Liuzza.*

Davide Fontano.

Davide Fontano of *Villermino,* a man exceeding aged and feeble, was maffacred in the Village of *Bezza,* and afterwards had his Body dragged up and down by the Souldiers in a moft unfeemly manner.

Giovanni Gaio.

Giovanni Gaio, Son of the afore deceafed *Antonio Gaio* of *Pravillerm,* who had formerly fled to *Villaro* for Refuge, was maffacred in his Flight towards the Mountains of *Balmedaut.*

Daniele Benech with his two fmall Children.

Daniele Benech, an Inhabitant of *Villaro,* was taken by the Souldiers in one of the Villages of *La Cercena,* who firft cut off his Nofe, his Ears, and other parts of his Body, till fuch time as they had difpatched him; and afterwards left the mangled pieces upon the Hedges and Bufhes of the faid place. There were alfo two fmall Children of the abovefaid *Daniele Benech* ftifled in the Snow at the fame time, for want of a Father to lead and conduct them.

Daniele Garre.

Daniele Garre, Son in Law to the Sieur *Mondonis,* was moft unmercifully murdered by the fame Souldiers, who had difpatched the abovefaid *Benech,* in the Village of *La Cercena.*

Maria Gril.

Maria Widow of the afore deceafed *Daniele Gril Bourgoin* of *Villaro,* was horribly murdered by the Souldiers at *Macanail* near *La Cercena,* whofe Body was afterwards eaten up and devoured by wilde Beafts.

Pietro Berardo.

Pietro Berardo of *Villaro,* being purfued hard by the Souldiers towards the Mountains of *Balmedaut,* his Foot unhappily flipt in a narrow paffage as he was flying, and fo he fell down the fide of an high Rock, where he was afterwards found dead.

Maria Pelanchion.

Maria the Widow of the afore deceafed *Daniele Pelanchion* of *Villaro,* being taken by the Souldiers at *La Combe delli Carbonieri,* after they had abufed her, they fhot her almoft to death, and then flung her into the River of *Valguichiart:* this poor Woman being not quite dead, with much pains and many fhifts, (very pitifull to behold) got out of the River again, and laid her felf down in the Sun, hoping by the heat thereof to be fomewhat revived and refrefhed; but the Souldiers

diers perceiving that, took her again, and faftening a Rope to her Feet, dragged her to the Bridg, and there they hung her up by the Feet ; in which pofture they fhot her to death, and afterwards left her ftark naked upon a Rock.

Maria Monino.

Maria the Wife of *Daniele Monino*, was taken by the Souldiers in the Village of *Liuzza*, who having broken her Jaws in pieces, and given her a very deep Cut in the Neck, fo that her Head was half on and half off, left her in this languifhing condition, where, after enduring unfpeakable Torments for divers days together, fhe departed this miferable life.

Maria Negrino and her Daughter.

Maria Widow of the afore deceafed *Davide Nigrino* (a poor Begget of *Villaro*) together with a Daughter of hers who was an Innocent, were both of them inhumanely maffacred in the Village of *Bozza*, and their dead Bodies afterwards thrown into the adjoyning Woods.

Anna Arduino.

Anna Widow of the afore deceafed *Arduino*, was maffacred in the Mountains of *Chiapelet*, where alfo her Body was left unburied.

Sufanna Bals.

Sufanna Widow of the afore deceafed *Samuele Bals* of *Villaro*, was taken by the Souldiers in the Village of *Balmedaut*, who after they had abufed her at their pleafure, fhut her up between two Stone Walls where fhe was miferably ftarved and pined to death.

Daniele Bert.

Daniele Bert of *Villaro*, endeavouring to defend his Wife from the Rage of the Souldiers, was by them maffacred in the Village of *Liuzza*.

Sufanna Calvio.

Sufanna the Wife of *Jacopo Calvio* of *Villaro*, being forely wounded by the Souldiers at *Cercena*, got into a Barn that was there clofe by ; which the Souldiers perceiving, they fet fire to the Barn, and fo burnt her Body to Afhes.

Faci Magnet.

Faci Magnet was murdered in the Village of *Pertufel*, at a certain place called *La Maifonetta*.

Daniele Pelanchion.

Daniele Pelanchion of *Villaro*, was maffacred in a certain Village called *Meinet*, clofe by *Brezza*.

Catharina

Catharina Fontano.

Catharina, Widow of the afore deceased *Daniele Fontano*, was massacred among the Villages of *Bezza*, where she was found afterwards with the very Sword wherewith she was killed, sticking in her bowels. It may be those that were so bloudy to thrust it in, had not the heart to pluck it out again.

Magdalena Roussa.

Magdalena Roussa, a poor Innocent, had her Head chopt off by the Souldiers upon the Mountains of *Chiapelet*.

Micheli Bertino.

Micheli Bertino, was cruelly murdered by the Souldiers upon the Mountains of *La Cercena*.

Stephano Perino.

Stephano Perino, a very aged man of *Villaro*, was massacred close by his own House, which in a manner adjoyned to the Town.

Daniele Bertino, his Childe.

A Childe of *Daniele Bertino*, who had been from the Womb both Dumb and an Innocent, was by the Enemy burnt in a Barn at *Balmedaut*.

A Woman and a young Childe whose Names are unknown.

A certain person who was living in the Year 1656. and an Inhabitant of *La Torre*, assured the Authour during his abode at *Geneva*, that being upon the Mountains of *Villaro*, he himself saw a young Infant not above three Moneths old, together with a Woman who was unknown to him, taken by those Murderers, and hurled down the Precipices of the Rocks, in a manner most barbarous and fearfull to behold.

Stephano Monino,
Giovanni Albareo,
Pietro Albareo,　} all massacred.
Giovanni Calve,
Pietro Bert.

Of

Of Bobio.

Giovanni di Savetto.

GIovanni di Savetto *della Combe, della Feriera,* in the Communalty of *Bobio,* was found dead upon the Snow, where he had been maffacred, with a little Infant (whom the Murderers, as it's probable, had fpared) fleeping in it's Fathers arms: and thus though the Father was murdered, yet the young Infant by a fpecial Providence was preferved.

Paolo Armand.

Paolo Armand, being extreme fick and weak, was taken by the Souldiers at a place called *La Vota di Crofouna,* and by them hackt in pieces.

Andrea Bertono and *Jofepho Catalino.*

Andrea Bertono, a very ancient and lame Man, was taken at a certain place called *Serre de Cruel,* where he had firft his Breafts cut off, and then he was cruelly murdered by thofe bloudy Butchers: and to teftifie their hatred againft him for his perfeverance in his Religion, they cut out his Bowels after his Death, and with their Halberds hacked his dead Body in pieces. And not far off from the place where this was done, *Jofepho Catalino* was alfo maffacred.

Daniele Michialino.

Daniele, the Son of *Davide Michialino,* in the very fame place where *Catalino* was maffacred, was taken by the Souldiers, and befides other ill and cruel ufage, had his Tongue plucked out with great violence and torments.

Martha Giraudina.

Martha Giraudina, an old Woman of about fourfcore years of age, had her Head chopt off by fome of the Maffacrers.

Conftantia Bellione.

Conftantia Bellione de Sibaud, after having had her Body hacked and mangled in moft parts thereof, was difpatched with feveral Bullets that were fhot into her Bowels; and after fhe was dead, they cleft her Head with a Hanger.

Juditha Mondon.

Juditha Mondon was beaten to death in a moft favage manner with Clubs and Staves.

Daniele

Daniele Bertinat.

Daniele Bertinate, (alias *Maxiet*) was cut in pieces at *Villa Nuova.*

A Childe of *Francisco Charboniero* massacred.

Davide Paglias, and *Paolo Genre,* with two Infants.

Davide Paglias and *Paolo Genre* endeavouring to escape each of them with a little Infant in their arms, were at last tired, and by that means overtaken by their Pursuers, and so both Men and Infants cruelly put to death.

Stephano Billior.

Stephano Billior, a poor old man of at least fourscore years of age was most barbarously killed in his Bed.

Giovanni Rovetto.

Giovanni Rovetto was massacred near the Fort of *Mireboc,* whose Corps lay a long time naked upon the Rock, and was afterwards thrown into the River.

Davide Pecole, Son of *Jacopo Pecole,*
Giovanni, Son of *Josepho Favatiero,* ⎫ shot to death by the Soul-
Jacopo, and *Pietro Biglior,* Brothers, ⎬ diers, and left upon the
Francisco Brother to *Paolo Genre,* ⎭ Snow.

Micheli Genre.

Micheli Genre, a young man of *Bobio,* was thrown off the Bridg of *La Torre,* down into the River of *Angrognia,* where, as he was praying with his Hands lift up to Heaven, he was partly stoned and partly drowned.

Francisco Genre.

Francisco Genre, having first received a Wound by a Shot in his Body, was thrown down the Rocks at a place called *Valguichiart.*

Stephano Baridono,
Moyse Bongiorno, ⎫
Daniele Gras Son of *Pietro Gras,* ⎬ all cruelly and barbarously
Catharina Gonetta, ⎭ massacred.
Susanna Vy, alias *Ruffit,*

Davide Armand.

Davide Armand, had his Head knocked and beaten with a Hammer till he died, with most sensible pains and torments.

Jacopo Baridono.

Jacopo Baridono, was taken Prisoner at *Villaro,* and from thence carried

ried to *La Torre,* where after the Tormenters had to their mindes sufficiently afflicted him with burning Matches between his Fingers, his
Lips, and other parts of his Body, till he died with meer pain and anguish, they caused his dead Corps to be carried out by two of his fellow prisoners, and by them to be thrown into the River of *Pelice;*
but afterwards, better bethinking themselves how they might be revenged against the dead Corps, and supposing the River too honourable a Burying place for an Heretick, they compelled those that cast it
in, to fetch it out again, and lay it at the Brink of the River, where,
after they had exposed the same to all manner of Ignominies, it was at
last eaten up by the Dogs.

In Roras.

The Wives of *Josepho Garniero, Josepho Pellenc,* and *Stephano Revellio.*

THe Wife of *Josepho Garniero,* the Wife of *Josepho Pellenc,* and
the Wife of *Stephano Revellio,* were all most prodigiously assas-
sinated and murdered at the time when the Army fell upon the Borders of *Roras;* where, among other passages, there was one very remarkable concerning *Marguerita* the Wife of *Josepho Garniero,* and
Sister to Captain *Josua Gianavel;* for she having received a Shot in
one of her Breasts, as she was giving Suck to a little Childe with the
other, was yet so hearty and couragious, that she exhorted her Husband with many pathetical expressions, to *endure the Cross with patience,*
and to *hold out to the end ;* neither did she at all desire any favour of the
Massacrers, save onely to spare the Life of her innocent Babe ; which
accordingly they did, but immediately gave the Mother another Shot
into her Body, whereof she died, and afterwards the Infant was found
alive in the dead Mothers arms, and so miraculously preserved.

Isaiah Mondon.

Isaiah Mondon, having a long time hid himself in the cleft of a Rock,
where for many days together he had nothing but a few leaves of un-
wholsom hearbs to feed upon, was at last found out by the Souldiers,
and near to the Bridge of the River called *La Lucerna,* was most unmercifully handled by them. From thence they dragg'd him (being no better then half dead) towards the Town of *Lucerna,* but the
poor man when he was able to march no further, fell down upon his
Knees, beseeching his Executioners to dispatch him speedily, who
accordingly were so civil as to gratifie him in his request, and thereupon
what with their Swords, and what with their Pistols, they soon ended his miserable dayes, crying out in a scoffing and deriding manner,
Kill this Barbet ! Kill this Barbet, who refuses to become a Christian.
All this was done near to the *Rocca di Lucerna.*

Ludovico

Ludovico Pellenco and his Wife,
Paolo Richardo,
Ludovico Torno and his Mother,
Maria, the Wife of *Jacopo Durando*, an old
 woman of fourfcore years and upwards,
Micheli Salvagiot,

} all of them horribly maffacred, and fome of their bodies cut and torn in pieces.

Giovanni Barrolino, and his Wife.

Giovanni Barrolino and his Wife, were caft alive into a Pond or Pool, where they were feveral times plunged and thruft under the water with Prongs and Pitch-forks, and at laft difpatched with Stones and Brick-batts.

Maria Revel.

Maria Revel, having received a fhot in her body, fell down in a manner dead, but afterwards recovering fo much ftrength as to get upon her Knees to pray unto God, the Enemy difpatched her.

Giovanni Salvagiot.

Giovanni Salvagiot, as he was returning from *Bagnol,* after the Peace was concluded, and paffing by a Chappel without pulling off his Hat, and making obeyfance thereto, was murthered, and his body left unburied.

Giovanni Gayo, and two of his children ; *Daniele Garniero* and his Son ; a Daughter of *Giovanni Morglio* ; *Giovanni Feliero, Giovanni Miroto, Bartholemi Morglio,* and *Giovanni Salvagiot,* another of the fame name with the abovefaid.

Giovanni Gayo, and all the reft above-named, were cruelly maffacred in a certain *Cave,* where they had hid themfelves, thinking to be more fecure in that place then any other. Thefe poor creatures finding themfelves difcovered, fell upon their Knees and begg'd their lives of their Maffacrers, of the moft of whom they had a long time before had a particular and perfonal knowledge, and who had always made profeffion to be their very good friends, for indeed they were no other then their neighbours of *Lucerna, Bubbiana, Barges, Bagnolo, Cavor,* and the adjacent parts. But the mercy of thofe men being altogether cruelty, the kindeft falute they could then afford their old acquaintance,was with Mufquets,Swords,and Piftols: which the poor people perceiving, and being not defirous to behold the lamentable fpectacle of each others mifery,kneeled down in a ring,and thruft all their heads (with their faces towards the ground) into certain Fearn-brakes and other fuch ftuff,which they had got into theCave,thinking to have lain thereupon inftead of beds, in which pofture they were all miferably fhot to death, and their dead bodies afterwards horribly mangled and cut to pieces.

In

In Roccapiatta.

Jacopo Barral, and his Wife.

JAcopo Barral and his Wife, having been taken prisoners by the Earl of *San Secondo*, were three or four dayes after carried out of the Prison to a certain place about a quarter of a *Piemont*-mile distant, and there were shot to death: The very same Executioners did also cut off the womans breasts.

Giovanni Bonino.

Giovanni Bonino (alias *Grangiot*) was taken in his flight by the French Troops, near *Val Perosa*, and there miserably hackt to pieces with their Hangers.

Antonio Guigou.

Antonio Guigou, being come to *Periero* with a designe to change his Religion at the instigation of *Conte Borichard*, it pleased God so to touch his heart that he repented him of his resolution, and thereupon endeavoured to make his escape. But being caught again by the Troops of the *Marquess* of *Galeas*, and handled with exceeding great cruelty because he would not yeeld to go to Mass, as they were carrying him prisoner towards *Prali*, and in their way passing by a Precipice, the poor man, to avoid the hands of his tormentors, leapt down the side of a Rock, and so was dasht to pieces.

Besides the above-named cruelties, there were brought to the Authors hands a multitude of other Relations, which, because he had them not sufficiently verified, he thought fit rather to omit, then to insert them among those whom he found to be undoubtedly true. Besides this, the ingenuous Reader can never expect that all those cruelties which were exercised upon those poor creatures in so many dark corners and by-places, should be brought to light. The truth is, these which are here set down may abundantly suffice to demonstrate the cursed and hellish cruelties of their Popish and bloudy Enemies. All therefore which I shall here add, shall be onely a Catalogue of the Names of some of those poor *Protestants*, who miserably perished in Prison, or in their own defence, together with the rest who were detained Prisoners; And all these in their order as follows.

A

A Catalogue or List of the Names of those poor *Protestants* in the Valleys of *Piemont*, who died in Prison at *Turin*, and other places, so far as they have come to the Authors hands.

Of *S. Giovanni*.

David Reymont, servant to the Marquess of *Lucerna*.
Giovanni Rosel, in the Prison of *Lucerna*.

Of *Angrognia*.

Giovanni Arnoul.
Giovanni Pietro Raggio.
Sidrac Buffa.
Giovanni Benech.
Magdalena Wife of *Stephano Odin*.
Stephano Mondon, with his Wife and three children.

Of *Pramol*.

Jacopo Colalino.
Captain *Bartholemi Jahiere*.
Giovanni his Son.
Jacopo Long.
Bertino Long.
Jacopo Jaquet.
Giovanni Bondrano.
Pietro Andrion.
Giovanni Collatino.
Giovanni Beus.
Giovanni Son of *Paolo Bormons*.
Michele Granget.

Of *Angrognia.*

Giovanni Arnold.
Giovanni Pietro Raggio.
Sidrac Buffa.
Two of the same Name, *viz. Giovanni Benech.*
Magdalena the Wife of *Stephano Odin.*

A Catalogue or List of the Names of those poor *Prote-stants* in the Valleys of *Piemont* who died in fight.

Of *S. Giovanni.*

Daniel Arnoul.
Bartholemi Mallanot.
Daniel Bouvier.
Giovanni Jaime.
Paolo Garniero.
Pietro Ollivet.
Bartholemi Mahet.
Jacopo Gayot.
Pietro Sibille.
Antonio Lantare.
Giovanni Danna.
Giovanni Brocher.
Josepho Chiayret.
Josepho Lantaré.
Giovanni Gonino.

Of *Angrognia.*

Captain *Michele Bertino.*
Giovanni Musseton, son of *David.*
Antonio Bertino.
Pietro Coissone.
Giovanni Bertot.
Battista Forniero.
Daniele Fraschia.
Bartholemi Mallan son of *Daniel.*
Stephano Junon.
A son of *Elias Gygnous.*

Of *La Torre.*

Pietro Chabriolo.
Jacopo Bonnetto.
Pietro Fine.
Giovanni Charbonnier.
Jacopo fon of *Giovanni of Glodo.*
Pietro Richiardon.
Stephano Meglie.
Bartholemi Grigl.
Giovanni Pilone.
Jacopo Roffane fon of the deceafed
   Elias.
Giovanni fon of *Pol Roftagn.*
Giovanni Morglie.
Mattheo Ejnard.
Jacopo Ugon.
Jofepho Chiarret.
David Copin.
Bartholomi Martina.
Paolo Belin.
Pol Bonetto fon of *Jacopo* an Elder.

Of *Villaro.*

Giovanni Brunerol Balls.
Giovanni Albareo.
Pietro Albareo.
Pietro Bert.
Stephano Monino.
Giovanni Calue.
Of *Bobio.*
Jacopo, and *Pietro,* the fons of
  Giovanni Biglior.
Two who went by the name of
Giovanni the fon of *Samuel Genre.*
  Giovanni Gras.
Jacopo Balma or *Caffarel.*
Stephano Grafs.
Pol Pontet, and his fon *Giovanni.*
David Pecoul.
Giovanni Faratier of *di Jofepho.*
Pietro Giaymonat.
Jofepho Arduino.
Stephano Gras, alias *Biglior.*
Giovanni Roet.

Of Roras.

Jannet Morgle.
Daniele Salvagiol and his fon.
Bartholomi Morglie.
Ludovico Tourn.
Bartholemi Durand, and *Ludevico* his Brother.
Daniel Revel.
Giovanni Parife.

Of Roccapiatta.

Daniele Cardon.
Two whofe names were *Auguftino Roftaino,* whereof one
    was the moft confiderable member of that Church.
Daniele Martinat and his two fons.
Daniele Bieynat.
Philippo Romans.
Giovanni Pafquet fon of *Peyret.*
Giovanni Giouve.

A Catalogue or Lift of the Names of thofe poor *Proteftants* in the Valleys of *Piemont,* who were detained
Prifoners and refufed to be reftored, or let at
liberty, notwithftanding all fupplications
or interceffions to that
purpofe.

Of S. Giovanni.

Maria daughter of *Daniele Filipet* at *Paifana.*
A fon of *Stephano Meli* an Elder.

Of Piemont.

Bartholomeo fon of *Daniele Beffon,* detained at *Foffan,* at
    Captain *Leuron's* houfe.
Maria daughter of *Laurentio Odin,* at *Turin.*
Maria daughter of *Jacopo Ricca,* at *Coni.*
Jeanna daughter of *Catherina Riqua,* at *Cavor.*
Two infants of *Giovanni Arnold* detained, one at *Turin,* and
    then ranfomed at *Lucerna* for a French-crown, by a foul-
    dier, who was a *Bavarian.*

Of *La Torre*.

Two daughters of the deceased Mr. *Gilles*,
With one daughter of the deceased *Daniel Pellin*..
One daughter of *Giovanni Chianforan*, detained at *Turin*.
Two daughters *de Baptiste Giovel*.
A son of *Bartholemi Arnoul*, detained at *Turin*.

Of *Villaro*.

Giovanni, son of the deceased *Daniele Marinet*, detained at *Scarnafix*.
Paolo Pelanchion, son of the deceased *Daniele*, detained by the Priests.
Susanne, daughter of the deceased *Giovanni Brunerol*, detained at *Villa France*.
Paolo, son of the deceased *Daniel Geimonat*, detained at *Raconis*.
David Combe Magne, detained at *Pignerolio*.
Maria, daughter of the deceased *David Fantino*.
Pietro Pelanchion, detained at *Queyras*.

Of *Bobio*.

Two male children of *David Charbonier*, alias *Feé*, detained at S. *Front*.
Catherina, daughter of *Stephano Barridon*, detained at the house of *Giovanni Caimus*.

Of *Roras*.

Anna, daughter of *Giovanni Aghit*.

The End of the Second Book.

Printed in the United States
53500LVS00003B/37